THINK
PSYCHOLOGY

ABIGAIL A. BAIRD
Vassar College

Prentice Hall
Upper Saddle River   London   Singapore
Toronto   Tokyo   Sydney   Hong Kong   Mexico City

Front cover:
A BP cleanup crew shovels oil from a beach on May 24, 2010 at Port Fourchon, Louisiana. Under-fire BP chief executive Tony Hayward admitted at a press conference on the beach that the British energy giant's reputation was on the line over the oil spill in the Gulf of Mexico.

Editorial Director: Craig Campanella
Editor in Chief: Jessica Mosher
Editorial Project Manager: Judy Casillo
Editorial Assistant: Jackie Moya
Director of Marketing: Brandy Dawson
Executive Marketing Manager: Jeanette Koskinas
Marketing Assistant: Shauna Fishweicher
Managing Editor: Maureen Richardson
Project Manager: Annemarie Franklin
Copy Editor: Gabrielle Durham/Words & Numbers
Proofreader: Words & Numbers
Senior Operations Supervisor: Sherry Lewis
Manager, Design Development: John Christiana

Interior Design: Kathy Mrozek and John Christiana
Cover Design: John Christiana
AV Project Manager: Maria Piper
Manager, Visual Research: Beth Brenzel
Photo Researcher: Words and Numbers
Manager, Rights and Permissions: Zina Arabia
Manager, Cover Visual Research and Permissions: Karen Sanatar
Cover Photo: AFP/Newscom
Full-Service Project Management: Lauren Pecarich, Matt Gardner, Matt Skalka, Russ Hall, and Patricia Gordon/Words & Numbers
Composition: Words & Numbers
Printer/Binder: Courier Companies, Inc.
Cover Printer: Lehigh-Phoenix Color

"for my children, Christopher and Phoebe, whose lives inspire mine"

Library of Congress Cataloging-in-Publication Data
Baird, Abigail A.
Think psychology/Abigail A. Baird.—2nd ed.
    p. cm.
Includes bibliographical references and index.
ISBN-13: 978-0-205-84202-5 (exam copy)
ISBN-10: 0-205-84202-X (exam copy)
ISBN-13: 978-0-13-212840-7 (student edition)
ISBN-10: 0-13-212840-3 (student edition)
1. Psychology—Practice. 2. Psychology—Research—Methodology. I. Title.
BF75.B35 2011
150—dc22   2010034972

10 9 8 7 6 5 4 3 2 1

Prentice Hall
is an imprint of

www.pearsonhighered.com

Exam Copy: ISBN-10:   0-205-84202-X
                  ISBN-13:   978-0-205-84202-5

Student Edition: ISBN-10:   0-13-212840-3
                  ISBN-13:   978-0-132-12840-7

BRIEF CONTENTS

CONTENTS

06 CONSCIOUSNESS

What Causes Us to Sleep, Dream, or Even Become Hypnotized? 86

07 LEARNING

What Are We Capable of Learning, and How Do We Learn It? 102

08 MEMORY

What Do We Store in the "Filing Cabinet" of the Brain? 118

09 COGNITION AND INTELLIGENCE

How Do We Communicate, Solve Problems, and Make Thoughtful Decisions? 134

10 HUMAN DEVELOPMENT I: PHYSICAL, COGNITIVE, AND LANGUAGE DEVELOPMENT

What Universal Changes Do We Experience as We Grow Older? 152

17

PSYCHOLOGICAL DISORDERS
How Can We Explain Mental Disorders? 262

18

PSYCHOLOGICAL THERAPIES
What Techniques Do Psychologists Use to
Treat Mental Illnesses? 280

ACKNOWLEDGMENTS

I am grateful to all who reviewed this book and the previous edition for their thoughtful comments and insights:

Gerard Hoefling, University of Delaware
Fred Whitford, Montana State University
Holly Beard, Midlands Technical College
David Brackin, Young Harris College
David Copeland, University of Nevada, Las Vegas
Vicki Dretchen, Volunteer State Community College
Christine Grela, McHenry County College
Nicole Cheri Kittrell, Manatee Community College
Nicole Korzetz, Lee College
Don Lucas, Northwest Vista College
Molly Lynch, Northern Virginia Community College
Laura May, University of South Carolina, Aiken
Brian Parry, Mesa State College
Patrick Saxe, State University of New York, New Paltz
David Shepard, South Texas College
Lawrence Venuk, Naugatuck Valley Community College
Jennifer Verive, Western Nevada College
Linda Veronie, Slippery Rock University
Lois Willoughby, Miami Dade College
Karen Yanowitz, Arkansas State University

A heartfelt thank you also goes to David Waxler of Widener University for his contributions to the end-of-chapter test questions.

I am also grateful to the many individuals at Pearson Education and at Words and Numbers, without whose assistance this book simply would not exist: Amber Mackey, Jeanette Koskinas, Judy Casillo, Jackie Moya, Shauna Fishweicher, Paige Clunie, Maureen Richardson, Annemarie Franklin, John Christiana, Kathy Mrozek, Beth Brenzel, and Sherri Lewis at Pearson; Lauren Pecarich, Matt Skalka, Matt Gardner, Russ Hall, and Patricia Gordon at Words & Numbers.

Finally, thank you to Jessica Mosher whose innovative vision for this project has made me enormously proud to be part of it.

ABOUT THE AUTHOR

 ABIGAIL A. BAIRD is a professor of Psychology at Vassar College. She earned her undergraduate degree from Vassar College and both an M.A. and Ph.D. from Harvard University. Following completion of her Ph.D., she was awarded a Post-Doctoral Fellowship at the Center for Cognitive Neuroscience at Dartmouth College. Her numerous articles and presentations have covered topics such as adolescent brain development, cognitive regulation of emotion, juvenile justice, and manifestations of racial bias in mind brain and behavior.

Abigail's research has received awards from Harvard University, the Society for Research on Psychopathology, and in 2008, the Association for Psychological Science named Abigail a "Rising Star in Psychological Science." Her research has also led her to be elected to several scientific societies including the International Society for Behavioral Neuroscience and the Gruter Institute for Law and Behavioral Research. Abigail has been repeatedly recognized for her excellence in teaching. In 2000, she received Harvard's George Goethals Teaching Prize, and in 2004, she was awarded the Class of 1962 Excellence in Teaching Fellowship by Dartmouth College. Her professional accomplishments also include serving as secretary of the Association for Psychological Science, Honorary Faculty Member for the Order of Omega National Honor Society, Invited Faculty to the New York State Judicial Institute, and advisory board member on the Campaign for Youth Justice.

THINK
PSYCHOLOGY

INTRODUCTION

WHAT IS PSYCHOLOGY AND WHY DC FASCINATE US?
HOW IS THE SCIENTIFIC METHOD USE STUDY PSYCHOLOGY?
WHAT IS THE HISTORY OF PSYCHOLC
WHAT MAJOR QUESTIONS DO PSYCHOLOGISTS SEEK TO ANSWER?
WHAT ARE SOME DIFFERENT SUBTYF PSYCHOLOGY?

When

pop superstar Michael Jackson died at the age of 50, shockwaves resonated throughout the Western world. As news of the star's death spread, Internet traffic on Yahoo! News spiked to an all-time high and radio stations began playing Michael Jackson songs around the clock. Within days, the media was full of salacious details about the entertainer's troubled life, eagerly provided by former friends and employees. But why were we, the public, so eager to listen to them? What enthralled us about the life of a man we probably never met, let alone knew well enough to pass judgment on? Why do we have such a fascination with celebrities and their lives?

Celebrity worship is not a new phenomenon—successful Roman gladiators were revered like gods, and 19th-century composers Frédéric Chopin and Franz Liszt had legions of female fans. In fact, psychologists believe there may be something in our DNA that encourages us to find an idol and follow him or her. Stuart Fischoff, professor emeritus of media psychology at California State University, Los Angeles, believes that, as a social animal, man is preprogrammed to follow the alpha males and alpha females of the pack. In today's society, those alpha males and alpha females are the Brad Pitts and Angelina Jolies of the world—the rich and famous celebrities whose lives we envy.

Some scientific research suggests that a mild dose of celebrity worship may actually be good for

us, providing us with a goal to strive for and increasing our self-esteem. Psychologist Shira Gabriel and her colleagues gave 348 college students (one-fifth of whom admitted to having a celebrity crush) a self-esteem questionnaire and ranked the participants according to their baseline level of self-esteem. She then asked the students to take five minutes to write an essay about their favorite celebrity. Finally, the students retook the self-esteem test. Gabriel noted that the students who initially scored the lowest on the self-esteem test scored much higher on the second test after they had written about their favorite celebrities. She speculated that the students had formed a bond with their chosen celebrity, assimilating some of the celebrity's characteristics in themselves and feeling better about themselves as a result (Gabriel, et al. 2008).

Although a little celebrity worship might be good for us, a lot is likely to be harmful. Researchers have coined the term "celebrity worship syndrome" to describe the condition in which idolatry takes over a person's life and becomes all-consuming. Fans with unhealthy obsessions may suffer from anxiety, depression, and social dysfunction. It seems that celebrity worship, much like everything else in life, is best enjoyed in moderation.

What Is Psychology?

Psychology is the scientific study of behavior—overt actions and reactions—and mental processes—covert internal activity in the mind. While philosophers might speculate on why people act as they do, psychologists use scientific methods to accurately describe, explain, predict, or control human and animal behavior. The scientific method has only fairly recently been applied to psychology; until approximately 130 years ago, psychology was considered to be a branch of philosophy. Throughout this chapter, we will examine the development of psychology as a formal discipline in its own right.

WHY STUDY PSYCHOLOGY?

What motivated you to study psychology? Maybe you are hoping to solve the "nature versus nurture" debate and learn whether environmental factors can truly ever trump genetics. Perhaps you are looking for tips on how to improve your relationships with your friends and family members, or maybe you're more interested in learning about how you can reduce stress and anxiety in your daily life. If you polled your fellow students about their reasons for studying psychology, you would likely discover that everyone has something in common—a fundamental curiosity about themselves and the world they live in. Among other things, studying psychology reduces our uncertainty about our own experiences by providing knowledge about ourselves (Why do I have short-term memory lapses? How can I increase my IQ level?), other people (Why do people suffer from mental disorders? Why do people have different personalities?), and the world (Do people from other countries perceive the world differently? How does culture affect personality?).

Psychology is the scientific study of behavior and mental processes.

Empiricism is the view that knowledge originates through experience.

Scientific method is a process for conducting an objective inquiry through data collection and analysis.

Psychology and the Scientific Method

FOLK PSYCHOLOGY

You may have encountered some skepticism from people who do not believe that psychology is a science. This is a fairly common misconception, born out of the fact that much of what psychologists study may be personally experienced. For example, you may believe that men are more aggressive than women because you have two older brothers who are constantly engaged in fistfights and a younger sister who always takes on the role of family pacifist. Your individual experience has given you a false sense of actual scientific data that may or may not be true of the population as a whole.

This type of misconception is less common in the physical sciences. Few people would claim to have personal insight about the behavior of accelerated electrons or the results of a chemical reaction between hydrogen and nitrogen. Before they state their theories as facts, physicists and chemists undergo careful scientific processes to prove or disprove their ideas. Although many people don't realize it, scientific processes are equally important in psychology. For example, the fact that you have personally encountered more aggressive males and less aggressive females does not necessarily indicate that everyone has had the same experiences. Maybe your family is atypical. Perhaps non-biological factors such as parental influence, social environment, or peer pressure have affected your siblings' behavior. There are limits to what we can intuit about our own behavior and

the behavior of others. Not only are we limited by the boundaries of our own experiences, we are also limited by the reliability of our memories and the dangers of our personal biases. In order to make generalized, objective, and well-supported statements about human nature, psychologists need to act as scientists rather than as casual observers.

Of course, casual observers are often on the right track: Many times, theories that seem like "common knowledge" are in fact supported by rigorous psychological research. (For example, several studies indicate that in general, men *are* naturally more aggressive than women are.) However, scientific psychological research also frequently disproves many of our culture's commonly held assumptions, highlighting the importance of critical, objective inquiry to the study of the human mind.

THE IMPORTANCE OF EMPIRICISM

Have you ever met someone for the first time and immediately made assumptions about him or her? Maybe you thought that because a stranger was wearing glasses, she must be intelligent, or maybe you connected a neighbor's playing music with violent lyrics to a violent worldview. When we make judgments like these, we rely on contextual assumptions and stereotypes to give us information about people, but more often than not, this information turns out to be at least slightly inaccurate. Like other scientists, psychologists aim to eliminate the effects of personal and cultural bias from their research. When psychologists draw conclusions about people, they do so through experimentation rather than through personalized judgments or stereotyping.

Most psychologists today believe in the importance of **empiricism,** or the view that knowledge originates through experience. In other words, information that you observe or collect yourself is more reliable

<<< Are men naturally more aggressive than women? Scientific investigations both prove and disprove common assumptions.

than information that you can't observe or that you hear third-hand. As a result, psychologists who perform experiments use the **scientific method,** a process for conducting an objective inquiry through data collection and analysis.

1 **Identify the problem.** The first step in a scientific inquiry is to notice something that you would like to explain or investigate. It is important to choose a problem that you are able to study empirically. For example, there is no point in asking tempting philosophical questions such as "Why are we here?" or "What is morality?" Although the answers to these types of questions would provide valuable and fascinating insight into human behavior and the human experience, they cannot be answered using the scientific method and thus do not fall into the psychological realm.

Once you have established a problem that can be studied empirically, you should ensure that there is only one factor, or variable, that changes throughout your experiment. Any other factors that might influence your results should be controlled. Let's say you are investigating how many times your siblings behave aggressively on an average day, so you observe them as they go about their daily business. Would this be a fair test? How would you make sure that all three siblings encounter the same potential stressors that might make them behave aggressively? How might factors such as traffic jams, disagreements with peers, and unpleasant chance encounters with strangers affect their behavior? Before you begin your research, it is important to consider how you will collect and measure your data so that your results are as accurate and reliable as possible.

2 **Conduct background research.** Has your question been studied before? If you are investigating a popular topic such as male and female aggression, there is probably already a great deal of research available that will give you further information about your topic of study. You can consult library and Internet resources to discover what research has already been done on your topic, how that research might be improved, and what areas might warrant further study.

3 **Formulate a hypothesis.** Based on your initial observations and your background

The Scientific Method

Identify a problem.

Conduct background research.

Formulate a hypothesis.

Think critically and try again.

Test the hypothesis.

Analyze your results.

Results support the hypothesis.

Results do not support the hypothesis.

Report results.

<<< Psychologists use the scientific method to reduce bias and error in their research.

research, you can make a hypothesis, or an educated guess about an explanation for your observations. Your hypothesis should be written as a statement that can either be proved or disproved. For example, you may have read several articles indicating that men are more likely to use aggressive actions than women, or that men are less patient than women when placed in stressful situations. Incorporating this research with your observations about your brothers and sister, you might hypothesize, "If a male is placed in a stressful situation, he will react more aggressively than a female who is placed in the same stressful situation would."

4 **Test the hypothesis.** Psychologists use a variety of research methods, including surveys, case studies, and observations in laboratories or natural environments (see Chapter 2). However, the most conclusive way to test a hypothesis is to conduct an experiment. By manipulating a single characteristic, a researcher can study how this particular characteristic affects a specific outcome. Depending on the experiment, this outcome may involve the behavior of a person, the behavior of a group, or even the behavior of the human brain. While undertaking this particular study, you would manipulate a particular situation and then examine the behavior of several individuals within that situation. For example, you might select a group of men and a group of women of similar age, education level, and cultural background and individually place them in the same stressful situation—asking them to solve an impossible puzzle, for example, or exposing them to a loud, annoying noise for an extended period of time. You would then find some way of measuring the aggressive behavior in each gender. You might, for instance, invite participants to take out their frustrations on a punching bag, and then record how many times each person chooses to hit it. By controlling the environment in which the stressful situation takes place and creating the same stressful situation each time, you can ensure that you are only changing one variable in your experiment.

5 **Analyze your results.** Once you have completed your experiment, you can analyze your results to determine whether they support your hypothesis. Psychologists use statistical analysis to help them summarize their data and determine how likely it is that the results were due to chance (see Chapter 2). It is often helpful to repeat an experiment several

Chapter 01

Critical thinking is a way of processing information in which a person examines assumptions, evaluates evidence, looks for hidden agendas, and assesses conclusions.

Dualism is the belief that the mind does not cease to exist when the body dies, and that thoughts and ideas can exist separately from the body.

Structuralism is a school of psychology concerned with the individual elements of consciousness and showing how they can be combined and integrated.

Functionalism is a school of psychology focused on how organisms use their learning and perceptual abilities to function in their environment.

times to demonstrate that the first set of results was not due to chance.

If your results do not support your hypothesis, you should consider whether there is another possible explanation for your observations and construct a new hypothesis. Maybe your brothers' aggression results from playing a lot of contact sports. Maybe your sister is studying Buddhism and has adopted some of the

religion's nonviolent beliefs. Scientists continually refine their hypotheses until they are satisfied that their theories can be tested and proven.

6 **Report your results.** Whether or not the results of your experiment support your hypothesis, it is important to share your results by making them available to others. Other researchers may be able to use your findings to learn from your mistakes, refine your hypothesis, or attempt to replicate your experiment to add support to your research. Once a research paper has been established as credible, researchers may use it to predict behavior based on the findings or use the results of the findings to modify or control behavior. Published research also becomes the background information that is read by others who are formulating and refining their own hypotheses, as described in step 2. Let's say that your research suggests that men do behave more aggressively than women in stressful situations. Other researchers may wonder whether this particular situation provokes a unique response in men and women, or whether other types of stress might have different effects.

The scientific method is not a hard and fast rulebook for every type of psychological study. For example, some studies collect data via observation rather than experimentation, and they follow different empirical procedures. These are discussed in detail in Chapter 2.

THE IMPORTANCE OF CRITICAL THINKING

It's important to approach scientific claims with an open but skeptical mind. "Where's the evidence?" is often the first question on the lips of someone adept at **critical thinking**—a way of processing information in which we examine assumptions, evaluate evidence, look for hidden agendas, and assess conclusions. Ask yourself whether the author had a motive for making a particular claim. Did he or she use reliable evidence to prove his or her theory? Might there be alternative explanations for the author's results? You may have personally experienced the same findings as the author of a particular paper (for example, a study claiming that the middle child in a family is more sociable than the eldest child may accurately reflect your own family), but it is important not to allow your personal experiences to increase the legitimacy of the results. A thorough examination of the author's use of the scientific process is required to determine whether the research is reliable.

Critical inquiry also requires a degree of humility: Scientists need to be able to reject their own theories and open their minds to unlikely findings. Imagine if fellow scientists had persistently rejected Copernicus's heliocentric theory because it was common knowledge that the Earth was the center of the universe and the mere suggestion that things could be any other way was preposterous. The use of critical inquiry has convincingly discredited more recent assumptions, including the idea that opposites attract (Rosenbaum, 1986) and the notion that people who talk in their sleep are verbalizing their dreams (Mahowald & Ettinger, 1990).

Do you believe everything you read? Critical thinkers evaluate and assess information with a degree of skepticism.

The History of Psychology

PRESCIENTIFIC PSYCHOLOGY

In the fifth century BC, Greek philosophers began to speculate about how the mind works and how it might affect behavior. Socrates (470–399 BC) and Plato (428–347 BC) believed that the mind did not cease to exist when the body died, and that thoughts and ideas could exist separately from the body, a concept known as **dualism.** They theorized that knowledge is built within us and that we gain access to it through logical reasoning.

Although Socrates and Plato's beliefs were developed nearly 2,500 years ago, it was not until the Scientific Revolution of the late Renaissance period that French philosopher René Descartes (1596–1650), a believer of Socrates' idea that mind is distinct from body, began to investigate how the two might be connected. By dissecting the brains of animals, Descartes concluded that the pineal gland at the base of the brain was the principal seat of the soul, where all thoughts were formed. He believed that the soul flowed through the body through hollow tubes and controlled muscle movement. Although anyone who still subscribes to Descartes' beliefs about the soul would probably fail a biology exam, the hollow tubes that Descartes noted were, among other things, important for controlling reflexes: We now know them as nerves.

Not all 17th century philosophers agreed with the theories of Socrates and Plato. British philosopher John Locke (1632–1704) believed that at birth, the human mind is a *tabula rasa*, a "blank slate," containing no innate knowledge. Locke proposed that people gain knowledge through their experiences by means of observation, laying the foundations for later studies in sensation and perception. His theory that knowledge is gained through careful external and internal observation planted the early seeds of empiricism and contributed to the development of the scientific method.

FOUNDATIONS OF SCIENTIFIC PSYCHOLOGY

Most psychologists agree that the birth of modern psychology occurred in a laboratory in Germany in 1879. The founder of the laboratory, Wilhelm Wundt (1832–1920), argued that the mind could be examined both scientifically and objectively, and he invited students from around the world to learn how to study the structure of the human mind. This was the first time anyone had attempted to incorporate objectivity and measurement into the field of psychology, earning Wundt the moniker "father of psychology." His lectures gained popularity throughout the 1880s, and before long, the new science of psychology had evolved into two early schools of thought: structuralism and functionalism.

> **Wundt's lectures gained popularity throughout the 1880s, and before long, the new science of psychology had evolved into two early schools of thought: structuralism and functionalism.**

Structuralism and Functionalism

One of Wundt's students, Edward Titchener (1867–1927), believed that experiences could be broken down into individual emotions and sensations, much as a chemist or a physician might analyze matter in terms of molecules and atoms. His school of thought, which focused on identifying individual elements of consciousness and showing how they could be combined and integrated, became known as **structuralism**. Titchener's approach was to engage people in introspection, or "looking inward," training them to report various elements of their experiences as they patted a dog, thought about the color blue, or smelled a flower. Introspection and structuralism were short-lived concepts, dying out in the early 1900s. Although they had little long-term effect on psychological science, the study of sensation and perception is still an important part of contemporary psychology (see Chapter 5).

Unlike Wundt and Titchener, American academic William James (1842–1910) believed that to break consciousness into individual elements was an act of impossibility. He saw consciousness as a continuing stream of ever-changing thoughts that could not be separated. Instead, James focused on how organisms use their learning and perceptual abilities to function in their environment, an approach that came to be known as **functionalism**. Influenced by Darwin's theories of evolution, James speculated that thinking developed because it is adaptive. He believed that useful behavioral traits (in addition to physical traits) could be passed from generation to generation.

Although functionalism is no longer a major perspective in psychology, elements of functionalist thought can still be seen in educational psychology and organizational psychology. For example, by emphasizing individual differences, functionalism influenced the theory that children

complex, or accused someone of using humor as a *defense mechanism*? If so, you can thank Freud for these terms and the psychological theories behind them.

An Austrian medical doctor who specialized in disorders of the nervous system, Freud believed that human beings are motivated by primitive sexual drives, forbidden desires, and traumatic childhood memories unavailable to the conscious mind. According to Freud, these repressed urges constantly impinge upon the conscious mind, expressing themselves through dreams, through slips of the tongue (now known as Freudian slips), or as symptoms of psychological disorders.

Freud's theories, which formulated the **psychodynamic approach** to psychology, were highly controversial. Many of his Victorian contemporaries were shocked, both by his focus on sexuality and by the implication that people are not always in control of their actions. However, Freud's theories were held in

ism faced similar challenges because they both involved the study of consciousness—internal processes that could not be measured or validated. John B. Watson (1878–1958), however, wanted to make scientific inquiry a primary focus in psychology. In the 1900s, he developed the **behavioral approach** to psychology, which concentrates on observable behavior that can be directly measured and recorded.

Watson's ideas were based on the work of Russian physiologist Ivan Pavlov, who showed that a reflex (an involuntary action) such as salivation could be trained (conditioned) to occur in response to a formerly unrelated stimulus, such as a ringing bell. Whereas Freud believed that behavior stemmed from unconscious motivation, Watson used Pavlov's research to argue that behavior can be learned. Watson and his colleague, Rosalie Rayner, famously proved that fear could be conditioned by teaching an 11-month-old child to fear a white rat. By repeatedly pairing the appearance of the rat with a loud, scary noise, the child eventually associated the rat with the noise and cried whenever he saw the creature (Watson & Rayner, 1920). Given the questionable ethics of this study, it is unlikely that Watson's experiment will ever be repeated, though similar results have been obtained using less damaging forms of conditioning. The ethical factors to consider when designing and carrying out an experiment are discussed in detail in Chapter 2.

Throughout the mid-20th century, behaviorism gained momentum through the work of B. F. Skinner, who supported Watson's idea of learning through conditioning. Skinner believed that behavior could be altered through reinforcement—rewarding or punishing a learner when he or she engages in a particular behavior. The ways in which Watson and Skinner influenced contemporary psychological approaches are discussed in Chapter 7.

should be taught at the level for which they, as individuals, are developmentally prepared.

Gestalt Psychology

In Germany, psychologists were also objecting to structuralism, albeit for different reasons. Max Wertheimer (1880–1943) believed that the acts of sensing and perceiving could not be broken into smaller elements and still be understood. When people look at a house, Wertheimer reasoned, they see a house, not a collection of doors, walls, and windows. Wertheimer and his colleagues believed that the act of perception entails more than just the sum of its parts. Their ideas developed into a school of thought known as **Gestalt psychology**. Roughly translated, *gestalt* means "whole" or "form." Gestalt psychologists believed that people naturally seek out patterns, or wholes, in the sensory information available to them. (See Chapter 5 for more information about Gestalt psychology.)

Psychodynamic Theory

If one of the hallmarks of fame is to have one's favorite terms and catchphrases become part of our everyday lexicon, then Sigmund Freud (1856–1939) has achieved the height of posthumous celebrity in the world of psychology. Have you ever described someone as *anal,* discussed the *Oedipus*

> "Freud believed that human beings are motivated by primitive sexual drives, forbidden desires, and traumatic childhood memories unavailable to the conscious mind. According to Freud, these repressed urges constantly impinge upon the conscious mind, expressing themselves through dreams, through slips of the tongue (now known as Freudian slips), or as symptoms of psychological disorders."

high regard and inspired many well-known researchers, including Swiss psychologist Carl Jung and Freud's daughter Anna Freud, to continue his work. Freud's ideas formed the basis of modern psychotherapy, the development of which is discussed in Chapter 16.

Behaviorism

One disadvantage of psychoanalytic theory is that it is difficult to test scientifically. For example, it is all but impossible to prove that a grown woman has relationship problems because she unconsciously resents her father for not being around when she was a child. The theories of structuralism and functional-

Humanistic Psychology

In the first half of the 20th century, psychoanalysis and behaviorism were the two primary approaches to psychology. However, neither of them put forth the suggestion that individuals have significant control over their own destinies. Behaviorists maintained that people's actions were learned responses to various stimuli, while psychoanalysts claimed that people were influenced by their unconscious desires.

In the 1950s, a new psychological perspective emerged. This perspective emphasized the importance of self-esteem, self-expression, and reaching one's potential. Supporters of the **humanistic approach**, as it came to be known, believed that people have free will and are able to control their own destinies. Two founding theorists of the humanistic approach were Abraham Maslow (1908–1970), who studied motivation and emotion, and Carl Rogers (1902–1987), who made significant contributions to the study of personality and the practice of psychotherapy. Maslow believed that people should strive for self-actualization—the achievement of one's full potential.

Although the humanistic approach has had a pervasive effect in many disciplines, critics argue that it can come across as vague and naively optimistic. Chapter 16 provides an in-depth discussion of the facets of humanistic theory.

Cognitive Psychology

By the 1960s, developments in linguistics, neurobiology, and computer science were providing new insight into the workings of the human mind. The development of computers, in particular, stimulated an interest in studying thought processes. Pioneers in the field of **cognitive psychology** focused on the workings of the human brain and sought to understand how we process the information that we collect from our environments.

Focusing on memory, perception, learning, intelligence, language, and problem solving, cognitive psychologists expanded the definition of psychology to incorporate the study of specific mental processes into the more general concept of behavior. Developments in brain-imaging techniques have enabled cognitive psychologists to examine neurological processes that previously mystified scientists, such as how we store memories or how damage to particular areas of the brain increases the likelihood of specific mental disorders. In a relatively short period of time, the cognitive perspective has become one of the most rapidly advancing perspectives in modern psychology.

Statistically, you are more likely to be killed in a jumbo jet crash than as a result of a snake bite, but our evolutionary instincts have yet to catch up with our natural phobias.

Evolutionary Psychology

Why are people commonly afraid of snakes and spiders but not of cars or trains? It's generally believed that through the evolutionary process, our ancestors developed a healthy fear of things that might harm them (Seligman, 1971). Whereas fearless warriors who took on rattlesnakes with their bare hands probably didn't make it very far along the evolutionary ladder, those with more cautious approaches toward reptiles tended to survive, passing on their genes and eventually producing an entire population of people who naturally fear snakes. Since cars and trains have not been around for long enough to pass on a fear of crashes, we are not yet genetically predisposed to fear them.

Based on Darwin's theory of natural selection, the **evolutionary approach** to psychology explores ways in which patterns of human behavior may be beneficial to our survival. Evolutionary psychologists study issues such as parenting, sexual attraction, and violence among different species and cultures to explain how people might be genetically pre-programmed to behave in a certain way. For example, a recent study indicates that men with a gene variant called "allele 334" may find it more difficult to remain monogamous than men without the allele (Walum et al., 2008). Researchers have long speculated that the stereotype of the male philanderer developed as a result of gender differences between the sexes, and evolutionary psychologists might argue that while women require consistent, stable relationships because they spend more time nurturing children, it is evolutionary beneficial for men to father as many children as possible.

Over the years, the field of psychology has grown as scientists discover new and valuable ways of examining thoughts, actions, and behaviors. Today, psychologists use all of the approaches mentioned here—and more—to study the workings of the human mind. Some psychological perspectives may seem to contradict each other, and there's no consensus in the psychological community about which approach is the "right" approach. Rather, each of the many diverse approaches to psychology sheds new light on the fundamental questions of the field: Why do we act the way we do? What really goes on in our minds? Each perspective offers its own answers to questions like these, and each perspective, in turn, raises new questions of its own.

Levels of Analysis

Choose any question or issue in psychology, and you will be able to look at it from a number of different angles. Philosophers observed a long time ago that a single issue can be examined at multiple **levels of analysis.** For example, let's say you are studying the effects of celebrity worship, as discussed in the beginning of the chapter. You might examine the phenomenon at the level of the brain (Do certain neurological structures contribute to intensity of fandom?), at the level of the person (How do people's beliefs and values change as a result of their media fascination?), or

at the level of the world (Does celebrity worship affect how some people interact with others around them?). Psychologist Stephen Kosslyn identified these three categories as the major levels of analysis, although there are many more angles from which to approach a particular psychological issue.

Sometimes, psychological issues are ideally suited to a particular level of analysis. For example, if you are studying personality, it makes sense to focus your study at the level of the person. How do individuals react in stressful situations? What gives people a sense of achievement? How stable are individual personalities? However, a comprehensive study should incorporate other levels of analysis. You might consider whether MRI scans have uncovered patterns that point to specific behavioral traits (the level of the brain), or you might study whether culture affects personality type (the level of the world). Many psychologists believe that it is only possible to understand events at one level of analysis if we take into account what is occurring at the other levels.

Nature vs. Nurture

Jeffrey was a happy, bubbly youngster who enjoyed riding his bike and playing with his pet dog, Frisky. Growing up in the 1960s, he had a stable family, with two loving parents and a younger brother. There was little in Jeffrey's upbringing to suggest that he should develop into anything other than a healthy, well-adjusted adult.

On July 22, 1991, Jeffrey Dahmer was arrested at his Milwaukee apartment. What police found inside was almost unspeakable. Gruesome photos of dismembered body parts, a severed head in the refrigerator, three more heads in the freezer—the list of atrocities went on and on. Further investigation revealed that Dahmer had killed 17 men and boys during a killing spree that went undetected for 13 years. Following a 160-page confession, Dahmer was sentenced to 15 consecutive life terms in prison. He was murdered in prison by a fellow inmate in 1994.

Levels Of Analysis

Level of Analysis	Causal Process Studied	Category
Neural	Brain	Biological
Genetic	Genes	
Evolutionary	Natural Selection	
Learning	Individual's prior experiences with the environment	Experiential
Cognitive	Individual's knowledge or beliefs	
Social	Influence of other people	
Cultural	Influence of the culture in which the individual develops	
Developmental	Age-related changes	

∧
∧ There are many different levels of analysis from which to examine a psychological issue.

The story of Jeffrey Dahmer underscores one of the biggest and most enduring issues faced by psychologists. Do our human traits develop through experience, or does a genetic blueprint determine who we will become? Are we primarily defined by **nature**—inherited characteristics that influence personality, physical growth, intellectual growth, and social interactions, or by **nurture**—environmental factors such as parental styles, physical surroundings, and economic issues? Although Dahmer was not subjected to the abuse or neglect that many serial killers experience during childhood, there were several incidents in his past that could have factored into his decline into sadism. A hernia operation at the age of six left him subdued and vulnerable, and he became increasingly isolated when his family moved to a new area. However, many people deal with far more traumatic childhood occurrences without resorting to murder. Was there something inherent in Dahmer's biological makeup that made his sadistic killing spree inevitable?

HISTORY OF THE NATURE-NURTURE DEBATE

The nature-nurture debate has been raging at least since the time of the ancient Greeks. Plato's beliefs—that knowledge is built within us and that character and intelligence are largely inherited—placed Plato firmly in the "nature" camp. Flying the "nurture" flag was Plato's student, Aristotle, who disagreed with his teacher and claimed that people acquire knowledge by observing the physical world and passing information into the mind via the senses. In the 1600s, Locke and Descartes reignited the debate, with Locke arguing that the mind is a blank slate waiting to be filled by experience, and Descartes countering that some ideas are innate.

When Darwin sailed around the world in 1831, he collected evidence that would lend support to Descartes' views. Darwin's theory of **natural selection**, outlined in his 1859 book, *The Origin of Species,* explained variation within species as the result of evolution. Nature selects features that best enable an organism to adapt to its environment, and these features are passed on to future generations. Darwin's ideas (discussed in Chapter 4) remain the fundamental principles of biology, and the concept that traits may be heritable has strongly influenced contemporary psychology.

After many years of scientific debate and research, most psychologists agree that

∧
∧ **Are National Spelling Bee contestants excellent
∧ spellers because of their genes, their environments, or both?**

we become the people we are through a unique combination of hereditary and environmental factors. It is almost impossible to think of a psychological issue that is exclusively dependent on nature or on nurture. However, the debate continues with regard to just how influential each factor may be. For example, the subject of intelligence is still a hot-button issue: To what extent is intelligence inherited, and to what extent is it learned? Some researchers assume that intelligence is primarily determined by genetic factors (Bouchard & Segal, 1985; Herrnstein & Murray, 1994; Jensen, 1969), while others believe that environmental factors such as culture, economics, childhood nutrition, and education have a stronger sway (Gardner et al., 1996, Rose et al., 1984; Wahlsten, 1997). Aspects of the nature-nurture debate may be addressed by considering multiple levels of analysis. For example, a psychologist studying intelligence levels might examine biological factors at the level of the brain by comparing MRI scans of the brains of people with different levels of intelligence. The psychologist may also examine environmental factors at

the level of the person by investigating people's educational histories and childhood environments.

The nature-nurture debate raises interesting questions for contemporary psychologists. Are people with mental illnesses predisposed to suffer particular conditions, or do stressful life events or other environmental factors trigger mental disorders? How do children learn language—through repetition and education, or via a preprogrammed mechanism that stimulates the development of grammar? The answers to one question in particular may have fascinating social implications: Can people change? Is there hope of rehabilitation for men like Jeffery Dahmer, or is a serial killer always a serial killer? Are men with the allele 334 gene variant destined to cheat on their wives, or can they overcome their natural urges? Could all Holocaust survivors have gone on to develop the mental fortitude and productivity displayed by author Elie Wiesel, or did something in Wiesel's biological makeup awaken in him a sense of determination rather than one of hopelessness? The nature-nurture debate rages on.

Types of Psychology

Based on the wide range of issues already mentioned in this chapter, you have probably figured out that the field of psychology is extremely diverse. The term *psychologist* describes everyone from the therapist listening to a client talking about his depression, to the researcher measuring how violent video games affect children's behavior, to the scientist examining the structure of a rat's brain. While these professions may seem unrelated, there is a glue that binds all psychologists together—an interest in human behaviors and the processes that influence them.

PSYCHOLOGICAL ORGANIZATIONS

Like most vocations, psychology has a number of professional bodies that promote specific interests and maintain standards within the industry. With 148,000 members, the American Psychological Association (APA) is the world's largest organization of professional psychologists. Founded in 1892, it aims to promote the interests of psychology both nationally and worldwide. The APA produces a number of books, research papers, and journals, including its official journal, *American Psychologist*. You may have written (or in the near future will write) papers using APA style, which is a formatting style commonly adopted in the social sciences.

Since the APA is primarily geared toward clinical psychology, several research-focused groups have formed their own organizations. The Association for Psychological Science (APS) specializes in scientific psychology. Founded in 1988, it has 20,000 members and produces science and research-based books and journals, including its flagship magazine, *Psychological Science*.

> **With an increasing demand for psychological services in schools, hospitals, social service agencies, mental health centers, and private companies, the employment prospects for a psychology graduate are high.**

The APA currently has 56 professional divisions, each specializing in a particular area of psychology. Examples of specific divisions include developmental psychology (the scientific study of education and child care) and health psychology (the understanding of health and illness through basic and clinical research). Members of each division receive regular newsletters providing them with information about upcoming conferences and interesting developments within their field of expertise.

CAREERS IN PSYCHOLOGY

With an increasing demand for psychological services in schools, hospitals, social service agencies, mental health centers, and private companies, the employment prospects for a psychology graduate are high. According to the Bureau of Labor Statistics, 166,000 psychologists were employed in 2006, and this employment rate is expected to rise 15 percent by 2016—faster than the average for all occupations. Job prospects are highest for people with a doctoral degree in an applied specialty, such as counseling or health, and for people with a specialist or doctoral degree in school psychology. The median salary of a clinical, counseling, or school psychologist in May 2006 was a very respectable $59,440, and if you relish the thought of making your own hours, there is even better news—about 34 percent of all psychologists are self-employed, compared to 8 percent of the rest of the working population.

Although the APA has 56 professional divisions, careers in psychology can be broadly divided into three main categories: clinical psychology, academic psychology, and applied psychology.

Clinical Psychology

Clinical psychologists diagnose and treat people with specific mental or behavioral problems, and the field of **clinical psychology** covers a wide variety of professions, ranging from mental health experts to family therapists. Clinical psychologists interview patients, give diagnostic tests, provide psychotherapy, and design and implement behavioral modification programs. Unlike psychiatrists, clinical psychologists are not medical doctors, and most do not have the ability to prescribe drugs. This is changing in some states; in 2002, specially trained and licensed psychologists in the state of New Mexico were granted the right to prescribe drugs, and psychologists in Louisiana are now permitted to write prescriptions after consulting with a psychiatrist.

Areas of specialization within clinical psychology include neuropsychology (studying the relationship between the brain and behavior), counseling (advising people on how to deal with problems of everyday living, such as career-related stress), social work (helping people resolve problems in their lives specifically related to poverty or oppression), psychiatric nursing (assessing mental

Employment Outcomes for Graduates with Psychology Degrees

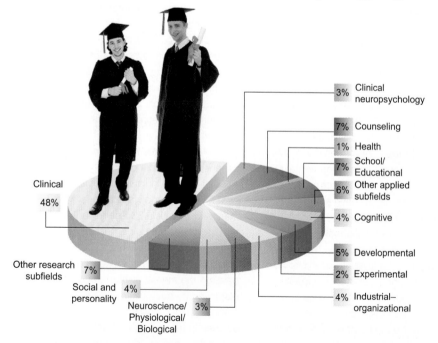

- 3% Clinical neuropsychology
- 7% Counseling
- 1% Health
- 7% School/Educational
- 6% Other applied subfields
- 4% Cognitive
- 5% Developmental
- 2% Experimental
- 4% Industrial–organizational
- Clinical 48%
- Other research subfields 7%
- Social and personality 4%
- Neuroscience/Physiological/Biological 3%

Source: 2005 Graduate Study in Psychology. Compiled by APA Center for Psychology Workforce Analysis and Research (CPWAR).

<<< This pie chart shows the specialty areas of psychologists who recently received their doctoral degrees.

health needs or diagnosing and treating people with mental disorders), and school psychology (addressing students' learning and behavioral problems). More psychology graduates gain employment in the field of clinical psychology than in any other subdiscipline.

Academic Psychology

Not all psychologists work directly with people who have mental or behavioral issues. If you talk to your psychology professors, you will probably learn that outside of the classroom, they each have specialty areas of interest in which they conduct research. **Academic psychologists** usually divide their time between supervising and teaching students, completing administrative tasks, and carrying out psychological research. The proportion of time that each psychologist devotes to each of these tasks depends on the nature of his or her academic institution; some academic psychologists spend the majority of their time teaching, while others, particularly at larger schools, devote more time to research. Teaching positions at universities are generally very competitive. According to a 1995 National Research Council survey of 3,200 graduates with PhDs, only 17.5 percent had firm teaching contracts, although 62 percent planned on an academic career.

Some areas of academic expertise include developmental psychology (the study of the social and mental development of human beings), cognitive psychology (the study of internal mental processes), abnormal psychology (the study of mental disorders and other abnormal thoughts and behaviors), personality psychology (the study of patterns of thought, feeling, and behavior that make a person unique), and social psychology (the study of group behavior and the influence of social factors on the individual). Academic psychologists who specialize in these and other areas often aim to publish their research in approved journals related to their field of study.

Applied Psychology

The term **applied psychology** refers to the use of psychological theory and practice to tackle real-world problems. For example, rather than simply examining whether there is a link between high stress levels and coronary heart disease, a health psychologist may work with patients at risk of coronary heart disease to reduce their stress levels. The field of applied psychology is not limited to any particular psychological discipline; it encompasses many different areas that share a common goal of using psychology in a practical form.

Imagine that you are an employer looking to select the best possible candidate for a position in your company. How can you guarantee that your interviewing strategies determine a person's true character? Once you have hired your new employee, how can you ensure that he or she thrives in a productive, enjoyable working environment? Industrial and organizational psychology is a form of applied psychology in which psychologists study behavior in the workplace and advise business owners based on their findings. An industrial/organizational (I/O) psychologist may conduct job analyses to determine candidates' suitability for a position, analyze fairness in employee compensation, use psychometric testing to assess employees' attitudes and morale, and train people to work more effectively in teams. Trends in the economic climate often play a vital part in determining the role of an I/O psychologist; in the current economic downturn, many are

> "Not all psychologists work directly with people who have mental or behavioral issues. If you talk to your psychology professors, you will probably learn that outside of the classroom, they each have specialty areas of interest in which they conduct research."

primarily involved with helping firms develop alternatives to employee downsizing or with managing layoffs in the most humane way possible.

Many businesses send their employees on annual team-building exercises to encourage bonding and teamwork in the office. Similar techniques are used in the rapidly growing field of sports psychology. If you were asked to name a film in which a new coach guides a poorly performing team to a seemingly impossible victory via a series of team-bonding exercises, you could probably rattle off several titles without trying very hard. Sports psychologists believe that it is not enough for athletes to train their bodies; athletes also need to have a healthy mindset in order to succeed. Techniques to help athletes achieve this mindset include setting clear short-term goals, holding positive thoughts,

using relaxation techniques, and visualizing a desired outcome, whether it be sinking a free throw or winning a race. If you're an athlete aiming for excellence, you might consider consulting a sports psychologist: Tiger Woods, perhaps the greatest golfer of all time, has been consulting one since age 13.

Although I/O psychology and sports psychology provide excellent examples of "real-world" psychology, applied psychology is useful in areas other than athletics and business, too. In fact, any subfield of psychology that has been mentioned in this chapter can be applied to real-world situations in some way. A personality psychologist may be consulted on the selection of a jury, for example, or an environmental psychologist might advise a town planning board. Contrary to the popular stereotype of a psychologist analyzing a patient on a couch, there are numerous industries to which psychologists can contribute their knowledge and insight.

∧
∧ Why might an I/O psychologist recommend that business employees participate in team-building activities together?

Chapter Summary

WHAT IS PSYCHOLOGY AND WHY DOES IT FASCINATE US? p. 4

- Psychology is the scientific study of behavior and mental processes.

- We study psychology in response to a fundamental curiosity about ourselves and our world.

HOW IS THE SCIENTIFIC METHOD USED TO STUDY PSYCHOLOGY? p. 4

- Scientists aim to reduce error and bias in their psychological studies by employing the principles of empiricism and the scientific method.

- The six steps of the scientific method that psychologists generally follow are identifying the problem, conducting background research, formulating a hypothesis, testing the hypothesis, analyzing the results, and reporting the results.

WHAT IS THE HISTORY OF PSYCHOLOGY? p. 7

- The Greek philosophers Socrates and Plato believed that knowledge is built within us, whereas John Locke (1632–1704) believed that the human mind is a blank slate at birth.

- William Wundt, the "father of psychology," set up his laboratory in 1879. His student, Edward Titchener, founded structuralism.

William James proposed functionalism, and Max Wertheimer put forth the concept of Gestalt psychology.
- Modern approaches to psychology include Freud's psychodynamic theory, behaviorism, the humanistic approach, cognitive psychology, and evolutionary psychology.

WHAT MAJOR QUESTIONS DO PSYCHOLOGISTS SEEK TO ANSWER? p. 11

- The question of whether our traits, behaviors, and mental processes are primarily the result of inherited characteristics (nature) or environmental factors (nurture) has been, and continues to be, a controversial topic in psychology.

- Most psychologists agree that humans are influenced by a unique combination of hereditary and environmental factors

WHAT ARE SOME DIFFERENT SUBTYPES OF PSYCHOLOGY? p. 12

- Clinical psychologists diagnose and treat people with mental or behavioral problems, while academic psychologists teach and carry out psychological research.

- Applied psychology refers to the use of psychological theory and practice to tackle real-world problems. Industrial organizational psychologists and sports psychologists are examples of people who use applied psychology day-to-day.

Test Your Understanding

1. Ashley is using the scientific method to test whether male children are more violent than female children. What will she most likely do first?

   a. research previous scientific studies about children, gender roles, and violence

   b. formulate a hypothesis stating that young males are more violent than young females

   c. select five male children and five female children and monitor their reaction to a violent video game

   d. perform statistical analysis to determine whether male children are more violent than female children

2. Which philosopher believed that the mind contains no innate knowledge?

   a. Socrates

   b. Plato

   c. Locke

   d. Descartes

3. Which of the following is a disadvantage of psychodynamic theory?

   a. It treats humans as mechanistic.

   b. It is considered naively optimistic.

   c. It is difficult to test scientifically.

   d. It does not emphasize individual differences.

4. Kyle wants to improve his class's attention span. Every week, he monitors which student works consistently for the longest period of time and rewards that student with a treat. Kyle is using:

   a. a humanistic approach.

   b. a cognitive approach.

   c. an evolutionary approach.

   d. a behavioral approach.

5. Which of the following statements would William Wundt most likely have agreed with?

   a. The mind can be studied scientifically.

   b. Advantageous behavioral traits can be inherited.

   c. At birth, the human mind is a blank slate.

   d. Repressed urges affect the conscious mind.

6. Leah is researching whether women smile more often than men. Having researched her topic and formed a hypothesis, she observes her female colleagues at work. She then meets her male friends for a drink after work and records their facial movements. What is the biggest problem with Leah's experiment?

   a. Her study has already been done before.

   b. She is changing more than one variable.

c. The hypothesis is too broad for one experiment.

d. She needs a second researcher to record the results.

7. Sigmund Freud believed that:

a. people control their own destinies.

b. consciousness cannot be measured.

c. people seek patterns in sensory information.

d. repressed urges affect the conscious mind.

8. Which approach to psychology has advanced rapidly in recent years due to improvements in brain-imaging techniques?

a. humanistic psychology

b. cognitive psychology

c. evolutionary psychology

d. Gestalt psychology

9. Raul is investigating the thought patterns of people afflicted with bipolar disorder. Which of the following represents a question Raul might ask at the level of the world?

a. How do a bipolar patient's thought patterns vary over the course of the day?

b. How are bipolar thought patterns reflected in brain activity?

c. How do a patient's thought patterns vary in response to different stimuli?

d. How do bipolar thought patterns vary across cultures?

10. Which of the following supports the "nurture" side of the nature vs. nurture debate?

a. Plato's ideas about intelligence

b. Darwin's theory of natural selection

c. Descartes' theory of knowledge

d. Aristotle's ideas about knowledge

11. Which of the following arguments is most likely based on ideas from the "nature" side of the nature vs. nurture debate?

a. Traumatic events during childhood can cause mental problems later in life.

b. Regularly practicing mental agility exercises can help to improve one's memory.

c. A person who is predisposed to have a mental illness is virtually guaranteed to develop that illness.

d. Children who perform poorly at failing schools will improve their performance if they are able to transfer to a more successful school.

12. Which of the following is true of the American Psychological Association (APA)?

a. It is geared toward psychological research.

b. It produces the journal *Psychological Science.*

c. It focuses primarily on developmental psychology.

d. It is the world's largest organization of professional psychologists.

13. Jenny is a firm believer in the ideas of Sigmund Freud, while Tom believes in the theories put forward by John B. Watson. Which of the following statements best summarizes their differences?

a. Jenny thinks that behavior stems from unconscious motivation, whereas Tom thinks that behavior can be learned.

b. Jenny thinks that behavior can be learned, whereas Tom thinks that behavior stems from unconscious motivation.

c. Jenny thinks that people should strive for self-actualization, whereas Tom thinks that people are not in control of their destinies.

d. Jenny thinks that people are not in control of their destinies, whereas Tom thinks that people should strive for self-actualization.

14. Psychiatric nurses and school psychologists are specialists within the field of:

a. academic psychology.

b. research psychology.

c. developmental psychology.

d. clinical psychology.

15. Mark, a professor of psychology, focuses much of his research on the study of group behavior and influence of social factors on the individual. Mark's academic specialty is:

a. cognitive psychology.

b. personality psychology.

c. social psychology.

16. Which of the following is NOT an example of applied psychology?

a. A health psychologist researches a potential link between depression and brain tumors.

b. A personality psychologist assists a prosecutor with the jury selection process for a trial.

c. An I/O psychologist performs individual assessments to determine whether candidates are suitable for a position.

d. A clinical psychologist teaches a patient to use breathing exercises to calm his anxiety.

17. Which of the following is an example of critical thinking?

a. researching facts about a topic

b. copying a previous experiment

c. accurately measuring and recording results

d. questioning a researcher's motive for making a claim

18. Which of these is NOT a role of a clinical psychologist?

a. interviewing patients

b. giving diagnostic tests

c. providing psychotherapy

d. carrying out psychological research

19. Which of the following statements is true about the nature-nurture debate?

a. Most psychologists agree that nature is more influential than nurture.

b. Most psychologists agree that nurture is more influential than nature.

c. Most psychologists agree that both nature and nurture are influential, but disagree on the extent of their influence.

d. Most psychologists agree that the nature-nurture debate was resolved when Darwin developed his theory of evolution.

20. Gemma is interested in studying the relationship between the brain and behavior. In which area of psychology should she aim to specialize?

a. neuropsychology

b. abnormal psychology

c. personality psychology

d. psychiatric nursing

Remember to check www.thethinkspot.com **for additional information, downloadable flashcards, and other helpful resources.**

Answers: 1) a; 2) c; 3) c; 4) d; 5) a; 6) b; 7) d; 8) b; 9) d; 10) d; 11) c; 12) d; 13) a; 14) d; 15) c; 16) a; 17) d; 18) d; 19) c; 20) a

RESEARCH
METHODS

WHY ARE RESEARCH METHODS IM
TO THE STUDY OF PSYCHOLOGY?

WHAT ARE SOME TYPES OF RESEARC
STRATEGIES?

HOW CAN STATISTICAL METHODS HE
GATHER AND ANALYZE DATA?

HOW CAN WE MINIMIZE BIAS?

WHAT ETHICAL ISSUES DO PSYCHOL
FACE?

When

American soldiers were accused of abusing Iraqi prisoners at Iraq's infamous Abu Ghraib prison in 2004, many people assumed that a "few bad apples" in the military were responsible for the shocking acts of torture and maltreatment. But the soldiers' claims that they were "just following orders" rang alarm bells among social psychologists familiar with the work of Stanley Milgram.

In the 1960s, Milgram, a professor at Yale University, conducted a series of experiments designed to test people's conformity to an authority figure. A research subject was told to act as a "teacher," presenting a series of questions to another person in the room: the "learner." Whenever the learner gave a wrong answer, the teacher was to administer an electric shock. The experimenter demanded that the teacher increase the intensity of the shock by 15 volts for every successive wrong answer, culminating in a 450-volt shock that was clearly marked on the machine as "XXX." As the voltage increased, the learner responded with loud screams of pain and begged to be let out of the room. If the subject questioned the experiment or tried to quit, the experimenter ordered him or her to continue.

Milgram's experiment was rigged: The learner was an actor, and no shocks were delivered. The true purpose of the experiment was to see how high a voltage subjects were willing to deliver. Milgram found that 65 percent of people were willing to render shock levels of 450 volts—a potentially lethal dose (though inflicting the shocks often caused them extreme discomfort). Race, class, and gender had no effect on the rate of compliance; given the right set of circumstances, people were willing to inflict pain on others purely because they were told to do so.

Milgram's experiments provided a fascinating insight into the darkest depths of the human mind and shed light on the behaviors of ordinary Germans during the Holocaust. However, the methods that he and other notable psychologists used before stringent American Psychological Association (APA) guidelines were imposed caused visible stress to participants, creating an ethical conundrum: How can psychologists study natural human impulses without the use of deception? Or if deception is used in a psychological study, how can psychologists ensure that it does not cause undue mental stress to participants? Under the current APA Ethical Principles of Psychologists and Code of Conduct, researchers must avoid the use of deception when research might reasonably be expected to cause physical harm or emotional distress.

In 2007, psychologist Jerry Burger managed to replicate Milgram's experiment within APA guidelines by stopping the procedure at 150 volts, carefully screening participants for any potential negative psychological reactions, reiterating that participants could withdraw from the study at any time, and immediately debriefing subjects at the end of the experiment. Burger's results were consistent with those recorded by Milgram nearly half a century earlier, and participants suffered no ill effects, proving that ethical research methods can achieve effective results without potentially damaging consequences.

<<< Milgram's studies demonstrated the power of human obedience. If ordered to, would ordinary citizens also perform forms of torture such as waterboarding or physical violence?

CHAPTER

Research Methods in Psychology

Because the study of psychology is scientific, it requires careful methods of observation and data collection. To answer questions about human behavior, we need to collect and analyze data as systematically and objectively as possible. Before psychologists perform a research study, they must first ask themselves several questions:

WHAT research strategies should I use to test my idea?

HOW can I guarantee that I obtain objective results?

HOW can I use statistics to analyze my results?

HOW can I ensure that people participating in my study are treated fairly?

WHY DO WE NEED SCIENTIFIC METHODS?

Hindsight Bias

Have you ever been described as a "Monday morning quarterback"? On Monday morning, it's easy to boast about how you would have played Sunday night's game differently. The other team's plays were so predictable that anyone should have been able to guess them easily! If you

find yourself making this claim, you're probably experiencing **hindsight bias**, or the belief that you knew something all along. Some observations made in hindsight seem so obvious that they are often mistaken for common sense. The risk of distributing numerous subprime mortgages seems obvious in hindsight, but didn't before the 2008 economic recession. Hindsight bias encourages us to see the world as more predictable than it actually is. That's one reason why scientists need to use sound research methods: Even psychologists can be susceptible to hindsight bias, and their biased preconceptions or interpretations of results can seriously hinder their research. Luckily, the scientific method can minimize the effect of that bias.

False Consensus Effect

Another pitfall for psychologists (and other humans) is the **false consensus effect** (Ross et al., 1977), or the tendency to overestimate the extent to which others share our beliefs and behaviors. Let's say you like to spend your free time chatting with like-minded friends on a political blog. It might seem to you and your fellow bloggers that your candidate of choice is practically guaranteed to win—after all, everyone supports him! Who wouldn't? Anyone with an ounce of common sense would agree with you that he's the best politician for the job. Or so it seems to you. However, it probably doesn't seem that way to your candidate's opponent or her supporters. In this case, your participation in the blogosphere, which in truth samples only a small portion of a self-selected population, has contributed to an occurrence of the false consensus effect. To minimize this type of problem—and avoid prejudice and bias—researchers try to gather a representative sample of people for their studies. Milgram found that variations in gender, class, and race made no difference in people's willingness to comply with authorized torture. How might his conclusions have differed if he'd only studied teenage males?

Critical Thinking

It's essential to think critically when carrying out scientific research. In other words, we need to examine our assumptions and

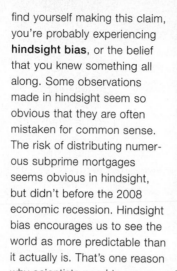

> ∧ ∧ ∧ **Economists debate whether the recent plunges in the stock market were foreseeable, while politicians are quick to point fingers at opposing party members for not taking the necessary preventive measures. Placing retrospective blame is a prime example of the dangers of hindsight bias.**

challenge our gut instincts rather than relying solely on intuition and common sense, which are sometimes proved to be wrong. Good researchers do not blindly accept theories, no matter how obvious they might seem—they use scientific methods to question and examine those theories.

EMPIRICISM

Empiricism is the belief that human knowledge is achieved through experience. Empiricists believe that we must observe the world in order to gain information about it. The birth of this philosophy marked a shift from **dogmatism**, a belief that requires people to accept information as irrefutable and refrain from questioning authority. Empiricism gained credibility during the experimental science age of the 18th and 19th centuries, when it laid the basis for contemporary scientific research.

Hindsight bias describes a person's erroneous belief that he or she knew something all along after an event has occurred.

False consensus effect describes a person's tendency to overestimate the extent to which others share his or her beliefs and behaviors.

Dogmatism describes a belief that requires people to accept information as irrefutable and to refrain from questioning authority.

Methods are rules or techniques that provide a framework for our observations.

Facts are objective statements made using direct observations.

Theories are ideas that help explain existing facts.

Hypotheses are predictions about new facts, based on existing theories.

Limitations of Empiricism

Empiricism does not guarantee that the information we acquire is completely accurate. Scientific studies are fallible and open to misinterpretation. To reduce the possibility of errors while conducting empirical research, it is important to have a **method**. Methods are rules or techniques that provide a framework for our observations. They enable us to avoid the types of mistakes we might make through simply observing our subjects. When Stanley Milgram conducted his famous study, he made sure to walk each volunteer through the exact same steps. The researcher's dialogue was scripted, as were the learner's cries of pain—for each shock level, the actor had a specific line to say. This ensured that every participant had the same experience, promoting empiricism and minimizing the potential for bias. By using a set method, Milgram made sure that his experiment contained as few errors as possible.

Empirical Challenges of Studying People

No matter how carefully we research our theory, or how closely we stick to our method, studying people is challenging. Why?

1 **People are complex.** We are not just a collection of cells that can be cultivated in a Petri dish and examined under a microscope. People have thoughts and feelings that affect their behavior.

2 **People are different.** The extent to which we vary from our fellow humans makes it hard for psychologists to make generalizations about our behavior.

3 **People react to situations differently.** We can't be pigeonholed into categories easily because our reactions might change from one day to the next.

THE STORY OF CLEVER HANS

Clever Hans was an Arabian stallion purchased in 1888 by German math teacher Wilhelm von Osten. Von Osten believed that, given the proper education, horses had the potential to be as intelligent as humans. He began to tutor Hans in simple arithmetic. Hans was taught to spell words by tapping his hooves to signify certain letters. He could also answer "yes or no" questions by moving his head up and down or back and forth. After four years of private tutoring, Hans could answer addition questions, figure out simple square root problems, and even tell time. Many professionals were astounded by Hans's apparent intelligence.

^
^
With results gleaned from earlier studies, scientists can formulate new facts, theories, and hypotheses and perpetuate the cycle of science.

FACT
Hans is correctly responding to basic arithmetic questions.

THEORY
Maybe Hans is taking clues from people around him.

Scientific Method

I predict that Hans will be unable to answer questions without visual aids.

HYPOTHESIS

FACT
Hans is unable to correctly respond to questions without visual aids.

I will take away visual clues from Hans to test his abilities.

STUDY

Hans's undoing came about as the result of an investigation by psychologist Oskar Pfungst. Pfungst believed that Hans was able to answer questions by responding to visual signals from his questioner. He began to test Hans by holding up numbered flashcards that Hans used for counting. First, von Osten was allowed to see the numbers on the flashcards before showing them to Hans. As usual, Hans tapped out the correct numbers with his hooves. Then, Pfungst asked von Osten to show Hans the cards without looking at them first. Hans was stumped. Pfungst began to study von Osten instead, and he noticed that von Osten made subtle unconscious gestures that cued Hans's correct responses. As Hans neared the correct number of hoof taps, von Osten would change his posture without realizing it. Hans was certainly clever, but his math skills left something to be desired.

Facts, Theories, and Hypotheses

The story of Hans demonstrates how **facts, theories,** and **hypotheses** function in scientific research.

Facts are objective statements made using direct observations. Theories are ideas that help explain existing facts. Hypotheses, based on existing theories, are predictions about new facts.

Researchers use operational definitions of concepts to allow others to replicate their findings. In other words, they give a clear definition of their research methods so that other people can conduct the exact same experiment as precisely as possible. If many different researchers come up with the same results, those results are more likely to be reliable.

What Can We Learn from Hans?

Clever Hans may not have been a stellar mathematician, but his story illustrates three important lessons of scientific research:

1 **Be skeptical.** Consider alternative explanations for what you are observing. Not all popular claims are accurate—if they were, we'd be living on a flat planet surrounded by vicious sea monsters. It is important to try to disprove theories, including your own. As Aristotle once said, "It is the mark of an educated mind to be able to entertain a thought without accepting it."

2 **Observe carefully in controlled conditions.** Pay close attention during your study. Pfungst was the first professional to notice the unconscious signals von Osten was giving Hans. Less observant researchers were ready to sign the horse up for ninth-grade math. Researchers need to control conditions so that only one factor varies at a time. The only thing that changed between Hans's first counting session with Pfungst and his second was von Osten's knowledge of what was written on the flashcards. This level of control made it easy for Pfungst to pinpoint the source of Hans's cleverness.

3 **Be aware of observer-expectancy effects.** Watch out for researchers or observers who inadvertently communicate their expectations to participants and affect their behavior as a result. Researchers must be careful when recruiting subjects as well—an improperly worded ad in the local newspaper or a campus announcement bearing value-laden statements can potentially bias the participants of an experiment.

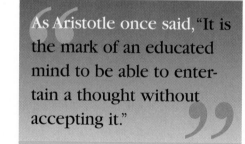

As Aristotle once said, "It is the mark of an educated mind to be able to entertain a thought without accepting it."

RESEARCH DESIGN: THE EXPERIMENT

Why do some people commit crimes? Why are teenagers often moody? Why do people sometimes become aggressive when they drink alcohol? Why do smart people sometimes do irrational things? The most conclusive way to test a hypothesis about human behavior is to conduct an experiment. In an experiment, a researcher can manipulate one **variable**—a characteristic that can vary, such as age, weight, or height—while all other variables remain constant. This makes it possible to see how the variable that is manipulated affects an aspect of behavior.

In 1956, Solomon Asch devised a series of simple experiments to test conformity among groups of people. He drew a standard line and asked his **participants** to determine which of three other lines it matched in length. Line C was clearly the correct response, but Asch wanted to see if people would give the correct answer under group pressure. He developed two conditions: In the first, he asked participants to answer the questions about line length alone. In the second, he put participants in groups with several **confederates,** people he'd previously instructed to give unanimous (and often incorrect) answers about the length of each line. The confederates served as the **independent variable,** or the variable that the researcher can manipulate: Their presence was the one factor that differed between the two conditions. The **dependent variable,** or the measurable response to the independent variable, was the number of correct

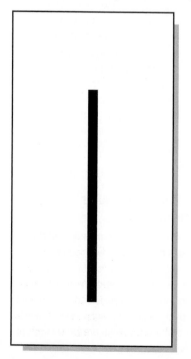

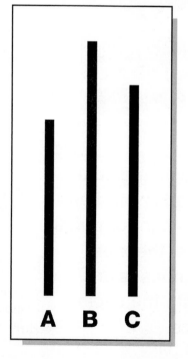

<<< This image is an example of the stimuli used in Asch's conformity experiments. Participants were asked to match the length of the standard line on the left to the length of line A, B, or C on the right.

responses that the participants gave. Asch discovered that when asked to identify matching lines individually, participants gave the correct response nearly 100 percent of the time. However, when placed in a group of confederates who all swore that line C was the correct answer even though it was clearly wrong, participants conformed to group pressure and gave incorrect responses more than one-third of the time.

Random Assignment

In some studies, each participant is exposed to several different independent variables. These studies are called **within-subject experiments.** Other studies, known as **between-group experiments,** expose different groups of participants to different independent variables. For example, many experiments feature an **experimental group**, which is subject to the independent variable, and a **control group,** which either gets no treatment or is given treatment that should have no effect (or a different effect than that caused by the independent variable). In a drug study, for example, the experimental group receives real medication while the control group might receive sugar pills. It's important to make sure that there are no major differences between these groups that may bias the results. This is achieved by **random assignment:**

When participants are assigned randomly to one of two groups, it is likely that, given enough people, the two groups will be roughly equivalent in terms of the ages, genders, and other characteristics of their members. Any differences between groups are the result of chance, and researchers use statistics to take chance into account when they analyze the resulting data.

RESEARCH DESIGN: THE CORRELATIONAL STUDY

In a correlational study, a researcher does not manipulate variables, but instead observes whether there is a relationship between variables. Correlational studies allow us to make predictions about one variable based on the knowledge of another. However, while good experimental studies can suggest cause and effect rela-

> **When participants are assigned randomly to one of two groups, it is likely that, given enough people, the two groups will be roughly equivalent in terms of the ages, genders, and other characteristics of their members. Any differences between groups are the result of chance, and researchers use statistics to take chance into account when they analyze the resulting data.**

Design an experiment
What do we want to find out?
What process can we use to get that information?

Select participants

Control group

Experimental group

Perform experiment
Independent variable is absent

Perform experiment
Independent variable is present

Collect data

Analyze data
What do our results mean?
Do we need to perform further research?

tionships, correlational studies do not usually indicate cause and effect: Correlation does not equal causation. For example, a correlational study might show a link between academic success and high self-esteem, but doing well in school may not necessarily cause high self-esteem. You might observe that increased child mortality rates are related to increased ice cream consumption. So is ice cream deadly? Before you put down your ice cream cone,

notice that both of these variables are also related to another factor—summer. In the summer, children eat more ice cream than they do during the rest of the year, and they are also more likely to get into accidents. Although both ice cream consumption and child mortality rise during the summer, neither of these variables causes the other to change. The third variable is, in fact, the actual cause of both events.

To prevent this so-called third variable problem, a researcher might choose research participants through the use of **matched samples** or **matched pairs.** Matched samples are two or more groups of people that are identical in terms of a third variable. For example, in a study to determine whether academic success is linked to high self-esteem, a researcher might want to reduce the effect of a third variable, age. It wouldn't make sense to compare third graders to college students, for example, because these two groups are at such different points in their lives that it would be hard for researchers to control all of the different variables in play. In order to reduce the effect of age, the researcher would create matched samples by ensuring that both sample groups are composed of similarly aged participants. Matched pairs take this principle to the next level—they ensure that each participant in one group is the same as a participant in another group in terms of a third variable. The self-esteem researcher might match a 15-year-old in one group with a 15-year-old in another group to create a matched pair.

RESEARCH DESIGN: THE DESCRIPTIVE STUDY

A descriptive study enables researchers to observe and describe behaviors without investigating the relationship between specific variables. Researchers may or may not use statistics to help them analyze their observations. Some descriptive studies have a narrow focus, such as observing how children react to a new environment or studying how adult males deal with confrontation. Other studies have a broader focus, such as observing the habits of animals in the wild. Descriptive studies may involve observing subjects (in either a natural habitat or a laboratory), using case studies, or conducting surveys.

Naturalistic Observation

We use **naturalistic observation** every day when we watch busy shoppers hurrying around the mall or observe children playing in the park. Naturalistic observation is the study of people or animals in their own environment. It enables researchers to get a realistic picture of how their subjects behave. Naturalistic observation is the primary research tool employed by scientists behind the hit TV show *Meerkat Manor*, which highlights the real-life adventures of African meerkats, seeks to learn more about their behavior, and features a "plot" worthy of a daytime soap. (While *Meerkat Manor's* narration may bias viewers to interpret the meerkats' behavior as more human than it really is, scientists who conduct naturalistic observation try not

to project human characteristics onto the animals they're studying.)

One disadvantage of naturalistic observation is the possibility of **observer bias.** This occurs when the observer expects to see a particular behavior and notices only actions that support that theory. One way to avoid observer bias is to use **blind observers,** or people who do not know what the research is about. It is also advisable to use more than one observer, to enable them to compare notes. Another disadvantage to naturalistic observation is that because it takes place in real life, there is no possibility of repeating individual scenarios. This makes it difficult for psychologists to make generalizations based entirely on information from natural observations.

Laboratory Observation

A **laboratory observation** enables a researcher to observe a person or an animal in a controlled setting. It is used when observing certain types of behavior is not practical in a natural setting. Milgram's shock experiment, for example, would not have been possible in a natural setting. Beyond the ethical ramifications, it's doubtful that such a real-world situation would present itself to be studied. But how did Milgram's team know if their subjects were acting normally? Could the unfamiliar environment have led them to follow the experimenters' instructions for longer than they would have outside of the lab? The disadvantage of laboratory observations is that participants' behavior, and therefore the results of the study, might be artificial.

Case Studies

During a **case study**, researchers will study one individual or a few individuals in depth. They may use real-life observations, interviews, or tests to obtain information about their subjects. Developmental psychologist Jean Piaget (1896–1980) famously studied his own children as they grew. He was able to make powerful discoveries about cognitive development as a result of his observations.

Case studies are useful for providing information that would otherwise not be possible—or ethical—to obtain. For example, no one's likely to conduct—or line up to participate in—an experiment that requires participants to undergo

^ ^ ^ What might a researcher learn from studying meerkats in their natural habitat?

severe brain damage. Enter the famous case study of Phineas Gage. Gage was a railway foreman who suffered severe brain trauma when an explosion propelled a metal spike through his skull—and the frontal lobes of his brain—in 1848. Amazingly, Gage recovered from his injuries, but he experienced drastic personality changes as a result of the accident. The case of Phineas Gage provided evidence that the frontal lobes play a role in personality and behavior (Damasio et al., 1994).

Case studies can reveal fascinating information that we might not otherwise be able to obtain, but they do have their drawbacks. For example, since a case study provides only a single example of a phenomenon, that example may be atypical. It can be dangerous to make generalizations based on a case study without conducting further research.

> " Gage was a railway foreman who suffered severe brain trauma when an explosion propelled a metal spike through his skull—and the frontal lobes of his brain— in 1848. Amazingly, Gage recovered from his injuries, but he experienced drastic personality changes as a result of the accident. "

Surveys

Have you ever gotten a phone call from a stranger who inquires, eagerly and persistently, about your opinion of everything from abortion to zero-emission engines? If so, you may have participated in a **survey.** To conduct a survey, a researcher will ask a series of questions about people's behavior or opinions, in the form of a questionnaire or interview. Surveys can be useful because they have the potential to access private information from a large number of people relatively easily. Researchers commonly use surveys in both descriptive and correlational studies.

Researchers have to think long and hard about how they word their questions when they create a survey. Take a look at the following examples:

> *Do you approve of guest workers being given permission to remain in the country?*
> *Do you believe that illegal immigrants are entitled to stay in the country?*

Both of these questions have a similar meaning, yet using one instead of the other is likely to alter the outcome of the survey. The words *guest workers* and *permission* have more positive connotations than the words *illegal immigrants* and *entitled* do, and this difference in wording could impact the survey's results in an uncontrolled way. Researchers also need to be aware that people do not always answer surveys honestly, either through fear of being judged, or by misremembering things.

Random sampling can help researchers make sure that their sample is representative of the general population. If you wanted to find out what people thought about gay marriage in California, you would get very different results if you interviewed only members of the gay community than if you surveyed only members of conservative religious groups. In any survey, it is important to question a cross-section of the entire group you're trying to learn about.

RESEARCH SETTINGS

All types of research can take place either in a laboratory or "in the field." In a **laboratory study,** participants are taken to a location that has been specifically set up to facilitate collection of data and allow control over environmental conditions. A **field study,** on the other hand, is conducted in a setting other than a laboratory. Naturalistic observation is a type of field study because people or animals are observed in their natural environment rather than in a controlled setting. To overcome the disadvantages of both laboratory studies and field studies, researchers sometimes conduct both a laboratory study and a field study to investigate the same question. If researchers arrive at the same conclusion using both methods, they can be more confident about the reliability of their findings. For example, in 2008, researchers at Auburn University asked participants to wear either sneakers or flip-flops as they walked on a special platform in a laboratory setting. After observing the flip-flop wearers' gaits, the researchers concluded that wearing flip-flops can cause injuries, specifically

Survey is a series of questions about people's behavior or opinions, in the form of a questionnaire or interview.

Random sampling is a technique in which the participants in a survey are chosen randomly so as to get a fair representation of a population.

Laboratory study is a study in which participants are taken to a location that has been specifically set up to facilitate collection of data and allow control over environmental conditions.

Field study is a study that is conducted in a setting other than a laboratory.

Self-report method is a form of data collection in which people are asked to rate or describe their own behavior or mental state.

Questionnaire is a series of questions with a strict purpose that has been developed using careful controls such as precise wording, carefully constructed questions, and random sampling.

Interview is a form of data collection in which people provide oral descriptions of themselves; this can be strictly structured, with a set list of questions, or loosely structured and more conversational.

sore feet, ankles, and legs. But are flip-flops in the lab the same as flip-flops in the wild? If the researchers had performed a field study by observing flip-flop wearers in their natural environment, they would have been able to collect further data to determine whether flip-flops are less supportive than other shoes on everyday surfaces like grass and asphalt.

The type of investigation usually determines the setting of the study. Experiments are often more effectively conducted in a laboratory because researchers have a higher level of control over the surroundings. Correlational and descriptive studies are usually performed in the field. However, the setting depends entirely on the individual investigation.

DATA COLLECTION METHODS

Self-report Methods

A **self-report method** is a form of data collection in which people are asked to rate or describe their own behavior or mental state. Studies are usually in the form of **questionnaires** or **interviews.** You may have recently evaluated, with the invaluable help of a glossy magazine, your emotional neediness or your ideal celebrity match. Psychological questionnaires are similar in some ways to those *Cosmo* quizzes, but they have a stricter purpose and use careful controls such as precise wording, carefully constructed questions, and random sampling. A survey is one type of questionnaire.

Observational methods are the processes of observing and recording a subject's behavior.

Testing is a type of observational method in which participants are provided with stimuli or problems to respond to and researchers collect data about how the participants perform a certain task.

Descriptive statistics are statistics researchers use to summarize data sets.

Inferential statistics are statistics that use probability laws to help researchers decide how likely it is that their results are due to chance and, as a result, how likely it is that the observed results apply to a broader population.

Measures of central tendency are the three most typical scores in a set of data: mean, median, and mode.

Mean is the arithmetic average of the scores in a data set, or the sum of all the scores divided by the number of scores.

Median is the middle score in a data set.

Mode is the most frequently occurring score in a data set.

Variability is the degree to which the numbers in a set of data differ from one another and the mean.

Range is the difference between the highest and lowest values in a data set.

Standard deviation is a measure of the dispersion of a set of values using information from each individual score.

Deviation score is the difference between an individual data point's actual value and the mean value of the whole data set.

Frequency distribution is a summary of how frequently each of the scores in a set of data occurs.

Bar graph is a representation of a frequency distribution in which vertical or horizontal bars are proportional in length to the value they represent.

Histogram is a representation of a frequency distribution using rectangles in which the width of a rectangle represents an interval and the area of a rectangle is proportional to the corresponding frequency.

Normal curve is a graphical representation of an evenly distributed data set in which the curve is symmetrical and bell-shaped due to the even distribution of results and the tendency of data to accumulate around the center of a set in an even distribution.

In an interview, people provide oral descriptions of themselves to the interviewer. Interviews can be either strictly structured, with a set list of questions, or loosely structured and more conversational. In some structured interviews, interviewers use numerical methods to score people's responses to questions. This technique allows researchers to make precise generalizations from their results.

Observational Methods

When a researcher uses **observational methods,** he or she observes and records a subject's behavior. Naturalistic observation is one example of an observational method. Another example is **testing.** By providing stimuli or problems for participants to respond to, researchers collect data about how participants complete a certain task. For example, if you participate in a research test, you might be asked to solve a logic puzzle or press a button every time you see a bulb light up.

Data Collection Pros and Cons

Frustratingly, no one method of data collection is perfect, and each has its advantages and disadvantages. Questionnaires and interviews are great for gathering private information, but there is no guarantee that people's responses are accurate. (Even those of us who are unfailingly honest don't have perfectly objective views of our own behavior.) Naturalistic observations allow researchers to observe participants' natural behavior firsthand, but it is difficult to observe behavior without disrupting it, and analyzing observed results statistically can be tricky. Tests are convenient and easily scored, but they can be artificial: Your ability to solve a logic puzzle in 5.2 minutes may have no relationship to your ability to be logical in your everyday life. When researchers choose an experimental design, they have to make sure that their method of data collection will give them useful information about the theory they're studying.

Statistical Methods in Psychology

Once researchers have collected their data, they use statistics to analyze that data and to look for significant patterns. There are two types of statistics: **descriptive statistics,** which researchers use to summarize data sets (for example, height, weight, or grade point average), and **inferential statistics,** which use probability laws to help researchers decide how likely it is that their results are due to chance and, as a result, how likely it is that the observed results apply to a broader population.

DESCRIPTIVE STATISTICS

Measures of Central Tendency

If you had to find out what the average gas price in your state was, or the average number of people who own hybrid cars in your community, what sorts of numbers would you be looking for? It all depends on your interpretation of the word *average.* There are three **measures of central tendency,** or most typical scores, in a set of data. The **mean** is the arithmetic average—the sum of all the scores divided by the number of scores. The **median** is the middle score in the data set: If all the scores were arranged in order from lowest to highest or highest to lowest, half of the scores would be above the median and half would be below it. The **mode** is the most frequently occurring score.

Measures of Variability

The measure of **variability** is the degree to which the numbers in a set of data differ from one another and from the mean. The simplest measure of variability is the **range,** which is the difference between the highest and lowest

Unlike most magazine quizzes, questionnaires used by psychologists are scientifically valid. >>>

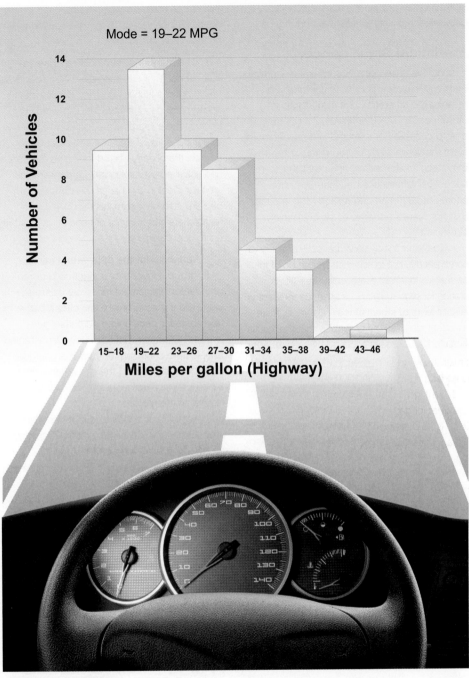

Gas Mileage of 2009 Toyota Vehicles

Mode = 19–22 MPG

Number of Vehicles (y-axis): 0, 2, 4, 6, 8, 10, 12, 14

Miles per gallon (Highway) (x-axis): 15–18, 19–22, 23–26, 27–30, 31–34, 35–38, 39–42, 43–46

Source: http://www.fueleconomy.gov

between the individual data point's actual value and the mean value of the whole data set. Calculating the standard deviation can give you a better idea of whether scores are closely packed together or spread out.

Frequency Distribution

Frequency distribution is a summary of how frequently each of the scores in a set of data occurs. To prepare a frequency distribution, researchers rank each data score from highest to lowest and group the data into intervals. They then create a frequency distribution table, putting the intervals in numerical order and identifying how many individual scores fall in each interval (or how many times each score appears in the data set). Finally, the researchers can create a graph to display the information. **Bar graphs** use vertical or horizontal bars that are proportional in length to the value they represent. A **histogram** is visually similar to a bar graph, but because it displays intervals on the x-axis and frequency on the y-axis, it is particularly well suited for graphing frequency distribution.

INFERENTIAL STATISTICS

It can be difficult to interpret data because there is always a possibility that the results you have collected are due to chance. Your measurements might not have been as accurate as you would have liked, your data may have been affected by uncontrollable variables, and your groups may not have been truly random. Can you account for these issues and still end up with useful data? Breathe easy—statistical methods have got you covered.

Normal Distribution and Skewed Distribution

In a set of data with an even distribution of results, a graphical representation of those results will show a **normal curve.** A normal

values in a data set. If gas hit a low price of $3.20 per gallon in December but skyrocketed to $4.50 by Memorial Day, the range of gas prices per gallon during that time period would be $1.30. A range is not always an accurate estimate of variation because it does not take the extreme nature of some scores into account. For example, imagine that the vast majority of gas station owners in America sell gas at $4.00 per gallon. However, one owner manages to cut her price to $2.50 per gallon, while another raises his price to $5.50 per gallon. These extreme changes in cost would create a deceptively high range in scores, even though the majority of scores are almost all the same.

A better measure of variation is **standard deviation.** Standard deviation takes into account the dispersion of a set of values by using information from each individual score. Each value is given a **deviation score,** which is the difference

> " He uses statistics as a drunken man uses lampposts—for support rather than for illumination."—Andrew Lang, Scottish scholar (1844-1912)

curve is symmetrical and bell-shaped, due to the fact that in a normally distributed data set, data tend to accumulate around the center of the set. On a normal curve, the mean, median, and mode are the same. In a set of data with unevenly distributed results, a graphical representation will show **skewed distribution,** with scores clustered together on one end rather than in the middle and a unique mean, median,

and mode. Most empirically collected data will not look particularly similar to the normal curve. However, we can use the normal curve to determine that data's statistical significance.

Statistical Significance

If there is a large difference between averages from two samples, and both samples are reliable, the difference has **statistical significance**—in other words, it's not simply due to chance. For example, if a psychologist tests the verbal skills of two different groups of college students, and finds that there are noticeable differences between average scores of freshmen and seniors, this means that her results are likely to be statistically significant.

The letter *p* may seem perfectly ordinary to some people, but to scientists, *p* can be of the utmost importance. Statistically, the letter *p* stands for probability and is used to represent an effect's **level of significance**, or *p*-value, a statistic that identifies the probability that the results of a study could have occurred by chance. A low *p*-value means that there is a low probability that the observed results were due to nothing more than chance. In other words, the lower the *p*-value, the more significant the results. Most researchers consider their results significant if the *p*-value of those results is less than 0.05 (5 percent). Therefore, if there is a 95 percent probability that the results of a college language study did not occur by chance, the results are significant.

When you determine a result's statistical significance, you'll need to take a few different factors into account:

1 **Size of the observed effect.** How big is the difference you've observed? Let's say your local car dealership, in an ecologically friendly effort to get ahead of its competitors, decides to offer a huge discount on hybrid vehicles. As a result, the dealership's sales increase. But how much do they increase? If there's a huge difference between the average number of cars sold

before the sale and the average number of cars sold during the sale, this difference is likely to be statistically significant. If the difference is minor, though, it may be caused by nothing more than chance.

2 **The number of subjects or observations.** It's pretty impressive if one car dealership notices a sharp increase in sales after offering a discount on hybrids. But wouldn't it be even more impressive—and even less likely to be caused by chance—if all the car dealerships in the country offered the same discount and achieved similar results? Larger samples are less affected by chance than smaller samples are, and large samples can give researchers a better idea of trends that affect an entire population.

3 **Variability of the data within each group.** How many uncontrolled or random factors influenced those car sales, anyway? Did the government just offer a bigger tax rebate for people who purchase new hybrids? Did it rain last Saturday, discouraging people from shopping for cars in an outdoor lot? The less variability there is within each group's results, the more significant those results are likely to be.

All other things being equal, if research produces a large observed effect, a large sample size, and little variability in data within groups, it's likely that the results of that research are statistically significant.

Use of Statistical Significance

When you look at statistical data, try not to put too much weight on the word *significance*. After all, data that's *statistically* significant may not actually have any *practical* significance or value. The tiniest and most irrelevant detail can have statistical significance if a big enough sample is taken.

Minimizing Bias in Psychological Research

ERROR

Imagine that a scientist inadvertently recruits participants for her study who lie in order to take part in the research. The results from these participants would introduce **error,** or random variability, into the results. Some degree of error is inevitable in psychological research because as hard as we try, we can't control every variable that might influence the behavior we're studying.

Normal Distribution

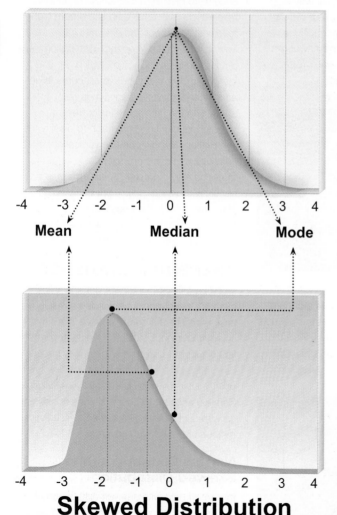

-4 -3 -2 -1 0 1 2 3 4

Mean   **Median**   **Mode**

-4 -3 -2 -1 0 1 2 3 4

Skewed Distribution

The presence of error doesn't necessarily mean that someone's made a mistake, and the consequences of error are relatively insignificant if the study is large enough. Researchers measure error by calculating the standard deviation of the relevant data. Then, they take this information into account when they perform a statistical analysis of the data.

BIAS

When Milgram and his colleagues interacted with the participants in their experiment, they had to be careful to avoid **bias.** What would have happened if they'd treated all the women normally but treated the uncomfortable male subjects with scorn, ridicule, or condescension? It's possible that the researchers' results would have been affected as a result of this unequal, biased treatment. Bias is a serious problem in psychological research because it cannot be identified and corrected using statistical procedures. Whereas error only reduces the chance that results may be statistically significant, bias can lead researchers to draw false conclusions. To address this bias, scientists use multiple researchers in their experiments, and they follow careful training procedures to make sure that all researchers are following the same valid experimental techniques.

Bias is not only a problem from the researcher's perspective. **Demand characteristics** are aspects of a setting that can cause participants in a study to behave as they believe the researcher wants them to, potentially invalidating the results of the study in the process.

Avoiding Biased Samples

A sample is biased when the people in it are not representative of the larger population being studied. When participants are randomly assigned into groups, their individual differences are the result of error and can be taken into account during statistical analysis of the results. However, when participants are not randomly assigned into groups, there may be elements of both error and bias. Another potential problem is self-selection: Sometimes, participants in a study create bias merely by choosing to take part in that study. For example, if a survey asks lots of personal questions, only people who feel comfortable answering personal questions will complete the survey. So what can we do to ensure an unbiased sample? The truth is that no matter how large a sample is, there will always be an element of bias. The trick is in keeping that bias as small and inconsequential as possible.

Avoiding Measurement Bias

A good researcher will check that his or her measurements are both reliable and valid. **Reliability** is the degree to which a measurement yields similar results every time it is used with a particular subject under particular conditions. A reliable measure may obtain different results from different participants, but if it is used with the same participant multiple times, it should get the same result every time.

Checking that a measurement is reliable pertains to error rather than bias because it is a researcher's responsibility to make sure he or she is consistent in his or her methods. If a measure-

ment has a low degree of reliability, it is unlikely that a study based on that measurement will have any statistical significance.

The **validity** of a measurement is the degree to which it measures what it is intended to measure. This is a more critical issue than reliability, because a procedure may be reliable, but if it is not valid then nothing has been achieved. There are several different categories of validity:

1 **Face validity.** Face validity is the extent to which a study superficially measures what it is intended to measure. Imagine that you are a participant in an experiment designed to test intelligence, and the researcher asks you whether you like ice cream. This question has no face validity because it's not immediately apparent that ice cream preference has anything to do with intelligence. In this case, a measurement with face validity might take the form of a logical problem that you're asked to solve.

2 **Criterion validity.** You may score off the charts on an intelligence test, but how can the researcher be sure that the test is actually measuring intelligence? Ideally, her test has **criterion validity,** a term that refers to how closely a measurement correlates with another criterion of the characteristic being studied. To determine that an intelligence test is valid, a researcher might compare the results of the test with results of another measure correlated with intelligence. For example, intelligence test scores are commonly compared with school achievement (Aiken & Groth-Marnat, 2005). If a large enough group of people who do well in school also perform well on an intelligence test, the test has criterion validity.

> **Bias** is a personal and sometimes unreasonable judgment that a researcher may make that could affect the results of an experiment.
>
> **Demand characteristics** are aspects of a setting that can cause participants in a study to behave as they believe the researcher wants them to.
>
> **Reliability** is the degree to which a measurement yields similar results every time it is used with a particular subject under particular conditions.
>
> **Validity** is the degree to which a measurement measures what it is intended to measure.
>
> **Face validity** is the extent to which a study superficially measures what it is intended to measure.
>
> **Criterion validity** is an indication of how closely a measurement correlates with another criterion of the characteristic being studied.

∧∧∧ **If a study proved that eating a pound of caviar a day could improve your brain power by one percent, but a pound of caviar costs $50,000, would this research be of any practical use?**

Predictive validity is a type of criterion validity in which you can use the results of a test to predict a person's score or performance in another area.

Construct validity is a type of validity that uses a specific procedure that measures or correlates with a theoretical or intangible concept.

Internal validity is a type of validity indicating that a researcher is able to control all extraneous values in a test so that the only variable influencing the results it of the study is the independent variable.

External validity is a type of validity indicating that a test can be generalized to the rest of the population.

Observer-expectancy effect see observer bias

Subject-expectancy effect is an occurrence where participants in a study expect to behave in a certain way as a result of their treatment, causing them to adjust their behavior.

Double-blind experiment is an experiment in which both the subject and the observer are kept blind, thus negating the observer-expectancy effect and the subject-expectancy effect.

Placebo is a substance or procedure which resembles medical therapy but has no intrinsic therapeutic value.

One type of criterion validity is **predictive validity.** If a test has predictive validity, you can use its results to predict a person's score or performance in another area. For instance, your career counselor might give you a test with predictive validity to determine how likely you are to do well in certain professions.

3 Construct validity. If a test has **construct validity,** it uses a specific procedure that measures or correlates with a theoretical or intangible concept. You can't take out your intelligence and weigh it on a scale or wrap a measuring tape around it. However, an intelligence test that has construct validity will be able to produce concrete results that correlate with intelligence.

4 Internal validity. A test has **internal validity** if the researcher is able to control all extraneous variables so that the only variable influencing the results of his or her study is the independent variable. Internal validity enables the researcher to prove there's a causal relationship between the dependent variable and the independent variable.

5 External validity. A test has **external validity** if it can be generalized to the rest of the population. If the researcher has used a representative sample in his or her study, the conclusions drawn should be applicable to any other group of people, and the study is likely to have external validity.

Avoiding Observer- and Subject-Expectancy Effects

Remember Clever Hans and his trainer? Researchers have desires or expectations during a study that they may inadvertently pass on to their participants, influencing the way participants behave. Wilhelm von Osten was providing Hans with subtle clues that biased the results of his "experiment." These expectations may also affect how the researcher perceives the participants' behavior. If Oskar Pfungst had expected Hans to be an equine Einstein, he wouldn't have been predisposed to notice von Osten's nonverbal cues. The **observer-expectancy effect,** or observer bias, is best overcome by using blind observers who are uninformed about the purpose of the study. In between-group experiments, a blind observer would also be unaware of which participants had received which treatments.

The **subject-expectancy effect** occurs when participants expect to behave a certain way as a result of their treatment, causing them to adjust their behavior. This is best avoided by keeping study participants blind, or unaware of the treatment they are receiving. For example, in 1971, psychologist Sandra Bem designed the Bem Sex Role Inventory to assess participants' gender identity as masculine, feminine, or androgynous. The inventory's instructions ask participants simply to answer questions about their personality. Participants are not aware that the inventory actually assesses gender identity—if they were, they might give very different responses.

In a **double-blind experiment**, both the subject and the observer are kept blind. In double-blind drug studies, some participants receive the drug being tested, while others receive a **placebo** (an inactive substance that looks like the drug). Since neither the participants nor the observers know which is being taken, any differences in behavior are more likely to be a result of the drug rather than a result of subject or observer expectations. This is how the now-famous impotency drug Viagra was tested. The results showed

The placebo effect can be powerful. What does its existence tell us about the power of the mind? >>>

that 69 percent of attempts at intercourse while using Viagra were successful, while only 22 percent of men using the placebo were able to successfully have sexual intercourse (Goldstein et al., 1998).

The double-blind procedure is not completely immune to subject and observer expectations, however. The **placebo effect**, an extreme example of the power of suggestion, occurs when individuals taking a placebo react as if they were receiving treatment, simply because they believe that they *are* receiving treatment. Researchers have observed the placebo effect in action during numerous trials, including studies of treatments for pain, depression, and anxiety (Kirsch & Saperstein, 1998).

Ethical Issues in Psychological Research

In 1971, psychologist Philip Zimbardo from Stanford University recruited about 70 young men, mostly college students, to participate in a study of the psychological effects of prison life. After completing diagnostic tests, 24 volunteers were offered $15 a day to participate in the two-week experiment. The participants were arbitrarily divided into two groups with the toss of a coin. Half were told they were now prison guards, and half were assigned the role of prisoner. The "prisoners" were booked at a real jail, blindfolded, and taken to a campus building that had been turned into a realistic prison environment with the help of a former convict. Upon arriving at the prison, each prisoner was stripped naked, searched, deloused with a spray, and forced to wear a uniform.

On the second day of the experiment, the prisoners staged a revolt that was quashed by the guards. The guards became more aggressive, forcing the prisoners to perform humiliating tasks such as cleaning toilet bowls with their bare hands. Five prisoners had to be released early because they were so emotionally distressed that they became physically ill. The experiment was eventually canceled on the fifth day (Zimbardo, 1971).

RESEARCH WITH HUMANS

Zimbardo certainly didn't set out to create an experiment that would harm its participants, but was the Stanford Prison Experiment ethical? When researchers conduct experiments on humans, they have to take three important issues into consideration:

1 **A person's right to privacy.** Researchers must obtain informed consent from each participant. Participants in a study must also be told that they do not need to share any information they are not comfortable sharing, and results must be kept anonymous.

2 **The possibility of discomfort or harm.** Zimbardo most likely wouldn't have gone ahead with his experiment if he had foreseen its outcome. Researchers have a responsibility to ensure that their participants are placed at minimal risk during a study and that any risk undertaken is outweighed by the potential human benefits. Participants must be aware that they are free to quit at any time (a questionable element of Zimbardo's study).

3 **The use of deception.** Some psychologists are opposed to any use of deception in a study because it undermines the concept of truly informed consent. Others believe that some processes cannot be studied without an

> "When researchers conduct experiments on humans, they have to take three important issues into consideration: A person's right to privacy, the possibility of discomfort or harm, and the use of deception."

element of deception involved. To avoid the use of deception, psychologists may **debrief** participants after the study by providing them with a verbal description of the true nature and purpose of the study.

RESEARCH WITH ANIMALS

Is it ethical to use animals in psychological research? Some people believe that procedures that cannot ethically be performed on humans may still be performed on animals. Many of the basic biological mechanisms underlying animal behavior are similar to those underlying human behavior, and animal

Placebo effect is a phenomenon in which participants taking a placebo react as if they were receiving treatment, simply because they believe they are actually receiving treatment.

Debrief is to give a verbal description of the true nature and purpose of a study after the study occurs.

American Psychological Association (APA) is a scientific and professional organization that represents psychologists in the United States.

Institutional Review Board (IRB) is an ethics review panel established by a publicly funded research institution to evaluate all proposed research by that institution.

research can provide valuable information. Much of what we know about perception, sensation, drugs, and the way the brain functions was gleaned from animal research (Carroll & Overmier, 2001).

However, is it ethical to use animals in studies when they cannot give their consent? Any suffering that is caused must be weighed against the potential benefits of the study. Would we object to growing tumors on mice if doing so enabled us to find a cure for cancer? Who decides whether the consequences are justified? Animal protection organizations such as Society & Animals Forum propose that animals be studied in their natural environments rather than tested in laboratory experiments. These groups' opponents claim that following this proposal would prevent valuable research opportunities.

HOW CAN WE ENSURE ETHICAL RESEARCH?

The **American Psychological Association (APA)** has established a code of ethics for psychological research. Researchers must abide by these rules if they wish to publish their work in APA journals. Furthermore, publicly funded research institutions are required by law to establish ethics review panels that evaluate all proposed research. These panels are commonly known as **Institutional Review Boards,** or **IRBs.** As a result of these safeguards and guidelines, panels now routinely turn down studies that would have once been deemed acceptable, and some "classic" studies cited in this book—such as the Stanford Prison Experiment—would not be approved today.

Summary

WHY ARE RESEARCH METHODS IMPORTANT TO THE STUDY OF PSYCHOLOGY? p. 18

• Psychologists use scientific methods to carry out research, reducing the problems of hindsight bias and the false consensus effect.

• When carrying out empirical research, psychologists use existing facts and theories to come up with new hypotheses.

WHAT ARE SOME TYPES OF RESEARCH STRATEGIES? p. 20

• Experiments, correlational studies, and descriptive studies (naturalistic observation, laboratory observation, case studies, and surveys) are used to conduct different types of research.
• Research can take place in a laboratory or in the field.
• Data collection may be self-reported or observational.

HOW CAN STATISTICAL METHODS HELP US GATHER AND ANALYZE DATA? p. 24

• Descriptive statistics are used to summarize data

sets and provide information about measures of central tendency, measures of variability, and frequency distribution.
• Inferential statistics are used to provide information about the statistical significance of data.

HOW CAN WE MINIMIZE BIAS? p. 27

• A degree of error is inevitable in any psychological research and is taken into account during statistical analysis.
• Researchers can minimize bias by using representative samples, taking reliable measurements, and avoiding subject- and observer-expectancy effects.

WHAT ETHICAL ISSUES DO PSYCHOLOGISTS FACE? p. 29

• When conducting a study, a psychologist needs to consider three issues: a person's right to privacy, the possibility of harm or discomfort, and the use of deception.

• Researchers must follow the American Psychological Association's code of ethics if they wish to publish their work in APA journals.

Test Your Understanding

1. Angel has never talked to his brothers about their political beliefs, but he assumes that they support the same candidates he does. Angel's belief is an example of:
   a. a theory.
   b. observer bias.
   c. the false consensus effect.
   d. hindsight bias.

2. Sarah sees an advertisement for a detergent that claims to remove any stain. However, Sarah is skeptical and wants to try the detergent herself before accepting the claim. Sarah is demonstrating:
   a. dogmatism.
   b. empiricism.
   c. the false consensus effect.
   d. statistical methods.

3. Phil wants the participants in his study's control group to be similar to the participants in the experimental group. In order to do this, he uses:
   a. an independent variable.
   b. a dependent variable.
   c. random assignment.
   d. a confederate.

4. Which of the following research studies would be best as a laboratory study?
   a. determining how families learn to cooperate when eating together
   b. identifying dating rituals of college students
   c. a comparison of male and female memory ability in which participants must repeat a number sequence after viewing it on a screen
   d. a study of self-knowledge in which participants, at various intervals over the course of five years, answer questions about their behaviors

5. Ari comes to the first class session thinking his professor will not like him, and he observes body language from his professor that suggests this. This is an example of:
   a. observer bias.
   b. blind observation.
   c. naturalistic observation.
   d. testing.

6. Jana conducts a study in which she calls participants and asks them questions about their opinions. She is conducting a:
   a. laboratory observation.
   b. survey.
   c. case study.
   d. biased study.

7. Daryl collects data on teen pregnancy rates in his city and finds that most teen pregnancies occur for women in a lower socio-economic bracket. Daryl can conclude that the relationship between teen pregnancy and socio-economic status is:

   a. causal.
   b. skewed.
   c. reliable.
   d. correlative.

8. Marc collects data on the age at which all of his married colleagues were wed. The ages are: 37, 36, 25, 25, 32, 24, 26, 36, 25, 31. The mode in his set of data is:

   a. 3.
   b. 25.
   c. 24.
   d. 36.

9. By today's ethical standards, the Stanford Prison Experiment would be rejected by an Institutional Review Board (IRB) because:

   a. participants were divided into study groups randomly.
   b. the study was conducted on a campus.
   c. the possibility of harm was too great.
   d. None of the above.

10. Which of the following is true about the use of deception in psychology experiments?

   a. Psychologists can never deceive participants.
   b. Participants are usually debriefed after a study that uses deception and told the true nature of the research.
   c. Participants must always be paid for their time if deception is used.
   d. The use of deception in psychological research is not generally considered an ethical problem.

11. Jay designs an experiment that has external validity. What does this imply about his experiment?

   a. It is a double-blind experiment.
   b. The results of the experiment can be generalized to the entire population.
   c. All extraneous variables are controlled for.
   d. The experiment appears to measure what it was intended to measure.

12. Kaya is conducting a study that tests intelligence in low-income families. One of the questions asks what political party the participant belongs to. This question:

   a. has no face validity.
   b. has no external validity.
   c. has no reliability.
   d. is biased.

13. Deborah participates in a study testing a drug used to quit smoking. She stops smoking, but was actually given an inactive substance and not the drug being tested. Her result may have been due to:

   a. hindsight bias.
   b. the false consensus effect.
   c. the placebo effect.
   d. observer bias.

14. Which of the following is a type of field study?

   a. correlational study
   b. laboratory observation
   c. experimental study
   d. naturalistic observation

15. Characteristics of study participants, such as reaction time, weight, and height, are called:

   a. dependent variables.
   b. independent variables.
   c. variables.
   d. controls.

16. Which combination of factors and results will make finding statistical significance the most likely?

   a. large observed effect, small sample size, little variability within groups
   b. large observed effect, large sample size, little variability within groups
   c. large observed effect, large sample size, high variability within groups
   d. small observed effect, large sample size, high variability within groups

17. Which of the following is NOT a measure of central tendency?

   a. range
   b. mean
   c. median
   d. mode

18. A set of data with a unique mean, median, and mode is likely to have a:

   a. normal distribution.
   b. skewed distribution.
   c. significant error.
   d. None of the above.

19. Using the scientific method can help minimize:

   a. hindsight bias.
   b. empiricism.
   c. hypotheses.
   d. external validity.

20. A person in a study who appears to be a subject, but is really working with the researcher is called:

   a. a confederate.
   b. a participant.
   c. a control.
   d. a variable.

Remember to check www.thethinkspot.com for additional information, downloadable flashcards, and other helpful resources.

PSYCHOLOGICAL SCIENCE

Short Report
A Picture's Worth
Partner Photographs Reduce Experimentally Induced Pain

Sarah L. Master, Naomi I. Eisenberger, Shelley E. Taylor, Bruce D. Naliboff, David Shirinyan, and Matthew D. Lieberman

University of California, Los Angeles

> The introduction explains what the study is testing. It also discusses previous findings that relate to the current study.

Social support is associated with reduced pain experience across several domains (Cogan & Spinnato, 1988; Kulik & Mahler, 1989; Zaza & Baine, 2002); intriguingly, a handful of experimental studies suggest that this connection may reflect a causal relationship. Participants who received interactive support during a cold pressor task reported less pain than participants who completed the task alone or engaged in nonsupportive interactions (Brown, Sheffield, Leary, & Robinson, 2003; Jackson, Iezzi, Chen, Ebnet, & Eglitis, 2005). Moreover, the mere presence of another supportive individual (vs. being alone) reduced pain ratings in a cold pressor task (Brown et al., 2003; but see McClelland & McCubbin, 2008) and reduced pain ratings among fibromyalgia patients following stimulation to a painful body site (Montoya, Larbig, Braun, Preissl, & Birbaumer, 2004).

Could the same pain-attenuating effects of social support be observed by merely activating the mental representation of a supportive other? Previous work has shown that activating mental representations of important others can produce effects similar to those created by the actual presence of these individuals (Fitzsimons & Bargh, 2003; Mikulincer & Shaver, 2001). Building on this research, the current study examined whether simply viewing a photograph of one's romantic partner could reduce physical pain experience. We examined how this condition compared with one that is more consistent with previous conceptualizations of social support—one in which the participant held her partner's hand.

METHOD

> The Method section describes what was done in the study. It explains who the participants were, and the steps that the researchers followed.

Participants were 28 right-handed women in long-term relationships (> 6 months). Three were excluded because of technical failures (final sample: n = 25). Upon arrival, each participant was taken into the testing room; her partner was taken to a separate room to have his photograph taken for later use.

After the participant provided consent, her pain threshold for thermal stimulation (a rating of 10, corresponding to moderate discomfort, on a scale from 0 to 20) was determined. She then placed her left arm behind an opaque curtain that was suspended from the ceiling. Throughout the study, a male experimenter behind the curtain delivered 6-s thermal stimulations to three alternating locations on the participant's left volar forearm, using a 9-cm^2 computer-controlled Peltier-type thermode (TSAII, Medoc Inc., Ramat Yishai, Israel).

Each participant received a total of 84 thermal stimulations: Six stimulations (separated by 20-s intervals) were given during each of seven task conditions, and each condition was presented twice. Unbeknownst to the participant, half of the stimulations were at her threshold temperature and half were at her threshold plus 1°C. The seven study conditions (each lasting 3 min 14 s) were as fol-

> In Chapter 2 (pp. 20-23), you read about various types of research strategies. Which is being used in this study?

What is the independent variable in this study? What is the dependent variable?

lows: (a) holding the hand of the partner (as he sat behind the curtain), (b) holding the hand of a male stranger (the experimenter behind the curtain),[1] (c) holding an object (a squeeze ball), (d) viewing the partner's photographs (taken upon his arrival) on a computer screen, (e) viewing photographs of a male stranger (ethnicity-matched to the participant's partner), (f) viewing photographs of an object (a chair), and (g) viewing a fixation crosshair (no manipulation). Half of the participants completed the hand- and object-holding conditions first, and half completed the photograph conditions first.[2]

The participant rated each stimulation's "unpleasantness" by pointing to a number on the Gracely Box Scale (Gracely, McGrath, & Dubner, 1978), which is a 21-box numerical descriptor scale anchored with previously quantified verbal descriptors of pain unpleasantness. A female experimenter (who was on the participant's side of the curtain) recorded the ratings. To address a competing hypothesis that social support reduces pain because it distracts one from pain (Hodes, Howland, Lightfoot, & Cleeland, 1990), we recorded participants' reaction times (i.e., the time it took them to press the space bar on the computer keyboard in front of them) to computer-generated beeps that were infrequently and randomly emitted throughout the study. This allowed us to assess whether participants were more distracted (as demonstrated by longer reaction times to the beeps) in the support conditions (partner hand-holding, partner photographs) than in the other conditions.

RESULTS AND DISCUSSION

Average reaction times to the computer-generated beeps during the seven conditions were submitted to a one-way repeated measures analysis of variance (ANOVA). The manipulations were not found to be differentially distracting, $F(6, 144) = 0.42$, $p = .87$, $p_{rep} = .21$; thus, it appears that social support was not confounded with distraction. For ease of interpretation, we calculated difference scores, subtracting mean pain ratings in the fixation condition from mean pain ratings in each of the other conditions. A one-way ANOVA showed a significant main effect of condition on pain scores, $F(5, 120) = 19.63$, $p_{rep} > .99$. Planned pair-wise comparisons revealed that, as expected, holding the partner's hand led to significantly lower pain ratings ($M = 0.48$, $SD = 1.97$) than holding an object ($M = 0.89$, $SD = 1.41$), $t(24) = 4.73$, $p_{rep} = .99$, $d = 0.80$, or holding a stranger's hand ($M = 1.55$, $SD = 1.47$), $t(24) = 5.33$, $p_{rep} = .99$, $d = 1.17$. Interestingly, the photograph conditions showed similar effects (Fig. 1)— viewing a partner's photographs led to significantly lower pain ratings ($M = -1.01$, $SD = 1.56$) than viewing photographs of an object ($M = 0.14$, $SD = 1.62$), $t(24) = 4.37$, $p_{rep} = .99$, $d = 0.72$, or viewing a stranger's photographs ($M = 0.22$, $SD = 0.84$), $t(24) = -5.09$, $p_{rep} = .99$, $d = 0.98$. In addition, pain ratings in the partner-photographs condition were marginally lower than those in the partner-handholding condition, $t(24) = -1.83$, $p = .08$, $p_{rep} = .84$.[3]

These findings confirm the notion that simply viewing a loved one's picture can have pain-attenuating effects, and they fit with social psychological research showing that being primed with a social construct is enough to activate associated mental representations and to bias behavior (Ferguson & Bargh, 2004). Thus, seeing photographs

p_{rep} indicates the probability that the results can be replicated. Since the p-rep is greater than .99, this means that there is more than a 99% likelihood that these results are accurate, and are not due to chance.

Think about what you learned in Chapter 2 about research methodology, especially controlled conditions and variables (p. 20). How is good research practice being demonstrated here?

[1]Although participants could not see behind the curtain, the experimenter told them whose hand they were holding—their partner's hand or a stranger's hand—in the respective conditions. All participants reported that they believed the experimenter.

[2]The fixation condition was randomly included with either the hand-holding/object-holding conditions or the photograph conditions, to form a set. The order of presentation was randomized within each set of three or four conditions.

[3]These effects of partner photographs are not likely due to expectancy effects; a separate sample of women who were in relationships (> 6 months; $n = 11$) and were asked to imagine that they had completed the study predicted that they would have felt significantly less pain (relative to fixation) when holding their partner's hand than when viewing his photograph, $t(10) = 3.24$, $p_{rep} = .95$, $d = 0.77$.

The Results section describes what the researchers found, while the Discussion section interprets these findings and compares them to other research.

THINK READINGS (CONTINUED)

Findings first introduced in academic journals are often discussed in the popular press. See here how the research findings from the journal Psychological Science are being discussed in this NY Times blog.

Why might loved ones vary in their ability to provide support to someone experiencing pain?

of loved ones may prime associated mental representations of being loved and supported, which may be sufficient to attenuate pain experience. The findings suggest that bringing loved ones' photographs to painful procedures may be beneficial, particularly if those individuals cannot be there. In fact, because loved ones vary in their ability to provide support, photographs may, in some cases, be more effective than in-person support. In sum, these findings challenge the notion that the beneficial effects of social support come solely from supportive social interactions and suggest that simple reminders of loved ones may be sufficient to engender feelings of support.

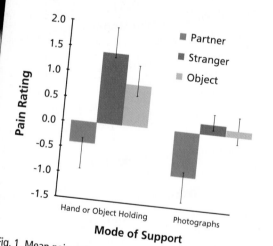

Fig. 1. Mean pain rating as a function of mode and source of support. Pain ratings on the ordinate are difference scores, which were calculated by subtracting mean pain ratings in the fixation condition from mean pain ratings in each of the other conditions. Thus, negative numbers indicate lower pain ratings during the condition of interest compared with fixation.

REFERENCES

Brown, J.L., Sheffield, D., Leary, M.R., & Robinson, M.E. (2003). Social support and experimental pain. *Psychosomatic Medicine*, 65, 276–283.

Cogan, R., & Spinnato, J.A. (1988). Social support during premature labor: Effects on labor and the newborn. *Journal of Psychosomatic Obstetrics and Gynecology*, 8, 209–216.

Ferguson, M.J., & Bargh, J.A. (2004). How social perception can automatically influence behavior. *Trends in Cognitive Sciences*, 8, 33–39.

Fitzsimons, G.M., & Bargh, J.A. (2003). Thinking of you: Nonconscious pursuit of interpersonal goals associated with Relationship partners. *Journal of Personality and Social Psychology*, 84, 148–164.

Gracely, R.H., McGrath, F., & Dubner, R. (1978). Ratio scales of sensory and affective verbal pain descriptors. *Pain*, 5, 5–18.

Hodes, R.L., Howland, E.W., Lightfoot, N., & Cleeland, C.S. (1990). The effects of distraction on responses to cold pressor pain. *Pain*, 41, 109–114.

Jackson, T., Iezzi, T., Chen, H., Ebnet, S., & Eglitis, K. (2005). Gender, interpersonal transactions, and the perception of pain: An experimental analysis. *The Journal of Pain*, 6, 228–236.

Kulik, J.A., & Mahler, H.I. (1989). Social support and recovery from surgery. *Health Psychology*, 8, 221–238.

McClelland, L.E., & McCubbin, J.A. (2008). Social influence and pain response in women and men. *Journal of Behavioral Medicine*, 31, 413–420.

Mikulincer, M., & Shaver, P.R. (2001). Attachment theory and intergroup bias: Evidence that priming the secure base schema attenuates negative reactions to out-groups. *Journal of Personality and Social Psychology*, 81, 97–115.

Montoya, P., Larbig, W., Braun, C., Preissl, H., & Birbaumer, N. (2004). Influence of social support and emotional context on pain processing and magnetic brain responses in fibromyalgia. *Arthritis and Rheumatism*, 50, 4035–4044.

Zaza, C., & Baine, N. (2002). Cancer pain and psychosocial factors: A critical review of the literature. *Journal of Pain and Symptom Management*, 24, 526–542.

Review the definitions on p. 22 in Chapter 2. What is being described here?

In Chapter 14 you'll read more about social psychology, including how it may be linked to our health (p. 207).

HOME PAGE   TODAY'S PAPER   VIDEO   MOST POPULAR   TIMES TOPICS

November 19, 2009, 1:59 PM

Pain Relief Through Photography

By RONI CARYN RABIN

Can looking at the photograph of a loved one make pain go away?

Numerous studies show that strong social connections have benefits for health. People who have active social lives seem to live longer than those who are isolated, and married cancer patients have a better outlook than divorced cancer patients. Now, a study [pdf] suggests that merely looking at a photograph of a loved one can relieve the sensation of physical pain.

Psychologists at the University of California, Los Angeles, recruited 25 women who had steady boyfriends. Using a tool that applied heat to the women's forearms, they turned up the temperature until it was slightly uncomfortable and asked the women to rate the pain they experienced on a scale of one to 20.

The researchers manipulated the heat and recorded the women's reactions under different conditions: while she was looking at a photo of her boyfriend, or a photo of a complete stranger and a chair. They also had the women rate the pain while they held the hand of a stranger hidden behind a curtain, and as they held their boyfriend's hand or a squeeze ball.

"We saw lower pain ratings on average when the women were holding their partner's hand compared with a stranger's hand or an object," said Sarah L. Master, the lead author of the paper, who did the study at U.C.L.A. as part of her doctoral research.

When the women looked at photographs of their boyfriends, they rated the pain lower than when they were staring at a photo of a stranger or a chair. Surprisingly, they even ranked the pain lower than they had while holding their boyfriend's hand.

"It's interesting that a physical sensation can actually become more manageable by just looking at a photo of someone you find supportive," Dr. Master said. The study appeared in the November issue of the journal Psychological Science.

Under certain circumstances, Dr. Master suggested, looking at a photo may have an even stronger effect than having the person physically present. "Having the actual person there might not be a good thing if the person is in a bad mood or not being supportive at that moment. A picture could be a better solution," she said.

Dr. Master said the mere reminder of the loved one may engender feelings of support, possibly by prompting the release of endogenous opioids, chemicals in the brain that have pain relief effects.

Add a comment   E-mail This   Print   Share

How does reading Dr. Master's thoughts on her study enhance your understanding of her work?

Dr. Master is making a prediction based on the results of her study. How might she test this hypothesis?

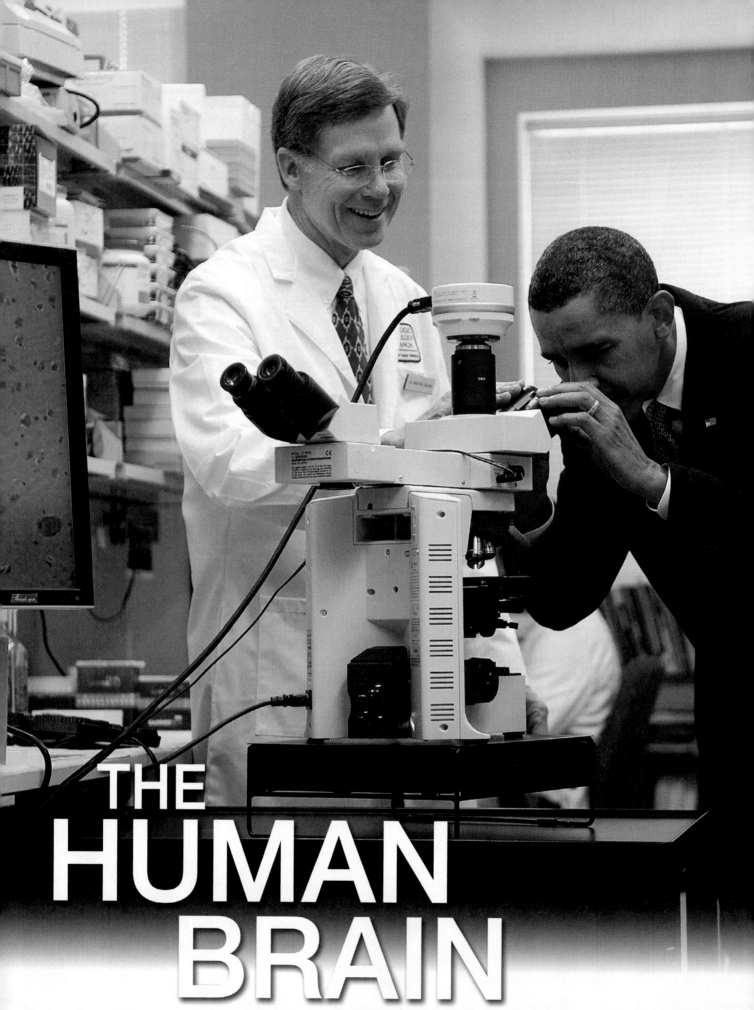

THE HUMAN BRAIN

WHAT CHARACTERISTICS DESCRIBE THE HUMAN BRAIN?

HOW IS THE NERVOUS SYSTEM ORGANIZED?

HOW DOES THE NERVOUS SYSTEM OPERATE AT THE CELLULAR LEVEL?

WHAT ARE THE DIFFERENT PARTS OF THE HUMAN BRAIN, AND WHAT ROLE DOES EACH PART PLAY?

Imagine

having prosthetic legs and taking a walk on the beach. How would the experience seem different to you if you could not feel warm sand between your toes or cool water and seaweed touching your skin? Researchers are on their way to helping amputees experience these kinds of tactile sensations—starting with a surgical technique called targeted muscle reinnervation (TMR) and the power of the human brain.

Study participants at the Research Institute of Chicago who had previously been amputated from either the shoulder or above the elbow were the first to experience this type of surgery. In it, nerves that used to be connected to the amputated limb are rerouted to large muscles that are near the point of amputation, in this case either in the upper arm or chest. The person only has to think of performing a movement with the prosthetic limb as if it were his or her own. When the rerouted nerve senses a contraction in the chest or arm muscle, sensors embedded in the muscle tissue send specific signals to the prosthetic limb, enabling the prosthesis to perform such actions as picking up a fork, catching a ball, or holding another person's hand. Even more amazingly, in the 2007–2008 study, the amputees completed specific movements with the robotic limb only

fractions of a second slower than nonamputated participants.

The surgeons have recently transplanted nerves that relay sensation to the brain and allow prosthetic limb users to mentally experience touch. Called targeted sensory reinnervation (TSR), the nerves from an amputated limb are rerouted to skin on the patient's chest. A patient who places an object against this area feels as if she is physically touching something with her hand. This technique is amazingly refined, allowing subjects to sense the difference between hot and cold, experience rough and smooth textures, and even feel sensations on individual fingers that correspond to different locations on their chests. In the future, researchers are hoping to develop new technologies that will allow the prosthetic limbs to send sensory signals to the rerouted nerves, enabling amputees to directly experience the environment through their hands once again. This remarkable advancement—centered around the functions of nerves and the brain's role in human experience—will not only restore amputees' sense of touch, but may also cause great changes in the ways they perceive themselves and are perceived by others.

CHAPTER **03**

The Brain in Context

WHY STUDY THE BRAIN?

To put it simply, the human brain enables behavior. Exactly how it does this, however, remains a mystery to scientists. At present, we can't draw simple relationships between brain events and

Central nervous system (CNS) is the largest part of the nervous system; it includes the spinal cord and the brain.

Peripheral nervous system (PNS) is the part of the nervous system that serves the limbs and organs.

Somatic nervous system is the part of the peripheral nervous system that picks up stimuli from the outside world, coordinates movements, and performs other consciously controlled tasks.

Autonomic nervous system is the part of the peripheral nervous system that performs tasks that are not consciously controlled.

Sympathetic nervous system is the part of the autonomic nervous system that is always active and acts as an accelerator for organs.

Parasympathetic nervous system is the part of the autonomic nervous system that is responsible for functions that do not require immediate action and acts as a brake for organs.

Neurons are excitable cells that receive different types of stimulation; the building blocks of the nervous system.

Dendrites are relatively short, bushy, branch-like structures that emerge from the neuron's cell body and receive signals from adjoining neurons.

Soma is the cell body of a neuron.

Axon is a cable-like extension that transmits a signal away from a neuron's soma toward the target of communication.

Myelin is a fatty substance that coats and insulates axons.

Terminal buttons are structures at the ends of the branches that extend from axons.

Sensory neurons carry information from the sensory receptors to the brain as a coded signal.

Motor neurons carry information away from the central nervous system to operate muscles and glands.

Interneurons carry information between sensory neurons and motor neurons.

Glial cells (glia) are cells that support neurons by, among other things, keeping neurons in place, creating myelin, and providing nutrition and insulation.

Blood-brain barrier is a fatty envelope that filters substances trying to leave the bloodstream and reach the brain.

Network is a large community of neurons.

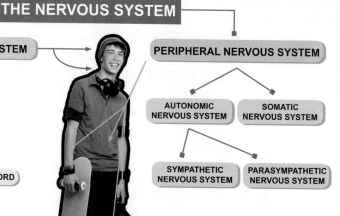

THE NERVOUS SYSTEM

CENTRAL NERVOUS SYSTEM → **PERIPHERAL NERVOUS SYSTEM**

BRAIN   **SPINAL CORD**

AUTONOMIC NERVOUS SYSTEM   **SOMATIC NERVOUS SYSTEM**

SYMPATHETIC NERVOUS SYSTEM   **PARASYMPATHETIC NERVOUS SYSTEM**

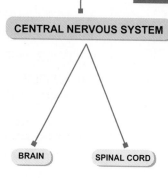

human behavior, but we can establish a number of consistent and predictable relationships between brain regions and classes of behavior. Understanding how the human brain works is crucial to understanding why we do what we do.

Speaking generally, the human brain has three major characteristics:

1 **Integration.** The brain's structures are constantly competing and cooperating.

2 **Sophistication.** Even the most high-tech computers can't match the human brain in complexity of thought and behavior.

3 **Adaptability.** The human brain is always working and constantly changing. The ability to control prosthetic limbs is an amazing illustration of the extent to which the brain can adapt and function fully under very unusual circumstances.

THE BRAIN AND THE NERVOUS SYSTEM

The nervous system is subdivided into two parts, the **central nervous system (CNS)** and the **peripheral nervous system (PNS)**. The central nervous system is the largest part of the nervous system and includes the spinal cord and the brain. The peripheral nervous system resides outside of the central nervous system and serves the limbs and organs.

The peripheral nervous system is further divided into the **somatic nervous system** and the **autonomic nervous system**. The somatic nervous system picks up stimuli from the outside world, coordinates our movements, and performs other tasks that we control consciously. The autonomic nervous system consists of the **sympathetic nervous system** and the **parasympathetic nervous system**. The sympathetic and parasympathetic nervous systems act in opposition to

each other and affect the same organs. In most situations, the sympathetic system acts as an accelerator for the organs, while the parasympathetic system acts as a brake. The parasympathetic system is responsible for functions that do not require immediate action. The sympathetic system, in contrast, is always active and becomes significantly more active during stress. The two systems have rhyming job descriptions: While the sympathetic system's job is "fight or flight," the parasympathetic system's priorities are "rest and digest."

Neurons: Their Anatomy and Function

Neurons are the building blocks of the nervous system. A neuron is an excitable cell that receives different types of stimulation, most often signals from other neurons. In response to a signal, a neuron can "fire" by passing the signal along to other neurons, but it can also hold its fire by not transmitting the signal. While neurons are binary in nature—they either fire or they don't—they can fire at various rates (from 100 to 1000 times a second) and thus pass on highly nuanced information to other neurons.

NEURON ANATOMY

Dendrites are relatively short, bushy, branch-like structures that emerge from the neuron's cell body and receive signals from adjoining neurons. A single neuron may have as many as 2000 connections to other neurons through its dendritic branches.

The neuron's cell body, the **soma**, contains the nucleus. All of the information collected by the dendrites converges in the soma, which processes this information. In effect, the soma calculates the sum of all incoming signals, and if the summed voltage is above a specific threshold, the neuron will fire and pass the signal along to the cells with which it connects.

When a neuron fires, the signal travels down the neuron's **axon**, a cable-like extension that transmits the signal away from the soma toward the target of communication. Axons "talk to" three different targets: muscles, glands, and dendrites of neighboring neurons. Axon length varies quite a bit among neurons. Some axons are relatively short, while others can extend from the base of the brain to the tips of the toes.

Most, but not all, axons are covered by a **myelin** sheath. A fatty substance that acts a lot like the plastic coating on electrical wires, myelin insulates the axon, thereby improving the strength and speed of signals traveling down its length.

Axons pass their signals to neighboring dendrites via **terminal buttons**, structures at the ends of the many branches that extend out from each axon. When they receive a signal, the terminal buttons release chemicals into the space between neurons and excite neighboring dendrites.

Types of Neurons

Although all neurons are generally similar in structure, they come in a variety of shapes and sizes. All neurons, however, fall into three categories, depending on their location and function in the nervous system:

- **Sensory neurons** carry information *toward* the central nervous system from the sensory organs (eyes, ears, nose, tongue, and skin).
- **Motor neurons** carry information *away from* the central nervous system in order to operate muscles and glands.
- **Interneurons** send information between sensory neurons and motor neurons.

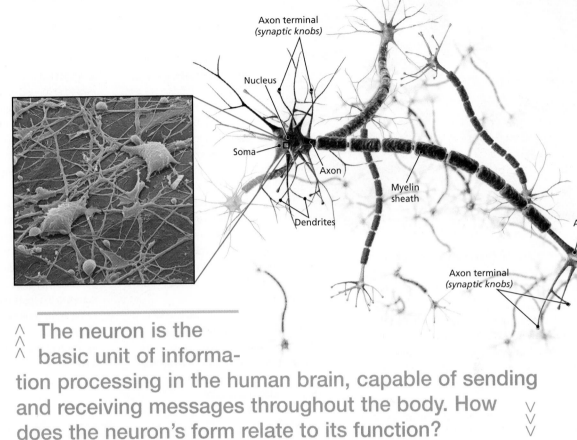

Axon terminal (*synaptic knobs*)

Nucleus

Soma

Axon

Myelin sheath

Dendrites

Axon

Axon terminal (*synaptic knobs*)

∧∧∧ The neuron is the basic unit of information processing in the human brain, capable of sending and receiving messages throughout the body. How does the neuron's form relate to its function? ∨∨∨

2 Sensory neurons excite interneurons in the dorsal gray portion of the spinal cord.

Sensory neuron

To the brain

3 Interneurons excite motor neurons in the ventral gray portion of the spinal cord.

4 Motor nerves exit the spinal cord, excite the muscle, and initiate a movement.

1 Flame stimulates pain receptors (sensory neurons).

Interneurons are the most numerous type of neuron in the human nervous system: There are millions of sensory and motor neurons, but there are about 100 billion interneurons. Located exclusively in the central nervous system, interneurons are capable of receiving and combining information from a variety of sources. As the

workforce of the CNS, these cells are responsible for generating perception from sensation, creating our internal mental worlds, and organizing and initiating behavioral actions.

Glia

What's the glue that holds neurons together? Look no further than the **glial cells**, also known simply as **glia**, the Greek word for *glue*. There are about 10 glial cells for every neuron in the human brain. Glia support those neurons in many ways: Among other tasks, they keep neurons in place, create myelin, and provide nutrition and insulation.

Additionally, a specialized form of glial cells, called astrocytes, surrounds the brain's blood vessels and creates what is known as the **blood-brain barrier**, a fatty envelope that filters substances trying to leave the bloodstream and reach the brain. Since many toxins and poisons are not soluble in fat, they cannot penetrate the blood-brain barrier and harm the brain.

COMMUNICATION BETWEEN NEURONS
To Fire or Not to Fire

Neurons are very social creatures. They live in large communities called **networks** and cluster

in tight groupings called **nerves**. Neurons depend on contact with one another for survival, and they work both as individuals and as part of larger groups.

Neurons communicate in much the same way people do when they have a bit of interesting gossip. Imagine an eighth grader tearing down the hallway of her middle school to tell her closest friend the "latest." Her excitement is palpable. Upon reaching her friend, she whispers in her ear; the friend shrieks in excitement and is off to tell the next student. Of course, neurons transmit information via energy rather than whispers, but their basic pattern of communication might seem familiar to a teenage social butterfly.

Neurons fire only when they are stimulated by a source, such as another neuron or a sensory receptor that has been stimulated by heat, light, or pressure. Many different neighboring cells can relay signals to a single neuron. Some cells instruct the neuron to fire—to transmit information to other neurons—while others tell the neuron not to fire (a process called **inhibition**). Faced with these conflicting messages, the neuron does something very social: It goes with the majority.

Every neuron has a specific **threshold** that must be reached in order for it to fire. Whether the number of positive inputs exceeds the threshold by 1 millivolt or 100, the result is the same: If the threshold is crossed, the cell will fire. This is called the **all-or-none**

principle. When you're standing on a high dive, you either jump or you don't; there is no "in between" state. The same is true for neurons.

When a neuron fires, the signal that the dendrites and cell body receive must travel down the axon to the terminal buttons at the opposite end of the neuronal cell. In order to accomplish this, the neuron creates an **action potential**, an electrochemical ripple that works its way from the cell body to the terminal buttons and terminates in the release of neurotransmitters that will stimulate the next neuron.

While at rest, a neuron's fluid interior contains more negatively charged particles than the external environment. This relatively negative state inside the neuron is called the **resting potential**. It's maintained by negatively charged protein molecules and chlorine atoms within the cell as well as by ion

pumps in the cell membrane that keep more potassium ions inside the neuron and more sodium ions outside the neuron. Not surprisingly, potassium and sodium ions use different channels to enter and exit the cell.

When the neuron is stimulated, the axonal membrane closest to the cell body selectively changes the status of its ion channels. As a result, potassium channels close and sodium channels open. Consequently, the amount of positively charged sodium ions inside the cell increases. This influx of sodium ions changes the internal state of the axon from negative to positive and propagates the action potential to the next section of the axon's membrane. The movement of sodium ions into the neuron and potassium ions out of the neuron, as well as the pumping that puts the ions back where they came from, continues down the axon, creating a moving electrical signal. This signal moves down the axon in the same way that a human wave at a sporting event travels around a stadium.

The self-propagating action potential works its way down the membrane to the terminal buttons, where it causes the release of chemicals that excite the neighboring neuron. Myelinated neurons are able to speed up this process. The myelin sheath that covers the axon is not continuous; rather, the glial cells that make up the myelin form insulated sections, leaving small bits of bare axon called the **nodes of Ranvier**. The action potential can jump from bare spot to bare spot. This jumping from node to node allows the signal to move down the axon with great speed.

The Synapse

Upon seeing **synapses** under his microscope, anatomist Santiago Ramón y Cajal (1937) nicknamed them "protoplasmic kisses." A synapse is a connection between two neurons through which information is transmitted. Often, the synapse is made up of a narrow space, or a **synaptic cleft**, between the transmitting neuron's terminal buttons and the

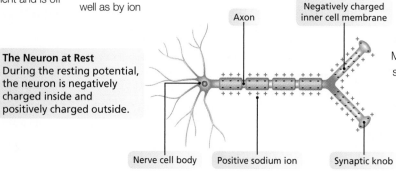

The Neuron at Rest
During the resting potential, the neuron is negatively charged inside and positively charged outside.

Axon · Negatively charged inner cell membrane · Nerve cell body · Positive sodium ion · Synaptic knob

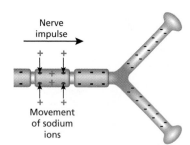

Nerve impulse

Movement of sodium ions

The Neural Impulse
The action potential occurs when positive sodium ions enter into the cell, causing a reversal of the electrical charge from negative to positive.

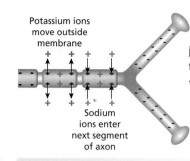

Potassium ions move outside membrane

Sodium ions enter next segment of axon

The Neural Impulse Continues
As the action potential moves down the axon toward the axon terminals, the cell areas behind the action potential return to their resting state of a negative charge as the positive potassium ions rapidly leave the inside of the cell.

∧∧∧ The movement of negatively and positively charged particles allows an electrical signal to travel down the axon.

receiving neuron's dendrites. The neuron that delivers the signal to the synapse is called the **pre-synaptic neuron**, and the neuron that receives the signal from the synapse is called the **post-synaptic neuron**. Synapses are also located between neurons and muscles as well as between neurons and gland cells.

Synapses convert the electric action potential that's traveled down the axon into a chemical message, called a **neurotransmitter**. When a neuron fires, its terminal buttons release neurotransmitters into the synaptic cleft. Some of those neurotransmitters then travel across the synapse and chemically stimulate the neighboring neuron. That neuron, in turn, converts the chemical signal back to an electrical signal.

Neurotransmitters don't stay in the synaptic cleft for long: A process called **reuptake** moves many of the released neurotransmitters back to the pre-synaptic neuron. (Recent research has shown that glia also play a role in removing neurotransmitters from the synapses (Volterra & Steinhäuser, 2004).) If a neurotransmitter doesn't quickly attach to a receptor on a neighboring neuron, it will fall victim to the reuptake process.

A specific class of drug designed to relieve symptoms of depression owes its effectiveness to this process: One theory of depression hypothesizes that a lack of a neurotransmitter called serotonin prevents cells from communicating the way they do in people without depression. Drugs called selective serotonin reuptake inhibitors, or SSRIs, block the reuptake of serotonin from the synaptic cleft. Because SSRIs prevent pre-synaptic neurons from rapidly reabsorbing serotonin, more neurotransmitters remain in the synaptic cleft longer, increasing the likelihood that they will stimulate the neighboring cells' post-synaptic receptors.

Synaptic Plasticity

As the research into prosthetic limbs reveals, one impressive characteristic of the brain is its **plasticity**, or its ability to adapt and change. This plasticity is evident not only in the brain as a whole but also at the cellular level. In 1949, Donald Hebb first proposed the idea of synaptic plasticity as a theoretical model to account for how the brain learns and retains memories. Hebb theorized that the more cells talk to one another, the more plentiful their synaptic connections become. In addition to providing a compelling model for learning and memory, this phenomenon helps us understand how individuals recover from damage to areas of the brain. There are two main theories. The first believes that since the brain cannot make new functional neurons, it recruits and fortifies smaller, previously underutilized connections. Recent discoveries further support Hebb's theory of synaptic plasticity. In one study, London taxi drivers exhibited increased hippocampus volume compared to similarly aged adults who were not taxi drivers. (The hippocampus is a structure critical to spatial memory that will be discussed in more detail later in this chapter.) Scientists believe that the drivers' increased hippocampus volume results from increased synaptic density, stimulated by learning numerous complicated driving routes (Maguire, Spiers, Good, Hartley, Frackowiak, & Burgess, 2003). The second theory regarding neural plasticity believes that the human brain does produce new neurons. In fact, there is now evidence suggesting that adult neurogenesis does occur in certain brain regions such as the hippocampus (Eriksson et al., 1998). If true, these cells are very likely to be involved with learning and memory, and brain plasticity in general.

Nerve is a tight grouping of neurons.

Inhibition is a process in which a neuron is instructed not to transmit information to other neurons.

Threshold is the number of positive inputs a neuron must receive before it transmits information.

All-or-none principle states that once the threshold for a particular neuron is reached, it will transmit all of its information, no matter how many more positive inputs it receives over that threshold.

Action potential is an electrochemical ripple that works its way from the cell body to the terminal buttons and terminates in the release of neurotransmitters that will stimulate the next neuron.

Resting potential is a relatively negative state inside a neuron in which the neuron's fluid interior contains a surplus of negatively charged particles.

Nodes of Ranvier are parts of an axon that are not insulated by myelin.

Synapse is the area between neurons across which nerve impulses travel.

Synaptic cleft is a narrow space between a transmitting neuron's terminal buttons and a receiving neuron's dendrites.

Pre-synaptic neuron is a neuron that delivers a signal to a synapse.

Post-synaptic neuron is a neuron that receives a signal from a synapse.

Neurotransmitter is a chemical message created by a synapse from an electric message transmitted by terminal buttons.

Reuptake is a process in which neurotransmitters are released back to a pre-synaptic neuron.

Plasticity describes a flexible ability to grow and change.

>>> Drugs like SSRIs are designed to affect the reuptake process and alter signal transmission across synapses. What might be the benefits and drawbacks of these drugs?

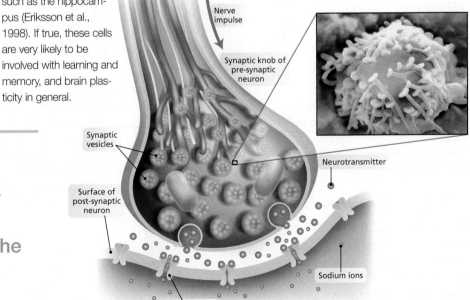

Nerve impulse

Synaptic knob of pre-synaptic neuron

Neurotransmitter

Synaptic vesicles

Surface of post-synaptic neuron

Sodium ions

Receptor site

The Central Nervous System: The Spinal Cord

The **spinal cord** connects the spinal nerves to the brain and organizes simple reflexes and rhythmic movements. It is organized in ascending and descending tracks: Ascending tracks carry sensory information from the body to the brain, while descending tracks deliver motor commands to the muscles from the brain.

THE JOB OF THE SPINAL CORD

Specifically designed to keep you alive, **reflexes** are rapid and automatic neuromuscular actions generated in response to a specific stimulus. Most often, the spinal cord organizes these automatic actions without the conscious participation of the brain. To produce a reflex, a sensory neuron must carry the stimulus to the spinal cord, where an interneuron enables connection to a motor neuron that produces a specific motor pattern. Consider the following example: You are walking barefoot on the beach when you begin to step on something sharp. The sensory neurons in your foot are immediately activated by the painful stimulus and send a signal to the interneurons in the spinal cord. Interneurons in turn answer this call by exciting the motor neurons leading to your foot. As a result, before you have time to really "think about it," your foot has jerked up off the sand, and you have avoided injury.

Have you ever felt like you don't have control over your body's movements? When it comes to reflexes, you *don't* have conscious control. It would be inefficient for a signal to travel all the way to the brain and back when only a simple movement is required. When there's the potential for harm, elaborate decision making becomes less important than

>>> The spinal cord connects the brain to the peripheral nervous system.

getting away from the stimulus as fast as possible. Of course, if you step on something sharp, the pain signal will eventually reach your brain, though the signal travels more slowly than the spinal reflex does. When the signal arrives, you will consciously experience pain, followed by the awareness of your own rapidly moved foot. But reflexes and conscious awareness aren't really connected: Although people with spinal cord injuries exhibit spinal reflexes, they have no conscious or sensory awareness of doing so.

DAMAGE TO THE SPINAL CORD

Unlike a great deal of tissue in the human body, the spinal cord is not able to repair itself following injury. The overwhelming majority of spinal cord injuries involve motor vehicle accidents and people between the ages of 16 and 30. Most frequently, damage to the bones of the spinal column severs or chokes the spine itself. Injuring the spine is like cutting a string of Christmas lights: All the bulbs that follow the cut will no longer light up. Similarly, a person may lose all of the functions controlled by the area of the spine below the injury. For example, damage to the cervical vertebrae can cause the brain to be out of touch with the body. This injury would paralyze the chest and lungs (requiring patients to rely on a machine to breathe) as well as the trunk and both arms and legs. In contrast, injury to the lumbar, or lower spine area, may result in hip and leg paralysis. The spinal cord is rarely completely severed, so some patients manage to

Brain (CNS)

Spinal cord (CNS)

Nerves (PNS)

recover certain aspects of function; however, complete recovery is unlikely.

The Central Nervous System: The Human Brain

All cells or structures found in humans are also found in other animals. Why, then, are humans fundamentally different from the vast majority of the animal kingdom? What gives rise to uniquely human thoughts and emotions like symbolic representation, empathy, and misanthropy? We don't really know the answers to these questions, but we do know that the structure of the human brain is not terribly unique. In fact, it shares a number of structures with the brains of animals farther down the evolutionary ladder. However, the ways in which these structures are used may be what makes the human brain truly unique.

Paul MacLean (1990) has written extensively about the "triune" brain. According to MacLean's model, the human brain is best understood within a socio-cognitive context by dividing it into three regions.

The primary and evolutionarily oldest part of the brain is the **brainstem**, which is responsible for survival-oriented functions such as breathing, cardiac function, and basic arousal. The second region, which emerged more recently in evolutionary terms, is the **limbic system**. Comprised of a number of structures that control social and emotional behavior, the limbic system also influences cognitive processes, most notably forms of memory. The evolutionarily newest part of the brain is the **neocortex**, specifically the **prefrontal**

>>>   How does MacLean's model of the triune brain illustrate the brain's sophistication, integration, and adaptability?

cortex. This advancement is credited with hurling humans up the evolutionary ladder by enabling symbolic representation, the cornerstone of most complex cognitive processes.

Following MacLean's model, we'll explore the human brain from the "bottom up," taking a look at the most basic and rudimentary structures before working our way to the more complex or "evolved" portions of the brain.

THE BRAINSTEM AND SUBCORTICAL STRUCTURES

The **brainstem** is exactly what it sounds like: the "stem" or base of the brain. Connected to the spinal cord, the brainstem houses the structures that control basic survival functions. Like the spinal cord, these structures are capable of reflexive action.

The brainstem has two main functions. First, it's a conduit for incoming sensory information and outgoing motor commands, much like the spinal cord. Second, it possesses integrative functions that are critical for cardiovascular system control, respiratory control, pain sensitivity control, alertness, and consciousness. Taking this information into consideration, it's easy to see why damage to the brainstem is often life-threatening.

Unfortunately, the brainstem is vulnerable to both direct and indirect damage. The adult skull is made of very hard bone with few openings. The largest opening is the **foramen magnum** at the base of the skull, which connects the

The Triune Brain

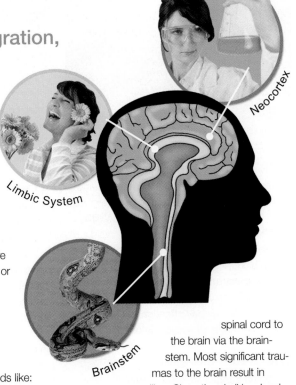

Limbic System

Neocortex

Brainstem

spinal cord to the brain via the brainstem. Most significant traumas to the brain result in swelling. Since the skull is a hardened sphere, the swollen brain has no place to expand other than through the large opening at the base of the skull. The "extra" volume of brain tissue creates a great deal of pressure at the base of the skull and can actually compress the brainstem enough to cause a coma. In the most dramatic case, swelling can disrupt the **medulla** and the **pons**, the centers that

regulate cardiac and respiratory function, causing death. While we know from the example of the civil servant that the brain is flexible and adaptable, it isn't always able to use these qualities to ward off serious damage to the vulnerable, valuable brainstem.

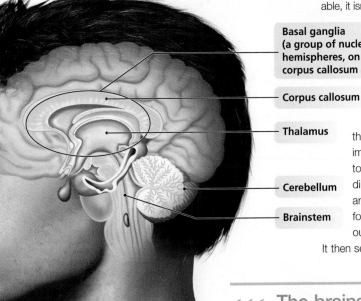

Basal ganglia (a group of nuclei located in both hemispheres, on either side of the corpus callosum and thalamus)

Corpus callosum

Thalamus

Cerebellum

Brainstem

The Thalamus

The **thalamus**, located just above the brainstem, has multiple critically important functions. It acts as a translator that receives sensory information directly from most of the sense organs and processes that information into a form that the **cerebral cortex**, or the outer part of the brain, can understand. It then sends that information to various parts

<<<   The brainstem controls basic survival functions.

Cerebellum is a part of the brain that coordinates muscle movements and maintains equilibrium. It is involved in conditioning and forming procedural memories and habits related to movement.

Basal ganglia are a set of interconnected structures in the brain that help with motor control, cognition, different forms of learning, and emotional processing. They are involved in forming procedural memories and habits related to movement.

Caudate is a part of the basal ganglia; involved in control of voluntary movement, and part of the brain's learning and memory system.

Putamen is a part of the basal ganglia; involved in reinforcement learning.

Globus pallidus is a part of the basal ganglia; relays information from the caudate and putamen to the thalamus.

Amygdala is a part of the limbic system; involved in fear detection and conditioning; it is essential for unconscious emotional responses such as the fight-or-flight response.

Hippocampus is a part of the brain involved in processing explicit memories, recognizing and recalling long-term memories, and conditioning.

Hypothalamus is a small structure in the brain that links the nervous system to the endocrine system.

Cingulate cortex is a part of the brain that is divided into four sections and is involved in various functions such as emotion, response selection, personal orientation, and memory formation and retrieval.

<<< The cerebellum helps athletes perform rapid, complex movements.

of the cerebral cortex. Additionally, the thalamus helps to regulate our states of arousal, sleep and wakefulness, and consciousness.

The Cerebellum

The "little brain," or **cerebellum**, in many ways resembles a smaller version of the cerebral cortex (e.g., it contains two distinct hemispheres) and is located just behind and underneath it. The cerebellum works as an integrator, allowing us to control and process our perceptions and motor movements. Many neural pathways link the cerebellum with both the cerebral motor cortex and the spinal cord. The cerebellum smoothly integrates these pathways, receiving feedback about the body's position and using this information to direct our movements.

Because the cerebellum *modifies* motor movement rather than producing it, damage to the cerebellum causes movement-related difficulties rather than paralysis. These difficulties tend to be most obvious during rapid, well-timed sequences of movements such as dialing a telephone, playing sports, or playing a musical instrument. Motor control isn't the cerebellum's only forte, however: The cerebellum also helps us pay attention to stimuli and process a variety of sensory information.

The Basal Ganglia

The **basal ganglia** are a set of interconnected structures (the **caudate**, **putamen**, and **globus pallidus**) next to the thalamus. The human basal ganglia are richly connected to the brainstem, thalamus, and cerebral cortex and are an essential participant in motor control, cognition, different forms of learning (particularly motor learning), and emotional processing. Illnesses that affect the

basal ganglia, such as Huntington's disease, often cause patients to experience muscle spasms in the arms, legs, or face. Damage to the basal ganglia may also cause poor coordination.

THE LIMBIC SYSTEM

The **limbic system**, which has rich reciprocal connections with both the brainstem and the neocortex (Davis, 1992), is responsible for a number of survival-related behaviors. Simply, the limbic system is a series of neural structures that are critical for human emotion, motivation, and some forms of emotional and social learning. There is, however, some disagreement with regard to which specific structures are included in the limbic system. Given the purpose of the present discussion, description of the limbic system will be limited to structures involved in emotionally driven behavior, including the **amygdala**, the **hippocampus**, the **hypothalamus**, and portions of the **cingulate cortex**.

The Amygdala

The amygdala (from the Greek word for *almond*, which describes its shape) is involved in fear detection and conditioning. Scientists describe this structure as "a neural system that evolved to detect danger and produce rapid protective responses without conscious participation" (LeDoux et al., 1994). Imagine that you awake in the middle of the night to hear banging against your window. Before you can understand what you are seeing or hearing, the amygdala has received a "rough copy" of this sensory information. If the amygdala appraises

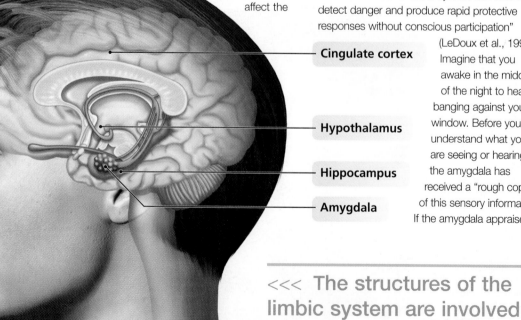

Cingulate cortex

Hypothalamus

Hippocampus

Amygdala

<<< The structures of the limbic system are involved in motivation and emotion.

the information it receives as threatening, then it will initiate a physiological response called the **fight or flight response** that prepares your body for action. You may notice that your heart is racing and that you suddenly feel wide awake. Meanwhile, a second, more detailed, message travels from your eyes and ears to the appropriate sensory cortex for more extensive processing and conscious perception. The banging sound you heard is analyzed in detail, using information from many parts of the brain. Once your brain has decided whether the threat is real or imagined, a message to this effect is sent back to the amygdala. If a burglar is entering your bedroom, your amygdala has prepared your body to react. If the sound you heard was a branch tapping against your window, the fear circuit is switched off and you are able to go back to sleep (although it may take you a while to relax).

The Hippocampus

The hippocampus, which means *seahorse* in Greek, is named for its curved shape when seen in cross-section. It is essential for creating and storing new memories. The hippocampus can be thought of as a top-notch administrative assistant in a very busy office. It is responsible for creating and logically storing memory "files," knowing where those files are, and retrieving them when necessary. Like a good administrative assistant, the hippocampus knows where everything is, meaning that it plays a critical role in a variety of memory processes, including spatial memory (remember the London taxi drivers described earlier?). Individuals with hippocampus damage are able to hold new information for a short time, but are unable to make enduring memories.

The Cingulate Cortex

The cingulate cortex lies along the midline of the brain in each hemisphere, just above the **corpus callosum**. The cingulate is functionally and anatomically segregated into four distinct regions (Vogt et al., 2005). The **anterior cingulate cortex**, closest to the forehead, has a primary role in emotion and in the integration of visceral and cognitive information. The **midcingulate cortex** lies just behind the anterior cingulate and is involved

with response selection, particularly among competing stimuli. The **posterior cingulate cortex**, closest to the back of the head, is closely tied to personal orientation: It not only helps you determine where you are in space, but also allows you to gauge your personal involvement and relevance in social situations. The final—and least understood—region of the cingulate cortex is the **retrosplenial cortex**, which is believed to be closely involved in memory formation and retrieval.

The Hypothalamus

The hypothalamus is a relatively small but critically important structure that links the nervous system to the **endocrine system**. It regulates body temperature, hunger, thirst, fatigue, anger, and circadian cycles. Located underneath the thalamus (*hypo* is Greek for "underneath"), the hypothalamus is situated directly above the **pituitary gland**, which regulates a number of other glands in the body. It is through these connections that the hypothalamus is able to regulate a vast number of body processes. Receiving its directives from above, the hypothalamus translates these instructions into chemical messages that are then sent out by the pituitary gland.

THE CEREBRAL CORTEX

The cerebral cortex is, evolutionarily speaking, the newest part of the human brain. Translated from Latin, *cerebral cortex* means "brain bark." This is an apt name, as the cortex itself is actually made up of **gray matter**, which is 1.5–5 millimeters thick and covers the cerebrum and cerebellum like bark covers a tree. Like bark, too, the cerebral cortex is ridged and wrinkled into bulges (called **gyri**) and grooves (called **sulci**). These folds aren't merely aesthetic: Because they increase the cortex's total surface area, they also increase its processing power. If you flattened out the entire cortex, it would cover approximately 2.5 square feet and would be much too large to fit in a human skull.

Motor cortex

Somatosensory cortex

Association cortex

Association cortex

Parietal lobe

Frontal lobe

Broca's area

Temporal lobe

Occipital lobe

Visual cortex

Wernicke's area

The cerebral cortex, the outermost portion of the brain, is packed full of neural connections.

White matter consists of myelinated axons that form the connections within the brain.

Primary cortex is a part of the cerebral cortex that serves basic sensory and motor functions; one exists in each lobe of the cerebral cortex.

Association cortex is a part of the cerebral cortex that helps basic sensory and motor information from a specific lobe integrate with information from the rest of the brain; one exists in each lobe of the cerebral cortex.

Occipital lobes are parts of the brain involved in visual processing; the smallest of the four lobes in the human brain.

Primary visual cortex is a part of the brain that receives input from the eyes and translates that input into what people see.

Temporal lobes are parts of the brain involved in auditory processing.

Parietal lobes are parts of the brain primarily concerned with bodily sensations, including those of touch, taste, and temperature.

Primary auditory cortex is a part of the brain involved in auditory processing.

Primary somatosensory cortex is a part of the brain that receives and interprets information about bodily sensations; located in the parietal lobe.

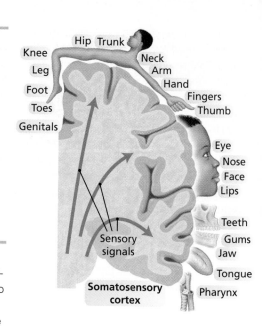

>>> This homunculus illustrates the somatosensory cortex. Why does the brain devote so much space to processing information about our hands and mouths?

The human brain is somewhat like an orange in its construction. The gray matter is like a thick orange peel, making up about two-thirds of the brain's total volume. The gray matter of the cortex is made up mostly of cell bodies, which give it its pinkish gray color. The interior of the cerebral cortex—where the blood supply meets the brain—contains the cell bodies that do the work of the brain. If you were to peel away the cortex (again, think of an orange), the remaining tissue would look white and shiny. You'd be looking at **white matter**, the myelinated axons that form the trillions of connections within the brain. It is these connections that enable the human brain to do some of the astounding things it does. Think of the gray matter as cities (where things are "happening") and the white matter as roads that connect the cities. Their functions are unique and equally vital.

The cerebral cortex is divided into two hemispheres, right and left. Each hemisphere is further divided into four lobes that have relatively specialized functions. The boundaries of the four lobes are created by particularly deep sulci on the brain surface. Each lobe contains an area of **primary cortex** (motor or sensory) that serves basic sensory and motor functions. Each lobe also contains an area of **association cortex** that helps basic sensory and motor information from a specific lobe integrate with information from the rest of the brain.

The Occipital Lobes

Located at the rearmost portion of the skull, the **occipital lobes** are the smallest of the four lobes in the human brain. The occipital lobe is known for its visual processing prowess. The **primary visual cortex** receives input from the eyes and is able to translate that input into things we "see." The occipital lobe's association cortex integrates the color, size, and movement of our visual perceptions so that visual stimuli become recognizable to us. The association cortex then shares this information with other regions of the brain. For example, it can send its results to the temporal lobe, which finds the stimulus's name, and to the parietal lobe, which determines where it's located in space.

The Temporal Lobes

The **temporal lobes** are located just in front of the occipital lobes and are primarily involved in auditory processing. They lie at the sides of the brain, beneath the **parietal lobes**. Seen in profile, the human brain looks something like a mitten. If you think of the brain this way, the temporal lobes are where you would expect the mitten's thumbs to be.

The temporal lobe is home to the **primary auditory cortex**. The association cortex that surrounds the auditory cortex is devoted to the complicated task of understanding language. Because the temporal lobe's association areas are so involved with language, they often contribute to visual tasks (such as naming observed objects) and memory-related tasks (such as creating narrative contexts for the information we want to remember).

The Parietal Lobes

The **parietal lobes** are located above the occipital lobes, just behind the frontal lobes. The **primary somatosensory cortex**, which receives and interprets information about all of our bodily sensations, is located within the parietal lobe. Strange (and gruesome) as it may seem, we can think of this area of the cortex as a homunculus, or "little man." The homunculus is a distorted body map, with each part of the body sized according to how much space the

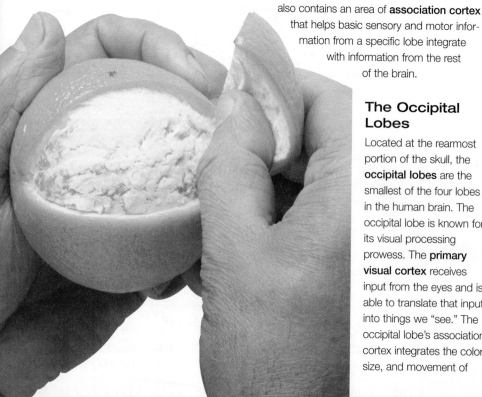

motion and sensory feedback is the process of human speech. A region within the frontal lobe, **Broca's area**, initiates the movements needed to produce speech, and it is the careful interplay of the motor and sensory cortices that keeps you from mispronouncing words.

The foremost portion of the frontal cortex is the brain's task-master. Providing the brain bases for overt attention and working memory, it makes sure the task at hand is attended to and completed. It also coordinates a vast amount of complicated information and supports processes like reasoning,

brain gives to processing information about that body part (Jasper & Penfield, 1954). For example, because so many neurons process information from the hands and lips, the homunculus's hands and lips are remarkably oversized. The primary somatosensory cortex doesn't literally look like an outlandish person, but its regions correspond to the regions of the homunculus: A lot of space in the cortex is devoted to the hands, while the area devoted to the hips doesn't take up much room.

The Frontal Lobes

The **frontal lobes** are the part of your brain that is behind your forehead. Often referred to as the "executive" or "conductor" of the brain, the frontal lobe performs a variety of integration and management functions. At the very back of the frontal lobes lies the **primary motor cortex**, which is responsible for generating the neural impulses that control the execution of movements. This is an extremely important function, as no behavior can "get out" of the human brain without some sort of action. The related association cortex is devoted to helping integrate and orchestrate movement. For example, the frontal lobe must work closely with the parietal lobe to make sure that movements are performed correctly within space and that visual information is translated into the appropriate movements. The portion of the cortex that controls motor movements is directly adjacent to the somatosensory cortex and has a nearly identical homunculus. This makes sense since all movements require immediate sensory feedback in order to confirm their proper execution. One of the most important examples of the interaction between

Left visual field
Right visual field

Optic nerves

Speech

Optic chiasm

Visual area of left hemisphere
Corpus callosum (split)
Visual area of right hemisphere

problem solving, and a variety of complex social behaviors.

THE DIVIDED BRAIN
Symmetry in the Brain

The brain is divided into two hemispheres that are connected by an enormous band of axons called the corpus callosum. A great number of brain functions, such as primary sensory and motor areas, are located in both the right and left cerebral hemispheres. What is interesting about this symmetry, however, is the fact that the brain and body are crisscrossed: For example, the motor cortex in the *right* hemisphere controls the movement of the *left* side of the body. This kind of connectivity can be described as **contralateral**. While the majority of brain-body connections are contralateral, there are also **ipsilateral** connections that link one side of the brain to the same side of the body. This division of labor may seem fairly straightforward, but in some areas of the brain, the relationship between mind and body gets infinitely more complicated.

Language and the Brain

The most ubiquitous and well-studied functional asymmetry in the human brain is language. Language is most commonly found in the left hemisphere, particularly among right-handed males. Left-handed people are more likely to have some language functioning in the right hemisphere, and women are more likely to have some language function in each hemisphere. However, it is nearly impossible to find a human who does not have some

∧
∧ **The corpus callosum is the largest band of**
∧ **axons in the human brain.**

language function in his or her left hemisphere. People who have suffered damage to the left hemisphere almost always have difficulty understanding or producing language as a result of the injury. Damage to comparable areas in the right hemisphere produces deficits in the performance of such tasks as reading maps, drawing shapes, and recognizing faces, all of which rely on perceiving and integrating the spatial relationships of stimuli. Speaking very generally, the left hemisphere is critical for language, while the right is critical for spatial relationships.

> "Speaking very generally, the left hemisphere is critical for language, while the right is critical for spatial relationships."

The Developing Brain

The way in which functions are distributed in the brain is largely a product of human development. Early in life, a great deal of the cortex is very flexible with regard to the types of functions it can perform. As a result, a significant number of developmental influences such as sex, gender, experiences, and culture—to name only a few—are capable of having a profound influence on the way the brain is organized. These

Picturing the Brain:

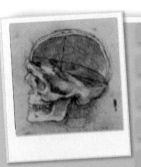

1489
Leonardo Da Vinci sketches the human brain.

1543
Artists in the Italian painter Titian's studio sketched detailed drawings of the brains of cadavers. This sketch appeared in a book by Dutch anatomist Andreas Vesalius which revolutionized the study of anatomy.

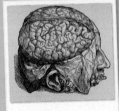

1861
French surgeon Paul Broca identified the speech center in the brain through autopsies.

1911
Santiago Ramón y Cajal's drawings and staining methods advanced those of Camillo Golgi for visualizing neurons, dendrites, and axons. Cajal promoted the "neuron theory," the fundamental principle of modern neuroscience, which holds that neurons are the basic unit of the central nervous system. More important, Cajal realized that neurons communicate across a small gap, or synapse.

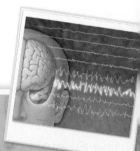

1929
Electroencephalograms (EEGs), which measure and record minute wavelike electrical signals produced by neurons as they "fire," are introduced.

Source: Adapted from *The Dana Sourcebook of Brain Science*, 3rd ed.

developmental influences make it hard for us to generalize about brain functions other than those that have been very well studied.

Of Two Minds?

Few have contributed as much to our understanding of the brain's asymmetries as Michael Gazzaniga and his colleagues. During the 1960s, doctors treated a group of patients with intractable epilepsy by cutting the corpus collosum in order to prevent seizures from spreading between the hemispheres. This surgery gave patients great relief from their epilepsy and did not seem to have much of an impact on their day-to-day living. Gazzaniga, however, was able to devise a series of tests that demonstrated two different minds, each with different abilities, in these patients. When common objects were presented to the left hemisphere of split-brain patients, the patients had no trouble telling the experimenter what they saw. This was not the case when objects were presented to the right hemisphere. Patients claimed that they had not seen anything, or they guessed randomly. Gazzaniga then had subjects use their right or left hands to identify the object (remember that the sensory cortex for each hand is contralateral). The startling result was that when patients were unable to use speech to identify the object they were seeing, they were able to select the same object using their left hand (right hemisphere). Gazzaniga interpreted this to mean that the right hemisphere can function well independently, but has no discernible access to language.

A Brain Imaging Timeline

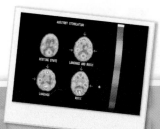

1973
The first computed tomography (CT) camera is created. This camera produces a composite image of the brain with a scanner that revolves around the skull, taking thousands of X-rays.

1975
The first positron emission tomography (PET) camera is unveiled. The PET camera uses the principle that blood is rushed to busy areas of the brain to deliver oxygen and nutrients to the neurons. Patients are injected with radioactive glucose, then scanned for the rays emitted as the solution metabolizes, highlighting neuronal activity.

1977
The first magnetic resonance imaging (MRI) camera produces images by subjecting the patient's head to a strong magnetic field, followed by several pulses of radio waves, producing three-dimensional computer-generated images.

1992
Functional magnetic resonance imaging (fMRI) is introduced. fMRI is used to map brain activity by detecting variations in the response of hydrogen atoms when oxygen is present in the blood.

2003
Peter Mansfield and Paul Lauterbur awarded Nobel Prize for their discoveries concerning MRI.

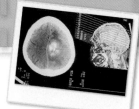

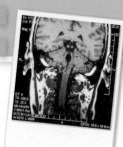

Summary

WHAT CHARACTERISTICS DESCRIBE THE HUMAN BRAIN? p. 38

• The human brain has three major characteristics: integration, sophistication, and adaptability.

HOW IS THE NERVOUS SYSTEM ORGANIZED? p. 38

• The nervous system consists of the central nervous system (the brain and the spinal cord) and the peripheral nervous system (the neurons and nerves that serve every other part of the body).

• The peripheral nervous system is divided into the somatic nervous system, which registers stimuli and regulates conscious actions, and the autonomic nervous system, which controls involuntary actions.

• Within the autonomic nervous system, the sympathetic system stimulates organs and responds to stress, and the parasympathetic system calms the organs and maintains normal functioning.

HOW DOES THE NERVOUS SYSTEM OPERATE AT THE CELLULAR LEVEL? p. 39

• The brain is made up of neurons and glial cells. Neurons are communication cells that receive, process, and pass on neural signals. Glia support and insulate neurons.

• Neuron signaling is an all-or-nothing event. When the number of positive inputs exceeds a certain threshold, the neuron fires an action potential—an electrochemical signal that travels down the axon. In the synapse, neurotransmitters pass on information to the next neuron or gland.

WHAT ARE THE DIFFERENT PARTS OF THE HUMAN BRAIN, AND WHAT ROLE DOES EACH PART PLAY? p. 42

• The brain stem is connected to the spinal cord and houses the structures that maintain basic life functions.

• The limbic system regulates emotion, motivation, and social and emotional learning.

• The cerebral cortex performs most information processing. It has four lobes: The occipital lobe processes visual information, the temporal lobe handles auditory input and language, the parietal lobe interprets sensory information, and the frontal lobe coordinates memory, reasoning, problem solving, social behavior, language, and movement.

Test Your Understanding

1. Which part of the nervous system is responsible for the "fight or flight" response?

   a. sympathetic
   b. central
   c. parasympathetic
   d. somatic

2. Which of the following is NOT part of a neuron?

   a. soma
   b. nucleus
   c. axon
   d. interneurons

3. Which of the following are support cells for neurons?

   a. glia
   b. dendrites
   c. terminal buttons
   d. nodes of Ranvier

4. Which of these processes involves returning neurotransmitters back into the pre-synaptic neuron?

   a. plasticity
   b. inhibition
   c. reuptake
   d. action potential

5. Which type of neuron is stimulated when you touch something so hot that you reflexively pull your hand away?

   a. sensory neurons
   b. interneurons
   c. motor neurons
   d. all of the above

6. The brain is most likely to be harmed by a toxin if it

   a. cannot pass the blood-brain barrier.
   b. is fat soluble.
   c. is not fat soluble.
   d. is injected directly into the blood.

7. When a small child steps on a sharp toy, why might he physically react before he begins to cry?

    a. Motor neurons are stimulated before the signal reaches the brain.

    b. When the brain receives the pain signal, it must then focus on controlling the muscle signal.

    c. A child has fewer neurons than an adult.

    d. A child has shorter neurons than an adult; therefore, the signals between neurons produce a reaction more quickly.

8. Following a stroke or other type of brain injury, not being able to quickly and smoothly pick up a pencil might indicate damage to what part of the brain?

    a. the hippocampus

    b. the cerebellum

    c. the amygdala

    d. the hypothalamus

9. The motor cortex in the right side of your brain controlling your left hand demonstrates what about the human brain?

    a. that it forms connections randomly

    b. that the right hemisphere controls all hand movement

    c. that it has contralateral connections

    d. that it has ipsilateral connections

10. What part of the brain may help you remember where you left your keys?

    a. the corpus callosum

    b. the basal ganglia

    c. the hippocampus

    d. the amygdala

11. Following a fight or argument, what part of the nervous system helps to calm you down?

    a. somatic

    b. the amygdala

    c. sympathetic

    d. parasympathetic

12. Named after the person who discovered it, which part of the brain helps coordinate pronunciation?

    a. Wernicke's area

    b. Broca's area

    c. Putamen

    d. Golgi

13. What part of the brain controls the most basic survival functions?

    a. the neocortex

    b. the cerebellum

    c. the limbic system

    d. the brainstem

14. Which part of the brain is involved in dreaming?

    a. the pons

    b. the medulla

    c. the cerebellum

    d. the basal ganglia

15. What are the connections that allow brain areas to communicate made of?

    a. sucli

    b. white matter

    c. gray matter

    d. gyri

16. Why is the brain wrinkled?

    a. There is fluid on the brain that causes it to wrinkle.

    b. Wrinkles in the cerebral cortex create folds for information to travel through.

    c. Wrinkles create more surface area, which gives the brain greater processing power.

    d. As the brain ages it becomes more wrinkled.

17. When neurons fire, they produce what kind of recordable signals?

    a. acoustic (sound) signals

    b. wavelike electrical signals

    c. light signals

    d. radio waves

18. What is true about a neuron at rest?

    a. The inside of the neuron is positively charged relative to the outside of the neuron.

    b. Sodium ions are rushing into the neuron.

    c. The neuron is firing.

    d. The inside of the neuron is negatively charged relative to the outside of the neuron.

19. Which of the following is an example of plasticity?

    a. the reuptake of neurotransmitters

    b. the brain's many contralateral connections

    c. Language is located primarily in the left hemisphere.

    d. When damage occurs to the brain, smaller and underutilized neurons may form new connections.

20. If a neuron receives a great number of inhibition signals from neighboring neurons, what is likely to happen?

    a. The neuron will fire.

    b. The neuron will not fire.

    c. The neuron will release neurotransmitters.

    d. the neuron will create an action potential.

Remember to check www.thethinkspot.com **for additional information, downloadable flashcards, and other helpful resources.**

Answers: 1) a; **2)** d; **3)** a; **4)** c; **5)** d; **6)** b; **7)** a; **8)** b; **9)** c; **10)** c; **11)** d; **12)** b; **13)** d; **14)** a; **15)** b; **16)** c; **17)** b; **18)** d; **19)** d; **20)** b

THINK READINGS

(facts & fictions in mental health)

Uncovering "Brainscams"

In which the authors debunk myths concerning the three-pound organ inside our head

BY SCOTT O. LILIENFELD AND HAL ARKOWITZ

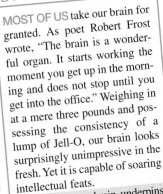

> Have you heard any common misconceptions about the brain? Were any of these misconceptions debunked in Chapter 3?

MOST OF US take our brain for granted. As poet Robert Frost wrote, "The brain is a wonderful organ. It starts working the moment you get up in the morning and does not stop until you get into the office." Weighing in at a mere three pounds and possessing the consistency of a lump of Jell-O, our brain looks surprisingly unimpressive in the fresh. Yet it is capable of soaring intellectual feats.

Although our brain underpins virtually every aspect of our thinking, personality and identity, it is the focus of a host of misconceptions. Without question, the world's expert on "neuromythology"—the study of myths regarding brain structure and function—was Simon Fraser University psychology professor Barry L. Beyerstein, who died last June at the age of 60. Barry coined the term "brainscams" in a 1990 article to draw attention to popular efforts to capitalize on the public's misunderstanding of the brain.

Barry was a friend of one of us (Lilienfeld) and a contributor to both *Scientific American* and *Scientific American Mind*. We thought it would be apropos to honor Barry's memory and contribution to neuromythology by dedicating this column to him and by examining three widespread brainscams that he helped to expose.

1. We use only 10 percent of our brain's capacity.

This misconception, about which Barry wrote on multiple occasions (including for an Ask the Experts column in the June 2004 issue of *Scientific American*), is among the most deeply entrenched in all of popular psychology. Its seductive appeal is understandable, as we would love to believe that our brain harbors an enormous reservoir of untapped potential. The 10 percent myth has contributed to a plethora of self-help books and self-improvement gadgets, including commercially available devices that supposedly enable us to harness our unrealized capacities.

Yet the scientific evidence against this myth is overwhelming. Functional brain-imaging studies have consistently failed to turn up any region of the brain that is perpetually inactive. Moreover, research on brain-damaged individuals reveals that a lesion to almost any brain area will produce at least some psychological deficits.

As Barry had noted, the 10 percent myth probably stemmed in part from a misinterpretation of the writings of William James, one of the founders of American psychology. In his musings around the turn of the 20th century, James wrote that

most of us actualize only a small portion of our intellectual potential, an assertion that may well possess some merit. But several popular authors including Lowell Thomas, who penned the foreword to Dale Carnegie's 1936 best-seller,

How to Win Friends and Influence People took liberties with James's writings by proposing that we use only about 10 percent of our brain. Further contributing to this notion's cachet were early studies suggesting that a substantial majority of the cerebral cortex is "silent." Yet because of advances in the measurement of brain activity, we now know that these areas are far from silent; they make up what neuroscientists term the brain's "association cortex," which plays a vital function in connecting perceptions, thoughts and emotions across diverse brain areas.

2. Some people are left-brained; others are right-brained.

Supposedly, left-brained people are analytical, logical and verbal, whereas right-brained people are creative, holistic and spatial. Scores of popular books have seized on this purported dichotomy. In his 1972 best-seller, *The Psychology of Consciousness*, Stanford University psychologist Robert Ornstein argued that

> For example, damage to the hippocampus can hamper long-term memory creation, and damage to the basal ganglia can cause muscle spasms or poor coordination (pp. 44–45).

> What have you learned about the cerebral cortex in Chapter 3 (pp. 45–46) that makes it difficult to believe this claim?

Western society places too great an emphasis on rational, left-brain thinking and not enough on intuitive, right-brain thinking. In 1979 artist and psychologist Betty Edwards's still popular book, *Drawing on the Right Side of the Brain*, similarly touted the benefits of more creative, right-brained forms of artistic expression.

Yet as Barry and University of Auckland psychologist Michael Corballis noted, the left-brained-versus-right-brained dichotomy is grossly oversimplified. For one thing, this distinction implies that people who are verbally gifted are not likely to be artistically talented, but research suggests otherwise. Moreover, neuroscience studies suggest that the brain's two hemispheres work in a highly coordinated fashion.

Like many brain myths, this one contains a kernel of truth. For several decades, beginning in the 1960s, neuroscientist Roger Sperry of the California Institute of Technology, psychologist Michael S. Gazzaniga of the University of California, Santa Barbara, and their colleagues studied patients who underwent surgery to sever the corpus callosum (the large band of neural fibers connecting the two hemispheres) in an effort to halt intractable epilepsy. The research showed that the left and right hemispheres are indeed different. In most of us, the left hemisphere is specialized for most aspects of language, whereas the right hemisphere is specialized for most visuospatial skills. Yet even these differences are only relative; for example, the right hemisphere tends to play a larger role than the left does in interpreting the vocal tone of spoken language. Moreover, because practi-

cally all of us have an intact corpus callosum, our hemispheres are continually interacting.

3. We can achieve a deeper sense of consciousness and relaxation by boosting our alpha waves.

Purveyors of "alpha consciousness" have encouraged people to undergo brain-wave biofeedback—in some cases using commercially available devices—to increase their production of alpha waves, brain waves that occur at a frequency of about eight to 13 cycles per second. Yet research shows alpha-wave output is largely or entirely unrelated to long-term personality traits and short-term states of contentment.

As Barry observed, the myth of alpha consciousness reflects a confusion between "correlation" and "causation." It is true that people tend to display a heightened proportion of alpha waves while meditating or relaxing deeply. But this fact does not mean that an increased production of alpha waves *causes* heightened relaxation. Moreover, research shows that elevated levels of alpha waves are found in some children with attention-deficit hyperactivity disorder, who are anything but relaxed.

These three myths barely scratch the surface of the sprawling field of neuromythology, but they give us a flavor of Barry's valuable role in combating the public's misconceptions about brain function. Fortunately, as readers of *Scientific American Mind* know, the facts about brain function are often far more interesting and surprising than

the fuctions. By helping laypersons better distinguish brain myths from brain realities, Barry Beyerstein was a pioneer in the ongoing effort to increase the public's scientific literacy. We will miss him.

SCOTT O. LILIENFELD and HAL ARKOWITZ serve on the board of advisers for *Scientific American Mind.* Lilienfeld is a psychology professor at Emory University and Arkowitz is a psychology professor at the University of Arizona. Send suggestions for column topics to editors@SciAmMind.com

(Further Reading)

• **Enhancing Human Performance: Issues, Theories, and Techniques.** Edited by D. Druckman and J. Swets. National Academy Press, 1988.

• **Brainscams: Neuromythologies of the New Age.** B. L. Beyerstein in *International Journal of Mental Health,* Vol. 19, No. 3, pages 27–36; 1990.

• **Mind Myths: Exploring Popular Assumptions about the Mind and Brain.** Edited by S. Della Salla. John Wiley & Sons, 1999.

• **Tall Tales about the Mind and Brain: Separating Fact from Fiction.** Edited by S. Della Salla. Oxford University Press, 2007.

© 2008 SCIENTIFIC AMERICAN, INC.

Your brain produces alpha waves when you are in a fully conscious, relaxed state. You can learn more about different frequencies of brain waves in Chapter 6 (p. 87).

To refresh your memory about the difference between correlation and causation, turn to Chapter 2 (p. 21).

We know the brain is sophisticated, highly integrated, and adaptable (p. 47–49). What evidence for these characteristics do neuroscience studies about the brain's two hemispheres provide?

Remember that many of us, including left-handed people and women, have at least some language functioning in the right hemisphere (pp. 47–48).

"The facts about brain function are often far more interesting and surprising than the functions."

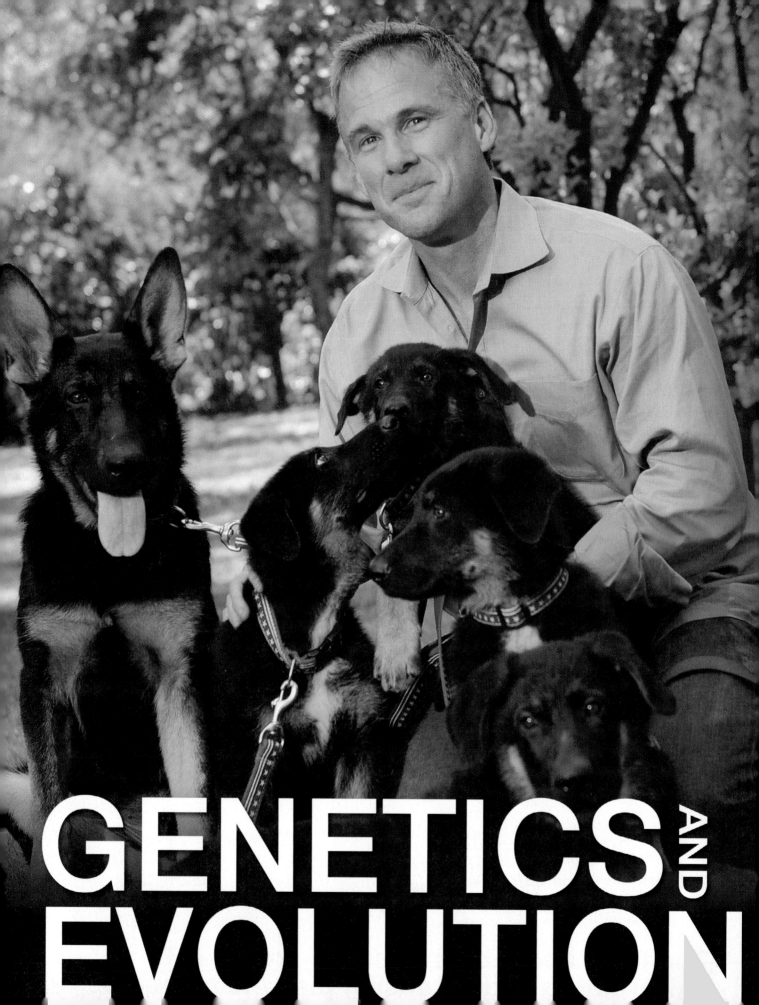

GENETICS AND EVOLUTION

WHAT ARE THE GENETIC MECHANISMS OF TRAIT INHERITANCE?

IN WHAT WAY DO GENES AND ENVIRONMENT INTERACT TO MAKE US WHO WE ARE?

HOW HAS THE IDEA OF EVOLUTION BY NATURAL SELECTION INFLUENCED THE STUDY OF HUMAN BEHAVIOR?

WHAT ARE THE TYPICAL MATING PATTERNS OF DIFFERENT SPECIES?

What if

we had the power to regrow our own organs? Although the possibility seems like the premise of a science-fiction movie or comic book, humans already have this capability, to an extent. Our skin, the largest organ of the human body and the one that holds us together, constantly regenerates and repairs itself. What if scientists could isolate the mechanism that allows this to happen and apply it to other organs? Might humans suffering from terminal diseases one day pick up their newly grown organs from a lab?

Scientists may have already, in fact, determined how to grow organs. Pioneering his research at Children's Hospital Boston, Dr. Anthony Atala—now at Wake Forest University—is the first scientist to successfully grow organs, with the achievement of bladder transplants using tissues grown in the laboratory. To grow the organs, Dr. Atala's lab seeded cells from damaged tissues in the patients' bladders onto collagen scaffolds shaped like bladders and allowed to reproduce through the normal process of cell division. They are then attached to the remains of the patients' bladders, where they continue to mature into a new organ. Because the cells are taken from the patients themselves, there is no risk that their immune systems will reject the organs, making the process both personal and efficient.

Dr. Atala's lab boasts not only scientifically grown bladders but also heart valves, blood vessels, and—helped along by their discovery of amniotic stem cells—tissues regenerated from pancreas, liver, and nerve cells (the three types of cells heretofore too difficult to culture in a petri dish). His lab has even created a two-chambered heart smaller than a human thumb by printing specific types of cells into a three-dimensional shape precisely where they would be found on a normal heart. Able to beat within four hours of creation, the lab-grown heart is at the cutting edge of a science that may hold the key to overcoming many terminal illnesses. As advances in medicine and technology render problems such as cardiovascular diseases and organ-specific cancers obsolete, do they eliminate the process of natural selection? In the future, will evolution be a thing of the past?

CHAPTER **04**

Natural Selection

In the mid-19th century, evolution was already the controversial topic; it continues to be today. When Charles Darwin began publishing his research in this area, he carefully avoided using the term "evolution" when drawing conclusions about the origins of humans. Despite these efforts, the public mocked what they assumed were his "man from monkey" ideas.

While controversy still surrounds these ideas, the concept of **natural selection** that Darwin introduced in his 1859 book *The Origin of Species* has become the guiding principle of biology and psychology. Darwin theorized that organisms with features best adapted to their environments were more likely to survive and reproduce. In other words, strong organisms are naturally selected for survival. As this process occurred, distinct species could evolve in response to different environmental pressures but would still resemble each other if they shared common ancestry. Humans share 99 percent of our genetic information with chimpanzees. According to evolutionary psychologist David Buss, "Humans are living fossils—collections of mechanisms produced by prior selection pressures" (1995).

Genetic Mechanisms

CHROMOSOMES, GENES, AND DNA

If Darwin had only known about genetic mechanisms such as chromosomes, genes,

> **Natural selection** is a theory that states that organisms best adapted to their environment tend to survive and transmit their genetic characteristics to succeeding generations.
>
> **Chromosomes** are long strands of genetic material found in the nuclei of all cells.
>
> **Chromatids** are pairs of duplicated chromosomes.
>
> **Centromere** is the place where two chromatids meet.
>
> **DNA** is a complex molecule that is the main ingredient of chromosomes; forms the code for all genetic information.
>
> **Genes** are sections of DNA that contain specific recipes to make proteins in the body.

Chromosomes are made up of long strands of DNA. Genes are sections of the DNA molecule, which has a double helix spiral form.

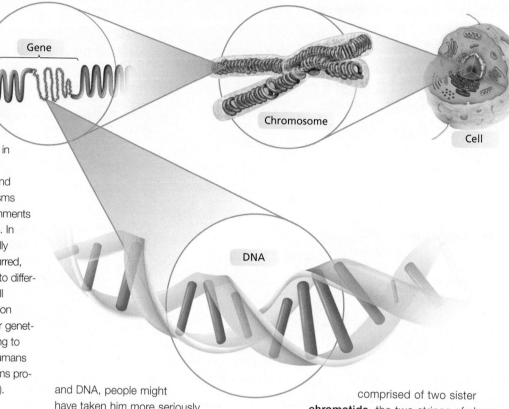

Gene

Chromosome

Cell

DNA

and DNA, people might have taken him more seriously. Twentieth-century discoveries not only have helped uphold Darwin's theories, but also have made for some high-tech drama in TV shows like *CSI* and *Cold Case*.

Chromosomes

To help solve crimes, investigators on TV and in real life analyze **chromosomes**, long strands of genetic material found in the nuclei of all cells. They are like biological blueprints that contain all the genetic information required to create each organism. Scientists study chromosomes to find out how closely different species are related, or in the case of a chimera, to determine how closely family members are related.

Normal human cells have 23 pairs of chromosomes, 46 in total. In addition to 22 true pairs, each cell also has an XX or XY pair that makes the individual female or male. Generally, chromosomes are spread throughout the nucleus and cannot be seen, but they become visible just before cell division. When chromosomes duplicate themselves, they form an X-like structure

comprised of two sister **chromatids**, the two strings of chromosomes, joined by a **centromere**, a place where the two strings meet.

Genes and DNA

The building blocks of chromosomes are **DNA**, or deoxyribonucleic acid. DNA molecules have a double helix form: They look like long, twisted ladders. **Genes** are sections of the DNA that contain specific recipes to make thousands of different proteins in the body. Because genes control the types of proteins in the nervous, sensory, and motor systems of an organism, they affect the individual's traits and behavior. James Symington's puppies had proteins designed by Trakr's genes, causing them to be clones of their father.

In organisms that reproduce sexually, the egg and sperm cells contain only half the number of chromosomes of all the other cells. During fertilization, the chromosomes of the mother pair up with those of the father to create a full set. As the fertilized egg divides, the DNA is replicated so that all cells contain the complete genetic information of that organism.

The Human Genome

Despite the observable cultural and physical differences between human beings, our common human **genome**—the complete instructions for making an organism—makes us very similar, behaviorally and biologically. No more than 5 percent of genetic differences arise from average population, racial, or ethnic group differences. Instead, 95 percent of genetic variation between individuals happens within the groups themselves. Such findings have fascinating implications for the many historical attempts that have been made to classify groups according to their genetic differences.

Since the discovery of chromosomes and DNA, scientists have been on a quest to map all of the genes in the human body, or the human genome. The U.S. government launched the Human Genome Project (HGP) in an attempt to map all 30,000 genes. Since the HGP finished its basic mapping in 2003, researchers have identified nearly all three billion units of DNA and have started identifying genes linked to various diseases and conditions. Scientists are continuing to find that genes often work in unison with each other, and the complexity of their interactions means that traits and diseases cannot always be traced to a single gene.

Genes and Environment

Recently, researchers have been working to identify the genetic roots of conditions as diverse as schizophrenia and obesity. But genes are not constant and unchanging; they work with the environment, self-regulate, and react by switching on and off, depending on the individual's environment.

> No more than 5 percent of genetic differences arise from average population, racial, or ethnic group differences. Instead, 95 percent of genetic variation between individuals happens within the groups themselves.

Environment includes everything around the organism and its surroundings, including an individual's life in utero.

Events and conditions in the individual's environment activate the genes that create proteins, which affect the individual's traits and behavior. The **external environment** includes what happens in the individual's outside world—the wealth or poverty of a nation, a loving or unloving family, a calm or stressful life. What happens inside

Genome is the complete set of instructions for making an organism.

External environment consists of events and conditions in the outside world.

Chemical environment consists of events and conditions inside an organism.

Genotype is the entire set of genes inherited by an organism.

Phenotype is the observable property that comes from a genotype.

the organism makes up the **chemical environment**. In a study of mice and nurturing, researchers found that mice who had not given birth normally avoided newborns, but would eventually begin to care for them after prolonged exposure. Their external environment activated a cluster of brain cells known to influence motivation to attend to young, showing that learning involves activation of genes (Johnston & Edwards, 2002).

Genotype and Phenotype

The entire set of genes inherited by an organism is its **genotype**; the observable properties that come from these genetics are **phenotypes**. Even if individuals have the same genotype, they can display different phenotypic characteristics or behaviors,

Are We Getting Smarter?

Average IQ Scores Over Time

100
95
90
85
80
75

1910   1930   1950   1970   1990

Year

<<< For at least 100 years, the IQ scores of people in developed countries have been steadily rising. Are "smart" genes increasing in the population of these countries, or have education, nutrition, and living conditions improved the genetic abilities that already existed? (Flynn, 1987, 1999)

comes in pairs, and one pair can dominate another. Today, we know that these factors are chromosomes. Genes located in the same position on the pair of chromosomes are called **alleles**. We also know that most genetic traits involve a more complicated interplay of multiple chromosomes.

Dominant and Recessive Genes

Identical pairs of alleles are **homozygous** and non-identical pairs are **heterozygous**. In heterozygous pairs, how does the body choose which gene to express? Like the round seeds of Mendel's pea plants, some genes are **dominant** and will always present themselves when paired with another gene that is **recessive**. For example, the widow's peak gene dominates other genes to produce a certain observable trait, or phenotype. If an individual's hairline has a widow's peak, he or she has at least one allele for the widow's peak. If paired heterozygously with a gene for a straight hairline, the widow's peak allele will ensure that the individual has a widow's peak.

Not all genes are either dominant or recessive. Some just blend with each other and combine the traits car-

ried by both genes. For instance, crossing red-petal four-o'clocks with white-petal four o'clocks will produce offspring with pink petals. Most traits come from a combination of multiple genes from one or more chromosomal pairs.

SEXUAL REPRODUCTION

Sexual reproduction combines the genetic information of one parent with that of the other to produce a new and unique combination of genes. Our reproductive cells—eggs and sperm—contain only half the genetic information of other cells in the body. When the sperm and egg successfully combine, they form a new cell called a **zygote**. The 23 pairs of chromosomes of one parent pair up with another set of 23 from the other parent, forming the necessary genetic component pairs that make a person uniquely who he or she is. The diversity of individuals created by this continual recombination of genes gives organisms that reproduce sexually a great evolutionary advantage. As genes rearrange themselves, new traits may arise that help the organism adapt to new environments.

Sibling and Twins

While gene recombination makes each person unique, family resemblances prove that human beings also share many inherited characteristics. You might share your high-pitched voice with your sister, your curly hair with your dad, or your short stature with your mom. People generally share only 50 percent of their genes with their siblings and parents, so you still have many differences. Identical, or **monozygotic**, twins are essentially individuals cloned by nature. After fertilization, the single zygote divides and separates into two zygotes that develop into separate fetuses with 100 percent identical genetic material. Fraternal, or **dizygotic**, twins come from two separate zygotes created from two different eggs that were fertilized by two different sperm cells around the same time. They are basically ordinary siblings born at the same time, so they share the same 50 percent of genetic material as any other set of siblings. As clones, Trustt, Solace, Prodigy, Valor, and Dejavu are essentially identical twins, whereas a normal litter of puppies would be considered fraternal twins.

depending on the environmental conditions they experience. The mice in the nurturance study who shared the same genotype would exhibit different observable behaviors depending on whether they had given birth or experienced prolonged exposure to newborns. These environmental factors changed the behavior of the rodents so that their genotype remained the same, but their phenotypes differed.

Mendelian Heredity

Have you ever wondered how traits pass from parents to children? Why do some people resemble their blood relatives more than others? In the mid-19th century, Gregor Mendel, an Austrian monk, cross-bred strains of round-seeded garden peas with wrinkled-seeded ones. When the offspring had round seeds, he concluded that inherited traits came from two factors and that the round-seeded factor dominated the wrinkled-seeded one. According to the idea of **Mendelian heredity,** a unit of heredity

∧
∧ Ben Affleck and his brother Casey both
∧ inherited cleft chins, a dominant trait.

Cell Division

An organism's reproductive cells are called **gametes**. Sexually reproducing organisms produce gametes through a special process of cell division, known as **meiosis**. During meiosis, chromosomes duplicate themselves, and the cell divides to form two new cells. These two cells divide a second time, distributing half the chromosomes to one cell and half to the other. The result is four new cells with half the number of chromosomes of the original. Each of these cells is now an egg or sperm cell, which combines with the sexual partner's gametes during conception. However, not all cells are designed to be reproductive cells; in fact, the vast majority of cells in the body reproduce through a more typical method of cell division—**mitosis**. During mitosis, chromosomes duplicate themselves before the cell divides, creating two cells genetically identical to the original.

At first glance, the first phase of cell division in meiosis seems a lot like mitosis, but in fact the initial division differs in an important way that adds significantly to the genetic diversity of the sexually reproducing organism. During the first division (meiosis I), sections of the duplicated chromosomes cross over and recombine to form new chromosomes. When these two new cells divide in meiosis II, the four new gametes contain chromosomes unlike the original parent cell and also

unlike the other gametes. Essentially, sexual reproduction shuffles the cards in the genetic deck twice, once during meiosis and once during fertilization. If for any reason the original parent cell mutates before meiosis, the mutation can also be passed on to the gametes, creating another opportunity for genetic variation. Hemophilia and color blindness occur in individuals that inherit the mutated gene for these conditions. Mutations can also occur during meiosis if chromatids do not separate properly, leaving more genetic information in one cell than in another. For example, an extra copy of chromosome 21 in the cell nucleus causes Down syndrome. Mutations can have positive effects as well. People with sickle-cell anemia have a mutation that causes their red blood cells to have a sickle shape. While this mutation inhibits the ability of their blood to carry oxygen, causing pain and fatigue, it also makes them resistant to malaria.

Gametes are reproductive cells in an organism.

Meiosis is the process of cell division in which chromosomes duplicate themselves and the cell divides to form two new cells; the two new cells then divide again, resulting in four new cells created from the original cell.

Mitosis is the process of cell division in which chromosomes duplicate themselves before the cell divides, creating two cells genetically identical to the original.

Gene complex is a group of genes acting together.

Polygenic means "coming from the interaction of several genes."

Continuous traits like height, weight, and skin color have a range of possible values.

Sexual selection refers to the process by which a mate is chosen.

Trait Inheritance: The Nature vs. Nurture Debate

SINGLE-GENE TRAITS

The theory of Mendelian heredity explains how single-gene traits pass from parents to offspring. Brothers Ben and Casey both have the unmistakable Affleck cleft chin because the gene for cleft chins dominates non-cleft chin genes. Like the cleft chin, cystic fibrosis, a disease that affects lung and digestive function, also originates in one specific gene. The recessive cystic fibrosis gene must be present in both alleles for an individual to develop the disease.

POLYGENIC TRAITS

Most traits do not correspond to a single gene pair, so scientists look for **gene complexes**, a group of genes acting together. Hair color, eye color, and height are all examples of **polygenic** characteristics, or characteristics resulting from more than one gene. Pigmentation or color traits like skin, hair, and eye color are known as **continuous traits** because they come not just in two colors but in a variety of shades along a spectrum.

Multiple genes also interact with the environment to produce certain characteristics. A person may have a genetic predisposition to grow to a certain height, but how tall that person actually becomes depends on growth hormones secreted by the pituitary glands and on the kind of nutrition received during childhood. Diseases with polygenic sources include heart disease and cancer. Multiple genes interact with environmental factors, such as diet and living conditions, to determine whether an individual will or will not develop the disease. As complex polygenic characteristics, intelligence and personality also vary widely in people. They do not appear in one single form or another, and they are influenced by environment.

SEXUAL SELECTION

Any experience with dating will tell you that all individuals do not attract mates equally. In humans and in other sexually reproducing species, this process of **sexual selection** affects which traits pass on to subsequent

<<< Although both Miley and her father Billy Ray Cyrus have similarly colored eyes and hair, no one gene is responsible for the resemblance.

generations. In species that emphasize mate selection, males often display distinctive and easily observable characteristics to attract females. Male birds with bright feathers can compete for females more effectively than their less colorful fellow birds. As a result, the genes for sexual characteristics, like colorful plumage or large antlers, continue into the next generation so that bigger antlers or brighter plumage may appear over the course of generations.

SELECTIVE BREEDING

Selection can also be done artificially through **selective breeding**. Varieties of dog breeds have all been produced by mating individuals with desired characteristics in order to select for those traits. Over time, dogs were bred specifically for hunting, following scents, or even for just being small and fluffy. In a famous 1940 study, Robert Tryon showed through selective breeding that genes can strongly influence behavioral traits. First Tryon identified two types of rats: those that made their way through a maze with few errors (maze bright) and those that made their way through with several errors (maze dull). Then Tryon mated rats that were maze bright with other maze bright rats, and he also mated maze-dull rats with other maze-dull rats. After more than 21 generations of breeding bright with bright and dull with dull, he created two genetically different types of rats. Almost all the bright rats made fewer errors than even the smartest dull rat, illustrating how traits develop over generations.

BEHAVIOR GENETICS

In the film *The Parent Trap*, Hallie and Annie, identical twins raised apart, meet at a summer camp and switch identities as a way to

∧
∧
∧ Skin pigmentation is one example of a continuous trait. Which of your other traits are continuous?

reconcile their divorced parents. The film's plot partly revolves around the opposite personalities of the two twins: Hallie, a casual California tomboy raised by her father, and Annie, a genteel and feminine English girl raised by her mother. It may seem surprising that individuals with identical DNA could be so different. But how much of a person's character comes from genetics and how much comes from environment?

Researchers in **behavior genetics** try to determine the relative effects of genes and environment on behavior and mental processes. Since Hallie and Annie have identical genes but different environments, a behavior geneticist could use their case

as evidence that personality is influenced more by an individual's environment than by an individual's genes. Although the real-life cases of identical twins raised separately are limited, behavior genetics relies on twin studies to compare twins raised together with twins raised separately. When twins raised separately show similar traits, researchers infer that these traits probably have genetic origins. When twins raised together show different traits, researchers infer that environmental factors may have affected these differences.

Twin Studies

When Elyse Schein went looking for her birth mother, she had no idea that she had a twin sister. The first time they met, Elyse and her sister Paula Bernstein noticed that they had many similarities. They shared similar speech rhythms, facial expressions, gestures, and medical conditions. Both Elyse and Paula had been the editors of their high school newspapers, and both had taken trips to Italy at the same age. They had both even studied film in New York. Like Elyse and Paula, identical twins raised apart have shown remarkable similarities in many areas such as career choice, food preferences, and gestures (Wolff, 2007). But identical twins raised apart have more dissimilar personalities than those raised in the same family (Pedersen et al., 1988). Like Annie and Hallie in the *The Parent Trap*, Elyse and Paula also had many personality differences, and they had led very different lives.

In an effort to reunite their parents, separated identical twins Annie and Hallie work out their differences and exploit their similarities. >>>

Adoption Studies

In addition to twin studies, behavior geneticists also use adoption studies to distinguish the degree of influence of nature and nurture. To calculate how particular traits are inherited, researchers compare the degree to which an individual's traits resemble those of biological parents as opposed to adoptive parents. Interestingly, adoptees have been found to resemble their biological parents more than their adoptive ones in certain preferences, personality, and behavior. Adoption studies have illustrated the genetic influence on conditions such as obesity and some forms of alcoholism (Cloninger, 1981).

Heritability

Heritability refers to the degree to which genetics explains the individual variations in observable traits. In similar environments, heritability is important in influencing individual differences. If environments vary or influence certain traits, heritability would explain individual differences to a lesser degree. A trait like eye color has a high heritability because differing genetics cause variations in eye color without any environmental influence. In contrast, intelligence has a much lower heritability because environmental factors also influence intelligence differences among individuals. Heritability does not tell us the percentage to which a trait is caused by genetics but rather the percentage to which variation among individuals can be attributed to genetic influence.

A hundred years ago, people had much less access to food and burned more calories in their daily activities. Today, with food available everywhere and few calories burned through activity, Americans as a group have become heavier and heavier. Since our genes have not changed, the environment must have a powerful impact even on traits with a strong genetic basis, such as weight. Even a temperament trait such as happiness has a genetic component, and some people are literally just naturally relatively happier people. Researchers found no concordance between dizygotic twins in their sense of happiness. But they found an 80 percent concordance rate in happiness ratings for monozygotic twins (Lykken & Tellegen, 1996). The heritability of schizophrenia has also been solidly established. If one identical twin has schizophrenia, the other twin has a 50 percent chance of developing the condition. If a fraternal twin has schizophrenia, the other twin has a 27 percent

chance of developing the disorder (Cardo & Gottesman, 2000).

MOLECULAR GENETICS

Suffering from problems in the lungs and digestive system, people with cystic fibrosis go through life malnourished and often die by the age of 30. But the outlook for treatment of this hereditary disease dramatically improved in 1989, when researchers in **molecular genetics** found the exact location of the cystic fibrosis gene on chromosome 7 (Hillier et al., 2003). Molecular geneticists study the molecular structure and function of genes and try to identify the specific genes responsible for a certain disease, trait, or behavior. Their work has led to genetic tests that can now predict which populations may be at risk for certain diseases. With advancing prenatal screening techniques, parents can receive an exact read-out of their child's genetic data, anomalies and all. While this new knowledge could lead to early treatment of certain diseases, it could also raise ethical issues in the distant future if parents are able to selectively abort fetuses to create "custom" babies with exactly the traits they prefer—a baby Mozart or a mini-Einstein.

Evolution by Natural Selection

EVOLUTIONARY PSYCHOLOGY

Like most people, you probably prefer eating sweet fruits to sucking on sour lemons and swallowing bitter medicines. Poisons often have a bitter taste, and food begins to taste sour as it spoils. Preferring sweet things to sour or bitter things probably helped our ancestors survive by

> *A trait like eye color has a high heritability because differing genetics cause variations in eye color without any environmental influence.* **In contrast, intelligence has a much lower heritability because environmental factors also influence intelligence differences among individuals.**

avoiding foods that could make them sick. Those individuals without the ability to distinguish among these tastes probably didn't live long enough to reproduce. Therefore, all of us now share this taste preference. Researchers in **evolutionary psychology** explain the development of our mind and behavior by studying how adaptive behaviors, such as certain taste preferences, helped our ancestors survive and reproduce.

Friendly Foxes: Man's New Best Friend?

One area of study that interests evolutionary psychologists is the domestication of wild animals. Russian researchers Belyaev and Trut set out to domesticate foxes and accomplished in a few decades behavioral changes that would naturally take thousands of years to develop. Over 30 generations of foxes, the scientists bred the tamest males with the tamest females. After 40 years, the wild and suspicious foxes had become a new breed of friendly, attention-loving foxes. The animals were so tame that the research institute even started selling them as house pets. By mating only the friendliest animals, the researchers essentially gave an evolutionary advantage to this character trait (Trut, 1999).

Innate Traits

Just having a particular trait does not necessarily make that trait **adaptive**, but many of our traits do help us adjust and function in our environment. All human babies turn toward the

---

Selective breeding is the process by which pairs of organisms of the same species with desirable characteristics are mated in order to select for those characteristics.

Behavior genetics is a field of study emphasizing the analysis of the effects of genes and environment on behavior and mental processes.

Heritability describes the degree to which a trait is able to be passed on genetically.

Molecular genetics is a field of study emphasizing the analysis of the molecular structure and function of genes to try to identify the specific genes responsible for a certain disease, trait, or behavior.

Evolutionary psychology is a branch of psychology involved with explaining the development of the human mind and behavior by studying how adaptive behaviors helped human ancestors survive and reproduce.

Adaptive refers to the ability to adjust and function according to one's environment.

cheek being stroked and suck objects put to their lips. Turning toward the touched cheek helps them make contact with the nipple, and automatic sucking ensures that babies will nurse and get the food they need to survive. Evolutionary psychologists study how innate traits such as **infant reflexes** evolved. They also consider whether common phobias have innate origins. Why do people fear spiders and snakes far more often than things more likely to harm them, like driving? Today, people in the developed world encounter more cars than spiders and snakes, but in our evolutionary past, spiders and snakes would have been the threat. In the past, the fear of snakes and spiders offered important protection, and its persistence is a good example of how long it takes for evolutionary processes to adjust our innate fears to new environments.

Issues with the Evolutionary Perspective

Critics of the evolutionary perspective claim that it starts with an effect or trait and works backward, so it cannot fail to explain a particular trait. To understand how a certain trait evolved, evolutionary psychologists must speculate about its cause, but they cannot prove that the explanation is correct. For example, some men may try to explain away their infidelity by claiming that it is an innate trait with an evolutionary advantage, but scientists have yet to identify a "cheater gene."

ACQUIRED CHARACTERISTICS: AN EARLY THEORY OF EVOLUTION

Before Darwin, a French biologist named Jean-Baptiste de Lamarck proposed a theory of evolution based on the inheritance of **acquired characteristics**. He argued that different species had common ancestry but evolved and changed into "higher" organisms by acquiring useful characteristics that they then passed to their offspring. Giraffes that could stretch their necks would produce offspring with longer necks, and over generations, the necks of giraffes would get longer. Lamarck's theories introduced the idea of evolution, but they did not adequately explain inheritance. An individual's use of a particular trait will not cause the trait to be passed onto

> Some men may try to explain away their infidelity by claiming that it is an innate trait with an evolutionary advantage, but scientists have yet to identify a "cheater gene."

offspring, just as its disuse won't prevent it. However, the utility of a trait could give the animal a better chance at survival and reproduction, and these are the ideas upon which Darwin expanded.

DARWIN AND SELECTIVE BREEDING

Darwin went much further than Lamarck in explaining how evolution actually occurred. Darwin explained that just as people use **artificial selection** to selectively breed livestock and crops for desired characteristics, nature also conducts a selective breeding process—natural selection. Unlike Lamarck, Darwin believed that inheritance does not happen because certain traits are useful but because the usefulness of the traits helps the organism survive and reproduce and allows those traits to pass on to the next generation. Although Darwin did not know about genetic mechanisms, he knew that new traits develop by chance. Advances in genetics tell us that this diversity occurs because of genetic reshuffling during meiosis and fertilization and because of mutations that happen during DNA replication.

ENVIRONMENTAL CHANGE

Climate change, catastrophic events, and even minor events mean that environments change continually. These changes in the environment promote evolution by natural selection. More than 100 years after Darwin, Peter and Rosemary Grant studied the same species of birds on the Galapagos Island to learn how environment affects natural selection (2002). When a drought left only large seeds, only birds with large beaks could break and eat these seeds, so more of the larger birds survived. Heavy rains created the opposite effect. Because of the many small seeds available, the birds with smaller beaks survived and became more numerous. Their small size allowed them to grow to adulthood and reproduce more quickly, so their numbers increased more than those of the large-beaked birds.

Misconceptions About Evolution

Evolution happens in response to environmental change and does not have foresight or a predetermined end. Species do not change in order to prepare for environmental changes or to become more "highly evolved" organisms. Finches could not develop larger or smaller beaks in anticipation of a drought or abundant rainfall. Different birds simply had different-sized beaks, and when conditions changed, those with the beaks most suited to that environment survived in the greatest numbers. Another misconception is that single-celled organisms such as amoebas are "less evolved" than human beings because of their lack of complexity. These single-celled organisms are equally well-adapted to their environments, and therefore not any less evolved.

HUMAN EVOLUTION: BIPEDALISM, ENCEPHALIZATION, AND LANGUAGE

The 1 percent–2 percent of human DNA that differs from that of chimps accounts for our exceptionally large brains, our ability to walk on two legs, and our capacity for language. Between five million and ten million years ago, our ancestors started walking on two legs instead of four. Between two million and three million years ago, our human genus, *Homo*, first started developing from our evolutionary family tree. **Bipedalism**, the ability to walk on two legs, let us use tools and manipulate our environment. **Encephalization**, the increase in our brain size, meant that we could better think, plan, and remember. Our unusual ability for abstract thought, which evolved in a way that is still unclear to scientists, allowed us to develop language. Being able to communicate through language meant that human beings could share knowledge with each other, cooperate, and pass information on to future generations.

Evolution of the Human Brain

In only tens of millions of years, an evolutionary blink of an eye, tremendous genetic changes produced our nervous system. Recent evidence has shown that the **phylogeny**—species development—of the human brain evolved far more quickly than the brains of other species. Specifically, the genes that design proteins in the nervous system evolved more quickly in our ancestral primates than in rodents and other animals. Scientists suspect our evolutionary speed may have something to do with an unusually large number of mutations in many genes and a selection for the mental abilities that these mutations allowed (Dorus et al., 2004).

Believe it or not, our species may be getting even smarter. Two separate genes that control brain size developed and spread as recently as 37,000 and 5,800 years ago (Evans et al., 2005;

Mekel-Bobrov et al., 2005). If we keep evolving at this rate, who knows where we'll be 100,000, or even 50,000,000 years from now. Just how big can our brains get before we have trouble holding up our heads or giving birth?

Species-Typical Behaviors

HUMAN BEHAVIOR

Cats climb trees, dogs bark, and squirrels hoard acorns. But dogs do not climb trees, cats do not hoard acorns, and squirrels do not bark. All animals have **species-typical behaviors**, instinctive or characteristic ways of behaving particular to a certain species. Smiling, talking, and walking on two legs are behaviors common to all human beings. Animals, including humans, communicate emotions through posture, movement, and facial expression. In *The Expression of the Emotions in Man and Animals* (1872), Darwin argued for the universality, and therefore genetic innateness, of facial expressions and the emotions they express.

Universality of Facial Expressions

In the 1960s, Paul Ekman and Wallace Friesen picked up on Darwin's idea and asserted that

humans across cultures share common facial expressions that communicate specific emotions. The researchers compiled an "atlas of emotions" of the numerous human facial expressions and identified the six universally recognized emotions as surprise, fear, disgust, sadness, anger, and happiness. In one study, they asked non-literate people from New Guinea to look at photos of actors making certain facial expressions and to identify the emotions. As in the other 31 cultures the researchers studied, the New Guineans identified the emotions correctly. Conversely, the researchers videotaped members of the New Guinea tribe making certain expressions and asked American college students to identify the corresponding emotions. Again, the college students identified the emotions correctly (Ekman & Friesen, 1975; Ekman, 1982).

But the universality of emotions seems to have its limits. Although people around the world recognize common expressions, they have an easier time identifying those of members within their cultural groups (Elfenbein & Ambady, 2002, 2003). Cultural variations in the way people express emotions give group members an "in-group advantage." Facial expressions may be universal because of genetic predisposition, common learned behavior, or a combination of the two, but if people within a cultural group recognize each other's emotions more easily, learning probably does play some role.

Role of Learning

Many species-typical behaviors based on predispositions become expressed only as a result of learning. Human beings have a genetic predisposition to walk on two legs, but babies are not born ready to walk. They learn it over time, and before they do, they practice balancing and taking steps. Similarly, humans also probably have a genetic predisposition to acquire language, but babies are not born speaking sentences or even articulating words; instead they come prepared to learn the language around them. They make nonsense

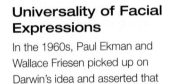

∧
∧ **Humans can identify the emotions behind a**
∧ **wide variety of facial expressions. What emotions do you think are conveyed in this photograph?**

sounds until they learn the phonemes (discrete sounds) of words in a specific language. Through learning, they start pronouncing words correctly and begin to develop the grammar and syntax of their native language.

Biological Preparedness

How does our biology control what we learn, as well as how and when? **Biological preparedness** refers to the extent to which biological features evolved to promote certain traits. Human beings are biologically prepared to walk on two legs. Physically, we have an upward tilted torso, strong hind limbs, and weak forelimbs. Our nervous system also prepares us to coordinate two-legged walking.

Through conditioning, animals can be trained to perform certain tricks or behaviors, as when four-legged animals walk on two legs, but they soon revert back to their original instinctive behaviors, a tendency known as **instinctual drift** (Breland & Breland, 1951, 1961). Raccoons taught to pick up a coin and drop it into a piggy bank would first rub the coins together, just as they would to remove shells from crayfish, before dropping it into the container. Pigs taught to do the same trick would drop the coins on the ground and root at them with their snouts, as they do to their food, before dropping the coins in the container. Despite conditioning, animals kept up these preliminary instinctual behaviors, and these tendencies even increase over time. Those behaviors that remained the longest were the ones for which the animals were more biologically prepared and likely had a strong genetic basis.

Mating Patterns

DIFFERENTIAL PARENTAL INVESTMENT THEORY

A familiar cliché says that women want commitment with one person while men want sex with many people. In looking for an evolutionary explanation for age-old patterns, evolutionary psychologist Robert Trivers found that mating patterns depend on gender differences in the amount of **parental investment** (1972). Parental investment includes the time, energy, and risk involved in producing and raising offspring. Which gender gets to choose a mate and which gender must compete for a mate depends on the amount of parental investment. The more invested gender will be choosier in picking a mate, and the less invested gender will have to compete against other individuals for the right to mate. This idea confirms the stereotype that women want to seek commitment with "Mr. Perfect" while men are content to compete with each other in order to gain that title. Of course, in highly developed Western societies, the availability of alternatives, such as artificial insemination and adoption and the presence of women in the workforce who can support

themselves, move us in the direction of making this point moot.

POLYGYNY: ONE MALE WITH MULTIPLE FEMALES

Most mammalian species are polygynous because females invest a great deal of time and effort in pregnancy and child care, whereas the work of males tends to be over after they impregnate the female. Long gestation and lactation periods limit the number of offspring females can produce. To maximize the genetic potential of their children, females have to choose the preferred mates with whom to combine their genes. On the other hand, males don't need to put much time or effort into raising children, so they can mate with as many females as they can. Increasing the number of offspring they produce means that more of those offspring may survive and the male's genes are passed on. Generally, the more polygynous a species, the greater the size difference between males and females. Large size makes a difference when males compete with each other over the right to mate, and not all males will win that right. For humans, it's important to keep in mind that our highly evolved brains override the pressure for males to be polygynous.

In 2008, the state of Texas raided the polygynist Yearning for Zion Ranch and took more than 400 children into custody. Officials believed that sexual abuse was so rampant that none of the members should be able to keep their children. With little evidence to support their claims, the children were returned to their families two months later.

POLYANDRY: ONE FEMALE WITH MULTIPLE MALES

Less common than polygyny, polyandry happens when females have less parental investment, as in some egg-laying fish and birds.

> **Male emperor penguins tend to incubation duties, and this species practices serial monogamy; they are faithful to a single mate for a year but won't necessarily wait around for the same partner when it's time to breed again the next year.**

Because the female has a short pregnancy and does not nurse, less of the reproductive cycle depends on her body. Once she lays the eggs, either parent can take care of the offspring. In these species, females have evolved to be larger, stronger, and often more brightly colored. Not surprisingly, they actively and aggressively court males. The female Northern Jacana bird keeps a large territory in which multiple males have smaller territories. She mates with each of the males and, within a few days, lays eggs that hatch into offspring that males raise (Ehrlich et al., 1988).

MONOGAMY: ONE MALE WITH ONE FEMALE

When individuals of both genders make an equal parental investment, a species tends to be monogamous. More than 90 percent of bird species are monogamous because offspring need the care of both parents. Although males and females pair up in family units and practice "social monogamy," sexual fidelity has not been known to be a part of any species' repertoire. In one study, female blackbirds whose mates had vasectomies still managed to produce hatchlings (Bray et al., 1975). Male emperor penguins tend to incubation duties, and this species practices serial monogamy; they are faithful to a single mate for a year but won't necessarily wait around for the same partner when it's time to breed again the next year. In mammals, monogamy tends to happen in species such as foxes and coyotes

that must provide their young with food other than milk. The offspring of certain species, particularly rodents like the prairie vole, also need the male parent to protect them from predators.

POLYGYNANDRY: MULTIPLE MALES WITH MULTIPLE FEMALES

Polygynandry characterizes species such as chimps and bonobo apes that live in large groups of two to three dozen individuals and share a communal parental investment. When females ovulate, they develop prominent pink swellings on their rumps, and they typically mate with all the males in the group. Unlike gorillas, male chimps and bonobos must compete less against each other for mating privileges, promoting harmony (De Waal, 1995). By preventing infanticide, paternity confusion also benefits the group as a whole. Conversely, male lions, like males of other species that put a premium on paternity, will kill the offspring of rival males (Packer & Pusey, 1983).

HUMAN MATING PATTERNS

Since males are slightly larger than females, it follows that humans tend to be primarily monogamous and slightly polygynous. While human mating patterns vary with culture, all cultures have some form of long-term mating bonds, often through socially recognized marriage contracts, and no human culture is as

> **Although we sometimes think of "survival of the fittest" as the very definition of natural selection, Darwin did not originate this idea. Instead, philosopher Herbert Spencer coined the phrase to explain his belief that society and culture evolved toward higher forms.**

promiscuous as our closest relatives, chimps and bonobos. Western culture has made polygyny illegal, but cultures with less Western influence tend to practice a mixture of monogamy and polygyny. However, many European cultures have an unspoken acceptance of extramarital relationships.

Monogamy makes sense for humans because human children, more than any other primate, need extended care. Across cultures, mothers provide most of the direct physical care

for children, whereas fathers indirectly provide food, shelter, and other provisions. But taking both direct and indirect care into account, male parental involvement lags behind female involvement. Romantic love and sexual jealousy, the biological preparedness for mating bonds, make human beings more similar to birds than chimps in their mating behavior. But biological preparedness also predisposes humans to seek sex outside the pair bond. Across different groups and cultures, 2 percent–10 percent of children in socially monogamous families have not been fathered by the husband (Marlowe, 2000).

Fallacies

By the late 19th century, Darwin's ideas had made such a great impact that philosophers and political thinkers tried to apply the idea of evolution to government, society, and all human relations. Often, they misunderstood Darwin's ideas or interpreted them in a way that suited their purposes. Although we sometimes think of "survival of the fittest" as the very definition of natural selection, Darwin did not originate this idea. Instead, philosopher Herbert Spencer coined the phrase to explain his belief that society and culture evolved toward higher forms. According to his theory of **social Darwinism,** individuals either adapted and survived or fell by the wayside, which supported his belief that governments should not aid those struggling with poverty or other social problems. Philosopher G. E. Moore later argued that Spencer had committed the **naturalistic fallacy** by equating the "natural" with the "good" or "right." Moore criticized Spencer for applying a natural explanation to the non-natural phenomena of society and government and also for presenting his personal ethical opinions as facts. At this point, we do not know if individualism and competition will be beneficial to the species in the long run.

With new genes being mapped continually and knowledge of genetics increasing dramatically, people sometimes make the **deterministic fallacy** and try to explain traits and behaviors entirely through genes. Genetics work with the environment to build or change the biological structures that then interact with the environment to produce behavior. While we know that genes are necessary, they are not sufficient to fully account for traits and behaviors. Genes may influence us, but they are not able to dictate who we are because, ultimately, humans can and do control their own behavior.

• Review

Summary

WHAT ARE THE GENETIC MECHANISMS OF TRAIT INHERITANCE? p. 56

• Made up of DNA, chromosomes inside cell nuclei contain all the genetic information needed to make an organism.

• Human cells contain 23 pairs of chromosomes, including an XX or XY pair that determines whether an individual is male or female.

• Egg and sperm cells contain half the genetic information of other cells. They combine during fertilization, passing on parents' genetic information in a new permutation.

IN WHAT WAY DO GENES AND ENVIRONMENT INTERACT TO MAKE US WHO WE ARE? p. 59

• Some traits, such as eye color, depend entirely on genetics. Others, such as height and weight, can be influenced by the environment.

• While genetics might predispose an individual to a certain trait, how that trait is expressed can depend on environmental factors.

• An environment may be external or chemical.

HOW HAS THE IDEA OF EVOLUTION BY NATURAL SELECTION INFLUENCED THE STUDY OF HUMAN BEHAVIOR? p. 61

• According to the theory of natural selection, organisms with features that best adapted to their environment are more likely to survive and reproduce.

• Some genes are dominant or recessive, affecting the likelihood that a particular trait will be passed on.

• Research in behavior genetics, molecular genetics, and evolutionary psychology has developed from the idea of natural selection.

WHAT ARE THE TYPICAL MATING PATTERNS OF DIFFERENT SPECIES? p. 64

• Mating patterns depend on gender differences in parental investment.

• There are four types of mating patterns: polygyny, polyandry, monogamy, and polygynandry.

Test Your Understanding

1. Which of the following helps explain why identifying a gene that causes a condition is difficult?

   a. Environment helps determine whether a gene is activated.

   b. Genes that contribute to a condition cannot be identified.

   c. Only five percent of differences among humans can be attributed to genes.

   d. Individuals with the same genotype always display the same phenotypes.

2. Which of the following traits has the lowest heritability?

   a. intelligence

   b. hair color

   c. eye color

   d. All of the above have equal heritability.

3. Which of the following statements helps explain how human genes contribute to our evolution?

   a. Offspring who possess genes that contribute to survival are more likely to pass their genes on through reproduction.

   b. An individual's genes change over his or her lifetime to help the species evolve.

   c. During reproduction, only the genes for adaptive traits are passed on.

   d. Only dominant genes are passed on during reproduction.

4. What factor(s) contribute to genetic variation between humans?

   a. meiosis

   b. mitosis and meiosis

   c. mitosis, fertilization, and mutations in DNA

   d. meiosis, fertilization, and mutations in DNA

5. A dog burying a bone in the backyard displays:

   a. phylogeny.

   b. a species-typical behavior.

   c. encephalization.

   d. artificial selection.

6. What explains why a wild animal raised as a domestic pet from birth might suddenly turn vicious on its caregivers?

   a. parental investment

   b. social Darwinism

   c. the naturalistic fallacy

   d. instinctual drift

7. All of Patty's siblings have high blood pressure. She does not, but she assumes that she will. Her belief demonstrates:

   a. the naturalistic fallacy.

   b. the deterministic fallacy.

   c. social Darwinism.

   d. biological preparedness.

8. What might contribute to why humans tend to be monogamous?

   a. Humans have a relatively long infancy and childhood period.

   b. Males must compete to mate with females.

   c. Females must compete to mate with males.

   d. Females have more parental involvement than males.

9. What theory helps explain why women might be choosy in dating partners?

   a. instinctual drift

   b. social Darwinism

   c. the differential parental investment theory

   d. artificial selection

10. A large number of genetic mutations occurring in a short time span might lead to:

   a. the evolution of a trait or characteristic.

   b. unnatural meiosis.

   c. unnatural selection.

   d. recessive selection.

11. Which of the following was NOT identified as a universally recognized emotion by researchers Ekman and Friesen?

   a. sadness

   b. anxiety

   c. anger

   d. disgust

12. What is a trigger for evolution?

   a. anticipation of the need for change

   b. environmental change

   c. natural selection

   d. artificial selection

13. Which of the following would NOT be considered an infant reflex?

   a. grasping

   b. sucking

   c. crying

   d. stacking blocks

14. If blue eyes are a recessive trait, the gene for blue eyes:

   a. must be inherited from one parent only in order for the phenotype to appear in an offspring.

   b. must be inherited from both parents in order for the phenotype to appear in an offspring.

   c. cannot be inherited from a brown-eyed parent.

   d. will become dominant in subsequent generations.

15. Which of the following research studies would an evolutionary psychologist be most likely to perform?

   a. testing whether small children who have never seen real or photographed spiders respond to spiders fearfully

   b. testing whether a new drug reduces symptoms in people with schizophrenia

   c. researching the relationship between insomnia and depression

   d. testing whether parrots can learn to count and use numbers

16. Four biological siblings in a family all have different colored hair from one another. Why might this have occurred?

   a. Hair color is a polygenic characteristic.

   b. Hair color is a recessive trait.

   c. Hair color is sexually selected.

   d. Hair color is not a heritable trait.

17. Kaya needs a kidney transplant. Why is there more of a chance that her sister will be an organ donor match than her stepmother?

   a. Siblings have more genes in common than biologically unrelated individuals do.

   b. A stepparent and child are further apart in age than what siblings are.

   c. The chromosomes that control organ compatibility are always the same among siblings.

   d. There is more of a likelihood that the stepmother's genes have mutated with age.

18. Which of the following helps explain why human children abandon crawling when they begin to walk, but a dog taught to walk on two legs does not abandon walking on four legs?

   a. biological preparedness

   b. parental investment

   c. encephalization

   d. acquired characteristics

19. Why might males of a species that practices polygynandry care for the offspring of others in the group?

   a. The females will kill a male who does not help take care of their offspring.

   b. The males are unsure which offspring are theirs and so it is necessary for them to ensure that any offspring who might be will survive.

   c. The males and females are closer to one another in size and so share more female characteristics.

   d. There is no competition for mating privileges, so the males can spend less time competing.

20. "Because humans have evolved to hunt and eat meat, it is morally correct to kill animals for food." This viewpoint might be considered:

   a. a naturalistic fallacy.

   b. a deterministic fallacy.

   c. social Darwinism.

   d. similar to natural selection.

Remember to check www.thethinkspot.com for additional information, downloadable flashcards, and other helpful resources.

SENSATION AND PERCEPTION

Imagine

if eating birthday cake was associated with taste sensations so intense that they made the experience entirely unpleasant. Scientists have discovered that some people have an unusually high number of taste buds, affecting not only their food preferences but also their food *experiences*. In the 1990s, Yale University researcher Linda Bartoshuk found that among American Caucasians, approximately 35 percent of women and 15 percent of men have higher densities of taste buds than the rest of the population. She named these sensory-gifted people "supertasters."

Many supertasters would dispute the notion that they are blessed with a gift. Since each taste bud is associated with clusters of pain fibers, people with high numbers of taste buds experience intensified taste sensations to the point of

pain. The burning sensation from a chile may be unbearable, while the feel of fat may irritate the touch sensors in the fungiform papillae (or, as they are more commonly known, the taste buds). For supertasters, eating a candy bar is an unpleasant and irritating chore rather than a pleasurable taste sensation.

Bartoshuk notes that because supertasters avoid certain foods, they are subject to long-term health risks. For example, although supertasters dislike the texture of fatty foods, they also find particular fruits and vegetables extremely bitter. A supertaster may therefore be slimmer and healthier than the average person because he or she avoids eating candy bars, but at a higher risk of developing diseases such as colon cancer that could be prevented by consuming a lot of fruit and vegetables.

How do our senses affect the ways in which we perceive the world? For some, a new culinary experience is an adventure, while for others it is a minefield of potentially unbearable dishes. We constantly use our senses to collect information about the world around us, but no two people experience the world in the same way.

Can a sense of smell save lives? More than 10 years after a [ci]il war, the South African country of Mozambique still faced [s]erious issue—land mines from the war were still hidden in [d]ensely populated areas, posing a grave threat to millions of [resi]dents. The solution? Indigenous rats, known for their highly [develop]ed sense of smell, were trained to sniff out the land mines. [Easy to] train and cheap to maintain, the mine-sniffing rats proved [use]ful in protecting the safety of Mozambique's citizens—and demonstrated just how vital our senses are to survival

Sensation

Sensory systems, the parts of the nervous system responsible for processing sensory information, allow people and animals to interpret stimuli from the outside world. These systems are essential for survival and reproduction. Imagine if our ancestors were unable to hear the snap of a twig to warn them of approaching danger. The human race would not have lasted long! Sensory systems are need-specific. In other words, each species has a unique sensory system according to its behavior and environment. For example, bats hunt in the dark of night, so they cannot rely on their eyesight. Instead their hearing is so finely attuned that they can use echolocation to track down prey the size of a mosquito.

Sensation is the process through which we detect physical energy from the environment and code that energy as neural signals. The way we select, organize, and interpret this sensory information is the process of **perception**. Sensation and perception work together to enable us to receive and interpret stimuli from the outside world.

Sensory Thresholds

PSYCHOPHYSICS

We are unable to detect much of the physical energy around us. For example, sound waves that have very low or very high frequencies are out of the human range of hearing. Every species has a different sensory threshold. This is why blowing a dog whistle has little effect on a person, but produces an instant response from any dog in the area.

Psychophysics is the study of the relationship between physical characteristics of stimuli and the sensory experiences that accompany them. It helps us know how much sensory stimulation is needed to see a candle in the distance, or to hear a mouse scamper across a kitchen floor.

Absolute Thresholds

An **absolute threshold** is the smallest amount of energy needed for a person to detect a stimulus (light, sound, pressure, taste, or odor) 50 percent of the time. Psychologists can establish an absolute threshold by presenting a stimulus at different intensities and asking people whether they sense anything. Adults generally have a higher absolute threshold than children, but all of us are remarkably sensitive to changes in the world around us. For example, a human being can smell a single drop of perfume in a three-room apartment (Galanter, 1962).

Signal Detection Theory

People are not always consistently able to detect stimuli. Awareness can depend on whether the individual is feeling tired or alert, whether the stimulus is expected, or the potential consequences of the stimulus. If you were told that your failure to detect the sound of a footstep would cause an explosion, you would probably be considerably more alert than usual. Psychologists using **signal detection theory** attempt to understand the differences between people's responses to different stimuli and how they vary depending on the circumstances. Signal detection theorists measure how often a person observes a weak stimulus by counting the number of successful detections compared to the number of false alarms.

> **People** are not always consistently able to detect stimuli. Awareness can depend on whether the individual is feeling tired or alert, whether the stimulus is expected, or the potential consequences of the stimulus.

Difference Thresholds

The **difference threshold**, or **just noticeable difference (jnd)**, is the minimum difference between two stimuli needed to detect the difference 50 percent of the time. This threshold increases with the size of one of the stimuli. For example, if you add a spoonful of sugar to a cup of tea, you will probably notice that it

---

Sensory system is the part of the nervous system responsible for processing sensory information.

Sensation describes the process through which we detect physical energy from the environment and code that energy as neural signals.

Perception describes the way a person selects, organizes, and interprets sensory information.

Psychophysics is the study of the relationship between physical characteristics of stimuli and the sensory experiences that accompany them.

Absolute threshold is the smallest amount of energy needed for a person to detect a stimulus 50 percent of the time.

Signal detection theory predicts how and when we detect the presence of a faint stimulus amid background stimulation.

Difference threshold or **just noticeable difference (jnd)** is the minimum difference between two stimuli needed to detect the difference 50 percent of the time.

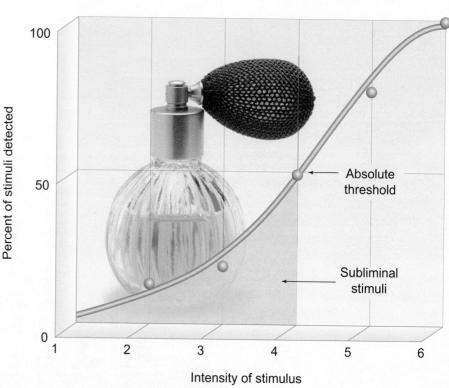

Percent of stimuli detected — 0, 50, 100

Intensity of stimulus — 1 2 3 4 5 6

Absolute threshold

Subliminal stimuli

	Respond "Absent"	Respond "Present"
Stimulus Present	Miss	Hit
Stimulus Absent	Correct rejection	False alarm

∧∧∧ A psychologist asks a man to nod every time he hears a beeping noise. Based on the man's response and the presence or absence of the noise, the psychologist will mark the man's response as a miss, a hit, a correct rejection, or a false alarm.

Weber's Law states that regardless of size, two stimuli must differ by a constant proportion for the difference to be noticeable.

Receptor cell is a specialized cell that responds to a particular type of energy.

Sensory neuron is a neuron that carries information from the sensory receptors to the brain as a coded signal.

Transduction is a process through which physical energy such as light or sound is converted into an electrical charge.

Sensory adaptation is a process in which sensory receptor cells become less responsive to an unchanging stimulus.

tastes sweeter. However, if you add a spoonful of sugar to an industrial-sized tea urn, you will probably not be able to tell the difference.

Ernst Weber (1795–1878) noticed that regardless of size, two stimuli must differ by a constant proportion for the difference to be noticeable. His principle became known as **Weber's Law**.

Sensory Processes

Psychologists are interested in analyzing the relationships between physical stimuli, our physiological responses to those stimuli, and the sensory experiences that result.

If someone asked you how many senses the human body possesses, you would probably think it was a trick question. But which sense tells the body when it is balanced? Or lets us know where our hands are in relation to our feet? We actually have many more senses than the traditionally studied five.

Sensation occurs when a **receptor cell** in one of the sense organs is stimulated by energy. When the energy level exceeds the absolute threshold, the receptor cell fires neural impulses. **Sensory neurons** carry information from the sensory receptors to the brain as a coded signal.

The process through which physical energy such as light or sound is converted into an electrical charge is known as **transduction**. The strength of the stimuli will affect how rapidly the sensory neurons fire. For example, a bright light may rapidly fire a set of sensory neurons, while a faint glow would set off a slower rate of neuronal firing. Each receptor cell is sensitive to a specific form of energy. Thus, receptor cells in the eye will respond only to light waves, while receptor cells in the ear will respond only to sound waves.

Think about the smell you encounter when you first walk into a barn, or drive past a chemical factory. At first, an unpleasant smell can be overpowering, but after a few minutes, we no longer notice it. This is because our sensory receptor cells become less responsive to an unchanging stimulus, a process called **sensory adaptation**. Sensory adaptation enables us to focus on changes in our environment. Without it, we would be constantly aware of the pressure of the ground under our feet or the humming of the air conditioner in the office.

Three factors control sensory adaptation: the number of receptor cells, the rate at which they fire, and the corresponding sensory cortex in your brain.

Is a soldier more likely to detect weak stimuli in wartime or peacetime? >>>

VISION

Which of your senses do you value the most? When faced with this question, many people choose vision. Although we could eventually adapt to navigating in a sightless world, most of us would find this adjustment a challenge. Vision is a key sense—but how does it work?

The Structure of the Eye

Focus your attention on an object within reach. Now look out of the window and focus on something in the distance. How is it possible that you can see both equally well? The lens adjusts in shape from thick to thin to enable us to focus on objects that are close by or far away. This process is called **visual accommodation**. Ask an elderly relative to try the same thing (without glasses!) and he or she will probably have difficulty with the task. As we grow older, the lens hardens and we are unable to accommodate for distance, a process known as presbyopia.

The **retina** is the multilayered tissue at the back of the eye that is responsible for visual transduction. Due to the size and structure of the eye's lens, images are projected onto the retina upside-down, which could lead to much confusion. Fortunately, receptor cells in the retina convert light energy into neural impulses, which are sent to the brain for processing. Here, they are constructed into an upright-seeming image, enabling us to see the world the right way around.

There are two types of photoreceptor cells in the retina: rods and cones. Named for their characteristic shapes, rods and cones each have specific parts to play in the visual process.

Rods respond to varying degrees of light and dark. They are found everywhere outside the **fovea**—a depressed spot in the retina that occupies the center of your visual field. Have you ever tried staring at a star at night, only to have it disappear

before your eyes? Try shifting your gaze to the side. Since rods are able to function in dim light, we are able to see objects in dim light clearer when the light hits just outside the fovea. This happens when we do not focus directly on the object, but instead look slightly off to the side.

Cones enable us to see color. They are primarily found in the fovea. Cones work best in bright light, which is why we cannot see colors in the dark. Cones are specialized for **acuity**, or sharpness of vision, and color perception. When you want to examine something carefully, do you move it into bright light, or turn the light off? Since cones are specialized for acuity and color perception, we need to use bright light in order to see things in detail.

VISUAL INFORMATION PROCESSING

The retina is actually an extension of the brain—during fetal development it moves from the brain to the eye. When we process an image, light waves hit the retina and are transmitted to the **ganglion cells**, whose axons make up the **optic nerve**. Light from the left side of each eye's retina translates into a neural message that travels along the optic nerve to the left visual cortex. Information from the right eye crosses to the left hemisphere at the **optic chiasm**. Similarly, messages from the right side of each eye's retina travel along the optic nerve to the right visual cortex. Information from the left eye crosses to the right hemisphere at the optic chiasm. The visual cortex at the back of the brain then processes this information.

Feature Detection

Nobel Prize winners David Hubel and Torsten Wiesel (1979) proved that the primary visual cortex has **feature detector** neurons that respond to specific types of features. They found that **simple cells** respond to a single feature, such as a vertical line, while **complex cells** respond to two features of a stimulus, such as a vertical line that moves in a horizontal direction.

Physiological response

Physical stimulus

Sensory experience

∧
∧
∧ **Our sensory systems work in a three-step process.**

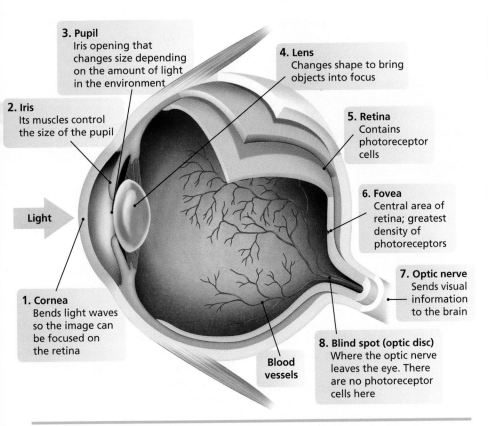

3. Pupil
Iris opening that changes size depending on the amount of light in the environment

4. Lens
Changes shape to bring objects into focus

2. Iris
Its muscles control the size of the pupil

5. Retina
Contains photoreceptor cells

Light

6. Fovea
Central area of retina; greatest density of photoreceptors

1. Cornea
Bends light waves so the image can be focused on the retina

7. Optic nerve
Sends visual information to the brain

Blood vessels

8. Blind spot (optic disc)
Where the optic nerve leaves the eye. There are no photoreceptor cells here

Hypercomplex cell is a feature detector that responds to multiple features of a stimulus.

Fusiform face area is an area of the visual cortex that specifically responds to and recognizes faces.

Parallel processing describes the process of doing several things at the same time.

Blindsight is a condition in which a person is not consciously aware of what he or she sees, but can still partially respond to visual information.

∧∧
∧ Light rays enter the eye through the cornea and the pupil. The light travels through the eye and is focused onto the retina by the lens. Visual information is then sent to the brain via the optic nerve.

Hypercomplex cells respond to multiple features of a stimulus, for example, a vertical line moving in a horizontal direction that is a particular length. When many neuron systems work together, we are able to perceive whole objects. Some areas of the brain are very good at perceiving specific types of objects. For example, one area of the visual cortex, just behind the right and left ears, specifically responds to and recognizes faces. This is known as the **fusiform face area**. This brain area is significantly more active on fMRI scans when pictures of faces are viewed.

Parallel Processing

Unlike a machine that works using a step-by-step process, our brains are able to do several things at once. In other words, the brain has a talent for **parallel processing**. When we view a painting, different areas of the brain process its color, depth, motion, and form (Livingstone & Hubel, 1988). Amazingly, we're able to reconstruct the image in our minds by pulling all of this information together in a fraction of a second. It's like putting together a jigsaw puzzle at record-breaking speed.

The concept of parallel processing explains why

brain damage can cause some unusual visual disabilities. Take Patient M, who suffered stroke damage near the rear of both sides of her brain, resulting in a loss of her ability to perceive movement. Pouring a cup of tea became more than a little tricky because the liquid appeared to be frozen in mid-air (Hoffman, 1998).

Brain damage (to the primary visual cortex) may also cause people to experience blindness in part of their field of vision, a concept known as **blindsight**. Despite having blind spots in which no stimuli can be consciously seen, patients are still able to maintain a high degree of accuracy when asked to guess about features of stimuli shown in their blind spots. For example, patients may not be able to see an object such as a rod in their blind field, but when asked about whether the rod is vertical or horizontal, these patients will nearly always make the correct determination.

For a visual experience to occur, messages must travel from the eyes to the visual cortex. >>>

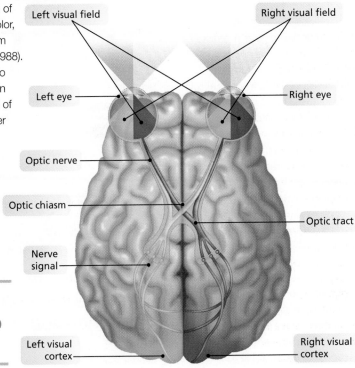

Left visual field

Right visual field

Left eye

Right eye

Optic nerve

Optic chiasm

Optic tract

Nerve signal

Left visual cortex

Right visual cortex

Hue is a particular color.

Saturation describes the intensity of a color.

Brightness describes the intensity of light waves.

Color constancy is the inclination to perceive familiar objects as retaining their color despite changes in sensory information.

Sound wave is a change in air pressure caused by molecules of air or fluid colliding and moving apart.

Frequency is the number of cycles per second in a wave.

Amplitude is the height of a wave.

Timbre is the quality and purity of the tone of a sound.

Tonotopic pertains to the way in which the primary auditory cortex is organized so that neurons that respond to particular frequencies are grouped together.

Sound shadow is an area of reduced sound intensity around the ear farther away from where a sound originates.

Echolocation is a process in which sound waves are emitted and the environment is analyzed by listening to the frequency of the waves that are reflected back.

COLOR VISION

Why is the sky blue? In a technical sense, the sky is every color but blue, because it reflects blue wavelengths. Light rays themselves are not colored; we create the experience of color in our brains. The human brain is able to distinguish 7 million different color variations (Geldard, 1972).

The wavelength of the light that reaches our eyes creates a particular color, or **hue**. The intensity, or purity, of the color is called its **saturation**. The intensity of the light waves affects the **brightness** of the color.

Look at the picture of the green cylinder on a chessboard at the top of the page. Square A is darker than square B, right? Surprisingly enough, squares A and B are actually the same shade. Our experience of color depends on context. We perceive familiar objects as having consistent color, despite lighting and wavelengths constantly changing. This phenomenon is known as **color constancy**.

Try wearing a pair of tinted sunglasses. Does everything still look brown after a couple of seconds, or are you able to distinguish the green grass from the blue water and the gray buildings? Our perception of an object's color is not an isolated phenomenon; it depends on the color of surrounding objects.

HEARING (AUDITION)

The average person may not be able to use echolocation like dolphins or bats, but our sense of hearing is still pretty amazing. With the help of our brains and ears, we gracefully convert sound waves— caused by the vibration of air—into meaningful noises.

<<< Which square is darker, A or B?

Sound Waves

If you traveled into deep space, you wouldn't hear a single sound. Why? A **sound wave** is a change in air pressure caused by molecules of air or fluid colliding and moving apart. In deep space, there are no molecules to collide with each other. Sound cannot exist in a vacuum (the next time you watch *Star Wars*, look out for inconsistencies!).

Sound can be represented as sine waves. Like light waves, sound waves have wavelength, amplitude, and purity.

The **frequency**, or pitch, of a sound wave is measured in cycles per second, or hertz (Hz). The first wave on the diagram might represent a trombone, or a tuba, while the third wave might show the high-pitched sound of a flute. The human ear is able to hear sounds that range from 20 to 20,000 Hz. This makes us practically pitch deaf compared to dolphins, who can hear up to an astonishing 200,000 Hz.

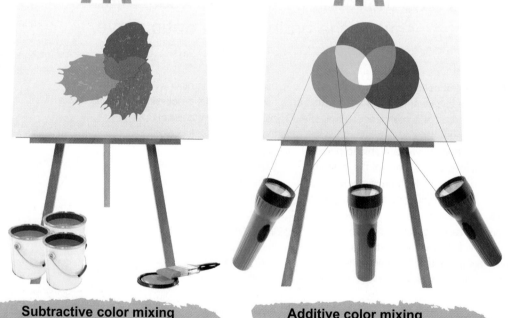

Subtractive color mixing

Additive color mixing

^^^^ **Subtractive color mixing** with paint results in a brown/ black color because each color's **wavelength** is absorbed by the others. **Additive color mixing** with light creates white light because **wavelengths** from each light reach the eye.

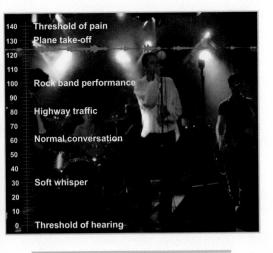

140	Threshold of pain
130	Plane take-off
120	
110	
100	Rock band performance
90	
80	Highway traffic
70	
60	Normal conversation
50	
40	
30	Soft whisper
20	
10	
0	Threshold of hearing

Locating Sounds

Have you ever wondered why our ears are on either side of our head, rather than at the front or back? It isn't just more aesthetically pleasing—the location of our ears enables us to hear stereophonically. When a dog to our left starts barking, the sound reaches our left ear a bit sooner and slightly more intensely than our right ear. Our heads cast a **sound shadow**, meaning that a sound has to go through or around the head in order to reach the other ear. As it travels, the sound weakens, providing an extra clue as to where the sound came from.

Few people can claim to be experts in sound location. However, if, somehow, we could teach ourselves **echolocation**, we'd be able to navigate by using sound. Animals with this talent include bats and dolphins. They send out sound signals to analyze and locate objects in their environment by listening to the frequency of the waves that reflect back to them.

∧∧∧ How much stress do you put on your ears every day?

The **amplitude**, or height, of a sound wave is interpreted as its volume—how loud or soft a sound is. Volume is measured in decibels. The absolute threshold for hearing is 0 decibels, and prolonged exposure to anything above 85 decibels can produce hearing loss. Some rock bands play at a whopping 140 decibels at close range, making it pretty amazing that they (and their die-hard fans) are able to hear at all.

Have you ever covered your ears in horror while listening to early *American Idol* auditions? The disillusioned contestants probably need to work on their **timbre**, or the quality and purity of their tone. A good musician will be able to judge the sound quality or resonance of a note. A poor musician will be labeled tone deaf and unceremoniously asked to leave the stage by Simon Cowell.

The inner ear is responsible for the transduction of sound energy. Sound waves move through the ear and are translated into neural signals by the receptor cells in the basilar membrane. The volume of a sound affects the number of hair cells that are activated. The brain can interpret the loudness of a sound from the number of activated hair cells. Too much noise can permanently damage hair cells by withering or fusing them.

The primary auditory cortex is organized in a **tonotopic** arrangement. This means that particular neurons respond to specific frequencies, and are grouped together according to their preferred frequencies.

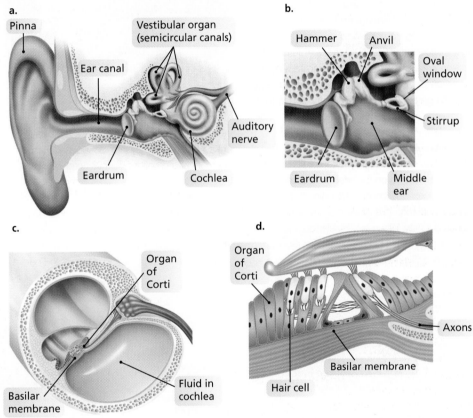

∧∧∧ The process of hearing: a. The outer ear acts as a funnel for sound waves, which travel to the ear drum, causing it to vibrate. b. The hammer, anvil, and stirrup strike each other, carrying the vibrations to the oval window and on to the cochlea in the inner ear. c. The fluid in the cochlea is moving, which causes ripples in the basilar membrane. d. The basilar membrane is lined with hair cells. Cilia on the tips of the hair cells stimulate the receptor cell axons to send messages via the auditory nerve to the temporal lobe's auditory cortex.

SMELL (OLFACTION)

Like taste, smell is a chemical sense. Molecules of a substance are carried through the air to the receptor cells at the top of our nasal cavities, meaning that we effectively inhale part of everything we smell. Not so bad if you are breathing in the scent of rose petals on a summer's day, but you might want to hold your breath the next time you drive past a sewage treatment plant.

Have you ever left the gas on by accident? Your sense of smell is an early warning system that helps you detect danger. The chemical senses are also used to attract partners, a concept that is persistently exploited by the multibillion-dollar-a-year perfume industry. Our sense of smell is not as acute as our eyesight or hearing, and it's downright embarrassing compared to the smelling abilities of dogs, who each possess at least 125 million scent receptors (compared to a paltry 5 million per human). However, human beings are still pretty impressive when it comes to smell: We're able to distinguish 10,000 different odors (Malnic et al., 1999).

As molecules travel to the top of our nasal cavity, they reach olfactory receptor sites—large protein molecules on the olfactory neurons that bind to specific odorants. We have 400 types of sensory neurons that work in a similar fashion to a lock and key. When a particular odor is encountered, it fits like a key into the receptor that is sensitive to that individual smell. Since we

do not have a distinct receptor for each of the 10,000 smells we encounter, it is likely that each odor triggers combinations of receptors.

Have you ever caught a whiff of a particular fragrance and been reminded of a happy occasion? Maybe the scent of laundry detergent loses you in the reverie of your first kiss, which happened to take place in the laundromat. The area of the brain that receives information from

> " Have you ever left the gas on by accident? **Your sense of smell is an early warning system that helps you detect danger.** "

receptor cells in the nasal cavities is closely linked to the limbic system associated with memory and emotion. Furthermore, smell signals don't have to travel through the thalamus; they have direct links to the brain's emotion and memory centers like the amygdala and the hippocampus. Thus, odors have the ability to evoke memories and feelings. Whether these memories are happy or sad depends on our

earliest experiences with the particular smell (Herz, 2001).

You have probably heard people with a cold complaining that everything tastes like cardboard. Our senses of smell and taste are inextricably linked because the back of the mouth cavity is connected to the nasal cavity. Pinch your nostrils, close your eyes and have a friend feed you chunks of apple and raw potato. You will probably find that you are unable to tell the difference.

Age and Sex Differences

Are you male? Over the age of 49? A smoker? If you answered "yes" to all three questions, you're in for a disappointing piece of career-related news: You are unlikely to be hired as a perfumer. Our ability to identify scents peaks in early adulthood. Women generally have a more acute sense of smell than men do, and their ability to identify odors increases with repeated exposure more than men's (Dalton et al., 2002). Our sense of smell is also negatively affected by smoking, alcoholism, Alzheimer's disease, and Parkinson's disease (Doty, 2001).

Communication and Pheromones

Some companies out there brag that one squirt of their pheromone spray will increase your sex appeal many times over.

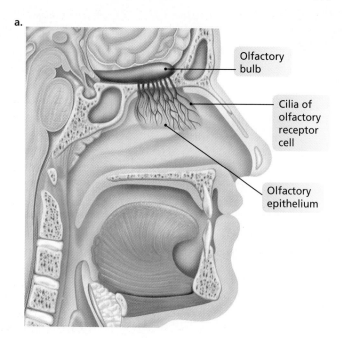

a.

Olfactory bulb

Cilia of olfactory receptor cell

Olfactory epithelium

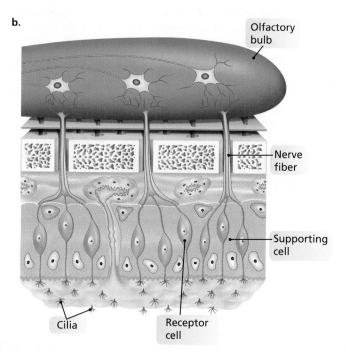

b.

Olfactory bulb

Nerve fiber

Supporting cell

Cilia

Receptor cell

∧
∧
∧ The olfactory system receptor cells in the nasal cavity send messages to the brain's olfactory bulb.

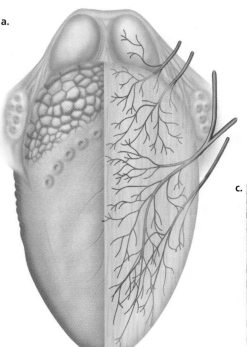

a.

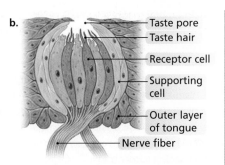

b.

- Taste pore
- Taste hair
- Receptor cell
- Supporting cell
- Outer layer of tongue
- Nerve fiber

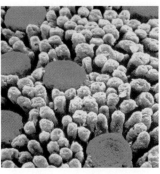

c.

> ∧
> ∧
> ∧ **Figure a shows the nerves in the tongue. Figure b shows the anatomy of a taste bud. Figure c shows a microphotograph of the surface of the tongue.**

Pheromones are a chemical substance released by an animal to trigger behavioral responses in other members of that species. Specialized cells in the nasal cavities of most mammals, called **vomeronasal organs**, detect pheromones and trigger responses through sexual, aggressive, or territorial behavior. Humans have the equipment needed to secrete pheromones, but before you rush for your credit card, there is no evidence that so-called sex sprays have any effect whatsoever. While we have the ability to secrete pheromones, the existence of a vomeronasal system in humans remains a subject of heated dispute among scientists.

TASTE (GUSTATION)

If our ancestors had enjoyed the taste of milkweed, we might not be around today. Fortunately, our natural inclination to avoid bitter-tasting foods developed as a result of the natural defense mechanism of many poisonous plants to produce a bitter-tasting substance. Chemical companies use the same technique when they introduce bitter-tasting chemicals into cleaning products to discourage people from ingesting them. Our sense of taste warns us when food may be unsafe to eat.

Taste receptor cells are located in the **taste buds**, which are embedded in the tongue's **papillae**—the bumps that you can see on your tongue. **Microvilli**—tiny hairs at the tips of the taste receptor cells—generate a nerve impulse, interpreted in the brain as a particular taste. When we eat, saliva dissolves the chemical substances in food, which slip between the papillae in order to reach the taste buds. Taste signals are passed to the limbic system and the cerebral cortex.

Psychologists now recognize five basic tastes: sweet, salty, sour, bitter, and umami (a Japanese word that describes the taste of foods such as soup, chicken, cheese and anything containing monosodium glutamate). Receptor cells for each taste are located throughout the tongue, mouth, and throat, with some types more prevalent than others in certain areas. (This often

leads to the myth you might have learned in elementary school, that different tastes correspond to different parts of your tongue.)

Our emotional responses to taste are hardwired. If you place a bitter substance on a newborn baby's tongue, the baby will react with a disgusted expression similar to one an adult might make (Bartoshuk, 1993).

BODY (SOMESTHETIC) AND SKIN (CUTANEOUS) SENSES

Our fifth sense is commonly known as touch, but it's actually a combination of several senses: the **skin senses**, which relate to pressure, touch, and pain; the **kinesthetic sense**, which relates to how our body parts interact with one another; and the **vestibular senses**, which relate to movement and body position.

Pain

Stefan Salvatore, one of the main characters in the TV show *The Vampire Diaries*, does not feel pain from injuries that would be intolerable to most people, resulting in his ability to perform an impressive array of death-defying stunts. To us mere humans, an inability to feel pain would eventually prove fatal. Pain is your body's way of telling you that placing your hand on a hot oven, or running into a brick wall, is a bad idea. It encourages us not to try those things again, which prolongs our survival. People who have rare genetic disorders that prevent them from detecting pain often die before they reach adulthood.

There are actually several different kinds of pain. **Nociceptive pain** is a negative feeling

gate-control theory (Melzack, 1980; Melzack & Katz, 2004). Pain signals pass through a "gate" in the spinal cord that either blocks the signals or allows them to pass to the brain. When pain signals reach the brain, they activate cells in the thalamus, somatosensory cortex, and limbic system. The brain interprets the messages and sends signals that either open the gate further, causing greater pain, or close it, preventing us from feeling further pain.

You have probably heard of an athlete managing to finish a race with a broken leg, or a football player completing a game with a broken collarbone and wondered why they weren't crumpled on the ground in a world of pain. **Endorphins**, the body's answer to morphine, inhibit the transmission of pain signals to the brain, enabling us to perform seemingly superhuman feats when we are under stress.

Touch

Did you know that you have about 21 square feet of skin on your body? That's a lot of receptor cells! We have several types of cells in layers of skin that process pain, pressure, and temperature.

Imagine a world in which you couldn't hold hands with a partner, kiss your parents hello, or console a friend with a hug. If it sounds like a terrible place to live, that's because it is—touch is necessary for our development and well-being. Infant rats deprived of maternal grooming produce less growth hormone and have a lower metabolic rate than their contemporaries (Schanberg, 1988). Infant monkeys not allowed to touch their mothers become desperately unhappy, while monkeys that are separated from their mothers by a screen that allows touching are far more content (Harlow, 1965).

caused by an external stimulus. If you sprain your ankle, bruise your arm, or burn yourself on a hot stove, you are feeling nociceptive pain. This type of pain is usually time limited; when the injury heals, the pain fades.

Neuropathic pain derives from a malfunction in the central nervous system. It may be triggered by an injury or through diseases such as cancer that disturb cellular functioning. Phantom limb pain is also an example of neuropathic pain—amputees sometimes feel pain or movement in nonexistent limbs (Melzack, 1992). Neuropathic pain is treated with drugs and therapies to calm abnormal cellular activity, but problems are often not fully reversible.

Referred pain occurs when sensory information from internal and external areas converges on the same nerve cells in the spinal cord. In other words, pain is experienced in a different part of the body than the location of the injury. The most common example of this is when heart attack victims experience pain in their shoulders or left arms.

Why do some people seem to feel pain more acutely than others? The best current explanation for the way we feel pain is the

Body Position and Movement

Our kinesthetic sense provides information to our brains about the positions and movements of our muscles and joints. Without it, we would be unable to walk in a straight line, raise a glass to our lips, or bend down to pick up a pencil. Signals from specialized nerve endings, or **proprioceptors**, provide a constant stream of information from our muscles through our spinal cords and on to the cortex of the parietal lobe.

The vestibular sense monitors the body's position in space. It originates in the inner ear, which is why you sometimes lose your sense of balance when you have an ear infection. Hair cells in the **semicircular canals** send messages to the brain as they move back and forth.

Movement also stimulates tiny crystals in the **vestibular sacs**, which connect the canals to the cochlea. The receptors send messages to the cerebellum, enabling it to maintain the body's sense of balance.

Labels: Hair; Sweat gland; Pressure-sensitive nerves; Subcutaneous fat; Pain-sensitive and touch-sensitive free nerve endings; Blood vessels; Skin layers; Skin surface

> ^^^ Skin has several layers. Some receptor cells are wrapped around the ends of the hairs on the dermis, some are located near the surface of the epidermis, and some are found under the top layer of tissue. The subcutaneous layer stores fats and lipids.

Perception

Perception is the way we organize and interpret sensory information from the outside world to give it meaning. No two people perceive the world the same way. Take the tattooed skinhead sitting at a bus stop. Some of us might hurriedly cross the road in an effort to avoid the brutal thug, while others may compliment the creative young man on his body art.

We perceive when we take the sensations we experience and interpret them as meaningful data. Rather than seeing patterns of light and darkness, we are able to perceive a frog hopping into a pond, or a car whizzing past us on the freeway. But how do we create meaning from the sensory data that bombards us every day?

Attention and Perception

Our conscious attention is selective—we are able to focus on only one perception at any given time, even though we know that alternative interpretations are possible. Try it yourself by staring at a Necker cube. You should find that your mind switches back and forth between images, never allowing you to see both interpretations at the same time.

Sometimes our attention is **endogenous**, or directed by our internal decisions. We make explicit choices to pay attention to particular stimuli. You might be making a conscious effort to pay attention to this book, rather than focusing on the new CD you are playing in the background.

At other times our attention is **exogenous,** or directed by external stimuli. If a plane crashes loudly outside your bedroom window, your attention will automatically be drawn to it, no

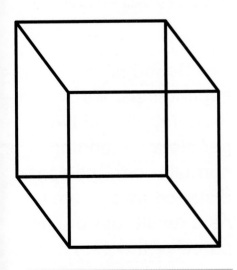

∧ ∧ Which way is the
∧ cube facing?

matter how fascinating the information in your textbook might be.

> Stimuli that are important or interesting to us are called pop-out stimuli— they "pop out" at us and keep our attention.

UNATTENDED STIMULI AND POP-OUT STIMULI

Since we are constantly being bombarded with stimuli, we are able to select just a few to process at any one time. This is why driving while talking on a cell phone is an extremely bad idea—if we are concentrating on last night's gossip, we are missing important traffic signals that would otherwise be the main focus of our attention. Our failure to perceive a given stimulus is known as **inattentional blindness**.

Would you notice if the person you were giving directions to suddenly changed his or her appearance? We like to think that we are observant, but most of us are subject to **change blindness**, or failure to detect drastic visual changes in a scene. In a 1998 study by Simons and Levin, an experimenter who was dressed as a construction worker stopped a person in the street and asked for directions. Workers carrying a door passed between the experimenter and the person giving directions, enabling another experimenter dressed as a construction worker to take the place of the first. In two-thirds of cases, the person continued to give directions without noticing that the construction worker had changed in appearance.

Similar examples of inattentional blindness can be observed with **change deafness**—the failure to detect drastic auditory changes, and **choice blindness**—the failure to detect alterations to choices we have made. For example, participants in a study were shown pairs of cards with photos of female faces on them and asked to pick which face they found more attractive. Once the participants chose a particular card, the experimenter handed them the other photo in a sleight of hand maneuver. The participants were then asked to justify their choice, even though the card they had been given was not the card they chose. Not only did most subjects fail to notice the switch, they also justified their "choice" using features of the non-preferred face (Johansson et al., 2005).

How are we able to carry out a conversation in a crowded room? The **cocktail party**

effect is a good example of how selective attention allows us to concentrate on one voice and ignore many others. Stimuli that are important or interesting to us are called **pop-out stimuli**— they "pop out" at us and keep our attention.

PREATTENTIVE PROCESSING

If you glance at an image for a fraction of a second, you will probably not be able to describe it in any great detail. However, you might know more about it than you think. **Preattentive processing** is the complex processing of information that occurs without our conscious awareness. If we are shown an image of a red dot in a grid of blue dots, even for a split second, we are likely to remember the red dot.

Preattentive processing enables us to analyze the images we see using a guided search process. We are able to quickly filter images through our brains by looking for particular features, such as color or shape.

MULTITASKING

While you are reading this textbook, you might be listening to the radio, or flicking between TV channels. You might have tried to read a page while having a phone conversation with your friend, or making a cup of tea. When you juggle independent sensory inputs, you are **multitasking**—a skill many people in today's fast-paced society pride themselves on. But are we really able to do more than one thing at a time?

Brain scan studies conducted on a particular form of sensory information, such as

Top-down processing refers to our use of beliefs, experiences, expectations, and other concepts to shape our view of the world.

Unconscious inference is a phenomenon in which a person's visual systems use sensory information to draw conclusions about what he or she sees.

Illusory contour is a visual illusion in which lines are perceived without actually being present.

Perceptual set is a mental disposition based on previous experiences and expectations that influences the way a person perceives things.

auditory, have demonstrated that when we focus on a noise, areas in the brain specialized for auditory processing increase in activity, while areas for other forms of sensory information, such as visual recognition, decrease.

These studies indicate that directing resources to one form of sensory information can drain resources from another, because there is a limited amount of blood circulating in the brain. Neuroscientists at Carnegie Mellon University in Pittsburgh proved that rather than double its level of activity, brain power decreases when we try to multitask, even when different parts of the brain are used for different tasks. This explains why talking on a cell phone inhibits our driving ability (Strayer & Johnston, 2001).

Theories of Perception

TOP-DOWN PROCESSING

The way we perceive the world is affected by our beliefs, experiences, and expectations—

Why do we perceive a white triangle in the center of this image when it is not really there?

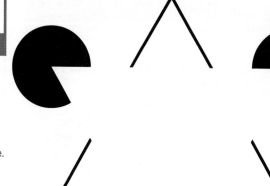

a concept psychologists call **top-down processing**. German physiologist Hermann von Helmholtz (1821–1894) argued that our conscious perceptions are determined by **unconscious inferences**, in which our visual systems use sensory information to draw conclusions about what we see. For example, when we hold a finger in front of the moon, how do we know that the finger and the moon are not the same size? Helmholtz

argued that we learn how to interpret spatial concepts through experience.

Our brains have a natural desire to create logic and order. Often, we create the perception of contours and borders to construct a logical form, even if it is not really there. An **illusory contour** is a visual illusion in which lines are perceived without actually being present. Researchers have discovered that illusory contour images activate specific regions in the visual cortex. Cells in these areas respond as though the contours were formed by real lines or edges (von der Heydt et al., 1984).

In White's illusion (shown at the top of p. 81), the gray rectangles on the left appear darker than the rectangles on the right. In actual fact, they are identical. Our perception of brightness depends on the context of a stimulus. The rectangles on the right are mostly surrounded by white, while the rectangles on the left are mostly surrounded by black. Our brains assess the relative reflection of light compared with surrounding objects.

Perceptual Sets

Our previous experiences and expectations give us a mental predisposition, or **perceptual set**, that influences the way we perceive things. For example, if a child hands you a page scrawled with scattered squiggles in brown crayon and tells you he has drawn a picture of a horse, you will be more likely to perceive the messy brown scribble as a horse. Top-down processing enables us to use preexisting knowledge to create a coherent image in our brains.

<<< Based on previous experiences, we assume that the two people are standing in a normal room, the same distance away from us. As a result, our brains perceive the person on the right to be much larger than the person on the left.

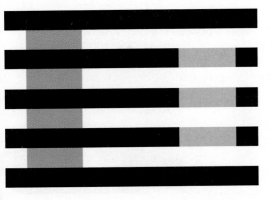

psychological terms, it refers to the way in which we naturally group objects together and perceive whole shapes, rather than a number of individual parts. For example, a Necker cube is really a series of converging lines, yet when we look at it, we see a three-dimensional object. Gestalt psychology developed in Germany at the beginning of the 20th century, partly as a reaction to the introspective methods used in structuralism.

Λ Λ Λ Which rectangles are darker?

Have you ever misheard something one of your friends said because you were expecting her to say something else? Perceptual sets are not just restricted to vision. We can play certain rock songs backward and not think anything of them. But if someone tells us that certain disturbing words or phrases can be heard among the backward sounds, we are far more likely to perceive the evil messages (Vokey & Read, 1985). Christian preacher Gary Greenwald maintained that Led Zeppelin's "Stairway to Heaven" when played backward, contained the phrase "There's no denying it, here's to my sweet Satan." When told what to listen for, Greenwald's religious supporters agreed that the song did in fact contain the heretical line. Similarly, once Joyce Simpson spotted Jesus in a forkful of spaghetti on a Pizza Hut billboard in Atlanta, Georgia, in 1991, perceptual set enabled others to perceive the image, sparking nationwide religious fervor.

Our perceptual set is determined by our previous experiences, through which we form schemas, or internal representations of an object. This can be influenced by culture. For example, Europeans and North Americans are likely to perceive diagrams differently than people in Native cultures. We can find evidence of this with a diagram commonly known as the "devil's trident." Europeans and Native Americans have a natural desire to interpret it as a three-dimensional object, yet people in native cultures are able to view the diagram as two-dimensional—just a series of lines and circles (Deregowski, 1969).

GESTALT PRINCIPLES

The German word *gestalt* means "form," or "whole." In

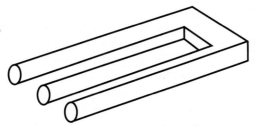

Λ Λ Λ How do you perceive the devil's trident?

Grouping

The main concept of Gestalt psychology is the **law of pragnanz** (German for *conciseness*), which says that we organize a stimulus into the simplest possible form. Six-month-old infants are already able to follow certain rules for grouping stimuli together (Quinn et al., 2002).

Proximity. We tend to perceive objects that are close to one another as part of the same group—a principle known as **proximity**.

Similarity. **Similarity** is the tendency to perceive objects that are the same shape, size, or color as part of a pattern. For example, members of a police force all wear the same uniform so that they are instantly recognizable as part of a group.

Closure. **Closure** is the tendency to perceive images as complete objects and overlook incompleteness. When shown a series of disconnected curved lines in a circular pattern, we will invariably describe it as a circle.

Continuity. **Continuity** is a tendency to view intersecting lines as part of a continuous pattern, rather than as a series of separate lines. A cross is usually perceived as two intersecting lines, rather than four lines that meet at a central point.

Symmetry. Our perceptual systems tend to organize objects in terms of symmetrical shapes that form around their center—the law of **symmetry**. When we see two unconnected but symmetrical shapes, we automatically perceive them as one object.

Common Fate. The law of **common fate** dictates that if the parts of a stimulus are all moving in the same direction, we perceive them as parts of a whole. If you see four people standing together at a party, and two of them walk toward the kitchen, while the other two head for the living room, you will no longer perceive them as a group of four, but rather as two pairs.

Figure–Ground Relationships

An important part of the perceptual process is being able to distinguish the object we are

Gestalt principles of perceptual organization V V V

Similarity

Proximity

Continuity

Closure

Symmetry

Figure is the object on which a person is focusing.

Ground is the environment surrounding the object of focus, or the figure.

Reversible figure refers to an illusion in which staring at an image long enough causes the figure and ground to reverse.

View-dependent pertains to the idea that previously seen objects are stored as a template that is compared to a viewed shape in the retinal image.

View-independent pertains to the idea that the visual system recognizes objects as a combination of their visual parts.

Distal stimulus is a stimulus from an object that exists in the surrounding environment.

Proximal stimulus is a pattern of physical energy created by the distal stimulus that stimulates a person's receptors.

Feature integration theory suggests that people organize stimuli based on knowledge of how their features should be combined.

Illusory conjunction results from mistakenly combining features of two different stimuli.

Geon is a simple three-dimensional shape that, with other geons, makes up all other objects.

Recognition-by-components is a theory that states that a person recognizes an unfamiliar object by piecing together the cylinder, cone, wedge, and brick shapes of which it is composed.

focusing on—the **figure**—from its surroundings—the **ground**. The figure–ground relationship relates to all of the senses, not just vision. For example, we might hear our name being called amid a cacophony of voices during a sports match, or be able to distinguish the smell of freshly baked bread among an array of scents we encounter on the street.

Sometimes it is tricky to distinguish the figure from the ground, as seen in **reversible figure** illusions such as the Rubin vase. When you first look at the image, you perceive the figure and the ground one way, but if you stare at the image long enough, your perception changes, reversing figure and ground. You'll find that it's not possible to perceive both at once.

OBJECT RECOGNITION

There are two main theories about how we recognize objects. According to supporters of **view-dependent** theories, previously seen objects are stored as a template, or mental representation, that is compared to a viewed shape in the retinal image. In contrast, proponents of **view-independent** theories propose that the visual system recognizes objects as a combination of their individual parts.

When we hear a dog barking, or see a bird sitting on a tree branch, we are using information from the **distal stimulus**—the barking of the dog, or the actual bird—to interpret the physical energy. The **proximal stimulus**—the barking sound stimulating our auditory receptors or the retinal image of the bird—recreates the distal stimuli in our minds.

Feature Integration Theory

How do we recognize a car even if we have never seen that particular model before? Psychologist Anne Treisman proposed the **feature integration theory**—that every stimulus can be broken down into primitive features, or simple parts that make up an object, and combined using a two-step process (Treisman & Gelade, 1980). According to Treisman, we first use parallel processing to detect visual features—our brains rapidly and preattentively scan an object for pop-out stimuli (such as the red dot in the grid of blue dots). Serial processing then takes place in which we combine features to form objects, often using our stored knowledge to help us determine what we are seeing.

Treisman's theory is supported by the fact that when we are not focusing our attention, and have no stored knowledge about an object, errors in feature combinations can occur to produce **illusory conjunctions**. Even though we have detected all the individual features, we combine them incorrectly during the serial pro-

cessing stage. The result is to perceive a blue *C* and a red *A* when you have actually been shown a red *C* and a blue *A*.

Components Theory

Irving Biederman proposed that all objects are composed of simplistic three-dimensional shapes called **geons**. According to his **recognition-by-components** theory, we recognize an unfamiliar object by piecing together the cylinder, cone, wedge, and brick shapes of which it is comprised (Biederman, 1987). Biederman's theory is supported by the fact that our ability to identify an object quickly depends on the clarity of its external edges, rather than features such as color or inner line detail.

Context and Motion

As you can see from the images above, it is much easier to identify parts of an object in context. Motion can also assist our perception. In 1973, psychologist Gunnar Johansson attached small lights to the major joints and head of a person who was filmed walking in the dark. When stationary, it was not possible to distinguish the person as a coherent form. However, while the person was moving, she could easily be recognized as a person walking, proving that we do not need to see a complete image as long as the unconnected points are moving in a recognizable manner (Johansson, 1973). We're also good at recognizing unique motions: If you've ever recognized a friend across the street by her distinctive walk, you're well aware that people's movements can be crucial clues to their identities.

1. Can you guess what this is? 2. How about now?

Do you see the silhouettes of two faces, or a goblet?

Perceptual Interpretation

Do we learn how to perceive the world through experience, or are we born with an innate ability

∧
∧ Did emotional deprivation
∧ drive him over the edge, or
was serial killer Charles
Manson born with a predisposition for violence?

to interpret our surroundings? Proving the answer to this question would make you an instant millionaire; it has been debated by philosophers for centuries. German philosopher Immanuel Kant (1724–1804) argued that perceptual knowledge exists at birth, while British philosopher John Locke (1632–1704) insisted that we learn through our experiences. The nature versus nurture debate still rages on today, influencing everything from crime prevention techniques to educational theory.

Are people who are born blind ever truly able to see, or does early sensory deprivation cause permanent damage? Studies suggest that there is a **critical period**, or optimal time period shortly after birth, during which normal sensory and perceptual development takes place. For example, adults who were born blind but later regained vision after having cataracts removed never enjoyed full sight. They were able to distinguish figure from ground, and could perceive brightness and color, but were unable to recognize objects (von Senden, 1932). Similar perceptual limitations are found with deprivation in other senses.

PERCEPTUAL ADAPTATION

While sensory adaptation allows us to adjust to changes in our environment, **perceptual**

adaptation helps us adjust to changes in the way we *experience* the environment. Have you ever tried on a friend's glasses? At first, the world seems blurry, but if you kept the glasses on for a day or two, your eyesight would adjust (although your friend might not be happy!). **Perceptual adaptation** enables us to adjust sensory input so that the world seems normal again. This is true even for radically altered visual fields. In a month-long study, Japanese psychologist Kaoru Sekiyama (2000) asked four students to wear prism glasses that reversed their left-right vision. While they were initially disoriented, within a few weeks the students were able to carry out tasks requiring complex coordination skills, such as riding a bicycle. At the end of the experiment, the students quickly readapted to normal vision.

SYNESTHESIA

Imagine being able to taste the words you speak, or hear a piece of music as a rainbow of different colors. People who interpret sense information as more than one sensation have a condition called **synesthesia**, in which signals from the sensory organs are processed in the wrong cortical areas of the brain. A common form of the disorder is **grapheme-color synesthesia**—the perception of letters as specific colors, for example thinking of *A* as red. Some synesthetes are **associators**—they might associate the letter *A* as being red, but they do not actually see the color red. A small number of people with the disorder are **projectors**—they actually view the letter *A* as red, even though they know that the type they are reading is black.

Researcher Danko Nikolic tested the authenticity of synesthesia by using a modified Stroop test. In a regular Stroop test, people are shown a word, such as *blue,* printed first in blue ink (a congruent condition) and then in red ink (an incongruent condition). When asked to identify the color of the word, people's reaction times are much quicker in a congruent condition

because their brains are not being given conflicting signals. To assess whether synesthetes achieve the same results, Nikolic presented congruent words according to the particular grapheme–color irregularity. For example, if the person viewed the letter *B* as green, a *B* presented as green would be congruent, while a *B* in any other color would be incongruent. Similar results to the regular Stroop test affirmed that synesthesia is an authentic phenomenon.

Did you know that pianist Duke Ellington was a synesthete? Rather than view their condition as a disorder, most synesthetes embrace the ability to see music in color or taste people's names. Many artists who have synesthesia use their abilities to create unique paintings or musical compositions.

Hip-hop artist Pharell Williams used synesthesia as the basis for N.E.R.D album Seeing Sounds. >>>

Critical period is the optimal time period shortly after birth during which normal sensory and perceptual development takes place.

Perceptual adaptation is a process in which a person adjusts to changes in the environment by adjusting sensory input.

Synesthesia is a condition in which signals from the sensory organs are processed in the wrong cortical areas of the brain.

Grapheme-color synesthesia is a condition in which a person perceives letters as specific colors.

Associator is a person who experiences synesthesia and only associates colors with letters; he or she does not actually see the color.

Projector is a person who experiences synesthesia and actually sees letters as being certain colors, even though he or she knows what color the type actually is.

Summary

WHAT ARE SENSORY THRESHOLDS? p. 70

• An absolute threshold is the smallest amount of energy needed to detect a stimulus such as light, sound, or pressure 50 percent of the time.

• A difference threshold is the minimum difference between two stimuli needed to detect the difference 50 percent of the time.

HOW DO WE PROCESS STIMULI FROM THE OUTSIDE WORLD? p. 71

• Sensation occurs when a receptor cell in one of the sense organs is stimulated by energy. Transduction is the process of converting physical energy into electrochemical codes.

• Light enters the eye through the cornea and pupil and is focused by the lens on the retina. Light waves are transmitted to the ganglion cells that make up the optic nerve. Neural messages travel along the optic nerve to the visual cortex.
• Sound waves cause the eardrum to vibrate. Vibrations are carried to the cochlea, causing ripples in the basilar membrane. Hair cells in the basilar membrane stimulate receptor cells to send messages to the auditory cortex.
• Airborne molecules stimulate receptor cells at the top of the nasal cavity, sending messages to the brain's olfactory bulb.
• Microvilli at the tips of receptor cells in the taste buds send messages to the limbic system and cerebral cortex. The five basic taste qualities are sweet, sour, salty, bitter, and umami.
• Receptor cells in skin process pain, pressure, and temperature. Pain is currently explained by the gate-control theory.
• The kinesthetic senses provide information about muscle movement and changes in posture. The vestibular senses provide information about the body's position in space.

WHY ARE WE ABLE TO EXPERIENCE ONLY ONE PERCEPTION AT A TIME? p. 79

• Perception is the brain's process of organizing and making sense of sensory information.

• Conscious attention is selective—we can only experience one perception at a time. Failure to perceive a stimulus is known as inattentional blindness.

WHAT ARE SOME MAJOR THEORIES OF PERCEPTION? p. 80

• Gestalt psychologists point out that we group stimuli together when the objects are near each other, are similar sizes, colors, and shapes, or complete a pattern.

• Treisman's feature integration theory proposes that we use parallel processing to detect visual features, then serial processing to combine them.

IS PERCEPTION DEVELOPED BY NATURE OR NURTURE? p. 83

• Normal sensory and perceptual development takes place during a critical period shortly after we are born.
• Perceptual adaptation enables us to adjust to changes in the way we perceive the environment.

Test Your Understanding

1. Alia can see the lights on the boats in a harbor at night. Although she cannot see the boats themselves, she perceives three of the lights as belonging to the same boat because they are close together and always move in unison as the boats rock. What Gestalt perceptual law or laws is Alia using?

   a. the law of common fate and the law of proximity
   b. the law of proximity and the law of continuity
   c. the law of continuity and the law of common fate
   d. the law of proximity

2. What theory states that we first identify features of an object (e.g., color, shape, size) and then combine those features to determine what the object is?

   a. the proximal stimulus theory
   b. the distal stimulus theory
   c. the feature integration theory
   d. the similarity theory

3. In experiments, subjects wearing glasses that flip the visual world upside-down have trouble performing even the simplest tasks at first. However, after several days, subjects no longer perceive their vision as inverted. This is an example of:

   a. sensory adaptation.
   b. synesthesia.
   c. perceptual adaptation.
   d. continuity.

4. Fiona's roommate decides to throw her a surprise party in their small apartment. All of Fiona's friends come to the party, so it is quite loud. Despite this, Fiona immediately notices her mother's voice when she arrives at the party. Why might Fiona be able to hear her mother's voice through all of the other voices?

   a. Fiona has undergone sensory adaptation to her mother's voice.
   b. Her mother's voice is a pop-out stimulus.
   c. Fiona's voice is an exogenous stimulus.
   d. Fiona is using echolocation.

5. Antonio is standing at an intersection when he hears a fire truck approaching from the distance. Without turning to look, he can tell that the fire truck is approaching from his left. It is likely that Antonio knows this because:

   a. the timbre of the siren is stronger in his left ear.
   b. the frequency of the siren is higher in his left ear.
   c. the sound of the siren is more intense in his left ear.
   d. the sound arrived at his right ear before it arrived at his left ear.

6. What chemicals released by the body help people to withstand pain?

   a. proprioceptors
   b. endorphins
   c. pheromones
   d. morphine

7. Anna is having an important phone conversation but sees smoke outside the window, and hangs up without saying goodbye. What happens to her attention that makes her discontinue the conversation?

   a. Her attention becomes exogenous.
   b. Her attention becomes endogenous.
   c. Her attention becomes inattentionally blind.
   d. Her attention exhibits choice blindness.

8. In order to catch a fly ball in baseball, a centerfielder must hold his or her glove in just the right position while not looking away from the baseball. What allows the player to know the position of his or her arm and glove without looking at them?

   a. the vestibular sense
   b. the kinesthetic sense
   c. the skin senses
   d. endorphins

9. Why are smells more likely than other sensory stimuli to trigger strong memories and emotions?

   a. Smell helps you detect danger.
   b. The sense of taste, which is connected to the sense of smell, evokes emotions.
   c. Olfaction (smell) is more sensitive than the other senses.
   d. Smell signals have a direct connection to emotion and memory centers in the brain.

10. When you alternate between looking at the speedometer and the road while driving, your eyes must quickly change focus between near and far objects. The process responsible for this is called:

   a. visual navigation.
   b. visual accommodation.
   c. feature detection.
   d. parallel processing.

11. A fly lands on the back of Jim's neck, but he doesn't feel it. Why not?

   a. The fly's weight is disproportionately small compared to Jim's weight.
   b. The fly's weight does not exceed Jim's difference threshold for touch.
   c. Jim is an adult, and children are more sensitive to touch.
   d. The fly's weight does not cross Jim's absolute threshold for touch.

12. Laura was very aware of how heavy her necklace was when she put it on in the morning. However, after a few minutes, she no longer felt the weight of the necklace around her neck. This is likely the result of:

   a. sensory adaptation.
   b. perceptual adaptation.

   c. transduction.
   d. Weber's law.

13. What is considered a "false alarm" in a sensory detection experiment?

   a. if there is no stimulus and the participant responds that there is
   b. if there is no stimulus and the participant responds that there is none
   c. if there is a stimulus and the participant responds that there is
   d. if there is a stimulus and the participant responds that there is none

14. What is the brain's ability to work on several parts of a task at once called?

   a. multiple processing
   b. parallel processing
   c. multitasking
   d. preattentive processing

15. In the eye, the greatest density of photoreceptors are found in the:

   a. fovea
   b. lens
   c. optic disc
   d. cornea

16. When multiple colors of paint are mixed together, why might the combined color appear brown?

   a. The colors absorb one another's wavelengths.
   b. The colors refract one another's wavelengths.
   c. The eye sees all of the wavelengths at once.
   d. The eye sees only the darker wavelengths.

17. Another way of referring to the purity of a color is:

   a. timbre.
   b. hue.
   c. saturation.
   d. color constancy.

18. Gabriel listens to his MP3 player at high volume for extended periods of time. If he continues this practice, he is likely to suffer permanent hearing loss caused by:

   a. damage to the hair cells.
   b. damage to the pinna.
   c. a blockage in one of his ears.
   d. swelling of the ear canal.

19. If you do not like the taste of a liquid medicine you must take, what technique might make the experience more bearable?

   a. Hold your breath while you take it.
   b. Warm the medicine to body temperature.
   c. Add a teaspoon of salt to it.
   d. Only allow the medicine to touch the tip of your tongue.

20. In handwritten notes, a single vertical line can represent the number one or a lowercase 'L.' If you were to see several vertical lines in a handwritten phone number, you would most likely perceive them as ones, and not letters, because you would not expect letters to appear in a phone number. This is an example of:

   a. an illusory contour.
   b. the law of pragnanz.
   c. synesthesia.
   d. top-down processing.

Remember to check www.thethinkspot.com **for additional information, downloadable flashcards, and other helpful resources.**

Answers: 1) a; 2) c; 3) c; 4) b; 5) c; 6) b; 7) a; 8) b; 9) d; 10) b; 11) d; 12) a; 13) a; 14) b; 15) a; 16) a; 17) c; 18) a; 19) a; 20) d

CONSCIOUSNESS

HOW DO DIFFERENT LEVELS OF CON
NESS FUNCTION?
HOW DOES CONSCIOUSNESS CHANG
WE SLEEP AND DREAM, AND WHY?
HOW CAN HYPNOSIS AND MEDITATIC
CONSCIOUSNESS?

Columbia

Daily Tribune sports editor Kent Heitholt was brutally attacked and murdered in the Missouri newspaper's parking lot shortly after finishing a late shift in October 2001. He was struck 11 times on the head with a metal object and strangled with his own belt. Although there was a mountain of physical evidence at the scene, including fingerprints, DNA, and a bloody hair in the victim's hand, police struggled to make an arrest.

Two years later, 19-year-old Charles Erickson, while under the influence of alcohol, began telling friends about a dream he'd had. The dream accompanied strong feelings that he and a classmate had been involved in a murder, although details were sketchy. After a friend reported Erickson's ramblings to the police, he was brought in for interrogation. Erickson could remember little about the night of the murder, and during questioning he appeared confused and unsure. Realizing that Erickson could provide no accurate details of the murder, police continuously prompted him—a fact that experts later argued could have enabled him to construct a narrative around the information. It was clear from the taped interrogation that Erickson simply went along while the interrogating officer supplied answers to his own questions.

Ryan Ferguson, Erickson's junior high school classmate, was arrested the same day, and bail was set at $20 million—the highest in U.S. history for one count of murder. Police found no physical evidence linking either Ferguson or Erickson to the crime, and a composite sketch of a man seen by an eyewitness bore no resemblance to either of them. During the trial, the defense called on memory expert Professor Elizabeth Loftus, who testified that, in her opinion, Erickson had made a false confession. She argued that it was extremely unlikely that a person would forget something as significant as a murder and suddenly remember it years later. Despite her testimony, in December 2005, Ferguson was convicted of murder and robbery and sentenced to 40 years in prison. He is currently appealing his sentence.

The Ferguson case raises several interesting questions about consciousness. Is it possible to suddenly recall an event that took place several years earlier? Can memories be recovered in a dream? Do our brains sometimes trick us into remembering things that never actually happened? If so, how can a jury distinguish between a false confession and a real one? An in-depth study of consciousness and the physiological changes the body goes through during altered states of consciousness may enable us to make more informed judgments.

ott Falater was an average man. He had a wife and family, was
n active member of the local church, and worked as a product
er at a nearby plant. However, on January 19, 1997, he brutally
stabbed his wife to death. A neighbor witnessed the scene and
ed police, who arrested Falater on the spot. In a strange twist,
er, Scott Falater claimed to have been sleepwalking during the
Officials were bewildered. No one could determine a motive for
deed, Falater's sister (pictured) and close friends of the family
ed the marriage as a happy one, and the relationship between
band and wife as warm and affectionate. But how could a man
t such a precise crime—even going so far as to hide the body
inate incriminating evidence—in his sleep? Was Scott Falater
hoping to escape charges through a bizarre lie, or does human
ess really have the power to drastically alter our awareness?

CHAPTER

Consciousness and Information Processing

Today, most psychologists define **consciousness** as our awareness of ourselves and our environment. This definition, however, may be deceptively straightforward. We each look at the world from a slightly different perspective, and our observations and experiences tend to be subjective. Since none of us see the world—or ourselves—in exactly the same way, it is likely that consciousness is a unique experience for each individual.

Phenomenology is the study of individual consciousness that addresses subjective experience. You know what the color red looks like, and if you pointed at a stop sign or a fire truck and asked your friend what color it was, she'd probably say, "It's red, of course." But how do you know that your friend's perception of red is identical to your perception of red? The color that your friend describes as red might actually look green or purple to you. Unfortunately, there's no way to determine whether your experience of the color red matches your friend's. This fundamental difficulty of trying to understand the consciousness of others is known as the **problem of other minds**: Because the nature of consciousness is internal, we can't possibly determine how similar or different another person's perceptions are to our own.

> **Consciousness** is a person's awareness of himself or herself and his or her environment.
>
> **Phenomenology** is the study of individual consciousness that addresses subjective experience.
>
> **Problem of other minds** states that because the nature of consciousness is internal, a person can't possibly determine how similar or different another person's perceptions are to his or her own.
>
> **Altered state of consciousness** is a state characterized by bizarre, disorganized, or dreamlike thought patterns.
>
> **Minimal consciousness** describes a relatively fragmented connection between self and environment in which a person might respond to a stimulus without being aware of it at a more thoughtful level.
>
> **Full consciousness** is a state of consciousness in which a person is aware of his or her own environment and also is aware of his or her mental state and is able to provide information about it.
>
> **Self-consciousness** is the most self-aware state of consciousness; it allows a person to focus on his or her individual self.

LEVELS OF CONSCIOUSNESS

Was Scott Falater consciously aware of stabbing his wife 44 times? If he was truly sleepwalking, it is possible that he was not functioning at the same level of awareness as a person in a wakened state. Someone who is not fully alert to his or her mental processes may be experiencing an **altered state of consciousness**—bizarre, disorganized, or dreamlike thought patterns. We enter these altered states naturally when we sleep or daydream, but they can also be purposely induced through drugs, meditation, or hypnosis.

When we sleep, we experience **minimal consciousness**—a relatively fragmented connection between self and environment in which we might respond to a stimulus without being aware of it at a more thoughtful level. Consider a sleeping person who rolls over, without waking up, in response to being nudged. This reaction is a function of minimal consciousness—the person is conscious enough to respond to the nudge by moving, but not conscious enough to respond in a more thoughtful way, and chances are good that he or she won't even remember that nudge in the morning.

Full consciousness, on the other hand, describes not only an awareness of one's environment but also an awareness of one's mental state and the ability to provide information about it. Metacognition, or thinking about thoughts, is a feature of this level. During Falater's trial, prosecutors argued that because he had the presence of mind to hide crucial evidence immediately following his wife's murder, he was clearly in a state of full consciousness—and thus criminally responsible for his actions.

The most self-aware state of consciousness, **self-consciousness**, allows us to focus on our individual selves. We enter a state of self-consciousness every time we examine ourselves in the mirror: Recognizing one's own reflection is a fairly advanced skill that requires self-consciousness to perform, and most animals can't achieve it. In fact, researchers have used mirror self-recognition tests to prove that humans, orangutans, and chimpanzees are

If you weren't self-conscious, how might you interpret what you see in the mirror?

among the relatively few species to possess some level of self-consciousness. In humans, this skill usually develops around the age of 18 months. Researchers have discovered that before this age, infants don't have the ability to recognize their mirror reflection as themselves (Lewis & Brookes-Gunn, 1979).

When we focus on ourselves, we tend to notice our successes and our shortcomings; self-evaluation and self-criticism are two aspects of self-consciousness. Unlike most animals, we have the capacity to congratulate ourselves on a job well done, but we're also capable of experiencing guilt and shame when we look in the mirror and think about the things we've done that we're less than proud of.

NONCONSCIOUS, PRECONSCIOUS, AND UNCONSCIOUS INFORMATION

Are we aware of everything we do? Not entirely. In fact, our brains store a significant amount of nonconscious, preconscious, and unconscious information. If you're skeptical of this claim, try to remember the last time you checked to make sure your heart kept beating while you were asleep. We don't consciously monitor and adjust our body's vital processes like blood flow, pulse rate, and oxygen intake, but we each carry out hundreds of these **nonconscious activities** every day. We are usually blissfully unaware of these processes, and they are rarely brought to consciousness, but they continue to operate even as you read this page.

> ❝Fortunately for us, we're able to focus our consciousness by paying attention only to the things that are most important at any given time.❞

Other types of information are **preconscious**, which means that we might not always be aware of them, but we can bring them into consciousness on demand. For example, with a little effort, we can bring preconscious memories into our conscious minds. A familiar scent or a vivid photograph can make old, preconscious memories memorable again; that's why a whiff of pumpkin pie can trigger memories of that long-ago Thanksgiving dinner you thought you'd forgotten. (For more information about memory, see Chapter 8.)

According to Sigmund Freud, some experiences, ideas, and motives are so threatening or unacceptable that we have permanently removed them from our consciousness. Freud believed that we bury this **unconscious information** through the process of repression (see Chapter 16). Contemporary psychologists have reinterpreted these ideas by developing the concept of a **cognitive unconscious**—a collection of mental processes that affect the way we feel or behave, even though we are not consciously aware of them. For example, if a photo of a smiling person flashes very briefly before your eyes, you may not even be aware that you've seen the picture. However, it's likely that you'll feel happier than you did before, even though you can't quite explain why. This process, which enables unconsciously perceived stimuli to affect our thoughts and feelings, is part of the cognitive unconscious.

SURVIVAL ADVANTAGES OF CONSCIOUSNESS

Our ability to be conscious of information on a number of different levels—and to move some pieces of information in and out of consciousness as necessary—gives us a significant advantage when it comes to survival. If we were completely unaware of ourselves and our environments, we wouldn't last long in a group of predators (or on a four-lane highway, for that matter). At the same time, if we were conscious of every single thing going on around and inside us, we would likely be completely overwhelmed and unable to function effectively. Fortunately for us, we're able to focus our consciousness by paying attention only to the things that are most important at any given time.

The Restrictive Function

Thanks to the **restrictive function** of consciousness, we don't waste our attention on information that is not immediately relevant to our situations. The restrictive function allows us to exercise selective attention, or a conscious focus on one stimulus or perception at a given time (see Chapter 5). For example, when you take an exam, the restrictive function of consciousness lets you focus on reading and answering the questions without becoming preoccupied by the feeling of your shirt against your skin or the pressure of the pencil against your finger. This function is also responsible for the cocktail party phenomenon, or our ability to selectively tune into particular messages while filtering out others in a crowded, noisy, or chaotic environment (see Chapter 8).

Selective Storage Function

Closely linked to the restrictive function, the **selective storage function** of consciousness allows us to selectively analyze, interpret, and act on stimuli. In

Nonconscious activity is a process that occurs in the body that people do not have to consciously monitor or regulate.

Preconscious information is usually outside a person's awareness, but is able to be brought into consciousness on demand.

Unconscious information consists of experiences, ideas, and motives that are so threatening or unacceptable that a person has permanently removed them from his or her consciousness.

Cognitive unconscious is a collection of mental processes that affect the way a person feels or behaves, even though he or she is not consciously aware of them.

Restrictive function is an aspect of consciousness that allows people to exercise selective attention, or a conscious focus on one stimulus or perception at a given time.

Selective storage function is an aspect of consciousness that allows people to selectively analyze, interpret, and act on stimuli.

other words, we are able to choose the sights, sounds, and other sensations that we want to pay particular attention to. For example, if you wore a special set of headphones designed to play two messages simultaneously, one in each ear, you would most likely be able to choose to listen only to the message in your right ear and ignore the message in your left. Then, if you decided to pay attention to the message in your left ear instead, you would be able to consciously refocus your attention.

The "selectivity" of the selective storage function can vary over time, as things to which we once devoted our attention become less important for us to think about consciously. When we first learn a novel, complex task—such as driving, for example—we must consciously focus on each aspect of the activity: switching gears, pressing the accelerator, or turning the wheel. During this learning period, other stimuli or thoughts—the sound of thunder in the

>>> **The restrictive function of consciousness allows you to focus awareness on the person you're talking to in a crowded room.**

distance, plans for the upcoming weekend—tend to be selectively restricted from our conscious awareness. As we gain mastery over the individual aspects of driving, it becomes an automatic process. This change "frees up" our consciousness to focus on other thoughts; we can simultaneously consider the weekend's events while safely navigating though traffic.

The Planning Function

Imagine that a friend breaks a promise to help you study, leaving you woefully unprepared for a big exam. You're furious, but rather than pummeling your friend with a physical or verbal assault, you express your frustration through pointed, but tactful, words. What helped you make this wise, conscious choice? The **planning function** of consciousness. The planning function helps us to inhibit urges we have that are not moral, ethical, or practical, and it equips us with the conscious self-awareness necessary to analyze and evaluate our thoughts before we act on them. This high-level conscious processing enables us to avoid saying or doing inappropriate things. While most people would agree that the planning

function is crucial, especially in social situations, it's not particularly speedy: Because it happens serially, or in sequence, rather than all at once, high-level conscious processing takes place relatively slowly compared to other types of information processing. If you want to confront your friend about his broken promise as coolly and rationally as possible, in other words, you might want to wait a few minutes to give your planning function a chance to step in.

Sleep

If you've ever tossed and turned in bed all night or nodded off in a lecture hall, you know that **sleep**—the natural loss of consciousness—often seems like it's beyond our control. In fact, this notion formed the basis of Scott Falater's defense against the murder charges filed against him: He claimed that he was not in control of, or responsible for, his actions while sleeping. However, Falater's claim begs the question: If our conscious minds aren't in control of our sleeping bodies' behaviors, what *is* in control?

> "Our temperatures rise in the morning, peak during the day, and decline both in early afternoon and before we go to sleep. Recent research suggests that thinking and memory peak consistently with circadian arousal."

CIRCADIAN RHYTHM

One force that controls our sleep patterns is the body's **circadian rhythm**, a biological clock that regulates body functions on a 24-hour cycle. Not only do our circadian rhythms affect whether we are awake or asleep, they're also responsible for changes in our body temperatures and levels of arousal during periods of sleep and wakefulness. Our temperatures rise in the morning, peak during the day, and decline both in early afternoon and before we go to sleep. Recent research suggests that thinking

and memory peak consistently with circadian arousal. While this peak occurs at different times for different people, it seems to occur at increasingly earlier times of day as we age (Roenneberg et al., 2004). This explains why many older adults rise at dawn, eat dinner by 5:00, and are asleep by 8:00 or 9:00 p.m. Moreover, research also indicates that young adults experience an improvement in performance throughout the day, but older adults experience a decline in performance throughout the day (May & Hasher, 1998). For college students, perhaps like yourself, who feel lively and energetic at night but struggle to make it to 9 a.m. classes, this likely comes as no surprise.

While circadian rhythms are an inherent part of our biology, they are not immune to effects from external factors. For example, light can alter or reset our circadian clocks. How? When light hits the eye, it activates light-sensitive proteins in the retina. These, in turn, signal the **suprachiasmatic nucleus**—the part of the hypothalamus that controls the circadian clock. The surprachiasmatic nucleus causes the pineal gland to either increase (in the evening) or decrease (in the morning) production of **melatonin,** a sleep-inducing hormone. When we stay up until 1:00 a.m. reading or socializing in a well-lit place, we're exposed to artificial light, which tricks our bodies into producing less melatonin at a time when it should be producing more, delaying sleep and pushing back our biological clocks (Oren & Terman, 1998). As a result, many young people today operate on a 25-hour cycle because they stay up late and don't rise until late morning or early afternoon. This doesn't just happen to humans: Most animals placed under a constant light source will develop a biological clock that ticks off more than 24 hours per day (DeCoursey, 1960).

Because the suprachiasmatic nucleus plays a key role in regulating sleep, damage to this area of the brain can have devastating effects, such as causing random periods of sleep throughout the day. You might think of damaging the suprachiasmatic nucleus as essentially equivalent to taking the batteries out of the circadian clock.

What else can influence our circadian rhythms? As anyone who has pulled an all-nighter likely knows, caffeine is one answer. Under normal circumstances, **adenosine**, another sleep-inducing hormone, increases as the night wears on, inhibiting certain neurons and making us drowsy. However, if we need to hold off adenosine's soporific effects late into the evening, we can block its activity by ingesting a few cups of coffee, a Red Bull, or any other potent source of caffeine.

SLEEP STAGES

Before the 1950s, scientists assumed that all sleep was essentially created equal; that is, they believed that there were no distinguishing physiological or psychological factors between the sleep you experience in the first ten minutes after lying down and the sleep that occurs in the middle of the night. In 1952, however, University of Chicago graduate student Eugene Aserinsky made a serendipitous discovery that paved the way for research into the distinct rhythms and patterns that characterize sleep. In an effort to repair a malfunctioning electroencephalogram (EEG) machine, Aserinsky decided to test the machine on his sleeping eight-year-old son, Armond. EEG machines collect amplified recordings of the brain's electrical activity through electrodes placed on a person's skull. After attaching the electrodes near Armond's eyes, Aserinsky was astounded to find the machine recording a dramatic zigzag pattern (Aserinsky, 1988; Seligman & Yellen, 1987). The pattern, which coincided with Armond's perceptible jerky eye movements, recurred several times throughout the night. Even more interestingly, when Armond was awakened during one of these periods, he told his father he had been in the middle of a dream. Aserinsky realized that the darting eyes, lively brain waves, and the dream were related and, most importantly, indicative of a distinct stage of sleep—**rapid eye movement (REM) sleep**, a recurring stage of sleep during which vivid dreams usually occur.

Aserinsky went on to collaborate with Nathaniel Kleitman on similar studies, and their research, among others, yielded the discovery of other sleep stages characterized by specific brain wave activity (Aserinsky & Kleitman, 1953). We now know, through the use of EEGs on sleeping participants, that sleep is comprised of five distinct stages that we cycle through every 90 minutes.

Stage 1 and Stage 2

If you used an EEG to measure the neural activity of someone who was on the verge of falling asleep, what would you discover? You'd most likely get evidence of a few different types of brain waves. As we prepare for sleep, our brains transition from producing the low-amplitude, fast, and irregular

beta waves

that characterize active wakefulness to producing the slower **alpha waves** that characterize a relaxed state of wakefulness. As we enter the first stage of sleep, alpha wave activity decreases and larger, slower **theta wave** activity increases. Stage 1 lasts approximately ten minutes on average.

> Some people report feeling as though they are floating weightlessly above the bed during the hypnagogic period. Although there's nothing otherworldly about these strange sensations, their existence may explain individuals' accounts of alleged alien abductions or other "supernatural" experiences (Moody & Perry, 1993).

Several strange, often disconcerting sensations can occur during **hypnagogia**, or the period of transition between wakefulness and sleep that typifies stage 1. One of these is the hypnagogic jerk—a sudden jerk of the body just as one is drifting off to sleep. A less common hypnagogic sensation is referred to as "exploding head syndrome," characterized by what sounds like a loud internal bang just as one falls asleep. Some people also report feeling as though they are floating weightlessly above the bed during the hypnagogic period. Although there's nothing otherworldly about these strange sensations, their existence may explain individuals' accounts of alleged alien abductions or other "supernatural" experiences (Moody & Perry, 1993).

As we continue to doze, we become increasingly relaxed, and soon we enter stage 2 of sleep. This stage lasts about 20 minutes and is marked by the periodic appearance of **K-complexes** and **sleep spindles**, which are bursts of fast, sharply pointed brain waves. Although the physiological roles of K-complexes and sleep spindles are still unclear, many researchers believe that their function is to inhibit conscious awareness to protect the sleeper from awakening (Hess, 1965). However, during stage 2, we can still be woken up fairly easily.

Stage 3 and Stage 4

Sleep stages 3 and 4 feature the kind of sleep most of us covet: deep, refreshing, and largely immune to disturbances. During the transitional stage 3, slow, irregular, high-amplitude **delta waves** begin to appear. These patterns continue into stage 4, another slow-wave, deep-sleep stage that lasts about 30 minutes (although it gets shorter and eventually disappears as the night progresses). People in stages 3 and 4 are usually difficult to wake up, and if they are awoken, they tend to be groggy and disoriented. For reasons that scientists don't completely understand, children who wet the bed or sleepwalk tend to do so at the end of stage 4. Approximately 20 percent of three- to 12-year-olds have at least one instance of sleepwalking that lasts two to ten minutes, and 5 percent have more than one episode (Giles et al., 1994). Because young children experience stage 4 sleep for longer periods of time than adults do, they are far more likely than adults to experience sleepwalking; sleepwalking after age 40 is quite rare. (This fact didn't prevent Scott Falater from blaming his criminal actions on sleepwalking, but it did raise questions as to the validity of such a defense.)

REM Sleep

About an hour after we fall asleep and complete one cycle of the four non-REM sleep stages, we return through stages 3 and 2 and enter REM sleep, which can last anywhere from a few minutes to an hour. We spend about 20 percent to 25 percent (about 100 minutes) of an average night in REM sleep.

At the beginning of REM sleep, our brain waves resemble those that appear during stage 1 sleep. In contrast to stage 1, however, the REM sleep stage is a time of physiological arousal rather than of increasing tranquility: Our heart rate increases, our breathing becomes rapid and irregular, and our eyes dark around behind our eyelids in quick bursts of activity about every 30 seconds. And yet, in the midst of all this excitement, our muscles remain relaxed. For this reason, REM sleep is also referred to as paradoxical sleep; even though the brain's motor cortex remains active, hyper-polarized, or overexcited, neurons in the brain-stem and spinal cord are unable to transmit messages to the rest of the body. This causes our muscles to be still to the point of paralysis. Researchers have discovered that glycine—the inhibitory neurotransmitter that causes muscle paralysis during sleep—does not inhibit the motor nuclei of the cranial nerves, explaining the occasional facial twitch during REM sleep. It is generally thought that REM-associated muscle paralysis occurs in order to prevent the body from acting out the dreams that occur during this stage, thus avoiding potential injuries while we ride purple horses or save the universe from robot aliens.

REM sleep is the primary venue for the often disjointed, hallucinatory imaginings we call dreams. Although about 37 percent of people claim they rarely or never dream, people, on average, spend about 600 hours each year dreaming and have more than 100,000 dreams over a typical lifetime (Moore, 2004). In fact, of those people who reported they never dreamed, a full 80 percent remembered a dream when woken during REM sleep.

Although some sleep researchers have suspected that the rapid eye movements character-istic of REM sleep are related to the visual aspects of dreaming, most scientists believe that these eye movements are a result of overflow to the active nervous system. Dreams that take place during REM tend to be narrative, emotion-al, and fantastical in quality (e.g., "My friend and I were taking a walk when all of a sudden we morphed into lions"), as opposed to the vague, impressionistic ones experienced at other stages (e.g., "I had left something somewhere").

As the night wears on, we tend to spend more time in REM sleep and less time in the stages of deep sleep, stages 3 and 4. Our periods of REM sleep generally increase in both duration and frequency the longer we sleep.

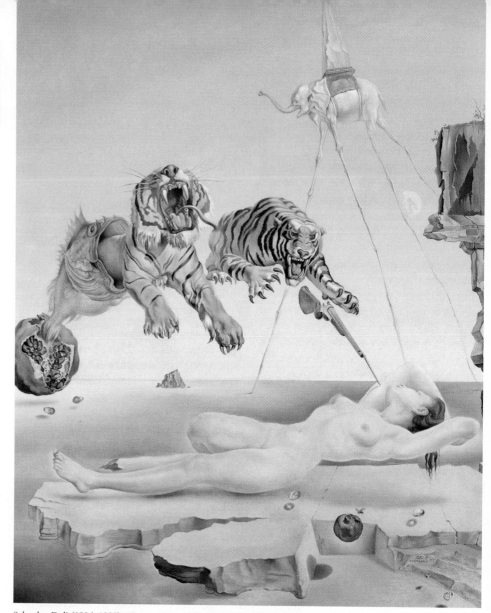

Salvador Dali (1904–1989), "Dream Caused by the Flight of a Bee around a Pomegranate One Second before Waking up", 1944, oil on panel/Thyssen-Bornemisza Collection, Madrid, Spain. © DACS/Lauros/Giraudon/The Bridgeman Art Library. (c) Salvador Dali, Gala-Salvador Dali Foundation/Artists Rights Society (ARS), New York.

∧
∧ One way to remember your dreams is to write
∧ them down as soon as you wake up. You could also paint them, like Salvador Dali did in his Dream Caused by the Flight of a Bee around a Pomegranate a Second Before Awakening.

STIMULI AWARENESS AND LEARNING

If you've ever seen a cat napping, you may have noticed that even while it's asleep, its ears con-tinue moving around in response to sounds. Since so much of our information processing takes place outside of conscious awareness, humans are also capable of processing certain stimuli while we sleep. EEG recordings show that the auditory cortex is responsive to sound stimuli while we sleep, which explains why we're able to awake from a deep sleep when someone calls our name or a baby cries in the next room (Kutas, 1990). We also manage to roll around while sleeping without falling out of bed or kicking the dog napping at our feet.

Some studies even make the case for **hypnopaedia**—learning while asleep. For example, participants in one study were able to link a certain sound to a mild electric shock during sleep (Graves et al., 2003), and others were able to stop problematic nail-biting after repeatedly hearing a phonograph recording of the phrase "My fingernails taste terribly bitter" during sleep (LeShan, 1942). While we may be able to engage in behavioral learning tasks like these while we sleep, it's less likely that we can engage in cognitive learning: Although it seems like it would be particularly convenient to listen to podcasts of study materials while we sleep, there is little evidence to support the notion that we can remember information we hear while we're sleeping. We also usually forget anything that happens during the five minutes just before we fall asleep or anything that wakes us briefly from sleep.

PURPOSE OF SLEEP

While psychologists have a fairly solid understanding of what happens in the brain and body as we sleep, exactly *why* we sleep remains a topic of debate. Several theories, summarized in the following table, attempt to shed light on this intriguing question. (See Chapter 13 for more on these theories.)

SLEEP NEEDS AND PATTERNS

It's generally believed that a "good night's sleep" should be about eight hours in duration, but the amount of sleep needed for optimal functioning varies across individuals. Some people are well rested from six hours of sleep each night, but others can't function on less than ten. Newborns spend about two-thirds of the day asleep, while most adults doze for about half that time. In rare cases, people known as **nonsomniacs** can sleep

> "It's generally believed that a "good night's sleep" should be about eight hours in duration, but the amount of sleep needed for optimal functioning varies across individuals. Some people are well rested from six hours of sleep each night, but others can't function on less than ten."

far less than what most would consider normal without feeling tired during the day. Domestic diva Martha Stewart and late-night talk show host Jay Leno, for example, reportedly get by on about four hours of sleep each night.

Our sleep patterns seem to have some genetic influence. When researchers studied the sleep patterns of identical and fraternal twins, they found that only the sleep patterns of identical twins were similar (Webb & Campbell, 1983). When allowed to sleep unhindered by alarm clocks, energetic children, or hungry pets, most people will sleep at least nine hours in a night; these people generally wake up invigorated and experience an overall boost in mood and performance (Coren, 1996). However, cultural habits can alter these natural patterns. Modern light bulbs, shift work, and social diversions have

created industrialized societies in which people sleep much less than they did a century ago.

SLEEP DEPRIVATION

Does sleep deprivation make you feel like a walking zombie most of the time? If it does, you're not alone; in fact, according to psychologist James Maas (1999), a sleep expert at Cornell University, the United States has become "a nation of walking zombies." Sleep deprivation is all too common and especially problematic not only because of how it affects our ability to function, but also because a sleep debt isn't easily paid off. Have you ever tried to make up for several nights of only five or so hours of sleep with one ten-hour doze? Unfortunately, this strategy doesn't usually work as well as we might like, and we're left feeling groggy even after a long sleep.

Young people, especially teenagers, are highly prone to skimping on sleep. Teenagers

THEORIES OF SLEEP

Theory	Description	Examples
Preservation and protection	Sleep is an evolutionary adaptation that keeps us out of harm's way when darkness sets in.	Different species sleep at different times of the day. In most mammalian species, infants sleep more than adults.
Body restoration	The body wears out during the day, and sleep is necessary for recuperation.	Brain tissue is repaired during sleep.
Memory	Sleep restores and rebuilds memories of the previous day's experiences	People who are trained to perform tasks do so better after a night's sleep than after several hours awake. People are able to more creatively solve a problem after sleeping on it than those who stay awake.
Growth	The pituitary gland releases growth hormone during deep sleep, so sleep plays an important role in the growth process.	Less of this hormone is released as adults grow older, and less time is spent in deep sleep.

need about eight to nine hours of sleep each night, but on average, they only get about seven hours—two hours less than teens got 80 years ago (Holden, 1993; Maas, 1999). Four in five American teens and three in five 18- to 29-year-olds wish they could get more sleep on weekdays (Mason, 2003, 2005). To make matters worse, teens who suffer from sleep deprivation during the day often get a "second wind" around 11 p.m., preventing them from going to bed earlier and getting more sleep. Stanford researcher William Dement (1997) reports that 80 percent of students are sleep deprived at dangerous levels that cause difficulty studying, irritability, fatigue, a lowered rate of productivity, and a tendency to make mistakes. Moreover, high-achieving secondary students with good grades average 25 more minutes of sleep each night and go to bed 40 minutes earlier than their lower-achieving counterparts. These results suggest that if maintaining a high G.P.A. is your goal, it's a good idea to make sleep a priority.

Dangers of Sleep Deprivation

Unfortunately, the effects of sleep deprivation are not limited to merely feeling lethargic or

> **Unfortunately, the effects of sleep deprivation are not limited to merely feeling lethargic or moody;** studies and examples show that sleep deprivation can, in fact, have tragic consequences.

moody; studies and examples show that sleep deprivation can, in fact, have tragic consequences. Traffic records suggest that car accidents are far more common during the morning after daylight savings time begins, when people change their clocks and lose an hour of sleep (Coren, 1996). Even without the effect of "springing forward," driver fatigue contributes to about 30 percent of American traffic accidents (United States Department of Transportation). Sleep deprivation leads to slowed reaction

times and increased errors on visual tasks, resulting in potentially catastrophic mishaps both for drivers and for those whose jobs rely on these skills: pilots, airport baggage screeners, surgeons, and X-ray technicians, to name a few (Horowitz et al., 2003). The 1989 Exxon Valdez oil spill; the 1984 Union Carbide Bhopal, India, disaster; the 1979 Three Mile Island nuclear accident; and the 1986 Chernobyl nuclear accident all occurred after midnight, when operators were likely to be most tired.

Sleep deprivation can have dire consequences for our general health, too. Older adults who have no difficulty falling or staying asleep and people who sleep seven to eight hours each night tend to live longer than those who are chronically sleep deprived (Dement, 1999; Dew et al., 2003). Sleep deprivation has also been shown to weaken the immune system, which explains why exhaustion and illness seem to go hand in hand, as well as why we sleep more when we feel sick (Beardsley, 1996; Irwin et al., 1994). Not only does sleep deprivation make us more susceptible to infection, but it can also make us feel and appear older.

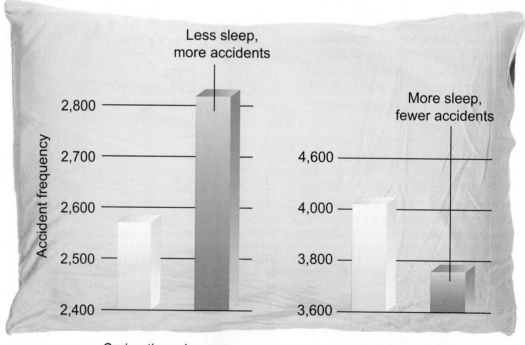

Canadian Traffic Accidents, 1991 and 1992

Less sleep, more accidents

More sleep, fewer accidents

Accident frequency

Spring time change (hour sleep lost)

Fall time change (hour sleep gained)

Monday before time change

Monday after time change

Source: Adapted from Coren, 1996.

When we don't get enough sleep, our metabolic and endocrine systems actually change in ways that resemble aging, making us more susceptible to obesity, hypertension, and memory loss (Spiegel et al., 1999; Taheri, 2004).

SLEEP DISORDERS

Often, sleep deprivation is a by-product of a busy schedule that allows little time for sleep. Sometimes, however, it is caused by **insomnia,** a sleep disorder characterized by recurring difficulty falling or staying asleep. About 10 percent to 15 percent of adults complain of insomnia, but they usually overestimate how long it takes them to fall asleep (by double) and underestimate how much sleep they actually get (by half) (Costa e Silva et al., 1996). If you sometimes have difficulty sleeping, or if anxiety or excitement keeps you awake from time to time, you shouldn't be alarmed—most people face occasional sleep issues like these, and unless these issues recur frequently, they usually aren't

As a child, you may have sent your parents into a panic by sitting bolt upright in bed, screaming, and uttering a stream of gibberish through ragged, frightened breaths. People who display these symptoms suffer from night terrors, a relatively benign, albeit disturbing, sleep disorder most common in young children.

symptomatic of insomnia. People who do experience insomnia, however, should avoid relying on "quick fixes" such as alcohol and sleeping pills, which can make the problem worse by reducing REM sleep and creating next-day fatigue. Moreover, people who use these substances on a regular basis can quickly build up a tolerance, leading to unpleasant withdrawal and worsening insomnia if and when the "sleep aids" are discontinued. Relaxing, exercising, abstaining from caffeine, and sticking to a regular sleep schedule are natural, effective treatments for insomnia.

In stark contrast to insomnia is **narcolepsy,** a sleep disorder characterized by periodic, uncontrollable sleep attacks. These unexpected periods of sleep usually last less than five minutes, but because they occur at unexpected times—in the middle of a conversation, for example, or while driving—they can seriously impair one's quality of life, not to mention safety (Dement, 1978, 1999). For the approximately one in 2,000 people suffering from narcolepsy (Stanford University Center for Narcolepsy, 2002), however, there is hope: Neuroscientists have found a relative absence of the hypothalamic neural center that produces **hypocretin**, an alerting neurotransmitter, in the brains of those afflicted. Armed with this knowledge, scientists are now working to develop a drug that mimics hypocretin and might relieve the symptoms of narcolepsy. Until such a drug is developed, narcoleptics must live their lives cautiously, lest they unexpectedly fall asleep while driving, cooking, or carrying out other potentially hazardous activities.

Sleep apnea, a disorder that literally leaves people breathless, affects 5 percent of the U.S. population. Those afflicted with sleep apnea intermittently stop breathing during sleep, which in turn causes the level of oxygen in the blood to plummet. As a result, sufferers may wake up around 400 times a night to gasp in air. These excessive, non-stop interruptions deprive sufferers of slow-wave sleep, leaving them chronically groggy and irritable during the day. Because they often don't remember waking up briefly during the night, many people suffering from sleep apnea don't even realize they have the disorder. Sleep apnea is particularly common among those who are obese, and as obesity rates have gone up in the United States, so too have the rates of sleep apnea. Treatment for sleep apnea usually involves wearing a masklike device that forces air into the lungs during sleep.

Some sleep disorders are most commonly observed in children. As a child, you may have sent your parents into a panic by sitting bolt upright in bed, screaming, and uttering a stream of gibberish through ragged, frightened breaths. People who display these symptoms suffer from **night terrors**, a relatively benign, albeit disturbing, sleep disorder most common in young children and characterized by episodes of high arousal and terrified appearance. Unlike nightmares, night terrors usually occur within two to three hours of falling asleep, during stage 4 sleep (Garland & Smith, 1991). Children rarely wake up during episodes of night terrors, and they tend not to remember these episodes the next morning. Because stage 4 sleep decreases in length as we age, so too do incidences of night terrors.

At least once in your life, you've probably woken from a memorable dream and wondered, "What was that about?" In their studies of dreams and dreaming, psychologists ask similar questions: What do we dream, and why?

Dreams

Dreams—the sequences of images, feelings, ideas, and impressions that pass through our minds as we sleep—are among the most fascinating aspects of human consciousness. They can leave us quaking with fear or with laughter, transport us through time, and make the impossible seem tantalizingly possible. Often, they're completely indecipherable. This fact hasn't stopped humans from *attempting* to decipher dreams, however: At least once in your life, you've probably woken from a memorable dream and wondered, "What was that about?" In their studies of dreams and dreaming, psychologists ask similar questions: What do we dream, and why?

DREAM CONTENT

As you've learned, dreams experienced during REM sleep tend to involve bizarre imagery and vivid, though highly illogical, plots. Nevertheless, when we dream, we uncritically accept these strange elements and, at times, even confuse them with reality. Our dreams often seem to be influenced by the events in our waking lives; for example, people tend to have nightmares after traumatic events, and in one study, psychologists found that people who played Tetris for seven hours before sleep were highly likely to report dreaming of images of falling blocks (Stickgold et al., 2001).

Sigmund Freud, who based much of his theory around the significance of dreams and dream analysis (see Chapters 16 and 18) classified the content of dreams into two sets: the manifest content and the latent content. **Manifest content** refers to what we explicitly remember about a dream—its storyline, characters, and details. Manifest content often includes pieces of experiences and concerns from daily life, such as having a meeting at work, taking an exam, or interacting with family members

(De Koninck, 2000). Manifest content also may incorporate sensory stimuli from the sleeper's environment. For instance, people who had cold water lightly sprayed on their faces while sleeping were more likely to dream about water (Dement & Wolpert, 1958). When your alarm clock goes off in the morning, you might find yourself incorporating its drone into your dream.

Studies of manifest content have found that our dreams follow certain trends, and those trends, unfortunately for us, can be a bit disturbing. For both men and women, eight in ten dreams are characterized by negative emotions, such as failing, experiencing misfortune, or being attacked, pursued, or rejected (Domhoff, 2002). Although many

people assume that sex dreams are frequent occurrences, only one in ten young men and one in 30 young women who were awakened during REM sleep reported dreams containing sexual imagery (Domhoff, 1996; Foulkes, 1982; Van de Castle, 1994). And researchers have noted one interesting gender difference: While women dream of men and women with equal frequency, 65 percent of the people in men's dreams are male (Domhoff, 1996).

Occasionally, we achieve an awareness of a dream as a dream while dreaming—a phenomenon known as **lucid dreaming** that's been illustrated in both Richard Linklater's 2001 rotoscoped film *Waking Life* and Cameron Crowe's film *Vanilla Sky.* Lucid dreamers can test whether or not they're dreaming by assessing the manifest content of their dream. Obviously dreamlike features (such as clocks that keep irregular time, an ability to fly, talking purple bananas, or light switches that don't work) allow lucid dreamers to determine that they're not actually awake.

THE PURPOSE OF DREAMS

Have you ever felt like a dream you had the previous night was trying to tell you something? Did it seem so cryptic that you decided it must have a deeper meaning and couldn't resist trying to decode it? Many believe that our dreams can help us solve the problems of our waking lives or give us clues about our futures. Just as several different theories attempt to explain why we sleep, there are

> "For both men and women, eight in ten dreams are characterized by negative emotions, such as failing, experiencing misfortune, or being attacked, pursued, or rejected (Domhoff, 2002)."

also many competing theories regarding the purpose of dreams.

Freud and The Interpretation of Dreams

In *The Interpretation of Dreams* (1900), Freud argues that dreams allow us to fulfill our wishes and express our unacceptable feelings in a safe environment. Freud believed that in addition to manifest content, dreams also contain **latent content**—the underlying meaning of the dream through which threatening or unacceptable drives and wishes are discharged. Freud theorized that most adults' wishes expressed through dreams are erotic, even when overt sexual imagery is not present. According to Freud, our inner conflicts and unconscious desires can be identified and analyzed through dream interpretation. There are plenty of critics of Freud's dream theory, however. Some of these critics point out that dreams can be interpreted to mean nearly anything, depending on the creativity of the interpreter; others argue that dreams don't hide anything below the surface and don't seem to contain subtle clues to our unconscious desires.

Information Processing

A more recent dream theory suggests that dreams help us sort and place the day's experiences into our memories. Deep, slow-wave REM sleep stabilizes our memories and experiences, converting them into long-term learning. One study of rats' brains illustrated this potential connection between dreams

<<< During a lucid dream, you can be pretty sure you're dreaming if your attempt to fly is successful.

and learning: Researchers measured rats' brain activity as they ran through two different mazes during the day. When researchers measured the rats' brain activity as the rats slept afterward, they noticed patterns that suggested the rats were not only dreaming of running through each of the mazes they had encountered that day, but also of a hybrid maze that seemed to synthesize characteristics of both mazes (Louie & Wilson, 2001; Maquet, 2001). These results suggest that dreams play a part in memory consolidation (see Chapter 8).

Activation Synthesis

We may be unconscious during sleep, but the neurons in our brain fire away even while we slumber. The **activation-synthesis theory** of dreaming states that dreams are the result of the brain's attempt to make sense of this random neural activity. PET scans of the brain during REM sleep show stimulation in the visual processing area of the brain, which is responsible for generating images, and the limbic system, which is linked to emotions (Maquet & Franck, 1996). According to the activation-synthesis theory, our brains produce dreams by weaving these image-based, emotion-laced signals into stories. Moreover, since the frontal-lobe regions of the brain (responsible for our powers of reason and logic) are largely inactive during sleep, dreams tend toward the nonsensical (Maquet et al., 1996). The activation-synthesis theory is further supported by research that indicates that damage to either the visual processing areas or the limbic system may lead to impairment in dreaming (Domhoff, 2003).

Development

Some psychologists theorize that dreams are not merely the fanciful inventions of a sleep-activated brain; instead, they may be key components in our cognitive development (Domhoff, 2003; Foulkes, 1999). The brain activity associated with dreaming may help to develop and preserve neural pathways, especially for infants, who spend ample time in REM sleep and who are also in a state of rapid neural development. The way dreams change over time also seems to indicate a developmental role. Up until about age nine, our dreams take the form of a series of individual scenes or images; only in late childhood and early adolescence do our dreams

come to resemble interconnected narratives. Eventually, dream content reflects our waking thoughts and intelligence, featuring coherent speech and drawing on our knowledge and learning.

Hypnosis

What comes to mind when you hear the term *hypnosis*? You might think of the carnival performer who dangles a pocket watch in front of his audience and proclaims that they are getting very sleepy, the stage-show magician who convinces her subjects to act like chickens, or the highway billboard that touts hypnosis as a quick fix for obesity or smoking. These popular conceptions of hypnosis—as a parlor game, a form of entertainment, and a miracle cure—can obscure the term's true meaning, and merits, within the field of psychology.

At its most basic level, **hypnosis** is an exercise in suggestion. During hypnosis, one person, the hypnotist, makes suggestions to another person, the subject, regarding the perceptions, feelings, thoughts, or behaviors that the subject can expect to experience. Austrian physician Anton Mesmer is credited with developing the techniques employed in modern hypnosis.

SUSCEPTIBILITY

Since hypnosis revolves around the power of suggestion, it makes sense that its effectiveness—that is, whether or not it

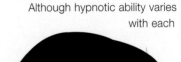

>>> **What aspects of hypnotism are probably more grounded in showmanship than in psychology?**

works for a given subject—is dependent on the subject's susceptibility to suggestion. That's not to say that highly hypnotizable people are especially gullible. Rather, those with **hypnotic ability**, or a high susceptibility to hypnotism, are able to focus their attention deeply and intensely on given tasks, to the point of absorption. Researchers have discovered that a person's susceptibility to hypnosis may be linked to the efficiency of the frontal system—the area of the brain associated with attentional action. According to Gruzelier's (1998) three-stage model of hypnosis, a person who is particularly susceptible to hypnosis is easily able to focus his attention. During the initial stages of hypnosis, the person pays close attention to the hypnotist, increasing activity in the frontal brain regions. The person then "lets go" of his controlled attention and gives executive control to the hypnotist, reducing frontal activity. During the third stage, the person engages in passive imagery, increasing posterior cortical activity. By exhausting his frontal abilities during the initial stages of hypnosis, the person becomes frontally impaired in a hypnotic state. Given that hypnosis enables people to entertain new and often bizarre possibilities, it's not surprising, then, that people with hypnotic ability tend to be highly imaginative and inventive in their thoughts, the types that easily become lost in the pages of a novel or transfixed by the images on a movie screen (Barnier & McConkey, 2004; Silva & Kirsch, 1992).

Although hypnotic ability varies with each

> "Given that hypnosis enables people to entertain new and often bizarre possibilities, it's not surprising, then, **that people with hypnotic ability tend to be highly imaginative and inventive in their thoughts.**"

individual, anyone who can turn his or her attention inward and imagine something—in other words, almost all of us—can experience some degree of hypnotism. Whether or not we realize it, we are all susceptible to suggestion in some ways. For example, it turns out that when people stand with their eyes closed and are told repeatedly that they are swaying, nearly everyone actually begins to sway. This test, called the postural sway test, is just one of the items on the Stanford Hypnotic Susceptibility Scale, which is used to assess individuals' relative degree of hypnotic ability. Other items on the scale—such as the spontaneous sensation of sweet and sour tastes on the tongue—are not as universal. Keep in mind, also, the power of expectation: People who believe that they can be hypnotized and who expect hypnotic responsiveness are far more likely to experience it than are determined doubters.

Proponents of hypnotism put forth myriad claims about its usefulness, and not all hypnotists have the same goals in mind. From memory recovery to smoking cessation to pain relief, hypnotism has many purported benefits, with varying evidence to support each promised result.

RECALL

Many people believe that hypnosis allows us to access the past, to recover long-buried memories from the annals of our brains (Johnson & Hauck, 1999). This belief has given rise to the use of hypnosis to induce "age regression" within a therapeutic setting, the goal being for clients to relive experiences from childhood in order to uncover and address the roots of psychological problems. However, research

demonstrates that claims of successful age regression are, in fact, questionable at best. As it turns out, age-regressed people under hypnosis tend to act as they *think* children of a certain age would act rather than how they *actually* act. For example, a client "hypnotized" to return to the age of four or five may start speaking in ungrammatical sentence fragments, not realizing that most four- and five-year-olds are highly adept at grammatical speech.

The use of hypnosis as a tool to aid (or not aid) memory also has implications for the legal system. It sounds great in theory—witnesses can't recall exactly what the perpetrator of a robbery looked like? Take them back to the scene of the crime, if only in their minds' eye, through hypnosis.

> " Many people believe that hypnosis allows us to access the past, to recover long-buried memories from the annals of our brains (Johnson & Hauck, 1999). This belief has given rise to the use of hypnosis to induce "age regression" within a therapeutic setting, the goal being for clients to relive experiences from childhood in order to uncover and address the roots of psychological problems. "

Unfortunately, not only does this method not work, but it can actually do more harm than good: It can cause people to develop false memories (see Chapter 8). Regardless of the best intentions of both hypnotist and subject, a hypnotist's questions can shape a subject's memory of an event simply through the power of suggestion. If a hypnotist asks, "What color was the burglar's beard?" the subject may falsely "remember" that the burglar had a beard, even if he was actually clean shaven. Due to the unreliability of hypnosis-induced "memories," court systems around the world, including those in the United States and United Kingdom, have begun banning testimony from witnesses who have been hypnotized (Druckman & Bjork, 1991; Gibson, 1995; McConkey, 1995).

THERAPY

Although the link between hypnosis and memory enhancement is largely unsubstantiated, hypnosis does have some real, valuable uses within a therapeutic environment. Hypnosis can, in fact, help people control undesirable behaviors or symptoms. Much of its success revolves around the implementation of **posthypnotic suggestion**—a suggestion made during hypnosis that is executed by the participant when he or she is no longer hypnotized. For example, a hypnotherapist might suggest that a client whose anxiety causes her to break out in unsightly hives imagine swimming in a pool of soothing, cleansing water whenever she becomes anxious. Posthypnotic suggestion has been shown to be effective in alleviating headaches, asthma, and stress-related skin disorders. Unfortunately, drug, alcohol, and smoking addictions do not respond well to hypnosis; however, hypnosis seems very helpful in the treatment of obesity (Nash, 2001).

PAIN RELIEF

Hypnosis also has promising implications in the area of pain relief. Hypnotic pain relief, known as **hypnotic analgesia**, can benefit about half of us, and 10 percent of people can become so hypnotized that major surgery can be performed on them without traditional anesthesia (Hilgard & LeBaron, 1984; Reeves et al., 1983). While the prospect of unmedicated surgery may seem rather ambitious, keep in mind that even light hypnosis can help calm us down and reduce our apprehension of (and subsequent oversensitivity to) pain. So if the mere thought of getting a tetanus shot or having a cavity filled makes you recoil, you might consider hypnosis. Perhaps due to the inhibition of pain-related brain activity, hypnotized people may even require less medication, recover more quickly, and leave hospitals sooner than people treated in a more traditional manner.

How does hypnotic analgesia work? One theory suggests that it causes **dissociation**—a split in consciousness that allows simultaneous thoughts and behaviors to occur apart from each other. Through hypnosis, the sensation of pain can be disconnected from the emotional suffering that characterizes the experience of pain. For example, in one study, participants were hypnotized to dissociate a typically painful stimulus—putting their arms in ice water—from the emotional reaction of discomfort that normally accompanies such an experience. The technique worked: Instead of screaming in pain after submerging their arms in the freezing water, the subjects tended to respond calmly and thoughtfully, saying things like, "Hmmm. That's very cold, but not really painful" (Miller & Bowers, 1993).

Hypnotic analgesia may owe its success in part to the power of selective attention. Think of athletes who sustain serious injuries during sporting events but who keep playing, claiming afterward that they didn't even feel the pain of the injury until the game was over. These athletes are often so focused on the competition that they easily ignore their injuries. Similarly, people treated with hypnotic analgesia may be so relaxed or distracted by the hypnosis process that they don't attend to their pain.

Although these theories attempt to explain how hypnosis relieves pain, they still assume that the participant experiences the pain stimulus at some level. This is supported by laboratory studies that show that participants who report feeling no pain from an electric shock still register increased heart rates. Moreover, PET scans of hypnotized people show reduced activity in the brain areas that process painful stimuli but not in the sensory cortex, which receives the raw sensory input (Rainville et al., 1997). It seems that although hypnosis can alter our perception of a painful stimulus, it's not powerful enough to block the sensory input itself.

Meditation

In the past, meditation—an altered state of consciousness that aims to enhance self-knowledge and well-being through an extreme sense of calm and relaxation—seemed, to many, a fringe practice reserved for "New Age" hippie types. In recent years, however, bolstered by high-profile celebrity endorsements (Sting and Madonna, for example) and, more importantly, scientific research findings, meditation has gone mainstream.

Valued by many Eastern cultures and religions as a way of directing consciousness away from worldly preoccupations, meditation may involve focused and regulated breathing, specific body positions, minimization of external distractions, mental imagery, and mental clarity. In a meditative state, sensory input is gradually diminished, creating what Carrington (1998) called a "mental isolation chamber." Although the person is awake, he or she is in a deeply relaxed state. During deep meditation, the brain shows similar brain wave activity to that seen during sleep. In concentrative meditation, participants attempt to achieve complete mental tranquility by focusing on something specific, such as a particular physical pose, mental picture, or word. Mindfulness meditation, on the other hand, involves a focused awareness of everything you experience, from walking to class to doing laundry to talking with friends. You might think of it as "being in the moment." (For more information about mindfulness meditation, see Chapter 18.)

Physiological changes resulting from meditation are well documented. EEGs show that meditation is associated with the alpha waves typical of a relaxed state, as well as with significantly low levels of activity in the posterior superior parietal lobe (Herzog et al., 1990/1991; Newberg et al., 2001). Meditating Buddhist monks have also been studied for their ability to use meditation to raise their body temperature and decrease their metabolism (Wallace & Benson, 1972). Some researchers have even found evidence of meditation's ability to increase intelligence and improve cognitive performance (So & Orme-Johnson, 2001).

The ultimate goal of many programs of meditation is enlightenment—a transcendent state of wisdom. While this might not necessarily seem practical or attainable, keep in mind that mediation, at the very least, can free your perceptions and thoughts, allowing you to see familiar things in new ways. Most scientists agree that it can be a powerful, natural antidote to anxiety and stress (Bahrke & Morgan, 1978; Kabat-Zinn et al., 1992).

>>> Specific body postures, or asanas, may be used during meditative yoga to help the practitioner focus attention inward.

06

Review

Summary

HOW DO DIFFERENT LEVELS OF CONSCIOUSNESS FUNCTION? p. 88

• During minimal consciousness, we only dimly perceive the environment and might respond to a stimulus without full awareness of it (for example, during sleep).

• During full consciousness, we are aware of our environment and of our own thoughts and mental state.

• Self-consciousness is the highest level of consciousness; it enables us to reflect on our own identity.

HOW DOES CONSCIOUSNESS CHANGE WHILE WE SLEEP AND DREAM, AND WHY? p. 90

• The body's circadian rhythm controls sleep patterns.

• The sleep cycle consists of several stages. Stage 1 is a very short period characterized by slow breathing and irregular brain waves, stage 2 is a brief period characterized by burst of brain activity, and stages 3 and 4 are longer periods of deep sleep.

• After we complete stage 4 sleep, we cycle back through stage 3 and 2 sleep and enter REM sleep, in which heart rate and breathing increase and brain waves become fast and irregular.

• This cycle occurs every 90 minutes throughout the night. Stage 3 and 4 sleep periods decrease in length and eventually disappear, while REM sleep periods lengthen over the course of the night.

HOW CAN HYPNOSIS AND MEDITATION ALTER CONSCIOUSNESS? p. 97

• Hypnosis is an altered state of consciousness achieved through social interaction. It may cause dissociation, a split in consciousness that allows some simultaneous thoughts and behaviors to occur separately from others.

• Meditation is a process by which people can achieve a state of deep mental calm through concentration or mindfulness.

Test Your Understanding

1. Which of the following demonstrates self-consciousness?

   a. A chimpanzee holding a hand-mirror opens her mouth and inspects the reflection of her tongue.

   b. A six-month-old baby makes grasping motions at its reflection in a mirror.

   c. A sleeping cat wakes up after being nudged.

   d. A sleepwalking boy is awakened by his mother.

2. Which of the following is a fundamental problem of phenomenology?

   a. It is impossible to study consciousness scientifically.

   b. Only humans show signs of self-consciousness.

   c. Because a person's consciousness can only be experienced by themselves, we cannot know what their subjective conscious experience feels like.

   d. Psychologists are not certain why we sleep.

3. Which of the following is a likely survival advantage of selective attention?

   a. Limiting which things we are consciously aware of allows us to focus on important stimuli.

   b. It prevents boredom because we can ignore things we are not interested in.

   c. It allows disturbing events or memories to be repressed into the unconscious.

   d. It allows us to fall asleep.

4. James feels himself getting angry as he waits in line to pay for a sandwich. He is about to complain, but then realizes the cashier is working hard and is not aware of how hungry he is. Which of the following aspects of consciousness does James employ?

   a. the circadian rhythm

   b. minimal consciousness

   c. the restrictive function

   d. the planning control function

5. A person living in a fallout shelter underground, in which there is constant artificial light, would most likely experience a change in:

   a. circadian rhythm.

   b. sleep apnea.

   c. planning function.

   d. consciousness.

6. On an EEG, which stage of sleep registers as having much slower and higher amplitude waves in comparison to a state of full consciousness or alertness?

   a. REM sleep

   b. both stages 3 and 4

   c. stage 1

   d. stage 2

7. Peter begins to fall asleep while watching television. His entire body jerks and he wakes up suddenly, though he is able to fall back asleep quickly. Peter is experiencing:

   a. a hypnagogic sensation.
   b. exploding head syndrome.
   c. sleep apnea.
   d. a change in his circadian rhythm.

8. Marlon reports a dream in which he is chasing flying horses through the desert when he sees the building that was his elementary school and walks into his old first grade classroom. What stage of sleep did the dream most likely occur in?

   a. stage 3
   b. stage 2
   c. REM sleep
   d. stage 4

9. Which of the following is NOT a theory about the purpose of sleep?

   a. People need sleep in order for the body to repair itself.
   b. Sleep helps to restore the day's memories.
   c. Sleep evolved as way to protect species from harm that might occur when it's dark.
   d. Sleep helps preserve the brain by allowing a period of time in which all brain activity ceases.

10. Amelia wakes up often during the night and feels tired all day long. Her husband says she often makes short snoring sounds as if she is trying to get air, which wake him up as well. Amelia is most likely experiencing:

    a. REM sleep.
    b. a sleep spindle.
    c. sleep apnea.
    d. a night terror.

11. Sam's cell phone rings early in the morning while he is still asleep. When Sam wakes up, he tells his wife that he dreamt fire engines were driving through the bedroom. This illustrates:

    a. lucid dreaming.
    b. incorporating sensory stimuli into the manifest content of a dream.
    c. latent feelings that Sam finds unacceptable in waking life.
    d. activation-synthesis theory.

12. Ronda has a dream that she is fishing and cannot reel in the fish. Which of the following is a possible example of latent content in the dream?

    a. The fishing episode represents sexual frustration.
    b. Ronda is still upset about a fish that got away.
    c. Ronda is nervous about her upcoming fishing competition.
    d. Ronda does not like to fish.

13. While Mark is sleeping, he listens to a tape that suggests he hates the taste of cigarettes. Mark is attempting:

    a. hypnosis.
    b. hypnopaedia.
    c. lucid dreaming.
    d. activation-synthesis.

14. Which of the following people would be the LEAST susceptible to hypnosis?

    a. Amy is strong-willed and is often distracted by her own thoughts.
    b. Cory daydreams about asking out a girl in his class.
    c. Aaron meditates daily and often engages in mindfulness meditation.
    d. Abigail is a research scientist and spends many hours per day focusing on single tasks.

15. What is a possible danger of hypnosis?

    a. Hypnotized individuals may develop false memories.
    b. Hypnotized individuals may age regress.
    c. Hypnotized individuals may access long-buried memories.
    d. Hypnotized individuals may not be able to treat addictions.

16. Maria is having major surgery without the use of anesthesia. Which of the following ways might she accomplish this?

    a. by having hypnotic analgesia
    b. by having post-hypnotic suggestion so that she experiences the surgery as if she were someone else
    c. by being hypnotized to a state of lucid dreaming
    d. by being hypnotized to a state of narcolepsy

17. Why has meditation been called a "mental isolation chamber"?

    a. It is only experienced sitting in a room alone.
    b. Attention is turned inward and sensory perception diminishes.
    c. It helps individuals live in solitude more peacefully.
    d. It increases intelligence and so it may sometimes alienate individuals.

18. Which of the following is NOT considered an altered state of consciousness?

    a. meditation
    b. metacognitive thinking
    c. daydreaming
    d. hypnosis

19. Matt's doctor suggests he try to reduce his anxiety. Which of the following would most likely help him to achieve this goal?

    a. hypocretin
    b. lucid dreaming
    c. meditation
    d. REM sleep

20. According to Freud, which of the following is most likely to be stored as unconscious information?

    a. witnessing abuse as a child
    b. an experience of self-consciousness in childhood
    c. dreams experienced during REM sleep
    d. memories about stimuli we do not have time to process

Remember to check www.thethinkspot.com **for additional information, downloadable flashcards, and other helpful resources.**

Answers: 1) a; 2) c; 3) a; 4) d; 5) d; 6) b; 7) a; 8) c; 9) d; 10) c; 11) b; 12) a; 13) b; 14) a; 15) a; 16) a; 17) b; 18) b; 19) c; 20) a

LEARNING

Have

you ever attempted to write backward? As a child, you may have tried this or something similar, such as writing with your nondominant hand or performing cartwheels by starting with a different hand and foot than usual. As an adult, many of us find that learning to do something in a new way is more difficult. Can your brain, which has already reached adult size, still help you adapt?

A recent study in which participants practiced mirror-reading a magazine article shows how learning specific tasks can physically change the brain. The cerebral cortex, the newest part of the brain in terms of its evolution, is made up of gray matter and makes up two-thirds of the brain's volume. This is the area where the brain's "work" is done. In the study, researchers gave male participants, aged 20 to 32, mirror-imaged magazine articles to read. Practicing 15 minutes per day for two weeks not only helped the men learn to read in a novel way, but

also resulted in physical changes to parts of the cerebral cortex that had been shown to be the most active in previous studies of mirror-reading. At the end of the two weeks, the researchers found that the men experienced significant increases in gray-matter density in their occipital cortexes. Researchers believe that changes in gray-matter density reflect an increased number of connections between brain cells—in other words, the ability to physically change your brain is necessary to learn new skills. Researchers noted that because of the short duration of practice time, changes in processing specific tasks likely cause the increase in gray matter. So, if you want to increase your brain's capability, don't just learn something new, but learn something in a new way.

The fact that we have the ability to change our brains in such a short period of time may feel disconcerting, but the study's findings have important implications for other research. What if some of the cognitive decline associated with aging or disease could be prevented—or even reversed—through engaging in specific tasks? Would learning to do something differently be a challenge you'd be up for?

<<< *Recent studies have shown that a small number of animals, such as dolphins and elephants, can learn to recognize themselves in mirrors. What does this mean? Researchers believe it's a sign of self-awareness—a realization that they are individuals, different from others around them. This may sound like a simple concept, but until now, only humans and certain apes have shown this ability. Can self-awareness be learned, or is it innate? Are there boundaries to the process of learning?*

CHAPTER 07

Principles of Learning

For psychologists, **learning** is the process through which experience results in a relatively permanent change in future behavior. Imagine never having learned that it is a bad idea to touch a pot of boiling water, step on a nail, or leave the front door unlocked. Learning is involved in nearly everything we do.

BEHAVIORISM

How should we study learning? Some early psychologists believed that we should focus on directly observable responses and discard any references to inner thoughts, feelings, and motives. This approach is known as **behaviorism.** Psychologists such as B. F. Skinner and John B. Watson believed that most behavior can be explained as the product of simple forms of learning. They maintained that introspection is too subjective to be scientifically viable, whereas observing behavior directly enables psychologists to analyze how organisms respond to stimuli in their environments. While few researchers today would agree that studying

mental processes is of little significance, nearly all would agree that observing behavior is a very important means by which to study learning.

SOME GENERAL TERMS
Learning-Performance Distinction

Imagine that you study hard for your next Psychology exam. By the time the day of the test rolls around, you've learned the material by heart. During the exam, however, you get so nervous that you end up skipping a line and filling in the bubbles wrong. Because of this, you fail the test. The difference between what you learned and its application on that particular day is known as a **learning-performance distinction.** Although learning gives us the capability to perform, we may not always be able to exercise this capability.

Associative Learning

Humans are not the only species with the capacity to learn. Have you ever watched a dolphin and its trainer at an aquarium? The dolphin will jump through hoops and balance a ball on its nose, knowing it will receive fish as a reward. By linking two events that occur together, the dolphin exhibits **associative learning.** We learn to associate certain stimuli all the time—a clap of thunder with a bolt of lightning, the smell of cooking with the possibility of food, an upturned nail on the floor with a sharp twinge of pain. This process of learning associations is known as **conditioning.**

Extinction and Spontaneous Recovery

What would happen if a dolphin trainer suddenly stopped rewarding Flipper for jumping through hoops? The dolphin would probably continue to perform for a while, but as the prospect of food became less likely, he would be less inclined to show off his trick. The gradual elimination of a learned response that occurs when an unconditioned stimulus such as a treat or reward is taken away is known as **extinction.**

Extinction does not completely erase what has been learned. A learned behavior may reoccur after a rest period—a phenomenon known as **spontaneous recovery.** Having refused to perform his trick for several

weeks, Flipper may decide to give it one more go in the hope of getting a treat.

If his trainer decided to reintroduce the treat, even after a long period without practice, Flipper would be able to perform the trick almost as well as he could originally. The ability to reacquire a learned behavior in a shorter period of time than it took to learn originally is known as **savings**.

Generalization and Discrimination

If a particular object or situation closely resembles another, a learner may react to both in the same way—a process known as **generalization.** A dog trained to fetch a ball when it hears a whistle may also fetch a ball if it hears a loud buzzer or bell. A child learning to speak may associate every woman she sees with the word *Mama*.

Psychologist Gregory Razran (1949) proved that we generalize not only objects that are physically similar, but also stimuli that have similar subjective meanings. When shown a list of words, adults will generalize the semantically related words *style* and *fashion,* rather than the phonetically similar words *stile* and *style,* even though the latter pair look and sound more alike. Razran's research suggests that we've learned to generalize words based on their meanings rather than on their sounds or appearances.

Some animals can be conditioned to associate performing tricks with receiving tasty rewards. ∨∨∨

Learning is the process by which experience results in a relatively permanent change in future behavior.

Behaviorism is a method of studying learning in which the researcher focuses solely on directly observable responses and discards any references to inner thoughts, feelings, and motives.

Learning-performance distinction is the difference between what a person learns and its application on that particular day.

Associative learning is learning characterized by linking two events that occur together.

Conditioning is a process of learning associations in which an implicit memory forms because of repeated exposure to a certain stimulus.

Extinction is the gradual elimination of a learned response that occurs when an unconditioned stimulus is taken away.

Spontaneous recovery is a reoccurrence of a learned behavior after extinction.

Savings refers to the ability to reacquire a learned behavior in a shorter period of time than it took to learn originally.

Generalization is a process in which a learner reacts to a particular object or situation in the same way that he or she reacts to one that resembles that object or situation.

Stimulus discrimination is a process in which a learner is trained to distinguish between similar but distinct stimuli.

● ● ●

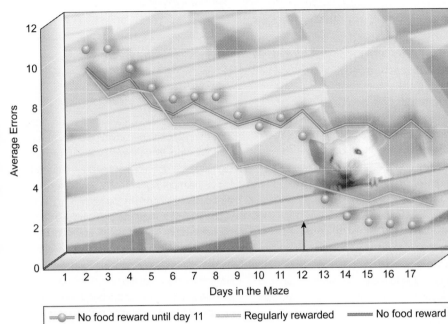

Evidence for Rats' Latent Learning in a Maze

Average Errors (y-axis): 0, 2, 4, 6, 8, 10, 12
Days in the Maze (x-axis): 1 through 17

Legend:
— No food reward until day 11
— Regularly rewarded
— No food reward

Source: After Tolman & Honzik, 1930

∧∧∧ The group of rats that is awarded food on Day 10 immediately begins to make fewer navigational errors, suggesting prior learning of the maze.

Through a process of **stimulus discrimination,** learners can be trained to distinguish between similar but distinct stimuli. The child who calls every woman *Mama* will learn to distinguish her actual mother by a process of positive reinforcement. She will be praised when she correctly identifies her mother and unrewarded when she incorrectly labels other female figures. The child's mother becomes a **discriminative stimulus**—a cue signaling that a particular response will be reinforced or punished.

Cognition and Learning

Just as behavioral conditioning is exhibited across different species, so too is cognitive learning. Researchers have found evidence of cognitive processes in animals by studying rats in mazes. Psychologist Edward Tolman performed an experiment in which he taught three groups of rats the same maze (Tolman & Honzik, 1930). Rats in the first group were individually placed in the maze and rewarded with food for making their way out the other side. The process was repeated over a period of several weeks. Rats in the second group were treated the same way but were not rewarded for making their way out of the maze until the tenth

day of the experiment. The third group, the control group, was not rewarded at all during the experiment.

Tolman discovered that the second group of rats, which appeared to be wandering aimlessly around the maze for the first nine days, immediately solved the puzzle once food was presented as a reward for escaping from the maze. He concluded that the rats had learned how to solve the maze but had no incentive to do so before they were rewarded for demonstrating their behavior. Learning that is exhibited only in the presence of an incentive is known as **latent learning.**

Just as London taxi drivers seem to create mental representations of the city in their brains, the rats appeared to develop **cognitive maps**, or mental representations of the maze. Tolman's experiment showed that learning can occur without reinforcement or punishment.

Motivation

Why do we behave as we do? Those of us who perform activities for their own sake are **intrinsically motivated**—we do things because they are interesting, satisfying, challenging, or enjoyable. **Extrinsic motivation** is the desire to complete a behavior because it will lead to a

reward or avoid punishment. Sometimes excessive rewards can undermine intrinsic motivation, a concept known as **overjustification**. Children promised a payoff for playing with a particular toy will play with that toy less than children who are not paid to play (Deci et al., 1999).

BIOLOGICAL PREDISPOSITIONS IN LEARNING

An animal's natural predispositions create a propensity for learning some kinds of associations rather than others. It is easy to teach a chicken to "dance" for treats because as the chicken waits for food, it naturally scratches at the ground in a manner that resembles (fairly bad) dancing. However, if you try to teach a chicken to stand still in order to obtain food, you will find the process much harder: Chickens are not biologically predisposed to wait patiently for dinner. The tendency for an animal to revert back to its instinctual behavior over time is known as **instinctual drift**.

Food Preferences

If you've ever gotten food poisoning from a bad hamburger and discovered afterward that you no longer have any interest in eating hamburgers, you've experienced **taste-aversion learning**, a form of conditioned learning in which exposure to a flavor paired with sickness will produce a consistent aversion to that flavor. Psychologist John Garcia discovered that rats given a sweetened liquid and then injected with a drug or exposed to

Classical conditioning is a phenomenon in which two stimuli are associated, thus creating a reflex response.

Unconditioned stimulus (US) is an original, unlearned stimulus that elicits a certain reflex action.

Unconditioned response (UR) is a reflex action elicited by an unconditioned stimulus.

Conditioned stimulus (CS) is an event that is repeatedly paired with a particular unconditioned stimulus.

Conditioned response (CR) is a learned reaction triggered by a conditioned stimulus, even in the absence of an associated unconditioned stimulus.

Delayed conditioning is a type of classical conditioning in which the conditioned stimulus is presented before the unconditioned stimulus, and the termination of the conditioned stimulus is delayed until the unconditioned stimulus is made available.

Trace conditioning is a type of classical conditioning in which the conditioned stimulus is discontinued before the unconditioned stimulus is presented.

Simultaneous conditioning is a type of classical conditioning in which the conditioned stimulus and unconditioned stimulus are presented at the same time.

Backward conditioning is a type of classical conditioning in which the conditioned stimulus is presented after the unconditioned stimulus.

Second-order conditioning is a type of classical conditioning in which the conditioned stimulus is paired with a neutral stimulus.

radiation that caused nausea would not touch the liquid again (Garcia & Koelling, 1966). Even if we ingest food several hours before we feel nauseated, we can still develop strong taste aversions.

If we are deprived of essential nutrients, do we automatically turn to foods that can provide us with the supplements we need? Studies of sodium-deprived and calcium-deprived rats show that the animals preferentially seek out foods rich in these minerals (Richter, 1936; Richter & Eckert, 1937). This is true even of rats that have never been exposed to sodium or calcium before, suggesting that the preference is an unlearned response.

However, food preference is not just a biological response; animals (including humans) also learn what's good to eat through social observation. Studies on Norway rats showed that the rodents expressed a preference for food that had already been successfully ingested by their fellow rats (Galef & Wigmore, 1983).

Fear-Related Learning Biases

Most of us have never been attacked by a shark, but plenty of people still hear the *Jaws* theme music in their heads every time they set foot in the ocean. Humans are biologically predisposed to acquire fears of situations and objects that posed a threat to our ancestors or that threaten our survival as a species. We quickly learn to fear storms, snakes, spiders, and cliffs, while our instincts leave us unprepared for modern dangers such as electricity and global warming, even though they now pose a bigger threat (Lumsden & Wilson, 1983).

Place-Learning Abilities

Some animals appear to have specialized learning abilities to help them locate important places. A squirrel is able to recall numerous locations of buried food stores, while salmon are biologically predisposed to return to their own hatching grounds when it is time to spawn. Although squirrels are known to have unusually large hippocampi, one study suggests that this might be seasonal. In spring and fall, when squirrels are actively gathering and retrieving nuts, they show a 15 percent increase in hippocampus size compared to the rest of the year (Lavenex et al., 2000).

∧
∧
∧
How does a squirrel remember where it stored all its nuts?

Classical Conditioning

Although the idea of learned associations was not new at the time, Russian physiologist Ivan Pavlov's classic studies in the early 20th century proved that it was possible to learn to associate two stimuli and thus create a reflex response. This phenomenon became known as **classical conditioning.** While Pavlov was studying canine digestion, he noticed that his dogs were salivating at the mere sight of food. Even the sound of a dog bowl clattering in the kitchen made them drool. Pavlov studied the dogs' reflexes by sounding a bell every time he was about to give them food. After many occasions of hearing the bell and immediately receiving food, the dogs learned to associate the two. They began to salivate at the sound of the bell, even in the absence of food, indicating that they had learned there was a connection between the bell's ring and the arrival of food (Pavlov, 1927).

The **unconditioned stimulus** (US) is the original, unlearned stimulus that elicits a certain reflex action, known as an **unconditioned response** (UR). In this case, the unconditioned stimulus is the food that the dogs expect to eat, while salivation is the unconditioned response. When a **conditioned stimulus (CS)**—an event that is repeatedly paired with the unconditioned stimulus—is introduced, it will eventually trigger a learned reaction even without the unconditioned stimulus. This is known as a **conditioned response (CR)**. Through a period of acquisition, Pavlov taught the dogs to associate the sound of a ringing bell with the expectation of food, causing the dogs to salivate whenever they heard a bell.

TYPES OF CLASSICAL CONDITIONING

Pavlov experimented with several types of classical conditioning. In **delayed conditioning**, the conditioned stimulus is presented before the unconditioned stimulus, and the termination of the conditioned stimulus is delayed until the unconditioned stimulus is made available. For example, Pavlov would continue ringing his bell until the dogs were able to see the food in front of them.

>>> 1. A neutral stimulus (NS) produces no salivation response. 2. An unconditioned stimulus (US) produces an unconditioned response (UR). 3. The unconditioned stimulus is repeatedly presented just after the neutral stimulus and continues to produce an unconditioned response. 4. The neutral stimulus produces a conditioned response without the unconditioned stimulus. The neutral stimulus becomes a conditioned stimulus (CS).

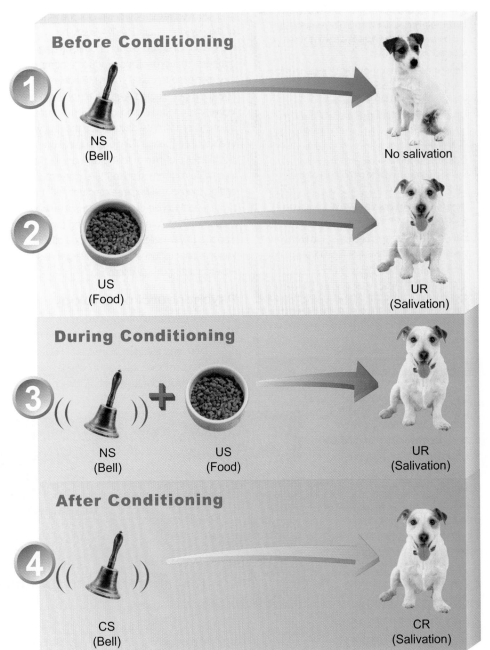

Before Conditioning

1 NS (Bell) → No salivation

2 US (Food) → UR (Salivation)

During Conditioning

3 NS (Bell) + US (Food) → UR (Salivation)

After Conditioning

4 CS (Bell) → CR (Salivation)

In **trace conditioning**, the conditioned stimulus is discontinued before the unconditioned stimulus is presented. For example, Pavlov would sound the bell once and then bring the food in after an interval with no stimuli. Pavlov found that the conditioned stimulus and unconditioned stimulus should occur within a few seconds of each other in order to work effectively.

In **simultaneous conditioning**, the conditioned stimulus and unconditioned stimulus are presented at the same time. Pavlov found this method to be ineffective: When the bell rang and the food appeared simultaneously, the dogs did not respond to conditioning (it's important to note that the dogs may have learned the association, but without a response, the amount of learning could not be assessed).

In the procedure called **backward conditioning**, the conditioned stimulus is presented after the unconditioned stimulus, signaling the end of the food. This rarely results in a response supporting the idea that classical conditioning is biologically adaptive—it helps organisms prepare for an event. It would be of little use to hear a footstep behind us in a dark alley (a conditioned stimulus that signals danger) if we have already been clonked over the head by an attacker (an unconditioned stimulus that causes a fight-or-flight reflex action).

Second-order conditioning occurs when a conditioned stimulus is paired with a neutral stimulus. It is possible for the neutral stimulus to become a second conditioned stimulus, even though it has never been directly related to the unconditioned stimulus. For example, Pavlov later paired the learned bell with a black square. Eventually, the dogs would salivate at the mere sight of the square, even though it had never been directly linked to food.

Fear Conditioning

Fear can be a biologically useful emotion; it alerts us to danger. But it can also be debilitating (imagine having an irrational fear of trees or bacteria). Using Pavlov's research, psychologists John Watson and Rosalie Rayner proved that it is possible to condition human emotions such as fear. They took an 11-month-old infant named Albert who, like most children, was afraid of loud noises but not of white rats. In an experiment sure to horrify most modern ethics boards, Watson and Rayner presented Albert with a white rat and, just as he was about to touch it, struck a hammer against a steel bar directly behind the infant's head. After this procedure had been repeated several times, Albert burst into tears at the mere sight of the rat (Watson & Rayner, 1920). Thanks to the principle of generalization, Albert also developed an unhealthy fear of all things furry: Rabbits, cotton wool, and even Santa Claus's beard caused the child to dissolve into tears.

Do we prepare ourselves for the ingestion of dangerous substances? A study by researcher Shepard Siegel and his colleagues suggests that organisms produce a compensatory response to certain drugs (Siegel et al., 1982). Siegel injected a group of rats with heroin every second day and gave them a sugar solution on alternate days. Once the rats were used to their routine, Siegel administered a double dose of heroin to the animals. He found that twice as many died in the sugar-expectant setting than in the heroin-expectant setting.

Repeated use of a particular substance produces **drug tolerance**, lessening the substance's physiological and behavioral effects. A frequent user requires larger and larger doses to experience the drug's effect.

Psychoneuroimmunology

Psychoneuroimmunology is the study of how psychology relates to events involving the nervous system and the immune system. Have you ever heard someone talk about head lice and immediately felt your scalp itch all over?

Fear conditioning is highly resistant to extinction. In severe cases, just one pairing of a neutral stimulus with an unconditioned stimulus can create a serious phobia. After the 9/11 attacks, tens of thousands of children in New York City experienced nightmares and fear of public places (Goodnough, 2002).

CLASSICAL CONDITIONING AND PHYSIOLOGICAL RESPONSES

Classical conditioning is present in at least two of our biological responses to stimuli: hunger and sexual arousal. We might not salivate as voraciously as Pavlov's dogs, but hunger is a conditioned stimulus that produces a number of biological functions. Our digestive juices secrete in the stomach, we produce more saliva, and our bodies release hormones that stimulate our appetites.

You may have had a romantic partner whom you associated with a particular sight, smell, or song. This association isn't unusual; in fact, it's another example of conditioning. Psychologist Michael Domjan (1992) demonstrated that after a female Japanese quail was paired several times with a red light, male quails became aroused simply by viewing the red light. Likewise, humans associate particular objects, sights, and smells with sexual pleasure.

> "We might not salivate as voraciously as Pavlov's dogs, but hunger is a conditioned stimulus that produces a number of biological functions. **Our digestive juices secrete in the stomach, we produce more saliva, and our bodies release hormones that stimulate our appetites.**"

Classical conditioning affects not only the body's physiological responses, but also its immune system. Consider the study by psychologist Robert Ader and immunologist Nicholas Cohen (1985). The researchers paired rats' drinking of saccharine-sweetened water with injections of a drug that suppressed immune functioning. After repeated pairings, the saccharine water alone triggered immune suppression, as if the drug had been given.

Operant Conditioning

Whereas classical conditioning occurs with reflexive, involuntary behavior, **operant conditioning** is a type of learning in which organisms associate their actions with consequences. This type of conditioning is active,

meaning it requires action from the organism. In classical conditioning, the organism is passive and simply learns to associate a stimulus with an outcome; it need not respond in any specific way. It is therefore more likely to repeat rewarded behaviors and less likely to continue performing actions that are punished.

OPERANT BEHAVIOR

Operant conditioning involves **operant behavior**—responses that an organism makes to produce an effect on the environment. According to Skinner, most of our behavior is a result of **reinforcement**—an act that causes the response to be more likely to recur.

Take Edward Thorndike's "puzzle box," for example. Thorndike placed a hungry cat in a wooden cage that required a simple act (such as pushing a lever) to open it. To heighten feline frustration and further motivate an escape attempt, he then placed a bowl of food just outside the door of the cage so that the cat could see it. To reach the food, the cat had to figure out how to press the lever to open the door, a process that Thorndike timed. After pushing and rubbing up against the walls of the cage, the cat accidentally stood on the lever, opening the door. The cat did not learn the connection between the lever and the road to freedom immediately. However, after numerous trials, the cat was able to open the door very quickly, demonstrating that it had learned an association between the lever and the path to food and freedom (1898).

Based on his research, Thorndike developed the **law of effect:** If a response produces a satisfying effect, it is likely to occur again.

PRINCIPLES OF REINFORCEMENT

Building on Thorndike's law of effect, Skinner developed some of the principles of behavior control. He developed his own version of a puzzle box, called a "Skinner box," or "operant-conditioning chamber." By pressing a bar in the chamber, a rat could release food pellets or water, while a device recorded the animal's responses.

Skinner believed that to analyze human and animal behavior, each act could be broken into three parts, known as a **three-term contingency.** This includes the discriminative stimulus (the bar to be pushed), the **operant response** (the act of pushing

People often choose the immediate gratification of risky, unprotected sex over the delayed gratification of safe sex or saved sex (Loewenstein & Furstenberg, 1991).

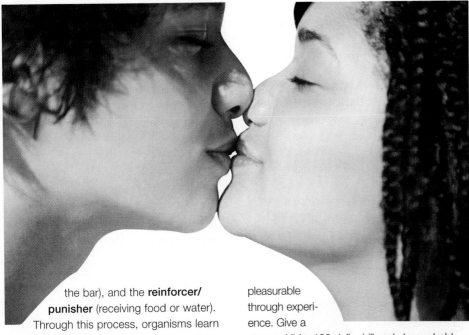

○ ● ○

Operant response is an act that causes a particular effect on the environment.

Reinforcer/punisher is a positive or negative consequence caused by an operant response.

Positive reinforcer strengthens a response by presenting a pleasurable consequence.

Negative reinforcer strengthens a response by removing an unpleasant consequence.

Primary reinforcer satisfies a basic biological need.

Secondary reinforcer becomes satisfying or pleasurable through experience.

Delayed reinforcement is a reward that does not immediately follow an action.

Continuous reinforcement is a method of reinforcement that ensures that a desired response is reinforced every time it occurs.

Partial (intermittent) reinforcement is a method of reinforcement in which responses are sometimes reinforced and sometimes not.

● ● ●

the bar), and the **reinforcer/ punisher** (receiving food or water).

Through this process, organisms learn that in the presence of certain stimuli, their behavior is likely to have a particular effect on the environment.

If you spend a few hours a week working out at the gym, what motivates you to go? Achieving a good level of personal fitness? Receiving compliments on your lean appearance? There are many health-related reasons to jump on a treadmill, but there are also fringe benefits such as spending time with your gym buddies or avoiding an unpleasant household chore. For every repeated action we take, there are different types of reinforcers.

Types of Reinforcers

Positive reinforcers strengthen a response by presenting a pleasurable consequence. We receive compliments for a job well done. We feel good about taking our recycling to the local recycling center or donating blood to the blood bank.

In contrast, **negative reinforcers** strengthen a response by removing an unpleasant consequence. We block our ears to shut out the piercing sound of a fire alarm. We rock a baby to sleep to stop it from crying.

A **primary reinforcer** satisfies a basic biological need, such as hunger or thirst. A **secondary reinforcer** becomes satisfying or

pleasurable through experience. Give a young child a 100 dollar bill and she probably won't have much of a reaction. But once she learns how many toys that 100 dollar bill could purchase, she will learn to appreciate money as a strong motivating factor.

Unlike other animals, humans have the ability to respond to **delayed reinforcement**, or a reward that does not immediately follow an action. We can wait a week or a month before we receive our paychecks, and we do not

> *Give a young child a 100 dollar bill and she probably won't have much of a reaction. But once she learns how many toys that 100 dollar bill could purchase, she will learn to appreciate money as a strong motivating factor.*

immediately demand to know an exam result at the end of a test. Even though we *can* respond to delayed reinforcement, however, we still often reject long-term, delayed consequences in favor of short-term, immediate pleasures. It's hard to convince ourselves to change our lifestyles dras-

tically in order to reduce our carbon footprint when we may not see any tangible environmental results of this decision for several years.

Reinforcement Schedules

Continuous reinforcement ensures that a desired response is reinforced every time it occurs. This schedule results in rapid learning, but if the reinforcement stops, extinction also occurs rapidly. If a rat suddenly stops receiving food pellets every time it presses a bar, it will soon stop pressing it.

Often, we do not experience continuous reinforcement in our daily lives. A telemarketer may be lucky if one person in a hundred gives him or her the time of day, and the people who create "junk" mail see the bulk of their labor immediately consigned to the nearest trash can. Yet if these people were completely unsuccessful, their companies would go out of business.

Partial (intermittent) reinforcement occurs when responses are sometimes reinforced and sometimes not. This produces slower initial learning, but the learning is more resistant to extinction. It seems that we are more persistent when we achieve rare but satisfying results. There are several types of partial reinforcement:

Fixed-ratio schedules. Behavior is reinforced after a set number of responses. For example, you might get one free latte after every ten purchases at the local coffee place. Fixed-rate schedules bring forth high rates of responding with only a brief pause following reinforcement.

Variable-ratio schedules. Behavior is reinforced after varying and unpredictable numbers

the hungry birds in individual cages containing food hoppers and dropped grains of food into each hopper at random intervals. The pigeons repeated whatever they had been doing just before the food was dropped into the cage—hopping from side to side, turning around, or making a pendulum-like motion with their heads. Although there was no actual link between the pigeons' actions and the outcome (just as your team is equally likely to win or lose regardless of whether you wear your lucky shirt), they continued to demonstrate the same behavior.

Attractive Rewards and Reward Expectations

Some theorists argue that the stimulus-response relationship is an oversimplification of the learning process, and suggest that there is a cognitive component involved with regard to the expectation of reward. For example, if a rat knows that it will receive a larger amount of food than usual when it completes a maze, will it be motivated to run faster? A sudden shift in the attractiveness of a reward is called a **reward**

contrast effect (Crespi, 1942, 1944). Response rates decrease when a strong reinforcer is exchanged for a weaker one, creating a negative contrast effect. Conversely, if a reward becomes more enticing, response rates will increase, creating a positive contrast effect. Institutions such as rehabilitation centers and psychiatric facilities use **token economies** to capitalize on this theory. Desired behaviors such as grooming and taking medication are rewarded with token payoffs such as free time or extra dessert.

Enticing rewards tend to be good motivators. The **Premack principle** states that a preferred activity can be used to reinforce a non-preferred task. For example, you might promise yourself a trip to the movies as a reward for finishing the paper that's been hanging over your head for weeks.

PUNISHMENT AND SHAPING

Most of us probably remember being sent to our rooms to "think about what we've done." Some of us may have even thought twice about locking our younger brother in the closet again. Whereas reinforcement increases a behavior, **punishment** decreases it. If a high school student cuts class, he or she might receive punishment in the form of weekend detention. Since most of us would prefer not to spend our sunny Saturday mornings sitting quietly in a classroom, we're likely to respond to this threat of punishment by making sure to show up for class.

Is it possible to gradually teach good table manners to a badly behaved child? The process of **shaping** behavior uses reinforcers to guide an organism's actions toward a desired behavior. This is achieved using **successive approximations,** or behaviors that are incrementally closer to the overall desired action. For example, on the first day, you might encourage the child to simply sit at the table for a short period of time

of responses. A gambler at a slot machine may put in thousands of coins and receive no payout, or insert a single quarter into the slot and win thousands of dollars. Variable-ratio schedules have high response rates and produce behavior that's difficult to extinguish.

Fixed-interval schedules. Behavior is reinforced for the first response after a fixed time period. If we know that our dinner is almost ready, we will check the oven more frequently, producing rapid responses at the expected time of reward and slower responses until then.

Variable-interval schedules. Behavior is reinforced after variable periods of time. We may obsessively check our e-mail for new messages and be rewarded for our efforts at varying time intervals. This generally produces slow and steady behavioral responses.

Accidental Reinforcement

Is behavior reinforced when it is accidentally linked to a fortunate outcome? You can probably answer this question by assessing your closet. If you have a "lucky" shirt that achieved its moniker because your team once made it to the championships while you were wearing it, you have experienced accidental reinforcement.

Skinner (1948) demonstrated similar "superstitious" behavior with pigeons. He placed

REINFORCEMENT

+ Adding something valuable or desirable

− Avoiding something unpleasant

PUNISHMENT

+ Adding something unpleasant (extra chores)

− Removing something valued or desired (such as playtime)

➕ POSITIVE   ➖ NEGATIVE

> ^ ^ ^ Reinforcement is generally acknowledged to be more effective than punishment when disciplining children.

before allowing him to watch TV. The next day, you might extend the time period, gradually moving to more complex behaviors such as using a napkin and not talking with a mouth full of food.

One method of shaping complex behavior is **chaining**, a process in which the final step in a sequence is reinforced first, becoming a conditioned reinforcer for the preceding response. This method is often used in animal training. For example, you might place a rat on a top platform in a cage where it is able to eat food. You might then place the rat on a lower platform so that it has to climb a ladder in order to reach the top platform and eat the food. These steps can be expanded to shape a complex chain of events. Skinner managed to train a rat to wait to hear the "Star-Spangled Banner" before sitting up on its hind legs, pulling a string to hoist the U.S. flag, and finally saluting the banner in a remarkable but atypical display of rodent patriotism.

APPLICATIONS OF OPERANT CONDITIONING

Skinner's theories that external influences shape behavior, as opposed to thoughts and feelings, were highly controversial. His critics argued that he dehumanized people by neglecting their personal freedom. Whatever the objections to Skinner's ideas, applications of operant conditioning are evident in schools, homes, and businesses.

Skinner believed that it was possible to achieve an ideal education. He stated: "Good instruction demands two things. Students must be told immediately whether what they do is right or wrong and, when right, they must be directed to the step to be taken next." We can see Skinner's vision to some extent in modern classrooms that use online learning programs and interactive student software.

Reinforcement principles have been shown to enhance athletic abilities. Thomas Simek and Richard O'Brien (1981, 1988) used these techniques to improve the performances of students learning to play golf and baseball. For example, golf students would start with very short putts and gradually increase their distance from the tee. This behavioral method of training showed faster skill improvement than students who had been taught using conventional methods.

Both punishment and reinforcement are most effective when they immediately follow the performed behavior. IBM bigwig Thomas Watson would immediately write an employee a

check whenever he spotted an achievement worthy of praise (Peters & Waterman, 1982). While it would be great to have such a generous boss, a simple "thank you" for a job well done is equally effective.

If you suddenly became responsible for the entire electricity bill in a shared house, would you be more careful about turning the lights off? You would probably find yourself

> Skinner's theories that external influences shape behavior, as opposed to thoughts and feelings, were highly controversial. His critics argued that he dehumanized people by neglecting their personal freedom.

painfully aware of how many lights your housemates were leaving on, too. Economists and psychologists believe that people's spending behavior is controlled by the consequences of that behavior. Al Gore (1992) pointed out that when the government decides to tax a commodity, people use less of that commodity (because they don't want to pay taxes), whereas when the government subsidizes a commodity, that commodity is more heavily used (because people want to take advantage of the relatively cheap price). He suggested that a good policy move would be to increase taxes on the burning of fossil fuels to encourage people to use less gas. Recent surges in fuel prices and the subsequent outcry suggests that there is a limit to how much Americans are willing to spend on their love of the open road.

Observational Learning

We didn't directly experience many of the behaviors we learned about as children. Instead, we learned by watching others. Take Michigan youngster Adrian Cole, who in 2005, at the age of four, was picked up by police officers in the middle of the night after driving his mother's car to the local video store. When the officers asked him how he learned to drive, Adrian told them that he just watched what his mom did. **Observational learning**, in which we observe and imitate others, plays a large part in our overall learning process.

ELEMENTS OF OBSERVATIONAL LEARNING

Stimulus enhancement is the tendency to pay attention to a particular place or object that someone else has shown interest in.

>>> If we are not willing to reduce our usage of fossil fuels for the good of the environment, should the government appeal to our wallets by increasing taxes at the pump? Environmentalists believe that these types of policies help promote sustainable living.

BANDURA'S EXPERIMENTS

How do children react when they see adults behaving aggressively? Psychologist Albert Bandura conducted a famous experiment in which he attempted to answer this question (Bandura et al., 1961). Using a group of preschool children, a researcher invited one child at a time to sit in a room and complete some artwork. Having shown the child how to design pictures with potato prints, the experimenter moved to the opposite side of the room and began playing with a Tinkertoy set and a five-foot inflatable Bobo doll. The experimenter then began acting aggressively toward the doll, using easily imitable actions such as placing the doll on its side and repeatedly punching it on the nose while chanting aggressive remarks.

After the child observed the aggressive outburst, the experimenter took the child to another room full of appealing toys. The

learning is not a good thing. Negative role models can create antisocial effects, encouraging crime and gang violence. Some studies conclude that violence seen on television and in the movies can have a negative impact on children's behavior (Comstock & Lindsey, 1975; Eron, 1987).

However, observational learning is not all bad news. **Prosocial** models—those that are positive and helpful—can have beneficial effects on people's behavior. Humanitarian figures such as Martin Luther King Jr. and Mahatma Gandhi used their influence to direct people's behavior through nonviolent action. Parents and teachers can also be strong role models, encouraging children through their own actions to be kind and helpful to others and to have a positive impact on the world.

Learning how to play a particular instrument will become more desirable if we see a friend or sibling playing that same instrument.

Our drive to receive the rewards we've obtained in the past is called **goal enhancement.** We are more motivated to act out behaviors that have previously resulted in being rewarded. An undesired piano lesson may become more appealing if previous lessons have ended with a trip to the movies, or if we have watched a sibling receive a treat for correctly reciting the scales.

To learn by observation, an organism must be able to reproduce the action that is being observed—a concept known as **modeling.** A toddler may be able to imitate a sibling drinking out of a cup, but more complex actions such as performing a back flip or reciting Beethoven's Fifth Symphony are generally not possible through mere observation.

Latent learning, which we discussed earlier, is another type of observational learning. Learning that an observer does not immediately demonstrate may still be added to his or her knowledge base. Observational learning helps us understand how the children of abusive parents may grow up to be more aggressive (Stith et al., 2000). These children may not necessarily display aggressive behavior at the time, but they are learning it through observation.

> " In nature, animals are active learners, acquiring new behaviors by observing others or simply by going about their day-to-day business. Both animals and humans learn via play and exploration. "

experimenter allowed the child to play for a few minutes before interrupting, explaining that these particular toys were reserved for other children. The frustrated child was then taken to another room that contained a few toys, including a Bobo doll. Making herself as inconspicuous as possible, the experimenter watched the child's reactions toward the doll.

Children that had been exposed to violent outbursts were much more likely to lash out at the doll. The experimenters noted that the children imitated the exact same acts that they had witnessed and used the same aggressive verbal remarks. Bandura concluded that children imitate violent behavior they see in adults, and he began to research links between children's exposure to violence on television and aggressive behavior toward others.

APPLICATIONS OF OBSERVATIONAL LEARNING

Based on Bandura's study, we might be tempted to conclude that observational

LEARNING-BASED ACTIVITIES

In nature, animals are active learners, acquiring new behaviors by observing others or simply by going about their day-to-day business. Both animals and humans learn via play and exploration.

Play

It is easy to dismiss play as a form of entertainment that serves no real purpose, but have you ever watched a kitten wiggle its rump and pounce on a piece of string or a dog's tail? This behavior is helping the kitten learn to hunt. Play activity in animals serves as natural training for behaviors that will prove useful in serious situations. Similarly, two young children role-playing nurturing games with dolls are actually learning important behavioral lessons that will improve their social development (see Chapter 12).

Exploration

If you place a rat in an unfamiliar cage and watch its reactions, you will probably see it scurry from corner to corner, as it assesses its new surroundings. Exploring an environment is generally considered to be more primitive and widespread than play behavior. New surroundings inspire both curiosity and fear in an organism.

Once the rat is satisfied that it has familiarized itself with its new environment, you may see it **patrolling**—periodically scanning the cage by rearing up on its hind legs to make sure that nothing has changed.

What skills might these children be learning as they play?

Learning in the Brain

EARLY STUDIES

What processes take place in the brain when we learn? Psychologist Karl Lashley (1950) approached this issue from an alternative angle and tried to discover what might prevent us from learning. Searching for the part of the brain that stored memory, he trained a group of rats to solve a maze and then cut out pieces of the rats' cortices before retesting their memory of the maze. From this research, Lashley developed the **mass action principle**, which states that reduction in learning is proportional to the amount of tissue destroyed. It did not matter where the lesions were made in the rats' brains: The more damage done, the less able the rats were to solve the maze. Lashley also noted that the more complex the task, the more disruptive the lesion became.

Eric Kandel and James Schwartz (1982) proved that even organisms with a simple nervous system of only a few thousand neurons could demonstrate rudimentary learning abilities. Take a few seconds to consider the Californian sea snail, *Aplysia*. When disturbed by a squirt of

water, the sea snail defensively withdraws its gill. If the squirts continue (as in rough water), the withdrawal response diminishes, because the response becomes habituated. But if the sea snail repeatedly receives an electric shock to the tail just after being squirted, its withdrawal response becomes stronger. This sensitization is

> The more we use the muscles in our bodies, the stronger they become. Is the same true of connections in our brain? Psychologist Donald Hebb (1949) theorized that if pre-synaptic and post-synaptic neurons are active at the same time, the synapses between them are strengthened.

associated with the release of the neurotransmitter serotonin at certain synapses. These synapses become more efficient at transmitting signals. If the shocks are repeated over a prolonged period, the sea snail's withdrawal reflex

may be enhanced for several weeks, effectively demonstrating long-term memory.

LONG-TERM POTENTIATION (LTP)

The more we use the muscles in our bodies, the stronger they become. Is the same true of connections in our brain? Psychologist Donald Hebb (1949) theorized that if pre-synaptic and post-synaptic neurons are active at the same time, the synapses between them are strengthened. This strengthening allows the post-synaptic neurons to respond to weaker stimuli, a process known as **long-term potentiation (LTP)**. Hebb proposed that memories were stored in networks of neurons called **cell assemblies.**

Studies have demonstrated that drugs that block LTP interfere with learning (Lynch & Staubli, 1991). Similarly, mice can be genetically engineered to have heightened learning capacities. By inserting an extra gene into fertilized mouse eggs, researchers increased the types of post-synaptic neurons that are effective at triggering LTP. The resulting "Doogie" mice (named after the brainy character on TV show *Doogie Howser, MD*) were able to remember the location of a hidden underwater platform and recognize cues that signaled an impending shock (Tsien, 2000).

The opposing process to LTP is **long-term depression**, the weakening of a neuronal synapse. Low-frequency stimulation over a long period of time reduces neuron sensitivity. Long-term depression is specific to the activated synapses, and there is some evidence that it can enhance LTP in neighboring synapses.

What Strengthens and Weakens LTP?

Do higher levels of stimulation improve our memory? Studies have demonstrated that rats living in enriched environments show enhanced post-synaptic potentials—a phenomenon that disappears when the rodents are placed in impoverished cages deprived of stimuli (Rosenzweig et al., 1972). Like the brains of the mirror-reading subjects mentioned in the beginning of this chapter, the structures of rats' brains alter with experience.

Missing an early morning lecture for a bit of extra sleep might actually improve your chances of graduating. Long-term potentiation is more difficult to induce following prolonged periods of wakefulness (Vyazovskiy et al., 2008). Wakefulness appears to be related to synaptic potentiation, whereas sleep may favor global

synaptic depression, preserving an overall balance of synaptic strength.

CONSOLIDATION IN LEARNING

How do we retain what we have learned? Sleep also plays an important role in the stabilization of long-term memory—after learning, we need sleep in order to consolidate the new information. Research has found that sleep deprivation can lead to the depletion of proteins that help neurons grow and survive (Sei et al., 2000) and can hinder the creation of cells in the hippocampus (Guzman-Marin et al., 2003). Sleep deprivation has also been found to impair subsequent learning (Yoo et al., 2007), making it a good idea to leave the Thursday night party relatively early if you want to retain any information from Friday's lecture.

Synaptic Consolidation vs. System Consolidation

Neurobiologists identify two types of memory consolidation. The first, known as **synaptic consolidation**, takes place within a few hours after learning. It involves the morphological changes necessary for the initial stabilization of memories, including protein synthesis.

The second type of memory consolidation takes place at a system level. **System consolidation** is a more gradual process (taking weeks or months), involving the reorganization of the brain regions that

support memory. According to **Ribot's law**, memory loss following brain damage affects recent memories to a greater extent than remote memories. Think of your brain as a computer saving a file—if the computer crashes, it will retain all the information on that file except for the most recent data that has not automatically been saved. Similarly, if the consolidation process is disrupted before your brain has had a chance to organize the information properly, the new memories that were being created may be lost.

COGNITIVE MAPS

From research conducted on squirrels, we know that there's a connection between spatial learning and the hippocampus. Expanding on this knowledge, psychologists John O'Keefe and Lynn Nadel (1978) proposed the **cognitive map theory**, in which the hippocampus provides a spatial framework, enabling us to create a mental map of our surroundings. O'Keefe and Nadel discovered that **place cells** in the hippocampus fire only when an organism is in a specific location in its natural environment.

In contrast, supporters of the **relational memory theory** suggest that the hippocampus processes events by linking them into relational frameworks (Cohen & Eichenbaum, 1993). For example, you might hear your favorite childhood TV show's theme song and suddenly be reminded of a multitude of associations—the characters on that show, what you liked to eat while you were watching it, the childhood friends who also used to watch the show and act out scenes with you at school the

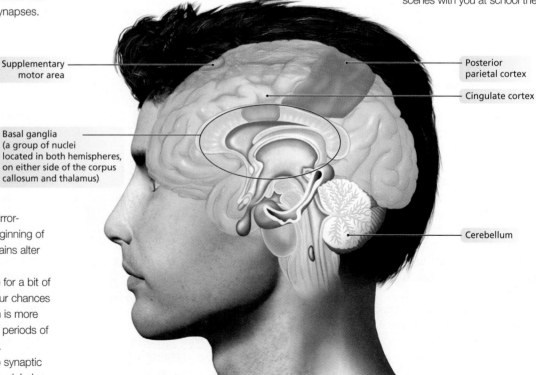

Supplementary motor area

Basal ganglia (a group of nuclei located in both hemispheres, on either side of the corpus callosum and thalamus)

Posterior parietal cortex

Cingulate cortex

Cerebellum

following day. This theory is supported by evidence suggesting that place cells represent not the global topology of the environment but rather the relationship of objects to each other within the environment.

SKILL LEARNING AND THE BASAL GANGLIA

Many studies have shown the cortical restructuring that occurs during skill learning. Neurobiologist Gregg Recanzone and his colleagues trained adult owl monkeys to detect the difference in frequency between two stimuli on a single finger (Recanzone et al., 1992). They found that with training, the area of the somatosensory cortices recruited for that finger increased significantly.

So which parts of the brain encourage cortical restructuring? The basal ganglia are often associated with the processes of reinforcement learning, or operant conditioning. Remember how the reward areas of a mother's brain light up on brain-scan images when she sees a photo of her smiling infant? Behavior that results in a reward causes dopamine neurons to fire in bursts. Conversely, if an expected reward is not received, the dopamine cells cease firing altogether. These dopamine bursts and lulls are believed to control changes in the strength of synaptic connections in the basal ganglia, reinforcing actions that are rewarded and discouraging actions that are not.

Our ability to learn motor skills is highly dependent on the basal ganglia (along with the posterior parietal cortex, supplementary motor area, cingulate cortex, and cerebellum). One of the primary roles of the basal ganglia in motor control is in the selection of responses via opposing excitatory and inhibitory effects on the thalamus.

There is also evidence that the brain can strengthen its perceptual abilities. Some studies show that the fusiform face area is not a space-specific module, but that it is also related to general visual expertise. For example, the fusiform face area in an auto mechanic may be

activated in response to images of cars, while the same area in a bird watcher may be activated by images of different birds (Gauthier et al., 2000).

> So which parts of the brain encourage cortical restructuring? The basal ganglia are often associated with the processes of reinforcement learning, or operant conditioning. Remember how the reward areas of a mother's brain light up on brain-scan images when she sees a photo of her smiling infant?

CONDITIONING

Little Albert, the toddler who was conditioned to fear white rats, developed an unhealthy fear of all things furry because he associated them with loud noises. But what area in his brain enabled such conditioning to take place? The answer is the amygdala—that small, almond-shaped structure deep within the temporal lobe. The central nucleus of the amygdala has been found to be critical for emotional conditioning, in particular fear conditioning.

Imagine a rat when it is frightened: It gets into a crouching position and sits motionless, a defensive reaction called **freezing**. Physiological reactions also take place, such as an increase in heart rate and blood pressure. If the rat is conditioned to fear a particular stimulus, both the behavioral and physiological reactions will occur. However, once certain connections from the amygdala to the midbrain are severed, these reactions no longer take place (Kim et al., 1993).

Most forms of conditioning also rely on the hippocampus, cerebellum, and basal ganglia. Depending on the demands of the

situation, the varying parts of the brain are used to different extents.

OTHER NEURAL MECHANISMS

When we learn through observation, are the processes in our brains similar to the processes that take place when we complete the task ourselves? Neuroscientists have discovered **mirror neurons** in the macaque monkey that respond both when a monkey performs a task, and when it watches another monkey perform the same task. These neurons are also present in humans, and they appear to serve the same functions in us as they do in macaques (Fabbri-Destro & Rizzolatti, 2008). Some scientists believe that these neurons, found in a frontal lobe area near the motor cortex, are important in behavior imitation and language acquisition (Ramachandran, 2000).

> ^ The amygdala is critical for emotional conditioning and damage to this area may cause a lack of fear. What disadvantages might you encounter if you became fearless?

Summary

WHAT ARE THE PRINCIPLES OF LEARNING? p.104

- Learning is the process through which experience results in a relatively permanent change in future behavior.

- Behaviorists B.F. Skinner and John B. Watson believed that most behavior can be explained as the product of simple forms of learning.

- Organisms have biological predispositions to learn certain types of associations such as natural fear of situations that threaten survival.

HOW DO REFLEXES CONDITION OUR RESPONSES TO STIMULI? p.106

- We naturally respond in certain ways to certain stimuli. Classical conditioning takes advantage of these reflexive responses by teaching us to respond reflexively to formerly neutral stimuli.

HOW DOES ASSOCIATION SHAPE OUR BEHAVIOR? p.108

- When we associate our actions with either positive or negative consequences, we undergo operant conditioning. We are likely to repeat behaviors that have positive consequences and abandon behaviors that have negative consequences.

WHAT CAN WE LEARN FROM WATCHING OTHERS? p.111

- We can learn to perform certain actions by watching others performing those actions and imitating their actions ourselves. This technique is known as observational learning.

- Through observational learning, we can learn both aggressive and prosocial behaviors.

WHAT BRAIN PROCESSES TAKE PLACE WHEN WE LEARN? p.113

- When we learn, neurons fire and the synaptic connections between those neurons become stronger. This process is known as long-term potentiation.

- There are two types of memory consolidation: synaptic consolidation, which takes place hours after learning, and system consolidation, which takes place days or weeks after learning. Sleep helps us retain new information.

Test Your Understanding

1. When Abner gets an A on his spelling test, he receives a gold star and is congratulated by his teacher in front of his classmates. What learning process is his teacher using?

   a. conditioning
   b. intrinsic motivation
   c. performance
   d. extinction

2. Which of the following scenarios illustrates the learning-performance distinction?

   a. Drew stubs his toe walking up the stairs too quickly and cringes in pain. The next time he walks up the stairs he does so slowly.
   b. Sanjana calls both of her parents "baba" until she is four years old and begins to call her mother "maa."
   c. Atticus' babysitter gives him a snack if he sits quietly while watching afternoon cartoons. When she takes a vacation for a week, a new babysitter takes care of him. The first two days he sits quietly while watching cartoons, but does not get a snack. The rest of the week he plays with a toy truck and makes loud beeping and revving noises during the cartoons.
   d. Tom knows all of the correct answers to the questions on his history test. However, he answers several questions incorrectly because he was distracted when taking the test.

3. Andy feels happy when he plays guitar. He plays every day, although he is not playing in a band. When he plays guitar, Andy exhibits:

   a. extrinsic motivation.
   b. latent learning.
   c. intrinsic motivation.
   d. overjustification.

4. Last semester, Anita sat next to a cute classmate in her psychology class who always wore a specific cologne. Every time she saw this classmate, Anita involuntarily blushed. A month after the semester ended, Anita was walking past the aftershave counter at a store and smelled the cologne her classmate used. Without even realizing it, Anita began to blush. Antia's blushing in the store is an example of:

   a. a conditioned stimulus.
   b. a conditioned response.
   c. an unconditioned stimulus.
   d. an unconditioned response.

5. In the scenario for question 4, the smell of the cologne is an example of:

   a. a conditioned stimulus.
   b. a conditioned response.

c. an unconditioned stimulus.

d. an unconditioned response.

6. Suppose a researcher rang a bell and then, after 10 seconds, gave a mild electrical shock to a subject. After a few trials, the subject began to tense up following the bell. This is an example of:

a. trace conditioning.

b. delayed conditioning.

c. simultaneous conditioning.

d. backward conditioning.

7. In question 6, suppose that the researcher then paired the ringing of the bell with a red light. After several trials, the subject began to tense up when the red light turned on, even though the red light and the electric shock had never been presented together. This is an example of:

a. delayed conditioning.

b. second-order conditioning.

c. trace conditioning.

d. backward conditioning.

8. Georgia's cat scratches the carpet with his claws. In order to save her carpet, Georgia squirts her cat with a water gun every time he scratches. After a week, the cat is no longer scratching the carpet. This is an example of:

a. operant conditioning.

b. reinforcement.

c. classical conditioning.

d. delayed reinforcement.

9. In question 8, spraying the cat with the water gun is an example of:

a. negative reinforcement.

b. positive punishment.

c. negative punishment.

d. positive reinforcement.

10. Maggie wants to teach her dog to lie down. She says the words "lie down" and places her hand on the ground in front of him. When he lies down near her hand, she gives him a dog biscuit. She asks him to lie down five times in a row and gives him a dog biscuit each time he does. In this example, the dog biscuit is:

a. a secondary reinforcer.

b. a positive reinforcer.

c. a negative reinforcer.

d. an operant response.

11. Regarding question 10, if Maggie asks her dog to lie down and mostly gives him a dog biscuit every two or three times he lies down, she would be demonstrating:

a. partial reinforcement on a fixed-ratio schedule.

b. partial reinforcement on a variable-ratio schedule.

c. partial reinforcement on a variable-interval schedule.

d. continuous reinforcement.

12. Soo Jin is writing a book but has been finding it difficult to devote time to writing. She would prefer to go with her friends to some new restaurants that have opened recently. Soo Jin decides that each week, if she has written 40 pages by Friday, she will go to one of the restaurants with a friend. This is an example of:

a. a token economy.

b. a reward contrast effect.

c. the Premack principle.

d. shaping.

13. On a visit to an art museum, Anthony sees a young women standing in front of a painting he has never noticed before. After she leaves, Anthony spends several minutes appreciating this painting. This is likely an example of:

a. successive approximations.

b. operant conditioning.

c. stimulus enhancement.

d. prosocial modeling.

14. While she watches her mother get ready to go on a date, Shauna plays dress up and tries on a pair of her mother's high heels. What type of observational learning is Shauna demonstrating?

a. latent learning

b. goal enhancement

c. modeling

d. exploration

15. Regarding question 14, if Shauna goes to a friend's house and they try on high heels and makeup and pretend they work in an office, Shauna is demonstrating:

a. goal enhancement.

b. patrolling.

c. shaping.

d. play.

16. The theory that the activity of neurons in the hippocampus represents a mental map that helps people and animals navigate their surroundings is called:

a. the cognitive map theory.

b. the relational memory theory.

c. long-term potentiation.

d. system consolidation.

17. A place cell in the hippocampus of a rat fires most often when:

a. the rat receives a reward.

b. the rat is in a specific location within its cage.

c. another rat enters its territory.

d. system consolidation is occurring.

18. Long-term potentation is:

a. a mechanism for strengthening the connections between neurons.

b. part of the mass action principle.

c. a lasting form of brain damage.

d. the weakening of a neuronal synapse.

19. Which of the following is a defensive response?

a. freezing

b. long-term depression

c. modeling

d. partial reinforcement

20. According to some researchers, which of the following is involved in the learning of new behaviors through imitation?

a. place cells

b. the amygdala

c. the hippocampus

d. mirror neurons

Remember to check www.thethinkspot.com for additional information, downloadable flashcards, and other helpful resources.

MEMORY

HOW IS MEMORY ORGANIZED?

WHAT ARE THE CHARACTERISTICS OF SENSORY, WORKING, AND LONG-TERM MEMORY?

HOW ARE MEMORIES ENCODED, STORED, AND RETRIEVED?

WHAT ARE THE WEAKNESSES AND LIMITATIONS OF MEMORY?

Jill Price

knows exactly what she was doing on the day that Elvis died. She remembers what she had for dinner on October 2, 1984. She could tell you every last detail about the final episode of the popular TV show *Dallas*, which aired in 1991. Ask Price any mundane detail about her daily life since the age of 14, and she will be able to recall the answer without hesitation. Price, a 43-year-old widow from California, has a rare neurological condition: Unlike most people's memories, which fade over time, Price's memory is nearly perfect—she cannot forget anything.

For some people, this may sound like a gift. Who among us wouldn't want to remember where we left our car keys or recall in perfect detail a wonderful memory from the past? But imagine having to relive every argument, every painful rejection, and every excruciatingly embarrassing incident over and over again. It may frustrate us when we can't remember the name of an acquaintance at a party, but forgetting is an essential part of psychological health. Time heals no wounds for Price, who likens her daily life to a split-screen television—on one side she can see her present activities, while on the other runs a constant loop of memories. Given a particular date, Price can replay the day in her mind as though she is watching a video recording filmed from her point of view.

In 2000, Price contacted neuroscientist Professor James McGaugh at the University of California, Irvine. After five years of psychological, neurological, and physiological tests, he coined a new term for her condition: *hyperthymestic syndrome*, meaning "overdeveloped memory." In Price's case, the overdevelopment is specific to her own experiences—she has no special ability to memorize a series of numbers or a book of poetry, and her ability to remember facts not directly related to everyday life is only average.

McGaugh discovered that parts of Price's brain are three times the size of those in other women her age. The enlarged parts of her brain are areas also associated with obsessive compulsive disorder (OCD)—a condition that often involves collecting and hoarding. Could Price be hoarding memories the same way she hoards Beanie Babies and other memorabilia? Doctors are hoping that through further research, Price may assist Alzheimer's patients and others by helping to answer some of the most enduring questions in cognitive psychology: How do we retrieve memories? How do we make memories that last? How do we know when and what to forget?

<<< "Super memory" is both a gift and a curse for Jill Price. While the process of remembering is important, so is the process of forgetting. It's natural for us to forget what we had for breakfast yesterday, or mistakenly remember the name of a past kindergarten teacher. But why does our memory behave this way? Are there methods available to increase our ability to remember—or to forget?

CHAPTER 08

The Function of Memory

As Jill Price knows all too well the things that we remember—and forget—can have a significant impact on our lives. **Memory**, our brain's system for filing away new information and retrieving previously learned data, is important to us both when it succeeds and when it fails. The ability to create and access memories is an evolutionary advantage; in fact, it's often necessary for survival. (Imagine trying to survive in a world in which none of us could remember our names, our families, or where we'd left our groceries.) Memory is an essential human attribute, but it can also be a flawed one. In terms of accuracy, memory is not a videotape: It doesn't always present us with a clear, factually accurate account of events. Like a videotape, though, our memories can be edited, tampered with, or lost forever.

Memory is the brain's system for filing away new information and retrieving previously learned data.

Sensory memory is a type of memory lasting no more than a few seconds in which the impression of a sensory stimulus is stored.

Working memory is a type of memory in which information for short-term use is stored.

Long-term memory is a type of memory in which information that can last a lifetime is stored.

Encoding is the process by which sensory information is converted into a form that can be stored.

Storage is the process by which encoded information is placed into memory.

Retrieval is the process by which previously stored information is moved from long-term memory to working memory.

Forgetting is the inability to retrieve information that has been previously stored.

Sensory registers are the parts of the brain that make up sensory memory.

Visual cortex is the part of the brain that mediates the human sense of sight by encoding visual information.

Auditory cortex is the part of the brain that mediates the human sense of hearing by encoding auditory information.

Sensory cortex is the part of the brain that mediates the human sense of touch by encoding tactile information.

Frontal lobe is a part of the brain involved in the encoding and storage of working and long-term memory and, to a lesser extent, in sensory memory processing.

Iconic memory is a type of sensory memory involving visual stimuli.

● ● ○

How Is Memory Organized?

TYPES OF MEMORY

Not all memories are created equal. There are three basic types of memory: **sensory memory**, **working memory**, and **long-term memory**. Sensory memories last no more than a few seconds. However, we can retain information we store in our working, or short-term, memory for longer periods of time. Our long-term memories can last our entire lives. These three types of memory can be further divided into subtypes:

Types and Subtypes of Memory

∧
∧
∧ **The process of memory encoding, storage, and retrieval is similar to a filing system. What kinds of memories might be stored in each "drawer"?**

Our brains can store many different types of information in memory. (You might remember where you live, your friend's phone number, and the muscle movements required for rollerblading, to name only a few possibilities.) Some memories are lost quickly, while others are more permanent; some memories are formed and stored consciously, while others are created without your conscious knowledge. Each of your day-to-day experiences, remarkable or mundane, has the potential to be preserved in your mind as a memory. Whenever you find yourself remembering the sight of exploding fireworks or the moves to a dance you choreographed, take a minute to appreciate your brain's remarkable capacity to process myriad types of memorable information.

INFORMATION PROCESSING: THE BACKBONE OF HUMAN MEMORY

How do we put our observations and experiences into memory, and how do we get them out later? Think of your memory as your own personal administrative assistant: Just as an assistant organizes hundreds of files, puts them away in specific filing cabinets, and finds your stored files for you when you need them, your memory encodes information, stores it away, and retrieves it for later use. This process of **encoding**, **storage**, and **retrieval** is known as the information-processing model of memory.

Although our memory's information-processing techniques consist of three basic steps, the work of memory isn't quite as easy as one, two, three. Sometimes, memory follows a basic three-stage processing model (first proposed by Atkinson and Shiffrin):

1) When you experience an event, your senses collect information about the event and hold those details in sensory memory.

2) Some of the sensory information you've collected is then encoded and stored in working memory.

3) If you need to remember the information for more than a few seconds or minutes, it can go through a second encoding process and become stored in your long-

Memory Processing Model

Sensory input → Attention

Unconscious Processing

External events → Sensory memory → Working memory → Long-term memory

Encoding

Encoding

Retrieving

Forgetting | Forgetting | Forgetting

<<< This modified three-stage of memory, based on Atkinson and Shiffrin's 1968 model, illustrates the process through which external events are transformed into long-term memories.

term memory. (You can later retrieve stored information from long-term memory and bring it back into working memory.)

The Atkinson-Shiffrin model isn't quite complete, however. For example, you may not be able to retrieve information you've previously stored. You probably know this phenomenon better as **forgetting**. Additionally, recent research has suggested that not all memories pass through working memory before arriving at long-term storage. Sometimes, without our conscious knowledge, our brains skip over the first two stages of the model and deposit information directly into long-term memory. As a basic framework, though, the three-stage model can help us understand the functions of—and connections between—our three types of memory.

Sensory Memory

THE SENSORY REGISTERS

No matter what its specific content, a memory is the product of a sensory experience—a series of images, sounds, tastes, smells, and feelings. We constantly use our five senses to collect information about the world around us. This information is the raw material from which memories are formed. It is transmitted from the senses into the brain's **sensory registers**, which together make up sensory memory. Each sense has its own register for holding information. These registers are capable of containing a large amount of

data, but if we don't pay attention to the information in our sensory registers, it disappears in less than a second.

SENSORY MEMORY AND THE BRAIN

We can think about sensory memory in a more concrete

way by taking a look at the human brain. Certain areas of the brain are active during the creation of sensory memory. These areas—the **visual cortex**, the **auditory cortex**, and the **sensory cortex**—receive input from the senses. When you listen to the radio, your auditory cortex is actively encoding the music you hear; when you look at a photograph, your visual cortex is hard at work processing the image. In short, when your senses encounter a stimulus, the corresponding sensory area of the brain processes that stimulus. While the **frontal lobe** plays a more prominent role in the encoding and storage of working and long-term memory, it is also involved to some extent in sensory memory processing.

ICONIC AND ECHOIC MEMORY

You've probably heard of "photographic memory," or the ability to accurately remember every detail in an image after looking at it for a short time. While research suggests that true photographic memory does not exist (not even for Jill Price), most people have the ability to recall exact images for very brief periods of time (a few tenths of a second). This ability is facilitated by a form of sensory memory called **iconic memory**. Research by George Sperling (1960) demonstrated that our visual registers are able to store accurate representations of images. Almost immediately, however,

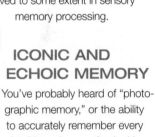

Somatosensory cortex

Auditory cortex

Frontal lobe

Visual cortex

∧∧∧ The visual cortex, the auditory cortex, the sensory cortex, and the frontal lobe all play a part in the processing of sensory memory.

Eidetic memory is the ability to recall detailed images vividly after looking at them for a short period of time.

Echoic memory is a type of sensory memory involving auditory stimuli.

Attention is the act of applying the mind to a sense or thought.

Conscious encoding s a process of encoding that involves paying specific attention to the information to be remembered.

Unconscious encoding is a process of encoding that does not involve any deliberate thought or action.

Visual encoding is the process of encoding images.

Auditory encoding is the process of encoding sounds.

Semantic encoding is the process of encoding meaning.

Chunking is the process of organizing large pieces of information into smaller pieces, or chunks.

Rote rehearsal is the process of repeating information, either out loud or silently, with the intent of learning that information.

these images are replaced by new images, so our "photographic memories" have severely limited life spans.

If photographic memory is a myth, then what's **eidetic memory**? A handful of people, known as "eidetikers," have the ability to recall detailed images vividly after looking at them for a short time (about 30 seconds in some experiments). As they describe the image they have just seen, eidetikers' eyes move as though they are looking at the image itself, suggesting that they are "seeing" their memories. According to psychologist Alan Searleman, however, eidetic memory isn't truly photographic: Eidetikers sometimes make errors, and unlike photographs, their vivid memories last only for a few minutes.

The other sensory register about which scientists have the most information is the auditory register. Our ability to briefly and accurately remember sounds is called **echoic memory**. Like iconic memory, echoic memory comes and goes quickly: If we are not paying attention to a sound, we are able to recall it

from our echoic memory only for the next three or four seconds before it disappears.

Working Memory

ENCODING INTO WORKING MEMORY

Attention

While most memories in the sensory registers are quickly overwritten, some of these memories are retained, encoded, and stored in working memory. But how do we determine which memories to store and which to discard?

The answer is **attention**. At any given moment, we are processing dozens of images, sounds, and other sensory information from our environment, but we're not paying attention to all of these sensory memories. When a sensation grabs our attention, however, we're likely to pay attention to it and transfer it to our working memory. This is particularly true for highly interesting or unusual events. For example, if you're asked to imagine and remember a bright pink chicken, this bizarre image is likely to capture your attention. Attention also takes center stage in the cocktail party effect mentioned in Chapter 5. When you're in a room full of laughing, chatting people, you're able to tune out the background chatter and pay attention only to the people who are talking to

you. You'll also probably notice if someone across the room says your name—it grabs your attention. Attention allows us to extract meaningful information from a background of sensory "noise."

Conscious and Unconscious Encoding

Information can be encoded for storage in working memory both consciously and unconsciously. **Conscious encoding**, also called effortful processing, requires paying explicit attention to the information to be remembered. This strategy is particularly useful when we need to remember novel information. When you meet a new acquaintance, for example, you have to pay attention to her name (and maybe repeat it silently to yourself once or twice) in order to remember that she's "Lara," not "Laura."

Unconscious encoding, also called automatic processing, refers to the fact that we often pay attention to certain things without being consciously aware that we are doing so. If someone asks you where you were at 6 p.m., you can say, "I was at dinner," even though it's unlikely that you took a few seconds at 6 p.m. to note and explicitly memorize your location. You're using automatic processing even as you read this paragraph: You can store the last few words you read in your working memory without even thinking about it.

Working Memory and the Frontal Lobe

Several areas of the brain contribute to the encoding and storage of working memory, but the frontal lobe presides over the process. Research has found that the frontal lobe becomes activated during challenging working-memory tasks. Furthermore, patients with damaged frontal lobes have difficulty performing a variety of memory tasks. These findings highlight the connection between the frontal lobe and the working memory process. While the frontal lobe is important to working memory, however, other areas of the brain may chip in as well, depending on the

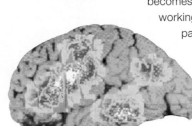

∧ ∧ **Different sensory stimuli activate different**
∧ ∧ **areas of the brain.**

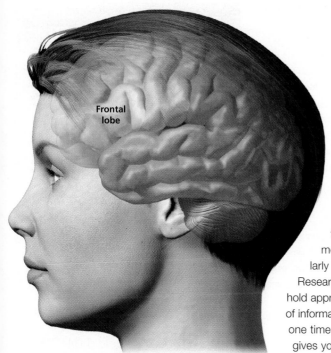

Frontal lobe

type of information being processed. Neuroimaging studies suggest that often one type of knowledge is stored across several different lobes in the brain; no one area is responsible for maintaining all of our working memories (Gabrieli, 1998).

What Do We Encode? Images, Sounds, and Meanings

The way in which our brains encode information depends on the type of information being processed. **Visual encoding** is the encoding of images, **auditory encoding** is the encoding of sounds, and **semantic encoding** is the encoding of meaning. Some pieces of information can be encoded in multiple ways: If you look at a pie chart that shows the results of a political poll, you can encode it both visually (by remembering what it looks like) and semantically (by thinking about what the poll results mean for each candidate).

Although we are capable of encoding images, sounds, and meanings, not all types of encoding are equally effective. In general, we find it easier to remember information that means something to us. A 20-letter sentence in a textbook, for example, is much easier for us to remember than a random, meaningless string of 20 letters. Experiments investigating the three types of encoding have demonstrated that semantically encoded information is likely to be retained longer than is information processed through visual or auditory encoding (Craik & Tulving, 1975).

STORAGE IN WORKING MEMORY

Although information remains in working memory longer than it can be held in the sensory registers, working memory does not have a particularly large capacity for storage. Research has found that people can hold approximately seven different pieces of information in working memory at any one time (Miller, 1956). If someone gives you a number that's seven digits long, you will most likely be able to remember all seven numbers for a short time, though it might be difficult to do so. If you need to remember a longer number, however, you may need to use a strategy for storing that number in your working memory.

Organization and Rehearsal

If we can hold only seven pieces of information in our working memory at one time, how are we able to remember ten-digit phone numbers? Why is 617-555-8342 easier to remember than 6175558342? Chalk it up to **chunking**. By organizing pieces of information into chunks, we can store more of that information in working memory. The phone number above consists of ten digits, but the digits are divided into three chunks, giving working memory only three pieces of information to store instead of ten. This strategy works only up to a point, however: The larger each chunk gets, the fewer chunks working memory can store.

We can use organizational strategies to remember things other than

numbers, of course. Words that are organized into categories, for example, are easier to remember than words listed in a random order (Bower et al., 1969).

Left untended, information is stored in working memory for only a few seconds. Through **rote rehearsal**, however, we can increase the length of time that information lingers in working memory. Rote rehearsal, also known as maintenance rehearsal, is the process of repeating information, either out loud or silently, with the intent of learning that information. When you "cram" for an exam, for example, you might use rote rehearsal to keep a long list of dates, facts, and historical figures in your memory. The intent to learn plays a large role here: If you repeat something over and over but are not paying attention to the information you are repeating, that information won't get stored in working memory (Nickerson & Adams, 1979). Rote rehearsal alone can't cause memories to last for years—when your exam is over, you probably won't be able to remember the material you memorized by "cramming"—but it is an effective strategy for keeping information in working memory for longer than a few seconds.

2008 U.S. Election Results

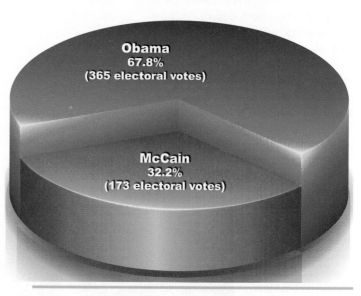

Obama
67.8%
(365 electoral votes)

McCain
32.2%
(173 electoral votes)

∧
∧ How would you encode this pie
∧ chart visually? How would you
encode it semantically?

Recency effect is the ability to recall information most recently stored when given a list of things to remember.

Primacy effect is the ability to recall information given first when given a list of things to remember.

Serial position effect is the ability to recall (or not recall) information in a list depending on that information's position in the list.

Pseudoforgetting is a a type of encoding interference in which information is never actually stored because of some kind of attention interference.

Cued forgetting is a type of forgetting in which a person is specifically told to forget certain information.

Explicit memories are memories of which a person is consciously aware.

Implicit memories are memories of which a person is not consciously aware.

Semantic means "containing factual and conceptual information that is not directly linked to life events."

Episodic memories are memories in which a person remembers an entire sequence of events.

Priming is the process of activating associations in memory just before starting a certain task.

RETRIEVAL FROM WORKING MEMORY

It's easy enough to store information in working memory, but what happens when you need to get that information back out? In general, items stored in working memory are fairly easy for us to retrieve. This is illustrated by the **recency effect**: When given a list of items to remember, we will be able to remember the last few items on the list without much difficulty. Since they were presented most recently, they are still in our working memory. We also won't have much trouble remembering the *first* few items on the list, thanks to the **primacy effect**: Since we had a lot of time to rehearse those first items, they have benefited the most from rote rehearsal and may have already moved into long-term memory. The items in the middle of the list are hardest to recall because they are no longer stored in working memory, but we didn't have the opportunity to rehearse them or move them to long-term memory. The middle items probably also suffered from a lack of attention: Since we were busy rehearsing the first few items on the list, we probably didn't

pay as much attention to the items that came after them. Our ability to recall (or not recall) items depending on their position in a list is known as the **serial position effect**.

While our long-term memories can sometimes seem almost impossible to retrieve, this isn't the case when it comes to working memory. For the short time during which memories are stored in working memory, they are "at the ready": We don't have to rack our brains or dig through metaphorical layers of sludge in order to retrieve them.

FORGETTING

Although our memories are easily accessible when they're in working memory, they're also easily lost. Working memory is limited not only in capacity but also in duration: Without rehearsal, information can be stored in working memory for about 15 or 20 seconds. Over a very short time, information in working memory decays until it's been forgotten altogether.

Interference with Encoding

When the encoding process does its job well, information from the sensory registers is stored in working memory. But what happens when something interferes with the encoding process? One cause of forgetting is ineffective or interrupted encoding of information (Brown & Craik, 2000). Say, for instance, that your friend is trying to tell you about his weekend plans while you're trying to read a novel. In psychological terms, your friend's story is interfering with your attention to your book. Since you're not really paying attention to your book, you'll probably find it hard to remember what you just read. Assuming you manage to encode any information from the book at all, you may be engaging in visual or auditory encoding rather than semantic encoding—you're processing the words themselves but not their meanings. Since these types of encoding aren't as effective as semantic encoding, you're more likely to forget the information you encoded.

It's possible, too, that while you think you're encoding information as you attempt to read, your

attention has been interfered with to the point that you're not actually storing any information in working memory at all. When you go to retrieve your memories and find them missing, it may be because they were never encoded into working memory in the first place. Technically, this isn't an example of forgetting information—it's impossible to forget something you never really knew. Rather, this type of encoding interference is called **pseudoforgetting**.

If, however, you're paying reasonably close attention to your book, you'll probably remember most of what you read. Do you remember which brightly colored animal was described a few pages ago?

Cued Forgetting

Some types of forgetting are intentional. If we don't intend to remember information, we usually have no trouble removing that information from working memory. **Cued forgetting** is one example of this process. Participants in cued

<<< What information might a blackjack player store in his or her working memory?

>>> The skills and movements necessary for riding a bicycle are stored in our brains as procedural memories.

forgetting studies are given information to study and told to remember some of that information and forget the rest. This instruction to forget is, generally speaking, quite effective: Participants do not remember the information that they are told to forget. Children, however, have more difficulty forgetting the "forget-cued" information than adults do, suggesting that as we grow older, we become more able to control (and inhibit) our own encoding processes (Cruz et al., 2003). A real-world example of this phenomenon is the experience of calling information for a phone number. Once the number is dialed and you hear the phone ringing, you might be cued to forget the number that the operator gave you.

While many of our memories are forgotten only seconds after they're formed, not all memories meet a tragic fate at the hands of forgetting. Some information is stored so effectively in working memory that it is transferred to a more secure place: long-term memory.

Long-Term Memory

ORGANIZATION OF LONG-TERM MEMORY

Memories that stay with us manifest themselves in two forms: explicit memories and implicit memories. You might explicitly remember the day you graduated from high school, but your implicit memories—such as a feeling of comfort, triggered by the smell of a cooking spice your grandmother used—are equally as important.

Explicit memories are memories of which we are consciously aware: We remember certain facts or experiences, and we are able to state that we remember these things. We are not consciously aware, however, of our **implicit memories**. When we remember information implicitly, that information is retained in our minds, but we are not necessarily aware that we have remembered it.

Explicit Memories

Some explicit memories are **semantic**—that is, they contain factual and conceptual information that is not directly linked to life events. If you bought a dozen pizzas for a party, how many pizzas did you buy? When you answered "12," you accessed a semantic memory: The word *dozen* means "12." This information is an example of one of the vast number of semantic facts stored in your long-term memory.

Often, though, we don't just remember bare-bones facts; we remember entire sequences of events, or episodes, as **episodic memories**. When you think about the process of solving a long division problem, you're accessing an episodic memory, or a specific sequence of events. Many episodic memories are autobiographical. If, for instance, you and your friends got unabashedly lost on the way to pick up your dozen pizzas, arriving at the pizza place so late that the party was already over and you had to eat most of the slices yourself, you would probably have a vivid personal memory

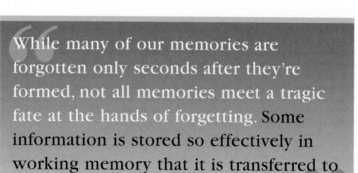

" While many of our memories are forgotten only seconds after they're formed, not all memories meet a tragic fate at the hands of forgetting. Some information is stored so effectively in working memory that it is transferred to a more secure place: long-term memory "

of this experience. Jill Price's "super memory" is mostly autobiographical, as she tests average for memorizing things not directly related to life events. This isn't surprising—since many autobiographical memories are particularly emotionally salient, they are often easier

for us to recall than episodic or semantic memories to which no particular emotion is attached. (We'll talk about the link between emotion and memory later in the chapter.)

Implicit Memories

Claiming that explicit memories exist is hardly controversial. After all, we are conscious of our memories of certain facts and events. But if we're not conscious of our own implicit memories, how do we know that implicit memories exist at all? Some evidence for the existence of implicit memory comes from the phenomenon of **priming**. In psychological studies, researchers prime subjects by presenting them with a stimulus (usually very quickly) before asking the subjects to complete a task. The stimulus is designed to activate certain unconscious associations in the subjects' minds. In their seminal research on priming and implicit memory, Graf and Schacter (1985) primed subjects with a list of words. Later, they gave the subjects several unfinished words and asked the subjects to complete the words. The results of the study

<<< Friend or foe? Your emotional reaction to this clown may be influenced by conditioning.

suggested that people who see the word *trees* on a list, for example, are likely to complete the word *tre___* as *trees*, even if they don't remember seeing *trees* on the original list. In other words, the priming process can form implicit memories.

One type of implicit memory, **procedural memory**, consists of habits and skills that we perform. Riding a bike and playing a musical instrument are both examples of procedural memory. Both of these skills take time and practice to learn, but once they're learned, they are stored in long-term memory, and we don't need to consciously access them. Additionally, in this case, the appearance of the behavior serves as evidence of the memory.

Other implicit memories are formed through **conditioning**. For example, let's say that you're scared of clowns: After watching a few horror movies featuring creepy supervillains decked out in red noses and floppy shoes (not to mention that harrowing trip to the circus when you were a kid), you've started to associate the sight of clowns with feelings of fear. The next time you see a real clown, you'll feel fearful, although you might not be aware of the source of your fear. There may be nothing inherently scary about a clown, but your implicit memories inform you that when a clown comes along, a scary situation won't be far behind.

How can you cure that fear of clowns? One way might be to start spending a lot of time in a tiny car with a few face-painted friends. Though it sounds paradoxical, this process is known as **habituation**. When a person is repeatedly exposed to a stimulus (such as a clown) over a period of time, the person's response to that stimulus eventually decreases over time. If you spend time with clowns that don't cause you to feel afraid, you may become habituated to their presence. Your implicit memories of clowns will cause you to feel calm around them rather than fearful. This result is an example of **extinction**: When we have become completely habituated to a stimulus, our original conditioned response to that stimulus diminishes.

ENCODING INTO LONG-TERM MEMORY

Just as information can be encoded into working memory both consciously and unconsciously, there are both conscious and unconscious processes for encoding long-term memories. Not all information passes through working memory before being stored in long-term memory. For example,

Which of these emotional events have you captured as flashbulb memories?

V V
V

September 11 2001
Al-Qaeda carries out terrorist attacks in the United States.

March 20 2003
Iraq War begins.

August 29 2005
Hurricane Katrina makes landfall in Louisiana.

April 16 2007
32 people are killed by a gunman at Virginia Tech.

December 27 2007
Benazir Bhutto is assassinated in Pakistan.

May 12 2008
Major earthquake strikes Sichuan Province, China.

January 20 2009
Democratic senator Barack Obama becomes the first black president in United States history.

particularly emotional events can become immediately seared into long-term memory as **flashbulb memories**. Flashbulb memories can be shared by many people, or they can be highly personal. Many people point to the terrorist attacks of September 11, 2001, as an example of a powerful, emotional event that most Americans remember vividly. You may also have a vivid memory of your first kiss, which was a highly unique and personally relevant event. Other (less dramatic) events and skills can also be encoded unconsciously into long-term memory.

If we could unconsciously store all the information we needed to remember in long-term memory, our lives might be a lot simpler. Some memories, however, need our conscious help in order to stick. Rote rehearsal can be useful for transferring information from working memory to long-term memory, but a much more effective strategy is **elaborative rehearsal**. When we elaborate, we give meaning to the information we want to memorize (even if the information itself is fairly meaningless). We also make connections between the new information and information that we already remember. This form of semantic encoding is particularly useful for getting information into long-term memory. If you wanted to memorize the first several digits of pi, rather than using rote rehearsal to repeat 3.14159265 over and over again, you could use elaborative rehearsal to attach meaning to the digits (your area code is 314; the year 1592 marked the hundredth anniversary of Christopher Columbus's voyage; your favorite aunt is 65 years old).

If your very educated mother has ever served you nine pizzas, you are probably familiar with **mnemonics**. Mnemonic devices are memory aids that give rhyme and reason to lists or other pieces of information. For example, before Pluto lost its planetary status, the phrase

My Very **E**ducated **M**other **J**ust **S**erved **U**s **N**ine **P**izzas was used to help students remember the order of the planets in the solar system. The first letter of each word in the phrase corresponds to the first letter of each planet's name (**M**ercury, **V**enus, **E**arth, etc.). Other mnemonics are short rhyming poems or memorable phrases. By arranging information in a meaningful order or a memorable context, we can help ourselves remember that information for years instead of seconds.

STORAGE IN LONG-TERM MEMORY

Levels of Processing

How long, exactly, is "long-term"? In other words, how long can we store information in our long-term memories? If we're lucky, some of our long-term memories can last our whole lives. We have the capacity to store vast amounts of information in long-term memory. However, the life span of any individual memory often depends on the way in which that memory has been encoded. Craik and Tulving reached this conclusion in a 1975 study in which they flashed words at people and asked people to think about the words' appearance (visual encoding), sound (auditory encoding), or meaning (semantic encoding). The researchers found that later, many people did not recognize the words they had encoded visually. Slightly more than half recognized acoustically encoded words, but nearly 90 percent recognized the words they'd encoded semantically.

Procedural memory is a type of implicit memory consisting of habits and skills people perform.

Conditioning is a process in which an implicit memory forms because of repeated exposure to a certain stimulus that causes a reaction in a person.

Habituation is a process in which repeated exposure to a stimulus reduces the response to that stimulus.

Extinction is the diminishing of a conditioned response, most often through the removal of the reinforcement associated with the response.

Flashbulb memories are memories that are immediately stored in long-term memory and that are caused by emotional events.

Elaborative rehearsal is a process in which a person gives meaning to information for the purpose of storing that information in long-term memory.

Mnemonics are memory aids that give rhyme and reason to lists or other pieces of information.

Shallow processing is a level of processing in which a word's sound or appearance is encoded.

Deep processing is a level of processing in which a word's meaning is encoded.

Hippocampus is a part of the brain involved in processing explicit memories, recognizing and recalling long-term memories, and conditioning.

These results led Craik and Tulving to propose that there are different levels of processing, and that **shallow processing** (encoding a word's sound or appearance) is not as effective for memory storage as **deep processing** (encoding a word's meaning).

Long-Term Memory Storage and the Brain

If you took a journey through the brain in search of a central long-term memory processing and storage center, you'd be searching for a long time. No single area of the brain is in charge of processing and storing long-term memories. A few areas, however, have been recognized as particularly crucial to memory formation.

Explicit and implicit long-term memories don't just seem different to us; they're actually processed in different areas of the brain. The **hippocampus** is largely responsible for processing our explicit memories, and it is assisted in memory formation by some areas of the frontal lobe. After semantic, episodic, and autobiographical memories are formed in the hippocampus, they are sent to other regions of

Basal ganglia (a group of nuclei located in both hemispheres, on either side of the corpus callosum and thalamus)

Frontal Lobe

Cerebellum

Hippocampus

>>> The hippocampus and frontal lobe process explicit memories, while the cerebellum and basal ganglia contribute to the creation of implicit memories.

the brain for storage. The hippocampus is also pivotal to the recognition and recall of long-term memories: People and animals with hippocampus damage struggle to remember explicit memories (Sherry & Vaccarino, 1989; Schacter, 1996).

If you want to boost your brain's memory storage, you might be wise to get some sleep. Several recent studies have suggested an exciting—and controversial—link between sleep and memory. For example, studies at M.I.T. revealed hippocampus activity in the brains of sleeping rats. Rather than suggesting rodent dreams, the rats' hippocampus activity was identical to the activity that occurred when those rats ran a maze during their waking hours. These results suggest that rats (and humans) replay daily events during sleep, strengthening the events' storage in memory.

In a study that supports these findings, researchers at Harvard found that people who sleep after studying images of Easter eggs remember the eggs' positions better than those who remain awake do. While we don't know everything about the link between sleep and memory, it seems likely that our brains remain focused on the task of processing and storing memories even when we're fast asleep.

Where are implicit memories processed and stored? Three regions of the brain—the hippocampus, the **cerebellum**, and the **basal ganglia**—play large roles in the formation and storage of implicit long-term memories. The hippocampus and cerebellum are essential for

successful conditioning, one process through which implicit memories are formed. Because both the cerebellum and the basal ganglia are linked to the development of motor skills, they are necessary for the formation of procedural memories and habits related to movement. The basal ganglia and the cerebellum may be linked to different types of motor skills, but patients with damage to either area have difficulty creating new procedural memories (Gabrieli, 1998).

Many parts of the brain are involved in long-term memory storage, but a significant amount of recent research has focused particularly on the **synapses** (the areas between neurons across which nerve impulses travel from one neuron to the next, as described in Chapter 3). When we learn, neurotransmitters travel across the synapses associated with the information we're learning. Each time we review that information, those specific neural connections are strengthened, and it becomes easier for neurotransmitters to travel across those certain synapses. In 1949, psychologist Donald Hebb theorized that a relationship existed between these strong neural connections and the creation and maintenance of memories. When Hebb's theory was confirmed in the 1970s, scientists dubbed this strengthening of neural connections **long-term potentiation (LTP)**. As Hebb suggested, LTP is a biological basis for memory: When memories form strong neural connections, we remember those memories more easily.

RETRIEVAL FROM LONG-TERM MEMORY

Recognition or Recall?

When you retrieve information from memory, you either recall it or recognize it. What's the difference between **recognition** and

recall? Say you're given a list of breakfast foods and asked to circle the foods you ate for breakfast that day. This exercise is an example of recognition: You are matching an external stimulus (a word on the list) to a stored memory (the contents of your breakfast). If, however, you're given a blank sheet of paper and asked to write down what you ate for breakfast, you are engaging in recall. You have no external cues or stimuli on which you can rely as you retrieve your breakfast memories.

Retrieval Cues

Assigned classroom seating: terrific or torturous? As it turns out, the monotony of having an assigned seat may be outweighed by the stellar grades you receive on the final exam—as long as you take that exam in that same assigned seat. When you encode information in a specific context, you are likely to find it easier to retrieve that information in the same context. So if you sit in one seat for every lecture and return to that seat for the exam, you will have an advantage when it comes to remembering the information you learned during those lectures. This **context effect** is one kind of **retrieval cue**—a stimulus that helps us retrieve information from memory. Like labels on the "file folders" in which your memories are stored, the pieces of information that you associate with a memory can help you access that memory later. Take the phenomenon of **state-dependent memory**, for example: If you learn something in one state (when you're deeply in love, scared to death, or just plain happy), you'll probably be able to recall that information more easily when you're in a similar state.

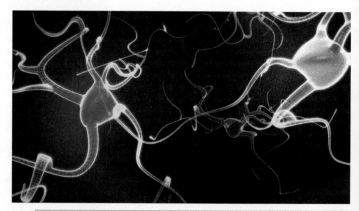

∧
∧
∧ **Connections between neurons serve as a biological basis for memory.**

RETRIEVAL FAILURE: FORGETTING

Despite our best efforts, not all information that we store in long-term memory can be retrieved. Do the memories that we forget disappear from our brains entirely? Or is the problem just that we can't figure out how to find the memories we've stashed away? In many cases, retrieval failure, or forgetting, occurs in long-term memory not because our memories have been "thrown away" or overwritten but because we are unable to access them.

Interference

Most of us have forgotten more than a handful of e-mail passwords, computer logons, and PINs in our lives. Maybe you just changed your e-mail password, and although you can't remember what your new password is, you have no trouble remembering the old one. This phenomenon is known as **proactive interference**, and it occurs when previously learned information interferes with your ability to recall new information. Conversely, maybe it's been a while since you've changed your password, and now that you've gotten used to the new code, you no longer remember what your old code was. This is an example of **retroactive interference**, which occurs when new information causes you to forget older memories.

Storage Decay

Interference isn't the only thing that causes us to forget the things we've learned. In 1885, German psychologist Hermann Ebbinghaus memorized a list of nonsense syllables and measured how many of those syllables he could recall over the next 30 days. His results, described graphically as the **forgetting curve**, suggest that we are quick to forget most things that we learn. After a few days, however, our rate of forgetting levels off: If we haven't forgotten something after 3 or 4 days, we're likely to remember it after 30 days as well. Ebbinghaus's findings have contributed to

the theory of forgetting known as **storage decay**. Simply put, many of our memories, like paintings or photographs, fade over time.

Memory Mishaps

When memory functions well, it's an invaluable resource. When things go wrong, however, the consequences can range from irritating (forgetting where you left your cell phone) to devastating (being haunted, as Jill Price is, by recurring memories). How do these memory mishaps occur?

EMOTION, STRESS, AND MEMORY

As the phenomenon of flashbulb memories illustrates, it's often very easy for us to remember emotional or stressful events. Arousal from heightened emotion or stress can facilitate the storage of information in long-term memory, while weaker emotions tend to create weaker memories. But stress isn't always so beneficial to the functions of memory: If you become too emotional or stressed, your capacity to recall information actually decreases. For example, if a traumatic event causes you to panic, you may go into a state of **hypervigilance**, in which your "fight or flight" response kicks into full gear. While a state of vigilance can actually facilitate memory storage and recovery, *hyper*vigilance tends to impair memory. This relationship is one incarnation of the **Yerkes-Dodson law**, which states in general that performance peaks with a moderate level of arousal (Yerkes & Dodson, 1908).

AMNESIA

"According to Hollywood," writes neuropsychologist Sallie Baxendale, "[amnesia] is something of an occupational hazard for professional assassins." Baxendale is referring to *The Bourne Identity* and other popular movies that, although they feature characters who struggle from various forms of memory loss, hardly ever present an accurate picture of

Proactive interference is a phenomenon in which previously learned information interferes with a person's ability to recall new information.

Retroactive interference is a phenomenon in which new information interferes with a person's ability to recall previously learned information.

Forgetting curve is a graphical representation of how quickly a person tends to forget information.

Storage decay is a phenomenon in which many of a person's memories fade over time.

Hypervigilance is a state in which a person's "fight or flight" response is fully activated.

Yerkes-Dodson law states in general that performance peaks with a moderate level of arousal.

Retrograde amnesia is memory loss characterized by the loss of past memories.

Anterograde amnesia is memory loss characterized by an inability to form new long-term memories.

Source amnesia is a phenomenon in which a person remembers information but forgets or misremembers where that information came from.

amnesia. Outside the borders of the silver screen, there are two distinct types of amnesia: **retrograde amnesia** and **anterograde amnesia**. Retrograde amnesia is characterized by the loss of past memories (usually memories formed before the time of the injury). Anterograde amnesia, in contrast, affects the future: Although people with anterograde amnesia can remember events from their past, they struggle to create new long-term memories. (Baxendale points to the 2000 movie *Memento* as a fairly accurate representation of anterograde amnesia.)

Both types of amnesia are linked to brain damage, which is often caused by accident, surgery, or illness. The type of amnesia a patient develops depends on the affected area of the brain: A patient with a disease like dementia that affects the whole brain (particularly the hippocampus) may show signs of retrograde amnesia, while someone who sustains frontal lobe injuries in a car accident will have difficulty encoding memories and may suffer from anterograde amnesia. The famous patient H. M. developed anterograde amnesia in 1953 when doctors removed his temporal lobes in an attempt to cure his severe epilepsy. H. M. could no longer create new long-term memories, but his working memory remained functional, as did many of his procedural memories. Although H. M. never knew it, his case was instrumental in leading scientists to research the biological connections between memory, memory loss, and the brain.

The 7 Seven Sins of MEMORY

Things to do today...
1.
2.
3.

In 1999, psychologist and memory expert Daniel Schacter put forth a description of the memory foibles that he calls the "seven sins of memory." Schacter explains that three of the sins are "sins of omission" that cause us to forget information. The other four are "sins of commission" that cause the memories we retrieve to be inaccurate or intrusive.

>>>

Three sins of forgetting:
absent-mindedness, transience, blocking

Three sins of distortion:
misattribution, suggestibility, bias

One sin of intrusion:
persistence

Three Sins of Forgetting

1   **Absent-mindedness.** As sins go, misplacing your sunglasses isn't so terrible. But it's caused by absent-mindedness, which occurs when we don't pay attention to what we're doing. This lack of attention results in a failure to encode information into working memory. (Schacter notes that in an impressive display of absent-mindedness, one musician left a priceless Stradivarius violin on the roof of his car and drove off.) Professors are also famous for this sin.

2   **Transience.** Most of our memories are not permanent; they fade over time. Schacter's second sin is tied to the concept of storage decay.

3   **Blocking.** Retrieval failure keeps us from accessing stored memories. If you've ever felt like the answer to a question was right on the tip of your tongue, but you couldn't quite remember it, you've experienced blocking.

Three Sins of Distortion

4 **Misattribution.** When we misattribute a memory, we may remember some parts of an event accurately but misremember their context. If you remember a joke your sister told you on the phone but think your roommate told you the joke at dinner, your memory has committed the sin of misattribution. This phenomenon is more specifically known as **source amnesia**. We remember information, but we forget or misremember its source.

5 **Suggestibility.** This fifth memory sin is one of the major causes of Sheri Storm's "brain stains." After Storm's psychiatrist suggested that she had endured traumatic experiences as a child, Storm began to create memories of these experiences. The brain has no filter for determining which memories are truly autobiographical and which are not; furthermore, it can be extremely prone to suggestion. Elizabeth Loftus, who researches false memories, performed a study in which participants were shown a film of a car accident. She then asked some of the participants how fast the cars were going when they "hit each other," and she asked other participants how fast the cars were going when they "smashed into each other." The participants who heard the word *smashed* reported that the cars were traveling faster than did participants who heard the word *hit* (Loftus & Palmer, 1974). By simply changing the phrasing of the question, Loftus implanted, or *suggested*, to the participants that the accident had taken place at higher ("smashed") or lower ("hit") rates of speed, when in fact that information was never explicitly given. Our memories can be tweaked, and false memories can be implanted, with only a few simple words and the power of suggestion.

6 **Bias.** Our memories reflect and support our personal biases, sometimes at the expense of accuracy. Say, for example, that you are an outspoken advocate of environmentalism. Although you've only recently realized the importance of being eco-friendly, you believe strongly in doing what you can to help the planet. Because your beliefs color your memories, you might remember recycling on a constant basis for the past five years, even if, in reality, you started recycling regularly only a year ago.

One Sin of Intrusion

7 **Persistence.** Both genuine and false memories can commit the sin of persistence. Often, these memories are painful, emotional, or disturbing. A soldier returning home from a tour in Iraq or Afghanistan with posttraumatic stress disorder, or PTSD, may experience vivid flashbacks of his or her wartime experiences. These memories cannot be brushed aside, and they can interfere significantly with day-to-day activities. People who struggle with PTSD must deal constantly with extremely vivid and painful memories they'd rather not remember at all.

> *"Our memories reflect and support our personal biases, sometimes at the expense of accuracy."*

Memory is critical to life as we know it, but the many benefits of memory are countered in part by the fact that memories are not always trustworthy. The Seven Sins of Memory illustrate memory's quirks, imperfections, and pitfalls, and they serve as a reminder that the world we perceive and the "real" world are not always one and the same.

Summary

HOW IS MEMORY ORGANIZED? p. 120

- There are three different types of memory: sensory memory, working memory, and long-term memory.
- According to the information-processing model, our brains encode information, store it as a memory, and retrieve it when we need to remember it.

WHAT ARE THE CHARACTERISTICS OF SENSORY, WORKING, AND LONG-TERM MEMORY? p. 121

- Sensory memory consists of sights, sounds, smells, and other information that the senses transmit to the corresponding sensory cortices in the brain. Sensory memories last for no more than a few seconds.
- Working memory contains memories that we can access immediately. Images, sounds, and meanings can all be encoded in working memory.
- Long-term memory includes both implicit and explicit memories. Meaningful or emotional information is often encoded into long-term memory. Long-term memories can last a lifetime but can be difficult to retrieve.

HOW ARE MEMORIES ENCODED, STORED, AND RETRIEVED? p. 122

- Attention enables us to consciously or unconsciously encode memories.
- We use rehearsal, mnemonics, and other organizational strategies to store memories.
- The frontal lobe, hippocampus, basal ganglia, and cerebellum are active in memory encoding and storage.
- Retrieval cues such as the context effect help us move long-term memories into working memory, where stored information is "at the ready."

WHAT ARE THE WEAKNESSES AND LIMITATIONS OF MEMORY? p. 129

- Stress can inhibit memory storage and recall.
- Brain damage can lead to retrograde and anterograde amnesia.
- Memories are easily forgotten and prone to distortion, and they can persist even when we try to forget them.

Test Your Understanding

1. Hannah can recall a vast amount of details in a painting she saw briefly at an exhibit, and describes it to her friends a minute later as if she is looking at it. Hannah is demonstrating:

   a. iconic memory.
   b. conscious encoding.
   c. eidetic memory.
   d. echoic memory.

2. Which of the following activities would rely the most on working memory?

   a. recalling your last birthday party
   b. writing long-hand during a test
   c. remembering two numbers while you calculate their sum in your head
   d. recalling your e-mail address

3. Which of the following is NOT a type of long-term memory?

   a. iconic memory
   b. implicit memory
   c. procedural memory
   d. semantic memory

4. Damage to which of the following areas of the brain would NOT be likely to result in the inability to process echoic memory?

   a. the auditory cortex
   b. the visual cortex
   c. the frontal lobe
   d. both B and C

5. Which of the following would make it likely that a memory is encoded into working memory from sensory memory?

   a. priming
   b. chunking
   c. paying attention to the thing being remembered
   d. rote rehearsal

6. Approximately how many items of information can be held in working memory at any given time?

   a. 5
   b. 7
   c. 20
   d. the storage capacity of working memory is unlimited

7. Patricia gets the phone number of a cute guy she meets at the store, but has no way to write the number down. What technique can she use to keep the phone number in working memory while she looks for a pen and paper?

   a. There is no way to increase the time information stays in working memory.
   b. chunking
   c. priming
   d. rote rehearsal

8. Aiden knows all of the U.S. state capitals. This is an example of:

a. episodic memory.
b. implicit memory.
c. procedural memory.
d. semantic memory.

9. Carla is taking a Calculus class. When her professor explains mathematical concepts to the class, he tells the students that the concepts won't be on the exam and that the students don't need to remember them. When Carla takes the exam, there is an extra credit question that asks students to list all of the mathematical concepts covered. Carla cannot remember any of them. She is exhibiting:

a. cued forgetting.
b. pseudoforgetting.
c. the primacy effect.
d. extinction.

10. Marco stops to get directions at a gas station. Unfortunately, after Marco leaves he realizes that he can only remember the first few turns, and has forgotten the rest of the directions. This is most likely an example of:

a. the primacy effect.
b. pseudoforgetting.
c. cued forgetting.
d. the recency effect.

11. In question 10, suppose Marco had instead forgotten the first part of the directions, but still remembered the last few street names the gas station attendant had told him. This would most likely be an example of:

a. the primacy effect.
b. the recency effect.
c. cued forgetting.
d. pseudoforgetting.

12. When visiting his grandmother's house, Benjy remembers the time he spilled grape juice on her carpet and then tried to clean it up with his grandmother's good towels. This is an example of:

a. a semantic memory.
b. an implicit memory.
c. a procedural memory.
d. an episodic memory.

13. Debbie has been driving a car for several years. Unlike when she first learned to drive, she can now control the car without thinking about which pedal to step on or how to turn the wheel. This is an example of:

a. extinction.
b. procedural memory.
c. semantic memory.
d. habituation.

14. Ashley is afraid to swim in lakes, and panics if she is in one. One summer, she decides to overcome her fear by putting a little more of her body in the lake each day. By the end of the summer she no longer feels afraid or panics when she swims in a lake. Ashley's lack of fear by the end of the summer is an example of:

a. extinction.
b. cued forgetting.
c. elaborative rehearsal.
d. deep processing.

15. Which of the following is most likely stored as a flashbulb memory?

a. taking a test
b. being robbed at gunpoint
c. playing an instrument you love
d. seeing a movie with your favorite actor in it

16. Students often remember the year of Christopher Columbus' first voyage by reciting the rhyme, "In 1492, Columbus sailed the ocean blue." This is an example of:

a. extinction.
b. a mnemonic.
c. deep processing.
d. chunking.

17. It is usually easier for people to memorize a list of words if they know the definitions of the words. One likely reason for this is:

a. Shallow processing leads to better memory than deep processing.
b. Deep processing leads to better memory than shallow processing.
c. Implicit memories are easier recall than explicit memories.
d. Explicit memories are easier recall than implicit memories.

18. If a person is in a bad mood when they study for an exam, they are likely to recall more of the information they studied if they are also in a bad mood when they take the exam. This is an example of:

a. state-dependent memory.
b. retroactive interference.
c. long-term potentiation.
d. the Yerkes-Dodson law.

19. Which of the following demonstrates proactive interference?

a. Julie can only think of her current zip code when she tries to remember her old zip code.
b. Patrick has a hard time remembering stories his mother told him as a child.
c. Sheila can remember events from her past, but has difficulties creating new memories.
d. A professor has trouble learning the names of his new students because he keeps confusing them with the names of his students from the previous semester.

20. Rebecca calls her mother to tell her she is going on vacation. Her mother said Rebecca already told her this. Rebecca is sure she didn't, but knows she told her brother. What might Rebecca's mother be experiencing?

a. absent-mindedness
b. misattribution
c. bias
d. persistence

Remember to check www.thethinkspot.com for additional information, downloadable flashcards, and other helpful resources.

Answers: 1) c; 2) c; 3) a; 4) b; 5) c; 6) b; 7) d; 8) d; 9) a; 10) a; 11) b; 12) d; 13) b; 14) a; 15) b; 16) b; 17) b; 18) a; 19) d; 20) b

COGNITION AND INTELLIGENCE

The word

"polyglot" may sound like a strange shape or animal, but if you were a polyglot yourself, you would already know the definition *and* could easily translate the word into multiple languages.

So what is a polyglot?

Polyglots—people who are fluent in four or more languages or dialects—abound in today's global society, in which jobs have become international and cell phones and the Internet connect people from all different places. With the speed at which the world is connecting, however, knowing four languages may soon not be anywhere near enough. Is there a way for humans to keep up and perhaps learn 20, 40, or even 100 or more languages?

Hyperpolyglots, who are fluent in record numbers of languages and dialects, are certainly rarer, but give interesting fodder to those studying the brain's capacity for language acquisition.

In history, famed hyperpolyglots include Cardinal Giuseppe Mezzofanti (1774–1849), who remained in Italy all his life yet, as head of the Vatican Library, claimed to know 78 separate languages and dialects; Sir Richard Francis Burton (1821–1890), a famous explorer and translator of the book *The Arabian Nights*; Emil Krebs (1867–1930), a German interpreter who understood approximately 100 languages; and others—including writer J. R. R. Tolkien (1892–1973). Krebs's brain was preserved upon his death and examined by German neuroscientists in 2003. The researchers found that Broca's region, which governs

speech, was organized differently in Krebs's brain than in the brains of 11 other men who had only known one language.

Although it cannot be determined if Krebs was simply born with outstanding language abilities or if his brain developed that way as a result of learning languages, living hyperpolyglots such as Ziad Fazah may help cognitive scientists understand how such people learn so many languages. Fazah, like others, will briefly refresh himself on a language he has not spoken recently before talking with a native speaker. In addition, he uses specific methods to learn languages, including listening to and studying the language for at least a half-hour a day and reciting it aloud for at least 15 minutes.

With this kind of information, some researchers have theorized that polyglots have found a way to identify the basic learning strategy in a language and, thus, learn a language from the inside out. These researchers maintain that, with the right discipline, any of us could become fluent in four or more languages. Others argue that the right environmental factors must be present. Humans possess a sensitivity for learning language before the age of 2, and with increased age comes an increased difficulty in acquiring new languages. Giuseppe Mezzofanti, for example, had already learned 10 languages by the time he was 12. Sir Richard Francis Burton knew French and Italian as well as Greek and Latin before the age of 20, and modern-day hyperpolyglot Ziad Fazah was raised as a child in a rich mix of Arabic, French, and English, personally learning 51 more tongues before his 18th birthday.

Regardless, language holds the key to communication and the ability to interact with others. Studying these individuals' rare abilities with language may provide us with insight into how to connect with people as well.

<<< *Studies have found that deaf children who receive instruction in both sign language and written/spoken language, such as the students at Al Amal Deaf School in Palestine, surpass both their hearing and hearing-impaired monolingual peers in the acquisition and use of language. Children who can hear react similarly to this bilingual instruction, leading scientists to theorize that increasing the use and scope of language increases the connections between the parts of the brain responsible for communication. It seems that learning a new language can increase your ability to communicate with the world around you—in more ways than one.*

CHAPTER 09

Cognitive Psychology

The science of studying what makes our minds work isn't new. Study of **cognition**, the mental activities associated with thinking, knowing, remembering, and communicating, has been going strong since the 1950s and 1960s (Miller, 2003). Before this, however, many psychologists were behaviorists who tended to dismiss the study of cognition. Instead they preferred the study of mental processes that are readily observable.

In opposition to the behaviorists before them, cognitive psychologists such as Chomsky and Piaget showed that we must understand cognition in order to understand behavior.

MENTAL PROCESSES

Think of all the stimuli around you when you are in class: the size of the room, familiar faces, the questions of the professor, the smell of the classroom, the sounds coming from outside. What if you had to give equal attention to all these stimuli at once? You couldn't possibly concentrate. Luckily, our minds use a variety of processes to take in and work with large doses of stimuli. Cognitive scientists have categorized processes in two general categories: (1) how much attention they involve and (2) whether they must be done in sequence rather than simultaneously.

The mental processes associated with seemingly simple tasks are surprisingly intricate. For example, a job requiring multitasking, such as a serving job at a restaurant, involves an average of six different forms of mental processing.

As you can probably tell by this point, our mental processes don't get much of a break in our day-to-day lives. Whether we're learning, creating, solving problems, reasoning, making judgments and decisions, or communicating, we rely on cognition to live our daily lives, go to school, do our jobs, and make sense of our world.

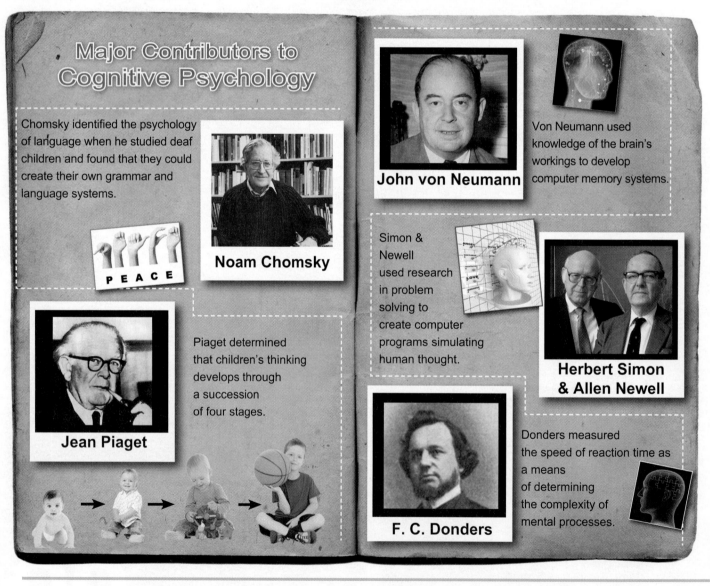

Major Contributors to Cognitive Psychology

Chomsky identified the psychology of language when he studied deaf children and found that they could create their own grammar and language systems.

Noam Chomsky

Piaget determined that children's thinking develops through a succession of four stages.

Jean Piaget

John von Neumann

Von Neumann used knowledge of the brain's workings to develop computer memory systems.

Simon & Newell used research in problem solving to create computer programs simulating human thought.

Herbert Simon & Allen Newell

Donders measured the speed of reaction time as a means of determining the complexity of mental processes.

F. C. Donders

How might these contributions help us understand human behavior and cognition?

Theories of Intelligence

Not everyone processes information the same way. Some of us are adept at solving complex math problems, while others are able to memorize mind-boggling amounts of text. Which skill is a better indication of mental prowess? For more than a century, psychologists have argued various theories of **intelligence**—the capacity to reason, solve problems, and acquire new knowledge. But is intelligence really that easy to define? How can we measure a person's intelligence level when different people have different areas of expertise? Is intelligence genetic, or does our environment play a role in determining our ability to organize, understand, and communicate information?

INTELLIGENCE TESTING

In 1904, French scientist Alfred Binet was asked to develop a test that could help teachers identify students with special needs. Binet developed a test that determined a child's **mental age**, or ability typical of a child of the same chronological age. The test was a great success and was administered throughout Europe and the United States. In 1916, Lewis Terman published an adaptation of Binet's test, called the Stanford-Binet Intelligence Scale. A mathematical formula

used the test score and the child's age to determine an intelligence quotient (IQ) score:

$$IQ = \frac{Mental\ age}{Chronological\ age} \times 100$$

Using this scale, if a child's mental age and chronological age are the same, the score is 100. This formula is particularly helpful in comparing children of various ages.

In response to the Stanford-Binet Intelligence Scale, David Weschler developed a derivative of the test to assist him in his work with adults at Bellevue Hospital in New York City. He first published the Weschler Adult Intelligence Scale (WAIS) in 1939. The scale contained fewer verbal items than Stanford-Binet, and it used **normal distribution** rather than IQ. According to normal distribution, scores are tracked on a bell-shaped curve with a concentration of data in the center.

Today's intelligence tests are often still referred to as IQ tests, yet for the most part they use deviation IQ scores. The tests are standardized so that the mean score will be 100, and the standard deviation will be 15. This allows scores from different IQ tests to be directly compared. Thus, someone with a score of 100 would be considered of average intelligence, while someone with a score of 125 would be considered above average, regardless of age.

Intelligence tests like these are designed to measure **aptitude**, which is a person's potential ability, rather than **achievement**, which is a

person's knowledge and progress. However, critics question if aptitude is really measurable. Test questions are inherently bound to tap into the subject's factual knowledge, despite efforts to mostly test common knowledge (Ackerman & Beier, 2005; Cianciolo & Sternberg, 2004). If a test taker shares the same knowledge as the test makers, then he or she will obviously perform exceedingly well. Despite criticism, psychologists perceive IQ results to be consistently reliable. Studies show that IQ test scores correlate relatively well with performance in academics and employment. However, these correlations are directly related to the type of work subjects do in these environments.

Cognition consists of mental activities associated with sensation, perception, thinking, knowing, remembering, and communicating.

Intelligence is the capacity to reason, solve problems, and acquire new knowledge.

Mental age refers to the level of ability typical of a child of the same chronological age.

Normal distribution is an instance of frequency distribution in which scores are tracked on a bell-shaped curve with a concentration of data in the center.

Aptitude is a person's potential ability.

Achievement is a person's knowledge and progress.

Routine
Mental
Processes
of a
Restaurant
Server

Mental Processes	Examples
Attentional: distribute resources to the most immediate or important needs	Greeting new customers is a server's most important task.
Serial: thoughts/actions that must be done consecutively	A server must take a customer's order before delivering food.
Parallel: able to be done simultaneously	A server can walk and carry beverages at the same time.
Controlled: require attention	Answering a customer's questions requires attention.
Automatic: do not generally require attention	Taking a customer's menu doesn't require attention.
Bottleneck: occurs when two processes cannot be done simultaneously and must be done serially	When serving a large party, a server may need to make two separate deliveries of food to the table.

What other types of jobs require multiple mental processes?

General intelligence is a common factor that underlies certain mental abilities.

g factor refers to the entire skill set of general intelligence that encompasses a range of abilities.

Fluid intelligence is the ability to process information and act accordingly.

Crystallized intelligence is mental ability derived from previous experience.

Central executive functioning is a set of mental processes that governs goals, strategies, and coordination of the mind's activities.

Prodigy is a person of normal intelligence who has an extraordinary ability.

Savant syndrome is a rare disorder that occasionally accompanies autism in which a person of below-average intelligence has an extraordinary ability.

Analytic intelligence is a type of intelligence generally assessed by intelligence tests that present well-defined problems with only one correct answer.

Creative intelligence is a type of intelligence characterized by the ability to adapt to new situations, come up with unique and unusual ideas, and think of novel solutions to problems.

Practical intelligence is the ability to find many solutions to complicated or poorly defined problems and use those solutions in practical, everyday situations.

Social intelligence is the ability to negotiate new social environments.

Emotional intelligence is a person's ability to perceive, understand, manage, and utilize his or her emotions.

GENERAL INTELLIGENCE

If you've seen the TV show *MacGyver*, you've witnessed MacGyver's amazing ability to solve problems by being resourceful. In any given episode, MacGyver might make explosives from a select combination of jungle weeds or repair a crashing helicopter with duct tape. MacGyver obviously exhibits a great amount of practical and scientific intelligence. Does this mean that he would also score well on the math section of the SAT?

Psychologist Charles Spearman would likely say yes. He identified **general intelligence** (or **g**) as a common factor that underlies certain mental abilities. Spearman might say that MacGyver's aptitude for scientific resourcefulness makes up an entire skill set, or **g factor**, that encompasses a range of other abilities, potentially stretching into mathematics and logic.

In contrast, psychologist Raymond Cattell argued that intelligence was not a single entity, but that different types of intelligence were, in fact, distinct from one another. He defined

fluid intelligence as the ability to process information and act accordingly and described **crystallized intelligence** as the mental ability derived directly from previous experience. Cattell's research found that as people age, they accumulate more crystallized knowledge, but their fluid intelligence levels decrease (Cattell, 1963; Horn, 1982).

In other attempts to identify what makes up general intelligence, psychologists have found that quick speeds in processing information often contribute to high IQ scores (Deary, 2001). The high capacity of a person's working memory has also been identified as an important factor in general intelligence (Kyllonen & Christal, 1990). Besides these factors, mental self-monitoring also plays a role. Researchers find that strong **central executive functioning**, the set of mental processes that governs goals, strategies, and coordination of the mind's activities, is related to higher intelligence (Duncan, 2000). They've been able to chart brain activity to support these ideas. Prefrontal cortex areas show an increased activity during taxing tasks. In addition, prefrontal cortex size is linked to IQ more closely than the size of any other area in the brain (Reiss et al., 1996).

NATURE OR NURTURE?

Parents might try to improve their children's intellect by reading to them and buying media like *Baby Mozart* and *Baby Einstein*. But to what degree is a child's intelligence predetermined by his or her genetics? In a study of

> It is important to remember that IQ tests are likely to be subject to cultural bias. People raised in a different culture or economic status from the person who designed the IQ test are likely to perform poorly on that particular test, meaning that group differences in scores are not necessarily reflective of group differences in intelligence.

> Every 30 years, IQ test scores have risen about 9–15 points. Scores measuring fluid intelligence have increased the most while scores reflecting school learning have seen the least change. With greater travel and communication opportunities in today's world, our enriched learning environment seems to be boosting our intelligence.

twins, siblings, and unrelated siblings raised in the same household (McGue et al., 1993), results indicated that genetics are ultimately more influential than environment. Identical twins raised in different households showed some difference in IQ score, indicating that environment plays a slight role. However, in cases of unrelated siblings raised in the same home, IQ correlations existed in childhood, but the correlation waned over time.

Do culture and socioeconomic status influence IQ scores? While some studies indicate that they do, it is important to remember that IQ tests are likely to be subject to cultural bias. People raised in a different culture or economic status from the person who designed the IQ test are likely to perform poorly on that particular test, meaning that group differences in scores are not necessarily reflective of group differences in intelligence. Many test designers have come to the conclusion that it may be impossible to create a test completely free of cultural bias (Carpenter et al, 1990). Instead, designers aim to create tests that are culturally fair, for example by minimizing or eliminating the use of language and downplaying skills and values that vary from culture to culture, such as speed.

Why are IQ scores currently on the rise? Environment may be playing a crucial role. Every 30 years, IQ test scores have risen about 9–15 points. Scores measuring fluid intelligence have increased the most while scores reflecting school learning have seen the least change. With greater travel and communication opportunities in today's world, our enriched learning environment seems to be boosting our intelligence.

DIFFERENT TYPES OF INTELLIGENCE

If you asked pro cyclist Lance Armstrong to make calculations for the launch of a NASA space shuttle or debate a noted Shakespearean scholar on the subject of *Hamlet*, he'd probably decline—after all, his intellectual abilities are just about par for the course. His cycling abilities, however, are famously phenomenal: From 1999 to 2005, he achived seven consecutive victories at the Tour de France, and came out of retirement in 2009 to once again tackle the grueling 2,000 mile race.

Cognitive scientists would call Armstrong a **prodigy**—a person of normal intelligence who has an extraordinary ability. No one would call Armstrong the next Einstein; his skill is in athletics rather than mathematics. But, some scholars would argue, athletic skill is simply one of many kinds of intelligence.

Prodigies are relatively rare, but other types of people have exceptional skills as well. Remember Dustin Hoffman's character in the film *Rain Man*? Although suffering from the developmental disorder autism, Hoffman's character also had incredible recall abilities, characteristic of **savant syndrome**—a rare disorder that occasionally accompanies autism. Unlike prodigies, people with savant syndrome have below-average intelligence, and they often suffer from developmental disorders like autism or disabilities like blindness. However, these setbacks don't prevent savants from having extraordinary abilities, such as being able to count cards in Las Vegas or memorize the phone book. Like prodigies, savants are talented in ways that our culture doesn't usually classify as "intelligence."

Sternberg's Triarchic Theory of Intelligence

So how many different types of intelligence exist? On this point, psychologists and other experts disagree. One psychologist, Robert Sternberg, identified three aspects of successful intelligence (1985). The aspect that most people probably think of when they hear the word *intelligence* is **analytic intelligence**, or academic problem-solving intelligence. This is the type of intelligence generally assessed by intelligence tests that present well-defined problems with only one correct answer. The second aspect, **creative intelligence**, isn't a skill that only people in the creative arts can tap into. If you're a creative thinker—if you can adapt to new situations, come up with unique, unusual ideas, and think of novel

solutions to problems—you have creative intelligence.

Practical intelligence, the third aspect in Sternberg's schema, is the ability to find many solutions to complicated or poorly defined problems and use those solutions in practical, everyday situations. For example, when you've discovered that the birthday bash you're hosting for a friend is the same day as your brother's college graduation, you might use practical intelligence to hash out a solution to your scheduling woes.

Gardner's Multiple Intelligences

Along with his Harvard colleagues, Howard Gardner developed a theory of multiple intelligences (1983, 2004) that's fairly well-known today. According to Gardner, there are eight different types of intelligence:

Each of Gardner's eight intelligences is distinct from the others, which means that we may be very talented in some of these areas and completely untalented in others. Someone who's a great dancer may have bodily–kinesthetic intelligence, musical intelligence, and spatial intelligence, but she might have difficulty making friends or interacting with people, meaning that interpersonal intelligence is probably not her strong suit. Gardner's theory is of particular interest to educators, who can tailor their lesson plans according to individual students' strengths and weaknesses. For example, a musical learner may find it easier to memorize facts if the teacher encourages that learner to create a song or rhyme incorporating the information.

Social Intelligence

Are you the life of the party? Can you squeeze yourself into any social group with ease? Lots of people can't, but all of us probably know a few individuals with these skills. This ability to negotiate new social environments is called **social intelligence** (Cantor & Kihlstrom, 1987). If you are socially intelligent, you can easily understand social situations and the part you should play in order to be a successful group member.

One important facet of social intelligence is **emotional intelligence**, or a person's ability to perceive, understand, manage, and utilize his or her emotions. People who exhibit a high degree of emotional intelligence are usually very self-aware. Interestingly, research has found that people who suffer brain damage that impairs their emotional intelligence tend to have unimpaired levels of cognitive intelligence (Bar-On et al., 2003). This finding provides biologically based support for the idea that we have many distinct and independent types of intelligence.

Gardner's Multiple Intelligences

Naturalistic

Linguistic

Logical/Mathematical

Intrapersonal

Interpersonal

Bodily/Kinesthetic

Musical

Spatial

NEUROLOGICAL MEASUREMENTS OF INTELLIGENCE

Since larger muscles often indicate greater strength, you might think that a larger brain indicates greater intelligence. In fact, several studies have indicated that there is a slight correlation between brain size and intelligence. However, uncontrolled variables such as nutrition and environmental stimulation could cause both above-average intelligence and large brains, so it's not clear that brain size has much to do with intelligence.

Instead, the neural component of intelligence might be more closely related to the brain's **plasticity**, or its flexible ability to grow and change (first discussed in Chapter 3). A study by neuroscientist Philip Shaw and his colleagues (2006) on a group of children who were "highly intelligent" according to intelligence tests revealed a link between the thickening and thinning rate of the brain's cortex and intelligence: Very intelligent children tended to have a thinner cortex than their peers during childhood, but the cortex thickened more rapidly during the preteen years. These results suggest that there's a relationship, at least in childhood, between the rate at which the brain matures and IQ.

Does intelligence reside in a particular part of the brain? Some believe that there is a "global workspace for organizing and coordinating information" in the brain's frontal lobe (Duncan, 2000), but this assertion is the subject of hot debate among intelligence researchers. However, there are a few correlations that may help us pin down the connections between intelligence and the brain. First of all, there are correlations between a person's intelligence test score and his or her **perceptual speed**, or the time it takes a

person to perceive and compare stimuli. People with higher scores tended to take in perceptual information more quickly than their lower-scoring counterparts. There also seems to be a relationship between high intelligence test scores and the speed and complexity of activity in the brain. People with high intelligence scores tended to exhibit complex, fast-moving brain wave activity in response to simple stimuli. While this finding

Some researchers believe that the prefrontal cortex is an area of the brain crucial to intelligence.

is certainly interesting, its significance is uncertain: We still don't know why fast reactions to simple tasks should be a good predictor of intelligence.

Problem Solving and Reasoning

CONCEPTS

Think about everything you've learned and all the information you've collected in your life

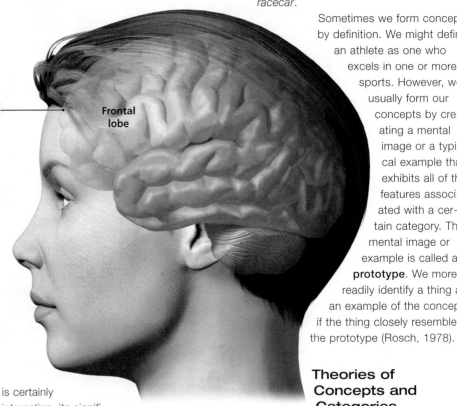

Prefrontal cortex

Frontal lobe

so far. Directions to the town recycling center, the poem you memorized when you were eight, the blog post about your cat that you're composing in your head, a litany of dates and facts and events. . . . How can we possibly keep track of everything that's stored in our brains?

For starters, we use **concepts**. Concepts are mental groupings of similar objects, events, and people. We are able to comprehend vast amounts of information with concepts by creating a mental representation that categorizes shared features of related objects, events, or other stimuli. For example, the concept *car* contains everything from a shiny BMW to a jalopy with a bad paint job to 2008's Batmobile. Once we form a concept category, we can classify it even more by organizing it into category **hierarchies**. The category *car* might contain the hierarchies *fuel-efficient*, *sedan*, and *racecar*.

Sometimes we form concepts by definition. We might define an athlete as one who excels in one or more sports. However, we usually form our concepts by creating a mental image or a typical example that exhibits all of the features associated with a certain category. This mental image or example is called a **prototype**. We more readily identify a thing as an example of the concept if the thing closely resembles the prototype (Rosch, 1978).

Theories of Concepts and Categories

We use categories to organize the world around us, but how exactly does this cognitive process work? Wittgenstein's **family resemblance theory** (1953) suggests that we put items in categories together if they share certain characteristics, even if not every member of the category has similar features. Wittgenstein used the example of games: Table tennis, poker, and hopscotch have very little in common, but they are united by a common thread—a family resemblance—that allows us to group them together in a single category.

^
^ While campaigning for president, Barack Obama
^ argued that although he didn't look like the men
on $1 and $5 bills, he was still capable of being
president. How does this statement invoke the
notion of prototypes?

Exemplar theory claims that people make category judgments by comparing new things they encounter with examples of other things they remember that fit into that category.

Problem solving is the act of combining current information with information stored in memory to find a solution to a task.

Initial state is a problem-solving state in which a person has incomplete or unsatisfactory information.

Goal state is a problem-solving state in which a person has all the information he or she needs.

Set of operations consists of the steps that a person needs to take to get from the initial state to the goal state.

Algorithm is a step-by-step procedure that a person can follow to arrive at a solution to a particular problem.

Mental set is a preexisting state of mind that a person uses to solve problems because that state has helped the person solve similar problems in the past.

Functional fixedness is a bias that limits a person's ability to think in unconventional ways.

Exemplar theory claims that we make category judgments by comparing new things that we encounter with examples of other things that we remember that fit into that category (Ashby, 1992). For example, your concept of a dog is informed not by a single prototype but rather by all the dogs you've ever interacted with.

PROBLEM SOLVING

Think about the last time you got lost. What did you do to find your way? You might have checked a map to get back on track. Maybe you used trial and error, trying different routes until you arrived at your destination. You may have just asked for directions. Whatever strategy you chose, you were probably ultimately able to reach your destination thanks to **problem solving**. Problem solving is the act of combining current information with information stored in your memory to find a solution to a task.

Newell and Simon examine a problem in terms of the **initial state**, the **goal state**, and the **set of operations** (1972). In the initial state, you have incomplete or unsatisfactory information. (You got lost on the way to Thanksgiving dinner at your aunt's house, and you don't know any of the roads in this part of town.) You're trying to reach the goal state, or the state in which you have all the information that you need. (You get a set of clear directions from your current location to your aunt's house.) The set of operations consists of the steps that you need to take to reach the goal state from the initial state. (You pull out your cell phone, call your aunt, ask her for directions, and write down her response.)

Problem-Solving Strategies

It's all well and good to identify a problem—to figure out your initial state and your goal state—but eventually, you're going to want to come up with a solution. We use a variety of different methods for solving different sorts of problems.

Algorithms are step-by-step procedures that we can follow in order to arrive at a solution to a particular problem. In order to do long division or decipher an encoded message, you might follow the steps of an algorithm. As long as you follow the correct process, you're sure to come up with the correct solution.

We all approach problems with a **mental set**, or a preexisting state of mind that we use to solve problems because it's helped us solve similar problems in the past. A mental set is especially helpful for simple, everyday tasks. However, our mental sets can sometimes interfere with problem solving. Try solving the problem below.

How'd you do? If you couldn't find the solution, you probably were a victim of **functional fixedness**, a bias that limits your ability to think in unconventional ways. You might not have considered an unconventional use of the pliers, which were the key to solving the problem.

>>> Can you find a way to tie the two strings together? You can use any of the objects in the room.

Insight refers to the sudden realization of the solution to a problem.

Reasoning is a cognitive process of organizing information or beliefs into a series of steps to reach conclusions.

Practical reasoning is a type of reasoning in which a person considers what to do or how to act.

Theoretical reasoning is a type of reasoning directed toward arriving at a belief or conclusion rather than at a practical decision.

Discursive reasoning see *theoretical reasoning*.

Syllogistic reasoning is a type of reasoning in which a person decides whether a conclusion logically follows from two or more statements that the person assumes to be true.

Syllogism is a deductive pattern of logic in which a conclusion is made based on two or more premises.

Deductive reasoning is a top-down method of arriving at a specific conclusion based on broader premises.

Inductive reasoning is a method of using specific examples to arrive at a general conclusion.

Overconfidence is a person's tendency to think that he or she is more knowledgeable or accurate than he or she really is.

Hindsight bias describes a person's erroneous belief that he or she knew something all along after an event has occurred.

By attaching the pliers to the end of one string, you could swing them like a pendulum to reach the other string and tie a knot (Maier, 1931).

As the "two strings" problem demonstrates, it can help to take a novel perspective or pay attention to unusual or seemingly unimportant elements when you're trying to solve a difficult problem. It also doesn't hurt to keep your chin up: Your mood can affect your success with a problem (Fredrickson, 2000). When you're in a bad mood, your perceptions and thoughts become restricted, and you'll probably find it harder to "think outside the box."

Sometimes, of course, we don't need to use algorithms or analyses or complicated methods in order to solve problems. On those rare and wonderful occasions, we experience **insight**: Without warning, the solution we've been looking for suddenly pops into our heads. If you've ever had a flash of inspiration while taking a test or struggling with a seemingly impossible project, you're probably familiar with the joys that insight can bring. It turns out that scientists can spot insight in the brain: Recently, psychologists used fMRI and EEG imaging technology to map the brains of participants who were solving word problems. The researchers noticed that when participants had an insight that helped them

solve a problem, there was increased activity in the participants' right temporal lobes (Jung-Beeman et al., 2004). Insight has also been connected to heightened brain activity in the cingulate, lateral, prefrontal, and posterior parietal cortices (Vogeley et al., 2001).

REASONING

Reasoning is the cognitive process of organizing information or beliefs into a series of steps to reach conclusions. When we reason, we generally think about facts we already know and use those facts to come up with new assumptions. There are a few different flavors of reasoning: We engage in **practical reasoning** when we consider what to do or how to act. **Theoretical reasoning**, or **discursive reasoning**, is directed toward arriving at a belief or conclusion rather than at a practical decision. Your religious beliefs might be shaped by theoretical reasoning. We use **syllogistic reasoning** when we decide whether a conclusion logically follows from two or more statements that we assume to be true. For example, assume that all professional baseball players have excellent hand-eye coordination. James is a professional baseball player. You should logically conclude that James has excellent hand-eye coordination. This pattern of logic is called a **syllogism**.

Syllogisms are a good example of **deductive reasoning**, a top-down method of

> Reasoning is the cognitive process of organizing information or beliefs into a series of steps to reach conclusions. When we reason, we generally think about facts we already know and use those facts to come up with new assumptions.

arriving at a specific conclusion based on broader premises. In the case of the example above, you can use two general pieces of information (baseball players have good hand-eye coordination and James is a baseball player) to arrive at a specific conclusion (James has good hand–eye coordination). Using deductive reasoning can be a bit like solving a math problem: When you follow certain rules in the proper order, you arrive at a correct and logical conclusion.

> Have you ever been 100 percent sure that you were right about something, only to find out that you were completely mistaken? It happens to the best of us: Sometimes, despite our best efforts, our reasoning can be quite faulty.

In contrast to deductive reasoning, which starts with generalizations and moves to specifics, **inductive reasoning** is a method of using specific examples to arrive at a general conclusion. For example, you may have noticed that all the ice you've ever seen in your life has been cold. Using inductive reasoning, you can logically conclude that all ice is cold. Inductive reasoning does leave some room for error, however: If you've observed only female field hockey players, you might reason that all field hockey players are female, but many male field hockey players around the world would beg to differ with you. When we use analogies to solve problems about unknown situations by comparing them to situations we've experienced in the past and drawing conclusions from those past situations, we're using inductive reasoning.

ERRORS IN REASONING

Have you ever been 100 percent sure that you were right about something, only to find out that you were completely mistaken? It happens to the best of us: Sometimes, despite our best efforts, our reasoning can be quite faulty.

Overconfidence

One common error in reasoning is **overconfidence**, or our tendency to think we are more knowledgeable or accurate than we really are. The subprime mortgage crisis that reared its head in 2008 was due in part to overconfidence on the part of both lenders and home buyers, many of whom were wrongly convinced that they'd be able to make payments on time or make huge amounts of money from home sales. Of course, many people who didn't get caught up in this housing debacle believed after the fact that they'd never have gotten involved in such a risky action, but this response may simply be an example of a form of overconfidence called **hindsight bias**, our tendency to overestimate our previous knowledge of situations (see Chapter 2).

Belief Bias

Logic is sometimes at odds with our reasoning. Consider the following statements:

- Premise 1: Women enjoy watching romantic comedies.
- Premise 2: Men are not women.
- Conclusion: Men do not enjoy watching romantic comedies.

Does this conclusion sound logical to you? If it does, you've fallen victim to **belief bias**, the effect that occurs when our beliefs distort our logical thinking. The two premises allow for the possibility that some men might like watching romantic comedies, but your own beliefs about men's preferred movies might have led you to conclude the opposite. Our beliefs have incredible power over our judgments and reasoning skills: Even when we are presented with evidence that refutes our beliefs, we find it difficult to abandon those beliefs. This tendency is known as **belief perseverance**.

Heuristics

Which is a more probable cause of death, a plane crash or a car crash? If you can, answer that question as quickly as possible, and try not to think too much about it. When you need to make a quick decision like this one, you often follow your intuition in lieu of extended logical analysis. In order to reach a quick solution, you use mental shortcuts called **heuristics**. Like rules of thumb, heuristics are informal rules that make the decision-making process quick and simple. We use them all the time; in fact, psychologists Daniel Kahneman and Amos Tversky argue that human judgment rests more heavily on heuristics than on purely rational analytic processes (1980). However, heuristics can easily lead us astray: While deaths from car accidents are actually far more common than deaths from airplane crashes, plane crashes are much more heavily reported in newspapers and on the 6 o'clock news, and we tend to remember them when we hear about them. If you said that dying in a plane crash was more likely than dying in a car crash, you were probably misled by the **availability heuristic**, which tells us that if we can bring examples of an event (like a plane crash) to mind easily, that event must be common. This rule of thumb, while true in many cases, is not always accurate.

Confirmation Bias

If you're a member of a political party, you probably laugh when you hear claims that the media are unbiased. It seems clear to you, if you're liberal, that news stories tend to have a conservative bent. On the other hand, if you're conservative, it's equally clear that reporters across the country have a distinct liberal bias.

When we already believe that something is true, we tend to look for evidence that proves our beliefs, and we tend not to notice evidence that disproves those beliefs. This phenomenon is known as **confirmation bias**—although we may think we're being objective, we're actually trying to confirm our previously held opinions. If you already think that the media are biased against your particular political beliefs, you're

>>> If you wanted to prove media bias, what evidence would you look for? What evidence might you unconsciously ignore?

more likely to notice those news stories that *are* biased against your beliefs, but you may not notice those stories that are unbiased or those that are biased *toward* your beliefs.

The Conjunction Fallacy

Gabe was a psychology major in college. He recently watched and enjoyed the documentary *An Inconvenient Truth*, about the dangers of global warming. Gabe takes cloth bags to the supermarket with him instead of using plastic bags to carry his groceries.

Which of the following statements is more likely?

- Gabe is a newspaper reporter.
- Gabe is a newspaper reporter who's active in an environmental group.

From what we know about Gabe, it's clear that he cares about the environment, so you might think that the second statement is more likely than the first. However, it's far more probable that Gabe is a reporter than it is that he is a

reporter *and* an environmentalist. Since the first statement is contained in the second, and the second statement includes additional pieces of information that may or may not be true, the first statement is more likely. If you thought otherwise, you experienced the **conjunction fallacy**, a phenomenon that causes people to believe that additional information increases the probability that a statement is true, even though that probability actually *decreases*.

Decision Making, Judgment, and Executive Control

Would you consider trying any of the language-learning techniques mentioned at the beginning of this chapter, or are you skeptical? You have probably formed an opinion about these methods using your **judgment**. Judgment is a skill that allows us to form opinions, reach conclusions, and evaluate situations objectively and critically.

DECISION MAKING

Judgment informs our **decision making**—the process of selecting and rejecting available options. The presentation, or **framing**, of an issue can greatly influence the decisions that

we make. For example, people are more likely to purchase ground beef that is "75% lean" rather than ground beef that's "25% fat" (Levin & Gaeth, 1988; Sanford et al., 2002). Sometimes, if we're presented with a decision that can be viewed through too many conflicting frames, or if we have too many alternatives to choose from, we develop **decision aversion**, the state of attempting to avoid making any decision at all.

Theories of Decision Making

Once we've been given a decision to make, how do we arrive at a conclusion? **Rational choice theory** states that we make decisions by determining how likely each outcome of that decision is, as well as the positive or negative value of each outcome. If you were asked to decide whether to purchase a Kindle, what would you do? According to rational choice theory, you'd determine the pros and cons of buying the device versus not buying it, as well as the likelihood of each of these pros and cons. Then, if the value of buying a Kindle outweighed the value of not buying one, you'd go online and make the purchase.

∧
∧
∧ **What outcomes would you consider before spending your money on a hot new gadget like this one?**

Kahneman and Tversky proposed an alternate decision-making theory called **prospect theory**, which describes how people make decisions in situations that involve elements of risk. In general, we avoid risk in situations where we stand to gain, but our behavior becomes more risk-seeking when we face a loss. Let's say you're a contestant on a game show. The host gives you a check for $1,000. You can either keep the check, netting a certain $1,000, or you can exchange the check for the envelope in the host's hand. There's a 50 percent chance that the envelope contains $2,500, but there's a 50 percent chance that the envelope contains nothing at all. In this situation, most people choose to avoid risk and stick with the $1,000 they're sure to win. However, try to imagine a slightly more sadistic game show: The host says that if you do nothing, he's going to take $1,000 from you. However, he offers you another envelope. There's a 50 percent chance that the envelope contains a card that will let you keep all your money, and there's a 50 percent chance that it contains a card that will allow the host to take $2,500 from you. Do you take the envelope? Faced with this decision, most people would rather run the risk of losing $2,500 in order to have a chance to keep all their money. Prospect theory suggests that we have different attitudes toward risk depending on the situation we're facing.

Neural Contributions to Decision Making

When your friend makes a decision that you don't agree with, you may wonder what could possibly have been going through her brain when she made that choice. What *was* going through her brain? One answer might be the neurotransmitter **dopamine**. Research has found that the presence of dopamine in the brain helps us make decisions that lead to good outcomes and avoid bad outcomes (St. Onge & Floresco, 2008). A large amount of dopamine is present in the basal ganglia, an area of the brain that seems to be crucial to decision making. When we're faced with a decision, activity in the basal ganglia picks up, and bursts of dopamine help us choose the most rewarding or favorable potential outcome.

> **Conscious attention is selective, meaning that although we are aware of alternative interpretations, we can experience only one perception at any given time.**

What happens, though, if a choice that makes us feel good isn't necessarily the best choice for us? For instance, if you want to eat more healthily, you probably don't want to decide to eat a delicious frosted cupcake, but the dopamine in your brain will cause you to identify that cupcake as a tasty reward. Luckily, your brain has **executive control systems** that inhibit the pleasurable response to the cupcake so you can stick to your original plan and snack on a salad instead. These systems are generally thought to be centered in the brain's frontal regions (with significant additional input from the thalamus). Specifically, the **ventromedial prefrontal cortex** helps us adhere to social and behavioral rules and plays a role in allowing us to link our behaviors to their potential consequences. The **dorsolateral prefrontal cortex** initiates our behavior, but it can also shift or inhibit that behavior based on the decisions we make. The **anterior cingulate cortex** is also involved in controlling our behavior, and the **parietal cortex** plays a critical role in directing our attention during the decision-making process.

Attention

How do you maintain focus when that all-important exam is approaching? Maybe you use coffee or energy drinks such as Red Bull to maintain alertness. Perhaps you listen to classical music to help you concentrate. Whatever method you choose, **attention**—the way the brain selectively processes important information—plays a vital role.

FOCUS OF ATTENTION

Conscious attention is selective, meaning that although we are aware of alternative interpretations, we can experience only one perception at any given time (see Chapter 5). According to one study, we consciously process about 40 of the 11,000,000 bits of information we receive per second (Wilson, 2002).

Cognitive scientists Corbetta and Schulman proposed that there are two types of attention, each with a distinct processing system (2002). In **goal-directed selection**, or **endogenous attention**, we make an explicit choice to pay attention to something—we look for a particular face in the crowd, or try to memorize a particular section of text. Endogenous attention uses the dorsal brain system (the part of the somatosensory system responsible for delivering sensory information from the external world to the brain).

Stimulus-driven capture, or **exogenous attention**, occurs when our attention is driven by external stimuli. When something novel or unexpected happens (a deer jumps through the living room window, for example), our attention is automatically drawn to the scene. Exogenous attention uses the right ventral brain system (the part of the somatosensory system that

transmits interpreted sensory information to the muscles via nerve impulses).

How do we decide how much attention to devote to a particular task? We might be able to keep up with a slow-moving romantic comedy while calling a friend for the latest gossip, but multitasking would not be recommended if our to-do list included cutting down a tree and writing a nuclear physics essay. **Perceptual load** is the level of processing difficulty or complexity of a task. Because human brains have limited resources, the perceptual load of a task often determines the amount of attention allocated to it.

<<< We are able to multitask if the perceptual load of each chore is fairly low.

> " Imagine that you are shown a series of words and told to remember every word that could be used to describe a tree. Pretty easy, right? But if you are shown the words *tall* and *leafy* within a very short period of time, you will be unable to recall seeing the second word. "

Inattentional Blindness

For a variety of reasons, we often fail to process certain stimuli, a concept known as inattentional blindness (see Chapter 5). One type of processing failure is called **attentional blink**. Imagine that you are shown a series of words and told to remember every word that could be used to describe a tree. Pretty easy, right? But if you are shown the words *tall* and *leafy* within a very short period of time, you will be unable to recall seeing the second word. This is due to the **psychological refractory period**—the interval during which your brain is too busy processing the first stimulus to comprehend the second.

FEATURE INTEGRATION

Since Broadbent developed his filter theory, many other models of attention have been proposed. Psychologist Anne Treisman developed the influential **feature integration theory,** suggesting that we organize stimuli based on knowledge about how their features should be combined (Treisman, 1987). Treisman argues that most stimuli are both similar and yet sufficiently different so that there are a limited number of sensible ways to combine their features (see Chapter 5). For example, while you may not have seen an Irish wolfhound before, you know that an animal with particular physical features is likely to be a dog. Previous sensory experience allows you to categorize the animal, while still being able to distinguish it from other four-legged creatures with a tail.

UNATTENDED STIMULI

Filter Theory

Our attention is limited to just a few stimuli at any one given time. So how do we choose what to concentrate on? Broadbent's **filter theory** (1958) proposed that we select stimuli early in the perception process, even before we assess the meaning of the input. When participants in a dichotic listening task use headphones to listen to two simultaneous messages, one in each ear, they are told to pay attention only to the message they hear in one ear. Then, they're able to repeat, or shadow, the words that they hear in that ear. The attended message is generally the only portion of the stimuli that can be reported. Broadbent suggested that two messages presented at the same time reach a **sensory buffer**, which holds information for a short time before it is accepted or rejected by the filter. One of the messages would then be allowed through the filter on the basis of its physical characteristics. For example, if participants have been told to listen to a male voice and the other voice on the tape is female, they can filter out the female voice fairly easily. When two messages are presented in the same tone with few physical differences, they become harder to separate (Cherry, 1953).

Both messages reach a sensory buffer and are temporarily stored, like ingredients being held in a mixing bowl. The messages are filtered according to their physical characteristics, as though they are sifted through a sieve. The desired physical characteristic is recognized. Attention is devoted to a single message, enabling focused conversation.

Broadbent's Filter Theory

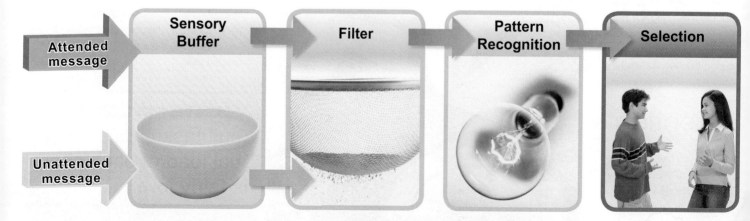

Attended message → Sensory Buffer → Filter → Pattern Recognition → Selection

Unattended message

Language and Verbal Cognition

Language—the system of symbols that enables us to communicate our ideas, thoughts, and feelings—plays a vital part in how we think. So does this mean that the language we use can shape our attitudes toward others? Do people who speak different languages also see the world a different way? What processes take place when we use language, and how are people able to comprehend more than one language?

MULTIPLE LANGUAGES

Polyglots such as Ziad Fazah often learn their second language at a young age. Children who acquire a new language before the age of seven can develop near-perfect fluency, and you would find it difficult to distinguish them from native speakers. Asian immigrants to the United States were given a grammar test, which showed that those who had arrived in the country as young children understood American English grammar as proficiently as native speakers (Johnson & Newport, 1991). However, fluency tends to decrease with age, even when learning sign language. Why is this? Research shows that some areas of the brain are more active in children than in adults during language-based tasks. This may account for some disparity in learning capacity between children and adults.

Adults can learn second languages after this critical period has passed. They use different cognitive strategies than babies and young children. Indeed, the brains of people who learn a second language late in life look different from the brains of people who are bilingual from infancy (Marian et al., 2007). Early bilingualism does not interfere with normal cognitive development. In fact, learning a second language early in life increases the density of

gray matter in the lower left parietal area. This area of the brain is associated with performance of verbal fluency tasks.

LANGUAGE PRODUCTION

You might have heard the expression, "Put your brain in gear before you put your mouth in action," meaning that we should think before we speak. But what actually does go through our minds the moment before we say something? Sociolinguist Allan Bell (1984) theorized that everything we say is directed to a particular audience, a concept known as **audience design**. Bell claimed that we adapt our style of speaking in accordance with the

> " Children who acquire a new language before the age of seven can develop near-perfect fluency, and you would find it difficult to distinguish them from native speakers. "

person we are talking to, either to express solidarity or to keep our distance. He called this habit **style-shifting**. You may have noticed the painfully awkward process of a parent trying to utilize modern slang in order to better relate to their teenage child.

Cognitive scientist H. P. Grice (1975) described the **cooperative principle**, which instructs speakers that utterances should be truthful, informative, relevant, and

Audience design is a concept that states that everything people say is directed to a particular audience.

Style-shifting describes the habit of a person to adapt his or her style of speaking in accordance with the person he or she is talking to, either to express solidarity or to maintain distance.

Cooperative principle instructs speakers that utterances should be truthful, informative, relevant, and clear.

>>> Style-shifting is not always effective if it comes across as false.

Marijuana Issue Sent to Joint Committee

clear. Both the speaker and the addressee have to follow certain semantic and syntactic rules in order to communicate effectively. Another critical consideration is whether a speaker has an accurate understanding of the listener's knowledge, enabling them to find "common ground" (Clark & Marshall, 1981). For example, it would be pointless to use the baseball metaphor "cover all your bases" in a conversation with someone who had never heard of the ball game.

Errors in speech are evidence that multiple levels of processing are at work during language production. A **spoonerism** is a common execution error in which a person exchanges the initial sounds of two or more words in a phrase, such as *cast far* instead of *fast car*. Studies suggest that spoonerisms are more likely to result when the exchanges result in actual words. Other errors, such as word switching, are more likely when two idioms from which the words are taken carry the same meaning. For example, a person might confuse *meet your maker* and *kick the bucket*, resulting in the befuddling expression *kick your maker*. **Opportunism**—the necessity of rapid speech production—is also the cause of many execution errors. Few of us can come up with a perfectly phrased witty retort on the spur of the moment, usually resulting in a poorly worded reply that has us kicking ourselves for the rest of the day as we think of increasingly eloquent responses.

LANGUAGE COMPREHENSION

The above headline, attributed to the *Toronto Star*, shows how even the experts struggle with **lexical ambiguity**—the multiple meanings of a word or phrase (in this case *joint*). We differentiate homonyms, such as *carrot* and *karat*, based on context and the relative frequency of the word's use. When resolving **structural ambiguity**—the multiple meaning of a sentence depending on syntax, we

> "Few of us can come up with a perfectly phrased witty retort on the spur of the moment, usually resulting in a poorly worded reply that has us kicking ourselves for the rest of the day as we think of increasingly eloquent responses."

differentiate between different possible sentence structures that produce different meanings. Take the following headline as an example: "Stolen painting found by tree." Did the tree find the painting? Probably not! Most of the time we are able to make logical inferences about the intended meaning of a word or sentence based on previous experience.

LANGUAGE AND THOUGHT

Do people from different cultures perceive the world differently? Many studies suggest that they do (Nisbett & Norenzayan, 2002; Peng & Nisbett, 1999). A group of Japanese and American students were shown an animated underwater scene in which one larger, "focal" fish swum among smaller fish and other aquatic life. When asked to describe what they saw, the Japanese students were much more likely to begin by describing the background and how the parts of the scene related to one another—the rocky pool, the color of the water, the fish swimming past seaweed. In contrast, American students were far more likely to begin by describing prominent individual aspects of the scene—the largest, fastest, brightest fish. Nisbett and his colleagues found that the Japanese were similarly sensitive to context in the social world and could pick up how situational pressures were affecting people's behavior far quicker than Americans. The results suggest that there are fundamental differences in the way Easterners and Westerners perceive the world.

Does language also affect the way we think? Linguists Edward Sapir and Benjamin Whorf proposed that the language we speak influences our conception of reality. Their ideas became known as the **linguistic relativity hypothesis** (Whorf, 1956). For example, English and other European languages have an egocentric frame of reference. In other words, space is represented with ourselves at the center. You might describe a local grocery store as being two miles from your house, whereas someone with an absolute frame of reference might give the specific geographic location. Similarly, the Japanese have many words for interpersonal emotions such as *sympathy*, while the English language contains many self-focused emotions, such as *anger* (Markus & Kitayama, 1991). Might this influence the differences in culture? Many bilingual speakers report feeling a different sense of self depending on which language they are using (Matsumoto, 1994).

Consider this riddle: A famous surgeon was a passenger in a car driven by his teenage son. "I'll drop you at the hospital, Dad," said the young man. "Fine, son," said his father. Those were his last words; a wildly careening convertible crossed the center strip and ran headlong into the car. At the emergency room the father was pronounced dead on arrival; the son was taken for emergency surgery. The surgeon called to the scene reached for a scalpel but paused: "I can't operate," the surgeon said; "this is my son." Is this possible?

Did you figure it out? If it took you more than a few seconds to work out that the surgeon was the boy's mother, some psychologists would argue that the generic use of *he* and *man* has influenced the way you perceive certain professions. Twenty studies have consistently found that the supposedly generic *he* is not interpreted as including women (Henley, 1989).

Linguistic determinism is the theory that different languages impose different conceptions of reality. However, some research undermines this theory. Whorf discovered that the Hopi Indian tribe had no words for *past*, *present*, or *future*, yet they still had a sense for the continuum of time. It's clear, though, that language and thought influence each other to a large degree: Our cognition shapes our language, and our language, in turn, may help to shape our cognition.

> "Think of a house you used to live in, or a favorite family vacation. You probably just conjured up a whole host of mental images. Visual representations are a useful way of helping us remember our experiences."

Visual Cognition

Think of a house you used to live in, or a favorite family vacation. You probably just conjured up a whole host of mental images. Visual representations are a useful way of helping us remember our experiences. Now try using visual images to think of a process or a concept. Not so easy, is it? According to Paivio's **dual-coding theory** (1986), concrete words are mentally represented both visually and verbally, whereas abstract terms, such as *choice*, are coded only verbally, requiring more complex coding and making them more difficult to retrieve. Event-related potential (ERP) studies, which measure electrical activity in the brain, indicate distinct patterns of brain activity when people are processing words that are easily visualized compared to words that are not (Kounios & Holcomb, 1994).

Studies of visual cognition have found that when imagining an activity, the same brain areas are activated as when physically performing the activity. We also think in images while we sleep. After learning something, such as the way through a maze, the mind retraces its steps during sleep (O'Neill et al., 2006). This behavior is a purported mechanism for learning (see Chapter 7), providing a convenient excuse for taking that afternoon nap.

∧∧∧ The Japanese have a proverb that says "The nail that sticks up gets hammered down," whereas Americans treasure individualism and the image of the lone cowboy hero. How might this affect cultural understanding?

Summary

WHAT IS COGNITIVE PSYCHOLOGY? p. 136

- Cognition comprises the mental activities associated with thinking, knowing, remembering, and communicating.

- Cognitive scientists assess the attention and steps associated with mental processes.

WHAT IS INTELLIGENCE, AND HOW CAN WE MEASURE IT? p. 137

- Intelligence is the capacity to reason, solve problems, and acquire new knowledge.

- Intelligence tests, such as the Weschler Adult Intelligence Scale, measure aptitude rather than achievement.

- Genetics are believed to influence intelligence levels more than environmental factors do.

- Many psychologists believe there are multiple types of intelligence.

HOW DO WE REASON, SOLVE PROBLEMS, AND MAKE DECISIONS? p. 140

- We use current and remembered information to find a solution to a task. We can use specific strategies (such as algorithms) to solve problems, and we occasionally experience insight.

- Reasoning is the process of organizing information into a series of steps to reach conclusions. Overconfidence, belief bias, confirmation bias, and the conjunction fallacy may all lead to errors in reasoning.
- Decision making is the process of selecting and rejecting available options. Rational choice theory and prospect theory both explain aspects of human decision making.

HOW DOES ATTENTION HELP US PROCESS INFORMATION? p. 145

- Attention—the way the brain selectively processes important information—is either endogenous (goal-directed) or exogenous (stimulus-driven).

- Our attention is limited to a few stimuli at any one given time.

HOW ARE VERBAL AND VISUAL COGNITION RELATED? pp. 147 & 149

- According to the linguistic relativity hypothesis, the language we speak influences the way in which we perceive the world.

- According to dual-coding theory, we process words for concrete concepts both visually and verbally, but we only code words for abstract concepts verbally.

Test Your Understanding

1. By design, what IQ score indicates average intelligence?
   - a. 15
   - b. 100
   - c. 150
   - d. 200

2. Which of the following is a change that might be made to an IQ test in order to minimize score differences based on culture or background?
   - a. eliminate a time limit for taking the test
   - b. focus most test questions on cultural references known by persons in the lower socio-economic bracket
   - c. focus most test questions on cultural references known by the persons in the upper socio-economic bracket
   - d. focus most test questions on vocabulary

3. Robby, who has autism, has difficulty with many simple tasks, but can tell you which day of the week any date falls on. Robby can be best described as someone with:
   - a. creative intelligence.
   - b. savant syndrome.
   - c. fluid intelligence.
   - d. practical intelligence.

4. Which of the following jobs would be most likely to require emotional intelligence?
   - a. acting
   - b. scientific research
   - c. construction
   - d. playing an instrument

5. Many people who succeed in one area are also successful in other, seemingly unrelated areas. For example, a math prodigy might also be an accomplished musician, or author. This supports the existence of:
   - a. general intelligence.
   - b. multiple intelligences.
   - c. crystallized intelligence.
   - d. social intelligence.

6. Carrie, who is six years old and seems like a normal child her age, can already draw and paint better than most adults. Abby would be considered:
   - a. someone with savant syndrome.
   - b. a prodigy.
   - c. emotionally intelligent.
   - d. to have perceptual speed.

7. Which of the following is NOT true about IQ scores and their correlation with other factors?

   a. In children, the rate at which the brain matures is correlated with their IQ scores.

   b. Brain wave activity is correlated with IQ scores.

   c. People with the ability to quickly perceive and compare stimuli tend to have higher IQ scores.

   d. Brain size is strongly correlated with intelligence.

8. Mickey has a lot of friends in various groups and age brackets. This likely indicates that he:

   a. has high kinesthetic intelligence.

   b. has high analytic intelligence.

   c. has high social intelligence.

   d. is a prodigy.

9. Although flutes, clarinets, saxophones, and bagpipes may not all share one common feature, they all belong to the woodwind category of musical instruments because, as a group, they share a common mechanism for creating sounds. This is an example of:

   a. the exemplar theory.

   b. prototypes.

   c. the family resemblance theory.

   d. the functional fixedness theory.

10. Suppose a young child sees a strange looking bird at the zoo. Despite never having seen this creature before, the child is able to correctly identify it as a bird by mentally comparing it to other birds she has seen before. This is an example of:

    a. the exemplar theory.

    b. a mental set.

    c. the family resemblance theory.

    d. functional fixedness.

11. Ellyn is trying to hang a picture in her office, but does not have a hammer to put the nail in the wall. It never occurs to Ellyn that her stapler could be used to hammer the nail into the wall. This is an example of:

    a. an algorithm.

    b. discursive reasoning.

    c. a heuristic.

    d. functional fixedness.

12. Mari is playing a computer game in which the letters of a phrase are mixed up. After a few moments of methodically trying to rearrange the letters, she suddenly knows what the phrase is. This demonstrates:

    a. an algorithm.

    b. insight.

    c. syllogistic reasoning.

    d. discursive reasoning.

13. When handing in his final exam, Karim tells his professor that he is confident that he answered at least 95 percent of the questions correctly. Karim later finds out that he only answered 70 percent correctly. This is an example of what kind of reasoning error?

    a. belief perseverance

    b. belief bias

    c. hindsight bias

    d. overconfidence

14. When Gabriel hears the word "Muslim," she quickly thinks of the Islamic terrorists she sees on the news. As a result, Gabriel falsely believes that most Muslims are terrorists. This is an example of:

    a. the belief bias.

    b. the availability heuristic.

    c. the confirmation bias.

    d. the conjunction fallacy.

15. The brain's executive control systems are believed to be located primarily in the:

    a. frontal cortex.

    b. temporal cortex.

    c. amygdala.

    d. the brainstem.

16. Mia is shopping for a dress, but the one she likes best comes in three colors that she can't decide between. She gets discouraged and goes home. What does Mia display?

    a. belief bias

    b. decision aversion

    c. discursive reasoning

    d. style-shifting

17. Gwyn speaks much more formally with her boss at work than she does with her friends. What is Gwyn displaying a tendency toward?

    a. cooperating

    b. style-shifting

    c. linguistic determination

    d. filtering

18. Suppose you met a person who spoke a language that has names for only a few basic colors. Based on the linguistic relativity hypothesis, they:

    a. might perceive two similar colors as the same, while you perceive them as different.

    b. will be surprised by the number of different colors Americans use.

    c. will find it difficult to learn English.

    d. will rely more on visual coding than verbal coding.

19. During a boxing match, the excited announcer accidentally says, "What a blushing crow!" when he meant to say, "What a crushing blow!" This is an example of:

    a. word switching.

    b. opportunism.

    c. a spoonerism.

    d. structural ambiguity.

20. Suppose you had to memorize a list of 30 words. Based on the dual-coding theory, which of the following words would be most difficult to recall from the list?

    a. pencil

    b. carrot

    c. reason

    d. leaf

Remember to check www.thethinkspot.com for additional information, downloadable flashcards, and other helpful resources.

Answers: 1) b; 2) a; 3) b; 4) a; 5) a; 6) b; 7) d; 8) c; 9) c; 10) a; 11) d; 12) b; 13) d; 14) b; 15) a; 16) b; 17) b; 18) a; 19) c; 20) c

DISNEP
baby
einstein.

Baby's First Sounds
Discoveries for Little Ears

m-nama

$19.99

BORDERS.
BABY EINSTEIN-FIRST SOUNDS

B
M5
Z

BABY EINST 9353400   1
Infant/ Toddler 9557   93009   57
96D 643620

AGES
6 Mos.
Plus

HUMAN DEVELOPMENT I

Physical, Cognitive, and Language Development

HOW DO OUR BIOLOGY AND OUR ENVIRONMENTS INFLUENCE OUR DEVELOPMENT?

WHAT UNIVERSAL CHANGES DO WE EXPERIENCE AT DIFFERENT STAGES IN OUR LIVES?

WHAT ARE SOME OF THE LANDMARKS OF PHYSICAL, COGNITIVE, AND LANGUAGE DEVELOPMENT?

HOW DO PSYCHOLOGISTS STUDY HUMAN DEVELOPMENT, AND WHAT QUESTIONS HAVE YET TO BE ANSWERED?

For many

harassed parents, the concept seemed like a dream come true: Sit your child in front of a video every day, and he or she will soon be at the top of his or her class. Over the past decade, educational products such as the Baby Einstein and Brainy Baby video series have become a $20-billion-a-year business, aided by parents anxious to give their children an early head start on the road to success. But are learning videos and DVDs a worthy substitute for real human interaction? Research suggests that when it comes to language development, infants primarily benefit from face-to-face learning.

Russian psychologist Lev Vygotsky (1896–1934) theorized that children learn through social interaction. A child will imitate his or her parents' speech and behavior and then internalize the information. In other words, the learning process occurs first between parent and child, and then within the individual.

Although little is known about the actual process through which infants acquire language, Vygotsky's theory is supported by a recent study at the University of Washington. Researchers exposed a group of 9-month-old American infants to native Mandarin Chinese speakers over a course of 12 language sessions. A separate set of infants were exposed to the same foreign-language speakers and materials, but only via audio or audiovisual recordings. A control group of infants also participated in 12 language sessions, but heard only English. The group of infants who had interpersonal interaction with the speakers demonstrated phonetic learning. However, the group that had only heard prerecorded language lessons showed no signs of phonetic learning.

Why does human interaction make a difference in language acquisition? Patricia Kuhl and her colleagues at the University of Washington speculated that the presence of a live person during the first set of lessons provided critical social cues, attracting infants' attention and motivating learning. The infants were also able to follow visual cues provided by the speaker. For example, when the speakers focused on pictures in the books that they were talking about, the infants were able to follow the speakers' gaze, helping them to identify the vocabulary word for the object in the picture and segment it from ongoing speech.

Although the results of Kuhl's study are unlikely to foreshadow the meltdown of a multibillion-dollar industry, it does raise some interesting questions. How do infants acquire language? Why does our ability to discriminate foreign-language sounds decline at an early age? Is there a limit to the number of languages we can learn? Theorists continue to argue over the internal processes involved in cognitive and linguistic development.

<<< In late 2009, the Walt Disney Company—threatened by lawsuits and facing a wave of bad publicity—announced customer refunds for its line of Baby Einstein tapes. These videos, estimated to be used in at least a third of infant households in the United States, are a hit with new parents who want to entertain their children in educational ways. However, like most successful marketing schemes, the concept of a "baby Einstein" is simply too good to be true. In fact, according to studies by the American Academy of Pediatrics, watching television before the age of 2 leads to a slower acquisition of language, as well as attention problems later on in childhood.

CHAPTER 10

What Is Developmental Psychology?

Somewhere in the back of the family vault you may find photo albums, films, and baby books that preserve important moments throughout your life so far: that first tentative step, your first lost baby tooth, a traumatic first day of school, that regrettable fourth-grade haircut. Just as parents sometimes track their children's progress, **developmental psychologists** study the physical, cognitive, and social changes that we experience throughout our life spans. While you might look back at your own development and wonder why your family dressed you in silly outfits when you were a baby, developmental psychologists frame their questions around three major issues:

- **Stability/Change:** What aspects of you are present throughout your life, and what aspects have changed across your development?

- **Nature/Nurture:** How do both your genetics and your life experiences influence your development?

- **Continuity/Stages:** Is development a continual, gradual process, or do we develop in a series of stages?

RESEARCH METHODS

To answer these questions, developmental psychologists conduct research that documents developmental changes in two ways: **Age changes** track how individuals change as they age, while **age differences** consider how people of varying ages differ from one another. However, age is only one element to consider; differences in experience play an even more important role. Researchers use **normative investigations** to determine the landmarks of development—characteristics present at certain ages or stages of development. By identifying norms, or standard development patterns, researchers can differentiate between **chronological age**—the amount of time someone has spent alive—and **developmental age**—the point at which someone falls among developmental stages. Developmental psychologists tend to rely on two types of studies to frame their research questions. **Cross-sectional studies** observe different individuals at different ages to track age differences. While these studies are relatively quick, inexpensive, and

easy to conduct, they can't control for differences among age groups being studied. **Longitudinal studies** observe the same individuals over a period of time to track age changes. While they often provide very valuable insights, longitudinal studies require a great deal of time, money, and effort.

Conception—2 Weeks

Starting at conception, your zygote—the cell resulting from sperm and egg fusion—entered the germinal stage, a 2 week period of rapid cell division during which your cells differentiated into structural and functional specializations. At 10 days, you attached to Mom's uterine wall, forming the placenta, through which she passed you nourishment. If you were an identical twin, your zygote would have split in half during this period.

CONCEPTION

2 Weeks—8 Weeks

During your 6 weeks in the embryonic stage, your organs began to form and function, and your heart began to beat. At the end of this stage, you were a whopping one inch long.

8 Weeks—Birth

The fetal stage lasts from 8 weeks until birth. During this time, you were responsive to sound: You could hear your mother's muffled voice (Ecklund-Flores, 1992) and kick in response. At 6 months, your organs were fully developed, and you would have had a chance at survival if born prematurely. From that point until birth, you grew rapidly in size and developed an insulating layer of fat beneath your skin. Maturation of the respiratory and digestive systems, as well as sensitive brain development, also occurred.

twinkle in her eye, your mother was born with all the immature eggs, or **ova,** she will ever have. Of these ova, only one in 5,000 are ever released from the ovaries. Mom's eggs are 85,000 times the size of one of Dad's sperm, but he beats her in quantity: starting at puberty, he produces sperm cells 24 hours a day for the rest of his life, and he releases an average of 200 million sperm during a single act of intercourse. Only a few make it to the egg, and they begin eating at its protective coating. As soon as one sperm penetrates, the egg blocks the others out and uses finger-like projections to pull the lucky guy in. In less than half a day, Dad's sperm and Mom's egg have fused into a single zygote: you.

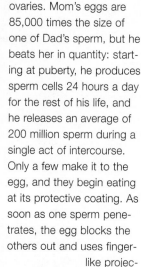

BIRTH

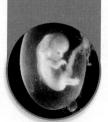

Stress and Harm

How much impact can a mother's lifestyle have on her unborn child? A pregnant woman's experiences are often shared with the developing life inside her. While the placenta blocks some harmful agents from passing from the mother to the embryo or fetus, other **teratogens** such as chemicals and viruses can infiltrate the womb and cause birth defects. Sounds like a good time to give up smoking!

Cigarettes aren't the only cause for concern during pregnancy—alcohol that a pregnant woman ingests can cause **fetal alcohol syndrome (FAS)**—physical and cognitive abnormalities in children resulting from a mother's heavy drinking. Researchers do not know how much alcohol at what point in the pregnancy can cause FAS; however, there is also no known "safe" amount of alcohol for a pregnant woman (Braun, 1996; Ikonomidou et al., 2000). FAS can cause noticeable facial misproportions and is the leading cause of mental retardation (Niccols, 1994; Streissguth et al., 1991).

If the thought of giving up smoking and drinking for nine months raises your blood pressure to dangerous levels, or you are

GERMINAL STAGE

EMBRYONIC STAGE

FETAL STAGE

Physical Development

PRENATAL DEVELOPMENT

We may not like to think about it, but for most of us, our development began during intercourse. Long before you were even a

prone to very high levels of stress, and you have two X chromosomes, you might want to reconsider having kids in the near future—a mother's psychological state and stress level are also believed to affect the fetus. Pregnant women with low self-esteem and high levels of pessimism, stress, and anxiety may be more likely to have premature births or babies with low birth weight (Rini et al., 1999).

Infant Reflexes

Even before you had much time to adjust to the world outside Mom's amniotic sac, you were hardwired to interact with it. At birth, your body began breathing air, regulating its temperature, and crying when hungry. The following table shows some of the reflexes that newborn babies exhibit. Doctors often check these reflexes to ensure the nervous system is functioning correctly.

INFANCY AND CHILDHOOD

Neural Development

Your head might be filled with years of knowledge and experience, but you actually had almost all of the brain cells you were ever going to get at birth. While in the womb, your body formed nearly a quarter of a million nerve cells a minute, while your brain cortex peaked in its production of neurons at 28 weeks, subsiding to a mere 23 billion cells when you were born.

Although your brain might have reached its full capacity of cells as a newborn, your nervous system was still immature. As you interacted more with the world around you, the neural networks that allowed you to walk, talk, and remember underwent a major growth spurt. From ages three to six years, your brain experienced the greatest growth spurt in the frontal lobes—the area of the brain associated

Developmental psychologists study the physical, cognitive, and social changes that people experience throughout their lives.

Age changes track how individuals change as they age.

Age differences consider how people of varying ages differ from one another.

Normative investigations consist of research conducted in order to establish norms.

Chronological age is the amount of time that has passed since a person was born.

Developmental age is the point at which someone falls among developmental stages; not necessarily related to chronological age.

Cross-sectional studies collect data from different individuals at different ages in order to track age differences.

Longitudinal studies collect data from the same individuals over a period of time to track age changes.

Ova are immature eggs

Teratogens are toxic substances that cross the placenta and may cause birth defects.

Fetal alcohol syndrome (FAS) consists of physical and cognitive abnormalities in children resulting from a mother's heavy drinking.

Motor development is the emergent ability to execute physical actions.

Cephalocaudal rule is the tendency for motor skills to emerge in sequence from top to bottom.

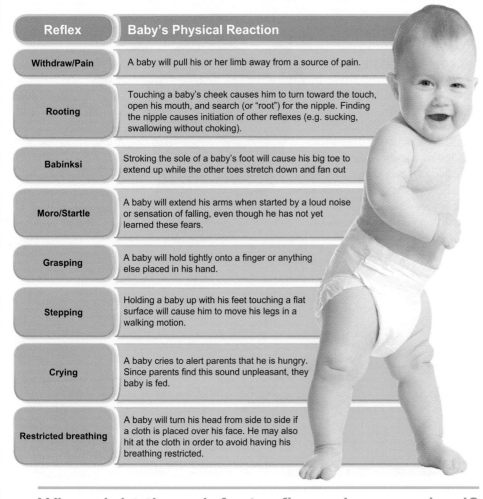

Reflex	Baby's Physical Reaction
Withdraw/Pain	A baby will pull his or her limb away from a source of pain.
Rooting	Touching a baby's cheek causes him to turn toward the touch, open his mouth, and search (or "root") for the nipple. Finding the nipple causes initiation of other reflexes (e.g. sucking, swallowing without choking).
Babinksi	Stroking the sole of a baby's foot will cause his big toe to extend up while the other toes stretch down and fan out
Moro/Startle	A baby will extend his arms when started by a loud noise or sensation of falling, even though he has not yet learned these fears.
Grasping	A baby will hold tightly onto a finger or anything else placed in his hand.
Stepping	Holding a baby up with his feet touching a flat surface will cause him to move his legs in a walking motion.
Crying	A baby cries to alert parents that he is hungry. Since parents find this sound unpleasant, they baby is fed.
Restricted breathing	A baby will turn his head from side to side if a cloth is placed over his face. He may also hit at the cloth in order to avoid having his breathing restricted.

∧
∧ Why might these infant reflexes have evolved?
∧ How might they have provided an evolutionary advantage?

with higher mental functions, such as personality and complex decision making—which continue to develop throughout your life span. Among the last areas of the cortex to develop are those associated with thinking, memory, and language.

Motor Development

As your muscles and nervous system developed, so too did your physical coordination. **Motor development**—the emergent ability to execute physical actions—tends to occur in a universal sequence. Like most other babies, you likely rolled over before you could sit up and crawled before you could walk. This sequence tends to be true for visually impaired children as well, suggesting that these behaviors do not merely reflect imitation.

Two general rules govern the development of motor skills. The **cephalocaudal rule** is the tendency for motor skills to emerge in sequence from top to bottom. Recall the rooting reflex, which causes the baby to move his or her head, open his or her mouth, and search for a nipple; as a baby, your head had very capable motor skills long before your legs would allow you to walk. The **proximodistal rule** is the tendency for motor skills to emerge in sequence from inside to outside. As a child, the center of your body possessed motor skills before the periphery. Do you remember learning to write? You probably started out by holding the pencil far from the tip because you initially used your shoulder to make the pencil move. The source of movement then worked its way down to your elbow, and finally to your fingers and thumb (Payne & Isaacs, 1987).

While the sequence of motor skill development is generally universal, the timing can vary based on an individual's genetics or experiences. The likelihood that identical twins sit up and walk on almost the same day suggests a genetic influence (Wilson, 1979). Experience may delay motor development: U.S. infants who are placed on their backs to sleep often

crawl later than infants placed on their stomachs, but the sleeping habit does not seem to affect onset of walking (Davis et al., 1998; Lipsitt, 2003). However, experience can do little to rush motor skills before adequate muscular and neural maturity have been reached. Most babies are ready to walk at around one year, when the cerebellum has developed enough to enable physical coordination. A parent could try to beg or cajole a six-month-old infant into walking earlier than his or her peers, but it will have little positive impact. Other physical skills, such as bowel and bladder control, are also resistant to being hurried along.

ADOLESCENCE

Puberty

After a period in childhood during which we grow and refine our skills, the onset of **adolescence**—the period of transition from childhood to adulthood—is marked by one of the most awkward periods of our lives: **puberty**. During this period, our bodies go through the physical changes that allow us to reproduce. These include growth spurts in height, changes in body shapes, and development of **primary sex characteristics**—reproductive organs and external genitalia—and **secondary sex characteristics**—nonreproductive traits, such as breasts and hips in girls, facial hair and deeper voices in boys, and pubic and underarm hair for both. As you may well remember, the landmarks of puberty are **menarche**—a girl's first menstruation—and **spermarche**—a boy's first ejaculation.

In North America, the average age for the onset of puberty is 10 for girls and 12 for boys. In preindustrial cultures, the growth spurt starts about four years later, consistent with North American trends 125 years ago. A similar trend is evident with menarche, which tends to occur between ages 12–13 in North America today and, consistent with 19th century onset, between ages 16–17 in some preindustrial cultures. Factors such as increased food intake and decreased incidence of disease are believed to contribute to the relatively early onset of puberty in North America.

Brain Development

If the awkwardness of puberty isn't enough of an explanation as to why adolescents are characteristically moody, emotionally immature, and all-around difficult, a look at what's going on with the brain during this period should provide more insight. Up until puberty, brain cells are increasing their connections, but during adolescence, the brain adopts a "use it or lose it" policy and selectively prunes neurons and connections that aren't being used (Durston et al., 2001).

Adolescents are also dealing with different rates of development in their brains. The maturation of the limbic system, which controls emotions, occurs more quickly than the maturation of the frontal lobe. Teens may feel like adults, but they lack the ability to make sensible,

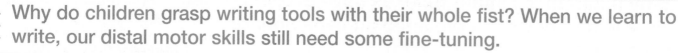

Why do children grasp writing tools with their whole fist? When we learn to write, our distal motor skills still need some fine-tuning.

well-thought-out decisions (Baird & Fugelsang, 2004). Couple this with surging hormones and you have a perfect storm, resulting in the impulsive and risky behaviors for which adolescents are infamous. Teenage immaturity can lead to significant consequences if adolescents go so far as to break the law. In 2005, however, a Supreme Court ruling against capital punishment for juveniles legally recognized a biological deficiency in their judgment. As the frontal lobes become more fully developed in the later teenage years and early 20s, most will experience a marked improvement in judgment, impulse control, and the ability to plan for the future (Bennett & Baird, 2006).

EARLY ADULTHOOD

If we manage to make it through the travails of adolescence, we are rewarded with the peak physical abilities of early adulthood. As with the onset of puberty, women tend to peak earlier than men. In our mid-20s, our muscles are strong, our reaction times are quick, and most of us barely notice the early signs of physical decline, such as wrinkles around the eyes and neck.

MIDDLE ADULTHOOD

As we move into middle adulthood, physical vigor becomes less to do with age and more to do with our health and exercise habits. No longer can we party until the early hours, eat pizza for breakfast three times a week, and still feel fit enough to run a marathon. Smokers, heavy drinkers, and sunbathers are more likely to look and feel older than those who avoid unhealthy behaviors, pay attention to nutrition, exercise, and reduce stress. However, there is generally little we can do to fully combat the inevitable declines in hearing, vision, metabolism, physical strength, and fertility.

Depending on how we perceive the aging process, physical changes can bring about varying psychological responses. Western cultures tend to view aging negatively—a perception that often causes the stereotypical midlife crisis. Ever seen a middle-aged man with hair plugs driving a convertible sports car? How about a woman whose breasts seem unnaturally perky for her age? They are likely experiencing a fear of aging. While research suggests that only 10 percent reported experiencing a midlife crisis

(Brim, 1999), an overall obsession with age is evident in TV shows like TLC's *10 Years Younger.* Participants stand inside a clear box in a public place while strangers guess their age. After the "glam squad" of doctors, dentists, and stylists attempt to take a decade off the participant's looks, the experiment is repeated. Still, others embrace aging for the wisdom and stability that often accompany it. In some Eastern cultures, with aging comes great respect and power.

Decline in Fertility

Tick-tock. Tick-tock. Despite advancements in gender equality and science, women in middle (and sometimes even early) adulthood have a hard time shutting out the sound of

> **Teenage immaturity can lead to significant consequences if adolescents go so far as to break the law. In 2005, however, a Supreme Court ruling against capital punishment for juveniles legally recognized a biological deficiency in their judgment.**

the ticking biological clock counting down their fertile years. For women between the ages of 35–39, a single act of intercourse is half as likely to result in pregnancy than it would be for a 19- to 26-year-old (Dunson et al., 2002). Within a few years of age 50, most women begin **menopause**—the end of the menstrual cycle and ability to bear children, accompanied by a reduction in estrogen, which can have uncomfortable effects, such as hot flashes.

As with aging in general, a woman's psychological response to menopause will depend on her attitude toward it. One study of postmenopausal women found that most of them recalled feeling "only relief" when their periods ceased, and only 2 percent felt "only regret" (Goode, 1999). Some women may lose a sense of their femininity and experience a decreased interest in sex, while others may celebrate that they no longer have to bother with feminine hygiene products and birth control methods.

Aging men experience more gradual sexual changes than women. What some call **andropause** (Carruthers, 2001) includes

decline in sperm count, testosterone level, and speed of erection and ejaculation. If testosterone levels decline too rapidly, men may experience depression, irritability, insomnia, impotence, or weakness—effects that can be treated with testosterone replacement therapy. For men, psychological reactions to a perceived decrease in virility may be tempered by the relatively long-term and subtle onset of these changes.

LATER ADULTHOOD

Life Expectancy

As worldwide life expectancy increases, from 49 in 1950 to 67 in 2004, and birth rates decrease, the portion of the population in later adulthood is growing. By the year 2050, approximately 35 percent of the European population will be over age 60 (Population Division of the Department of Economic and Social Affairs of the United Nations Secretariat, 2006). But don't assume they'll all be knitting in rockers. For both women and men, a decline in fertility does not necessarily mean a decline in sexuality. When the National Council of Aging surveyed adults over 60, they found that 39 percent reported they were satisfied with the amount of sex they were having, and 39 percent reported wanting to have more sex (Leary, 1998).

Movies often portray older women circling single elderly men in a nursing home like hungry sharks. Statistically, eligible bachelors over the age of 65 are a fairly rare breed—women outlive men by four years throughout the world and five to six years in the U.S., Canada, and Australia. At birth, there are 105 males for every 100 females. However, during the first year, the death rate for male infants is one-fourth more than that of female infants, and by age 100, women outnumber men five to one.

Few people live to be 100—in fact, if you are lucky enough to reach your centennial year in the U.K., you will receive a telegram from the Queen. However, the honor may come with a pretty steep price. The decline in our vision, muscle strength, reaction time, stamina, hearing, distance perception, and sense of smell make daily living rather challenging. The aging body is also vulnerable to many things it could have easily handled in youth, such as hot weather and falling. Although older people are less likely to suffer common short-term ailments because of all the antibodies they have accumulated over a lifetime, their ability to fight off other diseases makes them susceptible to life-threatening ailments like cancer and pneumonia.

Even if these and other ailments didn't exist and no one died before age 50, we would probably only ever top out at an average life expectancy of 85 years (Barinaga, 1991). Evolutionary biologists propose that the reason we eventually decline relates to the survival of our species. We are best able to pass on our genes when we raise young, then stop consuming resources, so younger generations are more likely to have what they need to reach child-bearing age and reproduce.

Brain Development

Like the body, the brain also declines with aging. Neural processing slows, and older adults take more time than younger adults to react, solve perceptual puzzles, and remember names. Memory decline may be partly explained by the gradual loss of brain cells that begins in early adulthood and causes an approximately 5 percent

>>> **Many studies have demonstrated that sedentary older adults show improvement in memory and judgment after adopting an aerobic exercise routine (Kramer et al., 1999).**

reduction in brain weight by age 80. The region of greatest cell loss tends to occur in the frontal lobes, which handle memory storage and other higher-mental functions. This decline is slower in women and active adults. Exercise, which causes increased oxygen and nutrient flow, not only enhances muscle strength, bone strength, and energy, as well as prevents obesity and heart disease, but also stimulates the development of brain cells and neural connections.

Cognitive Development

We now know the physical changes that the body experiences, from conception to old age. But how does our ability to develop thought materialize? When do we begin to remember our early experiences? How do we learn to communicate? Psychologists study **cognition**, the plethora of mental activities associated with sensation and perception, thinking, knowing, remembering, and communicating, to find answers.

INFANCY AND CHILDHOOD

Sensation and Perception

Although babies' sensory systems are functioning at birth, their vision is still immature, so research into this area of their cognitive development is challenging. Researchers have developed investigative techniques, such as eye-tracking machines and electronically wired pacifiers, to capitalize on the baby's ability to gaze, suck, and turn the head. Findings show that babies turn their heads in the direction of human voices, look longer at images that look like faces than images that look like other patterns (Fantz, 1961), and prefer to look at objects that are eight to 12 inches away, which is the approximate distance of the baby from the mother while nursing (Maurer & Maurer, 1988). These perceptual abilities develop rapidly; a few days after you were born, your neural networks had attuned to your mother's smell and voice. When placed between a gauze pad from the mother's bra and that of another nursing woman, a one-week-old nursing baby will turn toward that of his or her mother (MacFarlane, 1978). A three-week-old baby will suck on a pacifier more when recordings of his or her mother's voice are played than when those of a female stranger are played (Mills & Melhuish, 1974; Kisilevsky et al., 2003).

Stimuli Preferences

As with vision, speaking ability in infants is also immature, so they can't tell researchers why they do the things they do. Using several studies, researchers have inferred that babies have a preference for new stimuli and stimuli that they can control. The preference for new stimuli is associated with observed **habituation**—decreased responsiveness with repeated stimulation. Imagine that you came home from work to find a horse in your living room—you would probably react fairly strongly! But if the horse remained in your living room for several weeks, you would eventually get used to it being there when you came home and respond less dramatically. Infants who are repeatedly exposed to a familiar stimulus will begin looking away from it sooner than they previously did and are more likely to look longer at an unfamiliar stimulus than at a

familiar stimulus when presented with the option. This tendency suggests that babies have memory for the familiar stimulus and that they seek to learn from things that are new to them.

The tendency for five- to six-month-old babies to examine—manipulate and explore objects by holding them in front of the eyes, turning them around, and passing them from hand to hand—also appears to be related to a desire to learn. Examining, which seems to be an innate behavior that doesn't need to be learned and is present in every culture, also declines with an object's increased familiarity.

Interestingly, it seems we all start out with type-A tendencies: Babies display a particular interest in the parts of their environments that they can control. In one study, two-month-olds attended more to a

<<< Some of us continue to make this face throughout our lives when we don't have control over situations.

mobile they controlled with their own bodies than to a mobile they did not control (Watson & Ramey, 1972). They also learned to turn on a video and sound recording of the *Sesame Street* theme song by pulling a string attached to their wrists. When the device was disconnected and the babies could no longer control it, they showed facial expressions of anger. Follow-up research at four to five months revealed that babies showed the same facial expressions of anger and sadness when they couldn't control the video/sound recording

even if it still came on (but was instead under the experimenter's control) (Alessandri et al., 1990; Lewis et al., 1990).

Piaget's Theory of Cognitive Development

Jean Piaget's early 20th-century observations led him to believe that children didn't simply know less than adults, but that they instead understood the world around them differently. His revolutionary ideas presented children's minds not as miniature adult minds but rather as minds that develop in a series of stages, driven by an intrinsic motivation to explore and understand.

Piaget's theory described two processes by which we adjust our **schemas**—concepts or

Memory is one cognitive process that develops and changes during childhood.

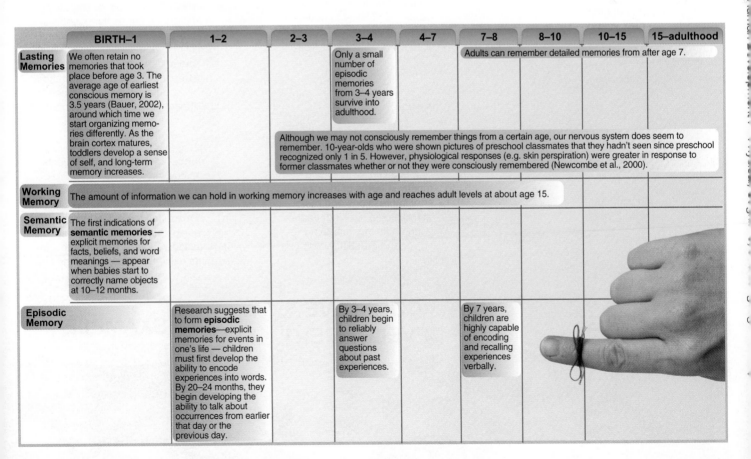

	BIRTH–1	1–2	2–3	3–4	4–7	7–8	8–10	10–15	15–adulthood
Lasting Memories	We often retain no memories that took place before age 3. The average age of earliest conscious memory is 3.5 years (Bauer, 2002), around which time we start organizing memories differently. As the brain cortex matures, toddlers develop a sense of self, and long-term memory increases.			Only a small number of episodic memories from 3–4 years survive into adulthood.	Adults can remember detailed memories from after age 7.				
			Although we may not consciously remember things from a certain age, our nervous system does seem to remember. 10-year-olds who were shown pictures of preschool classmates that they hadn't seen since preschool recognized only 1 in 5. However, physiological responses (e.g. skin perspiration) were greater in response to former classmates whether or not they were consciously remembered (Newcombe et al., 2000).					
Working Memory	The amount of information we can hold in working memory increases with age and reaches adult levels at about age 15.								
Semantic Memory	The first indications of **semantic memories** — explicit memories for facts, beliefs, and word meanings — appear when babies start to correctly name objects at 10–12 months.								
Episodic Memory		Research suggests that to form **episodic memories**—explicit memories for events in one's life — children must first develop the ability to encode experiences into words. By 20–24 months, they begin developing the ability to talk about occurrences from earlier that day or the previous day.		By 3–4 years, children begin to reliably answer questions about past experiences.		By 7 years, children are highly capable of encoding and recalling experiences verbally.			

frameworks around which we organize and interpret information. Using **assimilation**, we interpret new experiences in terms of existing schemas. Under this process, a child with a pet cat might see a dog for the first time and say "cat" because both animals have four legs and fur. However, once the child learns the differences between dogs and cats, he or she will use **accommodation** to adjust and refine his or her schema for cat in order to incorporate the new information he or she has learned about the differences between cats and dogs. The main idea of Piaget's theory is that mental development derives from children's interactions with the world around them. This idea implies an educational approach that is interactive and hands-on and that encourages (even the very youngest) students to think for themselves.

Piaget described this cognitive development as occurring in four stages from infancy to adulthood. These stages focus more on sequencing than the age at which milestones are reached. They are summarized in the following table:

Piaget's Stages of Cognitive Development

STAGE	COGNITIVE DEVELOPMENT	EXAMPLE
Formal Operational (12 years – adulthood)	People begin to think logically about abstract concepts.	Teenagers may get involved in **hypothetical thinking**—imagining possibilities or impossibilities.
Concrete Operational (7–12 years)	Children gain the mental operations that allow them to think logically about concrete events.	Children understand **conservation**—the principle that properties such as mass, volume, and number remain the same despite the objects' changes in the form.
Preoperational (2–7 years)	Children learn to use language but do not yet possess the abilities to understand mental operations of concrete logic.	Children exhibit **egocentrism**—not intentional selfishness, but difficulty taking another's point of view. As they develop **theory of mind**—ideas about their own versus others' mental states—they can infer others' feelings; tease, empathize, and persuade; explain people's behaviors in terms of perceptions, emotions, and desires (2–3 years); understand that thoughts may cause feelings; and understand that spontaneous self-produced thoughts may create feelings (5–8 years).
Sensorimotor (birth–2 years)	Infants know the world mostly in terms of their sensory impressions and motor activities (i.e. looking, hearing, touching, mouthing, and grasping).	Young infants lack **object permanence**—awareness that objects continue to exist when they are no longer perceived. Infants under 5 months may fail simple object permanence tests due to difficulty planning the correct movement of the hidden object. By 8 months, infants exhibit memory for things that are not perceived.

Reflections on Piaget's Theory

While Piaget's ideas about children learning through interacting with their environment have been widely adopted in the educational world, many researchers today understand cognitive development as more fluid and continuous than Piaget did. Many also believe that he may have underestimated children's cognitive abilities. While Piaget thought that babies couldn't think before age two, researchers have found that babies do possess some logic: They look longer at unexpected scenes, such as a car passing through a solid object (Baillargeon, 1995, 1998, 2004; Wellman & Gelman, 1992) or numerically impossible outcomes (Wynn, 1992, 2000). Researchers now disagree about whether the foundations of formal operational thinking emerge earlier than when children begin adolescence and whether Piaget may have underestimated the role of social interactions in cognitive development.

Vygotsky's Social Influence Theory

Leading the case for social influence on cognitive development was Russian psychologist Lev Vygotsky, who believed that development occurs on a social level before it occurs at the individual level. He considered the **zone of proximal development**—the difference between what a child can do alone versus what a child can do together with a more competent person. While learning in the zone of proximal development, dialogue can encourage critical thinking and revision and questioning of ideas so that they are either improved or discarded.

Unlike Piaget, who took the view of the child as a scientist with the goal of developing logic skills, Vygotsky believed the child was more like an apprentice with the goal of developing the ability to function effectively in adult society. According to Vygotsky, children want to participate in the activities that are central to their culture. As a result, the cognitive development of children is influenced by their specific cultural

experiences—their homes, schools, and meeting places. While a child in an industrialized country may learn math in a formal school environment, a child in a non-industrialized country may learn arithmetic through interactions with others in the community.

We can see Vygotsky's theories in practice when we watch babies using cues from adults to guide their behavior. At six months, they mimic adult's actions on objects, and from six to 12 months, they engage in **joint visual attention**—they look at the adult's eyes, follow the gaze, and then direct their own gaze toward whatever the adult is looking at (Corkum & Moore, 1998). This tendency helps babies learn what is of most interest to adults and aids in language development. By the end of the first year, babies engage in social referencing—they look at the emotional expressions of caregivers for cues about what may be dangerous (Rosen et al., 1992).

ADOLESCENCE
Reasoning

Teenagers are often stereotyped as moody and impulsive, and this stereotype isn't entirely unfair: While plenty of adolescents see themselves as completely grown up, our frontal lobes aren't fully developed until we reach our

---

Assimilation is a process in which a person interprets new experiences in terms of existing schemas.

Accommodation is a process in which a person adjusts and refines his or her schemas based on new information.

Zone of proximal development refers to the difference between what a child can do alone versus what a child can do together with a more competent person.

Joint visual attention describes a behavior in which a baby looks at an adult's eyes, follows the adult's gaze, and then directs his or her own gaze toward whatever the adult is looking at.

Reason is the skill of organizing information and beliefs into a series of steps leading to a conclusion.

" You may have felt a new kind of social awareness and moral judgment during adolescence. It's no coincidence that adolescents begin to think about and criticize society and to have strong opinions about, well, pretty much everything. Early adolescence typically focuses reasoning on the self. "

---

early 20s. As the frontal lobes develop, they enable us to **reason**—to organize information and beliefs into a series of steps leading to a conclusion. You may have felt a new kind of social awareness and moral judgment during adolescence. It's no coincidence that adolescents begin to think about and criticize society and to have strong opinions about, well, pretty much everything. Early adolescence typically focuses reasoning on the self. If you ever yelled something like "You don't understand what I'm going through!" and stormed off to your room, slamming the door and turning up your music, then you understand that adolescents often feel as though their experiences are utterly unique and earth-shatteringly significant.

Gradually, most adolescents reach the formal operational stage described earlier. As they become increasingly capable of abstract logic, they can reason hypothetically, reach conclusions, and identify flaws in others' opinions. Looking back, do you remember a point at which you suddenly had not only strong opinions but also the reasoning skills to back them up? This overlap can often be the cause

<<< "You don't understand what I'm going through!" Teenagers have a tendency to focus on the self.

longer than younger adults to produce their memories. **Prospective memory**—remembering to perform a specific action, such as calling someone back or bringing lunch to the office—remains strong if time management and reminder cues are used. Time-based and habitual tasks, however, are challenging. The good news for older adults is that their ability to learn and remember skills declines less than their verbal recall ability.

Intelligence

Understanding intelligence in later adulthood has been challenging and controversial. David Wechsler, who is perhaps best known for his intelligence scales, believed that deterioration of mental ability is an inherent part of aging. His cross-sectional study compared 70-year-olds and 30-year-olds from different eras, so his conclusions were based on confounded comparisons that failed to account for differences among **cohorts**— groups of people raised during the same time period.

Later longitudinal studies have brought down the myth of declining intelligence across the life span, with findings that intelligence remains stable and may even increase into later adulthood. However, these studies also have their pitfalls: It is possible that individuals who survived to the end of the studies were those with intelligence least likely to deteriorate.

Language Development

We might have an IQ of 130, but without the ability to talk, our genius would likely remain undiscovered. Language allows us to think in words rather than pictures, communicate our thoughts and feelings to others, and learn by asking questions. It is obviously a vital skill, but how does our ability to use language develop?

UNIVERSAL ELEMENTS OF HUMAN LANGUAGE

Although there are thousands of different languages across the world, several characteristics are common among them all. These similarities may account for the observed cross-cultural similarities in language development among humans. Every language has the same structure of units:

Morphemes are the smallest meaningful units that represent the objects, events, ideas, characteristics, and relationships in a language's vocabulary. **Phonemes** are the elementary vowel and consonant sounds that combine to form morphemes. Grammar governs the appropriate ways to arrange units at each level with rules of **phonology**—how phonemes may be arranged to produce morphemes, **morphology**—how morphemes may be arranged to form words, and **syntax**—how words may be arranged to produce phrases and sentences.

LANGUAGE DEVELOPMENT PROCESS

Cooing and Babbling

When you were born, you already had the capacity to communicate. You cried to communicate hunger and made other sounds to communicate distress. At about two months, you developed the capacity to make pleasant cooing sounds—repeated and drawn-out vowel sounds—to communicate happiness. At about six months, your cooing progressed to babbling—repeated consonant and vowel sounds. Cooing and babbling helped you develop and strengthen the muscle movements necessary for speech.

These early sounds appear not to depend on the spoken sounds an infant hears. Babbling is as likely to contain sounds of a foreign language as of a native one. Prior to 12 months, Japanese babies differentiate *ra* and *la* sounds, which are not present in their native language (Werker, 1989). By eight months, hearing infants

of conflict with parents and other authority figures, as adolescents develop their own thoughts and beliefs about the world.

ADULTHOOD
Memory

As with physical vigor, some types of learning and remembering peak in early adulthood. While younger adults have higher recall than older adults (for example, being asked to remember a list of words in a memory test), they don't have higher recognition (for example, being shown a list of words and asked to point out which words were in the memory test). Moreover, unless adults are given caffeine, recognition is better earlier rather than later in the day (Schonfield & Robertson, 1966).

Additionally, older people tend to make more errors than younger people when trying to recall meaningless information, such as nonsense syllables and unimportant events (Gordon & Clark, 1974). Although meaningful information is more easily remembered, older adults take

> "Although there are thousands of different languages across the world, several characteristics are common among them all."

But what exactly is intelligence? While generally conceived as the ability to learn from one's experiences, acquire knowledge, and use resources to adapt to new situations (Sternberg & Kaufman, 1998; Wechsler, 1975), intelligence is an imprecise catch-all term that describes many different traits, making intelligence studies extremely problematic. One of these traits, wisdom, describes the expertise in the fundamental practices of living acquired over a long and thoughtful life. Wisdom studies usually present participants with hypothetical situations and elicit think-aloud responses from them. Due to the subjectivity inherent in evaluating such questions and answers, as well as the presence of cultural biases, these studies often fail to provide conclusive results.

tend to babble in ways that mimic the language to which they are most exposed, and by 10 months their babbling resembles syllables and words of the native language. This change may result from parents reinforcing the babbling sounds that most mimic their adult language (Skinner, 1957). At 10 months, if hearing-impaired infants, who babble at the same time and in the same way as hearing infants, are exposed to sign language, they will begin "babbling" with their hands, repeating hand movements that resemble those of sign language (Petitto & Marentette, 1991).

Vocabulary Development

Before you could produce words, you were able to understand what some of them meant. By about nine months, you could respond to some common words by looking at the correct object that had been named and could follow simple commands (Balaban & Waxman, 1997; Benedict, 1979). Shortly thereafter, at around 10–12 months, you began producing your first recognizable words, and the rate of word acquisition accelerated from 15–20 months. At about 18 months, you went through a period of naming explosion during which you learned up to 45 new nouns each day to refer to the objects around you. Before you pat yourself on the back for your prolific rate of achievement, you probably hadn't yet perfected correct usage of all these words: You likely **overextended**—used common nouns more broadly than in the adult language would—or **underextended**—used them more narrowly than in the adult language would. Some research suggests that the latter is more common than the former (MacWhinney, 1998). How do these tendencies relate to Piaget's concepts of assimilation and accommodation?

Grammar

After a long period of one-word utterances, at about 18–24 months, you began to put together mostly **content words**—words that have meaning, as opposed to **grammatical words**, which provide structure. Your utterances probably contained mostly nouns and verbs along the lines of "kitty eat" and "doggy sleep." Before formal schooling began, you actively and unconsciously inferred grammatical rules from the language you heard. However, you probably overgeneralized the new rules you acquired, such as adding –s to pluralize. By age four, you had acquired much of the gram-

mar necessary to carry on meaningful conversations. Rules of grammar are encoded in implicit memory (memories that aren't easily brought into conscious awareness and are necessary to perform tasks, skills, habits, and learned reflexes) rather than explicit memory (memories of events from the external world that are easily brought from long-term storage to short-term memory), and people can often correctly apply grammatical rules that they can't name or describe.

THEORIES OF LANGUAGE ACQUISITION

Chomsky's Language Acquisition Device

In contrast to B. F. Skinner's ideas that children learn language through reinforcement, linguist

> " At 10 months, if hearing-impaired infants, who babble at the same time and in the same way as hearing infants, are exposed to sign language, they will begin "babbling" with their hands, repeating hand movements that resemble those of sign language (Petitto & Marentette, 1991). "

Noam Chomsky argued that children are born with a **language acquisition device (LAD)** that provides them an inherent foundation for the principles of universal grammar. In his book *Syntactic Structures*, he emphasized the hierarchical structure of sentences and argued that a person must have a meaningful representation of the sentence in mind before producing it and then must apply grammatical rules to that representation and fill out the lower levels of the hierarchy (Chomsky, 1957).

Critical Period

Similar to the way the senses must be used early on in life in order to function properly, language acquisition has a critical period—it is acquired most effectively in the years before puberty (Lenneberg, 1967). Therefore, children deprived of the opportunity to learn language during this time face major difficulties learning it later, and they never fully master the grammar. One famous case study is that of 13-year-old

Genie, a severely neglected teen who was rescued from an abusive home in Los Angeles, California, in 1970 (Curtiss et al., 1974). Initially unable to say more than a couple of words, Genie quickly acquired a large vocabulary. However, she was unable to comprehend the grammar needed to produce fluent sentences. Psychologists used Genie's case to prove the existence of a critical period, although critics argue that the severe trauma she suffered may have affected her learning.

People who learned their first language during the critical period are able to learn a second language reasonably well at any point in life. However, a second language is better learned during one's early years, as those who learn one after they are 10 or 11 years old almost always speak with an accent and don't acquire grammatical rules as fully or easily as those who learned the language when they were younger.

Social Environment

Psychologists widely agree that inborn mechanisms cannot fully account for language acquisition. Normal language development requires the **language-acquisition support system (LASS)**—the social environment into which the baby is born. In order to help children learn, adults often alter their speech into child-directed speech or "motherese," which features exaggerated, high-pitched intonation and may contain affective messages in order to grab infants' attention, keep them interested, provide support, and give warnings. However, children around the world acquire language at about the same rate, despite great differences in the nature and degree of adult verbal interactions with children.

10 Review

Summary

HOW DO OUR BIOLOGY AND OUR ENVIRONMENTS INFLUENCE OUR DEVELOPMENT? pp. 154 & 156

• During pregnancy, teratogens can pass through the placenta and cause irreparable harm to an embryo or fetus.

• Increased food intake and a decrease in disease may contribute to the earlier onset of puberty in industrialized countries.

WHAT UNIVERSAL CHANGES DO WE EXPERIENCE AT DIFFERENT STAGES IN OUR LIVES? pp. 155–158

• Newborn babies exhibit reflexes including rooting, sucking, swallowing, grasping, and stepping.

• Motor skills tend to develop in sequence from top to bottom and from inside to outside.

• During puberty, the body develops primary and secondary sex characteristics.

• The gradual loss of brain cells as we age leads to a decline in memory.

WHAT ARE SOME OF THE LANDMARKS OF PHYSICAL, COGNITIVE, AND LANGUAGE DEVELOPMENT? pp. 154, 160, & 162

• Physical landmarks include the germinal, embryonic, and fetal stages, newborn reflex actions, motor development, puberty, menopause and andropause, and the physical decline of old age.

• Piaget theorized that children use assimilation and accommodation to adjust their informational schemas. Vygotsky believed children's cognitive development is influenced by cultural experiences.

• Language development landmarks include cooing and babbling, producing vocabulary, and learning grammatical rules.

HOW DO PSYCHOLOGISTS STUDY HUMAN DEVELOPMENT, AND WHAT QUESTIONS HAVE YET TO BE ANSWERED? p. 154

• Developmental psychologists study the physical, cognitive, and social changes we experience by examining three issues: stability/change, nature/nurture, and continuity/stages.

• Researchers perform both cross-sectional and longitudinal developmental studies.

• Normative investigations enable researchers to distinguish between chronological age and developmental age.

Test Your Understanding

1. When a baby is held up in a standing position, what reflex does he or she exhibit?
   a. grasping
   b. crying
   c. rooting
   d. stepping

2. Starting when they are 6 months old, a researcher observes the same children once a month to determine at what age most children stop sucking their thumbs. This is:
   a. a cross-sectional study.
   b. a longitudinal study.
   c. a biased study.
   d. an age difference study.

3. Max, who is in high school, experiences a growth spurt later than all of his classmates of his same age. Max might have:
   a. an older chronological age than his developmental age.
   b. a younger chronological age than his developmental age.
   c. delayed motor development.
   d. a different cephalocaudal rule than his friends.

4. Babies almost always develop the motor skills necessary to grab objects with their hands before they learn to walk. This is an example of the:
   a. Babinksi reflex.
   b. rooting reflex.
   c. cephalocaudal rule.
   d. proximodistal rule.

5. Which of the following is NOT associated with puberty?
   a. changes in secondary sex characteristics
   b. spermarche
   c. menarche
   d. andropause

6. Which of the following is a cultural practice having to do with a secondary sex characteristic?
   a. shaving facial hair
   b. wearing tights or pants
   c. circumcision
   d. menstruation

7. Why are the cognitive and motor abilities of newborns limited?

   a. The birth process is stressful.

   b. They have fewer neurons than adults do.

   c. Their neurons are depolarized.

   d. Their brains and nervous systems are immature.

8. Which of the following might contribute to teenagers engaging in risky sexual activity?

   a. The frontal lobe of the brain does not reach maturity until a person is in his or her 20s.

   b. The limbic system of the brain does not reach maturity until a person is in his or her 20s.

   c. Teenagers have not yet reached the concrete operational stage.

   d. Teenagers do not understand the possible consequences of risky sex.

9. Men using prescription drugs to increase virility may be experiencing:

   a. secondary puberty.

   b. menopause.

   c. andropause.

   d. secondary sex characteristics.

10. Who of the following is most likely to live to 100?

    a. an average man

    b. an average woman

    c. conjoined twins

    d. people with few antibodies

11. Which of the following is NOT one of Piaget's stages of cognitive development?

    a. concrete operational

    b. sensorimotor

    c. conservation

    d. preoperational

12. If an infant is shown an old toy and a new toy, he or she will spend much more time looking at the new toy. The lack of interest in the old toy is an example of:

    a. habituation.

    b. memory loss.

    c. a type-A tendency.

    d. a type-B tendency.

13. Willa watches her father pour a half-full glass of apple juice into a smaller glass. Willa believes there is now more apple juice than before, because the new glass is completely full. Willa does not yet understand:

    a. conservation.

    b. egocentrism.

    c. object permanence.

    d. theory of mind.

14. Becky watches as her mother hides a doll under a blanket. She then immediately lifts up the blanket to get the doll. Becky is displaying:

    a. object permanence.

    b. egocentrism.

    c. hypothetical thinking.

    d. conservation.

15. Marco knows the word "milk." One day he points to a glass of orange juice and says "milk." According to Piaget, after his mother corrects him, Marco must adjust his schema for milk by using:

    a. assimilation.

    b. conservation.

    c. object permanence.

    d. accommodation.

16. A child struggles with putting his toys away on his own, but can do it when his mother helps him. The difference between what he can do on his own and what he can do with help is an example of:

    a. joint visual attention.

    b. the zone of proximal development.

    c. accommodation.

    d. assimilation.

17. Which of the following is a likely reason why babies babble early on (prior to eight months of age)?

    a. They are practicing pronouncing the words they hear.

    b. Babbling stimulates hearing development.

    c. It is a way to develop muscle coordination necessary for later speech development.

    d. From inside the womb, speech sounds like babble.

18. The sound "sh"is an example of a:

    a. morpheme.

    b. content word.

    c. phoneme.

    d. pronoun.

19. Which of the following is true regarding people who are not exposed to language until they are adults?

    a. It takes about the same amount of time for them to learn to speak as it takes infants.

    b. They often cannot master language.

    c. They acquire language faster than children normally do.

    d. They learn grammar rules easily, but have difficulty learning vocabulary words.

20. People who speak to their pets in childlike voices are demonstrating:

    a. being overextended.

    b. morphology.

    c. accommodation.

    d. motherese.

Remember to check www.thethinkspot.com **for additional information, downloadable flashcards, and other helpful resources.**

SEX AND GENDER

<<< As long as he could remember, Bangkok, Thailand, resident Punlop Tongchai wanted to be a woman. As a male child, he yearned to wear dresses and pursue a more feminine lifestyle, and at the age of 19, he began taking female hormones. Although he was now a female on the outside, at the age of 27, Tongchai decided to take the final step and rid himself of the male body parts he had hated for so long. Although Thailand has one of the largest transsexual populations in the world, laws are beginning to be put in place to make it harder for individuals to undergo sex-change operations. While the Thai government views this as a medical precaution to limit impulsive decisions and subpar facilities, many in Punlop Tonchai's position see it as a violation of their personal rights.

WHAT ARE THE BIOLOGICAL AND SOCIETAL INFLUENCES ON GENDER?

WHAT ARE THE TYPICAL AND ATYPICAL PROCESSES INVOLVED IN AN INDIVIDUAL'S DEVELOPMENT OF A GENDER IDENTITY?

WHAT SIMILARITIES AND DIFFERENCES BETWEEN THE GENDERS HAVE BEEN OBSERVED AND STUDIED?

WHAT DO WE KNOW ABOUT THE BIOLOGICAL AND SOCIETAL INFLUENCES ON SEXUAL ORIENTATION?

Thomas

and Nancy Beatie look like any other happily married couple with two young children. Strolling past the Beaties' home in Bend, Oregon, on a typical Sunday afternoon, you might see Thomas tending the garden while Nancy breast-feeds the couple's newborn baby boy. But for the Beatie family, the road to parenthood was anything but typical: Thomas, though legally a man, gave birth to both of the couple's children.

Thomas's story begins in Hawaii, where he grew up as a female named Tracy. Uncomfortable with his femininity from a young age, he began taking testosterone in 1998, had his sex officially changed from female to male in 2002, and legally married his wife, Nancy, a year later. Although he had chest-reconstruction surgery to remove his breasts, Thomas kept his female reproductive organs intact. When he and Nancy decided to start a family, they realized that they might have to consider a highly unusual possibility—since Nancy had undergone a hysterectomy, the only way they could have a biological child without using a surrogate was for Thomas to become pregnant.

Having made the decision to carry a child, Thomas stopped taking testosterone to enable his body to begin a regular menstrual cycle again. The couple conceived via artificial insemination with one of Thomas's eggs and donor sperm, which Nancy inserted into Thomas with a syringe-like device in the comfort of their own bedroom. Nine months later, on June 29, 2008, Thomas endured 40 hours of labor to give birth to a daughter the couple named Susan Juliette. He did not go back on the male hormone testosterone after the birth to enable the couple to try for a second child. Within just a few months, Thomas was pregnant with their son, who was born on June 9, 2009. During both of Thomas's pregnancies, Nancy's breasts inexplicably began lactating, enabling her to breast-feed both children.

Although the Beaties describe themselves as a traditional family, they have endured cruel taunts and even death threats. If you met Nancy and Thomas without knowing how their family was created, would they seem out of the ordinary? Why does knowing their story change so many people's perceptions of them? What factors influence gender identity and our perceptions of "male" and "female"? A look at the biological and societal influences on gender may help to answer some of these questions.

CHAPTER **11**

Sex and Gender

To lots of people, the words *sex* and *gender* mean pretty much the same thing. When we're asked to identify our sex or gender on a standardized test, many of us fill in the bubble marked *male* or *female* without much thought. But, as Thomas Beatie can probably attest, sex and gender are far from synonymous.

Our **sex** is our biological classification as either male or female based on the sex chromosomes contained in our DNA. Females have two **X chromosomes**, one from each parent. Males have an X chromosome, from the mother, and a **Y chromosome,** from the father.

Gender, on the other hand, is the set of behaviors and characteristics that define individuals as boys and men or girls and women in society. In other

words, while sex is a biological phenomenon, gender is psychological. Some have gone so far to say that a person's sex is located between their legs, while a person's gender is located between their ears. Identifying with a particular gender isn't usually as complicated for most of us as it was for Thomas, but the process does involve the influences of both biology and our interactions with society. In the vast majority of

> **"Thanks to new advances in surgical techniques and hormone treatments, those people who, like Thomas, face a conflict between sex and gender can modify their bodies to align with their genders, rather than the other way around."**

cases, gender is aligned with biological sex: Someone born with two X chromosomes will come to identify herself as female, and someone born with one X chromosome and one Y chromosome will come to identify himself as male. However, Thomas's case shows us that it doesn't always work out that easily: Some people with two X chromosomes feel more like men than women, and some people who are genetically male feel more comfortable identifying as female. Gender is not merely a stark division between male and female, either: It can be experienced on a continuum, and it's possible for people to feel varying degrees of gender intensity. Thanks to new advances in surgical techniques and hormone treatments, those people who, like Thomas, face a conflict between sex and gender can modify their bodies to align with their genders, rather than the other way around.

The Nature of Gender

PRIMARY SEX CHARACTERISTICS

The process of identifying with a gender begins long before we are aware of it. As soon as we are born and our **primary sex characteristics**— the sexual organs present at birth and directly involved in human reproduction—are visible to doctors, nurses, and parents, they begin to treat us a certain way. The minute we are swaddled in a pink or blue hat and a onesie embroidered with dainty butterflies or big,

tough fire trucks, we have not only a sex but a gender too.

Primary sex characteristics, including gonads, internal sex organs, and external genitalia, emphasize the main ways in which males and females are different—their roles in reproduction. However, you might be surprised at just how similar male and female primary sex characteristics are for much of prenatal development.

Gonads and Internal Sex Organs

The first sex organs to develop are the **gonads**, which are identical in male and female fetuses for the first four weeks of prenatal development. Then, if a Y chromosome is present, it activates the enzyme that turns gonads into testes for males. If the Y chromosome is absent, however, the fetus is female, and it begins to develop ovaries.

Until the third month of pregnancy, the fetus, regardless of its sex chromosomes, has both the **Müllerian system**—the precursor of female sex organs—and the **Wolffian system**—the precursor of male sex organs. During the third month, a male's testes will secrete **androgens**, or male hormones, to make the Wolffian system develop. They'll also produce an anti-Müllerian hormone to stop development of the female sex organs. In the absence of these androgens, the Müllerian system will develop and the Wolffian system will wither away; in other words, the fetus will develop female sex organs.

External Genitalia

The development of **external genitalia**—the penis and scrotum in males and the labia, clitoris, and external vagina in females—also depends on the presence or absence of androgens. In rare cases in which the fetus's receptors for androgens fail to function, **androgen insensitivity syndrome** causes a genetic male to develop external female genitalia. Varying degrees of androgen insensitivity can cause males' testes to develop internally or cause boys to develop breasts during puberty.

SECONDARY SEX CHARACTERISTICS

When we reach reproductive age, our bodies change to prepare for reproduction and alert others that we're physically ready to reproduce. These changes involve the development of **secondary sex characteristics**—sexual organs and traits that develop at puberty and are not directly involved in reproduction. Both sexes

---

Sex is a person's biological classification as either male or female based on the sex chromosomes contained in his or her DNA.

X chromosomes are sex chromosomes that exist as a matched pair in females and as part of an unmatched pair in males (the other part being a Y chromosome).

Y chromosomes are sex chromosomes that exist in males as part of an unmatched pair (the other part being an X chromosome).

Gender is a set of behaviors and characteristics that define individuals as boys and men or girls and women in society.

Primary sex characteristics are sexual organs present at birth and directly involved in human reproduction.

Gonads are the first sex organs to develop; these are identical in male and female fetuses for the first four weeks of prenatal development.

Müllerian system is the precursor of female sex organs.

Wolffian system is the precursor of male sex organs.

Androgens are male hormones.

External genitalia consist of the penis and scrotum in males and the labia, clitoris, and external vagina in females.

Androgen insensitivity syndrome is a condition in which a genetically male fetus's receptors for androgens fail to function, resulting in the development of external female genitalia.

Secondary sex characteristics are sexual organs and traits that develop at puberty and are not directly involved in reproduction.

begin to grow pubic hair and experience an overall growth spurt. Females begin this development about two years before males do, which explains why most of the girls towered over most of the boys at your seventh-grade dance. Females grow breasts and their hips widen to prepare for childbirth, while males grow facial hair and chest hair. Both males and females develop lower, more adult voices; this change is particularly noticeable in boys, who sometimes seem to change from sopranos to basses with astonishing speed.

HORMONES

As you've probably already figured out, hormones play a significant role in the development of our sex characteristics. The androgen **testosterone** is the principal male hormone. The male's Y chromosome includes a single gene that triggers the testes to produce testosterone. In females, the ovaries produce testosterone, but to a much lesser extent. Many studies have examined the impact of atypical concentrations of testosterone in genetic males and females on the development of **gender identity**—our sense of being a boy or girl, man or woman.

Evidence from several cases suggest that while excess androgens in female embryos may create more "masculine" girls, these male hormones don't cause girls to identify themselves as boys. If a female embryo exposed to excess androgens is born with male-looking genitals, doctors may surgically "correct" the genitals by making them appear female. Although these girls tend to be typical tomboys, act more physically aggressive than most girls, and play in ways more typical of boys than girls, their gender identification as girls is not altered by the excess male hormones (Berenbaum & Snyder, 1995; Money & Matthews, 1982; Money & Norman, 1987). Research into other species from rats to monkeys shows that female

embryos that are exposed to male hormones go on to develop a masculine appearance and act more aggressively than typical females of their species do (Brody, 1981).

Some genetic males with normal male hormones are born with penile deformity, causing some well-meaning parents to raise their sons as daughters. However, genetic males who are raised as females often come to reject their female gender identity. In the past, the medical community was quick to recommend sex reassignment surgery for genetic males born with deformed or very small penises. One study of 14 such cases found that six of these individuals later identified as men and five identified as women, while the remaining three had unclear gender identities (Reiner & Gearhart, 2004).

The case of David Reimer, whose story was told in *Rolling Stone* in 1997, convinced many readers of the biological basis of gender. David was born a normal genetic male with an identical twin, but his penis was destroyed in a botched circumcision. Doctors performed sexual reassignment surgery, and David was raised as a girl. Since David's twin provided a natural control, doctors followed the case for many years in an effort to prove that gender was entirely learned. Although David didn't learn of his history until age 14, and despite his parents' efforts to raise him as a girl, he always displayed typically masculine behaviors and preferences. When he did learn what had happened to him, he began to live as a man, but the experience took a tragic toll on David, and he eventually committed suicide (Colapinto, 1997, 2000; Walker, 2004). (Interestingly, David's twin brother had committed suicide two years prior.)

> ∧ ∧ ∧ **It's not unusual for girls who are tomboys as children to become more feminine as women.**

Testosterone is an androgen that is the principal male hormone.

Gender identity is a person's sense of being a boy or girl, man or woman.

Intersex refers to those people who are born with nonstandard male or female genitalia.

As researchers learn more about the biology of gender, sex reassignment surgery isn't taken as lightly as it once was. The Intersex Society of North America advocates for the rights of **intersex** individuals—those born with nonstandard male or female genitals—not to have surgical sex assignment forced upon them in infancy. As the medical community has come to understand more about the complexities of gender, doctors have become more willing to leave intersex individuals' genitalia intact and far less eager to surgically alter infants' anatomical features. Even when an individual chooses to have sex assignment (or reassignment) surgery performed as an adult, the process isn't undertaken hastily: Gender has such a powerful impact on our lives that people who choose to have this type of surgery must undergo extensive counseling to ensure that they are fully informed about—and comfortable with—their decision.

The Nurture of Gender

GENDER TYPING

It's hard to deny that we all have ideas about gender that go beyond just what nature determines. When we see a baby, we look for external clues about its gender so we know how we're supposed to act around it. If it's a girl, we're expected to gush over her beauty; if it's a boy, we're expected to marvel at how strong he looks. And if you've ever mistaken a baby girl for a baby boy, you know the wrath of the mother who corrects you while quickly searching for a

>>> **With his rugged virility, propensity for (often shirtless) athleticism, and Southern charm, Matthew McConaughey exhibits very masculine gender typing.**

feminine traits are **androgynous.** Bem and others believe that androgynous people are highly functioning and effective because, rather than limit themselves according to gender typing, they are comfortable displaying whatever behaviors and traits are most appropriate in a given situation (Bem, 1975, 1981, 1993). Imagine that a woman gets a flat tire on her way to the fabric store (a typically feminine locale). If she ranks high on the feminine scale and low on the masculine scale of the BSRI, she might find herself stranded if the idea of trying to change the flat herself (a traditionally masculine task) doesn't

way to clip a barrette to her baby daughter's hairless head. Gender ambiguity—whether a girl baby mistaken for a boy or a woman who becomes a man and gives birth—generally causes discomfort in a society in which gender is such a significant part of a person's identity.

Although it is clear that biology plays a part in our sense of gender identity, many of the behaviors and ideas associated with each gender are socially constructed. Women may be viewed as emotional, nurturing, and passive, while men may be viewed as rational, dominant, and aggressive. These associations are most apparent in people who are highly **gender typed**—boys and men who show traditionally masculine traits and behaviors, and girls and women who show traditionally feminine traits and behaviors.

ANDROGYNY

Although gender has traditionally been viewed as an either-or dichotomy, psychologist and gender studies researcher Sandra Bem developed a sex role inventory (known as the BSRI) to measure both the degree to which people are masculine and the degree to which they are feminine, rather than how far they lean in one direction or the other. Those who rate themselves equally on both masculine and

> "Although it is clear that biology plays a part in our sense of gender identity, many of the behaviors and ideas associated with each gender are socially constructed. Women may be viewed as emotional, nurturing, and passive, while men may be viewed as rational, dominant, and aggressive."

cross her mind. If she is androgynous—that is, if she ranks about equally on both the feminine and masculine scales—she might be more likely to change her own tire and still make it to the fabric store before closing time.

GENDER IDENTITY DISORDER

Unlike androgyny, which involves a healthy combination of masculinity and femininity, **gender identity disorder** causes a person to feel that he or she was born with the body of the wrong sex. Gender identity disorder has nothing to do with sexual orientation; people with gender identity disorder believe that their

gender does not match their body's anatomy, but this mismatch is not associated with sexual preference. These people, like Thomas Beatie, may seek sex reassignment surgery to "fix" what they feel was a biological error. The first widely known **transsexual**—a person who has had sex reassignment surgery and lives as a member of the "new" sex—was Christine Jorgensen, a former U.S. Army soldier who traveled to Denmark for her surgery in the early 1950s. Other transgender individuals—people who participate in any of a wide range of behaviors that in some way conform more to the opposite sex than the one they were born—may alternate between living dressed as men or women or, in the extreme, may dress as the opposite sex in order to perform in drag shows.

GENDER IN CHILDHOOD

The majority of people who deal with some sort of gender dissonance in adolescence or adulthood, including David Reimer and Christine Jorgensen, report having had such feelings since childhood. David's mother recalls him clawing at a dress the first time she dressed him in one, and his brother recalls David preferring the rough-and-tumble play of boys to dolls and tea parties (Colapinto, 1997). This early gender expression also suggests roots in both society and biology.

Babies are treated differently as soon as their sex is known. A father may talk to his son about cars while he's still in the womb, and a mother may read her *in utero* daughter stories about princesses. As infants, boys and girls are dressed and treated differently. Girls tend to be talked to more often and treated more gently than boys, who are played with more roughly (Maccoby, 1998). Children are given gendered toys to play with and may even be discouraged from playing with toys typical of the other gender. Recently, Disney Consumer Products created a pink, glitter-encrusted cash cow in the

<<< What factors might contribute to the gender gap in fields like math and science? What strategies might teachers and parents use to close this gap?

form of its bestselling Disney Princesses toys, which successfully play to the idea that all little girls love ball gowns, tiaras, and handsome princes. Disney's princess-based marketing plan clearly does not have boys in mind. Some researchers have found that male babies as young as one year show a preference for balls, guns, and trucks, while girls show a preference for dolls, stuffed animals, and cookware (Caldera et al., 1989). Studies with nonhuman primates have revealed similar preferences (Alexander & Hines, 2002). While these findings may suggest some biological influence, we are still left to wonder what use a female monkey of any age would have for cookware.

Perhaps more detrimental are the different assumptions that adults have about the interests and abilities of school-age boys and girls. These assumptions can lead to unequal treatment: For example, adults tend to offer more help and comfort to girls, while they expect boys to solve problems on their own (Maccoby, 1998). Boys often receive more encouragement and instruction in math and science than do girls (Sadker, 2000), who tend to pursue careers in these fields less often than their male counterparts (O'Rand, 2004). Proponents of single-gender education claim that without classroom competition between genders, both boys and girls receive equal opportunities and encouragement (Hughes, 2007).

THEORIES OF GENDER

Psychologists consider not only what aspects of gender are learned, but also how that learning occurs. The **social learning theory** assumes that children learn gendered behavior by observing and imitating adults and responding to rewards and punishments. The **gender schema theory**,

> **Adults** may not encourage girls to pursue math and science careers because of old assumptions or stereotypes that women will go on to raise children while their husbands serve as the breadwinners. This arrangement may work fine for the women and men who want to fill those roles, but it's important to recognize that this formula of male and female roles may be nothing more than a holdover from another time—especially in the 21st century, it doesn't work for everyone.

however, combines the social learning theory with the element of cognition. According to the gender schema theory, the process of gender differentiation begins at a very young age. Before age one, children learn to differentiate between male and female faces and voices (Martin et al., 2002). As children develop schemas for other things around them, they also begin to develop a schema for their gender and to adjust their behavior to align with it. As they begin to learn language, children are forced to organize words based on gender, whether through male and female pronouns or through masculine and feminine classifications. Studies show that by age three, children prefer to play with members of their own sex; they generally reach the peak of gender rigidity at age five or six (Bem, 1993).

GENDER ROLES IN SOCIETY

Children may be treated differently according to the **gender roles**—expectations about the way

Social learning theory emphasizes the role of cognition in motivation and the importance of expectations in shaping behavior.

Gender schema theory states that the process of gender differentiation begins at a very young age; as children develop schemas for other things around them, they also develop a schema for their gender and adjust their behavior to align with it.

Gender roles are expectations about the way men and women behave.

women and men behave—that they are expected to fill. Adults may not encourage girls to pursue math and science careers because of old assumptions or stereotypes that women will go on to raise children while their husbands serve as the breadwinners. This arrangement may work fine for the women and men who want to fill those roles, but it's important to recognize that this formula of male and female roles may be nothing more than a holdover from another time—especially in the 21st century, it doesn't work for everyone.

While those dissatisfied with limited gender roles may feel that it takes hundreds of years to change them, women's roles around the globe have changed vastly in just the last century. In the early 1900s, the only place where women had the right to vote was New Zealand, but by the end of the century, the only place where women didn't have the right to vote was Kuwait. In just 50 years, the number of U.S. law students who were women rose from 1 in 30 in 1960 to 1 in 2 in the early 21st century. In less than a decade, the percentage of women who agreed that married women should be full-time homemakers dropped from about 45 percent in 1967 to 15 percent in 1972 (Glater, 2001).

Several examples of a third gender exist throughout the world. In 2005, India included a designation on passports for the *Hijra*, a distinct gender that is neither man nor woman. *Hijra* are typically born male or intersex, and they adopt a feminine dress but reject both the terms *man* and *woman*. The *kathoeys* of Thailand and the *winkte* of indigenous North American cultures are other examples of third genders living in the world today. When not all males are men and not all females are women, it becomes easier to see how sex and gender don't always go hand in hand.

STEREOTYPES AND SEXISM

If you've logged on to the social networking Web site Facebook recently, you might have noticed ads on the margins of the site. Anyone

Kuwait finally gave women the right to vote in 2005. What cultural factors might have delayed equal voting rights for Kuwaiti women?

can buy ad space on Facebook and choose what type of person will see their ads—single women between the ages of 18 and 30, for example, or conservative Jewish students from Missouri. In 2008, some female Facebook users were less than thrilled to see weight-loss-centered ads popping up on their screens. They were even more chagrined when they learned that these ads were targeted only toward women: Their husbands, boyfriends, male friends, and other people who did not identify themselves as female on their Facebook profiles were never asked if they wanted to lose those extra 10 pounds. The ads in question offended many viewers because they implied that all women want to lose weight (or *should* want to lose weight), while no men want or need to slim down.

The idea of the weight-obsessed woman is just one of thousands of examples of gender stereotypes. A **gender stereotype** is a widely held concept about a person or group of people that is based only on gender. These stereotypes have both positive and negative characteristics. For example, in many cultures, women are commonly stereotyped as being nurturing and empathetic, but they are also stereotypically overly emotional and irrational. Stereotypes portray men as powerful and rational, but also as aggressive and inattentive.

These stereotypes often lead to **sexism**—prejudice and unfair treatment against men or women based on gender stereotypes. Schoolteachers who call on boys more often than girls in math and science classes may not even realize that their bias is a result of sexism. Sexism can be more blatant, too. During Hillary Clinton's run for the Democratic presidential nomination in 2008, the media and blogosphere

were rife with sexist claims against the feasibility of a female president. Arguably more attention was paid to what Clinton wore than what she stood for. Ben Barres, a transgendered Stanford neurobiology professor who attended MIT as Barbara Barres, knows all about sexism. According to Barres, his colleagues' treatment of him has changed noticeably since he changed his gender, and this change in treatment has led Barres to believe that sexism in the scientific community is likely responsible for the relatively small number of women who hold tenured academic positions in the sciences. Barres describes one fellow scientist who mentioned to him that Barres's work was much better than that of his "sister," Barbara. Barres's academic ability hadn't changed at all, but his change in gender altered people's perceptions of his work.

Another type of sexism is more insidious. **Benevolent sexism** is the acceptance of positive stereotypes or favorable biased behavior

∧∧∧ **Do you think female Olympic athletes should be required to undergo gender testing?**

that propagates unfairness and inequalities based on gender (Glick & Fiske, 2001). Certain aspects of chivalry could be considered examples of benevolent sexism. When men open doors for women and insist on footing the bill for every romantic evening out, both the men who act "chivalrously" and the women who expect them to do so are perpetuating the sexist idea that women are helpless, weak, and unable to provide for themselves. Of course, holding the door for someone isn't inherently sexist, but in order to eliminate the effects of benevolent sexism, both men and women should be willing to hold open doors for people of any gender.

Gender Similarities and Differences

Before the 2008 Beijing Olympics, organizers created a "gender determination lab" where female athletes could be given genetic tests to determine whether or not they were truly female. The decision to create this lab was most likely made in the spirit of fair play, based on the idea that men are generally physically stronger than women and would have an innate biological advantage if they posed as women and competed against female athletes. The mere fact that sporting events, including the Olympic games, are almost always divided into men's competitions and women's competitions reinforces this generalization. But are men and women really so different? And what are the ethical implications of testing athletes' genders? How do transgender athletes, intersex athletes, and others who blur boundaries of sex and gender fit into the picture? Even at the "gender determination lab," the question of differences and similarities between genders persists.

While much effort has been made to emphasize the equality of men and women, several studies have found ways in which they are consistently different. As with gender itself, these differences are likely not rooted in biology alone. After all, 45 of our 46 chromosomes are unisex. The way that parents, siblings, peers, and society as a whole treat people differently according to gender certainly has an influence on the ways in which they are different. Often, our expectations about the ways we think people will act become a self-fulfilling prophecy. We should also remember that variation among individuals is much greater than generalized variation between genders.

PHYSICAL DIFFERENCES AND PSYCHOLOGICAL VULNERABILITIES

Some differences between men and women are more clear-cut than others. The average woman has 70 percent more fat and 40 percent less

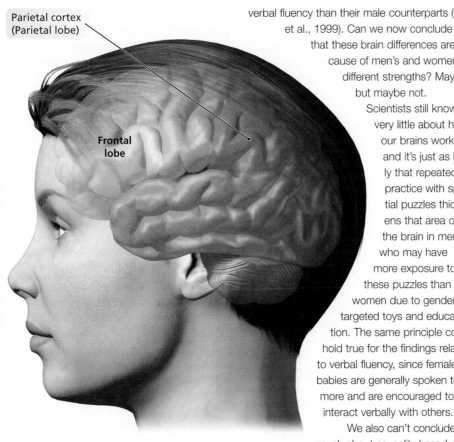

Parietal cortex
(Parietal lobe)

Frontal
lobe

verbal fluency than their male counterparts (Gur et al., 1999). Can we now conclude that these brain differences are the cause of men's and women's different strengths? Maybe, but maybe not.

Scientists still know very little about how our brains work, and it's just as likely that repeated practice with spatial puzzles thickens that area of the brain in men, who may have more exposure to these puzzles than women due to gender-targeted toys and education. The same principle could hold true for the findings related to verbal fluency, since female babies are generally spoken to more and are encouraged to interact verbally with others.

We also can't conclude much about causality based on the different vulnerabilities that are seen, on average, in men and women. Women are twice as likely to suffer from depression and ten times as likely to suffer from eating disorders (Weissman & Olfson, 1995). It certainly wouldn't be difficult to make a case for society's impact on eating disorders in young women, so this example clearly illustrates why we can't assume inherent causality just because something seems biologically based.

Men, on the other hand, are four times as likely to commit suicide (Centers for Disease Control and Prevention, 2005) and suffer from alcoholism (Schneider Institute for Health Policy, 2001). They are also more likely to be diagnosed with autism (Baron-Cohen, 2002), color-blindness, hyperactivity (Szatmari et al., 1989), and antisocial personality disorder (Torgersen et al., 2001). Again, notice that these are likelihoods of diagnosis and may not reflect actual prevalence. Remember, too, that the medical community is not immune from gender bias.

AGGRESSION AND POWER

Surveys, experiments, and observed cultural behaviors lend support to the idea that physical aggression is more prevalent in men than in women. One study found that men are more

∧
∧ Part of the parietal
∧ cortex is thicker in men than in women, and part of the frontal lobes is thicker in women than in men. Why can't we draw conclusions about causality based on brain differences?

muscle and is five inches shorter than the average man. She also enters puberty two years sooner and dies five years later. These findings are fairly innocuous in that they are unlikely to lead us to draw stereotypical conclusions. Studies of male and female brain differences, however, are more complicated.

Many studies have supported the popular ideas that men excel at spatial puzzles, while women are better with words. Researchers have found that, consistent with these generalizations, the part of the parietal cortex associated with spatial perception is thicker in adult men than it is in adult women, who have a thicker part of the frontal lobes associated with

Women and Men in the U.S. Senate, 2009

17   83

■ Women ■ Men   **Source:** http://www.senate.gov/artandhistory/history/common/briefing/women_senators.htm

∧
∧ Although women have made impressive gains
∧ in being elected to prominent national positions, men still significantly outnumber women in the United States Senate.

Male answer syndrome is a phenomenon in which males are more likely than females to guess at answers to difficult questions rather than reveal their uncertainty.

Sexual orientation describes enduring sexual attraction toward members of our own sex, the other sex, or both.

likely than women to administer what they believe are more painful shocks to another person (Bettencourt & Kernahan, 1997). Men also commit more violent crimes; the male-to-female arrest ratio is nine to one in the United States (FBI, 2004) and seven to one in Canada (Statistics Canada, 2003). A 2005 Gallup poll found that men expressed more support for the Iraq war than women did, and men are more likely to engage in hunting, fishing, and warring throughout the world (Wood & Eagly, 2002). Female adolescents, on the other hand, are more likely to engage in indirect or verbal aggression in the form of gossiping, spreading rumors, and revealing secrets about each other (Björkqvist et al., 1992).

Perhaps in line with their aggressive tendencies, men are also more socially dominant in most cultures. Not only do men tend to be leaders in groups, such as juries and companies (Colarelli et al., 2006), but they also held 84 percent of seats in the world's governing parliaments in 2005 (United Nations, 2005). Studies comparing male and female leaders have found that men tend to be more directive, autocratic, and opinionated and more likely to talk assertively, interrupt, initiate touching, and stare, and less likely to smile, while women tend to be more democratic, more welcoming of subordinates' participation in decision making, and more likely to express support (Aries, 1987; Eagly & Johnson, 1990; Hall, 1987; Major et al., 1990; van Engen & Willemsen, 2004; Wood, 1987).

SOCIAL CONNECTEDNESS

It seems to follow that if men are more aggressive and autocratic, then women are more affiliative and socially connected. Psychologist and feminist Carol Gilligan and her colleagues described the desire for social connectedness as largely female and the desire for a separate identity as largely male (1982, 1990). Many studies show how this pattern begins in childhood and persists throughout adulthood.

Childhood

Gender segregation in childhood play reaches its peak at ages eight through 11. It is reinforced not only by adults but also by other children who ridicule any peers who don't seem to buy into the dominant "girls versus boys" mind-set. The kinds of play seen in these separate groups are also distinct. Boys tend to play in large groups that focus on activity over discussion, while girls tend to play in smaller groups or pairs with little competitiveness and more focus on social relationships.

Adulthood

As the play of childhood gives way to the conversations of adulthood, men and women continue to show differences. Women are more receptive to feedback than men, many of whom suffer from a condition amusingly dubbed **male answer syndrome**: Men are more likely than women to guess at answers to difficult questions rather than reveal their uncertainty (Campbell, 1992). Women are also more interdependent; they use conversation to explore social relationships (Tannen, 1990) and to cope with stress (Tamres et al., 2002; Taylor, 2002). Interestingly, both women and men report having more intimate, enjoyable, and nurturing friendships with women (Hall, 1984).

SEXUAL EAGERNESS

The gender double standard regarding sexual activities isn't news to anyone. We've all witnessed the guy who gets pats on the back when people hear of his sexual endeavors and the girl who is deemed what your grandmother

> Perhaps in line with their aggressive tendencies, men are also more socially dominant in most cultures. Not only do men tend to be leaders in groups, such as juries and companies (Colarelli et al., 2006), but they also held 84 percent of seats in the world's governing parliaments in 2005 (United Nations, 2005).

might have called "loose" when people hear of hers. Encouraging boys to seek out and take pride in sexual adventures is a practice that seems to be true cross-culturally, not just in the United States. This observation begs investigation into possible biological influences.

Many theories based on evolutionary principles speculate that men are encouraged to seek out sex more often and with more people than women because of men's and women's differing reproductive roles. This argument generally states that men are biologically driven to propagate their genes as much as possible, and by impregnating many women, they are able to do just that. Men are also more likely to report being eager to have sex just for the sheer pleasure of it. Women, who take a more dominant role in raising children and are more likely to associate sex with love, prioritize finding one mate who will take care of his family (Gordon & Gilgun, 1987; Michael et al., 1994). Of course, the fact that these differences in gender exist does not mean that socially deviant actions such as rape and adulatory can be defended—no gene is powerful enough to overcome individual behavior in a deterministic way. Curiously enough, cross-cultural studies reveal that male and female promiscuity occurs more frequently in cultures in which men devote little time to caring for offspring, while male and female sexual restraint is more likely in cultures in which men spend more time caring for their children (Marlowe, 1999).

Sexual Orientation

While a lot of the research into sex and gender is based on heterosexual relationships and norms, there has also been research into the causes of alternative sexual orientations.

Sexual orientation refers to an enduring sexual attraction toward members of our own sex (homosexual), the other sex (heterosexual), or both (bisexual). Until 1973, homosexuality was listed as a mental illness by the American Psychiatric Association. This classification endured until 1993 at the World Health Organization, 1995 in China, and 2001 in Japan. While there are still groups out there claiming to "cure" homosexuality, psychologists now focus on conducting research to determine the environmental and biological factors related to a person's sexual orientation.

Early psychological research concluded that sexual orientation was entirely the result of one's upbringing: Childhood sexual abuse or, according to Freud, unresolved pre-Oedipal conflicts, for example. However, more recent and reliable research has failed to identify any aspect of parenting that significantly impacts sexual orientation, and there is little support for the idea that early sexual encounters leave a lasting impact on a person's sexual preferences, either. Current research tends to focus on potential biological factors that may affect sexual orientation.

But biology may be only part of the story. Social psychologist Daryl J. Bem put forth his exotic-becomes-erotic theory (1996), which posits that biology doesn't directly influence sexual orientation. Instead, our biology plays an indirect role by influencing our temperaments and determining the activities that we prefer. Children who follow behavior patterns that are typical of other children of their sex come to see their own sex as familiar and the opposite sex as unfamiliar. Children who follow sex-atypical behavior patterns, however, may see members of their own sex as unfamiliar. Bem's theory suggests that we're likely to feel romantically interested in the sex we view as more "exotic," or more different from ourselves. The exotic-becomes-erotic theory has come under fire from many critics who find it both insufficiently substantiated by scientific data and inaccurate in its explanation of homosexuality in both genders (Peplau et al, 1998; Stein, 1999).

There is still much we don't know about the origins of sexual orientation, and even determining the percentage of homosexuals in a given population is challenging and unreliable. One study found that sexual orientation may even function differently in men and women. Women may experience **erotic plasticity**: Their sexuality tends to be less strongly felt and can be more fluid than men's (Baumeister, 2000). One generally accepted idea is that sexual orientation is neither willfully chosen nor willfully changed.

THE ROLE OF GENETICS

Studies involving twins and family members consistently suggest that genes play at least some role in determining a person's sexual orientation. Male and female homosexuals tend to have a larger proportion of homosexual siblings than heterosexuals do (Bailey & Bell, 1993). Other studies have found that 33 out of 40 homosexual brothers had the same genes in common in one area of the X chromosome even though other genes on that chromosome were different (Hamer et al., 1993; Hu et al., 1995; Turner, 1995). Since males get their X chromosomes from their mothers, these studies are consistent with those that have found homosexual men to have more homosexual relatives on their mother's side of the family than on their father's side (Camperio-Ciani et al., 2004).

There is an even more compelling finding for the influence of genetics on sexual orientation: In male identical twins (whose DNA is identical), if one of the twins is gay, the other has a 50 percent chance of also being gay, while the fraternal twin or non-twin sibling of a gay man has only a 15 percent chance of also being gay (Bailey et al., 2000; Dawood et al., 2000). But those percentages mean that one identical twin can be homosexual and the other can be heterosexual, so we know for certain that there must be more to sexual orientation than genes.

Many researchers think that birth order can play a role in the determination of sexual orientation. According to the fraternal birth-order effect, each additional older brother that a male has increases the odds that the male is homosexual by 33 percent. The fraternal birth-order effect may be explained by a defensive maternal immune response to foreign substances produced by male fetuses that increases with each consecutive birth (Blanchard, 1997, 2001; Blanchard et al., 1998; Ellis & Blanchard, 2001).

BRAIN STRUCTURES AND SEXUAL ORIENTATION

Research into the biological origins of sexual orientation has also looked at structures in the brain. While brain structures can be altered by experience, observed differences in postmortem studies reveal certain correlations between some brain structures and sexual orientation. For example, a section of the anterior commissure, which connects the two hemispheres of the brain, is larger in homosexual men (Allen & Gorski, 1992), and a set of nodules in the hypothalamus called a hypothalamic cluster is reliably larger in heterosexual men than in homosexual men (LeVay, 1991). Another study has linked the hypothalamus to sexual orientation: In heterosexual women and homosexual men, the scent of the testosterone derivative AND, found in male sweat, activated a hypothalamic response that is commonly related to sexual behavior. In contrast, heterosexual men showed a similar sexually linked hypothalamic response to EST, an estrogen derivative present in female urine (Savic et al., 2005). Overall, postmortem studies have found more similarities between homosexual male brains and female brains than between homosexual male brains and heterosexual male brains. While few conclusions can be drawn based on these findings, they may eventually lead to a better understanding of the origins of sexual orientation.

> **Erotic plasticity** is the degree to which the sex drive is shaped by cultural, social, and situational factors.

∧
∧
∧
Several species have been known to engage in occasional same-sex relations, including grizzlies, gorillas, monkeys, flamingos, and owls. About 8 percent of rams are exclusively homosexual (Cloud, 2007).

Summary

WHAT ARE THE BIOLOGICAL AND SOCIETAL INFLUENCES ON GENDER? p. 168

• X and Y chromosomes control a person's sex—the biological categorization of that person as either male or female.

• Sex roles and conditioning affect the behaviors and characteristics that define gender, and a person's gender identity can be fluid.

WHAT ARE THE TYPICAL AND ATYPICAL PROCESSES INVOLVED IN AN INDIVIDUAL'S DEVELOPMENT OF A GENDER IDENTITY? pp. 168-169

• Typically, a child has male or female genitals at birth and develops secondary sexual characteristics during puberty. An individual identifies with either gender based on these biological characteristics and the responses they receive from others.
• Atypically, a person can be born with ambiguous genitalia. A person born with one set of sexual characteristics may identify with the opposite sex and choose gender reassignment surgery.

WHAT SIMILARITIES AND DIFFERENCES BETWEEN THE GENDERS HAVE BEEN OBSERVED AND STUDIED? p. 172

• Women tend to be shorter than men. They generally have more fat and less muscle than men do, and they tend to live longer.

• The male brain seems to be thicker in areas related to spatial abilities, while the female brain seems to be thicker in areas related to verbal abilities.
• In general, men tend to be aggressive and socially dominant, and women tend to value interdependence and social connectedness.

WHAT DO WE KNOW ABOUT THE BIOLOGICAL AND SOCIETAL INFLUENCES ON SEXUAL ORIENTATION? p. 174

• Early psychological research suggested that people's sexuality depended largely on their upbringing.
• Most current research suggests that sexual orientation is largely biological in origin, dependent on such factors as genetics and birth order.

Test Your Understanding

1. Which of the following is NOT caused by androgen insensitivity?
   a. males developing breasts during puberty
   b. females developing the Müllerian system
   c. males developing internal testes
   d. males developing external female genitalia

2. Which of the following is NOT a secondary sex characteristic?
   a. male testes
   b. facial hair
   c. female breasts
   d. wide hips

3. Which of the following is true regarding the terms "sex" and "gender"?
   a. Sex is a psychological phenomenon, while gender is a biological phenomenon.
   b. The terms "sex" and "gender" have identical meanings, and they can be used interchangeably.
   c. A person's sex is determined solely by their chromosomes.
   d. A person's gender is always either male or female, while a person's sex may be somewhere in-between.

4. Which of the following persons is most gender typed?
   a. a female truck driver
   b. a male nurse
   c. a boy who starts physical fights
   d. a girl who starts physical fights

5. A female born with male-looking genitals is considered:
   a. gender typed.
   b. intersex.
   c. transgendered.
   d. insensitive to androgens.

6. A person who has gender identity disorder and opts for sex reassignment surgery is called:
   a. intersex.
   b. a homosexual.
   c. androgynous.
   d. a transsexual.

7. Which of the following demonstrates gender typing?
   a. single-gender education
   b. single-sex education
   c. girls receiving dolls as gifts
   d. boys who like to read

8. Gema's friends make fun of her when she plays with trucks. She begins to prefer playing dress-up in her mother's clothes instead. This demonstrates:

   a. the gender schema theory of gender.
   b. the social learning theory of gender.
   c. gender identity disorder.
   d. transgendered teaching.

9. In India and neighboring countries, a person identifying themselves as a "hijra" is:

   a. a male homemaker.
   b. a female who does not take on traditional gender roles.
   c. a male who believes women should be subservient to men.
   d. considered neither male nor female.

10. Tom does not ask any of the girls in his math class to join his study group because he assumes none of them is very good at math. This is an example of:

    a. benevolent sexism.
    b. gender stereotyping.
    c. gender identity.
    d. gender typing.

11. Miriam applies for a job as a financial analyst on Wall Street, for which she is highly qualified. There are two positions open. She gets one of them, and a man who is not as qualified as Miriam gets the other. Miriam finds out that the man receives a starting salary that is 25 percent higher than what she receives. This demonstrates:

    a. benevolent sexism.
    b. sexism.
    c. gender typing.
    d. gender stereotyping.

12. Which of the following is likely an example of benevolent sexism?

    a. coed volleyball teams
    b. a boyfriend always carrying the bags when he and his girlfriend go shopping
    c. a woman being fired from a job if she demands equal pay as the men in her same position
    d. allowing women into the armed forces

13. The assumption that only women are obsessed with weight loss is:

    a. a gender stereotype.
    b. benevolent sexism.
    c. a true psychological difference.
    d. a psychological difference based on a physical difference.

14. Even though the part of the parietal cortex associated with spatial perception is thicker in men than in women, scientists cannot conclude whether men are innately better at spatial puzzles than women are because:

    a. Different parts of the brain may thicken due to use.
    b. The cortex of men's brains is generally thicker than in women.
    c. Cortical thickness is not related to ability or use.
    d. none of the above

15. Which of the following is true regarding the different rates of psychological problems for men and women?

    a. Women are more likely to suffer from alcoholism than men.
    b. On average, women are twice as likely to suffer from depression.
    c. Research shows that the higher rate of eating disorders in women is biologically based.
    d. Women are more likely to be diagnosed with antisocial personality disorder than men.

16. According to studies, which of the following is NOT generally true?

    a. Men tend to take a leadership role in groups.
    b. Adolescent girls engage in gossiping more than boys.
    c. More men than women are arrested for violent crimes.
    d. Women leaders are more opinionated than male leaders.

17. Gender-segregated play in childhood reinforces:

    a. gender typing.
    b. the male answer syndrome.
    c. same-sex attraction.
    d. erotic plasticity.

18. Which of the following is male sexual eagerness LEAST attributed to?

    a. gender typing
    b. desire to care and provide for children
    c. biology
    d. peer pressure

19. Which of the following BEST demonstrates that sexual orientation may be genetic?

    a. studies showing that male identical twins share the same sexual orientation more frequently than fraternal twins do
    b. the fraternal birth-order effect, which proposes that having an older brother increases the odds that a man will be gay
    c. children with atypical behavior patterns seeing their own sex as unfamiliar and thus becoming erotically attracted to members of their own sex
    d. some identical twins having opposite sexual orientations

20. Postmortem studies have found that the brains of homosexual males generally share the most similarities with the brains of:

    a. homosexual females.
    b. heterosexual males.
    c. heterosexual females.
    d. None of the above: Sexual orientation is not related to the brain.

Remember to check www.thethinkspot.com for additional information, downloadable flashcards, and other helpful resources.

HUMAN DEVELOPMENT II
Social Development

Megan Meier

was a shy 13-year-old girl from Missouri with a history of depression. Suffering from low self-esteem, she turned to the social networking site MySpace and the comforting world of cyber-friendships. When she was befriended online by a cute 16-year-old boy named Josh Evans, Megan's luck seemed to change. The pair began e-mailing back and forth, beginning an intense month-long relationship. Megan looked forward to her daily online chats with Josh, and her self-esteem began to improve.

Things were going well until October 2006, when Megan received a strange message from Josh, saying, "I don't know if I want to be friends with you anymore because I hear you're not very nice to your friends." Puzzled and upset, she tried to find out what he meant, but was bombarded with a series of hurtful messages and online postings. The final message she received said, "The world would be a better place without you." Unable to handle the rejection, Megan hung herself in

her bedroom closet. She died the next day, just a few weeks shy of her 14th birthday.

There was worse to come for Megan's parents, who discovered six weeks after their daughter's death that Josh Evans was not a 16-year-old boy at all. A neighborhood mom, Lori Drew, had set up a fictitious MySpace profile so that she could monitor what Megan was saying about her daughter online. Drew, 49, was later convicted of three misdemeanor charges of computer fraud.

Megan had never met Josh or even spoken to him on the phone, yet the bond she felt with her cyberspace friend was so intense that she was willing to lose her life rather than face the rejection of an online acquaintance. Social networking sites are relatively new methods of forming human attachments, and are particularly popular among impressionable teenagers who use peer relationships as a method of connection and an aid in forming a strong sense of self. When these bonds are threatened or severed, the results can be tragic. Broken friendships are the second-highest cause of suicide attempts among girls (Bearman & Moody, 2004). Why do social relationships hold this much power? How do the bonds of attachment form between people, and why are they so important to human development?

<<< Peer support is critical during adolescence. Far from being socially isolating, the Internet provides teens— and adults—widespread opportunities to connect with others. While our methods of communication may differ from those of the past, people today share the same basic social needs as those who lived 100, and even 10,000, years ago.

CHAPTER **12**

Attachment

As we develop, we become attuned to the behavioral norms within society. We may learn that getting a good education is a valuable asset, while being naked in public after the age of six or seven is a cultural no-no. This process of **socialization**, in which we shape our behavioral patterns according to the values of the society we live in, begins almost at birth. Our behavior is influenced both by people—our parents, relatives, friends, and teachers, and by institutions—our schools, places of worship, and workplaces.

The emotional bond that newborns share with their caregivers is called **attachment**, a term developed by psychologist John Bowlby in the 1950s. Bowlby believed that emotional ties between a child and caregiver developed out of instinct (Bowlby, 1969). Babies will smile and coo when they are near their caregivers, and whimper when the caregivers go away. They recognize familiar faces and voices and show preferences for them. At about eight months old, this preference becomes even stronger and develops into a fear of strangers, called **stranger anxiety**. If you have ever attempted to greet an infant sitting next to you in a restaurant and been met with loud, disapproving screams, you should not take it personally. Stranger anxiety is a survival strategy that enables babies to perceive unfamiliar faces as potentially threatening.

ORIGINS OF ATTACHMENT

Body Contact

Why do we bond with our caregivers? Psychologists initially believed that infants become attached to people who provide them with nourishment. However, a 1950s study by University of Wisconsin psychologist Harry Harlow showed otherwise.

While working with infant monkeys that had been separated from their mothers, Harlow noticed that the infants became strongly attached to the cloth pads used to cover the floors of their cages. When the cloths were taken away from the young monkeys, they threw violent temper tantrums. Infant monkeys raised in bare wire-mesh cages without a cloth pad survived with difficulty, if at all. Although the cloths provided no nourishment, they seemed to be important to the monkeys' development.

To test his theory, Harlow created two artificial mothers. One was a bare wire cylinder, while the other was a wooden cylinder covered in sponge rubber and soft terry cloth. Both types of surrogate mothers were placed in the monkeys' cages, but only one type provided nourishment. Harlow discovered that whether or not the cloth mother provided nourishment, the infant monkeys invariably preferred it, spending a greater amount of time clinging to the cloth surrogate than the wire surrogate. His results indicated the importance of body contact from a comforting caregiver (Harlow, 1958).

Human infants similarly become attached to parents who are soft and warm and who provide gentle contact. Emotional communication through touch not only facilitates attachment, but also is a vital part of our development.

Familiarity

Familiarity is also vital to attachment. You may remember from Chapter 5 that adults who are born blind and have cataracts removed later in life never fully regain their sight. In many animals, there is a similar **critical period**, during which exposure to certain stimuli produces proper development. For example, the first moving object that a gosling, duckling, or chick sees after it hatches is usually its mother. From this point onward, the young bird will follow her and only her. This process of early attachment is called **imprinting**.

But what if the first thing that a duckling sees is a car, or a sheepdog, or a young child on a tricycle? Konrad Lorenz (1937) explored this concept by ensuring that he was the first moving creature seen by newly hatched goslings. The

^ ^ ^ **Wherever Konrad Lorenz went, his gaggle of imprinted geese would follow.**

result was an instant team of devoted followers. Similar studies have proved that although birds imprint best to their own species, they will imprint to any number of moving objects, forming a bond that is difficult to break.

While children do not imprint, they do become attached to what they are familiar with. Mere exposure to a particular person or object encourages attachment. Former babysitters may recall being asked to read the same bedtime story, perform the same card trick, or sing the same song to their charges for the hundredth time. For children, familiarity is a sign of safety and contentment.

DIFFERENCES IN ATTACHMENT

Does the behavior of the main caregiver affect attachment? Psychologist Mary Ainsworth (1979) developed a "strange situation" test, in which one-year-old infants were briefly separated from their mothers and left to play in a new environment under a stranger's supervision. Watching how the infants responded to their mothers' return, Ainsworth noted several different types of attachment:

- **Secure:** The majority of infants that Ainsworth studied were labeled as secure. These children were quite happy to play in their new environment while their mothers were present, became upset when she left, but were soon comforted by parental contact upon their mother's return.

- **Anxious-ambivalent:** Ambivalent infants were ill-at-ease to begin with, and became extremely distressed when their mothers left the room. They were difficult to soothe, even when their mothers returned. Infants often displayed a mixed reaction to their mothers' return, simultaneously demanding to be picked up and pushing or kicking their mothers away.

- **Anxious-avoidant:** Avoidant children did not appear to be particularly distressed when their mothers left the room. Upon the mothers' return, infants actively ignored their mothers and instead focused on a toy or other object in the room.

Subsequent researchers added a further category to Ainsworth's findings (Main & Hesse, 1990):

- **Disorganized-disoriented:** Infants who were labeled disorganized did not have a consistent response to their mother's return. They seemed unable to decide how they should react, suggesting a lack of a coherent coping pattern.

Ainsworth's results correlated with the behavior of the infants' mothers. Mothers who were loving, warm, and sensitive to their child's needs had secure babies, while mothers who were unresponsive or insensitive had anxious, insecure children. Is it possible that the inattentive mothers' brain processes differed from their attentive counterparts? Further research may shed light on why some mothers do not bond as well with their children.

Limitations of the Strange-Situation Test

Critics of Ainsworth's test have pointed out that placing young children in an unfamiliar situation may not capture the interaction between mother and child in less stressful circumstances. The temperament of the infant may also affect the mother's reaction. For example, a child with a high reactive, or generally anxious, temperament is naturally hard to soothe, no matter how attentive the mother. Some Japanese researchers believe that the test is not a valid measurement of attachment in their culture because Japanese infants are rarely separated from their mothers (Miyake et al., 1985).

Relationships Throughout the Life Span

In most cultures, from the age of four or five onward, we spend more time with our peers than with our parents. Our relationships with the people we surround ourselves with play an important role in our social development.

> "Remember how you used to play "Duck, Duck, Goose"? Or the time you dressed up as your favorite superhero and saved the world with your trusty sidekick? You were actually learning important socialization skills. Children play in every culture, and the way they interact is surprisingly universal."

THE ROLE OF PLAY

Remember how you used to play "Duck, Duck, Goose"? Or the time you dressed up as your favorite superhero and saved the world with your trusty sidekick? You were actually learning important socialization skills. Children play in every culture, and the way they interact is surprisingly universal.

Gender Segregation

Children develop gender awareness at a very young age, and they play in groups segregated by sex. By doing so, they develop the gender-specific skills and attitudes of their culture. If you walk into an elementary school playground, you will most likely see large groups of boys playing competitive, rough-and-tumble games, while the groups of girls are generally smaller and geared toward maintaining group cohesion. It's a division psychologist Eleanor Maccoby describes as "the two cultures of childhood" (Maccoby, 1998).

Human-Specific Skills

Play helps children develop the skills they need in later life. A simple game of tag encourages physical stamina and

agility, while playing with dolls encourages a nurturing role. Both chase games and play nurturing are universal across cultures. Similarly, constructive play such as building brick towers or creating a play den out of boxes helps children develop skills in making things with their hands. Word play helps to develop language skills, while fantasy role-playing exercises children's imagination.

Cultural Skills and Values

If you study children playing in a particular culture, it is often possible to see how their play reflects the values and skills of the society they live in. Anthropologist Douglas Fry studied the behavior of children ages three to eight in two Zapotec communities in Mexico. While the play methods in the two villages were very similar—boys played with toy plows and girls made pretend tortillas—the communities differed in one crucial aspect. Villagers in La Paz valued peacefulness and discouraged play fighting. Children rarely witnessed violence between their parents. In San Andrés, however, violence was common. Children witnessed adults fighting each other at parties and siblings beating each other with sticks. Play fighting was actively encouraged and took place three times more often than in La Paz. Fry concluded that aggression was the result of learned social behavior, which begins in childhood (Fry, 1992).

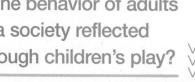

Is the behavior of adults in a society reflected through children's play?

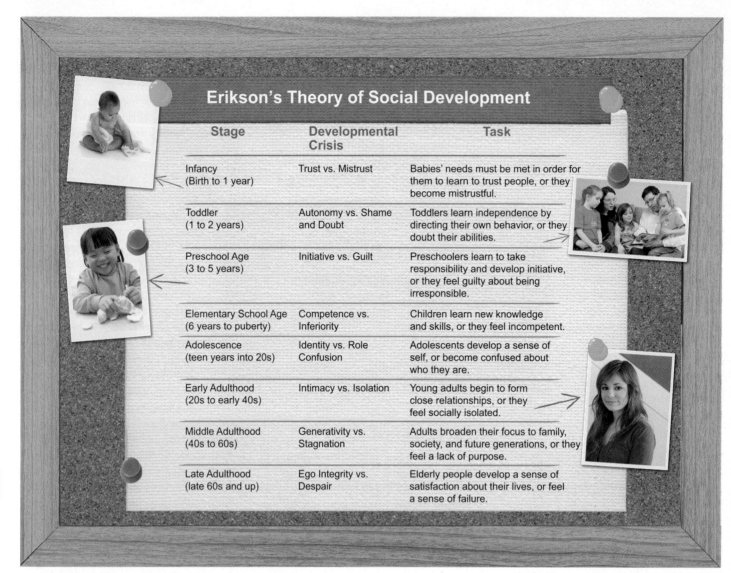

Erikson's Theory of Social Development

Stage	Developmental Crisis	Task
Infancy (Birth to 1 year)	Trust vs. Mistrust	Babies' needs must be met in order for them to learn to trust people, or they become mistrustful.
Toddler (1 to 2 years)	Autonomy vs. Shame and Doubt	Toddlers learn independence by directing their own behavior, or they doubt their abilities.
Preschool Age (3 to 5 years)	Initiative vs. Guilt	Preschoolers learn to take responsibility and develop initiative, or they feel guilty about being irresponsible.
Elementary School Age (6 years to puberty)	Competence vs. Inferiority	Children learn new knowledge and skills, or they feel incompetent.
Adolescence (teen years into 20s)	Identity vs. Role Confusion	Adolescents develop a sense of self, or become confused about who they are.
Early Adulthood (20s to early 40s)	Intimacy vs. Isolation	Young adults begin to form close relationships, or they feel socially isolated.
Middle Adulthood (40s to 60s)	Generativity vs. Stagnation	Adults broaden their focus to family, society, and future generations, or they feel a lack of purpose.
Late Adulthood (late 60s and up)	Ego Integrity vs. Despair	Elderly people develop a sense of satisfaction about their lives, or feel a sense of failure.

Learning Social Rules

How do we learn acceptable forms of behavior? Development psychologist Jean Piaget argued that unsupervised play with peers is critical to moral development (Piaget, 1932). It enables children to resolve their own conflicts and develop an understanding of social rules based on reasoning, rather than authority. In other words, little Jason learns to give the toy truck to little Tommy because he reasons that it is fair to take turns, not because his parents threaten to deny him his favorite TV show for three weeks if he doesn't comply. To further support Piaget's clams, psychologist Ann Kruger found that children's moral development is strengthened more when youngsters discuss social dilemmas with their peers than when they discuss them with their parents (Kruger, 1992).

Can playing by the rules develop our self-control? Russian psychologist Lev Vygotsky believed that children learn to control their natural impulses while playing by sticking to the rules of the game. For example, if a child imagines herself to be the mother and her doll to be the child, she will obey the rules of maternal behavior (Vygotsky, 1978). Play allows children to practice self-discipline, a concept known as **self-regulation**. In support of this idea, researchers have found that young children put a lot of effort into planning and reinforcing the rules in fantasy role-play. Good-humored babysitters may have found themselves clad in capes and leotards while playing dress-up with children, only to be scornfully informed by their charges that "Superman doesn't run like that." Despite their occasional criticism of their babysitters' acting skills, these types of kids are more likely to grow up to be well-adjusted members of society: Positive correlations have been found between the amount of social fantasy role-play children engage in and their subsequent levels of self-confidence and self-control (Elias & Berk, 2002).

Age-Mixed Play

Although the traditional, age- and grade-based educational system in the United States does not encourage age-mixed play, social interactions between younger and older children can have several advantages. Children of different ages tend to be less competitive with each other, and younger children are able to learn more advanced skills by watching their older peers (Brown and Palinscar, 1986). Conversely, older children learn how to nurture their younger counterparts by helping them, which promotes healthy social interaction (Ludeke and Hartup, 1983).

ADOLESCENCE

We've all been through it—one day everything makes sense and the next we're moody, we're confused, and our parents are threatening to put us up for adoption. Adolescence is the famously awkward period in life in which our **identity,** or our sense of self, becomes a critical part of our relationships with others. Psychologist Carl Jung believed that we do not establish a sense of self until we reach adolescence.

A Search for Identity

Do all teenagers go through an identity crisis? Theorist Erik Erikson (1963) believed that every stage of life has a crisis in need of a resolution and that the plight of the adolescent is to experience identity versus role confusion—establishing a sense of self by deciding on individual beliefs and value systems. Which political party should I support? What do I think about religion? Which career path should I choose? Adolescence is a time of transition and confusion.

To form an identity, most adolescents will find themselves trying out different roles—the diligent student at school, the clown among friends, the moody teenager at home. Eventually, as the adolescent develops a stronger sense of self, these roles fuse into one cohesive identity. However, Erikson noticed that some adolescents form their identities much earlier than others by taking on parents' values and expectations. Other adolescents adopt a negative identity that deliberately opposes their parents' views, while still others align themselves with a particular peer group, proving there is an element of truth to teen movies like *Mean Girls* that group together stereotypical goths, jocks, and geeks.

Erikson believed that once we have a clear and comfortable self, we are ready to develop intimacy—close relationships with others.

Conflict in Adolescence

Adolescence can be a difficult time, but are teenagers really as rebellious and scornful as pop culture suggests? Not exactly: Studies frequently demonstrate that most teens admire their parents and support their religious and political beliefs. Conflicts usually arise over deceptively minor topics such as hair styles and clothing, but these parent–child spats often boil down to a much more basic issue—control. Adolescents want to be treated as adults, while parents worry that allowing their teens too much freedom exposes them to alcohol, drugs, and other potential dangers. Intense conflict usually occurs during the early teen years. The battle for independence is usually resolved in the late teens, when many

adolescents and their parents manage to establish some sort of balance between childhood dependence and self-sufficiency.

Peer Support

If you got your heart broken in high school, it's likely that the first person you called to help you through that traumatic, near-death experience was a friend rather than a parent. Adolescents increasingly turn to their peers for emotional support, enabling greater independence from their parents and a stronger sense of self.

Australian researcher Dexter Dunphy (1963) identified two kinds of peer groups; cliques and crowds. **Cliques** are small, same-sex groups of three to nine members who share intimate secrets and see themselves as best friends. However, even if you pinky-swore to be best friends forever with Tori and Lisa in seventh grade, you may have found that by tenth grade, your soul mates had become mere passing acquaintances. Cliques tend to break down by mid-adolescence, giving way to more loosely associated groups. **Crowds** are

> For many parents, the possibility of negative peer pressure luring their child into a world of alcohol, drugs, and casual sex is a constant source of worry. Research suggests that these fears are well-founded—teenagers of the same friendship group usually indulge in similar risky behaviors, and teens who start smoking usually do so because one of their friends offered them cigarettes or made it look cool (Rose et al., 1999).

larger, mixed-sex groups who tend to get together socially on weekends, often for parties. Cliques of boys and girls interact, and the gender barriers that were so firmly established in childhood break down, increasing the number of opposite-sex peers in an adolescent's social network.

Peer Pressure

If you've ever been dumped by a former best friend or shunned in the cafeteria, you're well aware that social ostracism, especially among teens, can be vicious and painful. Being a social outcast as an adolescent is often seen as a fate worse than death, resulting in groups of teen clones all anxious to fit in by talking, dressing, and acting like their peers. For many parents, the possibility of negative peer pressure luring their child into a world of alcohol, drugs, and casual sex is a constant source of worry. Research suggests that these fears are well-founded—teenagers of the same friendship group usually indulge in similar risky behaviors, and teens who start

>>> Conforming to a particular peer group can help adolescents form a sense of identity.

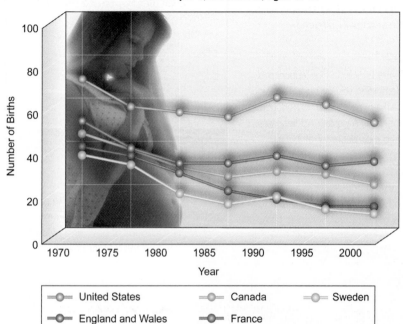

Births per 1,000 women, ages 15-19

Number of Births

100

80

60

40

20

0

1970   1975   1980   1985   1990   1995   2000

Year

United States   Canada   Sweden

England and Wales   France

Source: Darroch et al., 2001

<<< Even though the teen pregnancy rate is declining in the United States, the country still has the highest teen pregnancy rate in the Western world.

status, and less likely to sustain long-term marriages (Coley & Chase-Lansdale, 1998).

While these statistics may seem alarming, the teen pregnancy rate in the United States is actually the lowest it's been in the past 30 years. Research suggests this decrease is due primarily to an increase in the use of contraceptives (Santelli et al., 2007). Better sex education in schools, as well as parents' increased willingness to discuss sex openly with their children and teenagers, appear to be convincing adolescents to practice safe sex.

EMERGING ADULTHOOD

Recently the term "quarter-life crisis" was coined to capture that unsettled period in life between adolescence and early adulthood. The hit Broadway musical *Avenue Q* tapped into the psyche of a generation of twenty-somethings who had graduated college but had no idea what they wanted to do with their lives. A generation or two ago, people were expected to reach sexual maturity, find a job, get married, and have children, all within the space of a couple of years. But increasing opportunities for higher education, combined with numerous career choices, has meant that in industrialized cultures, adolescents are taking more time to finish college, fly the ever-comfortable nest, and establish their independence. In the United States, the average age for a first marriage has increased by more than 4 years since 1960 (to age 27 for men and age 25 for women).

It's not unusual for people in their 20s to ask their parents for a little help paying the rent, buying a car, or moving into a new apartment. As adolescents reach adulthood, emotional ties with parents loosen. But during their early 20s, many people still depend greatly on their parents for financial and emotional support. Throughout this phase of life, which some have dubbed **emerging adulthood** (Arnett, 2000), it is all too tempting to return to the family home when an exam result is not what we expected or we are having difficulty settling into a new job. This period of uncertainty is usually resolved by the later 20s, when people tend to achieve total independence from parental support and develop the ability to empathize with others as fellow adults.

smoking usually do so because one of their friends offered them cigarettes or made it look cool (Rose et al., 1999). While the selection effect—choosing friends who have similar interests and behaviors—partly explains peer similarities, friends usually become increasingly similar to each other in terms of frequent smoking, drinking, or other risky behavior.

Although peer pressure is usually seen in a negative light, it can have positive effects. For example, teens in China often meet to do homework together and encourage each other to do well academically. Parents and teachers in China view peer pressure as a positive influence.

Adolescent Sexuality

During elementary school, you probably viewed members of the opposite sex as the enemy, or at best ignored them completely. Then, all of a sudden, that red-haired guy in your art class started looking strangely attractive. While girls develop physically earlier than boys do, the onset of sexual interest occurs at the same time for both boys and girls. This suggests that **adrenal androgen,** the hormone that increases in production during puberty, plays an important role in the development of sexual interest.

Sexuality is a confusing issue for adolescents in industrialized cultures: Although teens have the ability to reproduce, they are not socially accepted as adults. While being bombarded with sexually suggestive advertisements, magazines, and television shows, teens are expected to abstain from sexual activity, and those who

are sexually active are often associated with delinquency.

The United States has the highest teen pregnancy rate in the Western world. Rates were on the decline since the 1990's, but in 2006, rates increased by 3 percent. We do not know yet if this is a short-term fluctuation or the beginning of a long-term increase (Guttmacher Institute, 2010). Most of these pregnancies occur outside of marriage, and nearly one-third end in abortion. The future of a young unmarried mother is generally bleaker than it is for women who delay pregnancy until later in life. Teen moms are less likely to graduate from high school, less likely to improve their economic

"What do you do with a B.A. in English? What is my life going to be? Four years of college and plenty of knowledge have earned me this useless degree. I can't pay the bills yet 'cause I have no skills yet. The world is a big scary place. But somehow I can't shake the feeling I might make a difference to the human race."
—*Avenue Q*, Broadway musical

ADULTHOOD

At what age do people buy their first house? How old are first-time parents? When should we aim to retire? Whereas childhood and adolescence are punctuated by formal rites of passage that occur at roughly the same time, adulthood is less predictable. Behavioral scientist Bernice Neugarten emphasized the difference between **chronological age**, the amount of time that has passed since we were born, and **social age**, our maturity level based on life experiences (Neugarten, 1996). In today's society, not everyone enters the workplace at 18 and retires at 65. Some people transition from adolescence to adulthood much later than others, while many continue working well into their 80s.

What defines an adult? Erikson's lifespan theory proposes that the ability to establish intimate, caring relationships and find fulfillment are primary tasks of early and middle adulthood. Similarly, Freud (1935) defined emotional maturity as the capacity to both love and work.

Love and Marriage

People are often said to be "insanely in love," a phrase that implies that romance and sanity aren't altogether compatible. While being in love won't actually drive you crazy, it does cause specific brain activity. Remember how a picture of a baby's smile can activate the reward centers of the mother's brain? The neural and hormonal mechanisms of mating bonds between two adults are similar to the bonds between an infant and a caregiver. Partners feel most secure and confident when they are together, and they may even show physiological evidence of distress when they are separated. It is not uncommon for elderly couples to die within a few days of each other, apparently unable to bear life alone.

Just as infants form different types of attachments with their caregivers, adult relationships can be characterized by partners' behaviors. In a **secure relationship**, both partners provide each other with comfort and security. An **anxious relationship** is characterized by worry about love or a lack of love from a partner. In an **avoidant relationship**, there is little expression of intimacy, and partners may be ambivalent about commitment.

Studies have shown that people's descriptions of their adult romantic attachments are closely related to their recollections of early relationships with their parents. For example, those

who were rated as having more positive, loving relationships with their mothers as children became more trusting adults. They were therefore more likely to seek comfort from their romantic partners and enjoy an honest, open relationship with them (Black & Schutte, 2006).

We usually consider marriages to be strong if they're based on emotional and material support, intimacy, and mutual shared interests, although long-term married couples may not necessarily share the same hobbies. Sometimes the strength of an emotional bond between partners is revealed only after a divorce or the death of a partner, when the remaining partner may experience long periods of grief and depression.

Why do some marriages work and others fail? In a country that suffers one divorce for every two marriages (Bureau of the Census, 2002), the answer to this question is hungrily sought after by everyone except divorce lawyers. Statistically, marriage is most likely to last when couples marry after the age of 20 and are well-educated. In interviews and on questionnaires, happily married couples also:

- consistently say they like each other
- use the term "we" rather than "I" when describing their activities
- value interdependence more than dependence
- discuss their individual commitments to the marriage
- argue as much as unhappily married couples, but do so constructively
- remain sensitive to the unspoken needs and feelings of their spouse

So how can we become part of a happily married couple? Many people think that testing a relationship by cohabiting before marriage is a good way to iron out any potential problems. Many couples happily cohabit, and those who do often get married, but studies have shown that couples who live together before marriage are more likely to divorce than non-cohabiting couples (Myers, 2000). Keep in mind that this finding is a correlation, not a causal link: Couples who choose not to cohabit due to strong religious or

moral beliefs may also be less likely to divorce based on those same beliefs, while couples who believe it's morally acceptable to cohabit may also find it easier to accept the idea of divorce if their marriages deteriorate.

What about having kids? As anyone who caught an episode of the 2008 reality show *The Baby Borrowers* can probably tell you, having children won't magically increase your marital satisfaction. While seeing a newborn baby may activate the pleasure centers in Mom's brain, research has shown that parents usually report a lower level of marital satisfaction than do non-parents, and that the more children a couple has, the less marital satisfaction they report. Employed women, who often find themselves overwhelmed with juggling their careers along with the bulk of household chores, are particularly likely to report marital discontent (Belsky et al., 1986).

>>> Wedded bliss increases our levels of overall contentment.

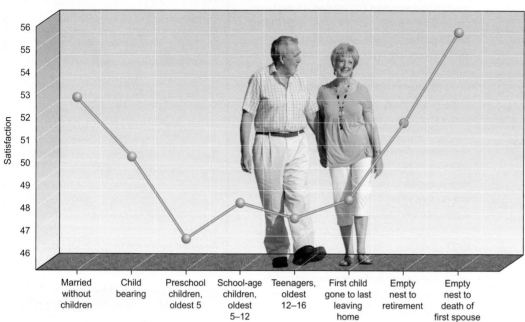

Marital Satisfaction Over the Life Span

Satisfaction (y-axis): 46, 47, 48, 49, 50, 51, 52, 53, 54, 55, 56

x-axis categories: Married without children | Child bearing | Preschool children, oldest 5 | School-age children, oldest 5–12 | Teenagers, oldest 12–16 | First child gone to last leaving home | Empty nest to retirement | Empty nest to death of first spouse

Source: Rollins & Feldman, 1970.

>>> Studies show that marital satisfaction starts out high, drops when children are first born, begins to recover, drops again when the children become adolescents, and reaches premarital levels when the children leave home.

Despite the odds being stacked against newly married couples, the institution of marriage is showing no signs of collapse. Far from being threatened by gloomy divorce statistics, many gay couples are currently campaigning for the right to marry. In Western cultures, three in four adults who divorce will remarry, and their second marriage is likely to be pretty much as happy as an average first marriage (Vemer et al., 1989).

In Baltimore, Maryland, billboards with images of smiling couples proclaim that "Marriage works." Launched by the Campaign for Our Children (CFOC), the advertisements are geared toward changing the attitudes of teens aged 15–19 by promoting the benefits of marriage. The organization has plenty of research to support its campaign: Marriage is a good general predictor of happiness, health, sexual satisfaction, and income level. Surveys of Americans since 1972 show that 40 percent of married adults report being "very happy," compared to only 23 percent of unmarried adults. Lesbian couples also report being happier than single lesbian women (Wayment & Peplau, 1995). And if you live in a neighborhood with a high marriage rate, you are likely to benefit from a low crime rate, few delinquent teenagers, and low numbers of children with emotional disorders (Myers, 2000).

Employment

People say that if you find a job you enjoy, you never have to work a day in your life. Since we spend about a third of our adult lives working, it makes sense to choose a job that doesn't fill us

> "Marriage is a good general predictor of happiness, health, sexual satisfaction, and income level."

with a growing sense of dread every Sunday evening at the thought of returning to the office the next day. At its best, work has the same psychological benefits for adults as play does for children. It brings people into social contact with peers outside of their family, presents problems to be solved, and offers us a chance to improve our physical and intellectual skills.

Most people report that they enjoy work if it is complex rather than simple, varied rather than

routine, and not closely supervised by another. Sociologist Melvin Kohn refers to these desired job characteristics as **occupational self-direction** (Kohn, 1977). Jobs with high occupational self-direction enable a worker to make many choices and decisions throughout the day. Surprisingly, despite the high demands that these jobs pose, most people find them less stressful than jobs in which workers make few decisions and are under c lose supervision.

Since it became socially acceptable in the 1960s for women to juggle a career and a family, the combination of raising children, completing housework, and holding down a paid job has become a fine balancing act. Although men are more involved in housework and childcare than they were 30 years ago, the bulk of household chores usually fall to women. The most recent figures from the University of Wisconsin's National Survey of Families and Households show that the average wife does 31 hours of housework per week, while the average husband does just 14 hours worth of household chores (Belkin, 2008). Despite the additional workload, most women report that having a paid job increases their self-esteem (Elliott, 1996), and most say that they would continue to work even if they didn't need the money (Schwartz, 1994).

GROWING OLDER

Baby boomers, those multitudes of Americans born between the end of World War II and the early 1960s, are throwing 60th birthday celebrations across the country even as you read this. Thanks to improved medical care, life expectancies in general are increasing. As a result of these factors, among others, the United States has a rapidly aging population. In 2000, 35 million Americans were over the age of 65 (U.S. Bureau of Census, 2001). This figure is expected to increase to more than 70 million people by the year 2030.

Ageism, or prejudice against the elderly, often leads to negative stereotyping that can cause isolation and poor self-image among members of the older community. When reporter Pat Moore disguised herself as an 85-year-old woman and wandered the streets of more than 100 cities in the

United States, she was ignored, treated rudely, and nearly beaten to death by a mugger, because she was seen as an easy target. Most people assumed she was hard of hearing and shouted at her, or pushed ahead of her in grocery store lines (Moore, 1985).

While aging does involve many losses—physical strength, agility, sensory acuity, and memory, as well as the loss of employability and other social roles—most elderly people report that old age isn't as bad as young people seem to think. Many assume that the years after age 65 are the worst time of life (Freedman, 1978); however, ratings of life satisfaction actually increase after middle

> "Age is an issue of mind over matter.
> If you don't mind, it doesn't matter."
> —*Mark Twain* (1835–1910), novelist

age (Mroczek, 2001). In a surprising "paradox of aging," elderly people report greater enjoyment of life than do middle-aged people, who in turn report greater enjoyment of life than do young adults. While you might regard old age as a long, slow walk to death, when you get there, the stroll might not actually be so bad.

Theories of Aging

What motivates us when we no longer have to get up for work in the morning? How do we feel when our children suddenly stop needing parental support? According to the **disengagement theory of aging** (Cumming & Henry, 1961), elderly people gradually and willingly withdraw themselves from the world around them. In preparation for death, members of the older generation sever all social ties and become increasingly preoccupied with their own memories, thoughts, and feelings. Cumming and Henry theorized that this enabled a transfer of power from the older generation to the younger generation, making it possible for society to continue functioning after its individual members die.

In contrast, the **activity theory of aging** (Havinghurst, 1957) suggests that elderly people are happiest when they stay active and involved in the community. Contrary to the view that the elderly willingly disengage themselves from the outside world, the activity theory proposes that disengagement takes place only when people are forced to retire or are no longer invited to social engagements.

Recent research has shifted from the question of whether elderly people prefer to be active to questions about the types of activities they choose and their reasons for choosing those activities. Laura Carstensen (1991) proposed the **socioemotional selectivity theory of aging**, suggesting that as people grow older and realize that the time they have left is limited, they focus on enjoying the present rather than looking to the future. Elderly people pay more attention to people with whom they have close emotional ties, and spend less time with casual acquaintances. Couples in long-term marriages become closer, marital satisfaction increases, and ties with children, grandchildren, and long-term friends are strengthened. Those who continue working into old age report a higher level of enjoyment than they did when they were younger because they are more interested in maintaining social relationships with colleagues than with career progression.

Memory and Mood

We might become more wrinkled and less inclined to go bungee jumping, but at least one good thing comes from aging—we begin to tune out bad memories. Carstensen and

her colleagues conducted a series of experiments in which they showed young adults (aged 18–29), middle adults (aged 41–53), and elderly adults (aged 65–80) pictures displaying positive, negative, and neutral scenes. Each group was then asked to recall and describe as many pictures from memory as possible. The results showed that older people recalled fewer scenes overall, indicating a decline in memory with age. However, whereas the younger group remembered both positive and negative scenes, the older group recalled more positive images than negative images, suggesting that as we age, we are able to pay selective attention to the positive (Munsey, 2007).

Occupational self-direction is a set of desirable characteristics for an occupation comprising work that is complex rather than simple, varied rather than routine, and not closely supervised by another.

Ageism is prejudice against the elderly.

Disengagement theory of aging states that elderly people gradually and willingly withdraw themselves from the world around them.

Activity theory of aging states that elderly people are happiest when they stay active and involved in the community.

Socioemotional selectivity theory of aging states that as people grow older and realize that the time they have left is limited, they focus on enjoying the present rather than looking to the future.

Why might older people report more satisfaction with their lives than younger people do?

Kohlberg's Ladder of Moral Reasoning

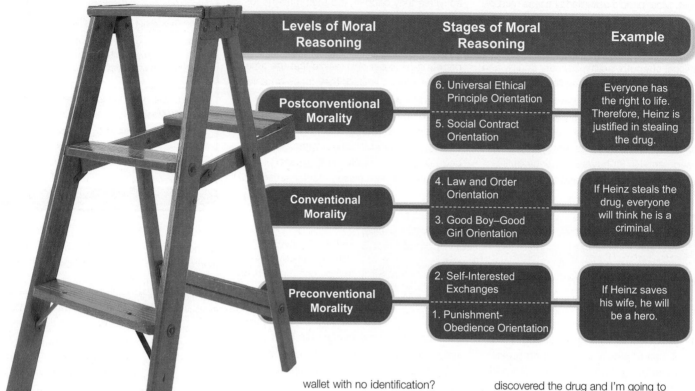

Levels of Moral Reasoning	Stages of Moral Reasoning	Example
Postconventional Morality	6. Universal Ethical Principle Orientation 5. Social Contract Orientation	Everyone has the right to life. Therefore, Heinz is justified in stealing the drug.
Conventional Morality	4. Law and Order Orientation 3. Good Boy–Good Girl Orientation	If Heinz steals the drug, everyone will think he is a criminal.
Preconventional Morality	2. Self-Interested Exchanges 1. Punishment-Obedience Orientation	If Heinz saves his wife, he will be a hero.

Neurological studies on the same topic show that although an older adult's amygdala, a center of emotion in the brain, is likely to show less activity in reaction to negative events than a younger adult's amygdala does, both elderly and younger brains show the same responsiveness to positive occurrences (Mather et al., 2004). In other words, it appears that as we get older, we learn not to let negative emotions drag us down.

Why do we rarely see elderly adults jumping up and down with excitement? It's not just due to older bodies—as we age, our moods become less extreme but more enduring. Whereas adolescents deal with emotions that quickly range from elation to despair, the mood swings of older people are much less extreme. Although they feel fewer periods of intense excitement, they also suffer from fewer periods of extreme depression (Costa et al., 1987).

Moral Development

If you found $20 on the street, would you keep it? What if the money were inside an unmarked wallet with no identification? Now imagine that you saw the money fall from a stranger's jacket. Would you pocket the cash or hand it back? Developing character and learning to distinguish between right and wrong is an important part of adolescence. Developmental psychologist Lawrence Kohlberg (1981, 1984) built on Piaget's idea that children's moral judgment is based on their cognitive development. He assessed moral reasoning by presenting people with hypothetical scenarios and asking them how they thought the person in the scenario should act. Here is one of Kohlberg's scenarios called the "Heinz Dilemma":

In Europe, a woman was near death from a special kind of cancer. There was one drug that the doctors thought might save her. It was a form of radium that a druggist in the same town had recently discovered. The drug was expensive to make, but the druggist was charging ten times what the drug cost him to make. He paid $200 for the radium and charged $2,000 for a small dose of the drug. The sick woman's husband, Heinz, went to everyone he knew to borrow the money, but he could only get together about $1,000 which is half of what it cost. He told the druggist that his wife was dying and asked him to sell it cheaper or let him pay later. But the druggist said: "No, I discovered the drug and I'm going to make money from it." So Heinz got desperate and broke into the man's store to steal the drug for his wife. (Kohlberg, 1969, p. 379)

Should Heinz have stolen the drug? Kohlberg was not interested in people's beliefs, but rather in how they reached their conclusions. He believed that moral reasoning developed through a series of six stages, progressing from simplistic and concrete to abstract and principled. To reach each stage, people had to progress through the stage before it. Kohlberg believed that not everyone reached the highest level of moral development, with most faltering at the fourth stage, and many not progressing beyond the second or third stage. While the stages of moral development were not linked to specific ages, Kohlberg proposed that adolescence and young adulthood were the most likely times in which a person may advance to higher levels.

Preconventional morality. Preadolescent children tend to view morality in terms of punishment and reward. Behavior that is rewarded is right, while behavior that is punished is wrong.

Conventional morality. By early adolescence, morality is defined by convention—caring for others and conforming to social laws is right simply because they are the rules within society.

Postconventional morality. The highest levels of moral reason are based on abstract principles such as justice, liberty, and equality. People who reach this level may not necessarily agree with societal norms, but follow their own personal set of ethics.

MORAL ACTION

If you are able to reason that handing a $20 bill back to a stranger is the right thing to do, does that necessarily make you a good person? Kohlberg recognized the differences between moral reasoning and moral action. It is often easy to theorize the correct moral choice, but it's not quite as simple in a real-world situation. How many Nazi concentration camp guards would have classified themselves as ordinary "moral" people before World War II? We all know that we should conserve natural resources, buy fair-trade products, and reduce our energy consumption, but how many of us actually live this way?

Today's character education programs focus on doing the right thing, as opposed to merely thinking in moral terms. For example, in cooperative learning schools, children are taught empathy for others' feelings, with the emphasis on group learning rather than competition. When group learning is of central importance, children become more socially responsible, academically successful, and accepting of other students (Leming, 1993). Many service learning programs engage students in community-spirited actions such as cleaning their neighborhoods, assisting the elderly, or volunteering in homeless shelters. Schools that participate in character education programs and promote service learning tend to have lower drop-out rates and improved attendance (Greenberg et al., 2003).

Moral Feeling

How do adolescents' thoughts and experiences contribute to their moral development? Psychologist Daniel Hart and his colleague studied 15 New Jersey youths from a low-income, inner-city neighborhood of Camden, who had been identified as morally exemplary by various community organizations. The teens had resisted involvement in criminal activities and spent much of their time volunteering in soup kitchens, shelters, counseling groups, and community gardens.

> *It is often easy to theorize the correct moral choice, but it's not quite as simple in a real-world situation.* **We all know that we should conserve natural resources, buy fair-trade products, and reduce our energy consumption, but how many of us actually live this way?**

According to Kohlberg's theory, the teens should have been motivated by abstract thoughts of right and wrong, but Hart discovered that the volunteers were motivated simply by wanting to do what was right. Part of their self-image was tied up with a desire to set a good example to others. Hart also noted that the teens' self-ideals were much closer to those of their parents than a matched comparison sample of peers who did not participate in

volunteer work (Hart & Fegley, 1995). This study suggests that social factors such as parental influence can contribute to moral development.

As members of industrialized countries, are we responsible for ensuring the basic rights of workers around the world? According to Jonathan Haidt's **social intuitionist** account of morality, you instantly thought of a "yes" or "no" response to that question and then justified it with reasons. Haidt theorized that we have an instant gut reaction to moral situations, which precedes moral reasoning (Haidt, 2001). He believed that our moral reasoning convinces us of what we feel intuitively.

Take one of Haidt's less than salubrious examples: A brother and a sister are on vacation in France. They drink some wine, one thing leads to another, and they decide they want to have sex. They use two different kinds of contraception and enjoy it, but decide they won't do it again. Haidt presented this scenario to people and asked for their reactions. Invariably, people said it was morally wrong and when pushed for a reason, most pointed to the possibility of birth defects. Upon being reminded that the brother and sister used two forms of contraception, the interviewees were stumped, but still adamant that the scenario was immoral. Haidt referred to this phenomenon as "moral dumbfounding," supporting his theory that we have an initial gut reaction to moral situations. Why might this be? Acceptable reactions to socially prohibited concepts such as incest are drilled into us from a very young age. We hear the negative comments of friends and family members and read terms such as *deviant* and *twisted* in the media. Over time, our responses of disgust become automatic, so that when given Haidt's scenario, we produce an instant gut reaction. Similarly, children of parents who consistently reiterate the values of honesty and integrity are more likely to hand back a $20 bill they saw falling out of a stranger's pocket than children who have been given mixed moral messages from their parents.

<<< **What motivates people to help others in their community?**

Summary

HOW DO WE FORM BONDS OF ATTACHMENT? p. 180

• Attachment is an emotional bond between a newborn and caregiver.

• Touch and familiarity are vital to attachment. Many animals have a critical period during which normal development takes place. In some species, this manifests through imprinting.

• According to Ainsworth's strange situation test, the behavior of a caregiver can determine whether an infant forms secure or insecure bonds of attachment.

WHAT ROLES DO PEERS PLAY IN SOCIAL DEVELOPMENT? p. 183

• Play is an important form of socialization for children. It is universally gender-specific, encourages skill development, and often reflects the values and skills of an individual culture.

• A sense of identity is established during adolescence. Adolescents form two kinds of peer groups: cliques and crowds. Until they have a firm sense of self, teenagers are subject to peer pressure that can result in risky behavior.

• Emotional ties with parents loosen during emerging adulthood. Adulthood is often characterized by the ability to establish intimate, caring relationships and find career fulfillment.

• According to the socioemotional selectivity theory of aging, as people get older, they focus on enjoying the present rather than looking to the future. They also pay closer attention to loved ones and less attention to casual acquaintances.

HOW DO WE DEVELOP MORALITY? p. 188

• Morality develops in adolescence and young adulthood. According to Kohlberg, moral reasoning develops through six stages. Few people progress beyond level four.

• Modern character education programs stress the difference between moral reasoning and moral action, encouraging young people to practice sharing, empathy, and social responsibility.

Test Your Understanding

1. Karen's 6-month-old daughter clearly recognizes her mother. While she will let other adults hold her, she is noticeably more comfortable with her mother. This is an example of:

    a. stranger anxiety.

    b. a critical period.

    c. socialization.

    d. attachment.

2. In a famous experiment, psychologist Harry Harlow showed that baby monkeys primarily developed an attachment to surrogate mothers that provided:

    a. food.

    b. water.

    c. soft body contact.

    d. comforting sounds.

3. Chris's mother decides to stay for his first day of preschool. While Chris's mother is in the room, Chris explores the room on his own and plays with other children. When Chris's mother leaves the room for a few minutes, he becomes worried, but soon returns to play once his mother returns. This behavior is typical of what type of attachment?

    a. anxious-ambivalent

    b. secure

    c. anxious-avoidant

    d. disorganized-disoriented

4. Which of the following is NOT a way human children become attached to their parents?

    a. body contact

    b. imprinting

    c. mere exposure to their parents

    d. All of the above are ways humans become attached to their parents.

5. Research comparing the children from two Zapotec villages in Mexico suggests that aggressive behavior:

    a. is mostly genetic.

    b. can be learned by children.

    c. is a child's natural response when they are provoked.

    d. is more common in boys that play with masculine objects like toy plows.

6. Stephanie goes to a babysitter who watches five children of different ages, of whom Stephanie is the youngest. Stephanie will most likely:

    a. learn to nurture others.

    b. learn advanced skills.

    c. feel lonely.

    d. feel confident.

7. According to Erikson, which of the following describes how adolescents form their own identities?

    a. They adopt identities similar to their parents' identities.

    b. They adopt identities opposite to their parents' identities.

c. They align their identity to a particular peer group.

d. All of the above are ways in which adolescents form their identities.

8. Which of the following is true regarding the relationship between adolescents and their parents?

   a. Most adolescents admire their parents and share many of their beliefs.

   b. Most adolescents dislike their parents.

   c. Most conflicts between adolescents and parents are about core values.

   d. Most conflicts center around the parents' desire for the adolescent to take on a more independent and adult role in the family.

9. Which of the following would be considered a crowd peer group?

   a. a large sports stadium full of diverse fans

   b. a family of 28 siblings

   c. a group of 20 to 30 high school students who all attend the same parties

   d. a close group of five girls who consider themselves "best friends"

10. Which of the following is true regarding peer groups?

    a. In China, peer pressure is considered particularly dangerous.

    b. Teenagers generally desire to stand out as individuals within their peer group.

    c. Teenagers in the same peer group tend to engage in the same risky behaviors.

    d. Teens in peer groups act similarly, not because of peer pressure, but because teens choose friends with similar interests and behaviors.

11. Which of the following is thought to contribute to the declining U.S. teen pregnancy rate?

    a. fewer teens having sex

    b. better sex education

    c. restrictions on sex education

    d. a decline in fertility

12. Mark lives with his parents until he is 30, when he secures a job that pays him enough to save money for a security deposit and rent. Mark is demonstrating:

    a. a greater social age than chronological age.

    b. the same social age as chronological age.

    c. a long period of emerging adulthood.

    d. a secure relationship with his parents.

13. Kyle does not like holding his girlfriend's hand or showing affection, even though they have been dating for five years. Both he and his girlfriend are not sure if they want to get married. Kyle and his girlfriend demonstrate what kind of relationship pattern?

    a. secure

    b. insecure

    c. anxious

    d. avoidant

14. According to the book, couples who live together before marriage are more likely than couples who did not cohabitate before marriage to:

    a. have few children.

    b. stay married.

    c. get divorced.

    d. have many children.

15. According to statistics in the text, who of the following would be most likely to report being happy?

    a. a married woman juggling a paid job with raising a family

    b. a married woman who does not work

    c. an unmarried woman who does not work

    d. an unmarried woman with a paid job

16. In his late 60s, Geraldo is recently retired. He used to be active, but now he chooses to stay inside his house more. He also calls his children less often than he once did. Geraldo's behavior is consistent with the:

    a. activity theory of aging.

    b. inactivity theory of aging.

    c. disengagement theory of aging.

    d. socio-emotional selectivity theory of aging.

17. Although Tim has worked all of his life to climb the corporate ladder, now that he is approaching retirement, he has decided to spend more time with his immediate family. When asked why he no longer spends long hours at work, Tim says that he is more interested in enjoying life now that he is getting older. This shift in Tim's priorities is consistent with the:

    a. socioemotional selectivity theory of aging.

    b. inactivity theory of aging.

    c. disengagement theory of aging.

    d. the activity theory of aging.

18. When compared to younger adults, older adults generally:

    a. experience good and bad emotions more intensely.

    b. suffer from greater periods of severe depression.

    c. experience good and bad emotions less intensely.

    d. have more confused emotional states.

19. "People do not use reasoning to decide what is and is not moral. Instead, people decide intuitively whether something is or is not moral, and then use reasoning to rationalize the decision they have already made." Which theory of morality does this describe?

    a. social intuitionist

    b. Kohlberg's ladder of moral reasoning

    c. preconventional

    d. postconventional

20. Anat's friend asks him if he would ever rob a bank. Anat says he would not because he might get caught and sent to jail. This is an example of what type of morality?

    a. social intuition

    b. conventional

    c. preconventional

    d. postconventional

Remember to check www.thethinkspot.com for additional information, downloadable flashcards, and other helpful resources.

EMOTION AND MOTIVATION

WHAT ARE THE COMPONENTS OF EMOTION AND MOTIVATION?

WHAT ARE THE DOMINANT THEORIES OF EMOTION AND MOTIVATION?

HOW DO WE EXPLAIN THE EMOTIONS OF FEAR, ANGER, AND HAPPINESS?

HOW DO WE UNDERSTAND HUNGER, SLEEP, SEXUALITY, BELONGING, AND WORK?

Imagine

a world of 10 billion people, a growing number of man-made products, and not enough ways to reduce, reuse, or recycle everyday waste and garbage. Sound disgusting? Unhealthy? Without recycling and efforts to educate consumers about reducing waste and reusing materials, that world could exist in your lifetime.

Unfortunately, the prospect of an overpopulated, overburdened planet has not been enough to motivate the number of individuals and governments needed to make a significant enough change. Research has found that people will recycle if they think it is effective, if they are knowledgeable about and believe in the benefits of recycling, if they are concerned about the environment, if they feel social pressure to recycle, and if there are financial reasons that motivate them. People don't recycle for a variety of reasons: Some fail to see its benefits to society, while others find it inconvenient. There is a misconception that recycling requires a large commitment of time and energy—who has time to flatten aluminum cans or separate different types of plastics? Many people aren't aware that these steps are no longer required.

Companies such as RecycleBank try to increase recycling levels by motivating people with money. To do so, they give out recycling bins that have radio frequency chips on them that contain customers'

account information. When a home's recycling is picked up, the truck weighs the amount recycled. The weight then gets converted to points that a customer can use to purchase items from RecycleBank's business partners.

Another way that people have been motivated to recycle is by seeing what they throw out. Waste-stream analysis, a method in which people sort and record information about the trash they produce, has been successful with groups such as high school students. Noticing how much reusable material gets thrown out can be a big motivator for recycling when coupled with the understanding of what each item is worth. Learning that a single glass bottle can save enough energy to run a laptop computer for a day can motivate a person to put the bottle in a recycling bin. Other motivations, such as offering fun activities as rewards, are especially great motivators for children.

Because governments need to meet both federal and state mandates for recycling, more ways to motivate people to recycle are quickly appearing. What ways can you think of to help keep the planet from becoming one giant landfill?

<<< What motivates a person to recycle? As students become more aware of the fragile state of the environment, the push to "go green" is slowly sweeping colleges around the nation. As conservation becomes the norm, the social pressure to recycle and reuse increases, motivating many to join in. Whether we're aware of them or not, our emotions often provide the physical and mental drive behind our actions.

CHAPTER **13**

Theories of Emotion

THE NATURE OF EMOTIONS

Laughing and crying are both expressions of emotions, but what do we mean when we talk about emotions themselves? Based on all the words we have for our emotions and all the artistic ways we express them, we know that emotions are complex. When we experience a subjective reaction to an object, event, person, or memory, we are experiencing **emotion**. Emotion includes an **affective component**, or the feelings associated with emotion. It also involves **mood**, a free-floating emotional feeling that does not relate directly to a stimulus.

Emotion includes three distinct but related parts: **physiological arousal**, **expressive behavior**, and **cognitive experience**. If your heart pounds in fear as you walk to the edge of a diving board or you feel choked up watching *Brokeback Mountain* or *Atonement*, you are experiencing physiological arousal. If you turn around and run back down the diving board ladder or cry during the film, you are exhibiting expressive behaviors. Your cognitive experience might include feeling embarrassed and deciding never to try diving off the high board again. On the other hand, you might feel moved and continue to rent sad movies.

THE UNIVERSALITY HYPOTHESIS

At some point in your life, you might have experienced emotions so painful that you wished you couldn't feel any emotions at all, but humans have evolved emotions in order to help us survive and reproduce. Fear might make us run away, anger might lead us to defend ourselves, and love might encourage us to bond with others. The facial expressions that indicate our emotions also help us communicate. In *The Expression of the Emotions in Man and Animals*, Charles Darwin's **universality hypothesis** supposes that facial expressions are understood across all cultures (1872/1965). For instance, a frown means sadness or disapproval in Japan, England, or Botswana, but gestures and other expressions of emotions can vary between cultures. But regardless of cultural norms, the expression of emotion seems fundamentally tied to the emotion itself.

THE JAMES-LANGE THEORY

Many psychologists have attempted to answer the question of whether the physiological experience, the expression, or the awareness of an emotion comes first and produces the other parts. At the end of the 19th century, American psychologist William James and Danish physiologist Carl Lange both simultaneously but independently arrived at the same theory of emotion. They believed that the physiological experience of emotion precedes our cognitive understanding of it. Instead of fear causing your heart to race or sadness causing tears to flow, the **James-Lange theory** proposes that the physiological experience of heart pounding or tears flowing causes you to feel afraid or sad (James, 1890/1950; Lange, 1887).

THE CANNON-BARD THEORY

Walter Cannon and Philip Bard, on the other hand, believed that physiological reactions did not precede emotions because sudden emotions don't allow for the delay in experiencing and then processing. According to the **Cannon-Bard theory**, the mental and physiological components of emotions happen simultaneously (Cannon, 1927).

When a 5.4 magnitude earthquake hit Los Angeles on July 30, 2008, Huntington Beach resident Danny Casler woke up from his sleep and ran out of the house in boxer shorts. According to the Cannon-Bard theory, Casler would have simultaneously felt fear and made the decision to run out of the house.

SCHACHTER AND SINGER'S TWO-FACTOR THEORY

In the 1960s Stanley Schachter and Jerome Singer developed the **Schachter and Singer two-factor theory**, which says that the cognitive evaluation happens alongside our physiological arousal to create the emotion we experience (1962). Labels become important since

> # Emotions involve physiological arousal, expressive behavior, and cognitive experience.

Emotion is a subjective reaction to an object, event, person, or memory.

Affective component describes feelings associated with emotion.

Mood is a free-floating emotional feeling that does not relate directly to a stimulus.

Physiological arousal is a heightened bodily reaction to a stimulus.

Expressive behavior is an outward sign that a person is experiencing an emotion.

Cognitive experience is the brain's remembered response to experiencing an emotion.

Universality hypothesis supposes that facial expressions are understood across all cultures.

James-Lange theory proposes that the physiological experience of heart pounding or tears flowing causes a person to feel afraid or sad.

Cannon-Bard theory proposes that the mental and physiological components of emotions happen simultaneously.

physiological experiences can be very similar. **Schachter's cognition-plus-feedback theory** says that how we perceive an environment feeds back into the physiological arousal and influences what we feel. During a pilgrimage to a temple in India in August 2008, a broken railing led pilgrims to believe they were experiencing a landslide. As the landslide rumor spread through the crowd, an environment of panic was created, and the pilgrims rushed down the hill, killing 145 people in the stampede.

ZAJONC AND THE MERE EXPOSURE EFFECT

While cognition may be part of emotion, Robert Zajonc believed that some emotional reactions can bypass our conscious minds (1980, 1984). A flashed image of a smiling or angry face influenced people's emotions, although they had no conscious awareness of having seen the face (Duckworth et al., 2002; Murphy et al., 1995). Prior experience of a stimulus causes an **exposure effect**; the familiarity of the stimulus primes us to react a certain way (Zajonc, 1968). Some messages can go directly to the **amygdala**, a structure in the brain essential for unconscious emotional responses such as the fight-or-flight response, leaving our cortex to process the information afterward. More messages go to the cortex from the amygdala than the other way around.

COGNITIVE APPRAISAL THEORY

In contrast to Zajonc, Richard Lazarus believes that we have to think about our physiological

> If you are taking an exam while sitting next to someone, you might think that you feel attracted to that person, when in fact you are simply terrified of failing the exam.

responses in order to develop an emotion (1991, 1998). According to the **cognitive-appraisal theory**, if you notice a particular physiological response, you first have to decide what it means before you can feel an emotion. For instance, your heart could be pounding because you're nervous that you didn't prepare for an exam or because you're excited that the person you went on a date with last weekend just walked into the room. Having to decide what emotion a physiological response indicates could lead to **misattribution**. If you are taking an exam while sitting next to someone, you might think that you feel attracted to that person, when in fact you are simply terrified of failing the exam.

PLUTCHIK'S MODEL OF PRIMARY EMOTIONS

Robert Plutchik proposed understanding emotions by organizing them around a wheel (1980). He believed that the eight primary emotions were fear, surprise, sadness, disgust, anger, anticipation, joy, and acceptance.

Schachter and Singer two-factor theory states that cognitive evaluation happens alongside a person's physiological arousal to create the emotion he or she experiences.

Schachter's cognition-plus-feedback theory states that how a person perceives an environment feeds back into physiological arousal and influences what the person feels.

Exposure effect is caused by the prior experience of a stimulus, and primes us to react a certain way.

Amygdala is part of the limbic system; involved in fear detection and conditioning; it is essential for unconscious emotional responses such as the fight-or-flight response.

Cognitive-appraisal theory states that if a person notices a particular physiological response, that person has to decide what it means before he or she can feel an emotion.

Misattribution is assigning the incorrect meaning to an emotion because of a particular physiological response.

Thalamus is part of the brain located just above the brainstem that receives sensory information, processes it, and sends it to the cerebral cortex; helps to regulate the states of arousal, sleep and wakefulness, and consciousness.

Rapid subcortical pathway is a pathway between the thalamus and amygdala through which the amygdala receives projections from sensory organs.

Emotions on the opposite ends of the wheel contrasted with each other just as colors on a color wheel. Joy would be the opposite of sadness, and disgust the opposite of acceptance. The pie shape of each emotional sector indicated that emotions could vary in intensity, and emotions such as anger and anticipation could combine to produce aggression.

Emotion and the Body

BRAIN STRUCTURES
The Amygdala

The amygdala, a small structure in the brain that assesses the emotional significance of stimuli, receives projections from sensory organs via the **thalamus**, the brain's message-directing center, by way of the **rapid subcortical pathway**. The amygdala can analyze sensory data even before it reaches the cortex. If you hear a loud noise, the thalamus may direct that message directly to the amygdala so that you feel startled and jump. You might turn around and see that the

Plutchik's Emotion Wheel

loud noise came from the wind slamming a door shut, and you would relax. In that case, the slower **cortical pathway** would have sent messages from the thalamus to the **visual cortex** and then back to the amygdala, allowing your perceptions to affect your emotions. When researchers removed monkeys' amygdalae and parts of their **temporal lobes**, the monkeys developed **psychic blindness**—they saw and approached objects that ordinarily would frighten them (e.g., a rubber snake) but seemed to feel no fear or anger and became indifferent to the object's emotional significance (Kluver & Bucy, 1937).

>>> Communication between the amygdala, thalamus, and cortex allows us to attach emotional significance to what we experience.

The Prefrontal Cortex

At the anterior of the frontal lobes, the **prefrontal cortex** is essential for the cognitive experience of emotion. As a treatment for severe mental disorders, from 1949 to 1952, about 50,000 people in the United States, including John F. Kennedy's sister Rosemary and actress Frances Farmer, received **prefrontal lobotomies**. Disabling the prefrontal area of the brain left people feeling less intense emotions but also unable to plan or manage their lives. Because the prefrontal cortex receives input from the amygdala and the somatosensory cortex in the parietal lobes, emotion may be essential to the prefrontal cortex's ability to carry out the life functions it controls, such as planning, setting goals, and reasoning.

AUTONOMIC NERVOUS SYSTEM

In situations such as fight-or-flight crises, the **autonomic nervous system (ANS)** prepares our bodies for action and controls unconscious processes such as perspiration and respiration. The two divisions of the autonomic nervous system help us prepare for and recover from emotionally charged actions.

Sympathetic Division

Imagine that you suddenly realize the building you're in is on fire, or the man who was walking behind you is attacking you, or the bus you need to catch is driving off. Your emotions are high, and you need to act. To prepare for action, the **sympathetic division** of the ANS initiates what is often called the "fight-or-flight response." This system does its work primarily through spinal neurons and connections to peripheral sympathetic

ganglia. When the sympathetic nervous system is stimulated, it induces a cascade of adrenaline from the adrenal medulla. The binding of adrenaline to adrenergic receptors throughout the body results in the fight-or-flight response. The firing of sympathetic neurons, along with the release of adrenaline, causes dilated pupils, decreased salivation, increased perspiration and respiration, accelerated heart rate, and inhibited digestion. These changes allow the body to focus on what it needs to do to get out of the building, fight the attacker, or catch the bus.

In general, this state of arousal aids performance on well-known tasks but hinders new or complex ones. At the 2008 Olympics in Beijing, swimmer Michael Phelps won an unprecedented eight gold medals. Since swimming is a well-learned task for Phelps, the excitement of the Olympics may make him even more likely to succeed. However, if he suddenly changed his sport to table tennis, the arousal would likely not have the same benefit and could create anxiety that would hinder his performance.

The Parasympathetic Division

Once the crisis is over, the **parasympathetic division** takes over and brings the body back to its resting rate. As the adrenal glands stop releasing stress hormones, the heart rate and breathing slow down, perspiration decreases, the pupils contract, and digestion resumes.

COMPARING SPECIFIC EMOTIONS

Just as your heart might pound as a result of nervousness over an exam or an attractive person, arousal levels for many emotions are similar. Many emotions have physiological similarities. Being ecstatic

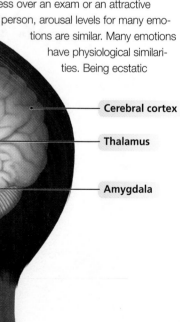

Cerebral cortex

Thalamus

Amygdala

about winning the lottery produces the same heart rate increase as the fear you might feel while running away from a wild animal. So how can you tell if you're feeling ecstatic or afraid?

You might want to think of emotions as recipes: Each emotion is made up of different physiological ingredients that set it apart. Anger changes finger temperature more than joy or sadness. Anger, fear, or sadness, will increase your heart rate far more than happiness, surprise, or disgust. Fear moves different muscles in the face than joy, and the amygdala becomes much more active in someone looking at a fearful rather than an angry face.

Positive and negative emotions also engage different sides of the brain. Negativity, such as resentment or guilt, activates the right side of the prefrontal cortex more than the left. Depressed people often show less activity in the left side of the frontal cortex, which is associated with positive emotions. Research has shown that a major factor in drug addiction involves the way that certain drugs are able to directly tap into the reward system that allows us to feel pleasure functions in a very particular way. Special neurons at the base of the brain send dopamine along a dopaminergic pathway to an area underneath the frontal cortex called the **nucleus accumbens** (Nestler & Malenka, 2004). Electrical stimulation of the nucleus accumbens in depressed people releases dopamine and triggers smiling and laughing.

LIE DETECTION

On the game show *The Moment of Truth,* contestants must answer questions truthfully in order to win prize money. In this case, "truth" depends on what they answered during a polygraph test taken before appear-

Emotionally charged stimulus

Hypothalamus releases epinephrine and norepinephrine

Pituitary gland releases thyrotrophic hormone

Adrenal glands release epinephrine and norepinephrine

Thyroid gland creates energy

Pupils dilate; salivation decreases; perspiration and respiration increase; heart rate accelerates; digestion is inhibited

Person reacts to stimulus

ing on the program. When someone lies, his or her body shows signs of arousal, which the polygraph test measures. Since many emotions evoke physiological arousal, a person feeling nervous or afraid may appear to be lying. Conversely, spies famously tricked lie detectors because they knew how to control their physiological reactions or confuse results by showing arousal for baseline questions. Thermal imaging can also reveal the different patterns of facial blood flow that accompany a lie. However, many of these techniques may be no more reliable than the polygraph tests we have today.

Nonverbal Emotional Expression

FACIAL EXPRESSION AND EYE CONTACT

It's impressive how much we're able to communicate to each other without words: With just a "look," two people who know each other well can communicate when they want to leave a party or if they've hit on the same idea. Interestingly, not all expressions draw our attention equally. We seem to have radar for threats and will more easily pick out angry faces from a set of different facial expressions (Fox et al., 2000; Hansen & Hansen, 1988). Experiences also influence which emotions we see more easily. When shown a picture of a face that combined fear, sadness, and anger, physically abused children more frequently classified the expression as angry.

GENDER DIFFERENCES

Gender also informs how we read and express emotions. In general, women can detect and interpret nonverbal cues better than men (Hall, 1984, 1987). When asked to express happiness, sadness, and anger, women expressed happiness better than men, and men expressed anger better than women (Coats & Feldman, 1996). Psychologist Monica Moore found that while flirting, women also communicate better nonverbally and use 52 recorded flirting behaviors, such as hair flipping, head tilting, and smiling coyly, to invite men to approach.

CULTURE

Drawing from Darwin's universality of emotion theory, other researchers have shown that people throughout the world use the same facial expressions to show anger, fear, disgust, surprise, happiness, and sadness (Ekman & Friesen,

<<< A polygraph test measures vital signs such as blood pressure, heart rate, respiration, and perspiration in order to determine stress levels.

1975; Ekman et al., 1987; Ekman, 1994). Blind children who have never seen facial expressions will express emotions with the same expressions as sighted people, a fact that argues for the innate biological basis of emotional expression. Although facial expressions seem to be universal, physical gestures and degree of emotional expression vary among cultures. Norwegians who saw President George Bush's 2005 inauguration interpreted his University of Texas "Hook 'em Horns" salute as the sign of the devil.

THE FACIAL FEEDBACK HYPOTHESIS AND FACIAL EXPRESSIONS

Darwin wrote in *The Expression of the Emotions in Man and Animals* that "free expression by outward signs of an emotion intensifies it" (1872). The **facial feedback hypothesis** says that a person who makes a certain facial expression will feel the corresponding emotion, as long as the person is not feeling some other competing emotion. When people were asked to

>>> In 2009, Michelle Obama shocked British viewers when she greeted Queen Elizabeth with a friendly embrace. How might different cultures interpret this gesture?

frown while watching sad films, they felt even sadder than they did while watching the films without frowning (Larsen et al., 1992). People who held pencils in their teeth, effectively forcing them to smile, while looking at cartoons reported that the cartoons were more amusing and enjoyable (Strack et al., 1988). Ekman and Friesen extensively studied the facial muscles involved in emotional expressions and found that the muscles make 46 unique movements, or **action units**. For instance, the zygomatic major on the cheek and orbicularis oculi around the eye move when we smile. These findings suggest that expressing emotions seems to intensify, not diminish, how we feel them.

DECEPTIVE EXPRESSION
Hiding Emotions

Although forcing yourself to smile might make you feel happy, true expressions actually differ from false ones. If you are pleased to see someone but act overjoyed, you're showing **intensification**, exaggerating your emotions. In public, someone feeling intense grief might find it necessary to use **deintensification,** to mute some of their emotions in order to be sociable. Showing one emotion while feeling another is **masking**; the runners-up at beauty pageants smile broadly while feeling miserable about losing the contest. Poker players routinely maintain the "poker face," **neutralizing** whatever they feel, so their opponents have no clues about their hands.

Detecting Emotions

Regardless of how much people hide their emotions, we can detect them if we know the signs of true and false emotions. False expressions involve different muscle groups than real ones, and studying their **morphology**, or shape, can tell us if the expressions are real. Sincere emotions have more symmetry than insincere ones, so both sides of the face show the same expression equally. Real expressions last about half a second; false ones can have a longer or shorter duration. Temporal patterning also differs in false and real emotions; sincere expressions come and go smoothly, but insincere ones start and end abruptly.

Experienced Emotion

COGNITION AND EMOTION

Cognition, or thought, can influence what we feel or believe we feel. Arousal from one event can spill over into the emotions we experience about other events. For example, if someone insults you just after you've completed a long run, you might react more angrily than usual because your body is aroused from physical exercise. Misattribution sometimes leads people to attribute their arousal to the wrong stimulus. When given an injection of epinephrine, a stimulating hormone, subjects attributed their arousal to an attraction to someone in the room (Schachter & Singer, 1962). Sometimes our emotions can influence what we choose to perceive through **mood-congruent processing**. Depressed patients noticed stimuli related to sadness more than to other emotions (Elliott et al., 2002; Erickson et al., 2005). In general, people will selectively perceive stimuli congruent with their emotional state (Ito, 2000).

Sometimes emotions do not reach our cognitive pathways or even have a cognitive element at all. People tend to prefer an image they have seen before, even if they didn't know they saw it (Elliott & Dolan, 1998). Since the message about the stimulus goes directly from the thalamic nuclei to the amygdala without reaching the cortex, the stimulus can elicit an emotional response without the element of cognition.

When we engage in **emotion regulation**, we use cognitive strategies to control and influence our own emotional responses. For example, if you see your boyfriend or girlfriend animatedly talking to another person, you could stop yourself from feeling jealous or worried by reappraising the situation and deciding that talking does not necessarily indicate romantic involvement. Thoughts can also help us make better decisions. You might have perused college Web sites to decide where to apply and imagined yourself as a student at each school.

If so, you engaged in **affective forecasting**, imagining how you would feel about something that might happen in the future.

VALENCE AND AROUSAL

All emotions have a **valence**, a positive or negative value along a continuum, and also vary in degree of arousal. An unpleasant feeling, fear has a negative valence. As a strong emotion, its high arousal makes you act quickly in a frightening situation. Because people don't enjoy feeling bored, boredom would have a negative valence but a low arousal, as a low-energy emotion. By contrast, elation has a positive valence and a high arousal; an elated person feels happy and excited. Sadness has a negative valence and low arousal, sadness feels unpleasant but does not feel particularly stimulating.

FEAR

Fear may not be a comfortable feeling, but it is an adaptive alarm system that prepares us for a fight-or-flight response when faced with danger. Children learn fear by watching others and by experiencing fear-inducing situations. But some fears, such as a fear of snakes and spiders, seem to be biologically hardwired into us. In a classic experiment of conditioning (that would never be conducted today), researchers Watson and Rayner taught an infant named Albert to transfer and generalize his fears (1920). Initially, the child showed fear of loud noises. The researchers synchronized loud noises with the presence of a rat, and the child gradually learned to feel frightened of the rat (as well as of all furry white things—for more on the "Little Albert" study, see Chapter 7). Likewise, children learn to fear heights by repeatedly falling or almost falling (Campos et al., 1992).

Physiologically, fear seems to be controlled largely by the amygdala, which receives input from the anterior cingulated cortex and sends projections to the brain areas involved in fear. People with damage to the amygdala showed more trust of scary-looking faces (Adolphs et al., 1998). Of course, some fears can be extreme. Phobias leave people so terrified of specific objects or situations that sufferers cannot function properly.

ANGER

Facial expressions of anger may be universal, but elements of anger expression can be culturally specific. To preserve group harmony, individuals from cultures that emphasize interdependence tend to express anger less often (Markus & Kitayama, 1991). Tahitians are particularly polite, and Japanese express anger less often than Westerners. In the West, the **catharsis theory**, the idea that expressing

emotions to prevent them from building up and exploding, is generally accepted. Many forms of therapy encourage expressions of anger to release pent-up feelings, but studies have shown that "venting" does not decrease rage and actually makes people angrier (Bushman et al., 1999). Venting may give temporary relief, but distracting yourself or redirecting feelings are more effective coping mechanisms.

> ❝Children learn fear by watching others and by experiencing fear-inducing situations. But some fears, such as a fear of snakes and spiders, seem to be biologically hardwired into us.❞

HAPPINESS

What's so great about happiness anyway? According to the **feel-good, do-good phenomenon**, when people are already happy, they are more likely to be helpful. Psychologists use **subjective well-being**—a person's self-perceived satisfaction with life—along with objective measures, such as income and health, to evaluate quality of life. Martin Seligman, one of the founders of a field known as positive psychology, believes that psychology should also study highly functioning, not just maladaptive, people. Positive psychology tries to determine the inner strengths, virtues, resources, and character traits that enable people to be happy. Studies have found that negative feelings caused by unpleasant daily events tend to last for a short period of time and often result in more positive feelings the next day (Affleck et al., 1994; Bolger et al., 1989; Stone & Neale, 1984). Similarly, an extremely positive event makes people feel only temporarily happier, and they soon return to their normal state (Brickman et al., 1978).

As the saying goes, money can't buy happiness. Those who value and pursue money often feel less happy than those who value love and friendship (Kasser, 2002; Perkins, 1991). People in affluent countries don't seem to be any happier than those in poor countries (Diener & Biswas-Diener, 2002; Eckersley, 2000). We tend to judge our present state by our previous ones, so because of the **adaptation-level phenomenon**, an elevated mood, more money, or greater prestige becomes the new norm (Campbell, 1975), and we start to want even more.

Our happiness also depends on how happy we perceive others to be. While not everyone rejoices in other people's miseries, most of us do judge our **relative deprivation** by comparing ourselves to others. When we compare ourselves to those of higher social standing, we feel worse; when we compare ourselves to those of lower social standing, we feel better. Similarly, soldiers in the WWII Army Air Corps felt more frustrated about their own prospects when they saw others being promoted quickly (Merton & Kitt, 1950).

So what does make people happy? Although the predictors for happiness vary somewhat by culture, they include optimism, close relationships, faith, meaningful work, good sleeping and eating patterns, and, in individualistic countries, high self-esteem. Age, gender, education levels, parenthood, and physical attractiveness are not reliable predictors of happiness (Diener et al., 2003).

Perspectives on Motivation, Drives, and Incentives

MOTIVATION

Early in 2008, the world found out that Jérôme Kerviel, a 31-year-old trader with the French bank Société Générale, had committed the largest banking fraud in history and racked up a $7.5 billion debt. Speculations about his motives

Motivation is a need or desire that energizes and directs behavior.

Dispositional forces are internal factors involved in motivation.

Situational forces are external factors involved in motivation.

Motivation states are internal conditions that make a person tend toward certain goals.

Drives are internal conditions that make a person tend toward certain goals; this is caused by a departure from optimal states.

Conscious motivation is a motivation that remains in a person's awareness.

Subconscious motivation is a motivation that is not in a person's awareness but can be easily accessed.

Unconscious motivation is a motivation that operates without a person's awareness.

Approach motivation is a motivation involved with striving to achieve a positive result.

Avoidance motivation is a motivation involved with striving to avoid a negative result.

Instincts are unlearned complex behaviors with a fixed pattern throughout a species.

Hedonic principle states that people want to experience pleasure and avoid pain.

Drive-reduction theory states that a person reacts when a physiological need creates an aroused state that drives him or her to reduce the need.

Homeostasis describes a steady and balanced inner state.

Regulatory drives seek to preserve homeostasis.

Nonregulatory drives initiate activities not required to preserve homeostasis.

Social learning theory emphasizes the role of cognition in motivation and the importance of expectations in shaping behavior.

Central-state theory explains drives by understanding them as corresponding to neural activity.

Central drive system is a set of neurons that create a drive.

Incentive is a positive or negative stimulus in the environment.

---

ranged from the recent death of his father and a bad break-up to his introverted personality and his overwhelming ambition. Why do we do the things we do? **Motivation** is the need or desire that energizes and directs behavior. It is made up of internal factors—**dispositional forces**—and external factors—**situational forces**—that drive us to do specific things in a particular situation.

Our **motivation states** and **drives** are internal conditions that make us tend toward certain goals, which may change over time. **Conscious motivations** remain in our awareness, but we can also be motivated by **subconscious motiva-** tions, which are not in our awareness but can be easily accessed, and **unconscious motivations**, which operate without our awareness. Studying to get a good grade on an exam—a positive result—is an example of **approach motivation**. **Avoidance motivation** would involve pulling an all-nighter so you don't fail. When we act to satisfy a requirement by eating a healthy meal, we fulfill a physical need and our drive for food. By eating ice cream after the meal, we satisfy a want, something not considered a requirement.

THEORIES OF MOTIVATION

As Darwin's theories of evolution became popular, so did labeling human instincts. William James believed that **instincts**—unlearned complex behaviors with a fixed pattern throughout a species—are purposeful in humans and other animals (1890). Sigmund Freud, who believed in the **hedonic principle**—that people want to experience pleasure and avoid pain—described the force of psychic energy initiated by drives as the root of life instincts (including sexuality).

According to Clark Hull's **drive-reduction theory**, we act when a physiological need creates an aroused state that drives us to reduce the need. If we feel tired, we take the action of going to bed to restore **homeostasis**—a steady and balanced inner state. Reducing the tension reinforces the behavior (Hull, 1943, 1952). Departures from optimal states create drives. **Regulatory drives**, such as hunger and thirst, preserve homeostasis. **Nonregulatory drives**, such as sex or social drives, initiate other activities. A drive to preserve safety motivates feelings of fear, anger, and even the need for sleep. Sexual drives and drives to protect offspring motivate sexual and family relationships. Social drives make people want to cooperate, and educational drives inspire curiosity and play, as well as the pursuit of art and literature.

Julian Rotter developed the **social learning theory** that emphasizes the role of cognition in motivation and the importance of expectations in shaping behavior (1954). Rogue trader Jérôme Kerviel may have engaged in risky trades with the expectation of making a lot of money because people do things based on the expectation of obtaining a goal and the importance of that goal to them. If individuals find that behaving in a specific way does not get them what they want, they might change their behavior. Kerviel's irrationality made him continue to trade despite his losses, instead of changing his behavior.

Central-state theory explains drives by understanding them as corresponding to neural activity. Different drives have different **central drive systems**—sets of neurons that create the drive. For example, hunger and sex have different but overlapping drive systems. Italian researchers have found a relationship between chocolate consumption and sexual desire, and women with low libido seem to become more interested in sex after eating chocolate.

Located in the base of the brain, the hypothalamus connects to the brainstem and the forebrain and plays a significant role in regulating many central drive systems. The hypothalamus is directly connected to nerves carrying input from internal organs and carrying autonomic motor output back to internal organs. The hypothalamus also connects to and works with the pituitary gland to control hormone release.

∧
∧ **Why might**
∧ **offering choco-**
late to a loved
one on Valentine's
Day make sense
physiologically?

INCENTIVES

You may buy a soda because you feel thirsty, but you might also buy it because you watched a commercial touting its refreshing qualities. In addition to drives, **incentives**—positive or negative stimuli in the environment—motivate us to act. A strong drive can increase an incentive's value. If you are thirsty, you feel more influenced by the appearance of a refreshing drink.

Achieving a reward or a goal also reinforces incentives. An **intrinsic reward**, such as a desire to help others or learn new skills, creates its own joy just in performing the action. An **extrinsic reward**, such as studying to get a good grade, means we are motivated to perform an action that produces a separate, tangible reward. Triathlete Julie Ertel remembers to "have fun" in her sport and says that athletes get so caught up in winning (extrinsic reward), that they miss out on having fun (intrinsic reward).

Wanting and Liking

Both winning and enjoying a sport give an athlete a feeling of **liking**—a subjective feeling of pleasure derived from a reward. **Wanting** to win a medal at the Olympics gives athletes the desire to work hard for the reward. **Reinforcement** is the effect of the reward on learning and explains why athletes continue the pursuit of their sports.

Animals with **reward neurons** that are missing or damaged will lose all motivation and die unless artificially fed. The **medial forebrain bundle**, the brain's reward pathway, winds from the midbrain through the hypothalamus into the nucleus accumbens, the synaptic terminal for medial forebrain neurons. Because

> Once an individual had met biological and safety needs, he or she would seek a feeling of belongingness—the need to feel loved and avoid alienation.

this pathway controls reward, animals will work long and hard to stimulate it. Rats with electrodes attached to the nucleus accumbens pressed a lever thousands of times to stimulate the brain reward areas (Wise, 1978).

The **liking system** involves pleasure and does not depend on dopamine. For instance, neuroscientists have found sweet tastes activate the liking system regardless of the level of dopamine. When rats received dopamine-reducing drugs, they still engaged in liking behaviors and only sought out rewards that were directly available. **Endorphins**, morphine-like substances released by the medial forebrain bundle, inhibit pain and may be involved in the immediate pleasure of rewards, such as the runner's high.

By contrast, the **wanting system** depends heavily on dopamine. Rats trained to press a lever for a reward have a short burst of dopamine activity in the nucleus accumbens just before but not after pressing the lever (Phillips et al., 2003). Dopamine also plays a role in learning. When rats are exposed to light just before they receive food, their dopamine activity starts occurring in response to the light. When they expect food, the rats start feeling an anticipation of reward, a feeling well-known to those with addictions.

Like a bad romantic relationship, an addiction creates "wanting" without much "liking." Addictions basically hijack the brain's reward

system. Cocaine, amphetamines, and narcotics imitate the effects of dopamine and endorphins in the nucleus accumbens. They also stimulate mechanisms that control reward-based learning that activate every time the drug is used, reinforcing the behavior. Gambling and games of chance also activate the nucleus accumbens and the reward pathway. Like the rats in the experiment, the simple anticipation of payoff causes dopaminergic activity and overrides dopamine conserving mechanisms. Kerviel's anticipation of huge profits from trades might also have fueled his behavior.

OPTIMAL AROUSAL

Olympic athletes need an **optimal arousal** that gives them enough motivation but not so much that they feel anxious and unable to perform. Sixteen-year-old gymnast Shawn Johnson feels anxiety at every competition, but performs with confidence by putting her feelings into the poetry she writes. At 41, Dara Torres has qualified for her fifth Olympics and says that she enjoys swimming and competing more than ever. The **Yerkes-Dodson law** states in general that performance peaks with a moderate level of arousal (Yerkes & Dodson, 1908). Described graphically, the Yerkes-Dodson law resembles an inverted U: Performance levels increase as arousal increases, but only up to a certain point (the peak of the inverted U). After that, performance levels decrease as arousal increases. Easier tasks have higher optimal levels of arousal, and more difficult tasks have lower optimal levels of arousal. Tasks requiring persistence also generally require more arousal than intellectual ones. Optimal arousal to compete in a sport would be higher than to play chess.

MASLOW'S HIERARCHY OF NEEDS

Abraham Maslow described motivation through a **hierarchy of needs** in which more basic levels had to be fulfilled before higher levels (1970). **Physiological needs**, such as hunger and thirst, appeared at the bottom of the hierarchy as the most basic level. **Safety**, a feeling of being in a secure and safe environment, came next on the hierarchy. Once an individual had met biological and safety needs, he or she would seek a feeling of **belongingness**—the need to feel loved and avoid alienation. Then come **esteem needs**, feelings of worthiness and achievement. At the very top of the hierarchy, Maslow placed **self-actualization**, a complete feeling of self-acceptance and an awareness of fulfilling one's unique potential (1971). (For more information about the hierarchy of needs, see Chapter 16.)

Intrinsic reward is a task that is pleasurable in and of itself.

Extrinsic reward is a reward that is achieved through the completion of a task.

Liking is a subjective feeling of pleasure derived from a reward.

Wanting is a desire to achieve a particular goal in order to receive a reward.

Reinforcement describes an act that causes a response to be more likely to recur.

Reward neurons are neurons involved with experiencing the positive emotions associated with receiving a reward.

Medial forebrain bundle is the brain's reward pathway.

Liking system is a system involved with experiencing pleasure; it does not depend on dopamine.

Endorphins are morphine-like chemicals that inhibit pain signals and are released by the medial forebrain bundle.

Wanting system is a system involved with achieving a goal to receive pleasure; depends heavily on dopamine.

Optimal arousal is an arousal state in which a person has enough motivation but not so much that he or she feels anxious and unable to perform.

Yerkes-Dodson law states in general that performance peaks with a moderate level of arousal.

Hierarchy of needs is a pyramidal structure that shows the five needs that must be satisfied for a person to achieve self-actualization.

Physiological needs are needs that affect a person's physiology, such as hunger and thirst.

Safety is a feeling of being in a secure and safe environment.

Belongingness is a need to feel loved and avoid alienation.

Esteem need is a need to feel achievement and self-worth.

Self-actualization is a complete feeling of self-acceptance and an awareness of fulfilling one's unique potential.

How might gambling addiction resemble drug addiction?

Hunger

THE PHYSIOLOGY OF HUNGER

If you've ever skipped breakfast before an early morning class, you've probably experienced the embarrassment of your stomach growling loud enough to alert everyone in the room of your hunger. A. L. Washburn swallowed a balloon to monitor stomach contractions and discovered that feelings of hunger did indeed correspond to stomach contractions (Cannon & Washburn, 1912). But removing the stomach in rats and humans did not eliminate hunger, leading to new theories about its source.

Hunger, Body Chemistry, and the Brain

The levels of **glucose**—blood sugar—help determine hunger and satiety. When glucose levels drop, we feel hungry. If glucose levels rise, the hormone **insulin** reduces them by telling the body to convert glucose to fat. As the body monitors these chemical levels, it sends messages to the brain about whether to eat or not.

Research has shown the role the hypothalamus plays in regulating hunger along a dual center model. The lateral hypothalamus secretes the hormone **orexin**, which brings on feelings of hunger, an orexogenic response. When the lateral hypothalamus was electrically stimulated, rats that already felt full started eating. When the area was damaged or removed, even starving rats had no desire to eat (Sakurai et al., 1998). The ventromedial hypothalamus suppresses hunger and sends out **anorexogenic** signals that stop an animal from eating. The hypothalamus's **arcuate nucleus** contains both appetite-stimulating and appetite-suppressing neurons.

Not all hunger originates in internal body states. Many people seem to have room for dessert even when they already feel full after a meal. In this case, the **gustatory sense**—taste—mediates hunger. Satiety, a feeling of satisfaction, also involves sensory stimuli in the environment. The dessert looks appetizing, so we feel like eating it. Animals that eat a certain food until they feel satisfied will eat again if introduced to a novel food or taste. The sweet taste of dessert presents a new taste compared to the savory one of the meal.

> **Many people seem to have room for dessert even when they already feel full after a meal. In this case, the gustatory sense—taste—mediates hunger.**

Sexual Motivation

SYNCHRONY

Most mammals' sexual drives synchronize with their hormonal levels and chemical signals. The female cyclic production of estrogen and progesterone is the menstrual cycle in humans and the estrous cycle in other animals. In female rats, the ventromedial area of the hypothalamus corresponds to the preoptic area in males. For female mammals, estrogen peaks at ovulation, when the female becomes sexually receptive. Testosterone levels in male mammals remain more constant but still influence sexual behavior.

The human female's sex drive synchronizes less with her hormonal levels than in most other mammals. The female sex drive increases somewhat during ovulation but has more to do with testosterone levels than estrogen levels (Harvey, 1987; Meston & Frohlich, 2000; Meuwissen & Over, 1992; Reichman, 1998). Testosterone therapy, such as the testosterone patch, increases sex drive in women who feel a reduced desire for sex due to removal of the ovaries or adrenal glands. In males, testosterone also controls sex drive.

CASTRATION

In 17th- and 18th-century Europe, prepubescent boys who were castrated to preserve their high singing voices did not develop adult male sex characteristics or sexual desire. The 1994 film *Farinelli* depicts the life of the most famous

> **Sleep seems to be necessary to consolidate memories of the things we learn during the day and to promote learning.**

18th-century castrato, Carlo Broschi, thought to be one of the greatest opera singers of all time. In 2006, researchers exhumed Broschi's body to study castration's effects on the human body. While the study has not been fully completed, particularities in the bones do indicate castration. Castrated adult males also lose their desire for sex as their testosterone levels decline. Male sexual offenders given Depo-Provera to reduce testosterone to prepubescent levels also report less interest in sex. Some studies show a decrease in repeat offenses, but others indicate that the treatment does not reduce the rapist's desire to express aggression through sex (Criminal Justice Special Report, 1988). Implanting a testosterone crystal in the preoptic area of the hypothalamus restores sex drive in castrated animals (Everitt & Stacey 1987).

Sleep Motivation

WHY DO WE SLEEP?

The **preservation and protection theory** explains sleep as a mechanism evolved to preserve energy and provide protection during the night, when danger from predators was low and opportunities to get food were few. Sleep patterns do not depend on an animal's physical exertion levels but on how the animal finds food and protects itself. If predators hunt an animal during the day, the animal would be more likely to be nocturnal and out of harm's way during the daylight hours. Similarly, visually reliant species, such as human beings, tend to be diurnal to take advantage of sunlight for daily activities.

The **body restoration theory** explains sleep as a time for necessary rest and recuperation. During sleep, the metabolic rate goes down, muscles relax, and the body secretes growth hormones to promote tissue repair. Rats deprived of sleep experience tissue breakdown and eventually die (Rechtschaffen & Bergman, 1965). Sleep-deprived humans also experience declines in health and functioning.

Sleep seems to be necessary to consolidate memories of the things we learn during the day and to promote learning (Guzman-Marin et al., 2005; Leproult et al., 1997). Memory storage requires **long-term potentiation (LTP)**, two neurons firing together to extend the communication at the synapse, the junction where neurons meet. Rats that had been kept awake showed less long-term potentiation than those that had been allowed to sleep (Vyazovskiy et al., 2008).

The **activation-synthesis theory** understands sleep as a side effect of the visual and motor area neurons firing during **REM sleep**, the stage of sleep characterized by rapid eye movements. Dreams occur because neurons in different parts of the brain fire randomly, and the cortex synthesizes them into some kind of coherent story, but activation theory does not attribute any purpose to dreams or argue against any psychoanalytic theories.

INDIVIDUAL VARIATION

Although most people require about eight hours of sleep, some people need to sleep nine or ten hours to feel alert and rested. Former British Prime Minister Margaret Thatcher claimed that she only slept four hours a night, but sleep researcher Ian Hindmarch says that many photos showed Thatcher asleep during the day. Florence Nightingale and Napoleon also reportedly slept only a few hours a night. **Nonsomniacs** are those rare people who require much less than eight hours of sleep (sometimes only one hour a night). **Insomniacs** need as much sleep as most people but, for various reasons, are unable to get it.

Belongingness

When high school students try to be part of a clique or adults join professional groups, they are responding to a human need to belong. In the *Nichomachean Ethics*, Aristotle called humans the "social animal." Belonging does not simply make life more fulfilling; social bonds may have evolved to boost our ancestors' survival rates. Attachments between parents and children keep children close and protected. The word *wretched* comes from the Middle English word *wrecche*, meaning to be without kin nearby. Early humans probably fought, hunted, and foraged together to give themselves protection against predators and enemies.

Wanting to belong seems to be a cross-cultural need. A Zulu saying goes, "Umuntu ngumntu ngabantu," meaning "a person is a person through other persons." We act to increase our social acceptance because self-esteem tends to waver based on how valued and

accepted we feel. Our need to maintain relationships means that we stay in close contact with our friends and relatives. Bill and Hillary Clinton's marital problems played out very publicly, but the former President and the current Secretary of State remain together.

Being excluded hurts, and groups use social ostracism as a means of control. An online study showed that even the mildest forms of ostracism can control behavior powerfully (Williams et al., 2000). Participants playing a virtual game felt upset as other (computer-generated) participants began excluding them. In a second study, the ostracized participants complied more readily on tasks. Rejection literally hurts; social pain causes increased activity in the **anterior cingulate cortex**, an area involved in physical pain (Eisenberger & Lieberman, 2004). University students told during an experiment that they would be excluded from a group started showing more self-defeating and destructive behaviors (Twenge et al., 2001, Twenge et al., 2002). Conversely, social safety nets and a sense of belonging can improve and preserve health.

Motivation at Work

JOB SATISFACTION

If you've worked at a job you hated, you know how important job satisfaction can be to overall happiness. Those who think of work as a job, something they do to pay the bills, report the lowest job satisfaction. People who see work as a long-term career feel more satisfied. Individuals who see work as a "calling," something intrinsically important, feel the most satisfied (Wrzesniewski et al., 1997). Mihaly Csikszentmihalyi defined the feeling of being fully and comfortably engaged in work as "flow" (1990, 1999). We experience flow when tasks absorb us completely and demand enough from us, not too much or too little. A musician playing onstage, a chef busily preparing

> **Long-term potentiation (LTP)** is the process in which neural connections are strengthened through the repetition of neurotransmitters traveling across the same synapses.
>
> **Activation-synthesis theory** is a theory that explains sleep as a side effect of the visual and motor area neurons firing during REM sleep. It states that dreams are the result of the brain's attempt to make sense of the random neural activity that occurs while a person sleeps.
>
> **REM sleep** is a recurring stage of sleep during which vivid dreams usually occur.
>
> **Nonsomniacs** are people who require much less than eight hours of sleep each day.
>
> **Insomniacs** are people who need as much sleep as most people but are unable to get it.
>
> **Anterior cingulate cortex** is an area of the brain that serves as an executive control system that helps control a person's behavior; it is involved in the perception of physical pain.
>
> **Equity theory** states that workers decide how satisfied they feel with their jobs by comparing themselves to others.
>
> **Expectancy theory** defines job satisfaction as a worker's sense of achieving a certain outcome based on expectancy, instrumentality, and valence.

a dish, or a scientist engaged in research may all experience flow.

EQUITY THEORY AND EXPECTANCY THEORY

According to **equity theory**, workers decide how satisfied they feel with their jobs by comparing themselves to others. If they notice that they do a certain amount of work and get a specific reward while others do less work and get the same reward, they may feel unfairly treated. They may ask for a raise, work less, or leave their positions.

Expectancy theory defines job satisfaction as a worker's sense of achieving a certain outcome based on expectancy, instrumentality, and valence (Harder, 1991; Porter & Lawler, 1968; Vroom, 1964). For example, American International Group has offered new CEO Robert Willumstad an $8 million bonus. His expectancy would have to do with his ability to lead the company successfully. Instrumentality would involve the bonus he expects to receive for achieving the result, and valence would be defined by the value of the reward, the actual size of the bonus.

Popular series like Twilight speak to a need to belong.

Summary

WHAT ARE THE COMPONENTS OF EMOTION AND MOTIVATION?
pp. 194 & 199

- Emotions are made up of three distinct but related parts: physiological arousal, expressive behavior, and cognitive experience.

- We are motivated by both dispositional forces (internal states and drives) and situational forces (external stimuli).

WHAT ARE THE DOMINANT THEORIES OF EMOTION AND MOTIVATION? pp. 194 & 200

- Theories of emotion are the James-Lange theory (physiological response precedes cognition), Cannon-Bard theory (physiology and cognition are simultaneous), Schachter-Singer two-factor theory (perception along with physiological response produces emotion), cognitive-appraisal theory (cognitive evaluation follows physiological response to produce emotion), and Plutchik's emotion wheel (eight primary emotions combine to form more complex emotions).

- Theories of motivation are drive-reduction theory (actions are motivated by a drive to reduce physiological need), social-learning theory (actions are motivated by the expectation of achieving goals), and central state theory (drives are created by neural systems).

HOW DO WE EXPLAIN THE EMOTIONS OF FEAR, ANGER, AND HAPPINESS? p. 199

- Fear protects us by initiating a flight-and-fight response. Controlled mostly by the amygdala, it is partially learned and partially innate.

- Anger is a universal emotion, but its expression is culturally specific.

- Happiness tends to be temporary, makes people helpful, depends on our sense of success relative to others, and does not depend on money.

HOW DO WE UNDERSTAND HUNGER, SLEEP, SEXUALITY, BELONGING, AND WORK? p. 202

- Hunger depends on stomach contractions, glucose levels, hypothalamic secretions of orexin, and the gustatory sense.

- Sleep protects us from predators and restores our minds and bodies.

- The levels of testosterone, estrogen, and other hormones in our bodies influence our sex drives.

- A feeling of belonging maximizes survival, and its absence resembles physical pain.

- People find intrinsically rewarding work to be most satisfying.

Test Your Understanding

1. Beth takes an inhaler for her asthma. One of the side effects of the medicine is that it makes her heart beat quickly. When this happens, Beth often feels anxious, even though there is nothing for her to feel anxious about. Beth's reaction to her inhaler is predicted by:
   a. the James-Lange theory.
   b. the Cannon-Bard theory.
   c. the mere exposure effect.
   d. the two-factor theory.

2. Lauren was surprised to hear that her best friend is moving, and also feels sad about it. According to Plutchik's emotion wheel, it is likely that Lauren is experiencing:
   a. awe.
   b. love.
   c. contempt.
   d. disappointment.

3. James punches a hole in the wall when he finds out he doesn't get the job he wants. The emotional component he is displaying is:
   a. cognitive experience.
   b. expressive behavior.
   c. physiological arousal.
   d. mood.

4. Melissa cries at her friend's wedding. Even though she just ended a relationship and has been crying for several days, she assumes she must be crying now because she loves weddings and is happy. Melissa may be demonstrating:
   a. the exposure effect.
   b. misattribution.
   c. psychic blindness.
   d. a negative mood.

5. Zach is camping and hears rustling in the woods near his tent. He begins to sweat and breathe more quickly. What is happening?
   a. He is developing psychic blindness.
   b. The sympathetic division of his nervous system is preparing him for flight or fight.
   c. His prefrontal cortex is malfunctioning.
   d. The parasympathetic division of his nervous system is highly activated.

6. Ashley's brother jumps out in front of her, yelling "Boo," and she screams before she realizes who it is. Ashley's scream is likely the result of:
   a. rapid subcortical pathway activity.
   b. cortical pathway activity.

c. psychic blindness.

d. parasympathetic activity.

7. When a person experiences an emotionally charged stimulus, epinephrine (adrenaline) is released by:

a. the prefrontal cortex.

b. the parasympathetic nervous system.

c. the pituitary gland.

d. the adrenal glands.

8. While their accuracy is controversial, polygraph machines are often used to determine if a person is lying. They work by detecting:

a. changes in brain waves.

b. physiological changes like heart rate and perspiration.

c. changes in body temperature.

d. changes in facial expression.

9. Janelle tries to make an effort to smile at parties so other people will think she is having a good time. As it turns out, Janelle usually has more fun at parties when she remembers to smile. This is likely an example of:

a. action units.

b. deintensification.

c. affective forecasting.

d. the facial feedback hypothesis.

10. Nancy's husband recently suffered a stroke and is in the hospital. Nancy is scared for him. When she goes to her daughter's house, she smiles and acts happy so that her daughter will not worry. What is Nancy doing?

a. neutralizing her emotions

b. deintensifying her emotions

c. masking her emotions

d. intensifying her emotions

11. Harold is clinically depressed. He watches a romantic comedy with his friends and cries during a scene in which the main characters break up. At the end of the movie, even though the main characters get married, Harold says it was a sad movie. Harold is demonstrating:

a. mood deintensification.

b. temporal patterning.

c. mood-congruent processing.

d. affective forecasting.

12. Max has been feeling depressed that he is unemployed and can't find work. He volunteers at a soup kitchen for the day feeding homeless families and feels better when he goes home. Which of the following might explain why Max felt better?

a. He re-evaluated his relative deprivation.

b. He engaged in affective forecasting.

c. He experienced the feel-good, do-good phenomenon.

d. He experienced the adaptation-level phenomenon.

13. Which of the following is a nonregulatory drive?

a. hunger

b. sex

c. thirst

d. all of the above

14. Which of the following does NOT demonstrate the hedonic principle?

a. an angry toddler hitting his head against the wall

b. a person trying to avoid hard work

c. a child refusing to eat foods he or she does not like

d. a person eating a large slice of pie

15. Which of the following LEAST demonstrates the concept of reinforcement?

a. teaching a dog to sit by giving it dog treats when it obeys

b. continuing to donate blood because it makes you feel good about yourself

c. giving your child money for receiving a good grade

d. yelling at a child for misbehaving

16. Which of the following is most likely to yield an intrinsic reward?

a. investing in the stock market

b. doing cartwheels

c. studying for a test

d. practicing for an ice-skating competition

17. A male with a low sex drive most likely has:

a. high estrogen levels.

b. low testosterone levels.

c. aggressive behavior issues.

d. high testosterone levels.

18. According to Maslow's hierarchy of needs, which of the following would a person make his first priority?

a. having a job

b. finding food

c. buying a house

d. being in a romantic relationship

19. Which of the following people are most likely to be tired during the day?

a. nonsomniacs

b. insomniacs

c. people given Depo-Provera shots

d. people with low testosterone

20. Which of the following most indicates an experience of "flow"?

a. the workday seeming to pass quickly

b. the workday seeming to drag on

c. keeping an eye on the clock to see how soon class gets out

d. looking around to see what everyone else is doing

Remember to check www.thethinkspot.com for additional information, downloadable flashcards, and other helpful resources.

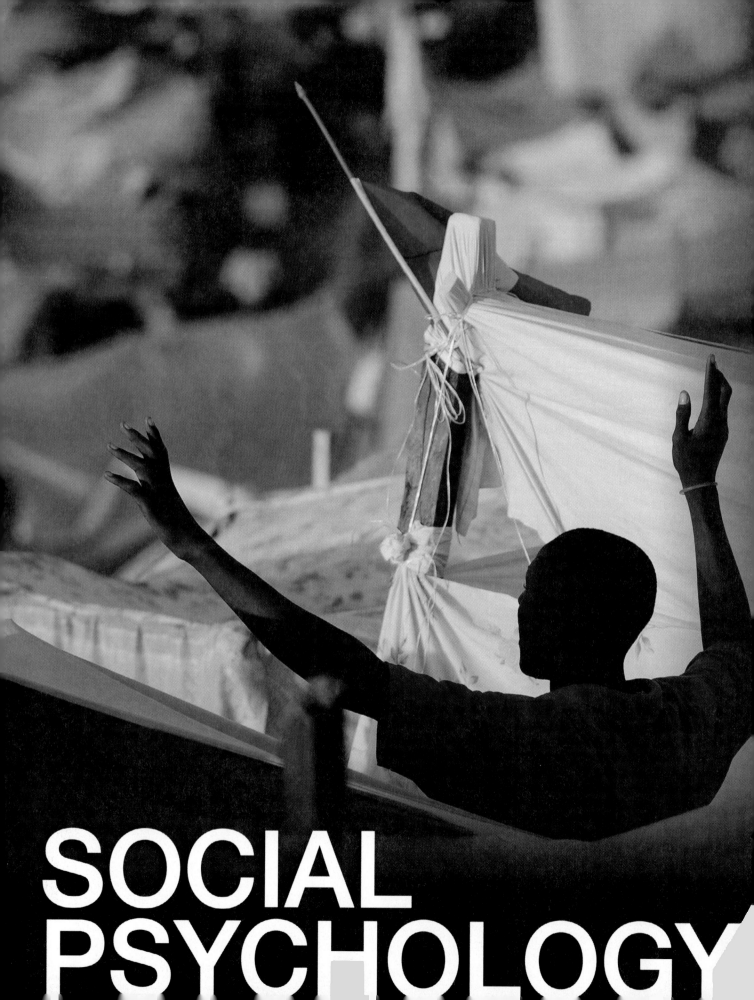

SOCIAL
PSYCHOLOGY

What if

you had only a half-hour to flee or find shelter before a devastating disaster wiped out your town? With no time to prepare, you would surely escape with nothing except the clothing on your back. This was the experience of many in the two-mile-wide town of Greensburg, Kansas, which was destroyed by a vicious tornado in May 2007. With 95 percent of the town completely destroyed, most of the 1,400 residents were left not only without their homes, but without jobs and schools as well.

Pulling together, the town decided to "go green" and rebuild with an emphasis on ecofriendly buildings and manufacturing. Although the difficulty of rebuilding not only the town but the townspeople's livelihood was immense, many in Greensburg made efforts to help rebuild green, including the General Motors and John Deere dealerships, local banks, the Baptist church, and the county hospital. The town has even constructed new "ecohomes" that are strong enough to survive future tornadoes, while conserving 70 percent more energy than the average house.

Rebuilding the town, however, is not just about encouraging people to go green, but also about sustaining the community and helping one another after an extreme loss. Although some longtime residents have left Greensburg, many are still waiting to return and build anew. Some who have lost everything in the recent disaster are hesitant about the changes, but city officials are confident that this type of community investment will bring new opportunities to ensure a bright future for those in Greensburg.

This emphasis on community well-being demonstrates particularly positive aspects of social psychology. The collectivism of the citizens of Greensburg—that is, everyone's willingness to contribute to the community as a whole—is the foundation of their success. Even though the grief and shock of the disaster might have overwhelmed Greensburg residents at first, this prosocial behavior has brought them together. The town has much to teach us about living harmoniously with the environment and each other.

<<< On January 12, 2010, a 7.0-magnitude earthquake struck the nation of Haiti, leaving much of the capital and beyond destroyed. As concerns over a shortage of food, water, and medical supplies mounted, members of the international community reached out to donate time and money to the Haitian relief effort. What motivates people to help others? Is there such a thing as true altruism? Social psychology addresses the nature of societal interactions and individual influences, allowing us to understand what it means to be human.

CHAPTER 14

Foundations of Social Psychology

Human beings may be individuals, but we are all individuals within a group. **Social psychologists** study how the thoughts, emotions, and behavior of individuals influence and are influenced by interactions between people. Our interactions with others (and sometimes with ourselves) depend to a great extent on our **social perception**, the process through which we understand and categorize the behavior of others.

ATTRIBUTION THEORY

The popularity of reality TV probably wouldn't surprise psychologist Fritz Heider. He believed that we are all "naive scientists," naturally interested in analyzing other people's personalities and attitudes. According to Heider's **attribution theory**, we understand the behavior of others by attributing their behavior either to their internal dispositions or their external situations (1958). Whether you think that *American Idol* judge Simon Cowell behaves rudely because he's naturally ill-tempered or because he thinks that acting nasty will land him in the limelight, you are making an **attribution**, a claim about the cause of his behavior.

When you attribute a person's behavior to his or her personality or characteristics, you are making a **dispositional attribution**. Alternatively, when you attribute behavior to external factors such as the person's situation or environment, you're making a **situational attribution**. When Senator John McCain's economic advisor, Phil Graham, dismissed the recent economic downturn and called the United States "a nation of whiners," he made a dispositional attribution about Americans' characteristics and personalities. When both President Obama and Senator McCain rebuked Mr. Graham by saying that "it isn't whining" to complain about "real difficulties," they made a situational attribution by claiming that Americans' behavior is caused by environmental factors rather than internal personality traits (Associated Press, 2008).

Often, we don't have enough information about people to determine why they act the way they do. Since we can't read other people's minds, we try to compensate by observing their behavior in a variety of situations and environments. Our observations are based on three characteristics: the behavior's distinctiveness (Is the behavior specific to a situation?), its consistency (Does the person usually behave this way?), and consensus (Do other people behave similarly in similar situations?). We can then use our observations to draw conclusions about why people act the way they do. This process of attribution is known as the **covariation principle** (Kelley, 1967).

The Fundamental Attribution Error

Both personal characteristics and external factors play an important role in determining our actions, but it turns out that most people tend to attribute behavior to character rather than the situation. Social psychologist Lee Ross (1977) has dubbed this phenomenon the **fundamental attribution error (FAE)**. Amazingly, studies have shown that even when people know that a situation has actually caused a certain behavior, they still make a dispositional attribution. Participants who were told that an experiment collaborator had been instructed to behave coldly or warmly toward them still persisted in believing that the behavior reflected the collaborator's real personality (Napolitan & Goethals, 1979). Of course, the attributions that we make about other people can have significant consequences for our own behavior: If your friend stands you up at the movie theater, you might attribute his or her behavior to thoughtlessness or cruelty and call him or her to leave a nasty message, not realizing that your friend has been delayed because of a parent's illness.

Bias in Attribution

Since we don't have a lot of information to go on when we make conclusions about other people, we take shortcuts by using our prior knowledge, personal beliefs, and biases to make assumptions about strangers. We all have **preexisting schemata**, sets of ideas or beliefs about

---

Social psychologist is a psychologist who studies how the thoughts, emotions, and behavior of individuals influence and are influenced by interactions between people.

Social perception is the process through which a person understands and categorizes the behavior of others.

Attribution theory states that a person understands other people by attributing their behavior either to their internal dispositions or their external situations.

Attribution is a claim about the cause of a person's behavior.

Dispositional attribution is an attribution based on a person's personality or characteristics.

Situational attribution is an attribution based on a person's situation or environment.

Covariation principle is a process of attribution in which behavior is observed based on three characteristics: the behavior's distinctiveness, it's consistency, and consensus.

Fundamental attribution error (FAE) is a phenomenon in which people make an attribution based on character, even when they know that the behavior is situational.

Preexisting schema is a set of ideas or beliefs about others that leads a person to perceive others in a way that conforms with that person's expectations.

∧
∧ **Whiners or hard workers? Although we do our**
∧ **best to understand others' behavior, we can't**
always truly know what people are thinking.

others that lead us to perceive people in a way that conforms with our expectations. For example, someone who believes that athletes are generally not as intelligent as non-athletes probably won't perceive the school's best football player as an academic superstar, even though that football player may graduate with honors and go on to receive a doctorate in astrophysics.

> "We often show a self-serving bias that causes us to attribute our failures to external events and our successes to our personal characteristics and skills (Gilovich, 1991)."

Although we know intellectually that appearances can be deceiving, we often subconsciously base our opinions about people on their physical appearance. An **attractiveness bias** leads us to rate physically attractive people as more intelligent, competent, sociable, and sensitive than their less attractive counterparts (Eagly et al., 1991; Feingold, 1992; Hatfield & Sprecher, 1986). And in both the United States and Korea, there is a "baby-face bias" that causes people to view baby-faced adults as more naive, honest, helpless, kind, and warm. This bias can even help baby-faced adults win in small-claims court (Zebrowitz & McDonald, 1991). As anyone who adores babies and puppies probably knows, humans instinctively respond to infant features with compassion and care (Lorenz, 1943).

CONSTRUCTING SOCIAL REALITY

We may make dispositional attributions when we judge other people's behavior, but when it comes to judging our *own* behavior, we tend to be a little kinder: We often show a **self-serving bias** that causes us to attribute our failures to external events and our successes to our personal characteristics and skills (Gilovich, 1991). When we get into a car accident or get rejected from a team, we keep our self-esteem intact by placing the blame on the other drivers on the road or the obviously inept coach.

In George Bernard Shaw's play *Pygmalion* (and the musical

version, *My Fair Lady*), arrogant linguist Professor Henry Higgins demonstrates that he can pass a London flower girl off as an aristocrat simply by changing the way she speaks. The **Pygmalion effect**, named after Shaw's play, describes people's tendency to behave in accordance with others' expectations: If you expect someone to be an aristocrat, she will behave in an aristocratic manner. The Pygmalion effect is one type of **self-fulfilling prophecy**, or a belief that causes itself to become true.

Social psychologists have noticed that these beliefs can be particularly powerful in the classroom. In one study, Robert Rosenthal told teachers at a Boston elementary school that certain students would bloom and show great progress in the school year. As a result, these randomly chosen students raised their IQ scores by 10 to 20 points (1974). Believing in the students' abilities, teachers encouraged them and expected more from them, producing a marked effect on student performance. This result is one example of **behavioral expectation confirmation** (Snyder, 1984), a phenomenon that enables us to influence other people to behave in accordance with our expectations. Behavioral expectation confirmation was at work in a study in which participants were told to choose a question to ask a shy person. Most of the participants chose questions that would confirm that person's shyness, such as "What factors make it hard for you to really open up to people?" and "What do you dislike about loud parties?" (Snyder & Swann, 1978).

Attractiveness bias is the tendency for a person to rate physically attractive people as more intelligent, competent, sociable, and sensitive than their less attractive counterparts.

Self-serving bias is the tendency for a person to attribute his or her failures to external events and his or her successes to personal characteristics and skills.

Pygmalion effect is the tendency for people to behave in accordance with others' expectations.

Self-fulfilling prophecy is a belief that causes itself to become true.

Behavioral expectation confirmation is a phenomenon that enables a person to influence other people to behave in accordance with his or her expectations

Social cognition refers to underlying processes, such as attention and memory, that make social behavior possible.

Fusiform face area is an area of the visual cortex that specifically responds to and recognizes faces.

Social Cognition

Research in **social cognition** focuses on the underlying processes, such as attention and memory, that make social behavior possible. As we expand our knowledge about the biology of the brain, social cognitive neuroscience has become increasingly important as a way to understand these processes. Biological structures and processes in the brain help us navigate our social environment, whether we're recognizing a friend's face in a crowd, making determinations about a person's age or race, or feeling empathy for others.

PERCEPTION OF SOCIAL CUES: FACIAL RECOGNITION

When you meet a person on the street, you can easily recognize that person as a friend or stranger. Just by looking at that person's face, you can probably tell what type of mood he or she's in and how he or she might feel about you. Face recognition forms an integral part of our social interactions. While debate in neuroscience rages about localized and generalized brain function, recent studies have shown that the **fusiform face area**, an area on the underside of the brain where the occipital lobe meets the temporal

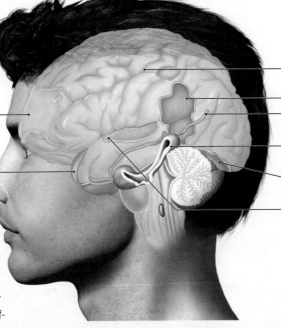

Posterior cingulate

Right inferior parietal
Superior temporal sulcus

Hippocampus

Fusiform face area

Lateral temporal neocortex

Frontopolar cortex

Temporal pole

∧
∧ **Several parts of the brain are active**
∧ **during the face-recognition process.**

lobe, plays an essential role in face recognition (Kanwisher et al., 1997). When we recognize a face, the fusiform face area becomes active and sends messages to the lateral temporal neocortex, where neurons specifically linked to face recognition fire (Gross & Sergent, 1992). The temporal pole at the back of the temporal lobe connects the visual information to emotional association (Olson et al., 2007). Finally, the hippocampus retrieves memories necessary for recognition (Rissman et al., 2008). These reciprocal exchanges of information between different areas of the brain happen so quickly that we can instantly distinguish a familiar face from an unfamiliar one. People with damage to the ventral region of the temporal lobe have difficulty processing information about facial features. This condition, known as **prosopagnosia**, prevents people from recognizing faces; however, these people can usually recognize facial expressions of emotion. Often,

> "Have you ever picked up a friend's belly laugh or favorite figure of speech without realizing what you were doing? **You weren't just being a copycat: When we mimic others, we are better able to understand what those others are feeling and thinking.**"

people with prosopagnosia are able to identify their loved ones using information from their voices or the way that they walk and move.

SOCIAL CATEGORIZATION

We often refer to social categories such as age, race, and gender, to make inferences about the people we meet. In fact, our brains are amazingly speedy when it comes to processing information about social categories: Researchers have measured electrophysiological responses in the brain and found that when we view faces of people of different ages and genders, our brains respond to these changing social categories in as little as 145 milliseconds (Mouchetant-Rostaing & Giard, 2003). While it might take us a while to determine someone's personal qualities (such as compassion, intelligence, or aggression) from his or her facial features, it usually doesn't take us long at all to categorize that person by age, race, and gender.

Can we learn about people's racial biases by observing their biological reactions? As recently as 2000 and 2003, researchers demonstrated how white participants asked to look at unfamiliar African American faces revealed an unconscious negative bias (Phelps et al., 2000; Richeson et al., 2003). When they looked at unfamiliar male African American faces, those participants who associated African American faces with negative traits also showed a stronger startle eye-blink response and greater amygdala activity than other participants did (Phelps et al., 2000). Since both amygdala activity and startle eye-blink response indicate fear, unfamiliar male African American faces probably evoked fear in these experiment participants. However, these results diverged completely from the participants' conscious or professed positive beliefs about African Americans, suggesting that it's possible for our biological responses to people to be at odds with our conscious, socially controlled responses (Richeson et al., 2003).

MENTALIZING

In order to empathize with others, neurologically speaking, we must walk a mile in their shoes. Experiencing empathy means feeling for others, understanding their position, and wanting to help them. It involves **mentalizing**, or understanding that our behavior and that of others reflects our mental states: our thoughts, beliefs, and feelings.

The brain assists us in this type of social cognition in several different ways. For example, mirror neurons in the brain fire both when we perform an action and when we

Social pressure has negative connotations, but can you think of any ways in which social pressure might be a positive influence?

watch others performing that same action, helping us relate our actions and intentions to those of others (Ferrari et al., 2005). We also have the mental flexibility to put ourselves in someone else's position and attempt to see things from his or her perspective. The brain's medial prefrontal cortex contributes to the self-awareness and self-regulation necessary to look at the world from another person's point of view (Decety & Moriguchi, 2007).

Social Influence

A presidential candidate asks for your vote; an animated gecko on television wants you to buy his company's car insurance; you want a friend to come out with you after work although she feels exhausted—every day we encounter and exert forms of **social influence**, or behavioral control. Closely related to the concept of social influence is **social pressure**, the real or imagined psychological forces that others exert over us through their example, judgments, and demands. Social pressure comes in too many forms to count, but when you face it, it can be hard to resist.

HEDONIC, APPROVAL, AND ACCURACY MOTIVES

"Call now!" the TV commercial begs you. "We'll even throw in an extra set of steak knives!" This tantalizing bargain is an example of one type of social influence called a **hedonic motive**, a pleasurable incentive or reward for acting in a certain way. Not all hedonic motives are as exciting as free steak knives, however: We can also be hedonically motivated by the threat of pain if we fail to act a certain way. (The traffic fine that doubles if you fail to pay it by a specific date is one such example.)

>>> Michelle Obama's fashion statements have been copied by hundreds of women across America. How might imitating others facilitate social behavior?

The **approval motive**, or the desire to be accepted by our peers, can also convince us to take action. Our love of social acceptance isn't superficial; in fact, being well-liked by others helps us survive. Research has found that social acceptance actually boosts our health, while isolation and loneliness can make us more vulnerable to illness (Pressman et al., 2005).

> *It appears that other people have a certain amount of influence on our own emotional states,* to the extent that catching a glimpse of a sad-looking person could put a slight frown on your face.

Since most of us don't enjoy being wrong, the **accuracy motive**, or our desire to be correct or accurate, can have a strong pull on our

Prosopagnosia is a condition caused by damage to the ventral region of the temporal lobe in which a person is unable to recognize faces.

Mentalizing is a person's understanding that his or her behavior and that of others reflects a person's mental states.

Social influence is behavioral control.

Social pressure consists of real or imagined psychological forces that people exert over others through their example, judgments, and demands.

Hedonic motive is a pleasurable incentive or an attempt to avoid pain that causes us to act in a certain way.

Approval motive is a person's desire to be accepted by his or her peers.

Accuracy motive is a person's desire to be correct or accurate.

Chameleon effect refers to a person's unconscious mimicry of other people's expressions, behaviors, and voice tones.

behavior. If you're in a group of people who are discussing their shared belief that the government should support the development of sustainable, renewable energy, you might listen to their opinions and decide to jump on the renewable-energy bandwagon because you've been persuaded that their position is the correct one.

CONTAGIOUS BEHAVIOR

As Elvis and Cher impersonators in Las Vegas know, human beings cannot help imitating each other. Even in countries like the United States, where individuality and independence are strong cultural values, there's a streak of imitation: When Michelle Obama appeared on a daytime talk show in a black-and-white floral dress, for example, the dress sold out in stores. But imitation isn't always a conscious choice. Take for example the **chameleon effect**, our unconscious mimicry of other people's expressions, behaviors, and voice tones (Chartrand & Bargh, 1999). Have you

> When Asch asked experiment participants to match the length of a stimulus line with the length of one of three other lines, they had no problem performing this matching task correctly. When they were asked to perform the same task in a group with experiment confederates who kept offering the wrong answer, however, participants changed their answers to conform with those of the group one third of the time.

ever picked up a friend's belly laugh or favorite figure of speech without realizing what you were doing? You weren't just being a copycat: When we mimic others, we are better able to understand what those others are feeling and thinking.

If you've ever met someone with "infectious enthusiasm," you know that emotions, like behaviors, can be contagious. Emotional contagion happens quickly and unconsciously. In fact, when researchers ran a study in which they flashed stimuli of emotional faces in front of participants, they discovered that although the participants were not consciously aware that they had seen facial expressions, the participants' faces took on the same expressions that they had unconsciously processed from the images (Dimberg et al.,

2000). It appears that other people have a certain amount of influence on our own emotional states, to the extent that catching a glimpse of a sad-looking person could put a slight frown on your face.

CONFORMITY

While imitation may be the sincerest form of flattery, **conformity** requires adjusting our behavior or thinking to conform to a group standard. We can feel the pressure to conform in a wide variety of situations, but certain conditions facilitate conformity: Whenever people conform by buying the latest style of jeans, joining a religious community, or ostracizing an outsider, social influence is at work. **Normative social influence**, influence that draws on our desire for others' approval and our longing to be part

of a group, can cause us to conform to the norms or social expectations about attitudes and behaviors that a group values. **Informational social influence**, influence exerted by information that others give us, can shed new light on the objective nature of an event or situation. Normative social influence appeals to the approval motive and our desire to be liked, while informational social influence appeals to the accuracy motive and our desire to obtain correct information.

Asch's Conformity Studies

Renowned social psychologist Solomon Asch showed how **suggestibility**, or susceptibility to the opinions of others, can cause people to conform (1940, 1956). When Asch asked

Conditions that

feelings of **incompetence** or **insecurity**

a group of **at least three people**

a unanimous group **without dissenters**

being among **admired** people

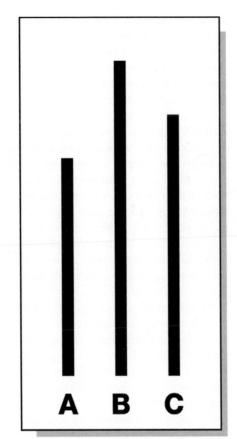

<<< Which of the three lines on the right matches the length of the line on the left?

(For more information about Asch's experiment, see Chapter 2.)

A B C

The Bystander Effect

We don't only conform to follow social norms in mundane places like the school cafeteria or the basketball bleachers. In emergency situations, socially accepted rules of behavior become particularly significant. After the 1964 rape and murder of Kitty Genovese, which allegedly took place in front of 38 witnesses, numerous studies have illustrated what's become known as the **bystander effect**: In a situation where someone requires help, the greater the number of bystanders present, the less likely any individual bystander is to help the person in need. Darley and Latané performed studies that suggested that most people intervene to help another person having an epileptic seizure when they believe they are the only person who can hear—and help—the seizing individual (1968). If they believe that other people can also hear the person in need, they are less likely to help. People also look to their **reference group**, those with whom they feel affiliated, to gauge how to behave. If they see people behaving indifferently, they tend to do the same, but if even one person chooses to help, the others will also tend to

experiment participants to match the length of a stimulus line with the length of one of three other lines, they had no problem performing this matching task correctly. When they were asked to perform the same task in a group with experiment confederates who kept offering the wrong answer, however, participants changed their answers to conform with those of the group one third of the time. Both normative and informational social influence may have played

a role in these results: Normative social influence may have caused participants to change their answers to match the group's answers, and informational social influence may have made the participants think that their original perceptions were factually incorrect: After all, if ten other people say two lines are the same and you are the only one who thinks the lines are different, it seems very likely that you've missed something that everyone else has seen.

Influence Conformity

lack of a **prior commitment** to a **particular response**

a **public setting**

a **culture** that **encourages adherence** to **social standards**

the **need** to make **difficult decisions** of high **personal relevance**

Total situation is a situation in which people are isolated from alternative viewpoints and given strict rewards and punishments from leaders.

Compliance is a change in a person's behavior that occurs in response to a direct request.

Cognitive dissonance is a disconnect between a person's internal attitudes and his or her external behavior.

Lowball technique encourages compliance by offering an attractive deal, only to change the terms of the deal later.

Bait-and-switch technique encourages people to comply with an attractive offer but substitutes that offer with a less attractive option once the person has agreed.

Foot-in-the-door technique involves asking people to comply with a small request and then making a much larger request, to raise funds.

Shared identity is a person's feeling that he or she is similar to other people in thought, feeling, and behavior.

Norm of reciprocity is a socialized norm that involves a person's tendency to desire to return favors.

Door-in-the-face technique is a procedure for gaining compliance that involves making a large request and then, when that request is refused, making a smaller request that seems reasonable in comparison.

people as "teachers" and instructed them to deliver an electric shock to learners for every wrong answer. The "learners," actually experiment confederates, voiced discomfort, pain, and even agony, but most of the teachers continued delivering progressively stronger shocks, despite having said explicitly that they would stop as soon as the learner experienced any discomfort. Even after the learner's voice became silent, suggesting that he had been severely injured by the shocks, the experimenter ordered participants to continue administering shocks, and although many of the participants seemed very uncomfortable about it, a surprisingly large number of them dutifully followed orders. As you'll remember, 65 percent of the participants showed total obedience by administering "lethal" shocks at the maximum level of 450 volts.

What allowed average people to behave like sadistic torturers? Milgram determined that certain conditions encouraged participants to follow commands. For example, we generally follow the norm of obeying legitimate authority figures such as the university psychologists who directed the experiment. The experimenter seemed self-assured and accepted responsibility for the outcome of the experiment, making participants feel less responsible for their actions. The experimenter also asked the participants to increase the shocks

We don't always behave the way others would like us to, but we make both small and large gestures of compliance all the time. Why are we so willing to change our behaviors because of other people's requests?

incrementally; once participants had agreed to give the "learner" a shock of 60 volts, it became more difficult for them to refuse to administer a 70-volt shock. Participants were placed in a separate room from the learner, increasing their psychological distance from the repercussions of their actions, and participants had no alternative models of behavior to follow—in other words, all they'd seen anyone do was comply with the experimenter's requests, so they didn't have a model for refusing to comply. Finally, demand characteristics, or the cues in the experimental setting that influenced participants' beliefs about their expected behavior, most likely played a role in participants' decisions to obey authority.

follow. As in Nazi Germany, **total situations**—situations in which people are isolated from alternative viewpoints and given strict rewards and punishments from leaders— also prompt people to follow social norms closely.

OBEDIENCE
Stanley Milgram and Obedience to Authority

The genocides in Cambodia, Bosnia, Rwanda, and Darfur have joined the Holocaust in Nazi Germany as testaments to the fact that ordinary human beings can perform extraordinarily inhuman acts. To understand how and why people obey immoral and unethical commands, Stanley Milgram conducted experiments that became some of the most famous and infamous in social psychology (1963, 1974). As you learned in Chapter 2, Milgram cast 1,000

Conditions that Influence Obedience

4 Participant does not have access to models of defiance.

3 Victim is depersonalized or kept at a distance.

5 An intermediary bystander is present.

2 Person giving orders is a legitimate authority figure supported by a prestigious institution.

6 Participant is affected by normative and informational influence.

1 Person giving orders is in physical proximity to the participant.

7 Participant's behavior is an ingrained habit.

150   600
750

AC VOLTS

Strengths and Weaknesses of Conformity and Obedience Studies

Conformity and obedience studies like Asch's and Milgram's have given us valuable insight into humans' susceptibility to social influence and provided information about why we sometimes accept false beliefs or capitulate to cruelty. However, Milgram's experiments also raised a number of criticisms. Today, ethical concerns about lasting damage suffered by participants coerced to harm others would have prevented these studies from being conducted. (It's worth noting, however, that 84 percent of participants in Milgram's experiments felt glad to have taken part in the study, and only 2 percent regretted it (Milgram, 1964; Errera, 1972). Critics also question the degree to which experimental results explain real-world crimes. It's possible that the participants' belief (warranted or not) that the experimenters would never allow them to severely harm others allowed the participants to follow instructions more easily (Orne & Holland, 1968). People who genuinely and purposefully harm others, however, obviously hold no such belief. While the scope of Milgram's results may be limited to the lab, his experiments do offer us clues about how ordinary people can obey orders to commit genocide and mass murder.

COMPLIANCE

If you wanted your friend to turn down his obnoxiously loud stereo or cheer up about his favorite football team's poor performance, you would need to figure out how to get your friend to comply with your wishes. **Compliance** is a change in a person's behavior that occurs in response to a direct request. We don't always behave the way others would like us to, but we make both small and large gestures of compliance all the time. Why are we so willing to change our behaviors because of other people's requests?

Cognitive Dissonance

Let's say you agreed to see a movie with friends even though you had no interest in watching a troop of robot overlords conquering the Earth. If you've ever experienced a disconnect between your internal attitudes and your external behavior, you've experienced **cognitive dissonance**. Social psychologist Leon Festinger (1957) coined the term, and he and others have shown that our desire to counteract cognitive dissonance can play a major role in the phenomenon of compliance: We often comply with requests in order to make our actions match our attitudes (or vice versa).

In what has become a classic study in social psychology, Festinger and his colleagues asked participants to undertake incredibly boring tasks such as putting spools into a tray and turning square pegs a quarter-turn at a time. The experimenter then asked each participant to tell the next participant that the tasks were enjoyable, intriguing, and exciting. Half of the participants were promised $20 in exchange for telling this lie; the other participants were offered $1. Festinger and his fellow researchers discovered that, after the participants had lied to their peers and received their money, the participants who had received $1 rated the tasks they'd performed as significantly more interesting than did the participants who had received $20. Festinger used his theory of cognitive dissonance to explain these results: If you say something you don't believe, but you don't have sufficient justification (such as a $20 bill) for saying it, you're likely to change your beliefs in order to reduce the effect of cognitive dissonance (Festinger & Carlsmith, 1959).

> "It's often all too easy to influence human behavior, and people with a vested interest in our compliance have come up with several time-honored methods for convincing people to act in certain ways. Credit card companies, for instance, often use the lowball technique, which encourages compliance by offering an attractive deal, only to change the terms of the deal later."

Motivations for Compliance

It's often all too easy to influence human behavior, and people with a vested interest in our compliance have come up with several time-honored methods for convincing people to act in certain ways. Credit card companies, for instance, often use the **lowball technique**, which encourages compliance by offering an attractive deal, only to change the terms of the deal later. You might agree to sign up for a credit card that offers no monthly fees through July, only to find out on August 1 that your monthly fees have skyrocketed. Since you've made a commitment to the credit card by that point, however, you're more likely to continue to use the card.

Advertisers and politicians use the discomfort created by cognitive dissonance to get people to try a new product or vote for a ballot initiative. For example, the **bait-and-switch technique** encourages people to comply with an attractive offer but substitutes that offer with a less attractive option once the person has agreed. During campaign season, a politician might promise not to raise taxes, but when he or she's in office, he or she may choose to keep taxes low only for people making a certain amount of money. In order to reduce cognitive dissonance, the people who complied with the politician's request for votes may convince themselves that the politician isn't breaking his or her promise.

Charities and public television stations that ask for small initial contributions and then follow up with larger and larger requests rely on the **foot-in-the-door technique**, a procedure that involves asking people to comply with a small request and then making a much larger request, to raise funds. Once we've given $10 to our favorite local radio station because we strongly believe in community-supported radio, it can feel inconsistent not to give the station the $100 they ask for in their next e-mail, so we adjust our actions to match our attitudes.

We often comply in order to reduce cognitive dissonance, but there are several other factors that encourage compliance. For instance, we tend to comply most easily with those with whom we feel a **shared identity** or with whom we've experienced a friendly conversation. On shows like *Survivor*, contestants who've formed strong alliances are often able to convince the members of their alliance to behave in a certain way or follow a specific voting pattern when it comes time to vote someone "off the island." Of course, when one contestant helps another, he or she tends to expect help in return. A socialized norm, the **norm of reciprocity**, means that we want to return favors, so people are more likely to comply with requests from others who have granted their requests in the past.

If a Girl Scout knocked on your door and asked you to buy 100 boxes of cookies, you'd probably refuse. But if she then said, "Okay, would you consider buying just three boxes?" you might comply with her request. This particular Girl Scout used the **door-in-the-face technique**, a procedure for gaining compliance that involves making a large request and then, when that request is refused, making a smaller request that seems reasonable in comparison.

Attitude is an evaluative belief or opinion about a person, object, or idea.

Explicit attitude is a belief or opinion that a person holds consciously and can report to others.

Implicit attitude is a belief or opinion that a person can't report and that will automatically influence his or her actions.

Persuasion is a deliberate effort to change an attitude or behavior.

Central route is a path to persuasion that involves paying careful attention to strong, well-presented arguments that are personally relevant and that appeal to reason.

Peripheral route is a path to persuasion that involves evaluating an argument based on tangential cues rather than on the argument's merits.

Elaboration-likelihood model states that people tend to be persuaded through the central route when their motivation and ability to understand and consider the persuasive message is high, while they are more likely to be persuaded by the peripheral route when their motivation is low or when they need to make a quick decision.

Perseverance effect is a phenomenon in which it is difficult for people to shake their initial impressions.

ATTITUDES AND ACTIONS

Attitudes, our evaluative beliefs or opinions about people, objects, and ideas, fundamentally affect our behaviors. We have both **explicit attitudes**, beliefs or opinions that we hold consciously and can report to others, and **implicit attitudes**, beliefs and opinions that we can't (or won't) report and that automatically influence our actions. All attitudes have three component parts: affect (our emotions or feelings), cognition (our thoughts), and behavior. Our feelings, thoughts, and behaviors work together to shape our attitudes. Attitudes can be formed in many ways, including through classical conditioning (see Chapter 7) and through the acceptance of social norms.

> *Your implicit attitudes during the 2008 election season probably matched your explicit attitudes, but maybe you decided to consciously fight a lifelong devotion to one political party and vote for McCain or Obama based on policy issues rather than on your gut instincts.*

Political elections can provide a wealth of examples of both explicit and implicit attitudes. If you have an explicit attitude about a candidate, you have consciously held opinions about him or her: Maybe, during the 2008 presidential campaign, you liked Barack Obama because of his positions on the economy and the environment, or maybe you disliked him because his social values differed from yours. Your implicit attitudes during the 2008 election season probably matched your explicit attitudes, but maybe you decided to consciously fight a lifelong devotion to one political party and vote for McCain or Obama based on policy issues rather than on your gut instincts.

In a 2008 study of Italian politics, researchers at the University of Padua discovered that implicit political attitudes can determine voters' behavior on election day. Voters who declared themselves "undecided" had no explicit attitude about the candidates, but they often had

implicit attitudes about the candidates or their political parties, and these voters tended to ultimately cast their ballots for the party they implicitly favored, even if they didn't consciously prefer either party (Arcuri et al., 2008).

PERSUASION

Some attitudes that we hold are stronger than others, but nearly all attitudes are susceptible to change. **Persuasion**, a deliberate effort to change an attitude or behavior, is indigenous to many areas of our lives, but it might help to consider it in one of its natural habitats: the courtroom. Attorneys commonly use persuasive techniques to get jury members on their side. The jury might be swayed through the **central route** to persuasion, which involves paying careful attention to strong, well-presented arguments that are personally relevant and that appeal to reason. Or they might be convinced through the **peripheral route** to persuasion, which involves evaluating an argument based on tangential cues rather than on the argument's merits. For example, a juror might be persuaded by a defense attorney's argument based on the attorney's good looks or sunny disposition rather than on the facts of the case. Emotional appeals can be just as persuasive as appeals to reason, but the former follow the peripheral route, while the latter follow the central route. According to the **elaboration-likelihood model** (Petty & Cacioppo, 1986), we tend to be persuaded through the central route when our motivation and ability to understand and consider the persuasive message is high. When our motivation is low, however, or when we need to reach a quick decision and we don't have time to think critically, we're more likely to be persuaded through the peripheral route.

When and where we learn information can also affect our ability to be persuaded by it. Our initial impressions are hard to shake, a phenomenon known as the **perseverance effect**. If a teacher

<<< What explicit and implicit attitudes might the American public have held about President Barack Obama and Vice President Joe Biden during the 2008 presidential campaign?

receives a stellar first paper from his or her student, he or she can probably be easily persuaded that the student's subsequent work is of the highest caliber even though unbiased teachers may not hold the same opinion of the student's performance. The **sleeper effect**, which occurs when we forget the unreliable source of a piece of information but remember the information itself and believe that it's trustworthy, can also affect our judgment and our ability to be persuaded by false statements.

GROUP INFLUENCE

Groups of people can influence individual behavior in powerful ways. In fact, the mere presence of others can affect how well we perform a task. When we're being observed by others, we perform better on easy tasks or ones we know well but worse on difficult or less familiar tasks (Guerin, 1986; Zajonc, 1965). When people believe that their individual efforts don't matter or that they are not personally responsible because they are only one member of a group, they tend to put less effort into a task, a phenomenon called **social loafing** (Harkins & Szymanski, 1989; Jackson & Williams, 1988; Kerr & Bruun, 1983; Latané, 1981).

You would probably not stand up by yourself and cheer loudly at a sporting event or concert, but you might do so very easily as part of a large cheering crowd. Being part of a group can make us feel less restrained and more aroused, a process of **deindividuation** that allows us relinquish personal responsibility and give ourselves over to the group experience.

Group Interactions and Minority Influence

The strength of group influence means that the more members of the group discuss similar opinions, the more extreme their positions become. This phenomenon, known as **group polarization**, strengthens resolve but can also create more radical behavior. Group interactions can also lead to **group think** when group members' opinions become so uniform that all dissent becomes impossible. Such uniformity of opinion may have been responsible for the Bay of Pigs operation in Cuba in 1961, when the members of the Kennedy administration felt so sure of themselves and their decisions that they authorized a botched attempt to overthrow the government of Fidel Castro (Janis, 1982).

While social control can be very powerful, committed individuals confident about their viewpoints have the power to influence the majority. **Minority influence**, the power of a few people, allowed Gandhi to lead the movement for the independence of India and civil rights leaders like Martin Luther King Jr. to press for desegregation in the American South.

Social Relations

EMOTIONAL FOUNDATIONS OF SOCIAL NATURE

Emotions affect how we behave with others, and social situations affect our emotions. As social animals, our emotions link inextricably with the social situations in which we find ourselves.

Ending a romantic relationship may hurt, and having a migraine headache can be very painful, but if you end a relationship while you have a migraine headache, your headache will be even more intense. At least, that's what researchers have found. If we lose a close personal relationship or

> " Emotions affect how we behave with others, and social situations affect our emotions. As social animals, our emotions link inextricably with the social situations in which we find ourselves. "

membership in a group, we feel **social pain**. The pain of rejection or loss feels as real as physical pain because it activates the same areas in the brain, the anterior cingulate cortex and the anterior insula (Eisenberger et al., 2003). If we happen to be experiencing physical pain, social pain will actually magnify our distress (Eisenberger & Lieberman, 2004).

Self-conscious emotions, such as guilt or shame, that relate to thoughts about ourselves and our own actions have important functions in social relations (Tangney, 1999). As a motivator for relationship repair, guilt can be an evolutionarily adaptive mechanism for preserving social cohesion, although it can be maladaptive if taken to extremes. Embarrassment motivates people to rectify

Sleeper effect is a phenomenon that occurs when a person forgets the unreliable source of a piece of information but remembers the information itself and believes that it's trustworthy.

Social loafing is a phenomenon that occurs when people believe that their individual efforts don't matter or that they are not personally responsible because they are only one member of a group, so they tend to put less effort into a task.

Deindividuation is a process that allows people in a group to relinquish personal responsibility and give themselves over to the group experience.

Group polarization is a phenomenon in which the more members of a group discuss similar opinions, the more extreme their positions become.

Group think is a phenomenon in which group members' opinions become so uniform that all dissent becomes impossible.

Minority influence refers to the power of a few people.

Social pain is the pain of rejection or loss brought on by losing a close personal relationship or membership in a group.

Self-conscious emotion is an emotion that relates to a person's thoughts about himself or herself and about his or her own actions.

awkward situations, and those who show embarrassment seem to appear more likable (Keltner & Anderson, 2000; Semin & Manstead, 1982). Shame leads to social withdrawal, especially when someone's failings have been publicly exposed. Notice how rarely the disgraced former New York Governor Eliot Spitzer appears in public. His apparent absence of guilt during the scandal did not help him repair his relationship with New Yorkers, and his lack of embarrassment did not make him appear more likable.

PREJUDICE

Prejudice is a negative learned attitude toward particular people or things. Although the detrimental effects of prejudice have been well documented, prejudice against individuals because of race, ethnicity, gender, or other factors still persists. Although most of us overtly deny having feelings of prejudice, many people still display prejudiced implicit attitudes. What causes this disconnection between our outward beliefs and our actions? Can well-intentioned, fair, considerate people still be unconsciously affected by powerful stereotypes?

Stereotypes

In and of themselves, **stereotypes**, or general beliefs about a group of people, can be useful schemas for interpreting the world around us. They can help us make rapid determinations about an individual, saving us cognitive time and energy. For example, if you see a man wearing a wedding ring and holding a baby, you might quickly intuit that the man is committed, mature, and caring—all positive stereotypes associated with married fathers. While stereotypes might provide us with some useful basic information, however, very often they can lead us to draw false conclusions and ultimately contribute to acts of prejudice and discrimination. Stereotypes can be hard to disprove: When we hold stereotypes about a certain group, we're likely to discredit information that does not support those stereotypes. Thanks to the confirmation bias (see Chapter 9), we tend to selectively accept only

> " **Tests have shown that while most people consciously believe that they are not racially prejudiced, many white students more quickly associate positive adjectives with white faces and negative adjectives with black faces.** "

information that supports our preconceived views (Munro & Ditto, 1997).

The mere existence of negative stereotypes can be harmful. Those subject to stereotyping may not be able to perform as well on tasks as they normally would because of **stereotype threat**, the knowledge that they must work against a negative stereotype (Steele & Aronson, 1995). For example, women who are aware of the stereotype that women are not supposed to be good at math and science may feel particularly pressured to perform well on a math test and disprove the stereotype, but the extra pressure they put on themselves may actually hurt their performance, leading them to inadvertently *support* the stereotype. Of course, a variety of other factors often contribute to the performance

gap between men and women in math and science; stereotype threat alone is only part of the complex picture.

When people hold an **explicit stereotype**, they consciously adhere to a set of beliefs about a group of people. But many beliefs actually operate as **implicit stereotypes**, an unconscious set of mental representations that guide attitudes and behaviors. Because of the way our implicit memories function, priming the mind with one concept facilitates the access of associated concepts. Tests have shown that while most people consciously believe that they are not racially prejudiced, many white students more quickly associate positive adjectives with white faces and negative adjectives with black faces, suggesting that these students hold implicit negative stereotypes about black people. Black students tend to show the inverse preference (Fazio et al., 1995). The Implicit Association Test, developed by Mahzarin Banaji and Tony Greenwald to access implicit attitudes by measuring the time required to pair certain concepts (such as "white" and "good"), has also revealed people's implicit beliefs about race and gender (Banaji & Greenwald, 1995; Greenwald et al., 1998, 2002).

Discrimination

The racial segregation practiced in parts of the United States until the 1950s showed how prejudiced attitudes lead to **discrimination**, negative behavior toward a group of people and its members. In the landmark Supreme Court case *Brown v. Board of Education*, Thurgood Marshall and other attorneys referred to studies by social psychologists Kenneth and Mamie Clark as evidence for the tremendously damaging effects of discrimination. During the "doll test," black children showed an overt preference for white dolls, and when asked to color pictures of children, they chose white or yellow crayons (Clark & Clark, 1947). By showing how the "separate but equal" education system fosters a sense of inferiority in children, the "doll test" helped end segregation in the United States.

Racism is hardly the only prominent form of discrimination. Unfortunately, in many countries,

<<< How might stereotype threat affect your life? How can it be combated?

People taking an Implicit Association Test might be asked to match African American faces with the word "good."

∨ ∨ ∨
∨ ∨

Ingroup is a group that a person is part of.

Outgroup is a group containing those people outside one's own group.

Just-world phenomenon is a phenomenon in which people convince themselves that they are doing well because they are good people, while those who are suffering are just getting what they deserve.

Mere exposure consists of simple contact between two individuals or groups.

Deprovincialization is a process in which learning more about an outgroup through friendship or collaborative efforts can make people more tolerant of the norms and customs of other groups.

Aggression is behavior intended to harm others.

discrimination is often conducted on the basis of gender, religion, or sexual preference, to name only a few categories.

Foundations of Prejudice

As social animals, human beings tend to form groups and derive some portion of their identity from these groups. They treat their own group as the **ingroup** and favor their group positions and members; those outside their group might be considered part of an **outgroup** (Tajfel, 1982; Wilder, 1981). When taken to extremes, the ingroup and outgroup dichotomy can erupt into violence, as happens during a time of war or even at sporting events when conflict erupts between supporters of rival teams.

Prejudice also often has an emotional basis, and our feelings of fear and anger are particularly likely to lead us toward discrimination. When we're frustrated by our own failings, we often look for scapegoats whom we can blame for our problems. Often, those scapegoats are outgroup members: After the attacks of September 11, 2001, for example, some

people's fears and feelings of anger led them to stereotype and act out against members of the worldwide Muslim community.

A number of cognitive processes help people justify both their position at the "top of the food chain" and their poor treatment of those who are worse off. For instance, the **just-world phenomenon** leads us to believe that the world is a fair place in which good people are rewarded and bad people are punished. If this is really the case, we convince ourselves, then we must be doing well because we are good people, while those who are suffering are simply getting what they deserve.

Reversing Prejudice

Although we might intuitively believe that contact between hostile groups should reduce prejudice, **mere exposure**, or simple contact between two groups, does not usually reverse prejudice unless groups cooperate with each other to achieve a common goal (Allport, 1954; Dovidio et al., 2003; Pettigrew & Tropp, 2006). This principle of cooperation also works to

soothe relationships in the classroom: In "jigsaw" classrooms, each student must manage one part of a project in order for the group to complete the entire assignment (Aronson & Gonzalez, 1988). Learning more about an outgroup through friendship or collaborative efforts can make people more tolerant of the norms and customs of other groups, a process called **deprovincialization**.

AGGRESSION
What Causes Aggressive Behavior?

Whether it occurs between warring nations, feuding first graders, or two *Big Brother* contestants cooped up with each other for weeks on end, any physical or verbal behavior intended to harm others qualifies as **aggression**. Given the pervasiveness of aggression in animals, it's no surprise that biology influences aggression. From an evolutionary perspective, we can explain aggression as a quality that has developed from a struggle for survival and resources. Aggression may also be influenced by genetics: If a child has a violent temper, his or her siblings are likely to be aggressive, too (Miles & Carey, 1997; Rowe et al., 1999). In the brain, the amygdala and other limbic structures help to initiate aggression, and it's likely that the frontal lobes play a role in controlling aggression as well (Lewis et al., 1986).

Alcohol and violence are commonly linked in the media, and it's true that the biological effects of alcohol can increase aggressive behavior. People prone to aggression are more likely to drink and become violent, and four out of ten violent crimes and three out of four cases of spousal abuse are committed by people who have recently been drinking (Greenfeld, 1998; White et al., 1993) This is likely because alcohol is known to reduce inhibition by compromising frontal lobe function.

While some factors that influence aggression are biological, others are linked to our environments and our external situations. Like many other violent criminals, Albert DeSalvo, better known as the "Boston Strangler" who confessed to murdering 13 women in the Boston area during the early '60s, had been severely abused as a child. When humans and other animals experience aversive events such as abuse, they tend to pay it forward (Berkowitz, 1983, 1989). Hot weather also seems to contribute to hot tempers, and a number of studies point to the influence of uncomfortable heat in aggressive acts (Anderson & Anderson, 1984). Anyone who has experienced road rage while stuck in traffic can agree with the **frustration-aggression hypothesis** that frustration occurs when people feel blocked in obtaining their goals (Dollard et al., 1939). Unemployment also creates economic frustration so that violence rates increase as unemployment rates rise, up to a given point. After that, the general anxiety over job loss supersedes aggressive feelings (Catalano et al., 1997, 2002).

Cultural Constraints

Cultural constraints about acceptable levels of aggression may control how much aggression we feel free to show. In one experiment, American children displayed more verbal aggression in hypothetical situations of conflict than did Japanese children (Zahn-Waxler et al., 1996). Even within the United States, acceptable levels of aggression vary regionally. Studies comparing responses to insults in the North and South revealed that the "culture of honor" prevalent in the South meant that "even small disputes become contests for reputation and social status" (Cohen et al., 1996; Nisbett & Cohen, 1996). Norms of aggression can also be set

> **Real-life models of violence seem to have more of an impact on behavior than do violent games or movies:** Children who have either experienced or watched physical abuse often become violent themselves (Berkowitz, 2003; Salzinger et al., 2006).

by models of aggression in everyday life. While there is no data to suggest that children's exposure to violent TV programs and video games leads to violent behavior later in life, the media and entertainment industries do provide numerous models of violence for children (Anderson & Bushman, 2001; Bushman & Anderson, 2002). Real-life models of violence seem to have more of an impact on behavior than do violent games or movies: Children who have either experienced or watched physical abuse often become violent themselves (Berkowitz, 2003; Salzinger et al., 2006).

CONFLICT

In September 2008, a crowd of protesters outside the Republican National Convention in St. Paul, Minnesota, clashed with police officers, who fired pepper spray, tear gas, and projectiles into the crowd in an attempt to make the protesters leave the scene. This is just one recent example of **conflict**, or a disparity between people's or groups' actions, goals, or ideas. We tend to engage in conflict in pursuit of our own self-interests, but the "winners" of a conflict don't always emerge from the fight in a better position than the one they started in. Sometimes, conflicting parties engage in mutually destructive behaviors, causing them to end

What might cause some conflicts to become physically violent?

up in a **social trap**: As everyone tries to win, no one actually does.

The Psychology of Genocide

On July 21, 2008, Radovan Karadzic, the Bosnian Serb president who presided over the genocide in Bosnia, was arrested after ten years in hiding. **Genocide**, the systematic destruction of one group by another, begins when living conditions become very strained, as they did after the breakup of Communist regimes in Eastern Europe. Faced with economic, social, and political uncertainty, old ethnic conflicts resurfaced as Bosnian Serbs identified themselves as the ingroup and Bosnian Muslims as a scapegoated outgroup. Feeling legitimized by the just-world phenomenon and under attack by Croatians and other outgroups, many Bosnian Serbs massacred their former neighbors, Bosnian Muslims. The lethargy of the world community in reacting to the genocide in Bosnia also reinforced feelings of righteousness among Serbians. Currently, the genocide in Darfur has also evoked little intervention by the United Nations and the international community.

Cooperation

Although we can easily think of recent examples of genocide, the picture isn't entirely bleak—some seemingly intractable conflicts have also been recently resolved. For example, positive political developments in Northern Ireland have proven that **cooperation**, or working together for the good of the group, can lead to more benefit than **defection**, promoting one's own interest at the expense of others. Cooperation is beneficial, but it isn't easy: We face a social dilemma when a certain course of action that benefits an individual hurts the group as a whole and will do more harm than good if everyone takes the same course. This dilemma often plays out on a global scale. Industrialized countries have about 20 percent of the world's population but produce about 40 percent of the global carbon emissions (Sierra Club, 2008). As China and India have also become increasingly industrialized and contribute more to carbon emissions, the entire planet suffers the consequences of each individual country promoting its own

economic interests with little regard for the environmental consequences.

There are plenty of factors that can convince us to cooperate with others, however. When people feel a high level of personal accountability, for example, they feel more inclined to cooperate. People may also cooperate in order to protect their reputation or follow the norms of reciprocity that dictate that we should help others if they have helped us. Norms of fairness (such as punishing cheaters and rewarding helpful individuals) can encourage cooperation, as can a shared social identity with a group. In the aftermath of the devastating 2010 earthquake in Haiti, international volunteers worked together and donated their time and money in order to help the Haitians in need.

It's hard to cooperate with someone else if you can't (or won't) communicate, so communication is a particularly crucial element of cooperation. When conflicting groups can't reach a mutually agreeable solution, mediators can help the groups communicate with each other and develop a plan that's beneficial to both sides.

> We face a social dilemma when a certain course of action that benefits an individual hurts the group as a whole and will do more harm than good as a whole if everyone takes the same course. This dilemma often plays out on a global scale.

ALTRUISM AND PROSOCIAL BEHAVIOR

What makes us put the interests of others first, even risking our own well-being in the process? **Prosocial behavior**, behavior carried out with the goal of helping others, becomes **altruism** when it is carried out without concern for one's own safety or self-interest. We don't gain any sort of advantage from performing an altruistic act; in fact, we might even put ourselves at a disadvantage. (Some psychologists and philosophers argue that if we feel good after performing an altruistic act, the act wasn't purely altruistic after all.) While displays of altruism don't commonly grip TV and movie audiences, it's important to remember that humans are capable of selfless social acts as well as selfish ones.

What might cause us to act altruistically? The theory of **reciprocal altruism** suggests that peo-

ple may carry out altruistic acts with the expectation of being the recipient of altruism at some point in the future or because they have been helped by altruism sometime in the past (Trivers, 1971). In general, people show altruism toward their relatives (nepotism), but perhaps we look after our families because we know that they will do the same for us (Burnstein et al., 1994). Altruism can even enhance our attractiveness: In one study, college women who perceived altruism in certain men evaluated those men as more physically and sexually attractive (Jensen-Campbell et al., 1995).

According to C. Daniel Batson, altruism constitutes only one motive for prosocial behavior (1994). Corporate sponsors who receive promotional benefits from charitable contributions practice **egoism**, doing something beneficial for others in the hopes of receiving something in return. Social security could be considered a form of **collectivism**: Everyone contributes to the community chest to help the group as a whole. Religious values that encourage helping others would count as examples of **principlism**, the desire to engage in prosocial behavior out of principle. No matter what drives us, however, our prosocial behavior helps us improve society and nurture and sustain our relationships.

Social trap is a situation in which conflicting parties all try to win a conflict by engaging in mutually destructive behaviors, resulting in no one winning.

Genocide is the systematic destruction of one group by another.

Cooperation is the act of working together for the good of the group.

Defection is the act of promoting one's own interest at the expense of others.

Prosocial behavior is behavior carried out with the goal of helping others.

Altruism is prosocial behavior that is carried out without concern for one's own safety or self-interest.

Reciprocal altruism is a theory that suggests that people may carry out altruistic acts with the expectation of being the recipient of altruism at some point in the future or because they have been helped by altruism sometime in the past.

Egoism describes the act of doing something beneficial for others in the hopes of receiving something in return.

Collectivism describes the act of contributing something beneficial to the whole group to which a person belongs.

Principlism is a desire to engage in prosocial behavior out of principle.

14

Summary

WHAT IS SOCIAL PSYCHOLOGY? p. 208

• Social psychology examines how the thoughts, actions, and behavior of individuals influence and are influenced by groups.

WHAT COGNITIVE PROCESSES UNDERLIE SOCIAL BEHAVIOR? p. 209

• Social cognition focuses on the underlying processes, such as attention and memory, that make social behavior possible. Biological structures and processes in the brain help us navigate our social environment.

• The fusiform face area of the brain allows us to recognize faces.
• The amygdala is involved in social category processing.
• The superior temporal sulcus processes biological motions.
• Mirror neurons in the inferior frontal gyrus help us feel empathy.

HOW DOES SOCIAL INFLUENCE AFFECT OUR THOUGHTS AND ACTIONS? p. 211

• Through social pressure, social influence can lead people to conform, obey, and mimic others.
• Social influence affects performance and plays a role in persuasion.

HOW ARE SOCIAL RELATIONS INFLUENCED BY PSYCHOLOGICAL PHENOMENA? p. 217

• Fear and anger can affect social relations through prejudice, stereotyping, and conflict.
• Self-conscious emotions such as guilt can lead to social repair.
• Group relations can be improved through cooperation and altruism.

Test Your Understanding

1. Becky e-mailed her professor two days ago but has not received a reply. Although it is possible that the professor is extremely busy or out of town, Becky assumes that the professor must be a rude person. This is an example of:

   a. a situational attribution.
   b. the fundamental attribution error (FAE).
   c. the attractiveness bias.
   d. the self-serving bias.

2. If you believe that you will never graduate and continually miss classes, you may be creating:

   a. a situational attribution.
   b. a self-fulfilling prophecy.
   c. a dispositional attribution.
   d. a self-serving bias.

3. The belief that women are more intelligent than men is:

   a. a type of preexisting schema.
   b. a fundamental attribution error (FAE).
   c. a situational attribution.
   d. a self-fulfilling prophecy.

4. Ellie lost a swim race to Matt. When they were each interviewed afterward, Ellie expressed that she would have won had she not had a cramp in her side. Matt expressed that he won because he trained hard and is lucky to be naturally fast. Both Ellie's and Matt's beliefs could be the result of:

   a. situational attributions.
   b. dispositional attributions.

   c. the Pygmalion effect.
   d. self-serving biases.

5. A group of friends who unintentionally make the same gestures and facial expressions as one another are likely displaying:

   a. prosopagnosia.
   b. the chameleon effect.
   c. the Pygmalion effect.
   d. an accuracy motive.

6. Cass brings Laura a gift every time he goes to her house. Cass's gesture is most likely a result of:

   a. a hedonic motive.
   b. an approval motive.
   c. an accuracy motive.
   d. the chameleon effect.

7. Which of the following is LEAST likely to cause a person to conform?

   a. feelings of insecurity
   b. a group of five people
   c. a private setting
   d. being with people whom one admires

8. In Solomon Asch's famous experiment (which involved comparing lines of various lengths), some subjects:

   a. refused to continue and walked out of the experiment.
   b. agreed with the group even when the answer was obviously incorrect.

c. convinced the confederates to change their answers.

d. had difficulty determining the length of the stimulus lines.

9. Which of the following is MOST likely to cause a person to disobey a command to inflict pain?

a. The person giving the command takes responsibility for the action.

b. The person being commanded knows the victim.

c. The person giving the command is a government official.

d. The person giving the command is in the room with the person he is commanding.

10. Jenny knows that her mother wouldn't give her $100 if she just asked for it. Instead, she gets her mother to give her $20. A few weeks later, Jenny asks her mother for $100, and her mother agrees to give it to her. This is an example of:

a. the bait-and-switch technique.

b. the foot-in-the-door technique.

c. the door-in-the-face technique.

d. the lowball technique.

11. Larry spent a lot of money on a trip to Paris. Unfortunately, it rained the entire time he was there, several museums he wanted to visit were closed, and his hotel room was dirty and small. Still, Larry believes that the trip was worth the money. Which of the following best explains Larry's attitude about his trip?

a. Believing the trip was worth the cost increases Larry's cognitive dissonance.

b. Believing the trip was worth the cost reduces Larry's cognitive dissonance.

c. Larry is highly suggestible.

d. Larry is following the norm of reciprocity.

12. Which of the following is NOT an example of the peripheral route to persuasion?

a. agreeing with someone because they are attractive

b. agreeing with a politician after studying the reasoning behind her argument

c. agreeing with your friend because you trust him

d. agreeing with a co-worker because you went to the same university

13. A witness testifies that she saw the defendant pull the trigger. Even though the witness's testimony is thrown out of the court because she was found to have lied about other details, and no other witnesses were present, the jury believes that the defendant was the murderer. This might be due to:

a. the bystander effect.

b. groupthink.

c. social loafing.

d. the sleeper effect.

14. Ben wears his roommate's suit without asking and gets a stain on it. Ben tells his roommate what happened and, after apologizing for not asking, offers to pay to have the suit dry-cleaned or replaced. Which of the following is the most likely reason why?

a. Ben experienced a self-conscious emotion that caused him to attempt reparations.

b. Ben experienced social pain as a result of abusing his friend's trust.

c. Ben experienced deindividuation.

d. Ben experienced social loafing and offers to pay for the suit to make up for it.

15. What process could help two cultural groups between whom violence has erupted eventually resolve their differences?

a. the just-world phenomenon

b. group polarization

c. deprovincialization

d. discrimination

16. Ryan, who is white, often notices that African Americans are not promoted as frequently in his company and are usually paid less than average. Because it upsets Ryan to think that his company treats people of unfairly because of their race, it is easier for Ryan to convince himself that the African Americans in his company must be inferior employees. Ryan's behavior is an example of:

a. the frustration-aggression hypothesis.

b. deindividuation.

c. the just-world phenomenon.

d. discrimination.

17. Which of the following people are most likely to be aggressive?

a. a person who was abused in childhood

b. a person who has experienced deprovincialization

c. an average person on a cold day

d. a scapegoat

18. A flight attendant notices that when bad weather forces a plane to divert to a city that was not the original destination, several of the passengers become angry and confrontational with her. The passengers' reaction is consistent with:

a. the mere exposure effect.

b. collectivism.

c. a stereotype threat.

d. the frustration-aggression hypothesis.

19. Which of the following is an altruistic act?

a. Becky studies with a friend so they will both do well on the test.

b. Sandy donates blood every year.

c. Ryan cheats on his girlfriend with his ex.

d. All of the employees in an office agree to pay $5 to purchase a new coffeemaker.

20. Which of the following is typically a reason people cooperate?

a. a feeling of personal accountability

b. to protect their reputations

c. norms of fairness

d. all of the above

Remember to check www.thethinkspot.com **for additional information, downloadable flashcards, and other helpful resources.**

Answers: 1)b; 2) b; 3) b; 4) a; 5) b; 6) b; 7) c; 8) b; 9) d; 10) b; 11) b; 12) b; 13) d; 14) a; 15) c; 16) c; 17) a; 18) d; 19) b; 20) d

THINK READINGS

Check out p. 214 for a visual representation of conditions that influence obedience.

POLICY FORUM

SOCIAL PSYCHOLOGY
Why Ordinary People Torture Enemy Prisoners

Susan T. Fiske, Lasana T. Harris, Amy J.C. Cuddy

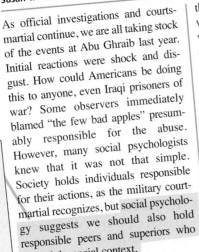

As you read this article, think about the concept of social influence discussed in Chapter 14 (pp. 211-217)

In Chapter 14 (p. 210), you read about social categorization. How is this related to the finding described here?

In Chapter 15, you'll read in detail about how stress affects mental and physical health.

As official investigations and courts-martial continue, we are all taking stock of the events at Abu Ghraib last year. Initial reactions were shock and disgust. How could Americans be doing this to anyone, even Iraqi prisoners of war? Some observers immediately blamed "the few bad apples" presumably responsible for the abuse. However, many social psychologists knew that it was not that simple. Society holds individuals responsible for their actions, as the military court-martial recognizes, but social psychology suggests we should also hold responsible peers and superiors who control the social context.

Social psychological evidence emphasizes the power of social context; in other words, the power of the interpersonal situation. Social psychology has accumulated a century of knowledge about how people influence each other for good or ill (1). Meta-analysis, the quantitative summary of findings across a variety of studies, reveals the size and consistency of such empirical results. Recent meta-analyses document reliable experimental evidence of social context effects across 25,000 studies of 8 million participants (2). Abu Ghraib resulted in part from ordinary social processes, not just extraordinary individual evil. This Policy Forum cites meta-analyses to describe how the right (or wrong) social context can make almost anyone aggress, oppress, conform, and obey.

Virtually anyone can be aggressive if sufficiently provoked, stressed, disgruntled, or hot (3–6). The situation of the 800th Military Police Brigade guarding Abu Ghraib prisoners fit all the social conditions known to cause aggression. The soldiers were certainly provoked and stressed: at war, in constant danger, taunted and harassed by some of the very citizens they were sent to save, and their comrades were dying daily and unpredictably. Their morale suffered, they were untrained for the job, their command climate was lax, their return home was a year overdue,

their identity as disciplined soldiers was gone, and their own amenities were scant (7). Heat and discomfort also doubtless contributed.

The fact that the prisoners were part of a group encountered as enemies would only exaggerate the tendency to feel spontaneous prejudice against outgroups. In this context, oppression and discrimination are synonymous. One of the most basic principles of social psychology is that people prefer their own group (8) and attribute bad behavior to outgroups (9). Prejudice especially festers if people see the outgroup as threatening cherished values (10–12). This would have certainly applied to the guards viewing their prisoners at Abu Ghraib, but it also applies in more "normal" situations. A recent sample of U.S. citizens on average viewed Muslims and Arabs as not sharing their interests and stereotyped them as not especially sincere, honest, friendly, or warm (13–15).

Even more potent predictors of discrimination are the emotional prejudices ("hot" affective feelings such as disgust or contempt) that operate in parallel with cognitive processes (16–18). Such emotional reactions appear rapidly, even in neuroimaging of brain activations to outgroups (19, 20). But even they can be affected by social context. Categorization of people as interchangeable members of an outgroup promotes an amygdala response characteristic of vigilance and alarm and an insula response characteristic of disgust or arousal, depending on social context; these effects dissipate when the same people are encountered as unique individuals (21, 22). According to our survey data (13, 14), the contemptible, disgusting kind of outgroup— low-status opponents—elicits a mix of active and passive harm: attacking and fighting, as well as excluding and demeaning. This certainly describes the Abu Ghraib abuse of captured enemies. It also fits our national sample of Americans (14) who reported that allegedly contemptible

outgroups such as homeless people, welfare recipients, Turks, and Arabs often are attacked or excluded (14).

Given an environment conducive to aggression and prisoners deemed disgusting and subhuman (23), well-established principles of conformity to peers (24, 25) and obedience to authority (26) may account for the widespread nature of the abuse. In combat, conformity to one's unit means survival, and ostracism is death. The social context apparently reflected the phenomenon of people trying to make sense of a complex, confusing, ambiguous situation by relying on their immediate social group (27). People rioted at St. Paul's Church, Bristol UK, in 1980, for example, in conformity to events they saw occurring in their immediate proximity (28). Guards abuse prisoners in conformity with what other guards do, in order to fulfill a potent role; this is illustrated by the Stanford Prison Study, in which ordinary college students, randomly assigned to be full-time guards and prisoners in a temporary prison, nevertheless behaved respectively as abusers and victims (29). Social psychology shows that, whatever their own good or bad choices, most people believe that others would do whatever they personally chose to do, a phenomenon termed false consensus (30, 31). Conformity to the perceived reactions of one's peers can be defined as good or bad, depending on how well the local norms fit those of larger society.

As every graduate of introductory psychology should know from the Milgram studies (32), ordinary people can engage in incredibly destructive behavior if so ordered by legitimate authority. In those studies, participants acting as teachers frequently followed an experimenter's orders to punish a supposed learner (actually a confederate) with electric shock, all the way to administering lethal levels. Obedience to authority sustains every culture (33). Firefighters heroically rushing into the flaming World Trade Center were partly obeying their superiors, partly conform-

Learn more about false consensus in Chapter 2 (p. 18).

Stanley Milgram's experiments are discussed in detail in Chapter 14 (p. 214).

ing to extraordinary group loyalty, and partly showing incredibly brave self-sacrifice. But obedience and conformity also motivated the terrorist hijackers and the Abu Ghraib guards, however much one might abhor their (vastly different) actions. Social conformity and obedience themselves are neutral, but their consequences can be heroic or evil. Torture is partly a crime of socialized obedience (34). Subordinates not only do what they are ordered to do, but what they think their superiors would order them to do, given their understanding of the authority's overall goals. For example, lynching represented ordinary people going beyond the law to enact their view of the community's will.

Social influence starts with small, apparently trivial actions (in this case, insulting epithets), followed by more serious actions (humiliation and abuse) (35–37), as novices overcome their hesitancy and learn by doing (38). The actions are always intentional, although the perpetrator may not be aware that those actions constitute evil. In fact, perpetra-

tors may see themselves as doing a great service by punishing and or eliminating a group that they perceive as deserving ill treatment (39).

In short, ordinary individuals under the influence of complex social forces may commit evil acts (40). Such actions are human behaviors that can and should be studied scientifically (41, 42). We need to understand more about the contexts that will promote aggression. We also need to understand the basis for exceptions—why, in the face of these social contexts, not all individuals succumb (43). Thus, although lay-observers may believe that explaining evil amounts to excusing it and absolving people of responsibility for their actions (44), in fact, explaining evils such as Abu Ghraib demonstrates scientific principles that could help to avert them.

Even one dissenting peer can undermine conformity (24). For example, whistle-blowers not only alert the authorities but also prevent their peers from continuing in unethical behavior. Authorities can restructure situations to allow communication. For

example, CEOs can either welcome or discourage a diversity of opinions. Contexts can undermine prejudice (1). Individual, extended, equal-status, constructive, cooperative contact between mutual outgroups (whether American blacks and whites in the military or American soldiers and Iraqi civilians) can improve mutual respect and even liking. It would be harder to dehumanize and abuse imprisoned Iraqis if one had friends among ordinary Iraqis. A difficult objective in wartime, but as some Iraqis work alongside their American counterparts, future abuse is less likely. The slippery slope to abuse can be avoided. The same social contexts that provoke and permit abuse can be harnessed to prevent it. To quote another report [(45), p. 94]: "All personnel who may be engaged in detention operations, from point of capture to final disposition, should participate in a professional ethics program that would equip them with a sharp moral compass for guidance in situations often riven with conflicting moral obligations."

Take a look back at Chapter 12 (p. 188) to review how morality is developed.

Can dissent become impossible? Recall what you read about group think in Chapter 14 (p. 217).

References and Notes

1. S. T. Fiske, *Social Beings* (Wiley, New York, 2004).
2. F. D. Richard, C. F. Bond, J. J. Stokes-Zoota, *Rev. Gen. Psychol.* 7, 331 (2003).
3. B. A. Bettencourt, N. Miller, *Psychol. Bull.* 119, 422 (1996).
4. M. Carlson, N. Miller, *Sociol. Soc. Res.* 72, 155 (1988).
5. M. Carlson, A. Marcus-Newhall, N. Miller, *Pers. Soc. Psychol. Bull.* 15, 377 (1989).
6. C. A. Anderson, B. J. Bushman, *Rev. Gen. Psychol.* 1, 19 (1997).
7. A. Taguba, "Article 15-6. Investigation of the 800th Military Police Brigade," accessed 30 June 2004 from www.npr.org/iraq/2004/prison_abuse_report.pdf
8. B. Mullen, R. Brown, C. Smith, *Eur. J. Soc. Psychol.* 22, 103 (1992).
9. B. Mullen, C. Johnson, *Br. J. Soc. Psychol.* 29, 11 (1990).
10. J. Duckitt, in *Advances in Experimental Social Psychology*, M. P. Zanna, Ed. (Academic Press, New York, 2001).
11. When their own mortality is salient, as in wartime, people particularly punish those from outgroups seen to threaten basic values (12).
12. S. Solomon, J. Greenberg, T. Pyszczynski, *Curr. Dir. Psychol. Sci.* 9, 200 (2000).
13. S. T. Fiske, A. J. Cuddy, P. Glick, J. Xu, *J. Person. Soc. Psychol.* 82, 878 (2002).
14. A. J. Cuddy, S. T. Fiske, P. Glick, "The BIAS map: Behaviors from intergroup affect and stereotypes," unpublished manuscript (Princeton University, Princeton, NJ, 2004).

15. L. J. Heller, thesis, Princeton University, 2002.
16. H. Schütz, B. Six, *Int. J. Intercult. Relat.* 20, 441 (1996).
17. J. F. Dovidio et al., in *Stereotypes and Stereotyping*, C. N. Macrae, C. Stangor, M. Hewstone, Ed. (Guilford, New York, 1996).
18. C. A. Talaska, S. T. Fiske, S. Chaiken, "Predicting discrimination: A meta-analysis of the racial attitudes– behavior literature," unpublished manuscript (Princeton University, Princeton, NJ, 2004).
19. A. J. Hart et al., *Neuroreport* 11, 2351 (2000).
20. E. A. Phelps et al., *J. Cogn. Neurosci.* 12, 729 (2000).
21. Neuroimaging data represent college student reactions to photographs of outgroup members. These data should not be interpreted to mean that such reactions are innate or "wired in"; they result from longterm social context (9) and vary depending on shortterm social context (46).
22. M. E. Wheeler, S. T. Fiske, *Psychol. Sci.*, in press.
23. J. P. Leyens et al., *Eur. J. Soc. Psychol.* 33, 703 (2003).
24. R. Bond, P. B. Smith, *Psychol. Bull.* 119, 111 (1996).
25. S. Tanford, S. Penrod, *Psychol. Bull.* 95, 189 (1984).
26. J. Tata et al., *J. Soc. Behav. Pers.* 11, 739 (1996).
27. J. C. Turner, *Social Influence* (Brooks/Cole, Pacific Grove, CA, 1991).
28. S. D. Reicher, *Eur. J. Soc. Psychol.* 14, 1 (1984).

29. C. Haney, C. Banks, P. Zimbardo, *Int. J. Criminol. Penol.* 1, 69 (1973).
30. B. Mullen et al., *J. Exp. Soc. Psychol.* 21, 262 (1985).
31. B. Mullen, L. Hu, *Br. J. Soc. Psychol.* 27, 333 (1988).
32. S. Milgram, *Obedience to Authority* (Harper & Row, New York, 1974).
33. T. Blass, *J. Appl. Soc. Psychol.* 29, 955 (1999).
34. H. C. Kelman, in *The Politics of Pain: Torturers and Their Masters*, R. D. Crelinsten, A. P. Schmidt, Eds. (Univ. of Leiden, Leiden, NL, 1991).
35. A. L. Beaman et al., *Pers. Soc. Psychol. Bull.* 9, 181 (1983).
36. A. L. Dillard, J. E. Hunter, M. Burgoon, *Hum. Commun. Res.* 10, 461 (1984).
37. E. F. Fern, K. B. Monroe, R. A. Avila, *J. Mark. Res.* 23, 144 (1986).
38. E. Staub, *Pers. Soc. Psychol. Rev.* 3, 179 (1999).
39. A. Bandura, *Pers. Soc. Psychol. Rev.* 3, 193 (1999).
40. L. Berkowitz, *Pers. Soc. Psychol. Rev.* 3, 246 (1999).
41. J. M. Darley, *Pers. Soc. Psychol. Rev.* 3, 269 (1999).
42. A. G. Miller, Ed., *The Social Psychology of Good and Evil* (Guilford, New York, 2004).
43. Although social context matters more than most people think, individual personality also matters, in accord with most people's intuitions: Social Dominance Orientation (SDO) describes a toughminded view that it is a zero-sum, dog-eat-dog world, where some

groups justifiably dominate other groups. People who score low on SDO tend to join helping professions, be more tolerant, and endorse less aggression; they might be less inclined to abuse. People choosing to join hierarchical institutions such as the military tend to score high on SDO, in contrast (47). Right-Wing Authoritarianism (RWA) entails conforming to conventional values, submitting to authority, and aggressing as sanctioned by authority. People who score low on RWA would be less prone to abuse. (48) High SDO and RWA both predict intolerance of outgroups, social groups outside one's own.
44. A. G. Miller, A. K. Gordon, A. M. Buddie, *Pers. Soc. Psychol. Rev.* 3, 254 (1999).
45. J. R. Schlesinger, H. Brown, T. K. Fowler, C. A. Homer, J. A. Blackwell Jr., *Final Report of the Independent Panel to Review DoD Detention Operations*, accessed 8 November 2004, from www.informationclearinghouse.info/article6785.htm
46. L. T. Harris, S. T. Fiske, unpublished data.
47. J. Sidanius, F. Pratto, *Social Dominance: An Intergroup Theory of Social Hierarchy and Oppression* (Cambridge Univ. Press, New York, 1999).
48. B. Altemeyer, *Enemies of Freedom: Understanding Right-Wing Authoritarianism* (Jossey-Bass, San Francisco, 1988).

HEALTH AND STRESS

HOW ARE PSYCHOLOGICAL STATES CONNECTED TO PHYSICAL REACTIONS?

HOW DOES STRESS AFFECT OUR IMMUNE SYSTEMS AND OUR OVERALL HEALTH?

WHAT ARE SOME OF THE DIFFERENT WAYS THAT PEOPLE COPE WITH STRESS?

WHAT TECHNIQUES CAN WE USE TO ALLEVIATE OR MANAGE STRESS?

You are about to

turn off the television and go to bed when you notice that a rerun of your favorite show is about to start. An hour less sleep won't make any difference, right? Surprisingly, it might. Researchers have discovered that people who skimp on sleep are at a much higher risk of obesity than those who get a good night's rest.

In 2004, Columbia University researchers Steven Heymsfield and James Gangwisch analyzed sleep patterns and obesity rates of more than 6,000 participants in the government's National Health and Nutrition Examination Survey. Looking at the results of the 1982–1984 survey, as well the results of a follow-up study in 1987, they discovered that people who get less than four hours sleep a night are 73 percent more likely to be obese than normal sleepers (those who sleep from seven to nine hours a night). The results also indicate that people who sleep for five hours a night are 50 percent more likely to become obese than normal sleepers, while those who receive six hours sleep a night are 23 percent more likely to suffer from obesity than normal sleepers.

So what links sleep deprivation to weight gain? The answer may lie in the hormones associated with

appetite regulation. Leptin is a chemical that effectively tells the brain when we are full, when it should burn calories, and when it should create energy for the body to use. Leptin levels usually increase during sleep, signaling to the brain that we have all the energy we require and do not need any more food. However, if we do not get enough sleep, leptin levels decrease. Our brains interpret this as a lack of energy, causing us to feel hungry, even though our bodies do not require food.

Conversely, the hormone ghrelin is an appetite suppressant that tells the brain when to eat, when to stop burning calories, and when to store energy. Ghrelin levels usually decrease during sleep because we require less energy than when we are awake. However, a lack of sleep may cause an increase in ghrelin, resulting in that familiar hungry feeling.

Stress may also play a vital role in the battle of the bulge, elevating levels of the hormone cortisol, which is secreted into the bloodstream from the adrenal glands when we are under stress—for example, it is released in higher amounts when the sympathetic "fight-or-flight" response is engaged. Because of this, cortisol is known as the "stress hormone." Too much cortisol prevents effective fat burning, leading to weight gain and an increased appetite.

So the next time you're tempted to stay awake all night worrying about your upcoming psychology exam, think of your waistline and get some zzzz's!

<<< *The "swine flu" scare of 2009 caused alarm around the world. In the United States, fears escalated with each report of a new outbreak, and panic spread with the slowly rising body count. Although the number of H1N1-related deaths was only one-fourth of the average yearly flu fatalities, individuals stood in line for hours hoping to receive one of the few vaccines made available to local clinics. Anxiety and stress negatively affect the immune system. Could the panic over H1N1 have actually led to poorer national health?*

CHAPTER **15**

The Mind–Body Connection

As the study of sleep deprivation and obesity demonstrates, there's a strong connection between our minds and our bodies. Many psychologists study this mind–body connection by examining the ways in which psychological states lead to physical reactions. Take, for example, the case of stress. While stress is a psychological state rather than a physiological ailment, it can significantly increase one's risk of developing any of the four leading causes of serious illness and death: heart disease, cancer, stroke, and chronic lung disease. The prognosis is even worse when people's feelings of stress are combined with unhealthy behaviors, such as smoking, excessive alcohol consumption, or lack of sleep. Unfortunately, as we feel more and more stress in our lives, we may be more likely to use smoking or alcohol as stress relievers, or we may attempt to reduce stress by staying up late and waking up early to get things done. In situations like these, our behaviors and our mental states work together to drag us into a vicious, unhealthy cycle.

How can we keep ourselves mentally and physically healthy in stressful situations or other cases in which our thoughts and behaviors can harm our health? The answer might lie in the field of **behavioral medicine**, an interdisciplinary approach to medical treatment that integrates behavioral, medical, and social knowledge to increase life expectancy and enhance quality of life. The psychologically based aspect of behavioral medicine, known as **health psychology**, is focused on the development of general strategies and specific tactics that people and their doctors can use to eliminate or reduce the

> " Unfortunately, as we feel more and more stress in our lives, we may be more likely to use smoking or alcohol as stress relievers, or we may attempt to reduce stress by staying up late and waking up early to get things done. In situations like these, our behaviors and our mental states work together to drag us into a vicious, unhealthy cycle. "

risk of illness. For example, health psychologists might develop stress-management techniques, weight-loss plans, or community support groups in an effort to encourage individuals to take a holistic approach to health. As the name of the field suggests, health psychology places emphasis on the idea that physical health and mental health are closely related: The mind–body connection is real and powerful, and our psychological states often contribute to our overall level of health.

Stress and Its Impact on Health

STRESS AND STRESSORS

You've got an exam coming up, you're trying to repair your less than cordial relationship with your old friend, and you're not sure how you're going to pay off your credit card this month. Even if you've never faced any of these particular circumstances, chances are good that you know what it feels like to be in a stressful situation. **Stress** describes the process by which we perceive and respond to **stressors**, events that we see as threatening or challenging. Not all stress is created equal. **Acute stress**, for example, is a temporary state of stress that varies in intensity, while **chronic stress** describes a long-lasting state of arousal during which we feel that we don't have the resources available to meet all of the demands placed upon us. If you've experienced either type of stress, you're far from alone: Almost 40 percent of Americans report frequently experiencing stress, and the same percentage report sometimes experiencing stress (Carroll, 2007).

As we begin to understand exactly how predominant stress can be in our daily lives, researchers are paying more attention to studying stress so that they can determine its negative effects on health and, ideally, find ways to reduce it. This increased focus on stress has opened doors to several new areas of study. For example, scientists fairly recently came to the realization that chronic stressors are often linked to specific environments, such as offices, cities, or schools. This discovery led to the development of **environmental psychology**, a field that investigates the physical environment's effects on behavior and health. For example, air pollution, excess noise, and metal toxins in the water are environmental stressors frequently associated with city living that can negatively affect people's well-being. Another stress-related field, psychoneuroimmunology, explores the ways in which external stressors alter the immune system's responses to internal stressors such as viruses and bacteria.

No matter where we encounter stress or how that stress manifests itself in our bodies, we tend to think of stress in negative terms. For most of us, stress is something to be avoided or overcome. However, while stress can potentially increase your risk for serious illnesses and other health-related problems, it can also help save your life. When stress is short-lived or perceived as a challenge that you feel capable of overcoming, it can have positive effects: It can help activate your immune system so that you can fight off an illness or heal a wound, it can motivate you to find solutions to problems, and it can teach you to become emotionally resilient. For example, feeling a little stressed out before a track meet isn't necessarily a bad thing—that stress might actually help you run faster. This positive type of stress is sometimes known as **eustress**. When stress is prolonged or perceived as a daunting obstacle, however, it is likely to have negative effects and is referred to as

---

Behavioral medicine is an interdisciplinary approach to medical treatment that integrates behavioral, medical, and social knowledge to increase life expectancy and enhance quality of life.

Health psychology is the psychologically based aspect of behavioral medicine.

Stress is a physical and mental response to threatening or challenging events.

Stressor is an event that a person perceives as threatening or challenging.

Acute stress is a temporary state of stress that varies in intensity.

Chronic stress is a long-lasting state of arousal during which a person feels that he or she doesn't have the resources available to meet all of the demands placed upon him or her.

Environmental psychology is a field that investigates the physical environment's effects on behavior and health.

Eustress is a low-level, positive type of stress that helps a person perform a task or achieve a goal.

distress. Children who suffer distress in the form of severe abuse may experience physiological reactions that lead to chronic disease later in life (Kendall-Tackett, 2000). Individuals who have posttraumatic stress responses are also at risk for serious diseases. For example, many veterans of the Vietnam War experienced posttraumatic stress as a result of their participation in heavy combat. Later, these same veterans were found to be more at risk for circulatory, digestive, respiratory, and infectious diseases than were their peers who had not experienced posttraumatic stress (Boscarino, 1997).

THE STRESS RESPONSE SYSTEM

We each perceive stressors differently, and each of us has our own strategies for coping with stress. However, we all have very similar immediate physiological responses to stress. Over the years, in an attempt to simplify and describe these responses, psychologists have developed several models of our stress response system.

Fight or Flight

In 1915, American physiologist Walter Cannon observed that extreme cold, lack of oxygen, and emotion-arousing incidents can trigger an increase in the release of the stress hormones epinephrine and norepinephrine from the adrenal glands. This observation demonstrated to Cannon that the stress response is a part of the mind–body system: Although stress is a mental state, it produces physical symptoms. Cannon dubbed the body's response to emotional arousal the **fight-or-flight response**, a term that describes our evolutionary options

when faced with a stressor—fighting back or fleeing to safety.

Cannon's description of the fight-or-flight response has become one of the most famous models used to explain animals' responses to stress, but chemically speaking, it doesn't tell the entire story. Following up on Cannon's research, physiologists have identified another stress response system that causes the outer part of the adrenal glands to secrete stress hormones such as cortisol. The stress

> No matter where we encounter stress or how that stress manifests itself in our bodies, we tend to think of stress in negative terms. For most of us, stress is something to be avoided or overcome.

hormones increase the concentration of glucose in the blood to make fuel available to the muscles. This finding bolsters Cannon's beliefs about humans' innate responses to stress: Whether we're preparing to fight or running to safer ground, our muscles need fuel to react appropriately, so the secretion of cortisol makes perfect sense in a fight-or-flight framework.

General Adaptation Syndrome

As popular as Cannon's theory is, it's not the only model of stress response. In the 1930s, endocrinologist Hans Selye developed the model of the **general adaptation syndrome (GAS)**, which describes how the body adaptively responds to stress in

three stages: alarm, resistance, and exhaustion. During the alarm stage, the body's initial reaction to a threat causes the heart rate to increase and blood to be diverted to the skeletal muscles. During the resistance stage, temperature, blood pressure, and respiration remain at high levels, hormones are suddenly released, and the body is ready to fight the challenge being encountered. The exhaustion stage occurs when persistent stress depletes the body of its reserves. During this final stage, the body is more vulnerable to illness and may even collapse or die.

Recent research confirms the implication's of the GAS's final stage: Prolonged stress can lead to physical deterioration and rapid aging. A 2008 study reported that young women who experience stressful events such as child abuse, violence at the hands of a partner, and increased responsibilities at an early age are more likely to begin menstruating earlier and to experience physical weathering, a term that describes accelerated aging and its associated symptoms (Foster et al., 2008).

Alternative Stress Responses

Sometimes, stress does not cause us to fight or flee; it causes us to withdraw. If someone close to you passes away, for example, you might respond to this stressful event by spending time alone and avoiding the outside world. Withdrawal may take the form of leaving a job or relationship or using drugs as a means of escape from reality. While withdrawal can be appealing because it allows us to avoid

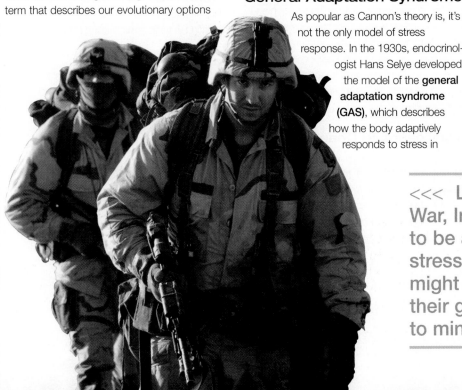

<<< Like veterans of the Vietnam War, Iraq War veterans are likely to be at an increased risk for stress-related problems. What might soldiers, their doctors, or their governments do to attempt to minimize this risk?

Catastrophe is an unpredictable, large-scale event.

Burnout is a state of physical, emotional, and mental exhaustion created by long-term involvement in an emotionally demanding situation and accompanied by lowered performance and motivation.

Hassle is a minor nuisance that, when combined with other small problems, can create a stressful environment.

"Thankfully, many people never experience catastrophic events firsthand. However, more mundane and common life events, such as moving out of a childhood home, getting married or divorced, losing a loved one, or changing career paths, can cause large amounts of stress in our lives."

stressors, it isn't necessarily an effective way to resolve stressful issues or improve emotional well-being.

Social psychologist Shelley Taylor's "tend and befriend" theory, named in homage to Cannon's original model, describes a more effective response to stress. The tend-and-befriend model, which is frequently used to explain women's behavior, describes our tendency to seek and give support in response to stress. Research has shown that people with support networks of friends and family are often better capable of handling stress than are people who do not have social support networks available.

"You may be surprised to discover that the cumulative impact of what we perceive to be minor stressors may be just as significant as the impact of one large-scale event."

STRESSFUL LIFE EVENTS

In our daily lives, we encounter stress in varying forms and degrees of severity. Which do you think would cause you more stress: surviving a plane crash, or surviving the traffic jams of your daily commute? Being displaced from your home when a hurricane causes your entire city to flood, or having your basement flood every time it rains? You may be surprised to discover that the cumulative impact of what we perceive to be minor stressors may be just as significant as the impact of one large-scale event.

Catastrophes

Major stressful life events are characterized as **catastrophes**—unpredictable, large-scale

events. The Iraq War and Hurricane Katrina are examples of catastrophes, as are the terrorist attacks of September 11, 2001. Catastrophic events like these can have extensive, far-reaching implications for people's stress levels and, subsequently, people's health. For example, after the 9/11 attacks, researchers found that many Americans' blood pressure had increased substantially as a result of the attacks and had remained at these increased levels for at least two months (Gerin et al., 2005). The New York area also saw a 28 percent increase in sleeping pill prescriptions after the attack (HMHL, 2002).

People who have experienced catastrophes on this scale may develop posttraumatic stress disorder (PTSD), a stress reaction caused by persistent reexperiencing of traumatic events (see Chapter 17). Symptoms of PTSD include sleep and concentration problems, anxiety, nightmares, and flashbacks. People may also react with residual stress patterns, which are more persistent and chronic but milder emotional responses of PTSD. When the stressor itself is chronic, stress reactions may be described as **burnout**—a state of physical, emotional, and mental exhaustion created by long-term involvement in an emotionally demanding situation and accompanied by lowered performance and motivation. Burnout is particularly common among those in emotionally stressful helping professions, such as social workers who frequently encounter child abuse cases or healthcare providers who treat casualties of war.

Significant Life Changes

Thankfully, many people never experience catastrophic events firsthand. However, more mundane and common life events, such as moving out of a childhood home, getting married or divorced, losing a loved one, or changing career paths, can cause large amounts of stress in our

lives. Many of these significant life changes tend to occur during young adulthood: In your late teens, twenties, and thirties, you may face the challenges and stressors that accompany leaving home for the first time, beginning a career, entering a long-term relationship, starting a family, and coping with the deaths of older relatives. In fact, young adults tend to experience so much change that the term "quarter-life crisis" was recently coined to describe the stressful, overwhelming feelings that people in their twenties commonly grapple with. Some statistics suggest that stress from significant life events decreases with age; for instance, half of American adults under age 50 report experiencing frequent stress, while less than 30 percent of Americans over age 50 report the same (Saad, 2001).

Like other stressful events, significant life changes can negatively affect your health. It's been found that people who have recently been widowed, fired, or divorced are more likely to become ill than are those people whose lives have been relatively stable and stress-free.

Daily Hassles

The most frequent and common stressors are daily **hassles**, which include such nuisances as sitting in traffic jams, waiting in long lines,

>>> **Minor hassles can add up to equal major stress.**

10 Leading Causes of Death in the USA

Systematic Infection 1.4%
Kidney Disease 1.9%
Influenza and Pneumonia 2.2%
Diabetes 2.9%
Alzheimer's 3.1%
Accidents 4.8%

Respiratory Disease 5.3%

Cerebrovascular Disease/
Stroke 5.5%

Cancer 23.1%

Heart Disease: 25.4%

Source: National Vital Statistics Report, Vol. 58, No. 1 (August 2009).

having an overly busy schedule, receiving too much e-mail spam, finding the office coffee pot always empty, tripping over your roommate's shoes every time you walk in the door, and so on. While these hassles may seem relatively minor, their effects on us can add up to create a significant amount of stress. This type of stress can be even more harmful when it is exacerbated by socioeconomic or safety-related factors such as struggling to pay rent or buy groceries, living in an impoverished or high-crime neighborhood, and experiencing the effects of racism and other types of prejudice. In lower socioeconomic areas, where the hassles of everyday life can be particularly stressful and dangerous, residents tend to show signs of high blood pressure, or hypertension—a physical symptom of a stressful environment, and a serious concern for those who are unable to afford or access appropriate medical care.

STRESS AND THE HEART

Just as sleep can improve our health, stress can cause our health to deteriorate. Unfortunately, it often seems as though we spend more time worrying about stressful situations than we do enjoying a good night's rest. The amount of stress in our lives may help to explain why North America's leading cause of death since the 1950s has been **coronary heart disease**, a condition characterized by

Coronary heart disease is a condition characterized by the clogging of the vessels that nourish the heart muscle.

Type A is a personality type characterized by a competitive, impatient, verbally aggressive, easily angered nature.

Type B is a personality type characterized by an easygoing, relaxed nature.

the clogging of the vessels that nourish the heart muscle. While several factors contribute to the development of coronary heart disease, scientists have found that heart disease and stress are often closely related.

Heart Disease and Personality

Every April 15, taxes are due in the United States . . . and every April 15, tax accountants' blood cholesterol climbs to dangerous levels. Is this relationship just a fluke, or could it be indicative of something more? That's the question that Meyer Friedman, Ray Rosenman, and their colleagues asked in the 1950s when they set out to discover whether stress was related to heart disease. They measured tax accountants' cholesterol levels and blood clotting speeds both during peak tax time (mid-April) and during less stressful times of year. The researchers discovered that while the accountants were relatively healthy before and after tax season, their cholesterol and clotting measures spiked around April 15 as they rushed to finish their clients' tax returns. In other words, the accountants' stress levels seemed to be directly correlated with their health (Friedman et al., 1958).

This research provided the basis for a classic investigation that studied more than 3,000 healthy men aged 35–59 for nine years. At the onset of the study, researchers interviewed the men to determine which of two personality types they displayed. The study included an approximately equal number of **Type A** men—competitive, impatient, verbally aggressive, easily angered men—and **Type B** men—easygoing, relaxed men. By the end of the study, 257 men in the sample had suffered heart attacks, and 69 percent of them were Type A. Possibly more impressive was the fact that the men who were the most laid-back and relaxed (the most "Type B-ish" of the Type B men) had all remained heart-attack-free (Rosenman et al., 1975).

What, then, makes the Type A personality so toxic? While Type A people and Type B people have similar levels of arousal in relaxed situations, Type As are more physiologically reactive when they are harassed, challenged, or

∧
∧
∧ **A stressful lifestyle may contribute to the onset of coronary heart disease, the number one cause of death in the United States.**

Lymphocyte is a type of white blood cell.

Somatoform disorder is a disorder characterized by physical symptoms that do not have an identifiable cause.

Psychophysiological ("mind–body") illness is a symptom such as chronic fatigue or hypertension that is caused by psychological reactions to stress.

Hypochondriasis is a disorder in which a person becomes so preoccupied with minor symptoms that he or she develops an exaggerated belief that the symptoms are indicative of a life-threatening illness.

Somatization disorder is a somatoform disorder characterized by vague, unverifiable symptoms such as dizziness and nausea.

Conversion disorder is a somatoform disorder characterized by the sudden, temporary loss of a sensory function.

Coping strategy is a strategy that helps a person reduce or minimize the effects of stressors.

STRESS AND THE IMMUNE SYSTEM

Your immune system is like your own built-in bodyguard—it protects you against damage from the diseases and injuries that try to attack it every day. Although the immune system is strong, it isn't invincible. Factors such as your age, your genetic background, your nutritional intake, and the amount of stress in your life can all influence your immune system's effectiveness. Based on what you already know about the effects of stress on your overall health, it probably comes as no surprise that when you're under stress, your immune system becomes less able to heal your body quickly and effectively.

Two types of white blood cells, or **lymphocytes**, play roles in the immune system. B lymphocytes form in your bone marrow and release antibodies that fight bacterial infections, while T lymphocytes form in your thymus and other lymphatic tissue and attack cancer cells, viruses, and foreign substances (including those substances that may not actually be enemies of the body, such as transplanted organs). When these lymphocytes do their job properly, they keep you healthy and heal your injuries. However, when your immune system isn't functioning properly, it can respond by either overreacting or underreacting. When it underreacts, it may, for example, fail to fight off those bacteria

> *Concentration camp survivors and prisoners of war have experienced some of the most extreme stress possible, but they do not exhibit a higher incidence of cancer than the regular population.*

disease-fighting activities of the B and T lymphocytes. Stress also causes the body to go into "panic mode" and divert much of its energy away from the immune system to the muscles and brain. This reaction to stress may cause surgical wounds to heal more slowly.

One study examined the effect of stress on people's susceptibility to colds. When a cold virus was dropped into the noses of higher-stressed and lower-stressed participants, 47 percent of the stressed participants and only 27 percent of the lower-stressed participants developed colds. Follow-up research demonstrated that the happiest and most relaxed people were significantly less vulnerable to an experimentally delivered cold virus (Cohen et al., 2003).

Stress and HIV/AIDS

When a person who is already immunosuppressed experiences stress, the effects of stress on the immune system are even greater. The mere diagnosis of an immunosuppressive disease, such as human immunodeficiency virus (HIV), can be a stressor. HIV, which is spread by the exchange of bodily fluids, such as semen and blood, can lead to acquired immune deficiency syndrome (AIDS). More than 30 million people worldwide are living with HIV (UNAIDS, 2008). Without regular testing for the disease, many remain unaware that they are infected and can therefore unknowingly transmit the disease to others. By definition, an immunosuppressive disease makes fighting off other diseases difficult, and people with HIV/AIDS commonly die as a result of these other diseases.

Researchers have found that stress and negative emotions correlate with the progression of HIV to AIDS and can speed the decline

threatened: Their hormonal secretions, pulse rate, and blood pressure increase drastically. The hormones cause plaque to accumulate more rapidly on artery walls, hardening the arteries, raising blood pressure, and increasing the risk of strokes and heart attacks. The active sympathetic nervous system redistributes blood flow to the muscles and away from internal organs such as the liver, which plays a key role in removing cholesterol and fat from the blood. As a result, the excess cholesterol and fat that the blood is carrying are deposited in the heart.

Negative emotions, especially aggressive anger, may also contribute to Type A toxicity. There are medical reasons why we shouldn't, in the words of one bestselling book's title, "sweat the small stuff": Adults who react angrily to minor problems or inconveniences are at a higher risk for cardiovascular disease than are their calmer counterparts. Another study found that middle-aged people with normal blood pressure who scored high on measures of anger were three times as likely to have had heart attacks, even after accounting for other risk factors such as smoking and high weight (Williams et al., 2000). And yet another study on the effects of pessimism on the heart found that pessimists were more than twice as likely as optimists to develop heart disease (Kubzansky, 2001). Both metaphorically and literally, stress and anger clearly don't do our hearts any favors.

> *A study found that middle-aged people with normal blood pressure who scored high on measures of anger were three times as likely to have had heart attacks, even after accounting for other risk factors such as smoking and high weight (Williams et al., 2000).*

that entered your body after you touched a dirty doorknob and then rubbed your eyes, or it may allow cancer cells to multiply. When it overreacts, your immune system may begin attacking your body's own tissues and could cause problems like arthritis, allergies, lupus, or multiple sclerosis. Since women tend to have stronger immune systems than men, women are generally less vulnerable to infections but more vulnerable to these self-attacking diseases.

How is stress related to the immune system's functions? During periods of stress, the brain causes increased secretion of stress hormones, which then suppress the

of those who already have AIDS. Stress-reduction techniques do seem to offer some hope in staving off this decline. For example, many people with HIV have benefited from educational initiatives, bereavement support groups, cognitive therapy, and exercise programs designed to relieve stress.

Stress and Cancer

While laughter and positive emotions can improve cancer patients' health and well-being, stress and negative emotions correlate with the *progression* of cancer. Researchers have conducted studies with rodents in which the rodents were either given carcinogens—cancer-causing substances—or transplanted with tumors and then exposed to uncontrollable stress, such as unavoidable electric shocks. They found that the rodents who were exposed to these stressors were more prone to tumors that grew larger and more quickly than those rodents who were given carcinogens or transplanted with tumors but were not exposed to uncontrollable stress (Sklar & Anisman, 1981). However, stress does not seem capable of causing cancer on its own. Concentration camp survivors and prisoners of war have experienced some of the most extreme stress possible, but they do not exhibit a higher incidence of cancer than the regular population. The developing view of the link between stress and cancer is that stress may affect the growth of cancer cells by weakening the body's immune system against a few malignant cells that are already present in the body.

STRESS AND SOMATOFORM DISORDERS

Some people react to stress by experiencing physical symptoms that are not fully explained by a general medical condition. As a group, the psychological disorders characterized by these symptoms are known as **somatoform disorders** (see Chapter 17). Although the physical symptoms related to these disorders have no physiological cause, people suffering from these symptoms experience them in a very real way.

Migraines, chronic fatigue, and hypertension are just a few of the real physical symptoms that can be caused or worsened by psychological reactions to stress. Once called psychosomatic symptoms, these stress-related symptoms are now referred to as **psychophysiological ("mind-body") illnesses**. It is important to note that, although these physical symptoms have psychological origins, they are not imaginary.

While other somatoform disorders seem less related to stress, it's possible that people develop these disorders partially in response to

>>> Even the most extreme stress can only worsen preex-isting cancer cells, not create them on its own.

stressful situations. One such disorder is **hypochondriasis**. People suffering from hypochondriasis become so pre-occupied with minor symptoms that they develop an exaggerated belief that the symptoms are indicative of a life-threatening illness. Similarly, people who suffer from **somatization disorder** display combinations of multiple physical complaints that have no medical explanation. Unlike someone with hypochondriasis, a person with somatization disorder may not exaggerate the seriousness of the symptoms.

Other people experience **conversion disorder**—the loss of motor or sensory functioning in response to current or imminent stressors, such as being called up for another tour of duty in Afghanistan. These symptoms, which may include blindness or paralysis, have no physical cause, but people with conversion disorder are not being intentionally deceitful. Although they may appear to be "acting out" symptoms, people suffering from blindness as a result of conversion disorder actually believe that they are blind.

SEEKING TREATMENT

Whether you have a stress-related illness or a common cold, visiting a doctor's office can be a stressful activity in and of itself. However, stress does have potential benefits when it comes to seeking treatment for illness. Some people are far more likely than others to notice physical symptoms of illness: While one person may not pay much attention to a headache or an upset stomach, another person might decide to see a doctor as soon as he or she notices these symptoms. What makes these two people react differently to the same symptoms? Stress may be part of the answer. People who notice physical symptoms and report those symptoms to doctors tend to be negative; they often describe themselves as anxious, depressed, and stressed. While no doctor would recommend that their patients strive to become anxious, depressed, and stressed, patients who do notice symptoms early on are more likely to receive early, effective

treatment. On the other hand, people who are insensitive to symptoms or who wait a while before seeking treatment are in danger of having their conditions worsen. Stress may cause a host of health problems, but it can also motivate you to see a doctor and improve your health.

Improving Health

COPING WITH STRESS

Take a moment to think about it: How do you cope with stress? Your answer is probably different from your friend's answer or your mother's answer. In fact, there are many different stress-management techniques, each with various advantages and disadvantages. **Coping strategies** help us to reduce or minimize the effect of stressors. People's methods of dealing with stress vary greatly, but common alleviating strategies include emotional, cognitive, and behavioral approaches.

Cognitive Appraisal

Often, we react negatively to stressors before we are able to think about them rationally. You might feel incredibly overwhelmed when you look at your schedule for next week and realize that you have three exams in one day, none of

Cognitive appraisal is a thoughtful interpretation and evaluation.

Primary appraisal is a person's initial evaluation of the seriousness of a stressor and the extent of the demands it will put on that person.

Secondary appraisal is a person's reassessment of a stressor that focuses on the actions he or she needs to take and the resources that will help him or her overcome the stressor.

Rational coping is a coping strategy that involves facing a stressor directly and working to overcome it.

Reframing is a coping strategy that involves finding a new or creative way to think about a stressor that reduces its threat.

Repressive coping is a coping strategy that involves maintaining an artificially positive viewpoint and trying not to think about a stressor.

Anticipatory coping is a coping strategy that involves a person's foreseeing a potential stressor and considering it in terms of how he or she has previously handled similar stressors, what he or she might do similarly in this situation, and what he or she has learned from past mistakes.

Problem-focused coping is a coping strategy that involves a person's attempting to alleviate stress directly, either by eliminating the source of a stressor or by changing the way he or she behaves in stressful situations.

Emotion-focused coping is a coping strategy that involves attempting to alleviate stress by avoiding the stressor and soothing stress-related emotions.

Stress inoculation is a therapeutic technique in which clients are taught how to evaluate and cope with various stressors and are then exposed to increasingly stressful situations in a controlled environment to strengthen these coping mechanisms.

reasonable way. You might realize that you have a three-day weekend before your exams, which will give you extra time to study, or you might decide to seek out study partners to make your exam preparation more effective and fun. By thinking rationally about a stressor and objectively evaluating the resources that are available to you, you may be able to quell your initial emotional reaction and replace it with a plan.

Rational Coping, Repressive Coping, and Reframing

When we make rational, thoughtful cognitive appraisals of stressors, we are engaging in **rational coping**—we're facing a stressor and working to overcome it. This hands-on approach to stress management tends to be effective, but it can also seem difficult and scary. When we choose not to cope rationally with a stressor, we may decide to use **repressive coping** or **reframing** techniques instead.

Repressive coping is like ignoring the elephant in the room: It involves maintaining an artificially positive viewpoint and trying not to think about the stressor. While some people believe that this method can be effective, especially under short-term circumstances, others worry that failing to adequately face, address, and deal with stressors can lead to long-term negative health consequences. One study found that a repressive coping style was more common

which you've begun to study for yet. However, stressors are often much more manageable than we originally assume they are. Just giving them some thought can help to minimize their harmful effects.

When we make a **cognitive appraisal** of a stressor, we thoughtfully interpret and evaluate it. Making a cognitive appraisal is usually a two-step process. First, we make a **primary appraisal**, or an initial evaluation of the seriousness of the stressor and the extent of the demands it will put on us. In your primary appraisal of the realization that you have three exams in one day, you may perceive the stressor either as an obstacle that will be impossible to overcome or as a challenge that will require effort to overcome. Later, however, you might make a **secondary appraisal**, or a reassessment that focuses on the actions you need to take and the resources that will help you overcome the stressor. A secondary appraisal can help you re-evaluate the stressor in a more informed and

> One study found that a repressive coping style was more common among women with a history of breast cancer and most common among women in advanced stages of breast cancer. Out of the eleven participants in the study who died from breast cancer, eight were repressive copers (Jensen, 1987).

among women with a history of breast cancer and most common among women in advanced stages of breast cancer. Out of the eleven participants in the study who died from breast cancer, eight were repressive copers (Jensen, 1987).

A more advantageous approach to stress is reframing—finding a new or creative way to think about a stressor that reduces its threat. When you use the reframing technique, you might see your three exams in one day as an opportunity to impress your professors, which will enable them to write you glowing letters of recommendation for graduate school. Or you might decide that it's much easier to get three exams over and done with in one day than to have them spread out over an entire week.

All stress-management techniques have their pros and cons, and you may find that different stressors require different approaches. A person who has recently suffered a heart attack may reframe his or her vulnerable health situation by speculating that a future attack would enable him or her to take some time off from work to spend with his or her family. However, it is probably best not to worry about future heart attacks at all. Researchers discovered that heart attack victims who constantly worried about a future attack were more likely to suffer from symptoms of posttraumatic stress, such as nightmares and insomnia (factors that actually increase the risk of heart attack), than were people who did not dwell on the possibility of future health problems (Ginzburg et al., 2003).

Anticipatory Coping

Worriers react to stressors before they are even a reality. They may anticipate hypothetical situations that might cause them stress in the future, and they tend to ponder the best way to handle potentially nonexistent problems. While this can be a tiresome way to live if taken to extremes, it can also be turned into a useful, proactive coping mechanism. **Anticipatory coping** involves foreseeing a potential stressor and considering it in terms of how you have previously handled similar stressors, what you might do similarly in this situation, and what you have learned from past mistakes. For example, if you were unable to cope with your workload last semester and can predict that your classes will be equally demanding this semester, you might minimize potential stress levels by cutting back on extracurricular activities. Like good Boy Scouts, people who use anticipatory coping mechanisms are always prepared.

Problem-Focused Coping

When a stressor is already a reality, attempts to alleviate it may be either problem-focused or emotion-focused. People who engage in **problem-focused coping** attempt to alleviate stress directly, either by eliminating the source of a stressor or by changing the way they behave in stressful situations. We tend to opt for this strategy when we feel a sense of control over a situation. If we feel capable of changing our circumstances or our behaviors in response to a problem, we are more likely to be able to tackle the problem itself. For example, if you are dealing with a particularly challenging project at work, you might talk with your supervisor to see if you can delegate some of your workload (changing the circumstances), or you might decide to work extra hours in order to get the job done (changing your behavior).

Emotion-Focused Coping

If we feel incapable of changing stressful circumstances, we may resort to **emotion-focused coping**—attempting to alleviate stress by avoiding the stressor and soothing our stress-related emotions. For example, if your relationship with your neighbor has become particularly stressful, you might try to avoid the neighbor and make yourself feel better by spending more time with your good friends instead. While this coping strategy can alleviate stress, it tends to be less effective than problem-focused coping in promoting a healthy, satisfying lifestyle. If you had addressed the problems with your neighbor directly, you might have learned useful strategies for getting along with others that could have helped you avoid the continuing stress of dealing with your neighbor.

Although emotion-focused coping isn't always the most effective way to deal with a stressor, it has certain benefits. For example, when cancer patients laugh, listen to jokes, or watch old comedies on television, they're using emotion-focused coping to alleviate stress. They don't have much control over cancer, but they can make themselves feel better by tending to their emotional well-being.

Stress Inoculation

Those who find dealing with stress especially difficult may seek the help of a therapist, who can assist in the development of effective strategies. One such strategy is **stress inoculation**. Developed by Donald Meichenbaum in the 1970s, stress inoculation is a three-step process during which one can evaluate, acquire, and apply effective responses to stress:

FACTORS THAT REDUCE STRESS

Perceived Control

In humans and nonhuman animals alike, threats and stressors over which we have no control produce stronger stress responses than do controllable threats. When we believe that we have no control over a situation, our stress hormone levels and blood pressure increase, and our immune responses decrease. These physiological responses help to explain how perceiving a loss of control over stressors in one's life can lead to increased vulnerability and poor health. When elderly residents in nursing homes have little perceived control over their activities, they tend to experience quicker declines in health and die faster than those who are given more control over their daily activities (Rodin, 1986). Having perceived control seems to be similarly important for people in their work environments: One study found that people who have the freedom to adjust their office furnishings and lighting, and who are able to control interruptions and distractions, experience less stress than do those who do not have control over their working environment (Wyon, 2000). If we believe that we have the power to control our lives and affect change, we are less likely to experience stress. In short, greater perceived control leads to lower stress levels and improved health.

The relationship between perceived control and stress helps to explain the link between economic status and longevity. High economic status is linked to lower risks for heart and respiratory diseases, infant mortality, low birth weight, smoking, and violence. While money doesn't necessarily lead to health, having enough money to live comfortably can significantly reduce your stress levels and increase your perceived control. If you

2
Skills Acquisition and Rehearsal
rehearsal of stress-reduction techniques, including positive coping statements, relaxation, and realistic appraisals of stressful situations

1
Conceptualization
identification of stressors and patient's response to stressors; evaluation of effectiveness of responses

3
Application and Follow-through
application of stress-reduction techniques in increasingly stressful real-world situations

STRESS INOCULATION PROCESS

∧
∧ Meichenbaum's stress
∧ inoculation strategy uses a three-step process to combat stress.

are fortunate enough to be relatively well off, you can afford to control several aspects of your life: For example, you can choose to live in a healthy neighborhood, go to a nice gym, and attend thriving schools.

Even if financial resources don't actually give people much control over their lives, it's *perceived* control that counts when it comes to stress reduction. Studies have found that the positive effects of perceived control over one's situation are very similar to the positive effects of actual control. You may face situations that are truly beyond your control, but if you believe that you can make a difference in those situations, you may reduce your stress levels and improve your overall health.

Explanatory Style

Do you have a fundamentally positive outlook on life? If so, you may find it relatively easy to cope with stress. One way in which we can try to reduce and combat stress in our lives is to make our **explanatory style**, or the way in which we explain events to ourselves, more optimistic.

Psychologists Michael Scheier and Charles Carver found that optimists have more perceived control, cope better with stressful events, and have better overall health than pessimists do (1992). The researchers also found that during the last month of a semester, optimistic students report less fatigue and fewer coughs, aches, and pains than do their more pessimistic peers, indicating that optimists may be experiencing less stress and, therefore, less illness and less sleeplessness.

Social Support

While laughing can be beneficial on its own, it's even better when you have a group of friends and family members to laugh with. Social support, in the form of an intimate network of supportive friends and family members, plays an important role in reducing stress and promoting happiness and health. In fact, people with good social support systems are less likely to die from illnesses or injuries than are those without a strong social network (Kulik & Mahler, 1993). While this correlation may be due in part to the stress relief that friends can provide,

> "We can only endure so much stress in a close relationship before it becomes harmful. How well a marriage functions is an important factor to consider—only a positive, happy, and supportive marriage will contribute to good health.

people with social support also tend to take better care of themselves in other ways. People with supportive friends and marriage partners tend to eat better, exercise more, sleep better, and smoke less—all of which are

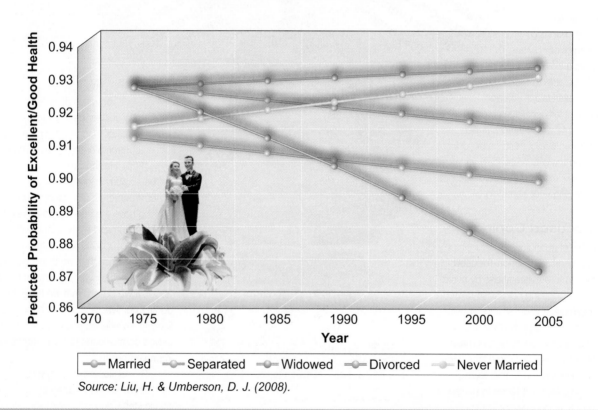

Estimated Trends in Self-Rated Health by Marital Status, 1972–2003

Source: Liu, H. & Umberson, D. J. (2008).

∧
∧ While studies consistently show that married people live longer than people
∧ who remain single, the gap has been closing in recent years. Why might this be the case?

activities that are conducive to coping with stress more effectively. One study also found that women who have social support networks are more likely to get breast cancer screenings (Messina et al., 2004).

You may be thinking about your turbulent romantic relationships, your nosy parents, and your argumentative siblings and wondering how relationships that sometimes cause so much stress could actually be helping you *cope* with stress. It is true that relationships can be stressful at times, especially when people live together in crowded conditions without much privacy. However, while family relationships are not always supportive or healthy, our close family members can provide us with comfort and love when we need it most.

Although marital relationships can be fraught with difficulties, they also happen to be positive predictors of health. The National Center for Health Statistics reported that regardless of age, sex, race, and income, married people tend to live longer, healthier lives than unmarried people do. Of course, we can only endure so much stress in a close relationship before it becomes harmful. How well a marriage functions is an important factor to consider—only a positive, happy, and supportive marriage will contribute to good health.

In successful relationships, a spouse often describes his or her partner as "my best friend." Researchers have found that having someone to confide in plays an important part in our overall well-being. James Pennebaker and Robin O'Heeron (1984) conducted research with the surviving spouses of people who had committed suicide or died in car accidents—events whose suddenness and unpredictability made them especially stressful. The researchers found that those surviving spouses who were unable to talk about their grief with others had more health problems than did those who had someone to confide in. Although talking about a stressful event may initially be awkward or difficult, the long-term effects can be beneficial. One study of Holocaust survivors found that when they shared their experiences with family friends in more detail than they ever had before, the survivors exhibited improved health after 14 months (Pennebaker et al., 1989).

People who don't feel able to share their close feelings with others sometimes benefit by writing about their

experiences. In one study, participants who wrote about personal trauma in a diary suffered fewer health problems in the following four to six months (Greenberg et al., 1996). For other people, man's best friend can provide stress relief, improved health, and slobbery smooches: One study found that Medicare patients who had a dog or other pet companion were less likely to need to see a doctor after stressful events than those without pets (Siegel, 1990).

People with pets tend to be happier and healthier. Many people would consider their pets important members of the family.

∨∨∨

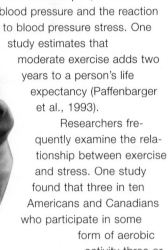

STRESS MANAGEMENT

In today's fast-paced society, sometimes it's just not possible to alleviate stress. We still have to face daily commutes, juggle work and family life, compete for scholarships and jobs, and tackle overflowing inboxes. However, a variety of stress-management techniques, including exercise, relaxation, and meditation, can make our bodies more resistant to the negative effects of stress.

Exercise

Regular **aerobic exercise**—sustained exercise that increases heart and lung fitness, such as jogging, swimming, and biking—not only is good for cardiovascular health but also has been shown to reduce stress, depression, and anxiety. Exercise has long been known to have a positive effect on health. It strengthens the heart, increases blood flow, keeps blood vessels open, and lowers blood pressure and the reaction to blood pressure stress. One study estimates that moderate exercise adds two years to a person's life expectancy (Paffenbarger et al., 1993).

Researchers frequently examine the relationship between exercise and stress. One study found that three in ten Americans and Canadians who participate in some form of aerobic activity three or more times each week manage stressful events better, display more self-confidence, feel more vigor, and experience depression and fatigue less frequently than those who exercise less (McMurray, 2004). Similarly, in 2002, a Gallup survey found that people who did not

How Americans Spend Their Free Time

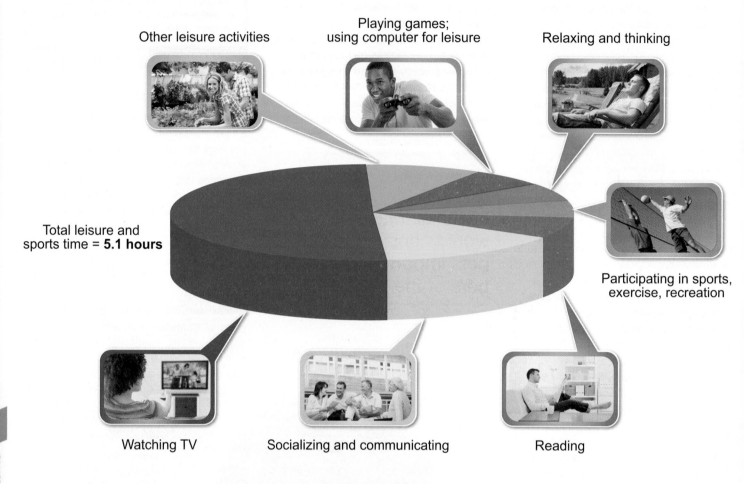

Other leisure activities

Playing games; using computer for leisure

Relaxing and thinking

Total leisure and sports time = **5.1 hours**

Participating in sports, exercise, recreation

Watching TV

Socializing and communicating

Reading

Note: Data include all persons age 15 and over. Data include all days of the week and are annual averages for 2006.

Source: Bureau of Labor Statistics.

∧
∧ Despite the proven benefits of regular aerobic exercise, most Americans
∧ spend about eight times longer watching television than they do participating
in sporting activities. How might this contribute to Americans' stress levels?

exercise were twice as likely as those who did exercise to report feeling "not too happy." One of the many excuses that people give for not exercising is that they can't find the time, but even a ten-minute walk can stimulate two hours of increased well-being by boosting energy levels and lowering tension levels (Thayer, 1978).

Other studies have considered the direction of cause and effect in the relationship between exercise and stress. Does exercise reduce stress, or are people with less stress more likely to exercise? In an

effort to find a causal relationship, Lisa McCann and David Holmes assigned mildly depressed female college students to one of three groups: a group required to perform aerobic exercise, a group required to perform relaxation exercises, and a control group that received no treatment. After ten weeks, the women who had been assigned to the aerobic exercise group displayed the greatest decrease in depression (1984). More than 150 studies have demonstrated that exercise reduces levels of depression and anxiety and is therefore

a useful tool to employ in combination with therapy and/or antidepressant drugs (see Chapter 18 for more information about treatment).

In addition to keeping our hearts healthy and reducing our chances of getting sick, exercise may improve our emotional state by releasing mood-enhancing hormones such as norepinephrine, serotonin, and endorphins. Exercise also helps us feel good by increasing our warmth and body arousal, helping us relax our muscles and sleep more soundly, improving our physical appearance, and giving us a sense of accomplishment. We can further enhance the benefits of exercise by taking advantage of diverse, interesting outdoor activities and exercising with members of our social support groups.

Biofeedback

While it may sound like a futuristic technique from a sci-fi movie, **biofeedback**, a system for measuring and reporting physiological states, is actually a mind-over-matter form of stress-management therapy. Biofeedback specialists use special electronic equipment to measure people's physiological states, such as blood pressure, heart rate, or muscle tension. The equipment then gives feedback designed to help people control their involuntary body functions and reduce stress. For example, a person may not be aware that he has particularly tense muscles, but when he sees a flashing light informing him that he is experiencing muscle tension, he may make a conscious effort to relax.

When biofeedback was first introduced in the 1960s, people were excited at the prospects of being able to control physiological responses and eliminate the use of certain types of drugs. However, about a decade later, researchers realized that the technique may have been overrated. While biofeedback may cure some people's tension headaches, for example, alternative medicine techniques such as acupuncture and meditation provide similar effects and often do not require expensive equipment.

Relaxation and Meditation

Although biofeedback did not live up to expectations, using relaxation techniques to control physiological responses continues to be a popular therapeutic approach to stress reduction. **Relaxation therapy**

involves alternately tensing and relaxing muscles in the body, and practicing breathing exercises in order to relieve tension. The aim of relaxation therapy is to achieve a **relaxation response**—a condition of reduced muscle tension, cortical activity, heart rate, breathing rate, and blood pressure. Brain scans of people achieving the relaxation response reveal that while the parietal lobe—the area involved in knowing where one is in space—is less active than

normal, the frontal lobe—the area involved in focusing attention—is more active than normal (Lazar, 2000). When Richard Davidson studied brain scans of Buddhist monks taken during meditation, he discovered that the monks showed increased levels of activity in the left frontal lobe—the area associated with positive emotion (Davidson, 2003).

> **Biofeedback** is a system for measuring and reporting physiological states.
>
> **Relaxation therapy** is a therapeutic technique that involves alternately tensing and relaxing muscles in the body and practicing breathing exercises in order to relieve tension.
>
> **Relaxation response** consists of reduced muscle tension, cortical activity, heart rate, breathing rate, and blood pressure.

> "If you ever feel guilty about taking a break, remember that relaxation has plenty of health benefits. Studies have shown that relaxation techniques can help alleviate headaches, hypertension, anxiety, and insomnia (Stetter & Kupper, 2002)."

If you ever feel guilty about taking a break, remember that relaxation has plenty of health benefits. Studies have shown that relaxation techniques can help alleviate headaches, hypertension, anxiety, and insomnia (Stetter & Kupper, 2002). In one study of Type A heart attack patients, all patients were given standard medical advice (take medications, eat right, and exercise), but some patients were also taught to become more relaxed and laid-back. Ultimately, the more relaxed patients experienced half as many repeat heart attacks as those patients who received only the standard advice (Friedman & Ulmer, 1984). If you want to reduce the negative health effects of stress, try to stay calm, exercise, emphasize the "Type B" aspects of your personality, and remind yourself that relaxation isn't an unnecessary luxury: On the contrary, it can promote both physical and mental health.

>>> Group motivation often encourages people to continue along the path to physical fitness.

Summary

HOW ARE PSYCHOLOGICAL STATES CONNECTED TO PHYSICAL REACTIONS? p. 228

- The field of health psychology places emphasis on the idea that physical health and mental health are closely related.

- Stress significantly increases a person's risk factor for the four leading causes of illness and death: heart disease, cancer, stroke, and chronic lung disease.

- When the body is emotionally aroused, it produces a fight-or-flight response by releasing stress hormones from the adrenal glands.

HOW DOES STRESS AFFECT OUR IMMUNE SYSTEMS AND OUR OVERALL HEALTH? p. 228

- Common stressors—events that we see as challenging or threatening—include catastrophes, significant life changes, and daily hassles.

- Stress is related to heart disease. Type A people are more likely than Type B people to suffer from heart attacks due to different physiological reactions to stress.

- Stress causes the brain to secrete stress hormones that suppress the immune system, making the body more vulnerable to illnesses, including the progression of cancer. Stress also correlates with the progression of HIV to AIDS.

WHAT ARE SOME OF THE DIFFERENT WAYS THAT PEOPLE COPE WITH STRESS? p. 233

- Coping strategies, including rational coping, repressive coping, and reframing, help to minimize the effects of stressors.

- Foreseeing a source of stress and considering how to deal with it in advance is known as anticipatory coping.

- Attempts to alleviate stress may be problem-focused (dealing directly with the source of the stress) or emotion-focused (avoiding the stressor).

WHAT TECHNIQUES CAN WE USE TO ALLEVIATE OR MANAGE STRESS? p. 237

- People who perceive that they have control over a stressor, who have a positive outlook, and who have social support are better able to deal with stress.

- Aerobic exercise, biofeedback, and relaxation and meditation techniques can help to relieve stress.

Test Your Understanding

1. Someone who studies the effects of living in the inner city on children's stress levels is most likely to be considered:
   a. a social psychologist.
   b. a behavioral medical doctor.
   c. a behavioral psychologist.
   d. an environmental psychologist.

2. A soldier stationed in a war zone who has not come under direct attack or experienced combat is most likely to feel:
   a. eustress.
   b. acute stress.
   c. chronic stress.
   d. hassled.

3. Which model predicts that the body's initial response to a stressful situation helps us cope with the stressor, but if the stressful situation persists, eventually the body's resources are depleted?
   a. flight or fight
   b. eustress
   c. cortisol secretion
   d. the general adaptation syndrome (GAS)

4. Molly found herself becoming closer to her friends following the death of her sister. This is an example of which reaction to stress?
   a. tend and befriend
   b. burnout
   c. hypochondriasis
   d. the general adaptation syndrome (GAS)

5. Which of the following people is LEAST likely to experience burnout?
   a. a rescue worker
   b. a person living with an alcoholic or drug addict
   c. a survivor of a car crash
   d. a person who counsels rape victims

6. Which of the following is believed to contribute to Type A-related health problems?
   a. Higher levels of certain hormones increase blood pressure, arterial hardening, and other factors that raise the risk of stroke or heart attack.
   b. Prolonged negative emotions can have a detrimental physiological effect on the body.

c. Excessive activation of the sympathetic nervous system redistributes blood away from the internal organs, which can increase cholesterol levels.

d. All of the above are likely to contribute to health problems in people with Type A personalities.

7. Which of the following would LEAST be considered a hassle?

a. getting divorced

b. cleaning up toys left out by the kids you normally babysit

c. cleaning up the dishes after your roommate

d. finding out that you are out of milk and cannot eat your cereal

8. Anup is the CEO of a banking company. He works long hours, often yells at his staff, and finds it difficult to relax when he does leave work. Anup is a good example of:

a. a burnout.

b. a Type B personality.

c. a Type A personality.

d. a somatoform disorder.

9. If several of your classmates have a cold virus, you are more at risk of catching and developing it if you:

a. have low lymphocyte levels.

b. have high lymphocyte levels.

c. have low stress.

d. are relaxed.

10. Patti gets migraine headaches in response to stressful events or situations. This is an example of:

a. a somatization disorder.

b. hypochondriasis.

c. conversion disorder.

d. a psychophysiological illness.

11. Harry's gums feel sensitive, he has a sharp pain in his neck, his feet keep falling asleep, and he is losing his hair. He goes to the hospital because he thinks his symptoms must indicate cancer. The doctors find nothing wrong, but Harry still believes he is dying. Harry is most likely demonstrating:

a. somatization disorder.

b. hypochondriasis.

c. a coping strategy.

d. conversion disorder.

12. Martha looks at her daily schedule and immediately thinks that she will never accomplish what she needs to. What might best help her to begin addressing the day's tasks?

a. making a primary appraisal

b. engaging in repressive coping

c. making a secondary appraisal

d. emotion-focused coping

13. The last time Kristine visited her parents, she found that the last few days of her five-day trip were very stressful. This year, Kristine plans to shorten the trip to three days to make the trip less stressful. This is an example of:

a. reframing.

b. anticipatory coping.

c. repressive coping.

d. primary appraisal.

14. Which stress-management technique involves a three-step process that can help people develop skills to better handle stressful experiences?

a. problem-focused coping

b. emotion-focused coping

c. anticipatory coping

d. stress inoculation

15. When things don't turn out how he wants them to, Andy tells himself that he is learning and that things will work out better the next time. What is most likely true about Andy?

a. He has an optimistic explanatory style.

b. He has a pessimistic explanatory style.

c. He has a Type A personality.

d. He is often sick and experiences sleeplessness.

16. Which of the following people is most likely to recover from stressful situations?

a. a woman who is recently divorced

b. a man living away from his family and friends for a year

c. a man who has undergone two separations with his wife but has been married for 25 years

d. a woman who is happily living with her long-term boyfriend, who also is her best friend

17. Which of the following is NOT a way that exercise may help to reduce stress?

a. It reduces levels of depression.

b. It releases mood-enhancing chemicals.

c. It increases warmth and bodily arousal, which helps to relax muscles.

d. It decreases blood flow and raises blood pressure.

18. An increase in frontal lobe activity is most likely responsible for what aspect of the relaxation response?

a. focused attention

b. a feeling of floating in space

c. decreased blood pressure

d. decreased heart rate

19. For 30 minutes each day, Pat attaches electrodes to his jaw that can detect muscle activity. Every time Pat clenches his jaw, the machine beeps, reminding him to relax. Over time, Pat hopes to reduce the amount of jaw pain he experiences when he is stressed. This is an example of:

a. biofeedback.

b. meditation.

c. relaxation therapy.

d. stress inoculation.

20. Which of the following is NOT supported by current research?

a. Laughter can improve the health of cancer patients.

b. Stress can increase the progression of cancer.

c. Stress may prevent the immune system from fighting cancer cells.

d. Stress may cause cancer.

Remember to check www.thethinkspot.com for additional information, downloadable flashcards, and other helpful resources.

PERSONALITY AND INDIVIDUAL DIFFERENCES

<<< In the world of pop music, Lady Gaga is known for her bizarre fashion sense and eccentric personality. From musician Ludwig van Beethoven to Grey Gardens' Big Edie and Little Edie, the general public often views those with unconventional characteristics with distaste and curiosity. What determines a person's individual personality and traits?

WHAT IS PERSONALITY, AND HOW IS IT STUDIED?

WHAT ARE THE MAJOR TRAIT THEORIES, HOW ARE TRAITS ASSESSED, AND HOW DO GENES AFFECT INDIVIDUALS' TRAITS?

HOW DID FREUD CONCEPTUALIZE HUMAN PERSONALITY, AND HOW HAS PSYCHODYNAMIC THEORY EVOLVED OVER THE YEARS?

WHAT ARE THE MAJOR TENETS OF THE HUMANISTIC APPROACH TO PERSONALITY?

HOW DO SOCIAL COGNITIVE THEORIES OF LEARNING AND BEHAVIOR APPLY TO THE STUDY OF PERSONALITY, AND HOW DO CONCEPTIONS OF PERSONALITY VARY ACROSS CULTURES?

In the

early 1970s, the lives of an eccentric mother and daughter were exposed to the public after the health department raided their property and articles about them appeared in the *New York Post* and *New York Magazine*. Edith "Big Edie" Ewing Bouvier Beale and her daughter Edith "Little Edie" Bouvier Beale—the aunt and first cousin of former First Lady Jacqueline Bouvier Kennedy Onassis—once were prominent in influential high-society circles, but they eventually turned to a reclusive life, letting their 28-room mansion in the affluent seaside town of East Hampton, on New York's Long Island, fall into extreme disrepair, overrun by cats, raccoons, and more than 1,000 pounds of garbage.

Big Edie and Little Edie, both known for having artistic talents, lived together for 37 years, ever since Little Edie gave up her dancing career and returned home at age 35. As Little Edie's father had left some 20 years before, the two women lived alone, with only each other for company. Their co-dependence was recorded in the documentary film *Grey Gardens*—titled after the name of the mansion property.

The personality traits that led to the two women to isolate themselves from society are well portrayed in the film. Little Edie dresses in a variety of unusual garb, including lace curtains and silk hair wraps, and feeds bread to the raccoons that have infested the attic, while Big Edie mostly remains in bed. The 1972 *New York Magazine* article—written by a neighbor about her first encounter with Little Edie around the time of the health department's raids on Grey Gardens—describes a woman who has hit her mid-50s, yet remains youthful. She is remarkably, perhaps overly, devoted to her mother, loves animals, sketches, writes poetry, swims in the ocean in the fall, and reminisces about her near engagement to the eldest Kennedy son, Joe Kennedy, Jr., who had been destined for politics before being killed while fighting in World War II.

In the film, Little Edie says, "It's very difficult to keep the line between the past and the present."

Is the eccentricity displayed by the mother and daughter indicative of mental disorders or just unusual personalities? Although the question remains unanswered, their marked difference from relatives and neighbors in choice of living arrangements is clear.

CHAPTER **16**

Introduction to Personality

In today's world, personality is an all-encompassing concept. Fashion magazines instruct us on how to "express our personalities" through clothing, while online dating Web sites promise to analyze the many dimensions of our personalities to successfully find our best romantic match. Perhaps you catch up on all the latest celebrity news and gossip by reading Walter Scott's *Personality Parade.* What, exactly, is personality?

In psychology, **personality** refers to the style in which we interact with the world, particularly with other people. Spending time with friends and family members, you've probably noticed that individual people's behavior tends to stay relatively consistent. You might have a friend who volunteers to take charge of every situation from working on a major class project to ordering pizza. You might know someone who is painfully shy and someone else who converses easily with anyone on any occasion. We are innately interested in and attuned to the ways in which people are different from ourselves and from one another. In addition, we tend to focus on the characteristics that make us different rather than those characteristics that we all share. This focus helps us to decide who we should choose as partners and friends, and it provides us with cues for interacting with specific individuals.

STRATEGIES FOR STUDYING PERSONALITY

In general, psychologists who study personality rely on five different sources of data, to

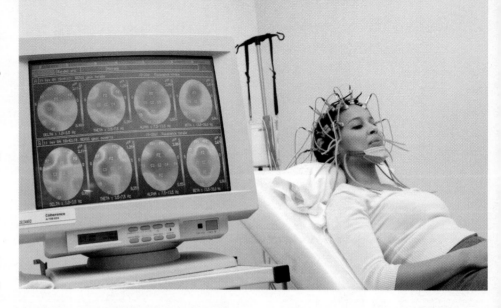

∧
∧ **One way psychologists study personality is
∧ through the use of physiological data. By measuring changes in brain waves or blood pressure in response to certain stimuli, psychologists aim to uncover patterns that point to specific personality tendencies or traits.**

varying degrees and in varying combinations: self-report data (information you provide about your own thoughts, feelings, behaviors, or qualities), observer-report data (information about you provided by friends or family), specific behavioral data (information about specific things you have done), life-events data (information about things that have happened to you), and physiological data (information about the goings-ons in your body, such as heart rate, blood pressure, and brain activity). In addition, psychologists interpret the data they collect through the use of two contrasting approaches. The **idiographic approach** is person-centered, focusing on how the unique parts of our personalities form a consistent whole. Studies that use this approach are primarily concerned with describing and analyzing individuals' personalities. In contrast, the **nomothetic approach** is variable-centered, focusing instead on finding consistent patterns of relationships among individuals' traits. Studies that use the nomothetic approach often involve many participants and are most concerned with determining general principles and theories of behavior. Both approaches have played, and continue to play, an important role in personality research.

Personality Traits

Quick—list a few words that describe your personality. What did you choose? Chances are good that the words you selected, whether they were *honest* and *kind* or *aggressive* and *ambitious*, are linked to certain personality traits. A **trait** is a relatively stable disposition to behave in a certain way. Traits are part of the person rather than part of the environment, although the environment, by triggering people to behave in certain ways, may play a key role in how traits are revealed. Although traits effectively describe how people are different, they do not offer explanations for what causes these differences.

An important distinction exists between traits and **states**. While both traits and states can be examined through someone's observable behavior, traits are lasting, while states are transient. Moreover, a trait can determine the likelihood that someone enters into a temporary state. For example, a person who possesses the trait of insecurity is more likely to enter a state of depression than is someone who is very secure.

In addition, traits are continuous characteristics, meaning that people can differ in the degree to which they express a trait. An

Personality is the style in which a person interacts with the world, particularly with other people.

Idiographic approach is a method of interpreting personality data that is person-centered and focuses on how the unique parts of a person's personality form a consistent whole.

Nomothetic approach is a method of interpreting personality data that is variable-centered and focuses on finding consistent patterns of relationships among individuals' traits.

Trait is a person's relatively stable disposition to behave in a certain way.

State is a person's transient disposition to behave in a certain way.

● ● ○

extremely sociable person may, for instance, have hundreds of friends, whereas a moderately sociable person could have a dozen.

TRAIT THEORIES

Since there are myriad traits and words to describe them, it can be challenging for psychologists to describe people's personalities briefly and consistently. That's why several researchers have come up with **trait theories**, sets of meaningful and distinct personality dimensions that can be used to describe how people differ from one another. In the 1930s, psychologist Gordon Allport became a pioneer in trait theory when he and his colleague H. S. Odbert attempted to identify all of the possible words in the dictionary that could be used to describe people's personality traits. It was a noble goal, but the results were a little overwhelming: They came up with a list of nearly 18,000 trait descriptors (Allport & Odbert, 1936).

Cattell's 16 Personality Factors

Psychologist Raymond Cattell (1965) developed the earliest well-known trait theory by first condensing Allport's extensive list of traits into about 170 distinct adjectives. Next, he had large

> While both traits and states can be examined through someone's observable behavior, traits are lasting, while states are transient. Moreover, a trait can determine the likelihood that someone enters into a temporary state. For example, a person who possesses the trait of insecurity is more likely to enter a state of depression than is someone who is very secure.

samples of people rate themselves on each of these adjectives. Cattell then used a statistical technique called **factor analysis** to identify patterns of correlations in these responses. He used these patterns to determine factors, areas in which certain responses tended to cluster. For example, Cattell found that individuals who rated themselves as given to perfectionism were also likely to describe themselves as organized and self-disciplined, but unlikely to be described as

impulsive or lax. Based on this research, Cattell identified 16 distinct personality dimensions, measured in the *16 PF Questionnaire* ("PF" stands for "Personality Factors"). In this questionnaire, there are almost 200 statements about specific aspects of behavior, such as "I plan my work carefully" and "I stay calm even when I'm angry," to which participants can respond *yes, occasionally,* or *no.* Psychologists still use the questionnaire today.

Eysenck and Gray's Two Central Dimensions

Psychologist Hans Eysenck (1967) believed that personality could be described in terms of two central dimensions: emotional stability vs. insta-

> Psychologist Hans Eysenck (1967) believed that personality could be described in terms of two central dimensions: emotional stability vs. instability and introversion vs. extroversion.

bility and introversion vs. extroversion. Emotional stability refers to our ability to cope with life's stressors in healthy ways and avoid extremes in mood or behavior, while introversion and extroversion refer to our tendency to be shy, serious, and reserved (introverted) or social, high-spirited, and affectionate (extroverted). Eysenck thought differences in introversion and extroversion stemmed from individual differences in alertness. He hypothesized that the **reticular formation**, a part of the brain that controls arousal, is more sensitive in outgoing people than in shy people.

Jeffrey Gray, another personality researcher, refined Eysenck's ideas, proposing that two basic brain systems are reflected in Eysenck's two personality dimensions. According to Gray, the **behavioral activation system (BAS)** activates approach behavior in response to the anticipation of a reward. For example, if a student expects to achieve a high grade by studying hard, activity in the BAS will cause the student to review thoroughly in order to move toward the goal. Gray believed that the BAS is also responsible for experiencing positive feelings such as hope, elation, and happiness. In contrast, the **behavioral inhibition system (BIS)** inhibits approach behavior in response to the anticipation of punishment (1972). Gray believed that the BIS is also responsible for experiencing negative feelings, such as fear, anxiety, frustration, and sadness. Gray's theory may help to

Trait theory states that a set of meaningful and distinct personality dimensions can be used to describe how people differ from one another.

Factor analysis is a statistical technique that is used to identify patterns of correlations in responses to questionnaires.

Reticular formation is a part of the brain that controls arousal.

Behavioral activation system (BAS) is a part of the brain that activates approach behavior in response to the anticipation of a reward.

Behavioral inhibition system (BIS) is a part of the brain that inhibits approach behavior in response to the anticipation of a punishment.

Five-factor model ("Big Five" theory) is a model that is used to describe personality by assessing a person's score on each of five dimensions: extraversion/introversion, agreeableness/antagonism, conscientiousness/undirectedness, emotional stability/instability, and openness to experience/non-openness.

explain certain personality traits. For example, a person with particularly high BIS sensitivity may be extremely anxious when faced with impending punishment (a parking ticket, for example), compared to someone with lower BIS sensitivity.

The Five-factor Model

The "Big Five" may sound like a global trade organization or a band of evildoers, but in fact, it's a popular trait theory. Robert McCrae and Paul Costa, who believe that Cattell's 16-factor theory is overly complex and redundant, reanalyzed Cattell's data and identified five factors of personality. According to this **five-factor model ("Big Five" theory)**, we can describe personality by assessing a person's score on each of five dimensions:

1. extraversion/introversion
2. agreeableness/antagonism
3. conscientiousness/undirectedness
4. emotional stability/instability
5. openness to experience/non-openness

In addition, each trait dimension consists of six facets, which correlate with one another. For example, agreeableness correlates with facets such as trust, straightforwardness, and modesty (McCrae & Costa, 1999). Although research into the psychology of personality continues, the Big Five theory has become a useful and generally accepted construct for describing personality within the field.

ASSESSING TRAITS

Have you ever taken a test to find out your ideal career or your dating style? You might think of these quizzes, some of which are more scientific than others, as "personality tests" that determine your traits and your strengths and weaknesses. In psychology, **personality inventories** refer to longer, more scientifically rigorous questionnaires that ask questions about many different behaviors and assess several traits at once. The most widely used and researched of all personality inventories is the **Minnesota Multiphasic Personality Inventory (MMPI)**. The MMPI was originally developed to identify emotional disorders, but it's now used for a variety of other purposes.

One major problem with virtually all personality questionnaires is that the questions tend to be transparent, meaning that it's possible for you to present yourself not as you are but as you'd like to be. Even if you have a quick temper, you might not be aware of your impressively short fuse, leading you to identify yourself as calm and cool on your personality test. The usefulness of a personality test's results depends on how honest and insightful the respondents are about their own behaviors and attitudes.

The Predictive Value of Personality Inventories

The validity of a personality measure is determined by the degree to which the scores for each trait correlate with the corresponding aspects of the person's actual behavior. For example, if world leaders like Vladimir Putin and Angela Merkel scored low on ambition and leadership qualities on a personality assessment, it would be clear that the inventory had failed to accurately describe them.

However, studies in which people fill out personality questionnaires, or are rated on personality characteristics by those who know them well, reveal that our personalities remain relatively stable throughout adulthood. Some studies demonstrate that personality

∧
∧ How might these prominent individuals describe themselves on personality inventories? Do you think this assessment would be accurate?

becomes increasingly stable with age, perhaps even constant by age 50 Asendorpf & Van-Aken, 2003; McCrae & Costa, 1999). So if you think your parents are becoming more set in their ways, you're probably right!

Researchers have also uncovered something called the **consistency paradox**—the observation that personality ratings are consistent across time and among different observers, but that behavior ratings are not (Mischel 1968, 1984, 2004). This accounts for how our actions vary, depending on the situation. A disciplined athlete who always shows up for practice on time might be late to a friend's party or a job interview. Although we have persistent underlying traits, people, like the situations we encounter, are dynamic.

THE EFFECTS OF GENETICS ON PERSONALITY

As modern twins research illustrates, **heritability**—the degree to which a trait is able to be passed on genetically—plays a significant role in personality. Researchers have discovered that traits identified by trait theories are relatively heritable. Because they share the same genes, identical twins are more likely than fraternal twins to have many similar personality traits. Psychologist David Lykken administered personality tests to twins raised in the same home and to twins who were separated at birth and raised in different homes (Lykken et al., 1988). He still found that identical twins were more similar than fraternal twins, regardless of whether the twins had been raised in the same home. It's estimated that genetic factors account for about 50 percent of individual differences for most traits, including the Big Five (Loehlin et al., 1998). Moreover, cross-cultural studies indicate that the Big Five personality traits exist in all human groups (McCrae et al., 2005). These traits even seem to persist across species; researchers have detected such traits in monkeys, dogs, cats, and pigs (Gosling & John, 1999).

How, then, do genes influence personality traits? Genes may impact the physiological characteristics of the nervous system, particularly neurotransmission in the brain. One theory is that genes influence our temperament—the characteristics and personality traits we are born with—which in turn influence the ways in which we behave. These behavioral

patterns and styles soon come to define our personalities.

EVALUATING THE TRAIT PERSPECTIVE

Looking at personality through the lens of the trait perspective can give us plenty of insight into the actions of our friends, our families, and ourselves—but traits have their limitations, too. While the trait perspective effectively describes *how* people are, it fails to offer much insight into *why* people are that way. And the question about whether people's behaviors are more influenced by situational factors than by personality traits, known as the **person-situation controversy,** persists. Although people's traits may endure over time, their specific behavior may vary in different situations, so traits alone may not always help us predict behavior.

> "Looking at personality through the lens of the trait perspective can give us plenty of insight into the actions of our friends, our families, and ourselves—but traits have their limitations, too. While the trait perspective effectively describes *how* people are, it fails to offer much insight into *why* people are that way."

The Psychodynamic Perspective

SIGMUND FREUD

Among his many accomplishments, famous psychologist Sigmund Freud pioneered the clinical approach to understanding personality. The image that many of us associate with psychological counseling—a bearded doctor asking his patient (who is, naturally, lying on a leather couch) to "Tell me about your mother"—originates here. A controversial figure who shocked Victorian Europe with his theories of sexual repression, Freud was initially ridiculed for his ideas. Today, his theories about the unconscious frequently

Heritability describes the degree to which a trait is able to be passed on genetically.

Person-situation controversy focuses on the question of whether people's behaviors are more influenced by situational factors than by personality traits.

Psychic determinism is the concept that unconscious processes underlie all conscious thoughts and actions.

Psychoanalysis is a type of psychotherapy that relates closely to Freudian concepts like the influence of the unconscious. It requires patients to talk to a psychiatrist about their lives while the psychiatrist listens, analyzes, and interprets each word.

Psychodynamic theory is a personality theory that focuses on the interaction of mental forces.

undergo similar tongue lashings from psychology students, and most professionals view his ideas with great skepticism. However, the influence Freud has had on the modern world is undeniable—ask any member of the public to explain a basic Freudian concept and they will most likely be able to do so. Despite the professional skepticism, many Freudian concepts still form a basis for modern personality theories.

Freud believed that our problems in adulthood are caused by our memories, especially disturbing ones from childhood. These memories, according to Freud, are impossible for us to access consciously—they're buried deep in the unconscious mind. Freud thought that in order to understand his patients' actions, problems, and personalities, he had to access the contents of their unconscious minds. This concept—that unconscious processes underlie all conscious thoughts and actions—is known as **psychic determinism**. The method of treatment that Freud invented, called **psychoanalysis**, requires patients to talk to a psychiatrist about their lives while the psychiatrist listens, analyzes, and interprets each word.

Freud's psychoanalytic theory was the first **psychodynamic theory**, a personality theory that focuses on the interaction of mental forces. Psychodynamic theories are based on two beliefs: We don't usually know what our true motives are, and we have defense mechanisms that keep our

contains our partly conscious perceptions, thoughts, judgments, and memories.

If the id represents some of your more devilish impulses, then the superego would be the opposite, the proverbial angel on your shoulder. The **superego** forces the ego to consider societal constraints and "acceptable" forms of behavior. Let's say that you're dying to have a shiny new car. If your superego didn't exist, you might steal the car from the lot, paying no attention to laws, social conventions, or a moral sense of right or wrong. Fortunately for you, your superego would probably step in, remind you that stealing is illegal and wrong, and then direct your ego to obtain the car in a realistic way: Get a job, earn enough money for a down payment, secure a loan, purchase the car, and continue to make monthly payments.

Freud's idea of the mind is often compared to an iceberg that's partly visible above the surface, which represents consciousness, but mostly hidden in the underwater depths of the unconscious mind. The id is a completely unconscious force, while the ego and superego have both conscious and unconscious components.

The Psychosexual Stages

You might have heard movies or books with sexual overtones or imagery referred to as "Freudian." This description is based on Freud's conception of the human personality as developing through a series of psychosexual stages. Freud believed that sex and aggression were important drives in the formation of our personalities; in fact, he thought that most of the things we do are thinly veiled demonstrations of sexual and aggressive concepts. As a result, the psychodynamic theory that he developed holds that personality differences are caused by the different ways in which people disguise and channel these drives.

Freud outlined five **psychosexual stages**, or developmental stages during which the id's desire for pleasure focuses on many of the body's erogenous zones in turn. According to Freud, anxiety or conflict of any sort could cause energy to become stalled at a particular stage, leading to **fixation**, or a focus on one particular area, during adulthood. For instance, Freud might trace a child's prolonged thumb-sucking to an oral fixation caused by being abruptly weaned as an infant. Someone who is rigidly organized or compulsively neat might be, in Freud's view, stalled at the anal stage as a result of overly strict toilet training. For Freud, personality was closely linked to childhood experiences.

unpleasant thoughts and motivations in our unconscious mind. How do these "mental forces" interact, why are we unaware of our motives, and what, exactly, are these defense mechanisms? Psychodynamic theory provides some interesting answers.

The Id, Ego, and Superego

Freud conceptualized the mind as three interacting systems: the id, the ego, and the superego. The **id** tries to satisfy our basic drives and survival instincts. It operates on the hedonistic **pleasure principle**: Seek immediate gratification and pay no attention to societal expectations or constraints. You might associate the id with the behavior of an infant, who cries when it needs something (even at a fancy dinner party or in a worship service) and stops when that need is fulfilled.

The **ego's** role is to identify the basic drive that the id wants to fulfill and come up with a realistic plan for satisfying that drive. In contrast to the id, the ego operates on the **reality principle**, meaning that it attempts to achieve the id's goals through actions that will be pleasurable rather than painful. The ego

Freud's Theory of the Mind

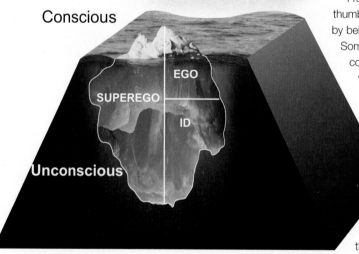

Conscious

EGO

SUPEREGO

ID

Unconscious

∧
∧ How is Freud's conception of the mind
∧ similar to an iceberg that is mostly — but
not entirely — underwater? What are some
limitations of this analogy?

Defense Mechanisms

According to Freud, we deal with feelings of anxiety through the unconscious use of **defense mechanisms**. These mechanisms (which Freud's daughter and fellow psychologist, Anna, played a major role in exploring) are mental processes of self-deception that help us alleviate our worry and anxiety. According to Freud, the way in which people use defense mechanisms also provides insight about their personality.

Repression is a process that blocks anxiety-provoking thoughts from our conscious minds. Freud believed repressed memories and thoughts often appeared in the form of dream symbols or "errors" in speech, known as **Freudian slips**. Former Secretary of State Condoleezza Rice made a ruckus in the gossip columns when she began to refer to President

> From a Freudian standpoint, a person who feels uncomfortable with his or her homosexual urges might engage in reaction formation and become homophobic.

George W. Bush as "my husband" before stopping to correct herself. If he'd been around, Freud might have thought (as plenty of eager columnists did) that Rice had committed a Freudian slip that suggested a repressed desire.

Regression is a retreat to an earlier stage of development, such as childhood or infancy. Have you ever crawled into bed and curled up in the fetal position at the end of a bad day? Freud might say you were seeking comfort through regression.

Displacement describes the process of redirecting an unconscious and unacceptable wish or drive toward a more acceptable alternative. If you have the urge to hit a family member, you might displace this unacceptable aggression by hitting a punching bag instead.

Sublimation occurs when displacement causes us to direct our energy into important or valuable activities. People who channel their internal angst into the creation of beautiful art might be considered "sublimators."

A **reaction formation** changes a wish into its more acceptable opposite. From a Freudian standpoint, a person who feels uncomfortable with his or her homosexual urges might engage in reaction formation and become homophobic.

Projection occurs when a person who unconsciously experiences an impulse attributes that impulse to someone else. For instance, for a person who projects feelings of sadness, "I feel depressed" might become, "My friend seems depressed."

Identification is the act of unconsciously taking on the characteristics of another person who seems better able to cope with feelings of threat and anxiety. Before giving a speech in front of a crowd, you might adopt the mannerisms of your fellow speechmaker, who seems much more calm and collected than you do.

Rationalization is the use of conscious reasoning to explain away anxiety-inducing thoughts and feelings. You might rationalize telling a white lie to a friend by saying that the lie is really for your friend's own good.

POST-FREUDIAN PSYCHODYNAMIC THEORISTS

Freud had a number of followers and disciples who helped propagate his ideas into future generations. At the same time, however, few of these disciples agreed with Freud on all points. Many prominent post-Freudian psychologists, including Carl Jung, Alfred Adler, Karen Horney, and Erik Erikson, modified or amended Freud's original theories to reflect their own beliefs and concepts regarding personality.

Carl Jung, for example, believed, like Freud, that human personality is strongly influenced by the unconscious. However, Jung placed less emphasis on sexual feelings and pioneered the concept of the **collective unconscious**, a shared pool of memories and images common to all humans. For example, the image of a mother as a caretaker and nurturer exemplifies a common idea persistent across time and cultures. Jung called such images **archetypes**.

> Adler believed people often strive for perfection and superiority throughout adulthood in an effort to compensate for feelings of both physical and mental inferiority rooted in childhood.

Alfred Adler developed the idea of the **inferiority complex** as being an important factor in human personality. Adler believed people often strive for perfection and superiority throughout adulthood in an effort to compensate for feelings of both physical and mental inferiority rooted in childhood.

Psychologist Karen Horney was deeply influenced by Freud's teachings, but she emphasized the importance of social factors,

Repression is a process that blocks anxiety-provoking thoughts from the conscious mind.

Freudian slip is an error in speech that represents the surfacing of repressed memories and thoughts.

Regression is a retreat to an earlier stage of development.

Displacement is the process of redirecting an unconscious and unacceptable wish or drive toward a more acceptable alternative.

Sublimation is the process that occurs when displacement causes a person to direct his or her energy into important or valuable activities.

Reaction formation is the process of changing a wish into its more acceptable opposite.

Projection is the process by which a person who unconsciously experiences an impulse attributes that impulse to someone else.

Identification is the act of unconsciously taking on the characteristics of another person who seems better able to cope with feelings of threat and anxiety.

Rationalization is the use of conscious reasoning to explain away anxiety-inducing thoughts and feelings.

Collective unconscious is a shared pool of memories and images common to all humans.

Archetype is a particular image, such as mother as caretaker and nurturer, persistent across time and cultures.

Inferiority complex is a drive for perfection and superiority throughout adulthood in an effort to compensate for feelings of both physical and mental inferiority rooted in childhood.

Thematic Apperception Test (TAT) presents a participant with a series of random, unfamiliar images and asks him or her to tell stories about them; these stories supposedly reflect the person's inner hopes, fears, and desires.

particularly anxiety, as a strong shaper of our personalities. According to Horney, some of us cope with anxiety by becoming submissive, others by becoming aggressive, and still others through detachment.

ASSESSING THE UNCONSCIOUS

Accessing, exploring, and assessing a person's unconscious processes sounds like a tall order, even for the most skilled clinician. Fortunately, a number of tests have been developed over the years to aid psychologists in this endeavor.

Many psychodynamic psychologists rely on projective tests when helping people understand their unconscious thoughts and feelings. These tests present an ambiguous stimulus and then ask the participant to describe it or tell a story about it. For example, the **Thematic Apperception Test (TAT)**, developed by Henry

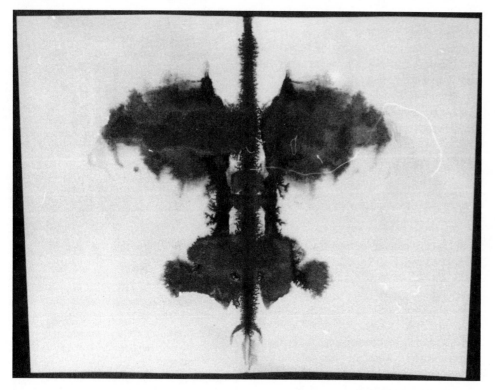

Murray, presents people with a series of random, unfamiliar images and asks them to tell stories about them. These stories supposedly reflect their inner hopes, fears, and desires.

Similarly, the **Rorschach inkblot test** presents a series of nebulous inkblots to participants, who are instructed to say whatever comes to mind upon viewing them. The test assumes that our interpretations of the inkblots are related to our unconscious thoughts. For example, if you see threatening storm clouds in the blurry inkblots, a psychologist might infer that you have feelings of fear or anxiety about something; if you see a dog, you might be longing for a best friend or trusty companion. While this may seem like an unreliable and subjective way to assess the unconscious mind, psychologists use a scoring system to measure participants' responses. For example, frequency tables indicate how often a particular response is given by the general population. Test administrators also look for qualities such as the vagueness of a response, rather than merely focusing on what participants see in the inkblot.

EVALUATING PSYCHODYNAMIC THEORY

Several of Freud's terms and theories have become familiar cultural mainstays, but how

popular is the Freudian approach to personality today? Given its emphasis on the unconscious, childhood, and sexuality and aggression, it's probably not too surprising that psychodynamic theory has remained controversial ever since Freud first introduced it to the world. While Freud's theory explains individuals' personality traits after they have developed, it offers no

> "The Rorschach inkblot test assumes that our interpretations of the inkblots are related to our unconscious thoughts. For example, if you see threatening storm clouds in the blurry inkblots, a psychologist might infer that you have feelings of fear or anxiety about something; if you see a dog, you might be longing for a best friend or trusty companion."

insight or methods to predict these qualities, making its usefulness more or less limited to after-the-fact analysis (Hall & Lindzey, 1978). Strangely, although Freudian theory is developmental, it's not supported by observations or studies of children. Many critics, including Karen Horney, point out that much of the theory seems to have a male-centered bias.

Despite these criticisms, however, Freudian-based, psychodynamic theories endure because both psychologists and people in general continue to see merit in many of their foundational concepts (Huprich & Keaschuk, 2006; Westen, 1998). The idea that we sometimes act in ways that we don't completely understand due to partially unconscious processes makes sense to most of us, as does the concept that our personalities are influenced, at least in part, by our early experiences as children. Although we might hesitate to look to Freud for all of the answers to our questions about why we are the way we are, we shouldn't write him off completely, either.

The Humanistic Approach

The humanistic approach represents yet another way psychologists attempt to understand and analyze human personality. **Humanistic theories** of personality emphasize people's conscious understanding of themselves and their abilities to attain self-fulfillment. Many humanistic theories were developed in the middle of the 20th century as a reaction to the dominance of psychodynamic theories like Freud's. With their emphasis on human capacity for generosity, self-improvement, high achievement, and happiness, humanistic theories tend to appeal to the optimists in all of us.

ROGERS AND SELF-CONCEPT

The humanistic approach to personality centers around the principle of **self-concept**, or a person's understanding of who he or she is. Humanistic theories contend that our self-concept comprises a key part of our reality. Take a moment to consider the question, *Who am I?* A college student, a son or daughter, a sister or brother, a friend? A kind person, a funny person, an ambitious person, a laid-back person? Answering this question can be a daunting task, and your responses will probably change depending on your mood and outlook. The way you think about yourself, however, represents your self-concept.

Psychologist Carl Rogers (1980) expanded on this idea to develop a theory of personality called **self theory**. Rogers believed that all people want to become their "real" selves. In order to achieve this goal, we need to live according to our own wishes rather than those of other people. At the same time, however, other people can help us become our real selves by accepting us, acting genuinely, and showing empathy. When people value us despite our problems and weaknesses, they show us **unconditional positive regard**, an ingredient that Rogers considered crucial to self-development.

For Rogers, our self-concept and access to unconditional positive regard is inextricably linked to our personalities and our interactions with the world at large. A positive self-concept, according to Rogers, manifests itself in positive interactions with the world, productive relationships, and personal satisfaction and happiness. Those people who lack unconditional positive regard and have a negative self-concept tend to struggle with feelings of anxiety or doubt.

MASLOW AND SELF-ACTUALIZATION

Humanistic theorists also believe in the importance of **self-actualization**, the experience of becoming your real self and realizing your full potential. Since everyone is individual and unique, everyone reaches self-actualization differently. However, whatever route you take toward self-actualization, it must be a route you've chosen for yourself. It makes sense: The

only person who can tell you how to become your real self is you!

That's not to say that external circumstances play no role in self-actualization. In fact, many humanists would argue that we need a nurturing environment in order to achieve full self-actualization. However, we alone are responsible for taking advantage of that environment and using its resources to help ourselves reach our goals.

Like Rogers, Abraham Maslow devoted a large portion of his career to developing the major tenets of humanistic psychology. Maslow (1954) believed that in order to self-actualize, we must satisfy five sets of needs. He envisioned this idea as a pyramidal structure, known as the **hierarchy of needs**.

Maslow's Hierarchy of Needs

Self-actualization needs, such as the needs for self-expression, creativity, and a broad sense of being connected to the world

Self-esteem needs, such as feelings of being competent

Attachment needs, such as love

Safety needs, such as protection from dangers in the environment

Physiological needs, such as the needs for water and food

According to Maslow, we can focus on higher needs only if our most basic needs have been satisfied. For example, you're unlikely to pay much attention to your need for love or self-expression if you are starving or desperate for a glass of water. Maslow's hierarchy makes sense from an evolutionary perspective: Our physiological and safety needs are the most basic because they are most immediately linked to survival.

In Maslow's view, some needs are more essential than others, but they are all nonetheless interconnected. Although you can technically live without friends, as opposed to food or water, maintaining strong social bonds actually helps you meet your physiological, safety, and reproductive needs. Additionally, you might think of self-actualization as the result of years of learning experiences. You acquire skills and knowledge through both formal education and activities like playing, exploring, and creating. These acquired skills not only help you self-actualize but also make it easier for you to get food, escape threats, and find a mate. Even your "less essential" needs turn out to be pretty essential after all.

By focusing on the capacity for psychologically healthy people to grow and achieve happiness, Maslow represented a marked shift from the psychodynamic emphasis on uncovering the roots of individual's psychological troubles. "Tell me about your mother" became "Tell me about yourself—your hopes, dreams, and vision of the future." From Maslow's perspective, our personalities are self-directed and self-determined. Those who strive for higher-level needs such as self-actualization, he found, tend to be more generous, accepting, and patient than those focused on satisfying only their basic needs.

McADAMS AND PSYCHOBIOGRAPHY

If you have the chance, ask an older family member to tell you his or her life story. You might not only learn some fascinating facts about your relative, but also delve a bit into **psychobiography**, the life-story conception of personality. Psychologist Dan McAdams (1988) believes that, although people's life stories are outwardly quite different, the stories' structures have several common links. For example, the stories we tell about ourselves usually feature themes and morals, characters who influence us, and conflicts that are ultimately resolved. We see our lives in narrative form, and we're able to relate our life events to broad themes and purposes.

McAdams and his psychobiographical approach rely on the idea that we are what we tell ourselves we are: Our life stories, and the facts and fictions that we tell about ourselves, determine who we are and what we would like to become.

EVALUATING THE HUMANISTIC APPROACH

If you start looking around for the humanistic perspective in your everyday life, you might start seeing it everywhere. Its ideas have influenced such diverse areas as counseling, education, childrearing, and management, not to mention contemporary pop psychology. Self-help books and upbeat magazines have probably urged you to read about "finding yourself," "getting in touch with the real *you,*" or "living the life you were meant to live." This type of language has become a ubiquitous part of self-help literature, talk show chatter, and general conversation. If you listen closely, you can hear the voices of humanistic psychology echoing in the background.

The appeal of the humanistic approach is obvious. It is person-centered, accessible to the masses, and refreshingly optimistic. Cultivating a positive self-concept is the key to being happy and successful, and most people think they're capable of seeing themselves in this positive light. In addition, humanists' focus on the individual self reinforces Western cultural values, so people in the Western world find it easy to relate to the humanist perspective.

Despite, or perhaps because of, its popularity, critics of the humanistic perspective have said that its concepts are vague and subjective. A self-actualized person sounds great in theory, but what, exactly, does this person look like? What evidence exists to differentiate that person from his or her non-self-actualized peers? Some psychologists also criticize the humanistic approach on the grounds that the individualism and focus on self that this perspective demands may lead to selfishness and narcissism. If realizing yourself, thinking well of yourself, and making yourself happy are all that you are

concerned about, critics argue, will you bother to think of the rest of the world? (Campbell & Specht, 1985; Wallach & Wallach, 1983).

Like any approach, the humanistic perspective has its limitations and nonbelievers. Nevertheless, humanists such as Rogers, Maslow, and McAdams, in their interpretation of humans as malleable, dynamic, and capable of great things, offer a hopeful view of personality.

The Social Cognitive Perspective

"You are the company you keep": Whoever first uttered this old saying would probably have been a proponent of the social cognitive perspective on personality. **Social cognitive theories** of personality place emphasis on the beliefs and habits of thought, both conscious

>>> Do you think the pop culture ubiquity of self-help messages based on humanistic principles is helpful or harmful?

and automatic, that we form through our interactions with society. Social cognitive theories overlap to some extent with humanistic ideas, but unlike most humanistic theories of personality, social cognitive theories rely heavily on laboratory research and are concerned with predicting people's behavior in specific situations rather than with predicting people's more general life choices.

Social cognitive theorists believe our behaviors can be traced to our attempts to model what we have observed others doing or to practice what we have learned through conditioning. We are fun-loving and affectionate because our parents were fun-loving and affectionate, and we naturally model their behavior. Or, we continue to be responsible because every time we have acted responsibly in the past, we were praised and rewarded.

Psychologists who support social cognitive theories generally believe that our unique perceptions and thinking—about ourselves and our situations—play a major role in determining our behavior. In their view, personality is less determined by underlying traits or childhood traumas than it is by the current situation, our acquired knowledge from past situations, and the way we think about both. For social cognitive psychologists, personality tends to be highly dynamic and reflective of a combination of social cues and norms as well as individual thought patterns.

ROTTER AND PERSONAL CONTROL

If you've ever felt like you have no control over a situation, you know that feeling this way can be depressing and difficult. One idea central to many social cognitive theories of personality is that of **personal control**, or our sense of controlling our environment rather than feeling helpless. Julian Rotter, one of the principal founders of the social cognitive perspective on personality, devoted much of his research to exploring the relationship between individuals' sense of personal control and their behaviors, personalities, and states of mind.

Do you act differently when you play a game of pool as opposed to a game of bingo? In one laboratory study, Rotter (1954) found that people behave differently at different tasks and games, depending on whether they believe that the game requires skill or luck. When we think a game requires skill, we work hard and improve our performance. When we think a game requires only luck, however, we believe that we can't control the game's outcome, so we don't work hard and we tend not to improve at all. Based on these findings, Rotter argued that our behavior depends on our perception of the amount of control that we have over a certain situation. He called this disposition the **locus of control**. According to Rotter, people with an **internal locus of control** believe that they control their own rewards and, therefore, their own fate. People who have an **external locus of control** believe that rewards and fate are controlled by outside forces. Rotter developed a locus-of-control

questionnaire (1966) that can be used to identify which locus of control an individual most displays.

Since Rotter's initial experiments, many studies have demonstrated links between scores on this questionnaire and actual behavior. People who demonstrate an internal locus of control are more likely to excel in school, take preventive healthcare measures, resist group pressure, and effectively deal with stress (Lachman & Weaver, 1998; Lefcourt, 1982; Presson & Benassi, 1996). In addition, people who demonstrate an internal locus of control tend to be less anxious and more content with life than people who demonstrate an external locus of control.

Recent research has explored the idea that we each have many different loci of control, each of which corresponds to a certain area of our lives. In other words, you may feel that your performance in school is entirely in your own hands, but your performance on the soccer team is more or less determined by fate. According to this theory, our **outcome expectancies**, or our assumptions about the consequences of our behavior, greatly influence the degree to which we may exhibit an internal or external locus of control.

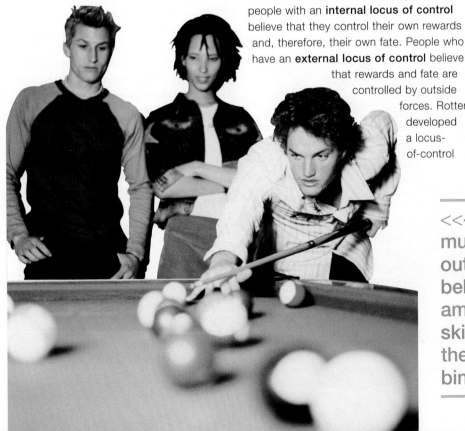

<<< Our perception of how much control we have on the outcome of a game affects our behavior. Many people devote ample time to improving their skills at pool. Would you do the same for a game like bingo? Why or why not?

Consistently being unable to control important situations may eventually cause us to develop **learned helplessness**, a feeling of hopelessness and passivity caused by being unable to avoid or control traumatic events. Psychologist Martin Seligman (1967) found that dogs, after being exposed to electric shocks with no chance to escape, did not even bother trying to escape later when put in the same situation, even when they had the opportunity to get away. Repeated exposure to painful or traumatic events can cause us to feel depressed and resigned to our fate.

BANDURA, RECIPROCAL DETERMINISM, AND SELF-EFFICACY

Albert Bandura was another pioneer of the social cognitive perspective. His cognitive social-learning theory emphasizes the cognitive processes that are involved in acquiring and maintaining patterns of behavior and, as a result, personality. At the center of this theory is the idea of **reciprocal determinism**, which provides a basis for understanding how environmental factors coexist with and influence personality, just as personality factors coexist with and influence the environment. Our personalities are a potent mix of our unique thought patterns, our environments, and our behaviors, all of which are engaged in a constant series of cyclical causes and effects. For example, you might love being in the limelight; you feel great when you're the center of attention. As a result, you sign up for a drama class and start hanging out with a group of gregarious friends. This new environment reinforces your thoughts and feelings, and soon enough, your behaviors reflect increased extroversion: You audition for *American Idol*; you perform at a local open mike night; you start conversations with strangers while standing in line. Your thoughts and personality helped you choose an environment, which in turn further shaped your thoughts, behaviors, and personality.

Much of Bandura's research also focused on self-efficacy (2003). **Self-efficacy**, a concept similar to self-confidence, describes people's expectations about their own abilities to perform certain tasks: The higher your level of self-efficacy, the greater your belief that you can perform a given task. Record-breaking 2008 Olympian Michael Phelps seems to have high self-efficacy when it comes to swimming. He also probably possesses an internal locus of control, believing that his outstanding swimming abilities, coupled with years of diligent training, will result in Olympic glory. Like locus of control, self-efficacy can refer to a specific task or to a large category of tasks: For example, Phelps might have a high sense of self-efficacy when it comes to swimming, but this sense might vary, up or down, for other sports or for athletics as a general category.

Self-efficacy consistently predicts high performance in areas like math, physical exertion, and pain tolerance. In fact, Bandura believed that high self-efficacy not only predicts high performance but also causes it. From Bandura's standpoint, the "I think I can" attitude results in

> From a social cognitive perspective, your feelings, your behavior, and your environment interact to determine your personality.

Reciprocal Determinism

BEHAVIOR

PERSONAL FACTORS (Thoughts and feelings)

ENVIRONMENT

Record-breaking 2008 Olympian Michael Phelps seems to have high self-efficacy when it comes to swimming. He also probably possesses an internal locus of control, believing that his outstanding swimming abilities, coupled with years of diligent training, will result in Olympic glory.

actual achievement (a comforting idea to keep in mind the next time you find yourself scaling a mountain, literally or figuratively).

THE POWER OF THINKING POSITIVELY

For some, the seemingly inexhaustible perkiness and cheer of daytime talk show hosts like Rachael Ray and Kelly Ripa is comforting and inspiring; for others, it can be grating and annoying. Nonetheless, psychological research shows that regardless of our feelings about these high-spirited, bubbly television personalities, we could all benefit from a healthy dose of optimism.

The roles that optimism and pessimism play in shaping personality are an important part of social cognitive theory. Psychologists have designed a number of different questionnaires that assess people's general ability to think either positively or negatively. For example, Rick Snyder and colleagues (1996) designed a questionnaire that assesses hope, and Martin Seligman designed a questionnaire that assesses how optimistically or pessimistically people explain negative events in their lives.

Questionnaires like these have been used in several correlational studies, which have found that optimistic people tend to cope more effectively with negative events than do people who tend to be pessimistic. For example, struggling students who adopt a positive attitude about school are more likely to start earning higher grades than are students who hold on to negative thought patterns like "This is too hard" or "I'm going to fail no matter what" (Noel et al., 1987; Peterson & Barrett, 1987). Optimism has other benefits, too: An optimistic state of mind benefits our health by giving the body's immune system its best chance at remaining strong. Research has even shown that optimists outlive pessimists and are generally healthier overall.

CROSS-CULTURAL DIFFERENCES IN PERSONALITY

If you grew up in Tokyo, Japan, would your personality be different than it would be if you grew up in rural Kansas? It's certainly possible. People around the world are exposed to a wide, rich variety of cultural values, philosophies, economic conditions, and expectations for how to behave. One major way in which cultures differ is the degree to which they are formed around collectivist or individualist ideals. **Collectivist cultures** emphasize people's interdependence: Our relationship to others is a defining aspect of our identities, and we all have responsibilities to our families and communities. The dominant cultures of East Asia, Africa, and South America tend to be collectivist. As a result, people raised in these cultures are likely to possess an **interdependent construal of self**, to see themselves as parts of a larger network of family and community members.

In contrast, **individualist cultures** place emphasis on each person's individual rights and freedoms and deemphasize the social roles that we play in relation to others. The dominant cultures of North America, Australia, and Western Europe tend to be individualist, and people who grow up in cultures like these tend to have an **independent construal of self**, viewing themselves as self-directed, self-contained entities.

What does all of this have to do with personality? If you exhibit a personality trait called **allocentrism**, you tend to think and act in a collectivist manner. If you exhibit **ideocentrism**, on the other hand, you tend to have a more individualistic focus. Allocentric people care deeply about their personal relationships and the interests of their friends, families, and other groups. They generally focus on the similarities between themselves and other group members, and they believe that their thoughts and actions are responses to their social environment.

Ideocentric people, on the other hand, tend to focus not on their roles in society but on their roles as individuals. These people see themselves as unique, and they believe that their personal hopes, dreams, and desires are the driving forces in their lives.

The culture in which we're raised affects not only our personality but also our views of the *concept* of personality. If you were raised in a collectivist culture, individualists' fascination with personality tests and "finding your true self" might seem bewildering to you, since people in collectivist cultures tend to believe that individual differences stem not from our deep-seated personality traits but from situational or environmental variations. And the cultural differences don't end there. For example, East Asians emphasize different personality trait dimensions than the dimensions that individualist cultures usually come up with. The Chinese believe in the importance of traits such as harmony (inner peace of mind and harmonious interactions with others), face (concern with maintaining reputation or dignity), and *ren quing* (emphasis on the mutual exchange of favors in relationships). You might notice that these traits don't correspond at all to

> "People around the world are exposed to a wide, rich variety of cultural values, philosophies, economic conditions, and expectations for how to behave. One major way in which cultures differ is the degree to which they are formed around collectivist or individualist ideals."

the dimensions described in the Big Five. This means that personality tests are not necessarily cross-culturally applicable: Fundamental differences in how Western and non-Western cultures understand personality prevent us from creating a truly global measure of personality.

EVALUATING THE SOCIAL COGNITIVE PERSPECTIVE

Critics charge that the social cognitive approach to personality places too much importance on external situations and does not fully appreciate the importance of the roles that biology and genetics play in establishing our inner traits. Some critics also point out that the social cognitive perspective often fails to account for the dramatically different ways in which people react to the same

Learned helplessness describes a feeling of hopelessness and passivity caused by being unable to avoid or control traumatic events.

Reciprocal determinism is a theory that states that a person's behavior is both influenced by and influences a person's personal factors.

Self-efficacy describes a person's expectations about his or her own ability to perform a certain task.

Collectivist culture is a culture that emphasizes people's interdependence.

Interdependent construal of self refers to a person's view of himself or herself as part of a larger network of family and community members.

Individualist culture is a culture that emphasizes each person's individual rights and freedoms and deemphasizes the social roles that people play in relation to others.

Independent construal of self refers to a person's view of himself or herself as a self-directed, self-contained entity.

Allocentrism is a personality trait exhibiting the tendency to think and act in a collectivist manner.

Ideocentrism is a personality trait exhibiting the tendency to think and act in an individualistic manner.

situations. For example, some people become panicked and uncontrollably anxious during emergency situations, while others are the picture of tranquility. Or consider the fact that identical twins score closer on personality tests than fraternal twins do, even if the twins have been raised in different households (Lykken et al., 1988).

Although the social cognitive approach to personality has its limitations, it's been embraced to some extent in popular culture. It gives us valuable insight into potential connections between our thoughts, our environments, and our actions. Even better, it offers us strategies for improving our lives: For example, the social cognitive perspective suggests that if we change the way we think, we can often change the way we act, effectively creating positive situations for ourselves. If you maintain a positive attitude about your upcoming exam, for example, you may be more likely to pass it with flying colors. Pop culture has picked up on this attractive theory, and Rhonda Byrne's best-selling book *The Secret* is based around this premise: If we think positively and expect great things, great things will come to us. Unfortunately, regardless of Byrne's claims, this approach is not foolproof; social cognitive theory isn't magic, after all. It is, however, a viable start for people who want to understand their personalities and improve their lives.

Summary

WHAT IS PERSONALITY, AND HOW IS IT STUDIED? p. 244

• Personality is the style in which one interacts with the world, particularly with other people.

• Researchers study personality by using either the ideographic or the nomothetic approach to examine self-report data, observer-report data, specific behavioral data, life-events data, and physiological data.

WHAT ARE THE MAJOR TRAIT THEORIES, HOW ARE TRAITS ASSESSED, AND HOW DO GENES AFFECT INDIVIDUALS' TRAITS? p. 244

• Trait theories are sets of meaningful and distinct personality dimensions that can be used to describe how people differ from one another.

• Research has shown that genetic factors account for roughly 50 percent of individual differences for most traits. Genes may impact the chemical makeup of the brain, which in turn influences behavioral patterns and personality.

HOW DID FREUD CONCEPTUALIZE HUMAN PERSONALITY, AND HOW HAS PSYCHODYNAMIC THEORY EVOLVED OVER THE YEARS? p. 247

• Freud believed the mind is comprised of three interacting systems: the id, the ego, and the superego.

• According to Freud, human personality develops through a series of psychosexual stages.
• Post-Freudian theorists include Carl Jung (collective unconscious), Alfred Adler (inferiority complex), and Karen Horney (social factors).

WHAT ARE THE MAJOR TENETS OF THE HUMANISTIC APPROACH TO PERSONALITY? p. 250

• Humanistic theories of personality emphasize people's conscious understanding of themselves and their abilities to attain self-fulfillment.

• Humanistic theorists include Carl Rogers (self theory), Abraham Maslow (hierarchy of needs), and Dan McAdams (psychobiography).

HOW DO SOCIAL COGNITIVE THEORIES OF LEARNING AND BEHAVIOR APPLY TO THE STUDY OF PERSONALITY, AND HOW DO CONCEPTIONS OF PERSONALITY VARY ACROSS CULTURES? p. 252

• Social cognitive theories hold that personality is a function of beliefs and habits of thought acquired through unique social experiences.

• People in collectivist cultures tend to have interdependent construals of self, while people in individualist cultures tend to have independent construals of self.

Test Your Understanding

1. Which of the following concepts best explains why a person who is abused by her partner fails to leave the relationship?
   a. learned helplessness **c.** identification
   b. self-efficacy **d.** regression

2. Albert eats breakfast, lunch, and dinner at an all-you-can-eat buffet and gorges himself by eating as much as he wants of everything available. According to Freud, Albert's eating is driven by:
   a. his ego. **c.** his id.
   b. his superego. **d.** the reality principle.

3. James compulsively bites his nails. Which of the following would Freud most likely have attributed this behavior to?
   a. His superego perceives nail biting as an acceptable form of pleasure.
   b. He is fixated at the oral psychosexual stage.
   c. He uses nail biting as a sublimation defense mechanism.
   d. His nail biting is a reaction formation.

4. Although Roger is usually a happy-go-lucky kind of person, on Sunday he was feeling sad, and nothing his friends did seemed to cheer him up. Roger's sadness is an example of:
   a. a personality. **c.** a state.
   b. a trait. **d.** a factor.

5. Which of the following statements about traits is true?
   a. Traits are temporary.
   b. Fraternal twins typically share more traits than identical twins do.
   c. There are only five traits.
   d. Traits may be inherited.

6. A researcher conducts a study identifying the relationship between personality traits in different cultural groups. What is the researcher using?
   a. the five-factor model **c.** the idiographic approach
   b. reticular formation **d.** the nomothetic approach

7. Michael is shy and will not ask out the girl he likes on a date because he is afraid she will say no. Which of the following is a possible explanation for his behavior?

   a. Michael is using the behavioral inhibition system (BIS) of his brain.
   b. Michael has a sensitive reticular formation area in his brain.
   c. Michael is using the behavioral activation system (BAS) of his brain.
   d. Michael uses projection as a defense mechanism.

8. Karen is a hiring manager at her workplace. She wants to assess whether the personalities of those she interviews are compatible with the company's work environment. Which of the following might she do to best assess the job compatibility of those she interviews?

   a. Assess their archetype.
   b. Assess their heritability for specific traits.
   c. Conduct factor analysis.
   d. Administer a personality inventory.

9. Axel considers himself an extremely caring person, and others believe him to be caring as well. He apologizes profusely when he does something that hurts a friend's feelings but will not apologize when he hurts his brother's feelings. This demonstrates:

   a. heritability.
   b. psychic determinism.
   c. the consistency paradox.
   d. the reality principle.

10. Ryan and Susan disagree about what causes some people to give a lot of money to charity. Ryan believes the most important factor is how much money a person has. Susan believes the most important factor is whether a person has a generous personality. Ryan and Susan's disagreement is an example of:

    a. the person-situation controversy.
    b. the nature versus nurture debate.
    c. the reality principle.
    d. factor analysis.

11. Tim and Tom are twins. Tim is introverted, but Tom is extroverted. Which of the following statements is true about them?

    a. Tim is agreeable while Tom is antagonistic.
    b. They are more likely to be fraternal twins than identical twins.
    c. Tom uses the behavioral inhibition system (BIS) while Tim uses the behavioral activation system (BAS).
    d. They are both likely to battle anxiety.

12. Mark teases Marion and calls her names, although he thinks about her a lot when he's not with her and likes spending time with her. Which of the following defense mechanisms might Mark be using?

    a. projection
    b. identification
    c. regression
    d. reaction formation

13. Erica is angry at her boyfriend. When her sister asks her if she is going to the mall today, Erica screams that it's none of her business. What defense mechanism might Erica be using?

    a. sublimation
    b. projection
    c. displacement
    d. identification

14. Which of the following is LEAST likely to be considered an archetype?

    a. the father
    b. the warrior
    c. the secretary
    d. the hero

15. Samantha wants to be the best at everything she does and often is competitive with others. Which of the following would best account for her personality?

    a. She has a highly evolved self-concept.
    b. She does not share in the collective unconscious.
    c. She has an inferiority complex.
    d. She has unconditional positive regard for others.

16. According to Carl Rogers's self theory, which of the following would LEAST help a person develop his or her "real" self?

    a. experiencing unconditional positive regard from others
    b. living according to his or her own wishes
    c. receiving empathy
    d. rejecting his or her desires

17. The quote from the theologian and scholar Erasmus, "When I have a little money I buy books … if any is left I buy food and clothes," could be best viewed as which of the following?

    a. strong self-esteem
    b. a quick progression through Maslow's hierarchy of needs
    c. an inversion of Maslow's hierarchy of needs
    d. an attachment need

18. Which of the following is NOT true of the humanistic approach to personality?

    a. It champions cultivating a positive-self concept.
    b. It views humans as dynamic.
    c. It focuses on the individual.
    d. It is based on psychodynamic theory.

19. Misha is strongly tied to his family and sends them money even though they live in another country. Which of the following is most likely true about Misha?

    a. He has an independent construal of self.
    b. He was raised in a collectivist culture.
    c. He has little self-efficacy.
    d. He is ideocentric.

20. Which of the following would a person who has a strong internal locus of control be most likely to do?

    a. watch a basketball game on television instead of studying
    b. practice throwing the ball with a fellow teammate before team practice begins
    c. blame his or her parents for his or her failures
    d. eat high-cholesterol foods

Remember to check www.thethinkspot.com for additional information, downloadable flashcards, and other helpful resources.

PSYCHOLOGICAL SCIENCE

Short Report

Facebook Profiles Reflect Actual Personality, Not Self-Idealization

Mitja D. Back, Juliane M. Stopfer, Simine Vazire, Sam Gaddis, Stefan C. Schmukle, Boris Egloff and Samuel D. Gosling

More than 700 million people worldwide now have profiles on on-line social networking sites (OSNs), such as MySpace and Facebook (ComScore, 2008); OSNs have become integrated into the milieu of modern-day social interactions and are widely used as a primary medium for communication and networking (boyd & Ellison, 2007; Valkenburg & Peter, 2009). Despite the increasing integration of OSN activity into everyday life, however, there has been no research on the most fundamental question about OSN profiles: Do they convey accurate impressions of profile owners?

A widely held assumption, supported by content analyses, suggests that OSN profiles are used to create and communicate idealized selves (Manago, Graham, Greenfield, & Salimkhan, 2008). According to this *idealized virtual-identity hypothesis,* profile owners display idealized characteristics that do not reflect their actual personalities. Thus, personality impressions based on OSN profiles should reflect profile owners' ideal-self views rather than what the owners are actually like.

A contrasting view holds that OSNs may constitute an extended social context in which to express one's actual personality characteristics, thus fostering accurate interpersonal perceptions. OSNs integrate various sources of personal information that mirror those found in personal environments, private thoughts, facial images, and social behavior, all of which are known to contain valid information about personality (Ambady & Skowronski, 2008; Funder, 1999; Hall & Bernieri, 2001; Kenny, 1994; Vazire & Gosling, 2004). Moreover, creating idealized identities should be hard to accomplish because (a) OSN profiles include information about one's reputation that is difficult to control (e.g., wall posts) and (b) friends provide accountability and subtle feedback on one's profile. Accordingly, the *extended real-life hypothesis* predicts that people use OSNs to communicate their real personality. If this supposition is true, lay observers should be able to infer the personality characteristics accurately of OSN profile owners. In the present study, we tested the two competing hypotheses.

Method

Participants

Participants were 236 OSN users (ages 17–22 years) from the most popular OSNs in the United States (Facebook; N = 133, 52 male, 81 female) and Germany (StudiVZ, SchuelerVZ; N = 103, 17 male, 86 female). In the United States, participants were recruited from the University of Texas campus, where flyers and candy were used to find volunteers for a laboratory-based study of personality judgment. Participants were compensated with a combination of money and course credit. In Germany, participants were recruited through advertisements for an on-line study on personality measurement. As compensation, they received individual feedback on their personality scores.

To ensure that participants did not alter their OSN profiles, we saved their profiles before the subject of OSNs was raised. Scores on all measures were normally distributed.

Measures

Accuracy criteria. Accuracy criteria (i.e., indices of what profile owners were actually like) were created by aggregating across multi-

In Chapter 16, you read about Maslow's Hierarchy of Needs (p. 251). What needs do social networking sites such as Facebook fulfill?

Think about what you learned about research methods in Chapter 2. How does this step demonstrate good research practice? What might have happened had the researchers not thought to do this?

Review the "Big Five" in Chapter 16 (p. 245).

ple personality reports, each of which measured the Big Five personality dimensions (John, Naumann, & Soto, 2008). In the U.S. sample, profile owners' self-reports and reports from four well-acquainted friends were obtained using the Ten Item Personality Inventory (TIPI; Gosling, Rentfrow, & Swann, 2003). In the German sample, self-reports on the short form of the Big Five Inventory (BFI-10; Rammstedt & John, 2007) and the NEO Five-Factor Inventory (Costa & McCrae, 1992) were combined.

Ideal-self ratings. We measured ideal-self perceptions by rephrasing the TIPI and the BFI-10 rating instructions: Participants were asked to "describe yourself as you ideally would like to be."

Observer ratings. Observer ratings (how profile owners were perceived) were obtained from 9 (U.S. sample) and 10 (German sample) undergraduate research assistants, who perused each OSN profile without time restrictions and then rated their impressions of the profile owners using an observer-report form of the TIPI (U.S. sample) or BFI-10 (German sample). Each observer rated only profiles of participants from his or her own country. Observer agreement (consensus) was calculated within each sample using intraclass correlations (ICCs) for both single, ICC(2,1), and aggregate, ICC(2, k), ratings. Consensus was then averaged across samples using Fisher's r-to-z transformation (see Table 1, column 1).

Analyses

In each sample, we determined accuracy by correlating the aggregated observer ratings with the accuracy criterion. To gauge the effect of self-idealization, we computed partial correlations between profile owners' ideal-self ratings and aggregated observer ratings, controlling for the accuracy criterion; this procedure removed the reality component from ideal-self ratings to leave a pure measure of self idealization.[1] To determine whether results were consistent across samples, we computed a dummy-coded variable, "U.S. versus German sample," and ran general linear models, including all interactive effects. No significant interactions emerged. Thus, to obtain the most robust estimates of the effect sizes, we first z-standardized all data within each sample, then combined the samples, and then ran the analyses again. To provide an estimate of accuracy and self-idealization effects for a single observer (not inflated by aggregation), we also calculated the effects separately for each observer and then averaged across observers using Fisher's r-to-z transformation (Hall & Bernieri, 2001). Significance testing was done by means of one-sample t tests, using observer as the unit of analysis.

Results and Discussion

Our results were consistent with the extended real-life hypothesis and contrary to the idealized virtual-identity hypothesis. Observer accuracy was found, but there was no evidence of self-idealization (see Table 1), and ideal-self ratings did not predict observer impressions above and beyond actual personality. In contrast, even when controlling for ideal-self ratings, the effect of actual personality on OSN impressions remained significant for nearly all analyses. Accuracy was strongest for extraversion (paralleling results from face-to-face encounters) and openness (similar to research on personal environments). Accuracy was lowest for neuroticism, which is consistent with previous research showing that neuroticism is difficult to detect in all zero-acquaintance contexts (Funder, 1999; Kenny, 1994). These results suggest that people are not using their OSN profiles to promote an idealized virtual identity. Instead, OSNs might be an efficient medium for expressing and communicating real personality, which may help explain their popularity.

Our findings represent a first look at the accuracy of people's self-portrayals on OSNs. To clarify the processes and moderating factors involved, future research should investigate (a) older users and other OSNs, (b) other personality traits, (c) other forms of impression management,

Neuroticism is a mental disorder accompanied by disturbances such as anxieties or phobias.

Experimenters compared average observer ratings with participants' ideal-self ratings to come to their conclusions.

Table 1 Consensus, Accuracy, and Self-Idealization: Agreement Among Observer Ratings Elicited by Facebook Profiles and Correlations With Actual Personality and the Ideal Self

Observer rating	ICC (consensus)	Actual personality			Ideal self $r_{partial}$ (self-idealization)
		r (accuracy)	$r_{partial}$	r	
Extraversion		.39***	.32***	.13	.01
Average observer	.81***	.25***	.21***	.08*	.00
Single observer	.31***				
Agreeableness		.22**	.20*	.16	.08
Average observer	.59***	.11**	.11**	.08*	.04
Single observer	.13***				
Conscientiousness		.27**	.26**	.05	-.02
Average observer	.77***	.17***	.16***	.03	-.01
Single observer	.27***				
Neuroticism		.13	.13	.12	.11
Average observer	.48***	.06	.06*	.04	.04
Single observer	.09***				
Openness		.41***	.37***	.24**	.11
Average observer	.72***	.24***	.21***	.14***	.06
Single observer	.23***				

Note: Consensus among observers was calculated using the intraclass correlation (ICC). Accuracy was determined by correlating observer ratings with the criterion measure of actual personality. The effect of self-idealization was determined by the partial correlation between the ideal-self ratings of the profile owners and observer ratings, controlling for the criterion measure of actual personality. In addition, the table shows simple correlations between the criterion measure of actual personality and observer ratings, as well as partial correlations between the criterion measure of actual personality and observer ratings, controlling for ideal-self ratings. In the case of single-observer scores, means of the correlations for single observers are presented.

* $p_{rep} > .95$. ** $p_{rep} > .99$. *** $p_{rep} > .999$.

(d) the role of specific profile components (e.g., photos, preferences), and (e) individual differences among targets (e.g., self-monitoring) and observers (e.g., OSN experience).

Declaration of Conflicting Interests

The authors declared that they had no conflicts of interests with respect to their authorship and/or the publication of this article.

Note

1. As expected, accuracy criteria and ideal-self ratings were moderately correlated, mean $r = .28$ (neuroticism: $r = .08$; extraversion: $r = .36$; openness: $r = .33$; agreeableness: $r = .22$; conscientiousness: $r = .26$).

In the first reading (p. 32), you learned the definition of "prep." What does it mean that these data have different prep? How might this affect the results of the study?

References

Ambady, N., & Skowronski, J. (Eds.). (2008). *First impressions*. New York: Guilford.

Boyd, D.M., & Ellison, N.B. (2007). Social network sites: Definition, history, and scholarship. *Journal of Computer-Mediated Communication, 13*, 210–230.

ComScore. (2008). *Social networking explodes worldwide as sites increase their focus on cultural relevance.* Retrieved August 12, 2008, from http://www.comscore.com/press/release.asp?press =2396

Costa, P.T., Jr., & McCrae, R.R. (1992). Revised *NEO Personality Inventory (NEO-PI-R) and NEO Five-Factor Inventory (NEOFFI) professional manual.* Odessa, FL: Psychological Assessment Resources.

Funder, D.C. (1999). *Personality judgment: A realistic approach to person perception.* San Diego, CA: Academic Press.

Gosling, S.D., Rentfrow, P.J., & Swann, W.B., Jr. (2003). A very brief measure of the Big Five personality domains. *Journal of Research in Personality, 37*, 504–528.

Hall, J.A., & Bernieri, F.J. (Eds.). (2001). *Interpersonal sensitivity: Theory and measurement.* New York: Erlbaum.

John, O.P., Naumann, L.P., & Soto, C.J. (2008). Paradigm shift to the integrative Big Five trait taxonomy: History, measurement, and conceptual issues. In O.P. John, R.W. Robins, & L.A. Pervin (Eds.), *Handbook of personality: Theory and research* (pp. 114–158). New York: Guilford.

Kenny, D.A. (1994). *Interpersonal perception: A social relations analysis.* New York: Guilford.

Manago, A.M., Graham, M.B., Greenfield, P.M., & Salimkhan, G. (2008). Self-presentation and gender on MySpace. *Journal of Applied Developmental Psychology, 29*, 446–458.

Rammstedt, B., & John, O.P. (2007). Measuring personality in one minute or less: A 10-item short version of the Big Five Inventory in English and German. *Journal of Research in Personality, 41*, 203–212.

Valkenburg, P.M., & Peter, J. (2009). Social consequences of the Internet for adolescents: A decade of research. *Current Directions in Psychological Science, 18*, 1–5.

Vazire, S., & Gosling, S.D. (2004). E-perceptions: Personality impressions based on personal websites. *Journal of Personality and Social Psychology, 87*, 123–132.

Online social networking sites might be an efficient medium for expressing and communicating real personality, which may help explain their popularity.

PSYCHOLOGICAL DISORDERS

WHAT ARE MENTAL DISORDERS?
WHAT ARE THE POSSIBLE CAUSES
OF MENTAL DISORDERS?
WHAT ARE THE MAJOR TYPES
OF MENTAL DISORDERS, AND
WHAT ARE THEIR CHARACTERISTICS?

Imagine

that, one by one, your friends and family are being replaced by imposters. They look the same and sound the same, but you are certain that these people are fraudsters who, for some reason, are impersonating your loved ones. Although this scenario may sound like the plot of the science-fiction movie *Invasion of the Body Snatchers*, it is all too real for people suffering from Capgras syndrome.

Named after French psychiatrist Jean Marie Joseph Capgras, who diagnosed the disorder in 1923, Capgras syndrome is a rare condition that causes people to suffer from the delusion that one or more of their close friends or family members has been replaced by an imposter. In 2005, *Saturday Night Live* actor and Capgras sufferer Tony Rosato was arrested for repeatedly complaining to police that his wife and daughter had gone missing and been replaced by doubles. Some sufferers even believe that they themselves have been duplicated, causing them to doubt their own identity when they look in a mirror. The disorder often occurs in

conjunction with traumatic brain injuries, although sufferers are often mentally lucid in all other respects.

Neuroscientist Vilayanur Ramachandran believes that Capgras syndrome may be caused by damage to the neural pathways leading from the fusiform gyrus (the area of the brain responsible for face recognition) to the amygdala (the part of the brain responsible for generating an emotional response to an event). Once damage occurs, the sufferer is able to recognize a person's face, but does not feel the emotional response usually associated with seeing a loved one. This emotional detachment leads them to believe that the person must be an imposter.

Capgras syndrome is rare, but like many disorders of its kind, we seek to understand it in order to bring us closer to understanding human nature. Each year, nearly 2.1 million people are admitted as inpatients to American mental hospitals and psychiatric units (U.S. Census Bureau, 2002). These persons suffer from a wide variety of psychological problems, such as depression and anxiety, which are more common than Capgras syndrome but no less debilitating. So how are psychological disorders categorized? What causes them, and how can they be identified?

<<< While many stars quickly deny accusations of mental illness, actress Glenn Close embraces them. She and her sister Jessie— founders of the "BringChange2Mind" campaign that works to abolish the stigma of mental disorders—are all too aware of the impact such illnesses can have on a family. Jessie suffers from bipolar disorder, an illness that went undiagnosed for 47 years due to a lack of knowledge and the shame associated with admitting that there was something "wrong." Jessie's son was later diagnosed with schizo-affective disorder. "What mental health needs," Close argues, "is more sunlight, more candor, more unashamed conversation about illnesses that affect

CHAPTER

Most people agree that a mother who throws herself in front of a train while holding her young child is not behaving normally. But how do we distinguish between someone who is temporarily unable to get out of bed after going through a traumatic divorce, and someone who is suffering from severe depression? How do we know which person is likely to recover after a period of grieving and which person needs immediate counseling? **Abnormal psychology**, or **psychopathology**, is the study of disorders of mind, mood, and behavior.

A precise definition for a psychological disorder is difficult to put into words—behavior that one person might see as a symptom of mental illness, another person may view as creative eccentricity. The American Psychiatric Association's (APA) *Diagnostic and Statistical Manual of Mental Disorders* (DSM-IV-TR) is the current authoritative scheme for classifying psychological disorders. It defines a mental disorder as a disturbance in a person's emotions, drives, thought processes, or behavior that:

- involves serious, prolonged distress
- impairs the person's ability to maintain social and occupational relationships
- is not a normal response to an event
- cannot be explained by poverty, prejudice, or other social forces
- is viewed by mental health professionals as persistently harmful, deviant, distressful, and dysfunctional.

characteristics of thought or behavior that indicate a potential mental disorder. A combination of interrelated symptoms observed in an individual is known as a **syndrome**. For example, a child with Asperger's syndrome might display symptoms such as performing repetitive rituals, interacting inappropriately with peers, and making clumsy, uncoordinated movements. A syndrome is considered to be a mental disorder if it involves impairment of functioning, is internally driven, and is not under voluntary control.

Sometimes a person may suffer from two or more mental disorders, a condition known as **comorbidity**. For example, a patient may simultaneously experience both depression and anxiety. Often, substance abuse problems such as alcoholism are linked to mental illness. Attempts to self-medicate symptoms of mental illness by abusing alcohol or prescription drugs are

existence of a mental disorder and substance abuse is referred to as **dual diagnosis**.

When a person is diagnosed with a physical or mental illness, he or she is given a **prognosis**—a prediction of the typical course of the disease and the likelihood of recovery. Just as some people respond to chemotherapy while others succumb to cancer, treatment of mental illness and subsequent recovery depends on a number of factors, including the individual patient and the severity of the disease.

DIAGNOSING PSYCHOLOGICAL DISORDERS

The *DSM-IV-TR* (the fourth edition of the manual, updated as a 2000 "text revision") is the American Psychiatric Association's current official guide for diagnosing mental disorders. (A fifth edition of this manual is scheduled to be released in early 2013.) It provides a complete list of approximately 250 disorders, each defined in terms of significant behavior patterns. Mental health professionals use this guide to give a **psychological diagnosis**, or assign a label to a person's mental disorder by identifying and classifying patterns of behavior. For example, a person who is hallucinating, talking incoherently, suffering from delusions, and acting socially withdrawn may be classified as schizophrenic. Classifying mental illnesses is helpful for clinicians who, thanks to the *DSM-*

Axes of Diagnosis

Chronic illnesses that may affect mental health

General Medical Conditions

Axis III

Maladaptive personality patterns

Personality Disorders/ Mental Retardation

Axis II

Problems in physical surroundings that may affect diagnosis, treatment, and outcome, e.g. death of loved one, loss of job

Psychosocial and Environmental Problems

Axis IV

Psychological disorders that impair functioning

Clinical Disorders

Axis I

Global Assessment of Functioning

Axis V

Overall judgment of current functioning, e.g. mental, social, occupational

The *DSM-IV-TR* divides mental health disorders into five categories, or axes.

IV-TR, have a common shorthand language, common understandings of the causes of particular mental disorders, and comprehensive treatment plans for each disorder. However, while they provide clinicians with a common language, labels do very little to describe a specific individual. Proper diagnosis and treatment must be centered around the careful understanding of every individual's situation.

LABELING PSYCHOLOGICAL DISORDERS

While it can be helpful for psychologists and psychiatrists to categorize psychological illnesses, labels can lead to damaging preconceptions. Psychologist David Rosenhan (1973) recruited eight mentally healthy volunteers and had them attempt to gain admission to various psychiatric facilities. The volunteers complained of hearing voices in their heads that were saying the words *empty*, *hollow*, and *thud*. The volunteers gave false names and occupations, but they answered all other questions truthfully, describing real relationships with friends, colleagues, and family members. All eight were admitted into the psychiatric facilities, and seven were diagnosed with schizophrenia. The clinicians later interpreted normal behavior, such as the volunteers' taking

notes or pacing the corridors out of boredom, as symptoms of mental illness.

Psychiatrist Thomas Szasz (1960) argued that the notion of mental illness is a myth. He believed that disease can affect only the body, whereas there is no evidence for the biological

> A precise definition for a psychological disorder is difficult to put into words—behavior that one person might see as a symptom of mental illness, another person may view as creative eccentricity.

Abnormal psychology is the study of disorders of mind, mood, and behavior.

Psychopathology see *abnormal psychology*.

Symptom is a characteristic of thought or behavior that indicates a potential mental disorder.

Syndrome is a combination of interrelated symptoms observed in an individual.

Comorbidity is a condition in which a person suffers from two or more mental disorders.

Dual diagnosis is the comorbid existence of a mental disorder and substance abuse.

Prognosis is a prediction of the typical course of a disease and the likelihood of recovery.

Psychological diagnosis is a label for a person's mental disorder assigned by identifying and classifying patterns of behavior.

Clinical disorders in Axis I and personality disorders in Axis II are further divided into diagnostic categories.

Disorder	Examples
Anxiety disorders	Phobias, panic disorder, posttraumatic stress disorder, obsessive–compulsive disorder
Mood disorders	Depression, mania, bipolar disorders
Somatoform disorders	Hypochondria, conversion disorders
Schizophrenia and psychotic disorders	Schizophrenia, delusional disorders
Dissociative disorders	Multiple personality, dissociative amnesia
Disorders usually diagnosed in infancy, childhood, or adolescence	ADHD, learning disabilities, autism, hyperactivity disorder
Delirium, dementia, amnesia, and other cognitive disorders	Alzheimer's, Parkinson's
Eating disorders	Anorexia nervosa, bulimia nervosa
Substance-related disorders	Alcohol dependence, nicotine dependence
Sexual and gender-identity disorders	Hypoactive sexual desire disorder, male erectile disorder, vaginismus
Impulse-control disorders not classified elsewhere	Kleptomania, pyromania, pathological gambling
Sleep disorders	Insomnia, sleepwalking, narcolepsy
Adjustment disorders	Mixed anxiety, conduct disturbance
Personality disorders	Borderline personality disorder, antisocial personality disorder, narcissistic personality disorder

causes of mental illness. According to Szasz, a person who is locked away because he is labeled as mentally ill is being locked away because he behaves differently from other people. Szasz argued that as long as people don't pose a threat to others, they should have the same rights and freedoms as everybody else. Some psychologists believe that labeling people as mad can suppress creativity and individuality: People who don't want to risk being thought of as "crazy" or "disturbed" aren't likely to put forward controversial or alternative ideas. Vincent van Gogh walked a fine line between genius and madness, but if he had been locked away without his art materials, the world would be deprived of several cultural masterpieces.

It's not uncommon for mental illness to walk hand in hand with cultural stigmas. When an associate of psychologist Stewart Page (1977) called 180 people in Toronto who were advertising rooms for rent, the rooms were nearly all still available. When the associate mentioned that she was about to be released from a mental health facility, 75 percent of the rooms were suddenly no longer vacant. Mysteriously, when a second person called back later, the rooms had become available again. Recently, however, the stigma associated with mental illness seems to be disappearing. Psychological disorders are now more widely recognized as diseases of the brain rather than character impediments (Solomon, 1996), and there has been a dramatic increase in the number of public figures willing to talk about their mental health disorders. Movie stars Brooke Shields and Gwyneth Paltrow have both publicly discussed their struggles with postpartum depression, a talk show topic that would have been unthinkable just a few years ago.

"Crazy" or just slightly eccentric? Actresses Jessica Lange and Drew Barrymore portray mother–daughter pair Big Edie and Little Edie Beale in the HBO movie *Grey Gardens*. ∨∨∨
∨
∨

CULTURAL VARIATIONS

What passes for normal behavior in one culture may look remarkably abnormal in another. **Cultural relativity** refers to the need to consider the individual characteristics of a culture in which a person with a disorder was raised in order to diagnose and treat it (Castillo, 1997). For example, in most Asian cultures, mental illness is considered shameful. As a result, many Asian people suffering from disorders such as depression or schizophrenia report bodily symptoms rather than mental ones because physical illness is more acceptable than mental illness (Federoff & MacFarlane, 1998).

Some disorders, known as **culture-bound syndromes**, are limited to specific cultural groups. For example, Koro is a psychological disorder primarily found in South Asian and East Asian countries in which the sufferer believes that his or her external genitals (or breasts in females) are retracting into the body, and that this will cause death. Tajin kyofusho (TKS) is a social anxiety disorder found primarily in Japan that causes people to fear they will do something inappropriate in public and cause embarrassment to others. Western cultures have unique disorders too—anorexia and bulimia nervosa are rarely found outside of North America and Western Europe.

Cultural values influence not only manifestations of particular disorders, but also their labels. It might seem difficult to believe now, but homosexuality was classified as a mental disorder by the American Psychiatric Association until 1973. In the 1940s, smoking was considered a harmless social pastime; less than forty years later, nicotine dependence was added to the APA's list of psychological disorders.

HISTORICAL PERSPECTIVES OF PSYCHOLOGICAL DISORDERS

People unlucky enough to be considered "mad" in the Middle Ages were caged, beaten, burned, exorcised, or castrated in vain attempts to cure them of their aberrant behaviors. Fortunately, the **medical model**—the concept that psychological abnormalities are diseases that, like biological diseases, have symptoms, causes, and cures—emerged in the 1800s. Reformers such as French physician Philippe Pinel (1745–1826) and German psychiatrist Emil Kraepelin (1856–1926) worked on developing a classification system of psychological disorders.

Contemporary Views of Psychopathology

There are a wide range of contemporary views of psychological disorders. A clinician taking the **biological approach** looks for physical problems as a root cause—structural abnormalities in the brain, biochemical processes, or hereditary factors. For example, depression is commonly thought to be caused by a chemical imbalance in the brain.

> **❝ Some psychologists believe that labeling people as mad can suppress creativity and individuality: People who don't want to risk being thought of as "crazy" or "disturbed" aren't likely to put forward controversial or alternative ideas. ❞**

A clinician using the **psychoanalytic approach** investigates unconscious conflicts and other possible underlying psychological factors. These factors can usually be traced back to childhood. A woman who was abandoned by her father when she was a young child may be clingy with romantic partners because she has an unconscious fear of being left alone again.

The **behavioral approach** focuses on people's current behavior and the learned responses that sustain this behavior. For example, a man who convinces himself that he is a poor communicator is less inclined to practice his public speaking skills. He flubs an important job interview because he hasn't rehearsed any practice questions, reinforcing his belief that he is a poor communicator. Behavioral therapists aim to modify people's dysfunctional behaviors by analyzing the self-fulfilling prophecies or reinforcements that cause them. Similarly, the **cognitive approach** focuses on thought processes that contribute to psychological distress, such as pessimism and poor self-esteem.

Today, most mental health workers have an interdisciplinary approach to psychological disorders, taking into account all of the aforementioned approaches, as well as the social context in which the disorder takes place. The **biopsychosocial approach** recognizes that it is not possible to separate body and mind—negative emotions can contribute to physical illness, while physical abnormalities may increase the likelihood of psychological disorders.

Possible Causes of Psychological Disorders

BRAIN DAMAGE

Irreversible brain damage can result in irreversible psychological damage and in some cases, the loss of ability to function in a normal social setting. Neuroscientist Antonio Damasio (1994) discovered that the removal of a brain tumor had left one patient, a corporate lawyer named Elliot, without any emotion. When shown disturbing images of injured people, destroyed communities, and natural disasters, Elliot reported feeling nothing. His

> " Most mental disorders are episodic—they recur and subside throughout a person's life. Why does this happen? Genetic, biological, and social circumstances all play a role. "

emotional detachment cost him his job and his marriage.

Alzheimer's disease, which primarily affects the elderly, is a degenerative memory disease resulting from a deterioration of neurons that produce the neurotransmitter acetylcholine. As the disease runs its course, the patient becomes emotionally flat, then disoriented, then incontinent, and finally mentally incapable of comprehending anything at all.

MULTIPLICITY OF CAUSES

Most mental disorders are episodic—they recur and subside throughout a person's life. Why does this happen? Genetic, biological, and social circumstances all play a role.

Predisposing causes are existing underlying factors that make an individual particularly susceptible to a certain disorder. Birth defects, environmentally damaging effects on the brain, toxins such as alcohol,

and viruses or bacteria can all be predisposing causes.

Let's say that you are predisposed to alcohol dependency and have a family history of alcoholism. You have been deliberately staying away from the liquor cabinet, but when your new job becomes overwhelming, you suddenly find it harder to resist the urge to drink. **Precipitating causes** are the events in our day-to-day lives that bring on a particular disorder.

Imagine that your alcohol consumption distracts you from pressures at work. You also gain attention of friends and family members, who notice that your drinking has increased and make a concerted effort to help you quit. **Perpetuating causes** are the consequences of a disorder that help keep it going once it has manifested. These can be positive (your behavior gains attention, so you continue to pursue it) or negative (excess drinking affects your performance at work, so you drink even more to numb the emotional pain of receiving a poor review).

GENDER DIFFERENCES

Statistically, women are more often diagnosed with depression and anxiety than men. However, this discrepancy does not indicate that women are more prone to mental disorders. In Western society, it's more culturally acceptable for women to discuss their emotional problems than it is for men, so women may be more likely to seek treatment. Conversely, men have higher rates of substance abuse and antisocial personality

Behavioral approach is an approach to psychology that concentrates on observable behavior that can be directly measured and recorded.

Cognitive approach is a method of analyzing a psychological disorder that focuses on thought processes that contribute to psychological distress.

Biopsychosocial approach is a method of analyzing a psychological disorder that recognizes that it is not possible to separate body and mind; negative emotions can contribute to physical illness, while physical abnormalities may increase the likelihood of psychological disorders.

Predisposing cause is an existing underlying factor that makes an individual particularly susceptible to a certain disorder.

Precipitating cause is an event in a person's day-to-day life that brings on a particular disorder.

Perpetuating cause is a consequence of a disorder that help keep it going once it has manifested.

> " Neuroscientist Antonio Damasio discovered that the removal of a brain tumor had left one patient, a corporate lawyer named Elliot, without any emotion. When shown disturbing images of injured people, destroyed communities, and natural disasters, Elliot reported feeling nothing. His emotional detachment cost him his job and his marriage. "

Rates of Psychological Disorders in Men and Women

Men	Disorder	Women
23.8%	Alcohol abuse or dependence	4.6%
10.4%	Phobias	17.7%
2.0%	Obsessive–compulsive disorder	3.0%
5.2%	Mood disorder	10.2%
1.2%	Schizophrenia	1.7%
4.5%	Antisocial personality	0.8%

Source: Robins & Regier, 1991.

∧
∧
∧ **Percentage of American men and women who have ever experienced psychological disorders.**

disorder (characterized by reckless and irresponsible behavior) than women do. When men behave abnormally, they are more likely to drink too much and display aggressive behavior, externalizing their stress, whereas women are more likely to become depressed and hopeless, internalizing their emotional pain. This distinction suggests that gender-based socialization often plays a significant role in the development and diagnosis of psychiatric disorders.

Diagnoses may also be influenced by clinicians' expectations of each gender. Maureen Ford and Thomas Widiger (1989) conducted a study in which they sent fictitious case studies to clinical psychologists for diagnosis. One case described a patient with antisocial personality disorder (usually diagnosed in males); the other described a patient with histrionic personality disorder (usually diagnosed in females). The subject of each case study was identified as male in some cases and female in others. Ford and Widiger discovered that when the antisocial personality disorder case was identified as male, most clinicians diagnosed it correctly. However,

when the subject was identified as female, most clinicians identified it as histrionic personality disorder. Similar results occurred in reverse with the histrionic personality disorder case indicating that, like the rest of us, clinicians are subject to expectation bias when it comes to gender.

> "When men behave abnormally, they are more likely to drink too much and display aggressive behavior, externalizing their stress, whereas women are more likely to become depressed and hopeless, internalizing their emotional pain."

Anxiety Disorders

Whether we're facing a tough exam or a sky-diving expedition, we all feel anxious or fearful from time to time. But what if we persistently feel anxious even though we cannot identify the source of our worries? This type of vague, unidentifiable, prolonged anxiety may be a symptom of an **anxiety disorder**.

GENERALIZED ANXIETY DISORDER (GAD)

People who are inexplicably and continually tense and uneasy may have **generalized anxiety disorder**. Sufferers worry about multiple issues and tend to experience muscle tension, irritability, difficulty sleeping, and occasional gastrointestinal upset as a result of an overactive autonomic nervous system. For diagnosis, a person must exhibit at least three of the symptoms listed above in addition to general feelings of anxiety.

Rates of GAD have dramatically increased in Western cultures since the middle of the 20th century. According to *DSM-IV*, approximately 5 percent of people will develop GAD at some point in their lives. Of these, 60 percent will also suffer from major depression—GAD typically precedes the onset of major depressive disorder. Two-thirds of people diagnosed with GAD are women.

PHOBIAS

Does the photo of the spider cause beads of sweat to appear on your forehead while your heart pounds furiously? If so, you may be arachnophobic. **Phobias** are persistent, irrational fears of specific objects, activities, or situations. While some species of spiders may be venomous, unless you live in the Amazon Rainforest you are unlikely to encounter one, making your debilitating fear of every eight-legged arachnid unreasonable (though fairly common). Specific phobias of objects or situations are more commonly diagnosed in women than men. To be classified as a phobia, the fear must be significant enough to disrupt everyday life in some way. Someone with a *fear* of thunderstorms would not spend a week inside after seeing an ominous weather report, but someone with a *phobia* of thunderstorms might. Other common specific phobias include fear of heights (acrophobia), confined spaces (claustrophobia), and snakes (ophidophobia). Psychologist Martin Seligman (1971) suggests that people are genetically predisposed to be wary of objects and situations that posed realistic threats to humans throughout evolutionary history.

Some people suffer from **social phobias**, irrational fears of being publicly humiliated or embarrassed. Common social phobias include speaking in public, using public restrooms, or meeting new people. Social phobias are diagnosed at about the same rate for men and women.

<<< Arachnophobia is an intense, irrational fear of spiders.

PANIC DISORDER

Many people who have a panic attack mistakenly believe they are having a heart attack: They suddenly experience chest pain, shortness of breath, heart palpitations, sweating, and an intense feeling of terror and panic. This attack usually lasts around ten to15 minutes. Recurring episodes lead to a diagnosis of **panic disorder**, a condition in which sufferers come to fear the possibility of another attack. Feelings of dread often last for days or even weeks after the original attack.

For some people, panic disorder can lead to **agoraphobia**, an intense fear of being in a situation from which they cannot escape. The fear of having a panic attack in public may cause sufferers to avoid being in crowds, traveling on trains or buses, or visiting unfamiliar places.

OBSESSIVE-COMPULSIVE DISORDER (OCD)

Most of us have probably had a sudden fear that we left our car unlocked or forgot to turn off the gas. A quick check is usually enough to put our minds at ease. For many people with **obsessive–compulsive disorder**, though, a quick check wouldn't be sufficient. Obsessions are disturbing and intrusive thoughts that repeatedly interrupt a person's consciousness even if the person knows these thoughts are irrational. Compulsions are repetitive, ritualistic behaviors usually performed in response to an obsession. Someone with OCD may need to repeatedly wash her hands, persistently check to make sure a task has been completed, or step in and out of a doorway a

certain number of times whenever she enters a room.

There is a fine line between normal behavior and OCD, and we cross it when our obsessions become so persistent that they disrupt our normal lives. It is estimated that 1 percent to 3 percent of the general population suffers from OCD, with the median age of onset being 19 (Kessler et al., 2005).

How does OCD develop? Trauma, poison, or disease can all initiate the onset of OCD, which seems to be closely linked to brain abnormalities in the portions of the frontal lobes

People with obsessive–compulsive disorder feel the urge to repeatedly perform certain tasks.

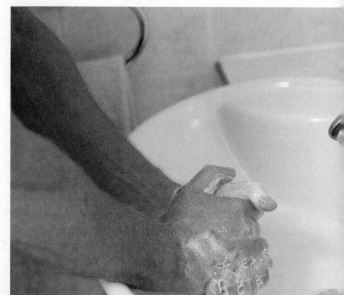

and parts of the limbic system and basal ganglia involved in the circuit controlling voluntary action. PET scans of people with OCD reveal unusually high activity in these areas (Rauch & Jenike, 1993). Sufferers report that they do not experience the normal sense of task completion when they carry out an action, prompting them to repeat it over and over again.

POSTTRAUMATIC STRESS DISORDER

Traumatic stress, caused by experiencing or witnessing out-of-control events with feelings of helplessness or fear, can cause **posttraumatic stress disorder**. Victims of abuse, accident and disaster survivors, people who live in war zones, and combat veterans are all likely to develop PTSD. A recent report by the RAND Corporation estimates that one in five American soldiers suffer from major depression or PTSD following service in Iraq or Afghanistan. The only anxiety disorder necessarily brought on by a particular traumatic experience, symptoms of PTSD will be directly linked to that trauma.

Sleeplessness, emotional numbing, high arousal, irritability, survivor's guilt and depression are all common symptoms that people suffering from PTSD experience. It is estimated that around 7 percent of the population suffers from the disorder at some point in their lives. Women are twice as likely as men to develop PTSD, a likelihood which increases if the traumatic event took place before the woman was 15 years old (Breslau et al., 1997, 1999).

EXPLAINING ANXIETY DISORDERS

We inherit Mom's green eyes and Dad's brown hair. Is it also possible to inherit tendencies toward particular psychological disorders? Evidence exists that biological factors contribute to anxiety disorders. Researchers have located specific genetic sites that may predispose people toward anxiety disorders (Goddard et al.,

2004; Hamilton et al., 2004). Twin studies also support this theory, although other research suggests that phobias are primarily caused by environmental factors rather than genetics (Skre et al., 1993).

The psychodynamic approach views anxiety as a signal that repressed urges are attempting to surface (Freud & Gay, 1977). According to this perspective, we transfer this anxiety to an outside object or situation, which then becomes the source of fear. Rather than viewing anxiety disorders as the result of unconscious fears, however, behaviorists believe that anxious behavior is learned. Remember Little Albert in Chapter 7 who was taught to fear white rats? The child's fear became a conditioned response once it was reinforced through repetition. Similarly, people with OCD find that their obsessive–compulsive habits reduce anxiety levels, reinforcing the behavior.

The dark winter months can initiate seasonal affective disorder, making us feel gloomy and lethargic.

V V V

Cognitive psychologists view anxiety disorders as the result of distorted negative thoughts. People with anxiety disorders tend to overestimate the dangers they are facing and underestimate their ability to cope with them, leading to complete avoidance of the perceived threat.

The precise cause of anxiety disorders continues to elude scientists, and is likely a complex interaction of genetics and environment that varies with each individual.

Mood Disorders

Although we can experience emotions ranging from deep despair to intense elation, we're usually somewhere in between these two extremes. People with **mood disorders**, however, experience these emotional extremes as a matter of course. Mood disorders come in two main forms: **depressive disorders**, characterized by prolonged or extreme periods of depression, and **bipolar disorders**, characterized by alternating episodes of depression and mania (a state of hyperactivity).

DEPRESSIVE DISORDERS

Clinical depression is different from the doldrums we all get into from time to time when nothing seems to be going right. Usually, people can snap out of a bad mood in a

> **Usually, people can snap out of a bad mood in a relatively short period of time, but when it lasts much longer and prevents everyday functioning, it is classified as a disorder.**

relatively short period of time, but when it lasts much longer and prevents everyday functioning, it is classified as a disorder. Because predispositions toward depression and anxiety are linked to the same genes, they are often comorbid. In one survey, 58 percent of patients diagnosed with major depression also had an anxiety disorder (Kessler et al., 2005).

There are several types of clinical depression. **Major depressive disorder (MDD)** is characterized by signs of severe depression that last for more than two weeks with no apparent cause. Symptoms include changes in appetite, sleep disturbances, feelings of guilt, poor concentration, or thoughts of suicide. MDD is the most commonly diagnosed mood disorder (21 percent of females and 13 percent of males experience it at some point in their lives).

Dysthymia, from the Greek words for "bad spirit," is a chronic, but less severe form of depression that lasts for two years or more. The lifetime risk for developing dysthymia is approximately 2 percent to 3 percent, with women again being twice as likely to suffer from the condition as men. Sometimes, bouts of major depression are superimposed over a chronic state of dysthymia, a condition known as **double depression**.

Some people find that they get depressed only at certain times of the year, particularly in the winter. This condition, known as **seasonal affective disorder (SAD)**, is characterized by increased appetite and general lethargy. It is caused by the body's reaction to low levels of light present during the winter months (Partonen & Lonnqvist, 1998). Shorter days and longer hours of darkness may cause decreased levels of serotonin—the hormone that helps to regulate a person's sleep-wake cycles, energy, and mood. Researchers believe that this may create the biological conditions for SAD.

BIPOLAR DISORDERS

What do novelists Virginia Woolf, Ernest Hemingway, and Edgar Allan Poe all have in

common? They all wrote their masterpieces while suffering from bipolar disorder. People with bipolar disorders suffer from alternating episodes of major depression and **mania**—periods of euphoria characterized by elevated self-esteem, increased talkativeness, enhanced energy, and a decreased need for sleep. People in a manic state may initially become more productive and creative but tend to suffer from poor judgment that can lead to reckless financial decisions, spending sprees, and unsafe sex. Cycles of at least one manic episode followed by at least one depressive episode are classified as Bipolar I disorder.

A milder form of mania, called **hypomania**, causes less severe mood elevations and does not interfere with normal daily functioning to the same extent as mania. People with milder forms of mania may find that increased energy levels fuel creativity, perpetuating the stereotype of the mad genius. Cycles of at least one episode of hypomania followed by at least one depressive episode are classified as Bipolar II disorder.

> **People in a manic state may initially become more productive and creative but tend to suffer from poor judgment that can lead to reckless financial decisions, spending sprees, and unsafe sex.**

People who suffer from more than four episodes of either mania or depression a year are said to go through **rapid cycling**, which occurs in approximately 10 percent of cases and is more common in women. Rapid cycling is sometimes attributed to the use of antidepressant drugs (Wehr et al., 1988).

EXPLAINING MOOD DISORDERS
Cognitive Theories of Depression

The rate of diagnosed depression is increasing with each successive generation. From 1936 to1945, the prevalence of major depression in the population was about 3 percent, with the onset of symptoms occurring around

Major depressive disorder (MDD) is a mood disorder characterized by signs of severe depression that last for more than two weeks with no apparent cause.

Dysthymia is a chronic, but less severe form of depression that lasts for two years or more.

Double depression is a condition in which bouts of major depression are superimposed over a state of dysthymia.

Seasonal affective disorder (SAD) is a mood disorder in which a person gets depressed only at certain times of the year.

Mania is a period of euphoria characterized by elevated self-esteem, increased talkativeness, enhanced energy, and a decreased need for sleep.

Hypomania is a milder form of mania that causes less severe mood elevations and does not interfere with normal daily functioning to the same extent as mania.

Rapid cycling occurs when a person with bipolar disorder experiences more than four episodes of either mania or depression a year.

Negative cognitive style describes a pattern of pessimistic or negative thoughts.

Attributional-style questionnaire is a type of questionnaire that seeks to assess how people view the events that happen in their lives based on three criteria: stability, globality, and locus.

the ages of 18 to 20. Between 1966 and 1975, rates of major depression had skyrocketed to about 23 percent, with the age of onset dropping to the early teens. What could be causing this trend? Many experts agree that depression is exacerbated, if not brought on, by **negative cognitive styles**, or patterns of thought.

Psychologist Aaron Beck (1967) noticed that depressed clients tended to negatively distort their perceptions of experiences. They made "mountains out of molehills" by viewing simple, everyday problems as major setbacks. Patients also anticipated that future events would turn out badly and had a habit of overgeneralizing, by interpreting one single negative event as a never-ending pattern of defeat. If you have a habit of using the phrase "Nothing ever goes right" whenever you lose your house keys or break a glass, you may be an occasional overgeneralizer.

Studies using **attributional-style questionnaires** support Beck's findings. Researchers gave people questionnaires containing 12 hypothetical events, half describing positive occurrences (a friend compliments you on your new haircut) and half describing negative incidents (you go

Learned helplessness describes a feeling of hopelessness and passivity caused by being unable to avoid or control traumatic events.

Schizophrenia is a mental disorder that causes a person to experience distorted perceptions, inappropriate emotions or reactions, and confusion.

Delusion is a persistent false belief.

Hallucination is a false sensory perception that a person believes to be real.

Positive symptom is a symptom that reflects an excess or distortion of normal functions, such as delusions and hallucinations.

Negative symptom is a symptom that indicates a decrease in normal functions such as attention or emotion.

these neurotransmitters by inhibiting their reabsorption into cells in the brain (see Figure 03–04 on pp. 269–273). However, while an SNRI will elevate a patient's norepinephrine and serotonin levels in only a few days, it won't cause noticeable behavioral changes for at least two weeks. Furthermore, the majority of depressed patients (approximately 75 percent) don't appear to have unusually low levels of either neurotransmitter, suggesting that there's more to depression than chemical imbalances (Valenstein, 1998).

Can ordering lox on our bagels improve our mental health? Recently, studies have linked depression to a low level of omega-3 fatty acids, typically found in cold water fish

Take the symptoms of seasonal affective disorder. Just as bears hibernate during the winter to conserve energy, humans could benefit evolutionarily from the increased appetite and extra sleep that characterize SAD during the winter months. The fact that SAD does not typically cause the levels of sadness, self-reproach, and crying characterized by other forms of depression supports the idea of an evolutionary basis (Keller & Nesse, 2005).

Have you ever seen a puppy roll onto its back with its legs in the air, in deference to its mother? Signals of helplessness by depressed people may similarly express submission and a need for care. People who are bereaved typically suffer from depressed moods characterized by sadness and crying—signs that they are looking for love and support from other people.

on a disastrous blind date). By asking people to assess the events in terms of stability (how likely they are to reoccur), globality (how important they are) and locus (who or what caused the events), the researchers were able to analyze people's attitudes. They discovered that negative thinking is not merely a symptom of depression—a depressive cognitive style can trigger the disorder (Peterson et al., 1982). Lyn Abramson, Gerald Metalsky, and Lauren Alloy (1989) proposed that negative thinking results in a sense of hopelessness. If you have a problem that you believe is permanent, will affect every other aspect of your life, and is entirely your own fault, you are more likely to become depressed.

So why can't people just "snap out of it" by thinking more positively? Martin Seligman theorized that depression can be explained by the idea of **learned helplessness**—the tendency to fail to attempt to escape a situation because of a history of repeated failures in the past (see Chapter 16). This sense of powerlessness may explain why people living in abusive households eventually stop trying to leave their abusers, even when given the opportunity.

The Depressed Brain

Depression seems to be at least partially related to the chemicals in our brains—it's often attributed to low levels of the neurotransmitters norepinephrine and serotonin. Antidepressant medications called serotonin and norepinephrine reuptake inhibitors (SNRIs) increase the levels of

> Have you ever seen a puppy roll onto its back with its legs in the air, in deference to its mother? Signals of helplessness by depressed people may similarly express submission and a need for care.

such as salmon and trout. Clinically depressed people often have a lower level of omega-3 levels in their blood, and several studies have shown that supplementing diets with omega-3 helps alleviate depression (Kiecolt-Glaser et al., 2007).

Neuroimaging studies have shown that localized areas in the brain are affected by depression. People with depression exhibit reduced activity in the left dorsolateral prefrontal cortex, while the right dorsolateral prefrontal cortex shows increased activation. Consistent with these results, studies also indicate that the brain may be bilaterally divided by positive and negative emotions, with the left hemisphere focusing on more positive feelings and the right hemisphere concentrating on negative reactions (Heller et al., 1998).

Evolutionary Bases of Depression

Are our ancestors to blame for modern mood disorders? Some psychologists believe that depression may have evolved from simple self-protective instincts into an extreme form of self-preservation. Depressive behavior can signal a lack of threat to others, invite care, and minimize unrealistic optimism.

Biological Causes of Depression and Bipolar Disorders

Although stressful experiences can bring on periods of depression, studies have also shown that some people are genetically predisposed to mood disorders. The risks of major depression and bipolar disorder increase if you have a depressed parent or sibling (Sullivan et al., 2000). Twin studies have shown that if one identical twin has major depression or bipolar disorder, the chances that the other twin will also develop a mood disorder are between 40 percent to 70 percent (Muller-Oerlinghausen et al., 2002). Women are twice as vulnerable to major depression as men, a discrepancy not yet fully understood but explained by psychologists as a combination of psychological, social, economic, and biological factors.

> Women are twice as vulnerable to major depression as men, a discrepancy not yet fully understood but explained by psychologists as a combination of psychological, social, economic, and biological factors.

Schizophrenia

Literally meaning "split mind," **schizophrenia** is often mistaken for dissociative identity disorder, a controversial condition in which people claim to have multiple personalities. However, schizophrenia actually refers to a person's split from reality, characterized by distorted perceptions, inappropriate emotions or reactions, and confusion.

To be diagnosed with schizophrenia, a person must display two or more symptoms for at least a month. People with schizophrenia often think or speak in ways that are disorganized, illogical, or incoherent. Schizophrenics may also suffer from **delusions**, persistent false beliefs. For example, patients may believe that they are being spied on, that someone is controlling their thoughts and actions, or that people are being unfaithful to them. These delusions may be supported by illogical thinking: Psychiatrist Silvano Arieti (1955) noted the huge gap in one patient's reasoning when she asserted "The Virgin Mary was a virgin. I am a virgin; therefore I am the Virgin Mary."

A third symptom of schizophrenia is the existence of **hallucinations**—false sensory perceptions that a person believes to be real. Hearing voices is the most common type of hallucination; many schizophrenics report that they hear insulting comments or receive orders from voices inside their heads. Research using fMRI scans shows that verbal hallucinations in schizophrenics are accompanied by activity in

> *Hearing voices is the most common type of hallucination;* many schizophrenics report that they hear insulting comments or receive orders from voices inside their heads.

the brain regions normally associated with thought processing (Shergill et al., 2000). While auditory hallucinations are most common, people may also see, feel, smell, or taste things that aren't really there.

Schizophrenics often have difficulty acting appropriately in social situations. They may become catatonic and remain motionless for several hours, or they may become wildly agitated and talk or shout constantly.

Clusters of symptoms can help to categorize schizophrenia. People who show **positive symptoms** reflect an excess or distortion of normal functions, such as delusions and hallucinations. These symptoms tend to appear and disappear as the disorder recurs and goes into remission. Disorganized symptoms, such as confused speech and flat emotion, follow the same pattern. However, schizophrenics who display **negative symptoms**,

or decreases in normal functions such as attention or emotion, tend to exhibit more constant symptoms that are less responsive to antipsychotic medications.

EXPLAINING SCHIZOPHRENIA
Cognitive and Neural Abnormalities

Cognitive deficits are a core feature of schizophrenia. People with schizophrenia tend to perform poorly on many information processing tasks, particularly activities that require sustained attention. Working memory is permanently and consistently impaired, while long-term memory involving the acquisition and recall of new information may be relatively severely impaired (Saykin et al., 1991). Since it is difficult for people with schizophrenia to remember the source of a piece of information, it is likely that they will be unable to distinguish between factual information and fiction or imagination, resulting in the delusions characteristic of the disorder.

Poor cognitive function may serve as an early warning system for diagnosing children with schizophrenia. Deficits in attention and memory in childhood correlate positively to the subsequent development of the disorder. One study found that children with early-onset schizophrenia display poorer verbal memory function than older adults with the disorder (Tuulio-Henriksson et al., 2004).

Can chemical imbalances in the brain explain schizophrenia? When researchers

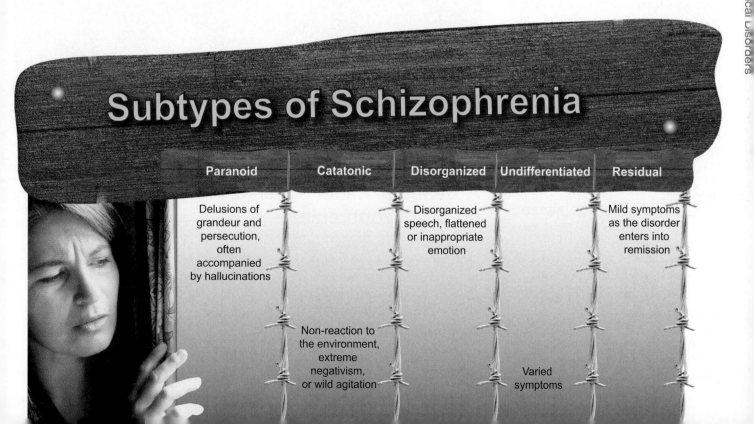

Subtypes of Schizophrenia

Paranoid	Catatonic	Disorganized	Undifferentiated	Residual
Delusions of grandeur and persecution, often accompanied by hallucinations		Disorganized speech, flattened or inappropriate emotion		Mild symptoms as the disorder enters into remission
	Non-reaction to the environment, extreme negativism, or wild agitation		Varied symptoms	

examined the brains of schizophrenic patients after death, they discovered up to six times the normal number of dopamine receptors (Seeman et al., 1993). The researchers believe that this elevated level of dopamine may intensify brain signals in schizophrenic patients, causing positive symptoms such as hallucinations and paranoia. Drugs that block dopamine transmission have proved effective at reducing many of the symptoms of schizophrenia, whereas drugs that increase dopamine action, such as cocaine or amphetamines, can exacerbate symptoms (Swerdlow & Koob, 1987).

Recent research suggests that defects in the major receptor molecules for glutamate, another neurotransmitter, may cause symptoms of schizophrenia. This would account for general cognitive defects, as well as explaining the effects of street drugs such as PCP (commonly known as "angel dust"), which interfere with glutamate transmission and temporarily induce schizophrenia-like symptoms in otherwise normal people.

Brain scans reveal that people with schizophrenia tend to have abnormal brain structures. Enlarged brain ventricles in some patients indicate a deficit in the volume of surrounding brain tissue. There is also evidence of abnormally low activity in the frontal lobes (Pettegrew et al., 1993). What is clear from studies of the schizophrenic brain is that there are clearly a number of brain regions whose compromise may contribute to schizophrenia.

Remember how the brain selectively prunes unused neurons and connections during adolescence? (See Chapter 10.) Some neuroscientists believe that abnormal pruning may lead to the loss of too many cell bodies, potentially causing symptoms of schizophrenia. Australian researcher Chris Pantelis and his colleagues took MRI scans of three groups of young people—one group of people who had recently been admitted to hospital with schizophrenia, one group of people without schizophrenia, and one group of people who had suffered from the disorder for around ten years. Pantelis discovered that the brains of the first group were shrinking at twice the rate of those without schizophrenia, suggesting that the normal developmental pruning process is accelerated in the brains of people with schizophrenia (Salleh, 2003).

^ ^ ^ Mathematician Dr. John Nash, who was played by Russell Crowe in the 2001 film *A Beautiful Mind,* suffered from a form of paranoid schizophrenia.

Genetics and Environment

Numerous studies indicate that schizophrenia has a strong genetic component. Irving Gottesman (1991) compiled data showing that the risk of developing schizophrenia increases with the degree of biological closeness to someone suffering from the disorder. While the general population has a 1 percent risk of developing schizophrenia, the chance of being diagnosed with the disorder increases to 9 percent if a sibling is afflicted. If an identical twin is diagnosed with schizophrenia, the likelihood of the other twin developing the disorder jumps to 50 percent.

The fact that dizygotic twins show a higher rate of concordance than non-twin siblings (17 percent compared to 9 percent) indicates that the prenatal environment may play a role in developing schizophrenia. Mothers who contract rubella or influenza during the second trimester of pregnancy are twice as likely to give birth to children who develop the disorder (Brown et al., 2000). However, whether this risk factor is due to the virus itself, the mother's immune response, medications taken to combat the virus, or another, unknown factor is still unclear.

If schizophrenia were entirely controlled by genes, the risk of two identical twins both developing the disorder should be close to 100 percent. That the concordance rate is half this suggests that both genetics and environment play significant roles in the development of schizophrenia. Some psychologists propose the **diathesis-stress hypothesis**, which suggests that people are genetically predisposed to a particular mental disorder but will develop the disorder only if they are exposed to environmental or emotional stress during critical developmental periods.

Personality Disorders

Personality disorders are rigid, maladaptive patterns of behavior that make it difficult for individuals to have normal social relationships. There are ten recognized types of personality disorders, divided into three clusters: odd or eccentric behaviors, dramatic or impulsive behaviors, and anxious, fearful behaviors.

ODD/ECCENTRIC PERSONALITY DISORDERS

People with eccentric personality disorders are classified as schizotypal, paranoid, or schizoid. Those with **schizotypal personality disorder** display peculiar or eccentric mannerisms, and find it difficult to form social relationships. They often hold peculiar or magical beliefs. Schizotypal personality disorder is often considered to be a mild form of schizophrenia and can occasionally develop into the full disorder.

Paranoid personality disorder is characterized by extreme suspicion and distrust of others. People with paranoid personality disorder are often jealous, critical of others, yet unable to accept criticism themselves. By quickly counterattacking perceived threats, people with this disorder may frequently become involved in legal disputes.

People with **schizoid personality disorder** are loners. Showing very little interest in others, they have few friendships and often do not marry. People with schizoid personality disorder often show emotional coldness or flattened affect.

> **People with paranoid personality disorder are often jealous, critical of others, yet unable to accept criticism themselves. By quickly counterattacking perceived threats, people with this disorder may frequently become involved in legal disputes.**

DRAMATIC/ERRATIC PERSONALITY DISORDERS

People with dramatic or erratic personality disorders exhibit impulsive behaviors. A person with **borderline personality disorder** may have unstable moods, intense, stormy personal relationships, and be manipulative and untrusting of others. Periods of depression, excessive spending, drug abuse, or suicidal behavior are also characteristic of the disorder. Lacking a sense of identity, the person may cling to others, often using suicidal behavior as a form of manipulation.

One of the most dangerous and well-researched personality disorders is **antisocial personality disorder**. Formerly called a sociopath or psychopath, a person with this disorder typically displays a complete lack of conscience by the age of 15. This usually leads to behaviors such as lying, stealing, cheating, or even murder, without remorse. Nearly three to six times as many males as females are

> **One of the most dangerous and well-researched personality disorders is antisocial personality disorder. Formerly called a sociopath or psychopath, a person with this disorder typically displays a complete lack of conscience by the age of 15.**

Diathesis-stress hypothesis suggests that people are genetically predisposed to a particular mental disorder but will develop the disorder only if exposed to environmental or emotional stress during critical developmental periods.

Personality disorder is a rigid, maladaptive pattern of behavior that makes it difficult for individuals to have normal social relationships.

Schizotypal personality disorder is characterized by peculiar or eccentric mannerisms and difficulty forming social relationships.

Paranoid personality disorder is characterized by extreme suspicion and distrust of others.

Schizoid personality disorder causes people to show very little interest in others and have few personal relationships.

Borderline personality disorder is characterized by unstable moods, instense and stormy relationships, and manipulation and distrust of others.

Antisocial personality disorder is characterized by a complete lack of conscience.

Histrionic personality disorder is characterized by a tendency to overreact to situations, excessive emotionality, and the use of manipulation to gain attention from others.

Narcissistic personality disorder is characterized by an inflated sense of self-importance and a deep need for admiration.

diagnosed with antisocial personality disorder (APA, 2000). Several brain-imaging studies have demonstrated that those who commit murder show reduced activity in their frontal lobes—the area that helps us control impulses. Adrian Raine (1999) compared PET scans of 41 murderers' brains and noted that this was especially true for those who murdered impulsively. In a follow-up study, Raine and his colleages (2000) discovered that criminals who repeatedly committed violent crimes had 11 percent less frontal lobe tissue than nonviolent control subjects, suggesting that they may have greater difficulty controlling their behavior than nonviolent criminals.

While antisocial personality disorder is primarily diagnosed in men, the frequency of **histrionic personality disorder** is two to three times greater in women (APA, 2000). Characterized by a tendency to overreact to situations, excessive emotionality, and the use of manipulation to gain attention from others, people with histrionic personality disorder often use sexually provocative behavior in order to be the center of attention.

Plenty of people believe they're more important than everyone else, but when this characteristic is taken to the extreme, it may be symptomatic of **narcissistic personality disorder**. People with this disorder have an

<<< A person who requires constant approval and reassurance may be suffering from dependent personality disorder.

Dissociative Disorders

If you have ever driven the familiar route home and then realized you can't remember anything of the journey, you are already familiar with dissociation. Our conscious minds are able to focus on the term paper due next week, while another part of our brains somehow navigates us through traffic lights and stop signs. **Dissociative disorders** are conditions in which the normal cognitive processes are fragmented, causing a sudden loss of memory or change in personality. These take several forms, and can vary in length from a matter of minutes to many years.

Dissociative amnesia is a disorder that causes sudden, selective memory loss. It is usually preempted by a traumatic event, such as rape or childhood abuse (Chu et al., 1999). Dissociative amnesia differs from retrograde amnesia (see Chapter 8), in which memory loss is typically caused by a blow to the head rather than psychological trauma.

Imagine waking up in a strange place with no idea who you were or how you got there. While it sounds like the plot to a bad Hollywood movie, **dissociative fugue** is a real condition, characterized by a sudden loss of memory accompanied by an abrupt departure from home. A person suffering from dissociative fugue may forget all personal history and take on a whole new identity.

Is it possible to have more than one personality? Psychologists are now debating the existence of **dissociative identity disorder**, formerly known as multiple personality disorder, in which a person seems to experience two or more personalities in one body. Each personality has its own voice and mannerisms, and may or may not be aware of the others. Skeptics find it suspicious that this disorder became so prevalent in the late 20th century, with the number of diagnosed cases in North America jumping from two per decade between 1930 and 1960 to more than 20,000 cases in the 1980s (McHugh, 1995). However, there are some neurological

inflated sense of self-importance and a deep need for admiration. They may have little regard for the feelings of others and be preoccupied with fantasies of their own success.

ANXIOUS/FEARFUL PERSONALITY DISORDERS

A person who consistently expresses feelings of anxiety may be suffering from an anxious or fearful personality disorder, categorized as avoidant, dependant, or obsessive–compulsive. **Avoidant personality disorder** is characterized by high levels of social anxiety and feelings of inadequacy. People with this disorder yearn for social interaction, but their extreme shyness and fear of rejection make it very difficult for them to socialize.

A person with a **dependent personality disorder** may display similar insecurities in the form of clingy, needy behavior. The person may require excessive approval and reassurance, ask others to make decisions for them, and have difficulty expressing disagreement with others in case of a loss of support or approval.

Anxiety that manifests in excessive orderliness may be a symptom of

obsessive–compulsive personality disorder. A person with this type of personality disorder may be obsessively neat, find it difficult to delegate tasks because of a fear they will be substandard, and become preoccupied with rules, schedules and order. However, people with this disorder do not feel the need to repeatedly complete ritualistic actions, distinguishing it from OCD.

> **"Is it possible to have more than one personality?** Psychologists are now debating the existence of dissociative identity disorder, formerly known as multiple personality disorder, in which a person seems to experience two or more personalities in one body."

findings that support the existence of dissociative identity disorder. Whether a person is right- or left-handed sometimes switches with personality (Henninger, 1992). In one study, ophthalmologists detected shifting visual acuity and eye-muscle balance as patients shifted between one patient and another—a change that control subjects simulating multiple personality were unable to achieve (Miller et al., 1991).

Somatoform Disorders

Somatoform disorders are characterized by physical symptoms that do not have an identifiable cause. For example, a person with **somatization disorder** may frequently and dramatically complain of vague, unverifiable symptoms such as dizziness and nausea. Although the person is not making up these symptoms, the ailments have no physical cause and treatment is often related to underlying psychological problems such as stress and depression.

    Conversion disorder is a somatoform disorder rarely seen in North America and Western Europe (although it was fairly common 100 years ago). Characterized by the sudden, temporary loss of a sensory function, a person may experience blindness, paralysis, deafness, or numbness of particular body parts. While none of the symptoms have physical causes, the disorder usually occurs when the person has been exposed to a traumatic event. For example, there was a high rate of psychological blindness among Cambodian women after the Khmer Rouge reign of terror in the 1970s.

> **A person with somatization disorder may frequently and dramatically complain of vague, unverifiable symptoms such as dizziness and nausea. Although the person is not making up these symptoms, the ailments have no physical cause and treatment is often related to underlying psychological problems such as stress and depression.**

Childhood Disorders

Some disorders are characteristic of children or may first be evident in childhood. The diagnostic criteria used to assess psychological disorders in children are less standardized and more contextualized than criteria used for adults, and diagnosis can be difficult because symptoms may differ in children and adults. According to the U.S. Surgeon General, one in five children in the United States suffers from a psychological disorder at any given time. The following disorders are just a few of the prevalent mental illnesses experienced or diagnosed in childhood.

ATTENTION-DEFICIT HYPERACTIVITY DISORDER (ADHD)

Children diagnosed with **attention-deficit hyperactivity disorder** typically find it difficult to focus their attention and are easily distracted. They may fidget, find it difficult to take turns, impulsively blurt out an answer before hearing the entire question, and consistently fail to remain seated. Affecting 3 percent to 5 percent of school-age children, ADHD is two to three times more prevalent in boys than girls. It is treated with stimulant drugs such as Ritalin or methylphenidate, which increase levels of dopamine in the brain, stimulating attentional and motivational circuits.

AUTISM

Children who fail to form normal attachments to their parents and withdraw into their own separate worlds may be suffering from **autism**, a developmental disorder that impedes social development and communication skills. Autistic children may display repetitive movements such as rocking back and forth, or self-abusive behavior such as head-banging.

    Researchers believe that autism is a polygenic disorder, meaning that when a number of particular genes combine, the risk of developing the disorder increases. In families with one autistic child, the risk of having a second child with the disorder is 3 percent to 8 percent higher than the risk for the general population. Autism has also been linked to underlying medical conditions, including metabolic disorders (untreated PKU), genetic disorders (fragile X syndrome), and developmental brain abnormalities (microcephaly). However, these disorders

Avoidant personality disorder is characterized by high levels of social anxiety and feelings of inadequacy.

Dependent personality disorder is characterized by clingy, needy behavior.

Obsessive–compulsive personality disorder is characterized by obsessive neatness, difficulty delegating tasks because of a fear the tasks will be completed in a substandard manner, and a preoccupation with rules, schedules, and order.

Dissociative disorder is a condition in which the normal cognitive processes are fragmented, causing a sudden loss of memory or change in personality.

Dissociative amnesia is a disorder that causes sudden, selective memory loss.

Dissociative fugue is a disorder characterized by a sudden loss of memory accompanied by an abrupt departure from home.

Dissociative identity disorder is a disorder in which a person seems to experience two or more personalities in one body.

Somatoform disorder is a disorder characterized by physical symptoms that do not have an identifiable cause.

Somatization disorder is a somatoform disorder characterized by vague, unverifiable symptoms such as dizziness and nausea.

Conversion disorder is a somatoform disorder characterized by the sudden, temporary loss of a sensory function.

Attention-deficit hyperactivity disorder (ADHD) is a disorder in which a person finds it difficult to focus his or her attention and is easily distracted.

Autism is a developmental disorder that impedes social development and communication skills.

Asperger syndrome is a syndrome in which a person has normal levels of intelligence and cognitive abilities but displays autistic-like social behaviors.

alone do not cause autism—most children with these conditions are not autistic.

ASPERGER SYNDROME

Autism has recently come to be viewed as part of a spectrum of disorders known as autism spectrum disorder (ASD). **Asperger syndrome**, named after Viennese physician Hans Asperger, is part of this spectrum. In 1944, Asperger wrote a paper about children who had normal levels of intelligence and cognitive abilities, but displayed autistic-like social behaviors. Often viewed as eccentric or odd, people with Asperger syndrome show marked deficiencies in social skills, have obsessive routines, and may be preoccupied with a particular subject they find interesting. The disorder was added to the *DSM-IV* in 1994.

17

Review

Summary

WHAT ARE MENTAL DISORDERS?
p. 264

● A mental disorder is a disturbance that impairs a person's ability to form social and occupational relationships, involves serious, prolonged distress, and is viewed by mental health professionals as harmful, deviant, and dysfunctional.

● Mental disorders may vary across cultures.

WHAT ARE THE POSSIBLE CAUSES OF MENTAL DISORDERS? p. 267

● Irreversible brain damage can cause psychological damage. Degenerative memory diseases such as Alzheimer's occur due to neuron deterioration in the brain.

● Predisposing factors such as genetics, birth defects, and toxins such as alcohol make individuals susceptible to particular psychological disorders.

● Environmental influences can trigger mental disorders in individuals who are biologically predisposed to develop those disorders.

WHAT ARE THE MAJOR TYPES OF MENTAL DISORDERS, AND WHAT ARE THEIR CHARACTERISTICS?
p. 268

● Anxiety disorders are characterized by persistent, often unidentifiable feelings of anxiety. Generalized anxiety disorder, phobias, panic disorder, obsessive–compulsive disorder, and post–traumatic stress disorder are all types of anxiety disorders.

● Mood disorders come in two main forms: depressive disorders, characterized by long, extreme periods of depression, and bipolar disorders, characterized by alternating episodes of depression and mania. Major depressive disorder, dysthymia, and seasonal affective disorder are all types of clinical depression.

● Schizophrenia is often characterized by delusions, hallucinations, and disorganized or catatonic behavior.

● Personality disorders are characterized by rigid, abnormal patterns of behavior that affect normal social functioning. There are three types of personality disorders: odd/eccentric, dramatic/erratic, and anxious/fearful.

● Dissociative disorders cause a sudden loss in memory or change of personality. Dissociative amnesia, dissociative fugue, and dissociative identity disorder are types of dissociative disorders.

● Somatoform disorders, including somatization disorder and conversion disorder, are characterized by physical symptoms without an identifiable cause.

● Childhood disorders are characteristic of children or first evident in childhood. Prevalent childhood disorders include ADHD, autism, and Asperger syndrome.

Test Your Understanding

1. Which of the following is an example of comorbidity?
   a. a person with undiagnosed schizophrenia
   b. a person with diagnosed schizophrenia
   c. drug abuse
   d. a person suffering from both bulimia and depression

2. The book most commonly used to diagnosis and classify mental disorders in the United States is called the:
   a. *Diagnostic and Statistical Manual of Mental Disorders*.
   b. *Axes of Diagnosis*.
   c. *Manual of Psychopathology*.
   d. *Guide to Abnormal Psychology*.

3. Prescribing medication to treat depression follows what approach related to psychopathology?
   a. the psychoanalytic approach   c. the biological approach
   b. the cognitive approach   d. the behavioral approach

4. Anya has suffered from severe depression most of her life. While still in her mother's womb, she was exposed to high levels of a chemical that affects brain development. If this exposure was a factor in Anya's later depression, the chemical Anya was exposed to may be considered what in relation to her depression?
   a. a biological circumstance   c. a precipitating cause
   b. a predisposing cause   d. a perpetuating cause

5. Kostas is addicted to gambling. He meets a lot of women at the casino he frequents who show interest in him when he wins, and this increases his desire to gamble. In relation to his gambling addiction, Kostas's winnings and the women he attracts are:
   a. precipitating causes.   c. predisposing causes.
   b. a comorbidity.   d. perpetuating causes.

6. Which of the following may contribute to the fact that women are more likely than men to be diagnosed as having some anxiety disorders?
   a. Clinical psychologists often expect women to have more anxiety problems than men, which biases their diagnoses.
   b. Women are more likely than men to seek help for their anxiety problems.
   c. Men often behave differently than women with the same anxiety problems.
   d. all of the above

7. Andy feels compelled to turn around five times when he enters a room. Which of the following might be true?

   a. He has panic disorder.
   b. He has agoraphobia.
   c. He has a social phobia.
   d. He has obsessive-compulsive disorder.

8. Which of the following is NOT true about posttraumatic stress disorder (PTSD)?

   a. Women are more likely than men to suffer from PTSD.
   b. People with PTSD may have a difficult time sleeping.
   c. PTSD can often develop without a precipitating traumatic event.
   d. Women are more likely to develop PTSD if a traumatic event occurs before they turn 15 years old.

9. Freda has felt generally sad for the past three years. However, for approximately three weeks she has felt much worse than usual and has not been eating. Freda most likely suffers from:

   a. dysthymia.
   b. major depressive disorder (MDD).
   c. double depression.
   d. rapid cycling.

10. Which of the following is true of mania?

   a. It depletes a person's sex drive.
   b. It increases a person's judgment capacity.
   c. It always accompanies rapid cycling.
   d. It may temporarily increase self-esteem.

11. Which of the following is NOT a potential cause of depression?

   a. learned helplessness
   b. high levels of omega-3 fatty acids
   c. low levels of norepinephrine
   d. a negative cognitive style

12. Ezekiel is schizophrenic and believes that government spies are trying to capture him because he is a secret agent. Ezekiel's beliefs are examples of:

   a. hallucinations.
   b. split personalities.
   c. negative symptoms.
   d. delusions.

13. Evie attempts to manipulate people who befriend her by telling them that she won't be their friend unless they do things that she wants. It is difficult to predict her moods, and she often becomes extremely angry at people with little reason. Of the following, she is most likely to suffer from:

   a. borderline personality disorder.
   b. schizotypal personality disorder.
   c. paranoid personality disorder.
   d. antisocial personality disorder.

14. Grady believes he is the smartest attorney in the law firm he just joined. He expects that he will be promoted to partner soon. When he expresses these thoughts to another attorney with whom he works, he scoffs that his colleague feels hurt by his statement and is shocked that she does not share his opinions. Which of the following disorders might Grady suffer from?

   a. narcissistic personality disorder
   b. schizoid personality disorder
   c. dissociative identity disorder
   d. dependent personality disorder

15. When Kathy and her boyfriend watch television together, he flips the channels on the remote control every 20 seconds. Kathy complains and says he must have attention deficit hyperactivity disorder (ADHD). Why does she make this statement?

   a. ADHD is characterized by an inability to focus attention.
   b. ADHD sufferers compulsively perform actions.
   c. ADHD is characterized by memory loss, which influences distractibility.
   d. ADHD is characterized by memory loss, which leads to fidgeting behavior.

16. A woman wakes up in a motel room with no idea of how she got there or who she is. Doctors examine her and find no evidence of physical trauma or damage. Which of the following is she most likely to be diagnosed as having?

   a. dissociative fugue
   b. conversion disorder
   c. retrograde amnesia
   d. dissociative identity disorder

17. Which of the following is a positive symptom of schizophrenia?

   a. auditory hallucinations
   b. decreased motivation
   c. lack of emotion
   d. There are no positive symptoms associated with schizophrenia.

18. Which of the following is NOT usually true of people with Asperger syndrome?

   a. They have below-average cognitive abilities.
   b. They can be obsessive about certain things.
   c. They have difficulty interacting with others.
   d. Their behavior sometimes seems strange.

19. Which of the following is true according to the diathesis-stress hypothesis?

   a. Mental disorder is determined solely by a person's genes.
   b. Mental disorder is determined solely by exposure to stress.
   c. People's genes predispose them to mental disorder, but they will only develop a disorder if they are also exposed to environmental or emotional stress.
   d. If one identical twin develops schizophrenia, then the other twin will also develop schizophrenia.

20. Candace suffers from panic attacks and is constantly worried that she will experience one in a crowded place where she will be unable to escape. As a result, she rarely visits malls, supermarkets, or theaters and only leaves her house for short periods. Which of the following is Candace most likely suffering from?

   a. generalized anxiety disorder
   b. a mood disorder
   c. posttraumatic stress disorder (PTSD)
   d. agoraphobia

Remember to check www.thethinkspot.com for additional information, downloadable flashcards, and other helpful resources.

PSYCHOLOGICAL THERAPIES

HOW HAS THE MENTAL HEALTH SYSTEM EVOLVED OVER THE YEARS, AND HOW IS IT STRUCTURED TODAY?

HOW DO BIOMEDICAL THERAPIES TREAT PSYCHOLOGICAL DISORDERS?

HOW DO PSYCHODYNAMIC AND HUMANISTIC THERAPIES TREAT PSYCHOLOGICAL DISORDERS?

HOW DO COGNITIVE AND BEHAVIORAL THERAPIES TREAT PSYCHOLOGICAL DISORDERS?

WHAT FACTORS MAKE PSYCHOTHERAPY AN EFFECTIVE TREATMENT, AND HOW DOES IT COMPARE IN USE TO BIOMEDICAL TREATMENTS?

In the

past, doctors often did not tell cancer patients their diagnoses. There was such discomfort surrounding the disease that those who had cancer and were treated for it were stigmatized and discriminated against. Can you imagine if your friends and family looked down upon because you were undergoing cancer treatment or treatment for another disease? Would it feel as if you wore a bright red A on your chest, similar to Hester Prynne in *The Scarlet Letter*?

Likewise, people receiving psychotherapy for depression and other mental illnesses are often looked upon as "crazy," as though they have something inherently wrong with them. To the contrary, those seeking therapy are positively and proactively helping themselves.

The good news is that the stigma surrounding psychotherapy may be alleviated with more awareness. Popular TV programs such as *Grey's Anatomy*, *Dr. Phil*, and *In Treatment* help make people aware of psychotherapy and psychological disorders. However, some have argued that these TV programs may lead to even more stigmatization by creating false conceptions of what psychotherapy is and what it can accomplish. With 24.3 million adults age 18 and older in the United States admitting to symptoms of one or more mental disorders, and the country's suicide rate nearly double the homicide rate, making treatment a hopeful prospect rather than a shameful one is imperative.

So who is working to make psychotherapy more widely accepted? In an odd twist of events, as a part of the October 2008 financial bailout, the U.S. government passed a mental-health parity law that forces insurance companies to provide the same coverage for mental-health treatment as for the treatment of other diseases and disorders. This law, disputed for 12 years after a similar one was rejected in the U.S. Senate, allows those who seek psychotherapy to get help without being discriminated against financially. Perhaps this move toward equality for mental-health patients will lead to even less stigmatization of treatment, and further aid in patients' paths to recovery.

CHAPTER **18**

Clinical Psychology and the Mental Health System

The character Paul Weston occupies a unique position in that he is both a patient and practitioner of **clinical psychology**, a field of practice and research that aims to help people suffering from psychological problems and disorders. When people find themselves struggling with the kinds of problems detailed in Chapter 17, they can turn to clinical psychology for help.

These days, seeking psychological help from a therapist is anything but uncommon. It's not unusual to hear people flippantly reference "getting their heads shrunk," or to even cite advice or directives from psychological professionals in casual conversations with friends. As you've likely noticed, therapists and therapy sessions also dot the cinematic and television landscape, from Meredith Grey discussing her commitment issues with Dr. McDreamy on *Grey's Anatomy* to Dr. Phil McGraw demanding that the troubled guests on his eponymous talk show "get real." Whether serious, as in Jamison's *An Unquiet Mind,* or tinged with humor, as in many contemporary movies and sitcoms, cultural references to psychological treatments have helped demystify and destigmatize such measures for many people. This represents a significant change,

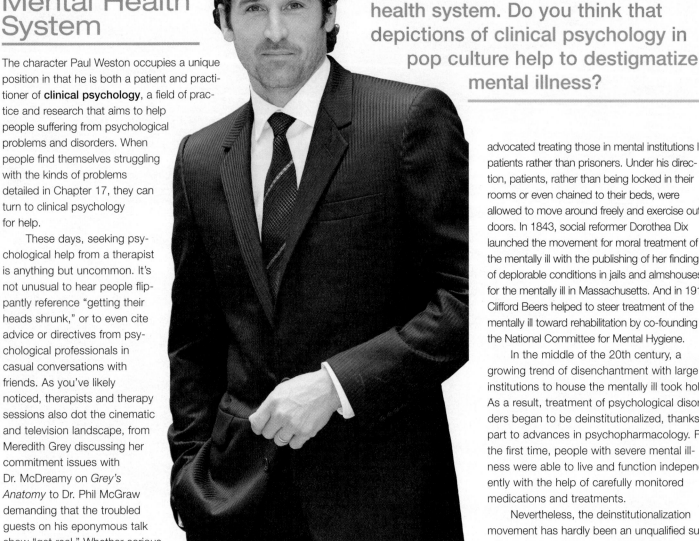

<<< Actor Patrick Dempsey stars on the hit show *Grey's Anatomy*, which occasionally dramatizes the mental health system. Do you think that depictions of clinical psychology in pop culture help to destigmatize mental illness?

and significant progress, within the realm of mental health.

THE HISTORY OF MENTAL HEALTH PRACTICES

From the middle ages through the 17th century, most people considered mental disorders to be a form of bedevilment or possession by evil spirits. As a result, treatment was ineffective—or worse. Many "treatment" methods, such as torture, hanging, and burning at the stake, were particularly cruel and inhumane. Some sufferers were even sent off in "ships of fools," relegated to a fate of either drowning or being miraculously saved by divine providence.

In 1792, Philippe Pinel, director of a large mental hospital in Paris, initiated the reform movement in the treatment of the mentally ill. He

advocated treating those in mental institutions like patients rather than prisoners. Under his direction, patients, rather than being locked in their rooms or even chained to their beds, were allowed to move around freely and exercise outdoors. In 1843, social reformer Dorothea Dix launched the movement for moral treatment of the mentally ill with the publishing of her findings of deplorable conditions in jails and almshouses for the mentally ill in Massachusetts. And in 1919, Clifford Beers helped to steer treatment of the mentally ill toward rehabilitation by co-founding the National Committee for Mental Hygiene.

In the middle of the 20th century, a growing trend of disenchantment with large institutions to house the mentally ill took hold. As a result, treatment of psychological disorders began to be deinstitutionalized, thanks in part to advances in psychopharmacology. For the first time, people with severe mental illness were able to live and function independently with the help of carefully monitored medications and treatments.

Nevertheless, the deinstitutionalization movement has hardly been an unqualified success. Lacking adequate transitional support, many patients stop taking necessary medication and end up unemployed, homeless, and unable to care for themselves. Assertive community treatments constitute a new approach toward managing the mental health system. These programs aim to help the severely mentally ill wherever they are in the community. Because each mentally ill person is assigned a multidisciplinary team including case manager, psychiatrist, nurses, and social workers, these programs are extremely expensive to maintain. However, because the programs keep mentally ill patients out of hospitals, they may actually save money in the long run.

THE STRUCTURE OF THE MENTAL HEALTH SYSTEM

When it comes to choosing a mental health professional, there is no shortage of choices.

Clinical psychology is a field of psychology that deals with the diagnosis and treatment of people with specific mental or behavioral problems.

Patient is a person with a psychological disorder who is being treated using a biomedical approach.

Client is a person with a psychological disorder who is being treated with the view that his or her psychological distress is caused by behavioral issues and faulty thought processes.

Mental health professionals take on a variety of titles and roles, depending on their education, training, expertise, and area of focus.

There is one additional distinction worth noting—that is, the one between **patient** and **client**. In general, professionals who take a biomedical approach to treating psychological disorders refer to those whom they treat as patients. In contrast, professionals who conceptualize psychological distress as "problems in living" (rather than as illness) call those who seek their help clients.

PSYCHIATRIST
Medical doctors who specialize in the treatment of psychological disorders. Because they have medical degrees, they can prescribe drugs. Some psychiatrists conduct psychotherapy sessions with patients.

PSYCHIATRIC NURSE
Have degrees in nursing with specific training for care of mental patients; generally work in hospitals or medical settings.

CLINICAL PSYCHOLOGIST
Specialists who hold doctoral degrees in psychology and have undergone extensive training in research and clinical practice.

COUNSELING PSYCHOLOGIST
Similar in training and degree to a clinical psychologist, with an emphasis on counseling.

COUNSELOR
Generally have master's degrees in counseling with less training in research and diagnostics than a clinical or counseling psychologist has; work primarily in school or institutional settings.

PSYCHIATRIC SOCIAL WORKER
Hold master's degrees in social work and have training and experience working with those with psychological problems. They usually are employed by public social-work agencies.

CLINICAL SOCIAL WORKER
Similar to psychiatric social workers, but have taken part in specialized training that has prepared them for working with psychiatrists, psychologists, and other mental health professionals.

PREVENTIVE CARE AND MENTAL HEALTH

In the past few decades, much of the focus in the field of psychiatric treatment has shifted toward preventive care—taking measures to prevent people from developing mental health problems in the first place by addressing the conditions thought to cause or contribute to them. For example, poverty, racism, and abusive households can have an enduring and significant effect on people's abilities to effectively cope with the stresses of life (Albee, 1986). Advocates for preventive care believe that reducing the incidence of these traumas in people's lives through social justice programs, community assistance, and educational opportunities will also decrease the number of people afflicted with psychological problems. Obviously, there are no easy solutions for complex social problems such as poverty; however, the investment of time, money, and resources into alleviating some of these issues is a worthy cause both from a social and mental health perspective.

The availability of care and treatment in the current mental health system remains a challenge for many people because of a shortage of qualified mental health professionals coupled with a difficult-to-navigate system that often neglects the underinsured or uninsured. Even people with health insurance often find that their insurance has strict limits on mental health care and doesn't cover treatments for certain psychological disorders. As a result, many people with psychological problems seek care and don't receive it to an adequate degree or, even worse, simply give up and continue suffering. As a result, these people's psychological problems often continue to deteriorate, with potentially tragic results. It's clear that there is still considerable room for improvement in the mental health system.

<<< Extreme poverty is just one of the social problems thought to contribute to mental illness. Do you think a difficult social environment contributes to a person's likelihood of developing psychological problems?

Biological Treatments: Biomedical Therapies

For some, biomedical therapies are a major part of an effective treatment plan. Over the past 50 years or so, **psychopharmacology**, the study of how drugs affect the mind and behavior, has led to the development of a wide array of **psychoactive medications**. These medications alleviate symptoms of mental disorders by acting on the bodily processes that may cause those symptoms.

ANTIPSYCHOTIC DRUGS

Antipsychotic drugs are a class of psychoactive medications used to treat disorders in which psychotic symptoms, such as hallucinations, paranoia, and delusions, predominate. There are two types: typical and atypical.

Although many typical antipsychotics have been around since the 1950s, they continue to be as effective as newer medications at treating psychotic illnesses such as schizophrenia. Examples of typical antipsychotics include chlorpromazine and haloperidol. These drugs effectively reduce or eliminate the positive symptoms of disorders like schizophrenia, such as delusions and hallucinations (see Chapter 17), by decreasing dopamine activity at certain synapses in the brain (Lehman et al., 1998; Lenzenweger et al., 1989). The relative effectiveness of these

drugs indicates that too much dopamine is at least partially responsible for schizophrenia (Pickar et al., 1984; Taubes, 1994). A notable limitation of typical antipsychotics, however, is that they do not treat negative symptoms. In addition, side effects of typical antipsychotics can include sluggishness, tremors, and even tardive dyskinesia, a serious and often irreversible motor disturbance in which the tongue, face, and other muscles involuntarily jerk or contract (Kaplan & Saddock, 1989). As a result of these potentially severe side effects, people with psychotic illnesses often find it difficult to continue taking antipsychotics for extended periods of time.

For those afflicted with negative symptoms of schizophrenia, such as apathy or prolonged lack of movement (see Chapter 17), atypical antipsychotics can provide relief. These newer medications can alleviate negative symptoms by altering the activity of other neurotransmitters, such as serotonin, in addition to dopamine. They are also less likely to produce the major side effects caused by typical antipsychotics because they target specific

dopamine receptors in the brain. Examples of atypical antipsychotics include clozapine, risperidone, and olanzapine. Although atypical antipsychotics generally produce fewer side effects than do typical antipsychotics, both types of drugs can cause symptoms such as dizziness, weight gain, constipation, sexual impotence in men, and nausea.

ANTIDEPRESSANTS

Given the prevalence of major depressive disorder in the United States—each year, it affects approximately 14.8 million American adults—it's no wonder that antidepressant medications have become well known to the general public in recent years (Kessler et al., 2005).

Antidepressants work to alleviate symptoms

of depression by altering how certain neurotransmitters—usually serotonin and norepinephrine—are circulated throughout the brain. Serotonin and norepinephrine are associated with arousal and feelings of well-being, and people suffering from depression often have serotonin or norepinephrine deficiencies.

The earliest form of antidepressants, most popular from the 1960s–1980s, are called tricyclics. Examples include imipramine (Tofranil) and amitriptyline (Elavil). Typically, serotonin and norepinephrine are reabsorbed by the synapses in the brain (see Chapter 3). By blocking the reuptake of these neurotransmitters, tricyclics can elevate patients' moods. However, tricyclics have a number of unpleasant side effects, including dry mouth, fatigue, and blurred vision, and are more likely to cause death in the case of an overdose than are other types of antidepressants (Anderson, 2000; Mulrow, 1999).

Selective serotonin reuptake inhibitors, or SSRIs, are a newer alternative to tricyclics. These antidepressants, which began appearing in the mid-1980s, only block the reuptake of serotonin in the brain and have relatively few side effects. Fluoxetine (Prozac), paroxetine (Paxil), and sertraline (Zoloft) are all SSRIs. Tricyclics and SSRIs tend to have similar effectiveness in treating depression, but because SSRIs have fewer unpleasant side effects, they are more popular. Testimonial evidence indicates that these drugs can be powerfully effective; ABC News political analyst George Stephanopoulos, actress Brooke Shields, and comedian Rosie O'Donnell have all publicly credited SSRIs with helping them reclaim their lives after bouts with depression. "The gray has gone away. I am living in bright Technicolor," O'Donnell wrote of her experience with the medication.

Monoamine oxidase (MAO) inhibitors are another type of antidepressant. MAO is an enzyme that metabolizes monoamines such as norepinephrine, so by inhibiting this enzyme, these drugs allow for increased amounts of norepinephrine in the brain.

Because they can have severe side effects, including lethal food and drug combinations, MAO inhibitors are usually used as a last resort, for people who don't respond to other drug therapies.

The newest types of antidepressants, atypical antidepressants, affect neurotransmitters (including serotonin, norepinephrine, and

> **"ABC News political analyst George Stephanopoulos, actress Brooke Shields, and comedian Rosie O'Donnell have all publicly credited SSRIs with helping them reclaim their lives after bouts with depression."**

dopamine) in specific combinations. Bupropion (Wellbutrin) and duloxetine hydrochloride (Cymbalta) are examples of these drugs. Interestingly, Wellbutrin, which works as an antidepressant by inhibiting the reuptake of norepinephrine and dopamine, has also been shown to be moderately effective in helping people quit smoking.

Millions of people have benefited from antidepressants—more than 38 million alone from Prozac (Goode, 2000). The title of journalist Elizabeth Wurtzel's 1994 memoir—*Prozac Nation*—serves as a facetious commentary on the pervasiveness of antidepressants in the United States. Indeed, our use of these drugs has become quite common over the last two decades, in part because of highly visible marketing campaigns. You're probably familiar with the cartoonish butterfly-chasing egg featured in Zoloft commercials or the emotionally wrought voiceovers that reverberate throughout Cymbalta ads. Some people even blithely refer to antidepressant medications as "happy pills." Yet the fact remains that antidepressants are serious, psychoactive medications. They are most effective and safe when they are used in conjunction with psychotherapy, and they should be taken only under close supervision of a physician who is hyperaware of the circumstances of treatment. Recent findings of a correlation between antidepressant use and increased suicide rates among children and young adolescents only strengthen the case for careful physician supervision (Olfson et al., 2006).

ANTI-ANXIETY MEDICATION

For those suffering from anxiety disorders, anti-anxiety medications can provide relief. These drugs reduce the symptoms, such as tension and nervousness, associated with many anxiety disorders by slowing down the central nervous system's activity. The first anti-anxiety drugs were barbiturates, commonly known as tranquilizers, and were highly addictive. **Benzodiazepines**, a safer class of drugs, largely replaced barbiturates during the 1960s. These medications, including Valium and Xanax, are mostly effective for treating generalized anxiety disorder and panic disorder. Side effects

can include drowsiness and a decline in motor coordination. Although benzodiazepines are less addictive than barbiturates, they have several unpleasant withdrawal symptoms. Furthermore, many practitioners believe that anti-anxiety drugs relieve the symptoms of the disorder without addressing the underlying causes; these practitioners often recommend treatment plans that consist of both medication and therapy. Other anxiety disorders, including OCD and PTSD, are more likely to be treated with antidepressants, specifically SSRIs.

Widespread advertising for antidepressant medications has helped make them acceptable to the mainstream. What do you think of such ads? Are they helpful or harmful?

MOOD-STABILIZING DRUGS

When people experience the rapid mood changes that are the hallmark of bipolar disorder, doctors often prescribe mood-stabilizing drugs—namely, lithium—in response. Lithium is a simple salt element that has been shown to benefit about seven in ten bipolar patients when

used on a long-term basis (Solomon et al., 1995). Exactly how and why the drug works remains a mystery to medical professionals. The important thing is, however, that it *does* work for so many afflicted with the disorder; journalist and television host Jane Pauley, diagnosed as bipolar in 2001, says of lithium: "It just is stabilizing. It allows me to be who I am."

ELECTROCONVULSIVE THERAPY

If you have ever read Ken Kesey's *One Flew Over the Cuckoo's Nest*, or seen the film adaptation, you likely have a very negative impression of **electroconvulsive therapy (ECT)**. Early uses of ECT—which involves sending electric shocks to patients' brains—were largely ineffective and, even worse, barbaric. However, with modern technology and careful medical supervision, ECT is now used to successfully treat people suffering from severe depression who do not respond to either psychotherapy or antidepressant medications.

ECT today is administered much differently than it used to be. Practitioners use muscle relaxants and other drugs to block nerve and muscle activity so the patient feels little pain and is not in danger of physical harm. Studies have shown that up to 80 percent of patients experience significant improvement in their depressive symptoms after six to 12 ECT sessions over the course of two to four weeks (Bergshlom et al., 1989; Coffey, 1993). Memory loss is typically the most troubling side effect; however, a new method called unilateral administration has helped to reduce its occurrence. During unilateral administration, physicians administer shocks only to the right hemisphere of patients' brains, lessening the treatment's impact on conscious, verbal memories.

As with lithium, the mechanism that makes ECT an effective treatment remains unknown. While ECT continues to be controversial, it is increasingly gaining a reputation as a promising, effective treatment option for those who have been unable to find relief from their depression elsewhere. (Consensus Conference, 1985; Parker et al., 1992; Glass, 2001).

PSYCHOSURGERY

Like ECT, psychosurgery, for many, conjures grotesque images of cruel, practically slapdash medical procedures from the past. Fortunately, modern medicine has ended the age of ill-advised lobotomies (a procedure that disconnects the frontal lobe from the rest of the brain and results in a near vegetative state) and transformed **psychosurgery**—in which parts of the brain are surgically altered to treat mental disorders—into a humane treatment option. These refined versions of psychosurgery are highly localized and targeted to specific areas of the brain. Because psychosurgery is irreversible and carries all of the risks of surgery, however, it is used only in rare or extreme cases.

For example, OCD that's untreatable by other means can sometimes be treated with psychosurgery. Doctors implant electrodes in areas of the brain shown to be overactive in OCD patients—the cingulum and basal ganglia—and then stimulate these electrodes with radio-frequency currents. Destroying these small segments of brain tissue can reduce OCD symptoms (Sachdev & Sachdev, 1997). In addition, a newer treatment called deep brain stimulation can be used for rare cases of otherwise untreatable OCD. Surgeons implant a thin wire electrode in the patient's brain; when activated, this electrode can stimulate (not destroy) neurons lying near it. Scientists believe this treatment effectively combats OCD by disrupting the ongoing neural loop that may underlie obsessions and compulsions.

Psychodynamic and Humanistic Psychotherapy

Psychotherapy refers to an interaction between a therapist and someone suffering from a psychological problem, the goal of which is to provide support or relief from the problem. Although some people view psychotherapy as an alternative to biomedical treatments, it is often used along with psychotropic drugs. This blended approach—the use of multifaceted treatments that vary depending on each person's unique problem and take into account biological, psychological, and social influences—is called **eclectic psychotherapy**, and it has becoming increasingly popular among therapists over the past two decades (Beitman et al., 1989; Castonguay & Goldfried, 1994).

> "Not all psychotherapies are the same. In fact, each approach to psychotherapy represents a different perspective on how the mind works and how to best address "problems of the mind.""

Not all psychotherapies are the same. In fact, each approach to psychotherapy represents a different perspective on how the mind works and how to best address "problems of the mind."

PSYCHODYNAMIC THERAPIES

Psychodynamic therapies are based on Freudian psychodynamics (see Chapter 16). According to psychodynamic theory, unconscious conflicts underlie mental disorders, and these conflicts make their way to the surface through our speech and behavior. This perspective leads psychodynamic therapists to tend to view the symptoms of a disorder as side effects of a deep, underlying problem that needs to be resolved. Psychodynamic therapists apply Freud's ideas not only to their view of psychological disorders but also to their treatments. They tend to trace their clients' problems to childhood or past experiences and focus strongly on understanding symptoms in the context of the client's important personal relationships.

Psychoanalysis

Although its popularity has waned considerably over the years due to its tendency to be expensive and time intensive (requiring several sessions a week for several years), some psychodynamic therapists still employ **psychoanalysis** when treating patients (Goode, 2003). Psychoanalysis is a type of psychotherapy that relates closely to Freudian concepts like the influence of the unconscious. It involves a number of specific techniques and concepts, all with the aim of helping clients "work through" their issues and resolve their psychological problems.

"I went to the zoo yesterday. . . elephants . . .gray . . . charcoal . . . campfire . . . oak tree." This seemingly random string of thoughts is an example of what might be produced during an exercise in **free association**. Free association is a psychoanalytic technique in which the therapist encourages the client to relax his or her mind and, starting from a recent experience, a memory, or a dream, report every image or idea that enters awareness, refraining from logic or self-editing. The therapist then tries to discern if these seemingly random associations point to particular underlying conflicts or anxiety in the client's unconscious mind.

Freud believed that dreams are the purest forms of free association, and dream analysis is another notable psychoanalytic technique. When analyzing clients' dreams,

> ∧
> ∧ Psychodynamic therapists may use
> ∧ psychoanalytic techniques including free
> association and dream analysis. Do you think
> these methods can produce great insights and
> relieve psychological problems?

therapists wade through the **manifest content**—the way the dream is experienced and remembered by the dreamer—in order to uncover the **latent content**, or the unconscious meaning of the dream.

Throughout sessions in psychoanalysis, therapists remain on the lookout for instances of resistance and transference in their clients. **Resistance** refers to a client's attempts to avoid doing therapeutic work. For example, a client might "forget" to go to sessions or refuse to talk about certain topics. During **transference**, a client's unconscious feelings about a significant person in his or her life are instead directed toward the therapist. From a psychoanalytic

perspective, a client who begins to resent her therapist might in fact be transferring her unconscious, unresolved resentment of her mother. By identifying these instances and analyzing their roots, therapists attempt to provide insights that will lead clients toward **catharsis**, or a healing emotional release.

Neo-Freudian Therapies

Several psychologists subscribe to Freud's fundamental ideas but have tweaked or amended his techniques to develop what are known as neo-Freudian therapies. Harry Sullivan, for example, believed that interpersonal relationships have a significant impact on psychological

problems. His philosophy contributed to the rise of **interpersonal psychotherapy**, which focuses on helping clients improve their relationships, particularly their current relationships, as a means to resolving their psychological problems. Like traditional psychoanalysis, interpersonal psychotherapy is based on the concept that patients need to uncover the roots of their problems, but it tends to be briefer, less intense, and more practical and immediate than psychoanalysis. This type of therapy seems to be particularly helpful for people suffering from depression (Weissman, 1999).

HUMANISTIC THERAPIES

If you believe that all people have the potential to grow, improve, and become their best selves, you might look at life from a humanistic perspective. The humanistic approach to psychology emphasizes humans' promise and our capacities for health, happiness, and generosity toward others (see Chapter 16). It makes sense, then, that humanistic therapies address psychological problems through a lens of positivity and optimism. Psychological problems are not necessarily *problems* at all, a humanistic therapist might say, but opportunities for us to pause, reflect on our lives, and make changes that enhance our potential. Humanistic therapies tend to focus not on treating illness but on achieving wellness, even greatness, and they're particularly concerned with recognizing and igniting individuals' inner potential for positive growth.

Humanistic therapies center on the notion that when it comes to happiness, the power lies with the people; that is, the choices we make regarding our own behavior can effectively promote our survival and well-being. Humanistic therapists aim to help their clients develop the self-awareness and self-confidence necessary to achieve happiness. They don't "fix" clients so much as show clients how to "fix" themselves. You might think of them as the unrelentingly upbeat cheerleaders of the psyche.

Person-Centered Therapy

Humanistic psychologist Carl Rogers believed that in order to feel motivated to move forward in life, we have to feel good about ourselves and feel accepted and approved of by others, regardless of our flaws. This principle underlies a popular humanistic therapy developed by Rogers (1961, 1980) called **person-centered**, or **client-centered**, **therapy**. In this model, the therapeutic process focuses squarely on the client's abilities and insights rather than the therapist's thoughts and skills. Person-centered therapists assume the roles of motivators, collaborators, and facilitators of their clients' mental health. They believe their clients are worthy and capable, even when the clients in question don't agree. The therapists' expressions of genuine acceptance are intended to help clients begin to feel more positive and self-confident, paving the way for clients to advance on their quest for personal fulfillment (Hill & Nakayama, 2000).

You might have heard a character on TV complain, "You're not really *hearing* me!" or you might have said something similar yourself once or twice. The idea of being "heard," or fully understood and listened to, comes from a key component of Rogers's person-centered therapy called active listening. When a therapist actively listens to a client, he or she tries to understand what the client is saying from the client's point of view, without judgment. Active listening involves echoing, restating, and seeking clarification of clients' statements. At the same time, therapists are careful to allow the client to maintain control of the discussion and direct its topics. An active listening session might sound something like this:

Client: Sometimes I feel like such a failure. Like I can't do anything right.

Therapist: So you feel like you're failing in some ways, that you can't do things right? Is that correct?

Client: Yeah, it's like every time I try to do something, I just mess it up.

Therapist: That sounds painful and frustrating. Is there an example you'd like to discuss?

According to Rogers, "hearing" clients in this fashion can be a powerful, uplifting force in the lives and minds of clients seeking help.

> Humanistic psychologist Carl Rogers believed that in order to feel motivated to move forward in life, we have to feel good about ourselves and feel accepted and approved of by others, regardless of our flaws.

Gestalt Therapy

Gestalt means "whole," so it makes sense that in **gestalt therapy**, another humanistic method, therapists aim to "fill in the holes . . . to make the person whole" (Perls, 1969). Developed by psychologist Fritz Perls, gestalt therapy helps clients become aware of, and take responsibility for, their thoughts, behaviors, experiences, and feelings. Gestalt therapists move their clients toward this goal by encouraging them to speak in the active voice ("I called my parents" rather than "my parents were called") and to confront their fears, conflicts, or other troubles head-on.

Group and Family Therapies

For some people, the prospect of sitting down one-on-one with a therapist is too

> Additionally, group therapy gives clients the opportunity to observe others, practice their interpersonal skills, and change their thinking and behaviors based on other people's influence and input. People often find that hearing about others' experiences dealing with similar problems can be enormously comforting and helpful.

intimidating to bear, no matter how open, accepting, and empathic the therapist may be. **Group therapy** can be an effective alternative for these people since it tends to be less threatening than a one-on-one session. Additionally, group therapy gives clients the opportunity to observe others, practice their interpersonal skills, and change their thinking and behaviors based on other people's influence and input. People often find that hearing about others' experiences dealing with similar problems can be enormously comforting and helpful. Community support groups and self-help groups, such as Alcoholics Anonymous, are examples of highly effective group therapies (Galanter et al., 2005; Kurtz, 2004; McKellar et al., 2003; Ouimette et al., 2001).

When families experience significant conflict or stress, they might look to a family therapist for help. **Family therapy** treats the family as a system or unit and can be an effective tool in helping families cope with and resolve conflict. The therapist focuses on how conflict or stress manifests itself in the relationships among the family members rather than on each individual's unique set of problems. Individual therapy often accompanies family therapy as part of the overall treatment plan.

Cognitive and Behavioral Psychotherapy

"I think, therefore I am": Even if you aren't an expert in philosophy, you're probably familiar with this statement from René Descartes, 17th century scholar and thinker. Although Descartes wasn't a psychologist, his belief about the interaction between thought, action, and existence is a convenient starting place for a discussion of cognitive and behavioral therapy as treatments for psychological disorders.

Cognitive and behavioral therapies are based on the idea that psychological problems are caused by faulty or irrational thinking, which in turn produces faulty or irrational behaviors. Essentially, you are what you think you are. As a result, cognitive and behavior therapies, which are often combined in the form of **cognitive–behavior therapy (CBT)**, try to get people to change the way they think (cognition) and the

way they act (behavior). This approach is significantly different from both the psychodynamic and humanistic approaches: The client's goal isn't to gain insights into the unconscious mind or to realize personal potential. Rather, CBT asks clients to identify the thought and behavior patterns that create their problems, and then make immediate, quantitative changes to break these patterns. Interestingly, the use of CBT to treat phobias has been shown to have similar brain effects to SSRI treatments: Both reduce amygdala and hippocampus reactivity or activation (Furmark et al., 2002). This finding indicates that there is a biophysiological aspect to CBT, and that changing the way you think and act can literally change your brain circuitry.

COGNITIVE THERAPY

Cognitive therapy, which can be either part of CBT or a stand-alone treatment option, first gained notice in the 1960s and is based on the theory that people's psychological problems can be traced to their own illogical or disturbed beliefs and thoughts. For example, people are depressed because they have depressive,

> **Cognitive-behavior therapy (CBT)** is a type of therapy centered on the idea that psychological problems are caused by faulty or irrational thinking, which in turn produces faulty or irrational behaviors; therefore, this type of therapy focuses on getting the client to change the way he or she thinks and behaves.
>
> **Cognitive therapy** is a type of therapy based on the theory that people's psychological problems can be traced to their own illogical or disturbed beliefs and thoughts; therefore, this type of therapy attempts to replace those cognitive patterns with healthier ones.
>
> **Cognitive restructuring** is a therapeutic technique in which therapists teach clients to question the automatic beliefs, assumptions, and predictions that often lead to negative emotional states and to replace negative thinking with realistic and positive thinking.

self-defeating, negative thoughts; people are anxious because they have apprehensive, fearful, panic-laced beliefs. Because these maladaptive thoughts and beliefs can make reality seem worse than it is, cognitive therapies attempt to replace them with healthier cognitive patterns.

Cognitive restructuring is an important part of most cognitive therapies. With this technique, therapists teach clients to question the automatic beliefs, assumptions, and predictions that often lead to negative emotional states and to replace negative thinking with realistic and positive thinking. Psychologist Aaron Beck and colleagues (1979) developed a widely used method based on this concept.

For instance, a client suffering from depression might be consumed by self-defeating thoughts like, "I failed that math exam, which means I'm going to fail the class, and I'll probably never get my degree or a decent job. I'm such a loser." A cognitive therapist applying Beck's technique would encourage the client to understand the illogical reasoning behind this "awfulizing" of an isolated situation: Failing one math exam doesn't make anyone a loser. "What does failing a math test have to do with your status as a human being? You made some mistakes in solving some math problems. Does that mean that everyone who struggles with math is a loser?" the therapist might say. The therapist would continue to work with the client to replace these thoughts with productive, effective ones grounded in reality: "I failed an exam, but it counts for only 10 percent of the final grade. If I work hard and ask the professor for extra help, I can still pass the class. Even if I don't, I can

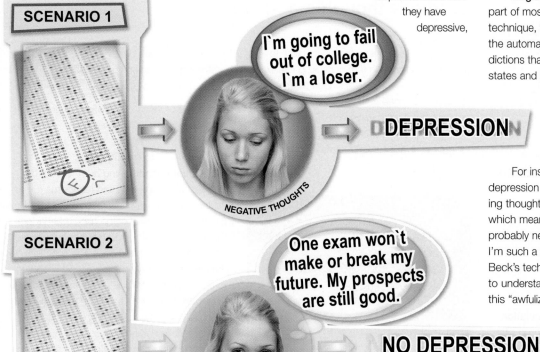

SCENARIO 1

I'm going to fail out of college. I'm a loser.

NEGATIVE THOUGHTS

DEPRESSION

SCENARIO 2

One exam won't make or break my future. My prospects are still good.

POSITIVE THOUGHTS

NO DEPRESSION

∧∧∧ Cognitive therapists work with clients to replace negative thought patterns with more adaptive ones that can help them avoid depression.

retake it in summer school. I'll still graduate on time. Failing one test is not going to destroy my future job prospects."

Once the client understands how harmful certain thought patterns can be, the therapist and client work together to create clear-cut, attainable goals as part of the treatment plan. These goals might include completing homework assignments like keeping a diary or filling out a form that describes troubling situations, thoughts, and emotions. The client and therapist discuss and analyze the results of the assignments in future sessions.

Sometimes, cognitive therapists encourage their clients to practice mindfulness meditation, a technique based on Buddhist teachings that emphasizes being fully present in each moment. When clients are acutely aware of their thoughts, feelings, and sensations, they can better detect symptoms before those symptoms become problems. According to psychologist Donald Meichenbaum (1977, 1985), this awareness can help people effectively self-edit their own harmful thoughts in negative situations. Meichenbaum called this **stress inoculation training**. For example, a client struggling with social anxiety may, at a party, begin to have doubts and fears: "Everyone is looking at me and judging me. They're wondering why I'm even here." Mindfulness meditation and stress inoculation training might allow the client to recognize these anxious thoughts and change them before they spiral out of control: "I feel anxious, but there's no reason to. I feel like people are judging me, but I realize that's probably not really true. People are more concerned with themselves than they are with me. I'm going to let go of my anxiety and enjoy the party."

> ∧
> ∧
> ∧ Mindfulness meditation, most often associated with Buddhist practices, has also found a place in cognitive therapy. Clients may work on gaining self-awareness through attending structured meditation sessions and paying close attention to their everyday thoughts and actions.

Ultimately, cognitive therapists hope to move from a teaching to a consulting role in their clients' lives. Therapists hope that with the techniques learned during the therapeutic process, clients can achieve self-directed control of their problems and rely on the therapist for guidance rather than treatment.

> " For Indiana Jones, receiving exposure treatment **might mean spending some serious quality time with snakes.** "

BEHAVIORAL THERAPY

The other half of CBT, as well as a treatment method in its own right, **behavioral therapy** attempts to change behaviors associated with psychological distress. This type of therapy has two foundational assumptions:

- The behaviors associated with psychological problems are not signs of a disorder or indications of an underlying issue; they *are* the problems themselves.

- Because these behaviors are learned, through conditioning or modeling, they can be "unlearned" through similar methods.

As a result of these assumptions, many of the treatment plans that behavioral therapists prescribe involve training the mind and body to react differently to various stimuli.

Counterconditioning is a process that involves replacing unwanted responses to particular situations with new responses. For example, if a child is afraid of the dark, a behavioral therapist might ask her to listen to her favorite song while sitting in the dark. The song makes the child feel happy and relaxed, and she begins to associate darkness with happiness and relaxation rather than with fear. Ideally, the child will eventually become completely habituated, or familiarized, to darkness. (For more information about conditioning and habituation, see Chapters 13 and 8.)

Exposure Treatments

Exposure treatment, a specific type of counterconditioning, takes the mantra "Face your fear" to a clinical level: Over several sessions, people who have a fear or phobia are repeatedly exposed to what they fear until they become so accustomed to it that they no longer fear it (Wolpe, 1958; Wolpe & Plaud, 1997). For Indiana Jones, receiving exposure treatment might mean spending some serious quality time with snakes.

Systematic desensitization is a variation of exposure treatment in which people, within a therapeutic environment, learn to pair states of deep relaxation with thoughts of anxiety-provoking situations. For example, a therapist might begin a systematic desensitization treatment for a client who's terrified of enclosed spaces by helping the client achieve a deeply relaxed, almost drowsy state. Then, the therapist might ask the person to engage in imaginative exposure by imagining a series of increasingly anxiety-inducing settings, from a large enclosed room, to a smaller enclosed room, to a car, to an elevator. The therapist would work with the client to replace any anxiety evoked by each image with relaxation, effectively "desensitizing" the client to the stimulus. Eventually, clients practice the desensitization by participating in real-life situations—such as riding in an elevator—that they previously feared and avoided.

For clients who have difficulty conjuring vivid imagery in their heads, virtual reality exposure provides a helpful alternative. Using computer simulations, clients can learn to be increasingly desensitized to anxiety-inducing situations, from speaking in public to taking an airplane ride. Systematic desensitization, whether through imaginative exposure or virtual reality exposure, has been shown to be an effective tool in the treatment of phobias (Hazel, 2005; McNeil & Zvolensky, 2000; Wang & Chen, 2000).

You might think of **implosion therapy** as the "tough love" approach to exposure treatment. While systematic desensitization eases clients gently into facing their phobias, implosion therapy does virtually the opposite: It habituates clients by exposing them to very intense stimuli. For example, a person afraid of spiders might be asked to imagine having hundreds of spiders crawling all over his body; all of a sudden, that lone arachnid in the bathroom sink doesn't seem so scary.

A technique called **flooding** takes implosion therapy a step further, exposing the client (with his or her permission) to the fear-inducing stimulus in a direct, intense way. Someone with an intense fear of dark underground spaces, for instance, might experience flooding in the form of spending several hours in a subway station.

What if you could overcome your deepest anxieties simply by moving your eyes? It sounds too good to be true, but it's the premise of a relatively new form of exposure therapy for phobias and PTSD called **eye movement desensitization and reprocessing (EMDR)**. EMDR therapists instruct clients to focus on a disturbing image or traumatic memory as they move their eyes back and forth. Studies conducted by psychologist Francine Shapiro (1989, 2002) have shown EMDR to be effective. However, additional studies have shown that clients tend to improve both with and without eye movements (Cahill et al., 1999; Davidson & Parker, 2001; Lohr et al., 1998). Skeptics suspect that the discussion of anxiety-provoking thoughts in a nurturing therapeutic environment, rather than the rapid eye movements, are responsible for the success of EMDR.

Aversive Conditioning

Therapists often use behavioral therapies to treat clients who have phobias, but what if phobias aren't at the root of your problem? People who struggle with alcoholism, for example, aren't confronting a phobic behavior; they're facing an addiction. In cases like these, therapists sometimes implement a treatment called **aversive conditioning.** The goal of aversive conditioning is to replace a positive response to a harmful stimulus, such as alcohol, with a negative response. For example, a therapist might pair a drink or a cigarette with a nausea-inducing chemical. When the client drinks or smokes, he

or she becomes violently ill and begins to associate drinking or smoking with feelings of sickness. Although aversive conditioning has been shown to treat alcoholism effectively in the short run, its long-term usefulness seems fairly limited (Wiens & Menustik, 1983).

Operant Conditioning

Operant conditioning, or behavior shaping, forms the basis of another category of behavior therapies. These therapies are centered on the idea that rewards (or a lack thereof) strongly influence our behavior. One strategy, **contingency management**, involves altering the relationship between a person's actions and those actions' consequences to replace unwanted behaviors with desirable ones. This type of technique can,

Systematic desensitization is a variation of exposure treatment in which people, within a therapeutic environment, learn to pair states of deep relaxation with thoughts of anxiety-provoking situations, with the goal of replacing the anxiety felt during these situations with relaxation.

Implosion therapy is a type of exposure treatment in which clients are exposed to very intense stimuli by being asked to imagine an extreme version of their fears or phobias.

Flooding is a type of exposure treatment in which clients are exposed to fear-inducing stimuli in an intense way by directly exposing them to the stimuli.

Eye movement desensitization and reprocessing (EMDR) is a form of exposure therapy in which therapists instruct clients to focus on a disturbing image or traumatic memory as they move their eyes back and forth, with the goal of helping them deal with the psychological issues brought on by the disturbing or traumatic event.

Aversive conditioning is a type of therapy in which a harmful stimulus is paired with a negative response, with the goal of replacing the usual positive response (such as the pleasure a client may feel when drinking alcohol or smoking) with the negative one.

Contingency management is an operant conditioning strategy that involves altering the relationship between a person's actions and those actions' consequences to replace unwanted behaviors with desirable ones.

<<< Therapists can use virtual reality exposure to treat people for their phobias and anxieties through a process of desensitization.

Token economy is a term for an operant conditioning procedure in which individuals earn tokens when they exhibit desirable behavior; later, people who've earned tokens can redeem them for privileges or treats.

Behavioral contract is an explicit agreement that thoroughly explains the consequences of several behaviors as well as expectations of the client and the therapist.

Social learning therapy is a type of therapy designed to modify clients' problematic behavior patterns through observation and behavior reinforcement.

among other outcomes, successfully change the behavior of withdrawn autistic children. For example, parents saw great improvements in the children's behavior and intellectual achievements after they reinforced their children's good behavior with attention and rewards and punished or ignored negative behaviors, such as hitting or screaming (Lovaas, 1987). In institutional settings, contingency management is sometimes enacted in **token economies**, an operant conditioning procedure in which individuals earn tokens when they exhibit desirable behavior. Later, people who've earned tokens can redeem them for privileges or treats.

In behavioral therapy based on operant conditioning, it's important for both the client and the therapist to reach a clear understanding about positive and negative behaviors and their consequences, so a therapist might draw up a **behavioral contract**, an explicit agreement that thoroughly explains the consequences of several behaviors as well as expectations of the client and the therapist.

Social Learning Therapy

Social learning therapy draws on the idea that we learn to act the way that we do through observing and modeling others' behavior. Based on psychologist Albert Bandura's research (see Chapter 7), social learning therapy is designed to modify clients' problematic behavior patterns through observation and behavior reinforcement. In a famous study, Bandura and his colleagues helped people overcome their phobia of snakes by watching films in which others interacted comfortably with snakes (Bandura, Blanchard, & Ritter, 1969). Clients learn to perform desirable behaviors by visualizing those behaviors and their consequences, and they receive positive reinforcement when they actually perform the behaviors themselves.

Evaluating Psychotherapies

Does talking with a therapist really work? Does it relieve psychological problems and help people achieve happier, healthier lives? And which therapy is best—psychodynamic, humanistic, cognitive, or behavioral? Are certain therapies more useful for certain types of disorders, or for certain types of people? And what about medications—where do they fit in?

There's plenty of controversy and debate in the world of psychology, and the field of treatment is no exception. Psychologists don't all agree as to whether any type of psychotherapy is effective, and each type of psychotherapy has its champions and skeptics. If you're wondering

> *If you're wondering which type of therapy is "best," however, there's only one safe answer: Each client, each therapist, and each disorder is different. As a result, the usefulness of any therapy depends on the client, the therapist, and the nature of their relationship.*

which type of therapy is "best," however, there's only one safe answer: Each client, each therapist, and each disorder is different. As a result, the usefulness of any therapy depends on the client, the therapist, and the nature of their relationship.

THE EFFICACY OF PSYCHOTHERAPY

Americans are turning to psychotherapy in increasing numbers, but is this growing confidence in the value of therapy justified? Research indicates that it is. In one classic study, psychologist R. B. Sloane and colleagues (1975) took a group of participants with generalized anxiety and assigned them to one of three groups: a control group that received no psychotherapy, a group that received psychodynamic psychotherapy, and a group that received behavioral psychotherapy. After the participants were double-blindly assessed both before and after treatment (or no treatment in the control group), Sloane found that although all groups improved, the two treatment groups improved significantly more than the control group did. Furthermore, although the behavioral group improved slightly more than the psychodynamic group, the difference was insignificant.

Other studies have confirmed these findings: In a meta-analysis of 475 investigations into the efficacy of psychotherapy, Mary Lee Smith and colleagues (1980) concluded that people who receive psychotherapy improve more than about 80 percent of people who do not receive this treatment. Recent studies have yielded similar results, showing that in general, most people who receive psychotherapy report improvement, and that some therapy appears to be better than no therapy at all (Nathan & Gorman, 2002; Shadish et al., 2000; Kopta et al., 1999). Additionally, a 1995 study of 7,000 *Consumer Reports* subscribers found that the longer people participated in therapy, the more they improved (Seligman, 1995).

It's important to keep a few points in mind in the context of these findings. In general, these experiments are carried out in research institutions with highly experienced, highly trained clinicians who are aware that they are also being assessed. This, in many instances, leads to optimal therapy conditions, which may or may not be available to the average person who seeks psychotherapy. In addition, the clients recruited to participate in these experiments may be a slightly biased group; their willingness to seek help may indicate an already existing belief that it can, and will, work.

It has been repeatedly shown that psychotherapy is effective for treating the conditions for which people most commonly seek help--generalized anxiety and major depression. Interestingly, however, research on the effectiveness of different therapeutic techniques has not discovered a single therapeutic strategy that is uniquely effective in treating all people with any disorder. However, some therapies do tend to treat certain disorders more effectively than others. For example, cognitive, interpersonal, and behavior therapy have been shown to be most effective in treating depression, while cognitive and exposure therapy have proven useful in anxiety treatment. Behavioral therapy tends to be effective for impulse-control disorders. For those struggling with bulimia, CBT is perhaps the best option (Chambless et al., 1997; Norcross, 2002).

FACTORS OF EFFECTIVE PSYCHOTHERAPY

What makes psychotherapy an effective treatment? Its success can be attributed to a number of identifiable factors (Frank, 1982; Goldfried & Padawer, 1982; Strupp, 1986; Wampold, 2001).

Support. For people struggling with depression and self-doubt, psychotherapy can provide a

Symptom Improvement as a Function of Time in Psychotherapy

Improvement Score

- 1 month: 201
- 1–2 month: 207
- 3–6 month: 217
- 7–11 month: 224
- 1–2 years: 226
- > 2 years: 241

Source: Seligman, M. E. P. (1995). The effectiveness of psychotherapy: The Consumer Reports study. American Psychologist, 50, 965–974.

∧∧∧∧ A 1995 *Consumer Reports* study directed by psychologist Martin Seligman found a strong link between the duration of therapy and participants' improvement scores.

welcome dose of acceptance, empathy, and encouragement. Studies have shown these qualities to be highly valuable in treatment success, and many therapists consider providing support to be the first and foremost task when treating clients (Blatt et al., 1996; Torrey, 1986).

Hope. Catching sight of a light at the end of the tunnel—the expectation that things can and will get better—can be enormously helpful and comforting to individuals in psychological distress. Therapy often provides clients with this sense of hope.

New perspective. Therapists can give their clients the ability to see alternative views of the situation at hand. A therapist's expertise and experience often allows clients to see themselves, and their problems, in ways they had never before consid-

ered. "I have a problem that no one else has and will never be fixed" can become, "I have a problem that many others have struggled with and overcome, and by implementing these strategies, I can overcome it, too."

Motivation. Therapists sometimes explain a client's lack of response to treatment by saying that the client was not "ready to do the work." Therapy is not a passive process, and the patient or client must be motivated to get better and be willing to put in the time and effort that such measures require.

PSYCHOTHERAPY VS. PHARMACOLOGY

The question of which is the most effective treatment for psychological problems—

psychotherapy or medications—can stir impassioned debate from both sides. Clearly, some conditions, such as schizophrenia and bipolar disorder, call for one above the other.

For other conditions, such as depression and anxiety, psychotherapy, medications, or both may prove to be the most effective treatment for a given patient. Some patients with depression respond immediately and enduringly to SSRIs; some don't. Some benefit greatly from a combination of SSRIs and humanistic therapy; some don't. Some can use what they learn in CBT to overcome their problems; some can't. Each person, each situation, and each treatment is different. As inexact as it may sound, it's the truth: When it comes to treatment of psychopathology, it just depends.

Summary

HOW HAS THE MENTAL HEALTH SYSTEM EVOLVED OVER THE YEARS, AND HOW IS IT STRUCTURED TODAY? p. 282

• Until the 17th century, the mentally ill were often treated in cruel and inhumane ways. Reformers such as Pinel campaigned for moral treatment.

• Today, clinical psychology, which aims to help people suffering from psychological disorders, lies at the center of the mental health system structure.

HOW DO BIOMEDICAL THERAPIES TREAT PSYCHOLOGICAL DISORDERS? p. 284

• Psychopharmacology, the study of how drugs affect the mind and behavior, has led to the development of a wide array of psychoactive medications.

• Antipsychotic drugs treat disorders such as schizophrenia. Typical antipsychotics (chlorpromazine and haloperidol) treat positive symptoms by decreasing dopamine activity. Atypical antipsychotics treat negative symptoms.

• Antidepressants alleviate depression by altering how neurotransmitters are circulated throughout the brain, usually serotonin and norepinephrine.

• Benzodiazepines treat anxiety disorders by slowing down the central nervous system, while lithium controls bipolar mood swings for many sufferers.

HOW DO PSYCHODYNAMIC AND HUMANISTIC THERAPIES TREAT PSYCHOLOGICAL DISORDERS? p. 286

• Psychodynamic therapies trace clients' problems to past experiences and focus on understanding symptoms through clients' personal relationships.

• Humanistic therapies aim to help people achieve self-awareness and positive self-regard so that they can effectively solve their own problems.

HOW DO COGNITIVE AND BEHAVIORAL THERAPIES TREAT PSYCHOLOGICAL DISORDERS? p. 289

• Cognitive–behavior therapy aims to help people change the way they think and act.

• With cognitive restructuring, therapists teach clients to replace negative thinking with realistic and positive thinking.

• Behavioral therapy seeks to change the behaviors associated with psychological problems using exposure treatments, such as systematic desensitization, implosion therapy, and flooding.

WHAT FACTORS MAKE PSYCHOTHERAPY AN EFFECTIVE TREATMENT, AND HOW DOES IT COMPARE IN USE TO BIOMEDICAL TREATMENTS? p. 292

• In general, most people who receive psychotherapy report improvement; some therapy appears to be better than no therapy.

• Psychotherapy often works because it provides clients support, hope, and a new perspective on their problems. Clients must be motivated to get better in order to improve.

Test Your Understanding

1. According to the reading, which of the following is a relatively new approach to helping those with severe mental illness?

   a. assertive community treatments
   b. mental institutions
   c. almshouses
   d. long-term hospitalization

2. Who of the following people is most likely to be able to prescribe drugs for his or her patients?

   a. a psychiatric nurse   c. a psychiatrist
   b. a clinical psychologist   d. a clinical social worker

3. Which of the following would LEAST be considered a preventive mental health measure?

   a. educating the public about the effects of alcoholism
   b. educating the public about ways to escape domestic abuse

   c. providing shelters for abused women and children
   d. providing work-life balance programs that attempt to reduce stress

4. Which of the following people would be most likely to refer to those they help with mental health concerns as "clients"?

   a. a psychiatrist
   b. a counselor
   c. a clinical psychologist specializing in the biology of mental illness
   d. a psychiatric nurse

5. Which of the following disorders is LEAST likely to be treated with an SSRI?

   a. depression
   b. obsessive–compulsive disorder (OCD)
   c. schizophrenia
   d. posttraumatic stress disorder (PTSD)

6. Who of the following people would be most likely to study the effects of psychotropic medications in children?

    a. a psychiatrist
    c. a psychopharmacologist
    b. a clinical psychologist
    d. a pharmacist

7. Which of the following is NOT a reason for the increase in antidepressant prescriptions?

    a. advertisements for antidepressant medications
    b. preventive mental health programs
    c. an increase in depression-related diagnoses
    d. a decrease in the severity of side effects related to antidepressants

8. Which treatment has largely replaced the used of barbiturates in treating anxiety disorders?

    a. electroconvulsive therapy (ECT)
    b. treatment with benzodiazepines
    c. treatment with MAO inhibitors
    d. deep brain stimulation

9. A psychologist who treats patients using a combination of free association and client-centered therapy is using what type of approach?

    a. psychoanalysis
    c. behavioral therapy
    b. humanistic psychotherapy
    d. eclectic psychotherapy

10. Lydia begins crying during therapy, stating that she is angry her mother left her family. According to the psychoanalytic perspective, what might Lydia be experiencing?

    a. transference
    c. resistance
    b. catharsis
    d. latency

11. In therapy, John discusses memories he has about his relationship with his father. He also discusses frustrations he has in his relationship with his partner, Cary. His counselor helps him come up with practical means to address his frustrations. What type of counseling might John be undergoing?

    a. traditional psychoanalysis
    c. cognitive restructuring
    b. gestalt therapy
    d. interpersonal psychotherapy

12. Marci is depressed over the breakup of a long-term relationship and feels that she was not good enough for her ex and that he must hate her. She has been calling him crying and on one occasion threatened suicide unless he said he still loved her. Marci's counselor works to help Marci understand that her ex's breaking up with her reflects his inability to commit. She also helps Marci think of actions she can take that demonstrate this new thought. Which of the following types of therapy is Marci most likely undergoing?

    a. humanistic therapy
    c. psychoanalysis
    b. gestalt therapy
    d. cognitive behavioral therapy

13. How might a counselor using flooding to treat a person who has a fear of heights?

    a. Make him stand on the roof of a tall building for an hour.
    b. Get him into a relaxed state, and then have him imagine being in a tall building.
    c. Guide him to visualize floating in outer space.
    d. Have him eat ice cream while standing on a ladder.

14. Which of the following is the best example of an aversive conditioning approach?

    a. putting mittens over a person's hands to prevent scratching
    b. putting a bitter liquid on a person's fingernails to prevent nail biting
    c. making a person listen to loud music while talking about a traumatic incident
    d. show images of snake bites to a person with a fear of snakes

15. Which of the following statements about psychotherapy is true?

    a. Psychotherapy is less effective the longer a person is in treatment.
    b. Behavioral therapy has been shown to be the most effective form of psychotherapy.
    c. While psychotherapy is typically more effective than no therapy, no one type of therapy is generally more effective than the rest.
    d. Psychoanalysis has been shown to be the most effective form of psychotherapy.

16. The drug lithium is used primarily to treat:

    a. schizophrenia.
    b. major depressive disorder.
    c. bipolar disorder.
    d. obsessive–compulsive disorder (OCD).

17. Which of the following statements is most likely to be used by a therapist or counselor using active listening?

    a. I hear what you are saying but I don't agree. Do you think you could look at the situation in a different way?
    b. It seems you are avoiding the topic. Do you want to talk about why?
    c. You seem tired. Can you explain why?
    d. I hear you say you feel tired all the time. Do you want to tell me about a specific situation?

18. To help her overcome her chronic self-doubt at work, Jasmine's therapist shows her movies in which women succeed at building careers. What kind of therapy or approach might Jasmine be engaging in?

    a. exposure treatment
    c. operant conditioning
    b. contingency management
    d. social learning therapy

19. Which of the following statements does NOT reflect the gestalt therapy approach?

    a. I feel sad that we have not spent time together recently.
    b. You haven't helped me feel better.
    c. I feel angry that you are not coming to the baseball game.
    d. I am happier when I express my feelings.

20. Kara's sixth-grade teacher gives her a star-shaped sticker every time she completes her homework. At the end of the week, if Kara has five or more stickers, she can trade them in for an extra 10 minutes of recess. Kara's teacher is using:

    a. a token economy.
    c. aversive conditioning.
    b. social learning theory.
    d. cognitive restructuring.

Remember to check www.thethinkspot.com **for additional information, downloadable flashcards, and other helpful resources.**

Answers: 1) a; 2) c; 3) c; 4) b; 5) b; 6) c; 7) b; 8) b; 9) d; 10) b; 11) d; 12) d; 13) a; 14) b; 15) c; 16) c; 17) d; 18) d; 19) b; 20) a

GLOSSARY

abnormal psychology   the study of disorders of mind, mood, and behavior (263)

absolute threshold   the smallest amount of energy needed for a person to detect a stimulus 50 percent of the time (70)

academic psychologist   a type of psychologist who divides his or her time between supervising and teaching students, completing administrative tasks, and carrying out psychological research (13)

accommodation   a process in which a person adjusts and refines his or her schemas based on new information (159)

accuracy motive   a person's desire to be correct or accurate (211)

achievement   a person's knowledge and progress (137)

acquired characteristics   useful traits acquired by an organism (62)

action potential   an electrochemical ripple that works its way from the cell body to the terminal buttons and terminates in the release of neurotransmitters that will stimulate the next neuron (41)

action unit   one of 46 unique movements involved in facial expressions that indicate emotion (198)

activation-synthesis theory   a theory that explains sleep as a side effect of the visual and motor area neurons firing during REM sleep It states that dreams are the result of the brain's attempt to make sense of the random neural activity that occurs while a person sleeps (96, 203)

activity theory of aging   theory that states that elderly people are happiest when they stay active and involved in the community (187)

acuity   sharpness of vision (72)

acute stress   a temporary state of stress that varies in intensity (228)

adaptation-level phenomenon   a phenomenon in which the things a person is currently experiencing become the norm for that person, causing the person to continually want more (199)

adaptive   able to adjust and function according to one's environment (61)

adenosine   a sleep-inducing hormone (90)

adolescence   the period of transition from childhood to adulthood (154)

adrenal androgen   a hormone that increases in production during puberty (185)

aerobic exercise   sustained exercise that increases heart and lung fitness, such as jogging, swimming, and biking (237)

affective component   feelings associated with emotion (194)

affective forecasting   a person's imagining how he or she would feel about something that might happen in the future (199)

age changes   developmental changes that track how individuals change as they age (153)

age differences   developmental changes that consider how people of varying ages differ from one another (153)

ageism   prejudice against the elderly (187)

aggression   behavior intended to harm others (219)

agoraphobia   intense fear of being in a situation from which there is no escape (269)

algorithm   a step-by-step procedure that a person can follow to arrive at a solution to a particular problem (141)

alleles   pairs of genes located in the same position on the pair of chromosomes in a unit of heredity (58)

allocentrism   a personality trait exhibiting the tendency to think and act in a collectivist manner (255)

all-or-none principle   a principle that states that once the threshold for a particular neuron is reached, it will transmit all of its information, no matter how many more positive inputs it receives over that threshold (41)

alpha wave   a type of brain wave that characterizes a relaxed state of wakefulness (90)

altered state of consciousness   a state characterized by bizarre, disorganized, or dreamlike thought patterns (88)

altruism   prosocial behavior that is carried out without concern for one's own safety or self-interest (221)

American Psychological Association (APA)   a scientific and professional organization that represents psychologists in the United States (29)

amplitude   the height of a wave (74)

amygdala   a part of the limbic system; involved in fear detection and conditioning; it is essential for unconscious emotional responses such as the fight-or-flight response (44, 195)

analytic intelligence   a type of intelligence generally assessed by intelligence tests that present well-defined problems with only one correct answer (138)

androgen insensitivity syndrome   a condition in which a genetically male fetus's receptors for androgens fail to function, resulting in the development of external female genitalia (168)

androgens   male hormones (168)

androgynous   neither specifically masculine or feminine (98)

andropause   gradual sexual changes in men as they age that include declines in sperm count, testosterone level, and speed of erection and ejaculation (154)

anorexogenic   signals that stop an animal from eating (202)

anterior cingulate cortex   an area of the brain that serves as an executive control system that helps control a person's behavior; it is involved in the perception of physical pain (45, 145)

anterograde amnesia   memory loss characterized by an inability to form new long-term memories (129)

anticipatory coping   a coping strategy that involves a person's foreseeing a potential stressor and considering it in terms of how he or she has previously handled similar stressors, what he or she might do similarly in this situation, and what he or she has learned from past mistakes (234)

antidepressant   a type of medication that works to alleviate symptoms of depression by altering how certain neurotransmitters—usually serotonin and norepinephrine—are circulated throughout the brain (284)

antipsychotic drugs   psychoactive medications used to treat disorders in which psychotic symptoms, such as hallucinations, paranoia, and delusions, predominate (284)

antisocial personality disorder a mental disorder characterized by a complete lack of conscience (273)

anxiety disorder a mental disorder in which a person feels anxious all the time without any identifiable reason (266)

anxious relationship an intimate relationship characterized by worry about love or lack of love from a partner (185)

applied psychology the use of psychological theory and practice to tackle real-world problems (13)

approach motivation a motivation involved with striving to achieve a positive result (200)

approval motive a person's desire to be accepted by his or her peers (211)

aptitude a person's potential ability (137)

archetype a particular image, such as mother as caretaker and nurturer, persistent across time and cultures (249)

arcuate nucleus a part of the hypothalamus that contains both appetite-stimulating and appetite-suppressing neurons (202)

artificial selection a concept that contrasts with natural selection in that humans are involved in selecting the desired characteristics to pass on to an organism's offspring (62)

Asperger syndrome a syndrome in which a person has normal levels of intelligence and cognitive abilities but displays autistic-like social behaviors (275)

assimilation a process in which a person interprets new experiences in terms of existing schemas (159)

association cortex a part of the cerebral cortex that helps basic sensory and motor information from a specific lobe integrate with information from the rest of the brain; one exists in each lobe of the cerebral cortex (46)

associative learning learning characterized by linking two events that occur together (104)

associator a person who experiences synesthesia and only associates colors with letters; he or she does not actually see the color (83)

attachment an emotional bond that newborns share with their caregivers (180)

attention the act of applying the mind selectively to a sense or thought (122, 145)

attentional blink a type of processing failure characterized by an inability to remember the second element in a pair of rapidly successive stimuli (146)

attention-deficit hyperactivity disorder (ADHD) a disorder in which a person finds it difficult to focus his or her attention and is easily distracted (249)

attitude an evaluative belief or opinion about a person, object, or idea (216)

attractiveness bias the tendency for a person to rate physically attractive people as more intelligent, competent, sociable, and sensitive than their less attractive counterparts (209)

attribution a claim about the cause of a person's behavior (208)

attribution theory a theory that states that a person understands other people by attributing their behavior either to their internal dispositions or their external situations (208)

attributional-style questionnaire a type of questionnaire that seeks to assess how people view the events that happen in their lives based on three criteria: stability, globality, and locus (269)

audience design a concept that states that everything people say is directed to a particular audience (147)

auditory cortex the part of the brain that mediates the human sense of hearing by encoding auditory information (120)

auditory encoding the process of encoding sounds (122)

autism a developmental disorder that impedes social development and communication skills (275)

autonomic nervous system the part of the peripheral nervous system that performs tasks that are not consciously controlled (38, 96)

availability heuristic a type of heuristic that tells a person that if he or she can bring examples of an event to mind easily, that event must be common (143)

aversive conditioning a type of therapy in which a harmful stimulus is paired with a negative response, with the goal of replacing the usual positive response (such as the pleasure a client may feel when drinking alcohol or smoking) with the negative one (291)

avoidance motivation a motivation involved with striving to avoid a negative result (200)

avoidant personality disorder a mental disorder characterized by high levels of social anxiety and feelings of inadequacy (249)

avoidant relationship an intimate relationship in which there is ambivalence about commitment and little expression of intimacy (185)

axon a cable-like extension that transmits a signal away from a neuron's soma toward the target of communication (38)

backward conditioning a type of classical conditioning in which the conditioned stimulus is presented after the unconditioned stimulus (106)

bait-and-switch technique a technique that encourages people to comply with an attractive offer but substitutes that offer with a less attractive option once the person has agreed (214)

bar graph a representation of a frequency distribution in which vertical or horizontal bars are proportional in length to the value they represent (24)

basal ganglia a set of interconnected structures in the brain that help with motor control, cognition, different forms of learning, and emotional processing They are involved in forming procedural memories and habits related to movement (44, 128)

behavior genetics a field of study emphasizing the analysis of the effects of genes and environment on behavior and mental processes (61)

behavioral activation system (BAS) a part of the brain that activates approach behavior in response to the anticipation of a reward (245)

behavioral approach an approach to psychology that concentrates on observable behavior that can be directly measured and recorded (8, 265)

behavioral contract an explicit agreement that thoroughly explains the consequences of several behaviors as well as expectations of the client and the therapist (292)

behavioral expectation confirmation a phenomenon that enables a person to influence other people to behave in accordance with his or her expectations (209)

behavioral inhibition system (BIS) a part of the brain that inhibits approach behavior in response to the anticipation of a punishment (245)

behavioral medicine an interdisciplinary approach to medical treatment that integrates behavioral, medical, and social knowledge to increase life expectancy and enhance quality of life (228)

behavioral therapy   a type of therapy that attempts to change behaviors associated with psychological distress (290)

behaviorism   a method of studying learning in which the researcher focuses solely on directly observable responses and discards any references to inner thoughts, feelings, and motives (104)

belief bias   the effect that occurs when a person's beliefs distort his or her logical thinking (143)

belief perseverance   a person's tendency to continue believing something even when presented with evidence refuting that belief (143)

belongingness   a need to feel loved and avoid alienation (201)

benevolent sexism   acceptance of positive stereotypes or favorable biased behavior that propagates unfairness and inequalities based on gender (172)

benzodiazepines   anti-anxiety medications used mainly to treat generalized anxiety disorder and panic disorder (285)

beta wave   a type of brain wave that characterizes active wakefulness (90)

between-group experiment   a study in which different groups of participants are exposed to different independent variables (21)

bias   a personal and sometimes unreasonable judgment that a researcher may make that could affect the results of an experiment (27)

biofeedback   a system for measuring and reporting physiological states (239)

biological approach   a method of analyzing a psychological disorder in which physical problems are looked for as the root cause (264)

biological preparedness   the extent to which biological features evolved to promote certain traits (64)

biopsychosocial approach   a method of analyzing a psychological disorder that recognizes that it is not possible to separate body and mind; negative emotions can contribute to physical illness, while physical abnormalities may increase the likelihood of psychological disorders (265)

bipedalism   the ability to walk on two legs (62)

bipolar disorder   a mood disorder characterized by alternating episodes of depression and mania (268)

blind observer   an observer who does not know what the research is about and is thus not subject to observer bias (22)

blindsight   a condition in which a person is not consciously aware of what he or she sees, but can still partially respond to visual information (73)

blood-brain barrier   a fatty envelope that filters substances trying to leave the bloodstream and reach the brain (38)

body restoration theory   a theory that explains sleep as a time for necessary rest and recuperation (202)

borderline personality disorder   a mental disorder characterized by unstable moods, intense and stormy relationships, and manipulation and distrust of others (273)

brainstem   the base of the brain; responsible for survival-oriented functions such as breathing, cardiac function, and basic arousal (43)

brightness   the intensity of light waves (74)

Broca's area   a part of the frontal lobe that initiates the movements needed to produce speech (47)

burnout   a state of physical, emotional, and mental exhaustion created by long-term involvement in an emotionally demanding situation and accompanied by lowered performance and motivation (230)

bystander effect   a phenomenon in which the likelihood that a person requiring help receives it from an individual bystander is inversely proportional to the number of bystanders present (212)

Cannon-Bard theory   a theory that proposes that the mental and physiological components of emotions happen simultaneously (194)

case study   an in-depth study of one individual or a few individuals (22)

catastrophe   an unpredictable, large-scale event (230)

catharsis   healing emotional release (287)

catharsis theory   a theory that states that a person should express emotions to prevent those emotions from building up and exploding (199)

caudate   part of the basal ganglia; involved in control of voluntary movement, and part of the brain's learning and memory system (44)

cell assembly   a network of neurons in which memories are stored (112)

central drive system   a set of neurons that create a drive (200)

central executive functioning   a set of mental processes that governs goals, strategies, and coordination of the mind's activities (138)

central nervous system (CNS)   the largest part of the nervous system; it includes the spinal cord and the brain (38)

central route   a path to persuasion that involves paying careful attention to strong, well-presented arguments that are personally relevant and that appeal to reason (216)

central-state theory   a theory that explains drives by understanding them as corresponding to neural activity (200)

centromere   the place where two chromatids meet (56)

cephalocaudal rule   the tendency for motor skills to emerge in sequence from top to bottom (153)

cerebellum   a part of the brain that coordinates muscle movements and maintains equilibrium; involved in conditioning and forming procedural memories and habits related to movement (44, 28)

cerebral cortex   an outer part of the brain that is mainly involved in the coordination of sensory and motor information (43)

chaining   a process in which the final step in a sequence is reinforced first, becoming a conditioned reinforcer for the preceding response (110)

chameleon effect   a person's unconscious mimicry of other people's expressions, behaviors, and voice tones (211)

change blindness   the failure to detect drastic visual changes in a scene (79)

change deafness   the failure to detect drastic auditory changes (79)

chemical environment   events and conditions inside an organism (57)

choice blindness   the failure to detect alterations to choices a person has made (79)

chromatids   pairs of duplicated chromosomes (56)

chromosomes   long strands of genetic material found in the nuclei of all cells (56)

chronic stress   a long-lasting state of arousal during which a person feels that he or she doesn't have the resources available to meet all of the demands placed upon him or her (228)

chronological age   the amount of time that has passed since a person was born (53, 185)

chunking the process of organizing large pieces of information into smaller pieces, or chunks (122)

cingulate cortex a part of the brain that is divided into four sections and is involved in various functions such as emotion, response selection, personal orientation, and memory formation and retrieval (44)

circadian rhythm a biological clock that regulates body functions on a 24-hour cycle (90)

classical conditioning a phenomenon in which two stimuli are associated, thus creating a reflex response (106)

client a person with a psychological disorder who is being treated with the view that his or her psychological distress is caused by behavioral issues and faulty thought processes (282)

client-centered therapy *see* **person-centered therapy** (288)

clinical psychology a field of psychology that deals with the diagnosis and treatment of people with specific mental or behavioral problems (13)

clique a small, same-sex group of three to nine members who share intimate secrets and see themselves as best friends (183)

closure the tendency to perceive images as complete objects and overlook incompleteness (81)

cocktail party effect a phenomenon in which selective attention allows a person to concentrate on one voice and ignore many others (79)

cognition mental activities associated with sensation, perception, thinking, knowing, remembering, and communicating (137, 156)

cognitive appraisal a thoughtful interpretation and evaluation (234)

cognitive approach a method of analyzing a psychological disorder that focuses on thought processes that contribute to psychological distress (265)

cognitive dissonance a disconnect between a person's internal attitudes and his or her external behavior (214)

cognitive experience the brain's remembered response to experiencing an emotion (194)

cognitive map a mental representation of an environment (155)

cognitive map theory a theory that states that the hippocampus provides a spatial framework that enables a person to create a mental map of his or her surroundings (114)

cognitive psychology a field of psychology focused on the workings of the human brain and seeking to understand how people process the information that they collect from their environments (8)

cognitive restructuring a therapeutic technique in which therapists teach clients to question the automatic beliefs, assumptions, and predictions that often lead to negative emotional states and to replace negative thinking with realistic and positive thinking (289)

cognitive therapy a type of therapy based on the theory that people's psychological problems can be traced to their own illogical or disturbed beliefs and thoughts; therefore, this type of therapy attempts to replace those cognitive patterns with healthier ones (289)

cognitive unconscious a collection of mental processes that affect the way a person feels or behaves, even though he or she is not consciously aware of them (89)

cognitive-appraisal theory a theory that states that if a person notices a particular physiological response, that person has to decide what it means before he or she can feel an emotion (195)

cognitive-behavior therapy (CBT) a type of therapy centered on the idea that psychological problems are caused by faulty or irrational thinking, which in turn produces faulty or irrational behaviors; therefore, this type of therapy focuses on getting the client to change the way he or she thinks and behaves (289)

cohorts groups of people raised during the same time period (160)

collective unconscious is a shared pool of memories and images common to all humans (249)

collectivism the act of contributing something beneficial to the whole group to which a person belongs (221)

collectivist culture a culture that emphasizes people's interdependence (255)

color constancy the inclination to perceive familiar objects as retaining their color despite changes in sensory information (74)

comorbidity a condition in which a person suffers from two or more mental disorders (263)

complex cell a feature detector that only responds to two features of a stimulus (72)

compliance a change in a person's behavior that occurs in response to a direct request (214)

concept a mental grouping of similar objects, events, and people (140)

conditioned response (CR) a learned reaction triggered by a conditioned stimulus, even in the absence of an associated unconditioned stimulus (106)

conditioned stimulus (CS) an event that is repeatedly paired with a particular unconditioned stimulus (106)

conditioning a process of learning associations in which an implicit memory forms because of repeated exposure to a certain stimulus (104, 127)

cone a photoreceptor cell in the retina that enables a person to see color (72)

confederate a person who takes part in an experiment who is seemingly a subject but is really working with the researcher (20)

confirmation bias a person's tendency to look for evidence that proves his or her beliefs and to ignore evidence that disproves those beliefs (143)

conflict the disparity between people's or groups' actions, goals, or ideas (220)

conformity a principle that requires people to adjust their behavior or thinking to match a group standard (212)

conjunction fallacy a phenomenon that causes people to believe that additional information increases the probability that a statement is true, even though that probability actually decreases (144)

conscious encoding a process of encoding that involves paying specific attention to the information to be remembered (122)

conscious motivation a motivation that remains in a person's awareness (200)

consciousness a person's awareness of himself or herself and his or her environment (88)

consistency paradox the observation that personality ratings are consistent across time and among different observers, but that behavior ratings are not (246)

construct validity a type of validity that uses a specific procedure that measures or correlates with a theoretical or intangible concept (28)

content words words that have meaning (160)

context effect   a person's ability to better retrieve information when in the same context in which the information was first encoded (128)

contingency management   an operant conditioning strategy that involves altering the relationship between a person's actions and those actions' consequences to replace unwanted behaviors with desirable ones (291)

continuity   the tendency to view intersecting lines as part of a continuous pattern (81)

continuous reinforcement   a method of reinforcement that ensures that a desired response is reinforced every time it occurs (109)

continuous traits   characteristics like height, weight, and skin color that have a range of possible values (59)

contralateral   describes a situation in which one side of something controls the opposite side of something else (47)

control group   a group of participants in an experiment who are either given no treatment or who are given treatment that should have no effect (21)

conversion disorder   a somatoform disorder characterized by the sudden, temporary loss of a sensory function (232, 275)

cooperation   the act of working together for the good of the group (221)

cooperative principle   a principle that instructs speakers that utterances should be truthful, informative, relevant, and clear (147)

coping strategy   a strategy that helps a person reduce or minimize the effects of stressors (232)

coronary heart disease   a condition characterized by the clogging of the vessels that nourish the heart muscle (231)

corpus callosum   a large band of axons connecting the two hemispheres of the brain (45)

counterconditioning   a process that involves replacing unwanted responses to particular situations with new responses (290)

covariation principle   a process of attribution in which behavior is observed based on three characteristics: the behavior's distinctiveness, it's consistency, and consensus (208)

creative intelligence   a type of intelligence characterized by the ability to adapt to new situations, come up with unique and unusual ideas, and think of novel solutions to problems (138)

criterion validity   an indication of how closely a measurement correlates with another criterion of the characteristic being studied (27)

critical period   the optimal time period shortly after birth during which normal sensory and perceptual development takes place (83, 180)

critical thinking   a way of processing information in which a person examines assumptions, evaluates evidence, looks for hidden agendas, and assesses conclusions (6)

cross-sectional studies   studies that collect data from different individuals at different ages in order to track age differences (153)

crowd   a large, mixed-sex group whose members get together socially (183)

crystallized intelligence   mental ability derived from previous experience (138)

cued forgetting   a type of forgetting in which a person is specifically told to forget certain information (124)

cultural relativity   the need to consider the individual characteristics of a culture in which a person with a disorder was raised in order to diagnose and treat the disorder (264)

culture-bound syndrome   any disorder that is limited to a particular cultural group (264)

debrief   give a verbal description of the true nature and purpose of a study after the study occurs (29)

decision aversion   the state of attempting to avoid making any decision at all (144)

decision making   the process of selecting and rejecting available options (144)

deductive reasoning   a top-down method of arriving at a specific conclusion based on broader premises (142)

deep processing   a level of processing in which a word's meaning is encoded (127)

defection   the act of promoting one's own interest at the expense of others (221)

defense mechanism   a mental process of self-deception that helps a person alleviate his or her worry or anxiety (248)

deindividualization   a process that allows people in a group to relinquish personal responsibility and give themselves over to the group experience (217)

deintensification   a muting of emotions (198)

delayed conditioning   a type of classical conditioning in which the conditioned stimulus is presented before the unconditioned stimulus, and the termination of the conditioned stimulus is delayed until the unconditioned stimulus is made available (106)

delayed reinforcement   a reward that does not immediately follow an action (109)

delta wave   a type of brain wave with a high amplitude that characterizes stage three (90)

delusion   a persistent false belief (270)

demand characteristic   an aspect of a setting that can cause participants in a study to behave as they believe a researcher wants them to (27)

dendrites   relatively short, bushy, branch-like structures that emerge from a neuron's cell body and receive signals from adjoining neurons (38)

dependent personality disorder   a mental disorder characterized by clingy, needy behavior (275)

dependent variable   a variable that is affected by the independent variable in an experiment (20)

depressive disorder   a mood disorder characterized by prolonged or extreme periods of depression (268)

deprovincialization   a process in which learning more about an outgroup through friendship or collaborative efforts can make people more tolerant of the norms and customs of other groups (219)

descriptive statistics   statistics researchers use to summarize data sets (24)

deterministic fallacy   the claim that traits and behaviors can be explained entirely through genetics (64)

developmental age   the point at which someone falls among developmental stages; not necessarily related to chronological age (153)

developmental psychologists   psychologists who study the physical, cognitive, and social changes that people experience throughout their lives (153)

deviation score   the difference between an individual data point's actual value and the mean value of the whole data set (24)

diathesis-stress hypothesis   a hypothesis that states that people are genetically predisposed to a particular mental disorder but will develop the disorder only if exposed to environmental or emotional stress during critical developmental periods (273)

difference threshold   the minimum difference between two stimuli needed to detect the difference 50 percent of the time (70)

discrimination   negative behavior toward a group of people and its members (218)

discriminative stimulus   a cue signaling that a particular response will be reinforced or punished (105)

discursive reasoning   *see* **theoretical reasoning** (142)

disengagement theory of aging   a theory that states that elderly people gradually and willingly withdraw themselves from the world around them (187)

displacement   the process of redirecting an unconscious and unacceptable wish or drive toward a more acceptable alternative (249)

dispositional attribution   an attribution based on a person's personality or characteristics (208)

dispositional force   an internal factor involved in motivation (200)

dissociation   a split in consciousness that allows simultaneous thoughts and behaviors to occur apart from each other (98)

dissociative amnesia   a disorder that causes sudden, selective memory loss (275)

dissociative disorder   a condition in which the normal cognitive processes are fragmented, causing a sudden loss of memory or change in personality (275)

dissociative fugue   a disorder characterized by a sudden loss of memory accompanied by an abrupt departure from home (275)

dissociative identity disorder   a disorder in which a person seems to experience two or more personalities in one body (249)

distal stimulus   a stimulus from an object that exists in the surrounding environment (82)

distress   a prolonged, negative type of stress characterized by a challenge being perceived as a daunting obstacle (229)

dizygotic twins   twins that come from two separate zygotes (58)

DNA   a complex molecule that is the main ingredient of chromosomes; forms the code for all genetic information (56)

dogmatism   a belief that requires people to accept information as irrefutable and to refrain from questioning authority (18)

dominant   suppressing the expression of the other gene in a pair of alleles (58)

door-in-the-face technique   a procedure for gaining compliance that involves making a large request and then, when that request is refused, making a smaller request that seems reasonable in comparison (214)

dopamine   a neurotransmitter that helps people make decisions that lead to good outcomes and avoid bad outcomes (144)

dorsolateral prefrontal cortex   an area of the brain that serves as an executive control system that initiates a person's behavior; it can also shift or inhibit that behavior based on the decisions the person makes (145)

double depression   a condition in which bouts of major depression are superimposed over a state of dysthymia (269)

double-blind experiment   an experiment in which both the subject and the observer are kept blind, thus negating the observer-expectancy effect and the subject-expectancy effect (28)

dream   a sequence of images, feelings, ideas, and impressions that pass through people's minds as they sleep (94)

drive   one of many internal conditions that make a person tend toward certain goals; this is caused by a departure from optimal states (200)

drive-reduction theory   a theory that states that a person reacts when a physiological need creates an aroused state that drives him or her to reduce the need (200)

drug tolerance   a lessening of physiological and behavioral effects caused by a drug through the repeated use of that drug (108)

dual diagnosis   the comorbid existence of a mental disorder and substance abuse (263)

dual-coding theory   a theory that states that concrete words are represented both visually and verbally, whereas abstract terms are coded only verbally, requiring more complex coding and making them more difficult to retrieve (148)

dualism   the belief that the mind does not cease to exist when the body dies, and that thoughts and ideas can exist separately from the body (6)

dysthymia   a chronic but less severe form of depression that lasts for two years or more (269)

echoic memory   a type of sensory memory involving auditory stimuli (122)

echolocation   a process in which sound waves are emitted and the environment is analyzed by listening to the frequency of the waves that are reflected back (74)

eclectic psychotherapy   a type of psychotherapy involving the use of multifaceted treatments that vary depending on each person's unique problem and take into account biological, psychological, and social influences (286)

ego   the part of the psyche that tries to identify the basic drive that the id wants to fulfill and to come up with a realistic plan for satisfying that drive (248)

egoism   the act of doing something beneficial for others in the hopes of receiving something in return (221)

eidetic memory   the ability to recall detailed images vividly after looking at them for a short period of time (122)

elaboration-likelihood model   a model that states that people tend to be persuaded through the central route when their motivation and ability to understand and consider the persuasive message is high, while they are more likely to be persuaded by the peripheral route when their motivation is low or when they need to make a quick decision (216)

elaborative rehearsal   a process in which a person gives meaning to information for the purpose of storing that information in long-term memory (127)

electroconvulsive therapy (ECT)   a type of therapy in which electric shocks are sent to patients' brains to treat certain psychological disorders in patients who don't respond to other treatment methods (285)

emerging adulthood   the period during a person's early 20s in which that person often still greatly depends on his or her parents for financial and emotional support (185)

emotion   a subjective reaction to an object, event, person, or memory (194)

emotion regulation   the use of cognitive strategies to control and influence a person's own emotional responses (198)

emotional intelligence   a person's ability to perceive, under-stand, manage, and utilize his or her emotions (138)

emotion-focused coping   a coping strategy that involves attempting to alleviate stress by avoiding the stressor and soothing stress-related emotions (234)

empiricism   the view that knowledge originates through experience (4)

encephalization   an increase in brain size (62)

encoding   the process by which sensory information is converted into a form that can be stored (120)

endocrine system   the system involved in the release of hormones that regulate metabolism, growth, development, tissue function, and mood (45)

endogenous   directed by a person's internal decisions (78)

endogenous attention   *see* **goal-directed selection** (145)

endorphin   a morphine-like chemical that inhibits pain signals and is released by the medial forebrain bundle (78, 201)

environmental psychology   a field that investigates the physical environment's effects on behavior and health (228)

episodic memories   memories in which a person remembers an entire sequence of events (124)

equity theory   a theory that states that workers decide how satisfied they feel with their jobs by comparing themselves to others (203)

erotic plasticity   the degree to which the sex drive is shaped by cultural, social, and situational factors (175)

error   random variability that is accidentally introduced into an experiment (26)

esteem need   a need to feel achievement and self-worth (201)

eustress   a low-level, positive type of stress that helps a person perform a task or achieve a goal (228)

evolutionary approach   an approach to psychology that explores ways in which patterns of human behavior may be beneficial to people's survival (8)

evolutionary psychology   a branch of psychology involved with explaining the development of the human mind and behavior by studying how adaptive behaviors helped human ancestors survive and reproduce (61)

executive control systems   parts of the brain that inhibit pleasurable responses so that people can avoid making decisions that feel good but are bad for them (145)

exemplar theory   a theory that claims that people make category judgments by comparing new things they encounter with examples of other things they remember that fit into that category (141)

exogenous   directed by external stimuli (79)

exogenous attention   *see* **stimulus-driven selection** (145)

expectancy theory   a theory that defines job satisfaction as a worker's sense of achieving a certain outcome based on expectancy, instrumentality, and valence (203)

experimental group   a group of participants in an experiment who are subject to an independent variable (21)

explanatory style   the way in which a person explains events to himself or herself (237)

explicit attitude   a belief or opinion that a person holds consciously and can report to others (216)

explicit memories   memories of which a person is consciously aware (124)

explicit stereotype   a stereotype that is consciously held (218)

exposure effect   an effect caused by the prior experience of a stimulus that primes us to react a certain way (195)

exposure treatment   a type of counterconditioning in which people who have a fear or phobia are repeatedly exposed to what they fear over several sessions until they become so accustomed to it that they no longer fear it (290)

expressive behavior   an outward sign that a person is experiencing an emotion (194)

external environment   events and conditions in the outside world (57)

external genitalia   the penis and scrotum in males and the labia, clitoris, and external vagina in females (168)

external locus of control   a person's tendency to believe that his or her rewards and fate are controlled by outside forces (252)

external validity   a type of validity indicating that a test can be generalized to the rest of the population (28)

extinction   the diminishing of a conditioned response, most often through the removal of the reinforcement associated with the response (104, 127)

extrinsic motivation   the desire to complete a behavior because it will lead to a reward or avoid punishment (155)

extrinsic reward   a reward that is achieved through the completion of a task (201)

eye movement desensitization and reprocessing (EMDR)   a form of exposure therapy in which therapists instruct clients to focus on a disturbing image or traumatic memory as they move their eyes back and forth, with the goal of helping them deal with the psychological issues brought on by the disturbing or traumatic event (291)

face validity   the extent to which a study superficially measures what it is intended to measure (27)

facial feedback hypothesis   a hypothesis that states that a person who makes a certain facial expression will feel the corresponding emotion, as long as the person is not feeling some other competing emotion (198)

fact   an objective statement made using direct observations (18)

factor analysis   a statistical technique that is used to identify patterns of correlations in responses to questionnaires (245)

false consensus effect   a person's tendency to overestimate the extent to which others share his or her beliefs and behaviors (18)

family resemblance theory   a theory that suggests that people put items in categories together if they share certain characteristics, even if not every member of the category has similar features (140)

family therapy   a type of therapy in which the therapist views the family as a single unit and attempts to resolve conflicts and stresses that arise among the family members (288)

feature detector   a specialized brain cell that only responds to particular elements in the visual field (72)

feature integration theory   a theory that states that people organize stimuli based on knowledge of how their features should be combined (82, 146)

feel-good, do-good phenomenon   the idea that if a person is already happy, he or she is more likely to be helpful (199)

fetal alcohol syndrome (FAS)   physical and cognitive abnormalities in children resulting from a mother's heavy drinking (153)

field study   a study that is conducted in a setting other than a laboratory (23)

fight-or-flight response   a physiological response to stressors, triggered by the amygdala, in which the body becomes prepared for action (45, 229)

figure   the object on which a person is focusing (82)

filter theory   a theory that states that a person selects stimuli early in the perception process, even before he or she assesses the meaning of the input (146)

five-factor model ("Big Five" theory) a model that is used to describe personality by assessing a person's score on each of five dimensions: extraversion/introversion, agreeableness/antagonism, conscientiousness/undirectedness, emotional stability/instability, and openness to experience/non-openness (245)

fixation a focus on one particular erogenous zone of the body (248)

flashbulb memories memories that are immediately stored in long-term memory and that are caused by emotional events (127)

flooding a type of exposure treatment in which clients are exposed to fear-inducing stimuli in an intense way by directly exposing them to the stimuli (291)

fluid intelligence the ability to process information and act accordingly (138)

foot-in-the-door technique a technique that involves asking people to comply with a small request and then making a much larger request, to raise funds (149)

foramen magnum the largest opening in the skull; allows the spinal cord to connect to the brain (43)

forgetting the inability to retrieve information that has been previously stored (170)

forgetting curve a graphical representation of how quickly a person tends to forget information (129)

fovea a depressed spot in the retina that occupies the center of a person's visual field (72)

framing the perspective from which people interpret information before making a decision (144)

free association a psychoanalytic technique in which the therapist encourages the client to relax his or her mind and, starting from a recent experience, a memory, or a dream, report every image or idea that enters awareness, refraining from logic or self-editing (286)

freezing a defensive reaction in which an organism remains motionless (114)

frequency the number of cycles per second in a wave (74)

frequency distribution a summary of how frequently each of the scores in a set of data occurs (24)

Freudian slip an error in speech that represents the surfacing of repressed memories and thoughts (249)

frontal lobe a part of the brain that performs a variety of integration and management functions It is involved in the encoding and storage of working and long-term memory and, to a lesser extent, in sensory memory processing (7, 120)

frustration-aggression hypothesis a hypothesis that states that frustration occurs when people feel blocked in obtaining their goals (220)

full consciousness a state of consciousness in which a person is aware of his or her own environment and also is aware of his or her mental state and is able to provide information about it (88)

functional fixedness a bias that limits a person's ability to think in unconventional ways (141)

functionalism a school of psychology focused on how organisms use their learning and perceptual abilities to function in their environment (6)

fundamental attribution error (FAE) a phenomenon in which people make an attribution based on character, even when they know that the behavior is situational (208)

fusiform face area an area of the visual cortex that specifically responds to and recognizes faces (73, 209)

g factor the entire skill set of general intelligence that encompasses a range of abilities (138)

gametes reproductive cells in an organism (59)

ganglion cell one of several neurons that connect the bipolar neurons in the eyes to the brain (72)

gate-control theory a theory that states that a "neurological gate" in the spinal cord controls the transmission of pain messages to the brain (78)

gender a set of behaviors and characteristics that define individuals as boys and men or girls and women in society (168)

gender identity a person's sense of being a boy or girl, man or woman (169)

gender identity disorder a condition in which a person feels he or she was born with the body of the wrong sex (170)

gender roles expectations about the way men and women behave (171)

gender schema theory a theory that states that the process of gender differentiation begins at a very young age; as a children develop schemas for other things around them, they also develop a schema for their gender and adjust their behavior to align with it (171)

gender stereotype a widely held concept about a person or group of people that is based only on gender (172)

gender typed referring to boys and men who show traditionally masculine traits and behaviors, and girls and women who show traditionally feminine traits and behaviors (170)

gene complex a group of genes acting together (59)

general adaptation syndrome (GAS) a response to stress that consists of three stages: alarm, resistance, and exhaustion (229)

general intelligence (g) a common factor that underlies certain mental abilities (138)

generalization a process in which a learner reacts to a particular object or situation in the same way that he or she reacts to one that resembles that object or situation (104)

generalized anxiety disorder a type of anxiety disorder in which a person feels inexplicably and continually tense and uneasy (266)

genes sections of DNA that contain specific recipes to make proteins in the body (56)

genocide the systematic destruction of one group by another (221)

genome the complete set of instructions for making an organism (57)

genotype the entire set of genes inherited by an organism (57)

geon a simple three-dimensional shape that, with other geons, makes up all other objects (82)

Gestalt psychology a school of psychology centered around the belief that people naturally seek out patterns, or wholes, in the sensory information available to them (8)

gestalt therapy is a type of humanistic therapy in which the therapist attempts to make the client feel whole by helping the client feel aware of and responsible for his or her thoughts, behaviors, experiences, and feelings (288)

glial cells (glia) cells that support neurons by, among other things, keeping neurons in place, creating myelin, and providing nutrition and insulation (38)

globus pallidus a part of the basal ganglia; relays information from the caudate and putamen to the thalamus (44)

glucose blood sugar (202)

goal enhancement the drive to receive the awards that have been obtained in the past (112)

goal state a problem-solving state in which a person has all the information he or she needs (141)

goal-directed selection a type of attention in which a person makes an explicit choice to pay attention to something (145)

gonads the first sex organs to develop; these are identical in male and female fetuses for the first four weeks of prenatal development (168)

grammatical words words that provide structure (160)

grapheme-color synesthesia a condition in which a person perceives letters as specific colors (83)

gray matter a substance that makes up the cerebral cortex; covers the cerebrum and cerebellum (45)

ground the environment surrounding the object of focus, or the figure (82)

group polarization a phenomenon in which the more members of a group discuss similar opinions, the more extreme their positions become (217)

group therapy a type of therapy that is led by a therapist and involves a group of clients experiencing psychological disorders (288)

groupthink a phenomenon in which group members' opinions become so uniform that all dissent becomes impossible (217)

gustatory sense the sense of taste (202)

gyri bulges in the cerebral cortex (45)

habituation a process in which repeated exposure to a stimulus reduces the response to that stimulus (127, 156)

hallucination a false sensory perception that a person believes to be real (270)

hassle a minor nuisance that, when combined with other small problems, can create a stressful environment (230)

health psychology the psychologically based aspect of behavioral medicine (228)

hedonic motive a pleasurable incentive or an attempt to avoid pain that causes us to act in a certain way (211)

hedonic principle a principle that states that people want to experience pleasure and avoid pain (200)

heritability the degree to which a trait is able to be passed on genetically (61, 247)

heterozygous having non-identical pairs of alleles (58)

heuristics informal rules that make the decision-making process quick and simple (143)

hierarchy a leveled or ranked organization of concept categories based on particular features (140)

hierarchy of needs a pyramidal structure that shows the five needs that must be satisfied for a person to achieve self-actualization (201, 251)

hindsight bias a person's erroneous belief that he or she knew something all along after an event has occurred (18, 142)

hippocampus a part of the brain involved in processing explicit memories, recognizing and recalling long-term memories, and conditioning (44, 27)

histogram a representation of a frequency distribution using rectangles in which the width of a rectangle represents an interval and the area of a rectangle is proportional to the corresponding frequency (24)

histrionic personality disorder a mental disorder characterized by a tendency to overreact to situations, excessive emotionality, and the use of manipulation to gain attention from others (273)

homeostasis a steady and balanced inner state (200)

homozygous having identical pairs of alleles (58)

hue a particular color (74)

humanistic approach an approach to psychology based on the belief that people have free will and are able to control their own destinies (8)

humanistic theory a type of personality theory that emphasizes people's conscious understanding of themselves and their abilities to attain self-fulfillment (251)

hypercomplex cell a feature detector that responds to multiple features of a stimulus (73)

hypervigilance a state in which a person's "fight or flight" response is fully activated (129)

hypnagogia a period of transition between wakefulness and sleep that typifies stage one (90)

hypnopaedia learning while asleep (92)

hypnosis an exercise in suggestion during which one person makes suggestions to another person regarding the perceptions, feelings, thoughts, or behaviors that the subject can expect to experience (96)

hypnotic ability high susceptibility to hypnotism (96)

hypnotic analgesia pain relief through hypnosis (98)

hypochondriasis a disorder in which a person becomes so preoccupied with minor symptoms that he or she develops an exaggerated belief that the symptoms are indicative of a life-threatening illness (232)

hypocretin an alerting neurotransmitter that stimulates wakefulness (94)

hypomania a milder form of mania that causes less severe mood elevations and does not interfere with normal daily functioning to the same extent as mania (269)

hypothalamus a small structure in the brain that links the nervous system to the endocrine system (44)

hypothesis a prediction, based on an existing theory, about a new fact (18)

iconic memory a type of sensory memory involving visual stimuli (120)

id the part of the psyche that tries to satisfy a person's basic drives and survival instincts (248)

identification the act of unconsciously taking on the characteristics of another person who seems better able to cope with feelings of threat and anxiety (249)

identity a person's sense of self (183)

ideocentrism a personality trait exhibiting the tendency to think and act in an individualistic manner (255)

idiographic approach a method of interpreting personality data that is person-centered and focuses on how the unique parts of a person's personality form a consistent whole (244)

illusory conjunction mistakenly combining features of two different stimuli (82)

illusory contour a visual illusion in which lines are perceived without actually being present (80)

implicit attitude a belief or opinion that a person can't report and that will automatically influence his or her actions (216)

implicit memories memories of which a person is not consciously aware (124)

implicit stereotype an unconscious set of mental representations that guide attitudes and behaviors (218)

implosion therapy a type of exposure treatment in which clients are exposed to very intense stimuli by being asked to imagine an extreme version of their fears or phobias (291)

imprinting a process of early attachment in which the first thing a newborn sees is considered its mother (180)

inattentional blindness the failure to perceive a given stimulus (79)

incentive   a positive or negative stimulus in the environment (200)

independent construal of self   a person's view of himself or herself as a self-directed, self-contained entity (255)

independent variable   a variable that a researcher can manipulate in an experiment (20)

individualist culture   a culture that emphasizes each person's individual rights and freedoms and deemphasizes the social roles that people play in relation to others (255)

inductive reasoning   a method of using specific examples to arrive at a general conclusion (142)

infant reflexes   a set of innate traits in humans (62)

inferential statistics   statistics that use probability laws to help researchers decide how likely it is that their results are due to chance and, as a result, how likely it is that the observed results apply to a broader population (24)

inferiority complex   a drive for perfection and superiority throughout adulthood in an effort to compensate for feelings of both physical and mental inferiority rooted in childhood (249)

informational social influence   influence exerted by information that others give a person (212)

ingroup   a group that a person is part of (219)

inhibition   a process in which a neuron is instructed not to transmit information to other neurons (41)

initial state   a problem-solving state in which a person has incomplete or unsatisfactory information (141)

insight   the sudden realization of the solution to a problem (142)

insomnia   a sleep disorder characterized by recurring difficulty falling or staying asleep (94)

insomniac   a person who need as much sleep as most people but is unable to get it (203)

instinct   an unlearned complex behavior with a fixed pattern throughout a species (200)

instinctual drift   the tendency for an organism to revert to instinctive behaviors after being trained to have new behaviors (64, 155)

Institutional Review Board (IRB)   an ethics review panel established by a publicly funded research institution to evaluate all proposed research by that institution (29)

insulin   a hormone that reduces the level of glucose in the blood (202)

intelligence   the capacity to reason, solve problems, and acquire new knowledge (137)

intensification   an exaggeration of emotions (198)

interdependent construal of self   a person's view of himself or herself as part of a larger network of family and community members (255)

internal locus of control   a person's tendency to believe that he or she controls his or her own rewards and fate (252)

internal validity   a type of validity indicating that a researcher is able to control all extraneous values in a test so that the only variable influencing the results it of the study is the independent variable (28)

interneurons   neurons that carry information between sensory neurons and motor neurons (38)

interpersonal psychotherapy   a type of psychotherapy that focuses on helping clients improve their relationships, particularly their current relationships, as a means to resolving their psychological problems (287)

intersex   referring to people who are born with non-standard male or female genitalia (169)

interview   a form of data collection in which people provide oral descriptions of themselves; this can be strictly structured, with a set list of questions, or loosely structured and more conversational (23)

intrinsic reward   a task that is pleasurable in and of itself (201)

intrinsically motivated   characterized by the desire to do things because they are interesting, challenging, satisfying, or enjoyable (155)

ipsilateral   describes a situation in which one side of something controls the same side of something else (47)

James-Lange theory   a theory that proposes that the physiological experience of heart pounding or tears flowing causes a person to feel afraid or sad (194)

joint visual attention   a behavior in which a baby looks at an adult's eyes, follows the adult's gaze, and then directs his or her own gaze toward whatever the adult is looking at (159)

judgment   a skill that allows people to form opinions, reach conclusions, and evaluate situations objectively and critically (144)

just noticeable difference (jnd)   *see* **difference threshold** (70)

just-world phenomenon   a phenomenon in which people convince themselves that they are doing well because they are good people, while those who are suffering are just getting what they deserve (219)

K-complex   a biphasic wave form that occurs spontaneously during sleep (90)

kinesthetic sense   is the sense relating to how a person's body parts interact with one another (77)

laboratory observation   the study of people or animals in a controlled setting (22)

laboratory study   a study in which participants are taken to a location that has been specifically set up to facilitate collection of data and allow control over environmental conditions (23)

language acquisition device (LAD)   a theoretical mechanism that provides children with an inherent foundation for the principles of universal grammar (160)

language-acquisition support system (LASS)   the social environment into which a baby is born (160)

latent content   the unconscious meaning of a dream (96, 287)

latent learning   learning that is exhibited only in the presence of an incentive (155)

law of common fate   a law that states that if the parts of a stimulus are all moving in the same direction, they are perceived as parts of a whole (81)

law of effect   a law that states that if a response produces a satisfying effect, it is likely to occur again (108)

law of pragnanz   a law that states that a person organizes a stimulus into the simplest possible form (81)

learned helplessness   a feeling of hopelessness and passivity caused by being unable to avoid or control traumatic events (255, 270)

learning   the process by which experience results in a relatively permanent change in future behavior (104)

learning-performance distinction   the difference between what a person learns and its application on that particular day (104)

level of significance   a statistic that identifies the probability that the results of a study could have occurred by chance (26)

levels of analysis   various ways that psychologists can look at a psychological issue, such as from the level of the brain, the level of the person, and the level of the world (10)

lexical ambiguity   confusion caused by multiple meanings of a word or phrase (148)

liking   a subjective feeling of pleasure derived from a reward (201)

liking system   a system involved with experiencing pleasure; it does not depend on dopamine (201)

limbic system   a system in the brain made up of a number of structures that control social and emotional behavior; influences cognitive processes, most notably forms of memory (43)

linguistic determinism   the belief that different languages impose different conceptions of reality (149)

linguistic relativity hypothesis   a hypothesis that states that the language a person speaks influences his or her conception of reality (148)

locus of control   a person's perception of whether he or she has control over a given situation (252)

longitudinal studies   studies that collect data from the same individuals over a period of time to track age changes (153)

long-term depression   the weakening of a neuronal synapse; the opposite of long-term potentiation (114)

long-term memory   a type of memory in which information that can last a lifetime is stored (120)

long-term potentiation (LTP)   the process in which neural connections are strengthened through the repetition of neurotransmitters traveling across the same synapses (112, 128, 203)

lowball technique   a technique that encourages compliance by offering an attractive deal, only to change the terms of the deal later (149)

lucid dreaming   a phenomenon in which a person achieves an awareness of a dream as a dream while dreaming (96)

lymphocyte   a type of white blood cell (232)

major depressive disorder (MDD)   a mood disorder characterized by signs of severe depression that last for more than two weeks with no apparent cause (269)

male answer syndrome   a phenomenon in which males are more likely than females to guess at answers to difficult questions rather than reveal their uncertainty (174)

mania   a period of euphoria characterized by elevated self-esteem, increased talkativeness, enhanced energy, and a decreased need for sleep (269)

manifest content   what a person explicitly remembers about a dream—its storyline, characters, and details (94, 287)

masking   showing one emotion while feeling another (198)

mass action principle   a principle that states that reduction in learning is proportional to the amount of brain tissue destroyed, no matter where in the brain the destruction occurs (112)

matched pair   a set of participants in an experiment, one from one group and the other from another group, who are identical in terms of a particular variable or set of variables (22)

matched sample   a group of participants in an experiment that is identical to at least one other group in terms of a particular variable or set of variables (22)

mean   the arithmetic average of the scores in a data set, or the sum of all the scores divided by the number of scores (24)

measures of central tendency   the three most typical scores in a set of data: mean, median, and mode (24)

medial forebrain bundle   the brain's reward pathway (201)

median   the middle score in a data set (24)

medical model   the concept that psychological abnormalities are diseases that, like biological diseases, have symptoms, causes, and cures (264)

medulla   a part of the brain that regulates cardiac and respiratory function (43)

meiosis   the process of cell division in which chromosomes duplicate themselves and the cell divides to form two new cells; the two new cells then divide again, resulting in four new cells created from the original cell (59)

melatonin   a sleep-inducing hormone (90)

memory   the brain's system for filing away new information and retrieving previously known data (120)

menarche   a girl's first menstruation (154)

Mendelian heredity   the idea that units of heredity come in pairs and one pair can dominate another (58)

menopause   the end of a woman's menstrual cycle and ability to bear children (154)

mental age   the level of ability typical of a child of the same chronological age (137)

mental set   a preexisting state of mind that a person uses to solve problems because that state has helped the person solve similar problems in the past (141)

mentalizing   a person's understanding that his or her behavior and that of others reflects a person's mental states (211)

mere exposure   simple contact between two individuals or groups (219)

method   a rule or technique that provides a framework for observations (18)

microvillus   a tiny hair at the tip of a taste receptor cell (77)

midcingulate cortex   part of the cingulate cortex; primarily involved in response selection (45)

minimal consciousness   a relatively fragmented connection between self and environment in which a person might respond to a stimulus without being aware of it at a more thoughtful level (88)

Minnesota Multiphasic Personality Inventory (MMPI)   the most widely used personality inventory, initially developed to identify emotional disorders but now used for a variety of other purposes (246)

minority influence   the power of a few people (217)

mirror neuron   a neuron that responds both when an organism performs a task and when it watches another organism perform the same task (114)

misattribution   assigning the incorrect meaning to an emotion because of a particular physiological response (195)

mitosis   the process of cell division in which chromosomes duplicate themselves before the cell divides, creating two cells genetically identical to the original (59)

mnemonics   memory aids that give rhyme and reason to lists or other pieces of information (127)

mode   the most frequently occurring score in a data set (24)

modeling   the ability to reproduce an action that is being observed (112)

molecular genetics   a field of study emphasizing the analysis of the molecular structure and function of genes to try to identify the specific genes responsible for a certain disease, trait, or behavior (61)

monozygotic twins   twins that come from a single zygote that divides and separates (58)

mood   a free-floating emotional feeling that does not relate directly to a stimulus (194)

mood disorder   a mental disorder in which a person regularly experiences emotional extremes (268)

mood-congruent processing   the selective perception of stimuli congruent with the emotional state of the person experiencing the stimuli (198)

morphemes   the smallest meaningful units of language that represent the objects, events, ideas, characteristics, and relationships in that language's vocabulary (160)

morphology   how morphemes may be arranged to form words (90); the form or shape of something (198)

motivation   a need or desire that energizes and directs behavior (200)

motivation state   one of many internal conditions that make a person tend toward certain goals (200)

motor development   the emergent ability to execute physical actions (153)

motor neurons   neurons that carry information away from the central nervous system to operate muscles and glands (38)

Müllerian system   the precursor of female sex organs (168)

multitasking   the act of juggling independent sensory inputs (79)

myelin   a fatty substance that coats and insulates axons (38)

narcissistic personality disorder   a mental disorder characterized by an inflated sense of self-importance and a deep need for admiration (273)

narcolepsy   a sleep disorder characterized by periodic, uncontrollable sleep attacks (94)

natural selection   a theory that states that organisms best adapted to their environment tend to survive and transmit their genetic characteristics to succeeding generations (10, 56)

naturalistic fallacy   the claim that whatever is natural is good or right (64)

naturalistic observation   the study of people or animals in their own environment (22)

nature   inherited characteristics that influence personality, physical growth, intellectual growth, and social interactions (11)

negative cognitive style   a pattern of pessimistic or negative thoughts (269)

negative reinforcer   something that strengthens a response by removing an unpleasant consequence (109)

negative symptom   a symptom that indicates a decrease in normal functions such as attention or emotion (270)

neocortex   the evolutionarily newest part of the brain; it enables symbolic representation (43)

nerve   a tight grouping of neurons (41)

network   a large community of neurons (38)

neurons   excitable cells that receive different types of stimulation; the building blocks of the nervous system (38)

neuropathic pain   a negative feeling caused by a malfunction in the central nervous system (78)

neurotransmitter   a chemical message created by a synapse from an electric message transmitted by terminal buttons (41)

neutralizing   showing no emotion, even though the person is actually feeling one (198)

night terrors   a relatively benign, albeit disturbing, sleep disorder most common in young children and characterized by episodes of high arousal and terrified appearance (94)

nociceptive pain   a negative feeling caused by an external stimulus (77)

nodes of Ranvier   parts of an axon that are not insulated by myelin (41)

nomothetic approach   a method of interpreting personality data that is variable-centered and focuses on finding consistent patterns of relationships among individuals' traits (244)

nonconscious activity   a process that occurs in the body that people do not have to consciously monitor or regulate (89)

non-regulatory drives   drives that initiate activities not required to preserve homeostasis (200)

nonsomniac   a person who require much less than eight hours of sleep each day (92, 203)

norm of reciprocity   a socialized norm that involves a person's tendency to desire to return favors (214)

normal curve   a graphical representation of an evenly distributed data set in which the curve is symmetrical and bell-shaped due to the even distribution of results and the tendency of data to accumulate around the center of a set in an even distribution (24)

normal distribution   an instance of frequency distribution in which scores are tracked on a bell-shaped curve with a concentration of data in the center (137)

normative investigations   research conducted in order to establish norms (153)

normative social influence   influence that draws on a person's desire for others' approval and his or her longing to be part of a group (212)

nucleus accumbens   an area of the brain underneath the frontal cortex that is involved in experiencing pleasure (196)

nurture   environmental factors such as parental styles, physical surroundings, and economic issues (10)

observational learning   a learning process in which a person observes and imitates others (111)

observational method   the process of observing and recording a subject's behavior (24)

observer bias   the effect that occurs when an observer expects to see a particular behavior and notices only actions that support that expectation (22)

observer-expectancy effect   *see* **observer bias** (28)

obsessive-compulsive disorder   an anxiety disorder in which a person feels driven to think disturbing thoughts or to perform senseless rituals (266)

obsessive-compulsive personality disorder   a mental disorder characterized by obsessive neatness, difficulty delegating tasks because of a fear the tasks will be completed in a substandard manner, and a preoccupation with rules, schedules, and order (275)

occipital lobes   parts of the brain involved in visual processing; the smallest of the four lobes in the human brain (46)

occupational self-direction   a set of desirable characteristics for an occupation comprising work that is complex rather than simple, varied rather than routine, and not closely supervised by another (187)

operant behavior   responses that an organism makes to produce an effect on the environment (108)

operant conditioning   a type of learning in which organisms associate their actions with consequences (108)

operant response   an act that causes a particular effect on the environment (109)

opportunism   the necessity of rapid speech production (148)

optic chasm   the point near the base of the brain where some fibers in the optic nerve from each eye cross to the opposite side of the brain (72)

optic nerve a bundle of axons of ganglion cells that carries neural messages from each eye to the brain (72)

optimal arousal an arousal state in which a person has enough motivation but not so much that he or she feels anxious and unable to perform (201)

orexin a hormone that brings on feelings of hunger (202)

outcome expectancy a person's assumption about the consequences of his or her own behavior (252)

outgroup a group containing those people outside one's own group (219)

ova immature eggs (83)

overconfidence a person's tendency to think that he or she is more knowledgeable or accurate than he or she really is (142)

overextended referring to the relatively broad use of common nouns (160)

overjustification the undermining of intrinsic motivation through excessive rewards (155)

panic disorder a condition in which sufferers come to fear the possibility of another panic attack following an initial attack (266)

papilla a bump on the tongue in which taste buds are embedded (77)

parallel processing the process of doing several things at the same time (73)

paranoid personality disorder a mental disorder characterized by extreme suspicion and distrust of others (273)

parasympathetic division *see* parasympathetic nervous system (196)

parasympathetic nervous system the part of the autonomic nervous system that is responsible for functions that do not require immediate action and acts as a brake for organs (38)

parental investment the time, energy, and risk involved in producing and raising offspring (64)

parietal cortex an area of the brain that serves as an executive control system that plays a critical role in directing a person's attention during the decision-making process (145)

parietal lobes parts of the brain primarily concerned with bodily sensations, including those of touch, taste, and temperature (46)

partial (intermittent) reinforcement a method of reinforcement in which responses are sometimes reinforced and sometimes not (109)

participant a person who takes part in an experiment as a subject (20)

patient a person with a psychological disorder who is being treated using a biomedical approach (282)

patrolling periodically scanning an environment to make sure that nothing in the environment has changed (112)

perception the way a person selects, organizes, and interprets sensory information (70)

perceptual adaptation a process in which a person adjusts to changes in the environment by adjusting sensory input (83)

perceptual load the processing difficulty or complexity of a task (145)

perceptual set a mental disposition based on previous experiences and expectations that influences the way a person perceives things (80)

perceptual speed the time it takes a person to perceive and compare stimuli (140)

peripheral nervous system (PNS) the part of the nervous system that serves the limbs and organs (38)

peripheral route a path to persuasion that involves evaluating an argument based on tangential cues rather than on the argument's merits (216)

perpetuating cause a consequence of a disorder that help keep it going once it has manifested (265)

perseverance effect a phenomenon in which it is difficult for people to shake their initial impressions (216)

personal control a person's sense of controlling his or her environment rather than feeling helpless (252)

personality the style in which a person interacts with the world, particularly with other people (244)

personality disorder a rigid, maladaptive pattern of behavior that makes it difficult for individuals to have normal social relationships (273)

personality inventory a long, scientifically rigorous questionnaire that asks questions about many different behaviors and assesses several traits at once (246)

person-centered therapy a type of humanistic therapy in which the therapeutic process focuses squarely on the client's abilities and insights rather than the therapist's thoughts and skills (288)

person-situation controversy the question of whether people's behaviors are more influenced by situational factors than by personality traits (247)

persuasion a deliberate effort to change an attitude or behavior (216)

phenomenology the study of individual consciousness that addresses subjective experience (88)

phenotype the observable property that comes from a genotype (57)

pheromone a chemical substance released by an animal to trigger behavioral responses in other members of that species (77)

phobia a persistent, irrational fear of a specific object, activity, or situation (266)

phonemes elementary vowel and consonant sounds that combine to form morphemes (160)

phonology how phonemes may be arranged to produce morphemes (160)

phylogeny the development of a species (62)

physiological arousal a heightened bodily reaction to a stimulus (194)

physiological need a need that affects a person's physiology, such as hunger and thirst (201)

pituitary gland a gland that secretes human growth hormone and influences all other hormone-secreting glands (45)

place cell a cell in the hippocampus that only fires when an organism is in a specific location in its natural environment (114)

placebo a substance or procedure which resembles medical therapy but has no intrinsic therapeutic value (28)

placebo effect a phenomenon in which participants taking a placebo react as if they were receiving treatment, simply because they believe they are actually receiving treatment (29)

planning function is an aspect of consciousness that helps people inhibit urges they have that are not moral, ethical, or practical; it equips people with the conscious self-awareness necessary to analyze and evaluate their thoughts before they act on those thoughts. (90)

plasticity a flexible ability to grow and change (41, 140)

pleasure principle a principle that states that a person should seek immediate gratification and pay no attention to societal expectations or constraints (248)

polygenic coming from the interaction of several genes (59)

pons is a part of the brain that is involved in sleep, dreaming, left-right body coordination, and arousal (43)

pop-out stimulus a stimulus that is important or interesting to a person (79)

positive reinforcer something that strengthens a response by presenting a pleasurable consequence (109)

positive symptom a symptom that reflects an excess or distortion of normal functions, such as delusions and hallucinations (270)

posterior cingulate cortex part of the cingulate cortex; primarily involved in personal orientation (45)

posthypnotic suggestion a suggestion made during hypnosis that is executed by the participant when he or she is no longer hypnotized (98)

post-synaptic neuron a neuron that receives a signal from a synapse (41)

post-traumatic stress disorder an anxiety disorder caused by experiencing or witnessing out-of-control events with feelings of helplessness and fear (268)

practical intelligence the ability to find many solutions to complicated or poorly defined problems and use those solutions in practical, everyday situations (139)

practical reasoning a type of reasoning in which a person considers what to do or how to act (142)

preattentive processing a complex processing of information that occurs without a person's conscious awareness (79)

precipitating cause an event in a person's day-to-day life that brings on a particular disorder (265)

preconscious information information that is usually outside a person's awareness but is able to be brought into consciousness on demand (89)

predictive validity a type of criterion validity in which you can use the results of a test to predict a person's score or performance in another area (28)

predisposing cause an existing underlying factor that makes an individual particularly susceptible to a certain disorder (265)

preexisting schema a set of ideas or beliefs about others that leads a person to perceive others in a way that conforms with that person's expectations (208)

prefrontal cortex the very front of the brain and part of the neocortex; responsible for the executive functions, such as mediating conflicting thoughts and making choices between right and wrong It is essential for the cognitive experience of emotion (43, 196)

prefrontal lobotomy a type of surgery in which the prefrontal area of the brain is disabled, causing people to feel less intense emotions but also leaving them unable to plan or manage their lives (196)

Premack principle a principle that states that a preferred activity can be used to reinforce a non-preferred task (110)

preservation and protection theory a theory that explains sleep as a mechanism evolved to preserve energy and provide protection during the night (202)

pre-synaptic neuron a neuron that delivers a signal to a synapse (41)

primacy effect the ability to recall information given first when given a list of things to remember (124)

primary appraisal a person's initial evaluation of the seriousness of a stressor and the extent of the demands it will put on that person (234)

primary auditory cortex a part of the brain involved in auditory processing (46)

primary cortex a part of the cerebral cortex that serves basic sensory and motor functions; one exists in each lobe of the cerebral cortex (46)

primary motor cortex a part of the brain that is responsible for generating the neural impulses that control the execution of movements (47)

primary reinforcer something that satisfies a basic biological need (109)

primary sex characteristics sexual organs present at birth and directly involved in human reproduction (154, 168)

primary somatosensory cortex a part of the brain that receives and interprets information about bodily sensations; located in the parietal lobe (46)

primary visual cortex a part of the brain that receives input from the eyes and translate that input into what people see (46)

priming the process of activating associations in memory just before starting a certain task (124)

principlism a desire to engage in prosocial behavior out of principle (221)

proactive interference a phenomenon in which previously learned information interferes with a person's ability to recall new information (129)

problem of other minds the observation that because the nature of consciousness is internal, a person can't possibly determine how similar or different another person's perceptions are to his or her own (88)

problem solving the act of combining current information with information stored in memory to find a solution to a task (141)

problem-focused coping a coping strategy that involves a person's attempting to alleviate stress directly, either by eliminating the source of a stressor or by changing the way he or she behaves in stressful situations (234)

procedural memory a type of implicit memory consisting of habits and skills people perform (127)

prodigy a person of normal intelligence who has an extraordinary ability (138)

prognosis a prediction of the typical course of a disease and the likelihood of recovery (263)

projection the process by which a person who unconsciously experiences an impulse attributes that impulse to someone else (249)

projector a person who experiences synesthesia and actually sees letters as being certain colors, even though he or she knows what color the type actually is (83)

proprioceptor a specialized nerve ending that provides a constant stream of information from a person's muscles through the spinal cord and on to the cortex of the parietal lobe (78)

prosocial positive and helpful (112)

prosocial behavior behavior carried out with the goal of helping others (221)

prosopagnosia a condition caused by damage to the ventral region of the temporal lobe in which a person is unable to recognize faces (211)

prospect theory a theory that states that people will more likely avoid risk in situations where they stand to gain but will seek risk when they stand to lose something (144)

prospective memory remembering to perform a specific action (160)

prototype a mental image or typical example that exhibits all the features associated with a concept (140)

proximal stimulus   a pattern of physical energy created by the distal stimulus that stimulates a person's receptors (82)

proximity   the tendency to perceive objects that are close to one another as part of the same group (81)

proximodistal rule   the tendency for motor skills to emerge in sequence from inside to outside (154)

pseudoforgetting   a type of encoding interference in which information is never actually stored because of some kind of attention interference (124)

psychic blindness   the inability to interpret the significance of a sensory stimulus because of an inability to experience the correct emotional response (196)

psychic determinism   the concept that unconscious processes underlie all conscious thoughts and actions (247)

psychoactive medication   a type of drug that alleviates symptoms of mental disorders by acting on the bodily processes that may cause those symptoms (284)

psychoanalysis   a type of psychotherapy that relates closely to Freudian concepts like the influence of the unconscious It requires patients to talk to a psychiatrist about their lives while the psychiatrist listens, analyzes, and interprets each word (247, 286)

psychoanalytic approach   a method of analyzing a psychological disorder in which unconscious conflicts and other possible underlying psychological factors are examined (264)

psychobiography   a life-story conception of personality (252)

psychodynamic approach   an approach to psychology based on the belief that behaviors are motivated by internal factors unavailable to the conscious mind (8)

psychodynamic theory   a personality theory that focuses on the interaction of mental forces (247)

psychodynamic therapy   a type of therapy based on Freudian psychodynamics, the theory of which states that unconscious conflicts underlie mental disorders, and these conflicts make their way to the surface through a person's speech and behavior (286)

psychological diagnosis   a label for a person's mental disorder assigned by identifying and classifying patterns of behavior (263)

psychological refractory period   the interval during which the brain is too busy processing a stimulus to comprehend a second stimulus (146)

psychology   the scientific study of behavior and mental processes (4)

psychoneuroimmunology   the study of how psychology relates to events involving the nervous system and immune system (108)

psychopathology   see **abnormal psychology** (263)

psychopharmacology   the study of how drugs affect the mind and behavior (284)

psychophysics   the study of the relationship between physical characteristics of stimuli and the sensory experiences that accompany them (70)

psychophysiological ("mind-body") illness   a symptom such as chronic fatigue or hypertension that is caused by psychological reactions to stress (232)

psychosexual stages   developmental stages during which the id's desire for pleasure focuses on many of the body's erogenous zones in turn (248)

psychosurgery   a treatment method in which parts of the brain are surgically altered to treat mental disorders (286)

psychotherapy   the interaction between a therapist and someone suffering from a psychological problem, the

goal of which is to provide support or relief from the problem (286)

puberty   the period in which a person's body goes through the changes that allow him or her to reproduce (154)

punishment   a penalty given in an attempt to decrease the occurrence of a certain behavior (110)

putamen   a part of the basal ganglia; involved in reinforcement learning (44)

Pygmalion effect   the tendency for people to behave in accordance with others' expectations (209)

questionnaire   a series of questions with a strict purpose that has been developed using careful controls such as precise wording, carefully constructed questions, and random sampling (23)

random assignment   the process by which participants in an experiment are randomly placed into groups (21)

random sampling   a technique in which the participants in a survey are chosen randomly so as to get a fair representation of a population (23)

range   the difference between the highest and lowest values in a data set (24)

rapid cycling   an incidence of a person with bipolar disorder experiencing more than four episodes of either mania or depression a year (269)

rapid eye movement (REM) sleep   a recurring stage of sleep during which vivid dreams usually occur (90)

rapid subcortical pathway   a pathway between the thalamus and amygdala through which the amygdala receives projections from sensory organs (195)

rational choice theory   a theory that states that people make decisions by determining how likely each outcome of that decision is, as well as the positive or negative value of each outcome (144)

rational coping   a coping strategy that involves facing a stressor directly and working to overcome it (234)

rationalization   the use of conscious reasoning to explain away anxiety-inducing thoughts and feelings (249)

reaction formation   the process of changing a wish into its more acceptable opposite (249)

reality principle   a principle that states that basic drives and survival instincts should be achieved through actions that will be will be pleasurable rather than painful (248)

reason   the skill of organizing information and beliefs into a series of steps leading to a conclusion (159)

reasoning   a cognitive process of organizing information or beliefs into a series of steps to reach conclusions (142)

recall   the process of retrieving a stored memory in the absence of external stimuli (128)

recency effect   the ability to recall information most recently stored when given a list of things to remember (124)

receptor cell   a specialized cell that responds to a particular type of energy (71)

recessive   being suppressed by the dominant gene in a pair of alleles (58)

reciprocal altruism   a theory that suggests that people may carry out altruistic acts with the expectation of being the recipient of altruism at some point in the future or because they have been helped by altruism sometime in the past (221)

reciprocal determinism   a theory that states that a person's behavior is both influenced by and influences a person's personal factors (255)

recognition   the process of matching an external stimulus to a stored memory (128)

recognition-by-components   a theory that states that a person recognizes an unfamiliar object by piecing together the cylinder, cone, wedge, and brick shapes of which it is composed (82)

reference group   those people to whom a person feels affiliated (212)

referred pain   a negative feeling that occurs when sensory information from internal and external areas converges on the same nerve cells in the spinal cord (78)

reflexes   rapid and automatic neuromuscular actions generated in response to a specific stimulus (43)

reframing   a coping strategy that involves finding a new or creative way to think about a stressor that reduces its threat (234)

regression   a retreat to an earlier stage of development (249)

regulatory drives   drives that seek to preserve homeostasis (200)

reinforcement   an act that causes a response to be more likely to recur (108, 201)

reinforcer/punisher   a positive or negative consequence caused by an operant response (109)

relational memory theory   a theory that states that the hippocampus processes events by linking them into relational frameworks (114)

relative deprivation   a person's comparison of himself or herself to others; when the person compares himself or herself to someone of higher social standing, he or she feels worse, and when the person compares himself or herself to someone of lower social standing, he or she feels better (199)

relaxation response   reduced muscle tension, cortical activity, heart rate, breathing rate, and blood pressure (239)

relaxation therapy   a therapeutic technique that involves alternately tensing and relaxing muscles in the body and practicing breathing exercises in order to relieve tension (239)

reliability   the degree to which a measurement yields similar results every time it is used with a particular subject under particular conditions (27)

repression   a process that blocks anxiety-provoking thoughts from the conscious mind (249)

repressive coping   a coping strategy that involves maintaining an artificially positive viewpoint and trying not to think about a stressor (234)

resistance   a client's attempt to avoid doing therapeutic work (287)

resting potential   a relatively negative state inside a neuron in which the neuron's fluid interior contains a surplus of negatively charged particles (41)

restrictive function   an aspect of consciousness that allows people to exercise selective attention, or a conscious focus on one stimulus or perception at a given time (89)

reticular formation   a part of the brain that controls arousal (245)

retina   a multilayered tissue at the back of the eye that is responsible for visual transduction (72)

retrieval   the process by which previously stored information is moved from long-term memory to working memory (170)

retrieval cue   a stimulus that helps a person retrieve information from memory (128)

retroactive interference   is a phenomenon in which new information interferes with a person's ability to recall previously learned information (129)

retrograde amnesia   memory loss characterized by the loss of past memories (129)

retrosplenial cortex   part of the cingulate cortex; primarily involved in memory formation and retrieval (45)

reuptake   a process in which neurotransmitters are released back to a pre-synaptic neuron (41)

reversible figure   an illusion in which staring at an image long enough causes the figure and ground to reverse (82)

reward contrast effect   a sudden shift in the attractiveness of a reward (110)

reward neuron   a neuron involved with experiencing the positive emotions associated with receiving a reward (201)

Ribot's law   a law that states that memory loss following brain damage affects recent memories to a greater extent than remote memories (114)

rod   a photoreceptor cell in the retina that responds to varying degrees of light and dark (72)

Rorschach inkblot test   a test that presents a participant with a series of nebulous inkblots and asks him or her to say whatever comes to mind upon viewing the inkblots; interpretations of the inkblots supposedly are related to the viewer's unconscious thoughts (251)

rote (or maintenance) rehearsal   the process of repeating information, either out loud or silently, with the intent of learning that information (123)

safety   a feeling of being in a secure and safe environment (201)

saturation   the intensity of a color (74)

savant syndrome   a rare disorder that occasionally accompanies autism in which a person of below-average intelligence has an extraordinary ability (138)

savings   the ability to reacquire a learned behavior in a shorter period of time than it took to learn originally (104)

Schachter and Singer two-factor theory   a theory that states that cognitive evaluation happens alongside a person's physiological arousal to create the emotion he or she experiences (123)

Schachter's cognition-plus-feedback theory   a theory that states that how a person perceives an environment feeds back into physiological arousal and influences what the person feels (195)

schemas   concepts or frameworks around which people organize and interpret information (156)

schizoid personality disorder   a mental disorder that causes people to show very little interest in others and have few personal relationships (273)

schizophrenia   a mental disorder that causes a person to experience distorted perceptions, inappropriate emotions or reactions, and confusion (270)

schizotypal personality disorder   a mental disorder characterized by peculiar or eccentric mannerisms and difficulty forming social relationships (273)

scientific method   a process for conducting an objective inquiry through data collection and analysis (4)

seasonal affective disorder (SAD)   a mood disorder in which a person gets depressed only at certain times of the year (269)

secondary appraisal   a person's reassessment of a stressor that focuses on the actions he or she needs to take and the resources that will help him or her overcome the stressor (234)

secondary reinforcer   something that becomes satisfying or pleasurable through experience (109)

GLOSSARY

secondary sex characteristics   sexual organs and traits that develop at puberty and are not directly involved in reproduction (154, 168)

second-order conditioning   a type of classical conditioning in which the conditioned stimulus is paired with a neutral stimulus (106)

secure relationship   an intimate relationship in which both partners provide each other with comfort and security (185)

selective breeding   the process by which pairs of organisms of the same species with desirable characteristics are mated in order to select for those characteristics (61)

selective storage function   an aspect of consciousness that allows people to selectively analyze, interpret, and act on stimuli (89)

self theory   a personality theory that states that all people want to become their "real" selves; to do so, people need to live according to their own wishes rather than those of other people (251)

self-actualization   a complete feeling of self-acceptance and an awareness of fulfilling one's unique potential (201, 251)

self-concept   a person's understanding of who he or she is (251)

self-conscious emotion   an emotion that relates to a person's thoughts about himself or herself and about his or her own actions (217)

self-consciousness   the most self-aware state of consciousness; it allows a person to focus on his or her individual self (88)

self-efficacy   a person's expectations about his or her own ability to perform a certain task (255)

self-fulfilling prophecy   a belief that causes itself to become true (209)

self-regulation   the process of practicing self-discipline (183)

self-report method   a form of data collection in which people are asked to describe their own behavior or mental state (23)

self-serving bias   the tendency for a person to attribute his or her failures to external events and his or her successes to personal characteristics and skills (209)

semantic   containing factual and conceptual information that is not directly linked to life events (124)

semantic encoding   the process of encoding meaning (122)

semicircular canal   a tube located in the inner ear that helps to monitor the body's position in space (78)

sensation   the process through which we detect physical energy from the environment and code that energy as neural signals (70)

sensory adaptation   a process in which sensory receptor cells become less responsive to an unchanging stimulus (71)

sensory buffer   part of the perceptual system that holds information for a short time before it is accepted or rejected by a filter (146)

sensory cortex   the part of the brain that mediates the human sense of touch by encoding tactile information (120)

sensory memory   a type of memory lasting no more than a few seconds in which the impression of a sensory stimulus is stored (120)

sensory neuron   a neuron that carries information from the sensory receptors to the brain as a coded signal (38, 71)

sensory registers   the parts of the brain that make up sensory memory (120)

sensory system   the part of the nervous system responsible for processing sensory information (70)

serial position effect   the ability to recall (or not recall) information in a list depending on that information's position in the list (124)

set of operations   the steps that a person needs to take to get from the initial state to the goal state (141)

sex   a person's biological classification as either male or female based on the sex chromosomes contained in his or her DNA (168)

sexism   prejudice and unfair treatment against men or women based on gender stereotypes (172)

sexual orientation   enduring sexual attraction toward members of our own sex, the other sex, or both (174)

sexual selection   the process by which a mate is chosen (59)

shallow processing   a level of processing in which a word's sound or appearance is encoded (127)

shaping   a process in which reinforcers are used to guide an organism's actions toward a desired behavior (110)

shared identity   a person's feeling that he or she is similar to other people in thought, feeling, and behavior (214)

signal detection theory   a theory that predicts how and when we detect the presence of a faint stimulus amid background stimulation (70)

similarity   the tendency to perceive objects that are the same shape, size, or color as part of a pattern (81)

simple cell   a feature detector that only responds to a single feature of a stimulus (72)

simultaneous conditioning   a type of classical conditioning in which the conditioned stimulus and unconditioned stimulus are presented at the same time (106)

situational attribution   an attribution based on a person's situation or environment (208)

situational force   an external factor involved in motivation (200)

skewed distribution   a graphical representation of an unevenly distributed data set in which scores cluster together on one end rather than in the middle (26)

skin sense   the sense relating to pressure, touch, and pain (77)

sleep   a natural loss of consciousness (90)

sleep apnea   a sleep disorder in which people intermittently stop breathing during sleep, which in turn causes the level of oxygen in the blood to plummet (94)

sleep spindle   a burst of fast, sharply pointed brain waves (90)

sleeper effect   a phenomenon that occurs when a person forgets the unreliable source of a piece of information but remembers the information itself and believes that it's trustworthy (217)

slower cortical pathway   a pathway that sends messages from the thalamus to the visual cortex and then back to the amygdala, allowing a person's perceptions to affect his or her emotions (196)

social age   a person's maturity level based on his or her life experiences (185)

social cognition   underlying processes, such as attention and memory, that make social behavior possible (209)

social cognitive theory   a type of personality theory that places emphasis on the beliefs and habits of thought, both conscious and automatic, that a person forms through interactions with society (252)

social Darwinism   a theory that states that society and culture evolved toward higher forms through the process of individuals adapting to hardship by either adapting and surviving or falling by the wayside (64)

social influence   behavioral control (211)

social intuitionist account of morality a theory that states that a person has an instant gut reaction to moral situations that precedes moral reasoning (189)

social intelligence the ability to negotiate new social environments (138)

social learning theory a theory that emphasizes the role of cognition in motivation and the importance of expectations in shaping behavior (171, 200)

social learning therapy a type of therapy designed to modify clients' problematic behavior patterns through observation and behavior reinforcement (292)

social loafing a phenomenon that occurs when people believe that their individual efforts don't matter or that they are not personally responsible because they are only one member of a group, so they tend to put less effort into a task (217)

social pain the pain of rejection or loss brought on by losing a close personal relationship or membership in a group (217)

social perception the process through which a person understands and categorizes the behavior of others (202)

social phobia an irrational fear of being publicly humiliated or embarrassed (266)

social pressure real or imagined psychological forces that people exert over others through their example, judgments, and demands (211)

social psychologist a psychologist who studies how the thoughts, emotions, and behavior of individuals influence and are influenced by interactions between people (208)

social trap a situation in which conflicting parties all try to win a conflict by engaging in mutually destructive behaviors, resulting in no one winning (221)

socialization the process through which a person shapes his or her behavioral patterns according to the society he or she lives in (180)

socioemotional selectivity theory of aging a theory that states that as people grow older and realize that the time they have left is limited, they focus on enjoying the present rather than looking to the future (187)

soma the cell body of a neuron (38)

somatic nervous system the part of the peripheral nervous system that picks up stimuli from the outside world, coordinates movements, and performs other consciously controlled tasks (38)

somatization disorder a somatoform disorder characterized by vague, unverifiable symptoms such as dizziness and nausea (232, 275)

somatoform disorder a disorder characterized by physical symptoms that do not have an identifiable cause (232, 275)

sound shadow an area of reduced sound intensity around the ear farther away from where a sound originates (74)

sound wave a change in air pressure caused by molecules of air or fluid colliding and moving apart (74)

source amnesia a phenomenon in which a person remembers information but forgets or misremembers where that information came from (129)

species-typical behaviors instinctive or characteristic ways of behaving particular to a certain species (62)

spermarche a boy's first ejaculation (15)

spinal cord a cord that connects the spinal nerves to the brain and organizes simple reflexes and rhythmic movements (43)

spontaneous recovery a reoccurrence of a learned behavior after extinction (104)

spoonerism a common execution error in which a person exchanges the initial sounds of two or more words in a phrase (148)

standard deviation a measure of the dispersion of a set of values using information from each individual score (24)

state a person's transient disposition to behave in a certain way (244)

state-dependent memory a stored memory that is more easily retrieved when a person is in the same state as they were when the information was first encoded (128)

statistical significance an indication that the difference between the average scores from two reliable samples is not simply due to chance (26)

stereotype a general belief about a group of people (218)

stereotype threat a stereotyped group's knowledge that they must work against a negative stereotype (218)

stimulus discrimination a process in which a learner is trained to distinguish between similar but distinct stimuli (104)

stimulus enhancement a person's tendency to pay attention to a particular place or object in which someone else has shown interest (111)

stimulus-driven capture a type of attention that is motivated by external factors (145)

storage the process by which encoded information is placed into memory (120)

storage decay a phenomenon in which many of a person's memories fade over time (129)

stranger anxiety fear of strangers (180)

stress a physical and mental response to threatening or challenging events (228)

stress inoculation a therapeutic technique in which clients are taught how to evaluate and cope with various stressors and are then exposed to increasingly stressful situations in a controlled environment to strengthen these coping mechanisms (234)

stressor an event that a person perceives as threatening or challenging (228)

structural ambiguity confusion that occurs when syntax causes a sentence to have multiple meanings (148)

structuralism a school of psychology concerned with the individual elements of consciousness and showing how they can be combined and integrated (6)

style-shifting the habit of a person to adapt his or her style of speaking in accordance with the person he or she is talking to, either to express solidarity or to maintain distance (147)

subconscious motivation is a motivation that is not in a person's awareness but can be easily accessed (200)

subject-expectancy effect an occurrence where participants in a study expect to behave in a certain way as a result of their treatment, causing them to adjust their behavior (28)

subjective well-being a person's self-perceived satisfaction with life (199)

sublimation the process that occurs when displacement causes a person to direct his or her energy into important or valuable activities (249)

successive approximations behaviors that are incrementally closer to the overall desired action (110)

suggestibility a person's susceptibility to the opinions of others (212)

sulci grooves in the cerebral cortex (45)

superego the part of the psyche that forces the ego to consider societal constraints and acceptable forms of behavior (248)

suprachiasmatic nucleus the part of the hypothalamus that controls the circadian clock (90)

survey a series of questions about people's behavior or opinions, in the form of a questionnaire or interview (23)

syllogism a deductive pattern of logic in which a conclusion is made based on two or more premises (142)

syllogistic reasoning a type of reasoning in which a person decides whether a conclusion logically follows from two or more statements that the person assumes to be true (142)

symmetry the tendency to perceive two unconnected but symmetrical shapes as one object (81)

sympathetic division *see* **sympathetic nervous system** (196)

sympathetic nervous system the part of the autonomic nervous system that is always active and acts as an accelerator for organs (38)

symptom a characteristic of thought or behavior that indicates a potential mental disorder (263)

synapse the area between neurons across which nerve impulses travel (41, 128)

synaptic cleft a narrow space between a transmitting neuron's terminal buttons and a receiving neuron's dendrites (41)

synaptic consolidation memory consolidation that takes place within a few hours after learning (114)

syndrome a combination of interrelated symptoms observed in an individual (263)

synesthesia a condition in which signals from the sensory organs are processed in the wrong cortical areas of the brain (83)

syntax how words may be arranged to produce phrases and sentences (160)

system consolidation gradual memory consolidation that takes weeks or months and involves the reorganization of the brain regions that support memory (114)

systematic desensitization a variation of exposure treatment in which people, within a therapeutic environment, learn to pair states of deep relaxation with thoughts of anxiety-provoking situations, with the goal of replacing the anxiety felt during these situations with relaxation (291)

taste bud a structure on the tongue that contains the receptor cells for taste (77)

taste-aversion learning a form of conditioned learning in which exposure to a flavor paired with sickness will produce a consistent aversion to that flavor (155)

temporal lobe a part of the brain involved in auditory processing (46, 196)

teratogens toxic substances that crosses the placenta and may cause birth defects (153)

terminal buttons structures at the ends of the branches that extend from axons (38)

testing a type of observational method in which participants are provided with stimuli or problems to respond to and researchers collect data about how the participants perform a certain task (24)

testosterone an androgen that is the principal male hormone (169)

thalamus a part of the brain located just above the brainstem that receives sensory information, processes it, and sends it to the cerebral cortex; helps to regulate the states of arousal, sleep and wakefulness, and consciousness (43, 195)

Thematic Apperception Test (TAT) a test that presents a participant with a series of random, unfamiliar images and asks him or her to tell stories about them; these stories supposedly reflect the person's inner hopes, fears, and desires (249)

theoretical reasoning a type of reasoning directed toward arriving at a belief or conclusion rather than at a practical decision (142)

theory an idea that helps explain an existing fact (18)

theta wave a type of brain wave that characterizes the first stage of sleep (90)

three-term contingency a three-part process in which organisms learn that in the presence of certain stimuli, their behavior is likely to have a particular effect on the environment; the three parts are the discriminative stimulus, the operant response, and the reinforcer/punisher (108)

threshold the number of positive inputs a neuron must receive before it transmits information (41)

timbre the quality and purity of the tone of a sound (74)

token economy a term for an operant conditioning procedure in which individuals earn tokens when they exhibit desirable behavior; later, people who've earned tokens can redeem them for privileges or treats (110, 292)

tonotopic pertaining to the way in which the primary auditory cortex is organized so that neurons that respond to particular frequencies are grouped together (74)

top-down processing our use of beliefs, experiences, expectations, and other concepts to shape our view of the world (80)

total situation a situation in which people are isolated from alternative viewpoints and given strict rewards and punishments from leaders (214)

trace conditioning a type of classical conditioning in which the conditioned stimulus is discontinued before the unconditioned stimulus is presented (106)

trait a person's relatively stable disposition to behave in a certain way (244)

trait theory a theory that states that a set of meaningful and distinct personality dimensions can be used to describe how people differ from one another (245)

transduction a process through which physical energy such as light or sound is converted into an electrical charge (71)

transference an instance in which a client's unconscious feelings about a significant person in his or her life are instead directed toward the therapist (287)

transsexual a person who has had sex reassignment surgery (170)

Type A a personality type characterized by a competitive, impatient, verbally aggressive, easily angered nature (231)

Type B a personality type character by an easygoing, relaxed nature (231)

unconditional positive regard valuing a person despite his or her problems and weaknesses (251)

unconditioned response (UR) a reflex action elicited by an unconditioned stimulus (106)

unconditioned stimulus (US) an original, unlearned stimulus that elicits a certain reflex action (106)

unconscious encoding a process of encoding that does not involve any deliberate thought or action (122)

unconscious inference a phenomenon in which a person's visual systems use sensory information to draw conclusions about what he or she sees (80)

unconscious information experiences, ideas, and motives that are so threatening or unacceptable that a person has permanently removed them from his or her consciousness (89)

unconscious motivation a motivation that operates without a person's awareness (200)

underextended referring to the relatively narrow use of common nouns (160)

universality hypothesis a hypothesis that states that facial expressions are understood across all cultures (194)

valence a positive or negative value along a continuum (199)

validity the degree to which a measurement measures what it is intended to measure (27)

variability the degree to which the numbers in a set of data differ from one another and the mean (24)

variable a characteristic that can vary, such as age, weight, or height (20)

ventromedial prefrontal cortex an area of the brain that serves as an executive control system that helps a person adhere to social and behavioral rules; it also plays a role in allowing a person to link his or her behavior to its potential consequences (145)

vestibular sac a group of cells that connect the semicircular canals to the cochlea (78)

vestibular sense the sense relating to movement and body position (77)

view-dependent pertaining to the idea that previously seen objects are stored as a template that is compared to a viewed shape in the retinal image (62)

view-independent pertaining to the idea that the visual system recognizes objects as a combination of their visual parts (82)

visual accomodation a process in which the lens adjusts in shape from thick to thin to enable a person to focus on objects that are close by or far away (72)

visual cortex a part of the brain that mediates the human sense of sight by encoding visual information (120, 196)

visual encoding the process of encoding images (122)

vomeronasal organ a specialized cell in the nasal cavities of most animals that detects pheromones and triggers a response (77)

wanting a desire to achieve a particular goal in order to receive a reward (201)

wanting system a system involved with achieving a goal to receive pleasure; depends heavily on dopamine (201)

Weber's law a law that states that regardless of size, two stimuli must differ by a constant proportion for the difference to be noticeable (71)

white matter myelinated axons that form the connections within the brain (46)

within-subject experiment a study in which each participant is exposed to several different independent variables (21)

Wolffian system the precursor of male sex organs (168)

working memory a type of memory in which information for short-term use is stored (120)

X chromosomes sex chromosomes that exist as a matched pair in females and part of an unmatched pair in males (the other part being a Y chromosome) (168)

Y chromosomes sex chromosomes that exist in males as part of an unmatched pair (the other part being an X chromosome) (168)

Yerkes-Dodson law a law that states in general that performance peaks with a moderate level of arousal (129, 201)

zone of proximal development the difference between what a child can do alone and what a child can do together with a more competent person (159)

zygote a cell formed from the combination of a sperm and an egg (58)

ABEND, L. (2008, July 18). In Spain, human rights for apes. *Time*. Retrieved October 13, 2008 from http://www.time.com

ABRAMSON, L. Y., METALSKY, G. I., & ALLOY, L. B. (1989). Hopelessness depression: A theory-based subtype. *Psychological Review, 96*, 358-372.

AC NIELSEN SURVEY. (2007, January 29). Global warming: A self-inflicted, very serious problem, according to more than half the world's online population. Retrieved July 18, 2008, from http://www.marketresearchworld.net/index.php?option= content&task=view&id=1264&Itemid=

ACETI ASSOCIATES. (2002). Recycling: Why people participate; Why they don't. Retrieved from http://www.acetiassociates.com/pubs/curbside.pdf

ACKERMAN, P. L., & BEIER, M. E. (2005). Knowledge and intelligence. In O. Wilhelm & R. W. Engle (Eds.), *Handbook of understanding and measuring intelligence*. Thousand Oaks, CA: Sage.

ADAMS, W. L. (2006, March/April). The truth about photographic memory. *Psychology Today*.

ADAMS, W. L. (2006, March 1). Could You Learn 40 Languages? *Psychology Today*. Retrieved February 16, 2010, from http://www.psychologytoday.com/articles/200605/could-you-learn-40-languages

ADER, R., & COHEN, N. (1985). CNS-immune system interactions: Conditioning phenomena. *Behavioral and Brain Sciences, 8*, 379-394.

ADLER, J. (2008, May 19). Unable to Forget. *Newsweek*. Retrieved February 16, 2010, from http://www.newsweek.com/id/136334

ADOLPHS, R., TRANEL, D., & DAMASIO, A. R. (1998). The human amygdala in social judgment. *Nature, 393*, 470-474.

AFFLECK, G., TENNEN, H., URROWS, S., & HIGGINS, P. (1994). Person and contextual features of daily stress reactivity: individual differences in relations of undesirable daily events with mood disturbance and chronic pain intensity. *Journal of Personality and Social Psychology, 66*, 329-340.

AIG SETS PAY, BONUS TARGET FOR NEW CEO WILLUMSTAD. (2008, July 21). *Insurance Journal*. Retrieved August 4, 2008, from http://www.insurancejournal.com/news/national/2008/07/21/92040.htm

AIKEN, L. R., & GROTH-MARNAT, G. (2005). *Psychological testing and assessment* (12th ed.). Boston: Allyn & Bacon.

AINSWORTH, C. (2003, November 15). The stranger within. *New Scientist, 180*(2421), 34.

AINSWORTH, M. D. S. (1979). Infant-mother attachment. *American Psychologist, 34*, 932-937.

ALBEE, G. W. (1986). Toward a just society: Lessons from observations on the primary prevention of psychopathology. *American Psychologist, 41*, 891-898.

ALESSADRI, S. M., SULLIVAN, M. W., & LEWIS, M. (1990). Violation of expectancy and frustration in early infancy. *Developmental Psychology, 26*, 738-744.

ALEXANDER, G., & HINES, M. (2002). Sex differences in response to children's toys in nonhuman primates (Cercopithecus aethiops sabaeus). *Evolution and Human Behavior, 23*(6), 467-479.

ALEXANDER, J. (2007, July 22). One Murder, Two Victims: The Wrongful Conviction of Ryan Ferguson. *Crime Magazine*. Retrieved February 16, 2010, from http://crimemagazine.com/07/ryan_ferguson,0722-7.htm

ALLEN, L. S., & GORSKI, R. A. (1992). Sexual orientation and the size of the anterior commissure in the human brain. *Proceedings of the National Academy of Sciences of the United States of America, 89*(15), 7199-7202.

ALLPORT, G. W. (1954). *The nature of prejudice*. Cambridge, MA: Addison-Wesley.

ALLPORT, G. W., & ODBERT, H. S. (1936). Trait names: A psycholexical study. *Psychological Monographs, 47*(1, Whole No. 211).

AMERICAN ACADEMY OF ACHIEVEMENT. (2005). *Elie Wiesel Biography*. Retrieved October 7, 2008, from http://www.achievement.org/autodoc/page/wie0bio-1

AMERICAN PSYCHIATRIC ASSOCIATION. (1994). *Diagnostic and statistical manual of mental disorders (Fourth Edition)*. Washington, DC: American Psychiatric Press.

AMERICAN PSYCHOLOGICAL ASSOCIATION, (2003, June 1). Ethical Principles of Psychologists and Code of Conduct. Retrieved February 5, 2010, from http://www.apa.org/ethics/code2002.html

AMUNTS, K., SCHLEICHERB, A., & ZILLESA, K. (2004). Outstanding language competence and sytoarchitecture in Broca's speech region. *Brain and Language, 89*(2): 346-353.

ANDERSON, C. A., & ANDERSON, D. C. (1984). Ambient temperature and violent crime: Tests of the linear and curvilinear hypothesis. *Journal of Personality and Social Psychology, 46*, 91-97.

ANDERSON, C. A., & BUSHMAN, B. J. (2001). Effects of violent video games on aggressive behavior, aggressive cognition, aggressive affect, physiological arousal and prosocial behavior: A meta-analytic review of the scientific literature. *Psychological Science, 12*, 353-359.

ANDERSON, I. M. (2000). Selective serotonin reuptake inhibitors versus tricyclic antidepressants: A meta-analysis of efficacy and tolerability. *Journal of Affective Disorders, 58*, 19-36.

ANGOLD, A., ERKANLI, A., EGGER, H. L., & COSTELLO, E. J. (2000). Stimulant treatment for children: A community perspective. *Journal of the American Academy of Child & Adolescent Psychiatry, 39*, 975-984.

ARCURI, L., CASTELLI, L., GALDI, S., ZOGMAISTER, C., & AMADORI, A. (2008). Predicting the vote: Implicit attitudes as predictors of the future behavior of decided and undecided voters. *Political Psychology, 29*, 369-387.

ARIES, E. (1987). Gender and communication. In P. Shaver & C. Hendrick (Eds.), *Review of Personality and Social Psychology, 7*, 149-176.

ARIETI, S. (1955). *Interpretations of schizophrenia*. New York: Brunner, p.195.

ARISTOTLE. (1908). *Nicomachean ethics*. Translated by W. D. Ross. Oxford: Clarendon Press. (Original work published in 350 BCE)

ARNETT, J. J. (2000). Emerging adulthood: A theory of development from the late teens through the twenties. *American Psychologist, 55*, 469-480.

ARONSON, E., & GONZALEZ, A. (1988). Desegregation, jigsaw, and the Mexican-American experience. In P. A. Katz & D. A. Taylor, (Eds.), *Eliminating racism: Profiles in controversy*. New York: Plenum Press.

ASCH, S. E. (1940). Studies in the principles of judgment and attitudes: II. Determination of judgments by group and ego standards. *Journal of Social Psychology, S.P.S.S.I. Bulletin, 12*, 433-465.

ASCH, S. E. (1956). Studies of independence and conformity: A minority of one against a unanimous majority. *Psychological Monographs, 70* (9, Whole no. 416).

ASENDORPF, J. B., & VAN-AKEN, M. A. G. (2003). Validity of Big Five personality judgments in childhood: A 9-year longitudinal study. *European Journal of Personality, 17*, 1-17.

ASERINSKY, E. (1988, January 17). Personal communication.

ASERINSKY, E., & KLEITMAN, N. (1953). Regularly occurring periods of eye motility, and concomitant phenomena, during sleep. *Science, 118*, 273-274.

ASHBY, F. G., & MADDOX, W. T. (1992). Complex decision rules in categorization: Contrasting novice and experienced performance. *Journal of Experimental Psychology: Human Perception of Performance, 18*, 50-71.

ASSOCIATED PRESS. (2008, May 2). Greensburg rises after tornado and goes green. *MSNBC.com*. Retrieved from http://www.msnbc.msn.com/id/24416341

ASSOCIATION FOR PSYCHOLOGICAL SCIENCE. (2007, July 26). Hearing Colors and Seeing Sounds: How Real Is Synesthesia? *Science Daily*. Retrieved July 10, 2008, from http://www.sciencedaily.com/releases/2007/07/070724113711.htm

ATKINSON, R. C., & SHIFFRIN, R. M. (1968). Human memory: A control system and its control processes. In K. Spence (Ed.), *The psychology of learning and motivation* (Vol. 2). New York: Academic Press.

ATLANTA JOURNAL-CONSTITUTION. (2009, June 26). The psychology of celebrity worship. Retrieved February 2, 2010, from http://www.ajc.com/health/content/shared-auto/healthnews/bhvr/628510.html

AVANIR PHARMACEUTICALS. (2006). Understanding involuntary emotional expression disorder. Retrieved July 21, 2008, from http://www.pbainfo.org/userfiles/File/IEED_ReviewPaper.pdf

AVANIR PHARMACEUTICALS. Patients' stories. Retrieved July 21, 2008, from http://www.pbainfo.org/pc/stories/

BABIES AND SIGN LANGUAGE. Creating a bilingual family. Retrieved December 16, 2009, from http://www.babies-and-sign-language.com/bilingual-children-family.html

BACK, M. D., SCHMUKLE, S. C., & EGLOFF, B. (2008). Becoming friends by chance. *Psychological Science, 19,* 439-440.

BAHRKE, M. S., & MORGAN, W. P. (1978). Anxiety reduction following exercise and meditation. *Cognitive Therapy and Research, 2*(4), 323-333.

BAILEY, J. M., & BELL, A. P. (1993). Familiality of female and male homosexuality. *Behavior Genetics, 23*(4), 313-322.

BAILEY, J. M., DUNNE, M. P., & MARTIN, N. G. (2000). Genetic and environmental influences on sexual orientation and its correlates in an Australian twin sample. *Journal of Personality and Social Psychology, 78*(3), 524-536.

BAILLARGEON, R. (1995). A model of physical reasoning in infancy. In C. Rovee-Collier & L. P. Lipsitt (Eds.), *Advances in infancy research* (Vol. 9). Stamford, CT: Ablex.

BAILLARGEON, R. (1998). Infants' understanding of the physical world. In M. Sabourin, F. I. M. Craik & M. Roberts (Eds.), *Advances in psychological science: Vol. 2. Biological and cognitive aspects.* Hove, England: Psychology Press.

BAILLARGEON, R. (2004). Infants' physical world. *Current Directions in Psychological Science, 13,* 89-94.

BAIRD, A. A., & FUGELSANG, J. A. (2004). The emergence of consequential thought: Evidence from neuroscience. *Proceedings of the Royal Society, B, Biological Sciences, 359,* 1797-1804. Reprinted in O. Goodenough and S. Zeki (Eds.), (2006), *Law and the Brain* (pp. 245-259). Oxford, UK: Oxford University Press.

BALABAN, M. T., & WAXMAN, S. R. (1997). Do words facilitate object categorization in 9-month-old infants? *Journal of Experimental Child Psychology, 64,* 3-26.

BANAJI, M. R., & GREENWALD, A. G. (1995). Implicit gender stereotyping in judgments of fame. *Journal of Personality and Social Psychology, 68,* 181-198.

BANDURA, A. (1986). *Social foundations of thought and action: A social cognitive theory.* Englewood Cliffs, NJ: Prentice Hall.

BANDURA, A. (1997). *Self-efficacy: The exercise of control.* New York: Freeman.

BANDURA, A. (1999). Social cognitive theory of personality. In L. A. Pervin and O. P. John (Eds.), *Handbook of personality: Theory and research* (2nd ed., pp. 54-196), New York: Guilford Press.

BANDURA, A., BLANCHARD, E. B., & RITTER, B. (1969). Relative efficacy of desensitization and modeling approaches for inducing behavioral, affective, and attitudinal changes. *Journal of Personality and Social Psychology, 13,* 173-199.

BANDURA, A., ROSS, D., & ROSS, S. A. (1961). Transmission of aggression through imitation of aggressive models. *Journal of Abnormal and Social Psychology, 63,* 575-582.

BANERJEE, S. (2008, June 8) Pregnant man Thomas Beatie may have more children. *Telegraph.* Retrieved September 2, 2008, from http://www.telegraph.co.uk/news/newstopics/howaboutthat/2093580/Pregnant-man-Thomas-Beatie-may-have-more-children.html

BARINAGA, M. (1991). How long is the human life span? *Science, 254,* 936-938.

BARNIER A. J., & MCCONKEY, K. M. (2004). Defining and identifying the highly hypnotizable person. In M. Heap, R. J. Brown, & D. A. Oakley (Eds.), *High hypnotisability: Theoretical, experimental and clinical issues.* London: Brunner-Routledge.

BAR-ON, R., TRANEL, D., DENBURG, N. L., BECHARA, A. (2003). Exploring the neurological substrate of emotional and social intelligence. *Brain, 126*(Pt 8), 1790-1800.

BARON-COHEN, S. (2002). The extreme male brain theory of autism. *Trends in Cognitive Sciences, 6*(6), 248-254.

BARTOSHUK, L. M. (1993). The wisdom of the body: Using case studies to teach sensation and perception. Paper presented to the National Institute on the Teaching of Psychology, St. Petersburg Beach, FL.

BATSON, C. D. (1994). Why act for the public good? Four answers. *Personality and Social Psychology Bulletin, 20,* 603-610.

BAUER, P. J. (2002). Long-term recall memory: Behavioral and neurondevelopmental changes in the first 2 years of life. *Current Directions in Psychology, 11,* 137-141.

BAUMEISTER, R. F. (2000). Gender differences in erotic plasticity: The female sex drive as socially flexible and responsive. *Psychological Bulletin, 126,* 347-374.

BAXENDALE, S. (2004). Memories aren't made of this: Amnesia at the movies. *British Medical Journal, 329,* 1480-1483.

BEARDSLEY, T. (1996, July). Waking up. *Scientific American, 14,* 18.

BECK, A. T. (1967). *Depression: Clinical, experimental, and theoretical aspects.* New York: Hoeber Medical Division, Harper & Row.

BECK, A. T., RUSH, A. J., SHAW, B. F., & EMERY, G. (1979). *Cognitive therapy of depression.* New York: Guilford Press.

BECKMAN, H., REGIER, N., & YOUNG, J. L. (2007). Effect of workplace laugher groups on personal efficacy beliefs. *Journal of Primary Prevention, 28,* 167-182.

BEITMAN, B. D., GOLDFRIED, M. R., & NORCROSS, J. C. (1989). The movement toward integrating the psychotherapies: An overview. *American Journal of Psychiatry, 146,* 138-147.

BEKES, S. (2000). How many languages can a person speak? Records of multilinguality. Λογοι.com. Retrieved February 16, 2010, from http://www.logoi.com/notes/polyglots.html

BELKIN, L. (2008, June 15). When mom and dad share it all. New York Times. Retrieved August 14, 2008, from http://www.nytimes.com/2008/06/15/magazine/15parenting-t.html

BELL, A. (1984). Language style as audience design. *Language in Society, 13*(2), 145-204.

BELSKY, J., LANG, M., & HUSTON, T. L. (1986). Sex typing and division of labor as determinants of marital change across the transition to parenthood. *Journal of Personality and Social Psychology, 50,* 517-522.

BEM, D. J. (1996). Exotic becomes erotic: A developmental theory of sexual orientation. *Psychological Review, 103,* 320-335.

BEM, S. L. (1974). The measurement of psychological androgyny. *Journal of Consulting and Clinical Psychology, 42,* 155-162.

BEM, S. L. (1975). Sex role adaptability: The consequence of psychological androgyny. *Journal of Personality and Social Psychology, 31,* 634-643.

BEM, S. L. (1981). Gender schema theory: A cognitive account of sex typing. *Psychological Review, 88,* 354-364.

BEM, S. L. (1993). *The lenses of gender: Transforming the debate on sexual inequality.* New Haven: Yale University Press.

BENEDICT, H. (1979). Early lexical development A: Comprehension and production. *Journal of Child Language, 6,* 183-200.

BENNET, M. P., ZELLER, J. M., ROSENBERG, L., & MCCANN, J. (2003). The effect of mirthful laughter on stress and natural killer cell activity. *Alternative Therapies in Health and Medicine, 9*(2), 38-45.

BENNETT, C. M., & BAIRD, A. A. (2006). Anatomical changes in the emerging adult brain: A Voxel-based morphometry study. *Human Brain Mapping, 27*(9), 766-777.

BERENBAUM, S. A., & SNYDER, E. (1995). Early hormonal influences on childhood sex-typed activity and playmate preferences: Implications for the development of sexual orientation. *Developmental Psychology, 31,* 31-42.

BERGSHLOM, P., LARSEN, J. L., ROSENDAHL, K., & HOLSTEN, F. (1989). Electroconvulsive therapy and cerebral computed tomography. *Acta Psychiatrica Scandinavia, 80,* 566-572.

BERKOWITZ, L. (1983). Aversively stimulated aggression: Some parallels and differences in research with animals and humans. *American Psychologist, 38,* 1135-1144.

BERKOWITZ, L. (1989). Frustration-aggression hypothesis: Examination and reformulation. *Psychological Bulletin, 106,* 59-73.

BERKOWITZ, S. J. (2003). Children exposed to community violence: The rationale for early intervention. *Clinical Child and Family Psychology Review, 6,* 293-302.

BERRIDGE, K. (2004, November). Simple pleasures. American Psychological Association. Retrieved August 4, 2008, from http://www.apa.org/science/psa/sb-berridge.html

BÉRTOLO, H., PAIVA, T., PESSOA, L., MESTRE, T., MARQUES, R., & SANTOS, R. (2003). Visual dream content, graphical representation and EEG alpha activity in congenitally blind subjects. *Cognitive Brain Research, 15,* 277-284.

BETTENCOURT, A. B., & KERNAHAN, C. (1997). A meta-analysis of aggression in the presence of violent cues: Effects of gender differences and aversive provocation. *Aggressive Behavior, 23*(6), 447-456.

BEY, L. (1996, August 17). Gorilla rescues boy: Child hurt in Brookfield fall. *Chicago Sun-Times.* Retrieved October 13, 2008 from http://www.suntimes.com

BIEDERMAN, I. (1987). Recognition-by-components: A theory of human image understanding. *Psychological Review, 94,* 115-147.

BJÖRKQVIST, K., LAGERSPETZ, K. M. J., & KAUKIAINEN, A. (1992). Do girls manipulate and boys fight? Developmental trends in regard to direct and indirect aggression. *Aggressive Behavior, 18,* 117-127.

BLACK, K. A., & SCHUTTE, E. D. (2006). Recollections of being loved: Implications of childhood experiences with parents for young adults' romantic relationships. *Journal of Family Issues, 27*(10), 1459-1480.

BLANCHARD, R. (1997). Birth order and sibling sex ration in homosexual versus heterosexual males and females. *Annual Review of Sex Research, 8,* 27-67.

BLANCHARD, R. (2001). Fraternal birth order and the maternal immune hypothesis of male homosexuality. *Hormones and Behavior, 40,* 105-114.

BLANCHARD, R., ZUCKER, K. J., SIEGELMAN, M., DICKEY, R., & KLASSEN, P. (1998). The relation of birth order to sexual orientation in men and women. *Journal of Biosocial Science, 30,* 511-519.

BLATT, S. J., SANISLOW, C. A., III, ZUROFF, D. C., PILKONIS, P. (1996). Characteristics of effective therapists: Further analyses of data from the national Institute of Mental Health Treatment of Depression Collaborative Research Program. *Journal of Consulting and Clinical Psychology, 64,* 1276-1284.

BLOOD, LEXINGTON. (2008, April 10). RecycleBank: Good Business, Green Motivation. *TriplePundit.* Retrieved February 16, 2010, from http://www .triplepundit.com/pages/recycle-bank-go.php

BOBOILA, C. (2004). From 'supertaster' to the taste-blind. *Yale Scientific.* Retrieved February 16, 2010, from http://research.yale.edu/ysm/article .jsp?articleID=77.

BOLGER, N., DELONGIS, A., KESSLER, R. C., & SCHILLING, E. A. (1989). Effects of daily stress on negative mood. *Journal of Personality and Social Psychology, 57,* 808-818.

BONE, J. (2008, March 26). Thomas Beatie, a married man who used to be a woman, is pregnant with a baby girl. *The Times.* Retrieved September 2, 2008, from http://www.timesonline.co.uk/tol/news/world/us_and_ americas/article3628860.ece

BORCHARD, T. J. (2009, October 29). Glenn Close tackles mental illness. Retrieved from http://psychcentral.com/blog/archives/2009/10/24/ glenn-close-tackles-mental-illness-thank-you.

BOSCARINO, J. A. (1997). Diseases among men 20 years after exposure to severe stress: Implications for clinical research and medical care. *Psychosomatic Medicine, 59,* 605-614.

BOSNIA WAR CRIME SUSPECT KARADZIC ARRESTED. (2008, July 21). CNN. Retrieved August 20, 2008, from http://www.cnn.com/2008/WORLD/ europe/07/21/serb.arrest/

BOUCHARD, T. J., & SEGAL, N. L. (1985). Environment and IQ. In B. B. Wolman (Ed.), *Handbook of intelligence: Theories, measurements, and applications* (pp. 391-464). New York: John Wiley.

BOWER, G. H., CLARK, M. C., LESGOLD, A. M., & WINZENZ, D. (1969). Hierarchical retrieval schemes in recall of categorized word lists. *Journal of Verbal Learning and Verbal Behavior, 8,* 323-343.

BOWLBY, J. (1969). *Attachment and loss:* Vol. 1. *Attachment.* London: Hogarth.

BRAUN, S. (1996). New experiments underscore warnings on maternal drinking. *Science, 273,* 738-739.

BRAY, O., KENNELLY, J. J., & GUARINO, J. L. (1975). Fertility of eggs produced on territories of vasectomized red-winged blackbirds. *The Wilson Bulletin, 87,* 187-195.

BRELAND, K., & BRELAND, M. (1951). A field of applied animal psychology. *American Psychologist, 6,* 202-204.

BRELAND, K., & BRELAND, M. (1961). The misbehavior of organisms. *American Psychologist, 16,* 681-684.

BRESLAU, N., CHILCOT, H. D., KESSLER, R. C., PETERSON, E. L., & LUCIA, V. C. (1999). Vulnerability to assaultive violence: Further specification of the sex difference in posttraumatic stress disorder. *Psychological Medicine, 29,* 813-821.

BRESLAU, N., DAVIS, G. C., ANDRESKI, P., & PETERSON, E. L. (1997). Sex differences in posttraumatic stress disorder. *Archives of General Psychiatry, 54*(11), 1044-1048.

BRICKMAN, P., COATES, D., & JANOFF-BULMAN, R. J. (1978). Lottery winners and accident victims: Is happiness relative? *Journal of Personality and Social Psychology, 36,* 917-927.

BRIM, O. (1999). *The McArthur Foundation study of midlife development.* Vero Beach, FL: The McArthur Foundation.

BROADBENT, D. E. (1958). *Perception and communication.* Oxford: Pergamon.

BRODY, J. E. (1981, March 7). Male hormone tied to aggressive acts. *The New York Times.* Retrieved August 26, 2008, from http://query.nytimes.com/ gst/fullpage.html?res=9F0DE6DD1539F934A35750C0A967948260&sec =health&spon=

BROWN, A. J., & PALINSCAR, A. (1986). Guided cooperative learning and individual knowledge acquisition. In L. B. Resnik (Ed.) *Knowing, learning, and instruction* (pp. 393-451). Hillsdale, NJ: Erlbaum.

BROWN, A. S., SCHAEFER, C. A., WYATT, R. J., GOETZ, R., BEGG, M. D., GORMAN, J. M., & SUSSER, E. S. (2000). Maternal exposure to respiratory infections and adult schizophrenia spectrum disorders: A prospective birth cohort study. *Schizophrenia Bulletin, 26,* 287-295.

BROWN, S. C., & CRAIK, F. I. M. (2000). Encoding and retrieval of information. In E. Tulving & F. I. M. Craik (Eds.), *The Oxford handbook of memory* (pp. 93-108). New York: Oxford University Press.

BUREAU OF THE CENSUS. (2002). *Statistical abstract of the United States, 2002.* Washington, DC: U.S. Government Printing Office.

BUREAU OF LABOR STATISTICS, U.S. DEPARTMENT OF LABOR. (2008). *Occupational Outlook Handbook, 2008-09 Edition, Psychologists.* Retrieved September 22, 2008, from http://www.bls.gov/oco/ocos056.htm

BURGER, J. (2007). Replicating Milgram. *Association for Psychological Science Observer, 20,* 15-17.

BURKE, D. (2008, April 1). Poll: 1 in 10 think Obama is Muslim. *USA Today.* Retrieved August 12, 2008, from http://www.usatoday.com/news/ religion/2008-04-01-obama-muslim_N.htm

BURNSTEIN, E., CRANDALL, C., & KITAYAMA, S. (1994). Some neo-Darwinian decision rules for altruism: Weighing clues for inclusive fitness as a function of the biological importance of the decision. *Journal of Personality and Social Psychology, 67,* 773-789.

BUSH SHOCKS FOREIGNERS WITH 'SATANIC' SIGN. (2005, January 21). Fox News. Retrieved August 2, 2008, from http://www.foxnews.com/story/ 0,2933,145062,00.html

BUSHMAN, B. J., & ANDERSON, C. J. (2002). Violent video games and hostile expectations: A test of the general aggression model. *Personality and Social Psychology Bulletin, 28,* 1679-1686.

BUSHMAN, B. J., BAUMEISTER, R. F., & STACK, A. D. (1999). Catharsis, aggression, and persuasive influence: self-fulfilling or self-defeating prophecies? *Journal of Personality and Social Psychology, 76,* 367-376.

BUSS, D. M. (1995). Evolutionary Psychology: A new paradigm for psychological science. *Psychological Inquiry, 6,* 1-30.

CAHILL, S. P., CARRIGAN, M. H., & CHRISTOPHER, F. (1999). Does EMDR work? And if so, why?: A critical review of controlled outcome and dismantling research. *Journal of Anxiety Disorders, 13,* 5-33.

CALDERA, Y. M., HUSTON, A. C., & O'BRIEN, M. (1989). Social interactions and play patterns of parents and toddlers with feminine, masculine, and neutral toys. *Child Development, 60*(1), 70-76.

CAMPBELL, D. T. (1975). On the conflicts between biological and social evolution and between psychology and moral tradition. *American Psychologist, 30,* 1103-1126.

CAMPBELL, D. T., & SPECHT, J. (1985). Altruism: Biology, culture, and religion. *Journal of Social and Clinical Psychology, 3,* 33-42.

CAMPBELL, J. (1992). Male answer syndrome: Why men always have opinions, even on subjects they know nothing about. *Utne Reader, 49,* 107-108.

CAMPERIO-CIANI, A., CORNA, F., & CAPILUPPI, C. (2004). Evidence for maternally inherited factors favouring male homosexuality and promoting female fecundity. Proceedings of the Royal Society: Biological Sciences, *271*(1554), 2217-21.

CAMPOS, J. J., BERTENTHAL, B. I., & KERMOIAN, R. (1992). Early experience and emotional development: The emergence of wariness and heights. *Psychological Science, 3,* 61-64.

CANNON, W. B. (1915). *Bodily changes in pain, hunger, fear, and rage: An account of recent researches into the function of emotional excitement.* New York: Appleton.

CANNON, W. B., & WASHBURN, A. (1912). An explanation of hunger. *American Journal of Physiology, 29,* 441-454.

CANNON, W. B. (1927). The James-Lange theory of emotion: A critical examination and an alternative theory. *American Journal of Psychology, 39,* 10-124.

CANTOR, N., & KIHLSTROM, J. R. (1987). *Personality and social intelligence.* Englewood Cliffs, NJ: Prentice Hall.

CAPRARA, G. V., BARBARANELLI, C., & ZIMBARDO, P. G. (1996). Understanding the complexity of human aggression: Affective, cognitive, and social dimensions of individual differences in propensity toward aggression. *European Journal of Personality, 10,* 133-155.

CARDO, A. G., & GOTTESMAN, I. I. (2000). Twin studies of schizophrenia: From bow-and-arrow concordances to star wars Mx and functional genomics. *American Journal of Medical Genetics, 97*(1), 12-7.

CAREY, B. (2007, October 23). An active, purposeful machine that comes out at night to play. *The New York Times.*

CAREY, B. (2008, July 1). Decades later, still asking: Would I pull that switch? *The New York Times.* Retrieved October 17, 2008, from http://www .nytimes.com/2008/07/01/health/research/01mind.html?_r=1&emc= eta1&oref=slogin

Carnegie Mellon University. (2001, July 27). Carnegie Mellon study provides conclusive evidence that cell phones distract drivers. *Science Daily*. Retrieved July 10, 2008, from http://www.sciencedaily.com/releases/2001/07/010727094311.htm

Carpenter, P. A., Just, M. A., & Shell, P. (1990). What one intelligence test measures: A theoretical account of the processing in the Raven Progressive Matrices test. *Psychological Review, 97*(3), 404-431.

Carrington, P. (1998). *The book of meditation: The complete guide to modern meditation* (revised ed.). New York: Element Books.

Carroll, J. (2007, January 24). Stress more common among younger Americans, parents, workers. *Gallup Poll*. Retrieved September 25, 2008, from http://www. gallup.com/poll/26242/Stress-More-Common-Among-Younger-Americans-Parents-Workers.aspx

Carroll, M. E., & Overmier, J. B. (2001). *Animal research and human health: Advancing human welfare through behavioral science*. Washington, DC: American Psychological Association.

Carroll, R. (2010, January 24). Haiti earthquake death toll rises to 150,000 and could double. *Guardian.co.uk*. Retrieved February 16, 2010, from http://www.guardian.co.uk/world/2010/jan/24/haiti-earthquake-death-toll-rises

Carruthers, M. (2001). A multifactorial approach to understanding andropause. *Journal of Sexual and Reproductive Medicine, 1*, 69-74.

Carstensen, L. L. (1991). Selectivity theory: Social activity in life-span context. *Annual Review of Gerontology and Geriatrics, 11*, 195-217.

Castillo, R. J. (1997). Eating disorders. In R. J. Castillo (Ed.), *Culture and mental illness: A client-centered approach* (p. 152). Pacific Grove, CA: Brooks/Cole Publishing.

Castonguay, L. G., & Goldfried, M. R. (1994). Psychotherapy integration: An idea whose time has come. *Applied & Preventive Psychology, 3*, 159-172.

Catalano, R., Novaco, R. W., & McConnell, W. (1997). A model of the net effect of job loss on violence. *Journal of Personality and Social Psychology, 72*, 1440-1447.

Catalano, R., Novaco, R. W., & McConnell, W. (2002). Layoffs and violence revisited. *Aggressive Behavior, 28*, 233-247.

Cattell, R. B. (1963). Theory of fluid and crystallized intelligence: A critical experiment. *Journal of Educational Psychology, 54*, 1-22.

Cattell, R. B. (1965). *The scientific analysis of personality*. Baltimore: Penguin.

Celizic, M. (2008, June 27). Michael Phelps: Greatest Olympian ever? *MSNBC*. Retrieved August 4, 2008, from http://www.msnbc.msn.com/id/25396030/

Centers for Disease Control and Prevention. (2009). H1N1 flu. Retrieved December 17, 2009, from http://www.cdc.gov/h1n1flu/estimates_2009_h1n1.htm

Centers for Disease Control and Prevention. (2009). Seasonal influenza (Flu). Retrieved December 17, 2009, from http://www.cdc.gov/flu/about/disease/us_flu-related_deaths.htm

Centers for Disease Control and Prevention, National Center for Injury Prevention and Control. (2005). Suicide: facts at a glance. *Web-based Injury Statistics Query and Reporting System (WISQARS)*. Retrieved August 1, 2008, from http://www.cdc.gov/ncipc/dvp/Suicide/suicide_data_sheet.pdf

Central Virginia Waste Management Authority. (2010). Why recycle? Retrieved from http://www.cvwma.com/why_recycle.wbp.

Chambless, D. L., Baker, M. J., Baucom, D. H., Beutler, L. E., Calhoun, K. S., Crits-Christoph, P., Daiuto, A., DeRubeis, R., Detweiler, J., Haaga, D. A. F., Johnson, S. B., McCurry, S., Mueser, K. T., Pope, K. S., Sanderson, W. C., Shoham, V., Stickle, T., Williams, D. A., & Woody, S. R. (1997). Update on empirically validated therapies, II. *The Clinical Psychologist, 51*(1), 3-16.

Chang, M. (1996, October 4). Joined for life: Co-joined six-year-old Hensel twins share many body parts. *Science World*. Retrieved August 11, 2008, from http://wwww.findarticles.com[0]

Chapoval, Tova. World's greatest living polyglot: Brazilian makes his point in a mere 56 languages. *Reuters*, Retrieved February 16, 2010, from http://www.spidra.com/fazah.html

Chartrand, T. L., & Bargh, J. A. (1999). The chameleon effect: The perception-behavior link and social interaction. *Journal of Personality and Social Psychology, 76*(6), 893-910.

Cherry, E. C. (1953). Some experiments on the recognition of speech, with one and two ears. *Journal of the Acoustical Society of America, 25*, 975-979.

Chomsky, N. (1957). *Syntactic Structures*. The Hague: Mouton.

Christie, W., & Moore, C. (2005). The impact of humor on patients with cancer. *Clinical Journal of Oncological Nursing, 9*(2), 211-218.

Chu, J. A., Frey, L. M., Ganzel, B. L., & Matthews, J. A. (1999). Memories of childhood abuse: Dissociation, amnesia, and corroboration. *American Journal of Psychiatry, 156*, 749-755.

Cialdini, R. B. (2001). *Influence: Science and practice* (4th ed.). Boston: Allyn & Bacon.

Cianciolo, A. T., & Sternberg, R. J. (2004). *Intelligence: A brief history*. Malden, MA: Blackwell Publishing.

Clancy, S. A., McNally, R. J., Schacter, D. L., Lenzenweger, M. F., & Pitman, R. K. (2002). Memory distortion in people reporting abduction by aliens. *Journal of Abnormal Psychology, 111*(3), 455-461.

Clark, C. (2008, July 23). The former pregnant man debuts his baby. *People*. Retrieved September 2, 2008, from http://www.people.com/people/article/0,,20214360,00.html

Clark, H., & Marshall, C. (1981). Definite reference and mutual knowledge. In A. K. Joshi, B. L. Webber, & I. A. Sag (Eds.), *Elements of discourse understanding* (pp. 10-63). NY: Cambridge University Press.

Clark, K. B., & Clark, M. P. (1947). Racial self-identification and preference in negro children. In T. M. Newcomb & E. L. Hartley (Eds.), *Readings in social psychology* (pp. 169-178). New York: Henry Holt.

Cloninger, C. R., Bohman, M., & Sigvardsson, S. (1981). Inheritance of alcohol abuse. *Archives of General Psychiatry, 38*, 861-868.

Close, Glenn. (2009, October 21). Mental illness: The stigma of silence. Retrieved February 16, 2010, from http://www.huffingtonpost.com/glenn-close/mental-illness-the-stigma_b_328591.html

Cloud, J. (2007). Yep, they're gay. *Time*. Retrieved September 2, 2008, from http://www.time.com/time/magazine/article/0,9171,1582336,00.html

Coats, E. J., & Feldman, R. S. (1996). Gender differences in nonverbal correlates of social status. *Personality and Social Psychology Bulletin, 22*(10) 1014-1022.

Coffey, C. E. (Ed.). (1993). *Clinical science of electroconvulsive therapy*. Washington, DC: American Psychiatric Press.

Cohen, D., Nisbett, R. E., Bowdle, B. R., & Schwarz, N. (1996). Insult, aggression, and the southern culture of honor: "An experimental ethnography." *Journal of Personality and Social Psychology, 70*, 945-960.

Cohen, N. J., & Eichenbaum, H. (1993). *Memory, amnesia, and the hippocampal system*. Cambridge, MA: MIT.

Cohen, S., Doyle, W. J., Turner, R., Alper, C. M., Skoner, D. P. (2003). Sociability and susceptibility to the common cold. *Psychological Science, 14*, 389-395.

Colapinto, J. (1997, December 11). The true story of John/Joan. *Rolling Stone*, 54-97.

Colapinto, J. (2000). *As nature made him: The boy who was raised as a girl*. New York: HarperCollins.

Colarelli, S. M., Spranger, J. L., & Hechanova, M. R. (2006). Women, power, and sex composition in small groups: An evolutionary perspective. *Journal of Organizational Behavior, 27*(2), 163-184.

Colbin, A. (2005, June 1). The cholesterol controversy. *Alternative and Complementary Therapies, 11*(3), 126-130.

Coley, R. L., & Chase-Lansdale, L. (1998). Adolescent pregnancy and parenthood: Recent evidence and future directions. *American Psychologist, 53*, 152-166.

College of Charleston and the National Museum of Language. (2005). How many languages is it possible for a person to speak? *The 5-Minute Linguist*. Retrieved February 16, 2010, from http://www.cofc.edu/linguist/archives/2005/11/how_many_langua_1.html

Comstock, G., & Lindsey, G. (1975). *Television and human behavior: The research horizon, future and present*. Santa Monica, CA: Rand.

Conlin, M. America's reality-TV addiction. (2003, January 30). *Business Week*. Retrieved August 8, 2008, from http://www.businessweek.com/bwdaily/dnflash/jan2003/nf20030130_8408.htm

Consensus Conference. (1985). Electroconvulsive therapy. *Journal of the American Medical Association, 254*, 2103-2108.

Coolidge, F. L., & Wynn, T. (2006, April). The effects of the tree-to-ground transition in the evolution of cognition in early *Homo*. *Before Farming*, 1-18.

Corbetta, M., & Schulman, G. L. (2002). Control of goal-directed and stimulus-driven attention in the brain. *Nature Reviews Neuroscience, 3*, 201-15.

Coren, S. (1996, April 4). Daylight savings time and traffic accidents. *The New England Journal of Medicine, 334*(14), 924-925.

Coren, S. (1996). *Sleep thieves: An eye-opening exploration into the science and mysteries of sleep*. New York: The Free Press.

CORKUM, V., & MOORE, C. (1998). The origins of joint visual attention in infants. *Developmental Psychology, 34,* 28–38.

CORRELL, J., PARK, B., JUDD, C. M., & WITTENBRINK, B. (2002). The police officer's dilemma: Using ethnicity to disambiguate potentially threatening individuals. *Journal of Personality and Social Psychology, 83,* 1314–1329.

COSTA, P.T., JR., ZONDERMAN, A. B., MCCRAE, R. R., CORNONI-HUNTLEY, J., LOCKE, B. Z., & BARBANO, H. E. (1987). Longitudinal analyses of psychological well-being in a national sample: Stability of mean levels. *Journal of Gerontology, 42,* 50–55.

COSTA E SILVA, J. A., CHASE, M., SARTORIUS, N., & ROTH, T. (1996 June). Special report from a symposium held by the World Health Organization and the World Federation of Sleep Research Societies: An overview of insomnias and related disorders—recognition, epidemiology, and rational management. *Sleep, 19*(5), 412–416.

COUGHLAN, S. (2006, September 28). All you need is ubuntu. *BBC News.* Retrieved August 7, 2008, from http://news.bbc.co.uk/2/hi/uk_news/magazine/5388182.stm

COWAN, N. (1988). Evolving conceptions of memory storage, selective attention, and their mutual constraints within the human information-processing system. *Psychological Bulletin, 104,* 163–191.

CRAIK, F. I. M., & TULVING, E. (1975). Depth of processing and the retention of words in episodic memory. *Journal of Experimental Psychology: General, 104,* 268–294.

CRESPI, L. (1942). Quantitative variation of incentive and performance in the white rat. *American Journal Psychology, 55,* 467–517.

CRESPI, L. (1944). Amount of reinforcement and level of performance. *Psychology Review, 51,* 341–357.

CRIMINAL JUSTICE: NEW TECHNOLOGIES AND THE CONSTITUTION. (1988, May). Retrieved August 25, 2008, from http://books.google.com/books?id=W40kUdI8bGoC&pg=PA41&lpg=PA41&dq=Male+sexual+offenders+given+Depo-Provera&source=web&ots=SfAUAFOPf&sig=ES1IuOM8VzeUg427QoAzKN6E2qk&hl=en&sa=X&oi=book_result&resnum=3&ct=result#PPA41,M1

CRITERION. (2001). *Grey Gardens.* Dir. Ellen Hovde, Albert Maysles, David Maysles, Muffie Meyer, DVD.

CRUZ, C. A., HALL, L. C., LEHMAN, E. B., RENKEY, M. E., & SROKOWSKI, S. A. (2003). Directed forgetting of related words: Evidence for the inefficient inhibition hypothesis. *The Journal of General Psychology, 130,* 380–398.

CSIKSZENTMIHALYI, M. (1990). *Flow: the psychology of optimal experience.* New York: Harper & Row.

CSIKSZENTMIHALYI, M. (1999). If we are so rich, why aren't we happy? *American Psychologist, 54,* 821–827.

CUMMING, E., & HENRY, W. E. (1961). *Growing old: The process of disengagement.* New York: Basic Books.

CURTISS, S., FROMKIN, V., KRASHEN, S., RIGLER, D., & RIGLER, M. (1974, September). The linguistic development of Genie. *Language: Journal of the Linguistic Society of America, 50*(3), 528–554.

DALTON, P., DOOLITTLE, N., & BRESLIN, P. A. S. (2002). Gender-specific induction of enhanced sensitivity to odors. *Nature Neuroscience, 5,* 199–202.

DAMASIO, A. R. (1994). *Descartes error: Emotion, reason, and the human brain.* New York: Grossett/Putnam & Sons.

DAMASIO, H., GRABOWSKI, T., FRANK, R., GALABURDA, A. M., & DAMASIO, A. R. (1994). The return of Phineas Gage: Clues about the brain from the skull of a famous patient. *Science, 264,* 1102–1105.

THE DANA FOUNDATION. (2003). *The Dana Sourcebook of Brain Science* (3rd ed.). New York: Dana Press.

DARLEY, J. M., & LATANÉ, B. (1968). Bystander intervention in emergencies: Diffusion of responsibility. *Journal of Personality and Social Psychology, 8,* 377–383.

DARROCH, J. E., FROST, J. J., SINGH, S., & THE STUDY TEAM. (2001, November). *Teenage Sexual and Reproductive Behavior in Developed Countries: Can More Progress Be Made?* Occasional Report, New York: AGI.

DARWIN, C. (1964). *On the origin of species.* Cambridge, MA: Harvard University Press. (Original work published 1859)

DARWIN, C. (1965). *The expression of the emotions in man and animals.* Chicago: The University of Chicago Press. (Original work published 1872)

DAVIDSON, R. J., KABAT-ZINN, J., SCHUMACHER, J., ROSENKRANZ, M., MULLER, D., SANTORELLI, S. F., URBANOWSKI, F., ET AL. (2003). Alterations in brain and immune function produced by mindfulness meditation. *Psychosomatic Medicine, 65*(4), 564–570.

DAVIDSON, P. R., & PARKER, K. C. H. (2001). Eye movement desensitization and reprocessing (EMDR): A meta-analysis. *Journal of Consulting and Clinical Psychology, 69,* 305–316.

DAVIS, B. E., MOON, R. Y., SACHS, H. C., & OTTOLINI, M. C. (1998). Effects of sleep position on infant motor development. *Pediatrics, 102,* 1135–1140.

DAWOOD, K., PILLARD, R. C., HORVATH, C., REVELLE, W., & BAILEY, J. M. (2000). Familial aspects of male homosexuality. *Archives of Sexual Behavior, 29*(2), 155–163.

DEAN, J. (2008, June). Which cognitive enhancers really work: Brain training, drugs, vitamins, meditation or exercise? Retrieved August 28, 2008, from http://www. spring.org.uk/2008/06/which-cognitive-enhancers-really-work.php

DEARY, I. J. (2001). Human intelligence differences: Towards a combined experimental-differential approach. *Trends in Cognitive Sciences, 5,* 164–170.

DECETY, J., & MORIGUCHI, Y. (2007). The empathic brain and its dysfunction in psychiatric populations: Implications for intervention across different clinical conditions. *Biopsychosocial Medicine, 1*:21. Retrieved August 11, 2008, from http://www.bpsmedicine.com/content/1/1/22

DECI, E. L., KOESTNER, R., & RYAN, R. M. (1999, November). A meta-analytic review of experiments examining the effects of extrinsic rewards on intrinsic motivation. *Psychological Bulletin, 125*(6), 627–668.

DECOURSEY, P. J. (1960, January). Daily light sensitivity rhythm in a rodent. *Science, 131*(3392), 33–35.

DE KONINCK, J. (2000). Waking experiences and dreaming. In M. Kryger, T. Roth, & W. Dement (Eds.), *Principles and practice of sleep medicine* (3rd ed). Philadelphia: Saunders.

DEMENT, W. C. (1978) *Some must watch while some must sleep.* New York: Norton.

DEMENT, W. C. (1997). What all undergraduates should know about how their sleeping lives affect their waking lives. Retrieved October 7, 2008, from http://www.stanford.edu/~dement/sleepless.html

DEMENT, W. C. (1999). *The promise of sleep: A pioneer in sleep medicine explores the vital connection between health, happiness, and a good night's sleep.* New York: Delacorte.

DEMENT, W. C., & WOLPERT, E. A. (1958, June). The relation of eye movements, body motility, and external stimuli to dream content. *Journal of Experimental Psychology, 55*(6), 543–553.

DEREGOWSKI, J. B. (1969). Perception of the two-pronged trident by two- and three-dimensional perceivers. *Journal of Experimental Psychology, 82,* 9–13.

DERRICK, J. L., GABRIEL, S., & TIPPIN, P. (2008). Parasocial relationships and self-discrepancies: Faux relationships have benefits for low self-esteem individuals. *Personal Relationships, 15*(2): 261–280.

DEW, M. A., HOCH, C. C., BUYSSE, D. J., MONK, H., BEGLEY, A. E., HOUCK, P. R., HALL, M., KUPFER, D. J., & REYNOLDS, C. F, III (2003). Healthy older adults' sleep predicts all-cause mortality at 4 to 19 years of follow-up. *Psychosomatic Medicine, 65,* 63–73.

DE WAAL, F. B. M. (1995, March). Bonobo sex and society: The behavior of a close relative challenges assumptions about male supremacy in human evolution. *Scientific American, 272*(3), 82–88.

DIENER, E., & BISWAS-DIENER, R. (2002). Will money increase subjective well-being? A literature review and guide to needed research. *Social Indicators Research, 57,* 119–169.

DIENER, E., OISHI, S., & LUCAS, R. E. (2003). Personality, culture, and subjective well-being: emotional and cognitive evaluations of life. *Annual Review of Psychology, 54,* 403–425.

DIMBERG, U., THUNBERG, M., & ELMEHED, K. (2000). Unconscious facial reactions to emotional facial expressions. *Psychological Science, 11,* 86–89.

DOLLARD, J., DOOB, L. W., MILLER, N. E., MOWRER, O. H., & SEARS, R. R. (1939). *Frustration and aggression.* New Haven: Yale University Press.

DOMHOFF, G. W. (1996). *Finding meaning in dreams: A quantitative approach.* New York: Plenum Publishing Co.

DOMHOFF, G. W. (2002). Using content analysis to study dreams: Applications and implications for the humanities. In K. Bulkeley (Ed.), *Dreams: A reader on the religious, cultural, and psychological dimensions of dreaming* (pp. 307–319). New York: Palgrave.

DOMHOFF, G. W. (2003). *The scientific study of dreams: Neural networks, cognitive development, and content analysis.* Washington, DC: APA Books.

DOMJAN, M. (1992). Adult learning and mate choice: Possibilities and experimental evidence. *American Zoologist, 32,* 48–61.

DONN, JEFF. (2006, April 3). Medical breakthrough: Doctors can grow human organs. *redOrbit.com.* Retrieved February 16, 2010, from http://www.redorbit.com/news/health/455900/medical_breakthrough_doctors_can_grow_human_organs

DORUS, S., VALLENDER, E., EVANS, P., ANDERSON, J., GILBERT, S., MAHOWALD, M., ET AL. (2004). Accelerated evolution of nervous system genes in the origin of *Homo sapiens*. *Cell, 119*(7), 1027-1040.

DOTY, R. L. (2001). Olfaction. *Annual Review of Psychology, 52*, 423-452.

DOVE, L., & PRICE, A. (1995). *Memory made manifest: The United States Holocaust Memorial Museum.* Retrieved October 7, 2008, from http://xroads.virginia.edu/~cap/holo/eliebio.htm.

DOVIDIO, J. F., GAERTNER, S. L., & KAWAKAMI, K. (2003). Intergroup contact: The past, present and the future. *Group Processes & Intergroup Relations, 6*, 5-21.

DOVIDIO, J. F., KAWAKAMI, K., JOHNSON, C., JOHNSON, B., & HOWARD, A. (1997). On the nature of prejudice: automatic and controlled processes. *Journal of Experimental Social Psychology, 33*, 510-540.

DRUCKMAN, D., & BJORK, R. A. (1991). *In the mind's eye: Enhancing human performance.* Washington, DC: National Academy Press.

DUCKWORTH, K. L., BARGH, J. A., GARCIA, M., & CHAIKEN, S. (2002). The automatic evaluation of novel stimuli. *Psychological Science, 13*(6), 513-519.

DUNCAN, J., & OWEN, A. M. (2000). Common regions of the human frontal lobe recruited by diverse cognitive demands. *Trends in Neurosciences, 23*, 475-483.

DUNPHY, D. C. (1963, June). The social structure of urban adolescent peer groups. *Sociometry, 26*, 230-246.

DUNSON, D. B., COLOMBO, B., & BAIRD, D. D. (2002). Changes with age in the level and duration of fertility in the menstrual cycle. *Human Reproduction, 17*, 1399-1403.

DURSTON, S., HULSHOFF, P., HILLEKE, E., CASEY, B. J., GIEDD, J. N., BUITELAAR, J. K., ET AL. (2001). Anatomical MRI of the developing human brain: What have we learned? *Journal of the American Academy of Child and Adolescent Psychiatry, 40*, 1012-1020.

EAGLY, A. H., & JOHNSON, B. T. (1990). Gender and leadership style: A meta-analysis. *Psychological Bulletin, 108*(2), 233-256.

EAGLY, A. H., ASHMORE, R. D., MAKHIJANI, M., & KENNEDY, L. C. (1991). What is beautiful is good, but... : A meta-analytic review of research on the physical attractiveness stereotype. *Psychological Bulletin, 110*, 109-128.

EBBINGHAUS, H. (1885/1913). *Memory: A contribution to experimental psychology* (tr. by H. A. Ruger & C. E. Bussenius). New York: Teachers College, Columbia University.

ECKERSLEY, R. (2000). The mixed blessings of material progress: diminishing returns in the pursuit of happiness. *Journal of Happiness Studies, 1*, 267-292.

ECKLUND-FLORES, L. (1992). The infant as a model for the teaching on introductory psychology. Paper presented to the American Psychological Association annual convention.

EHRLICH, P. R., DOBKIN, D. S., & WHEYE, D. (1988). Polyandry. Retrieved July 16, 2008 from Stanford University, Birds of Stanford Web site: http://www.stanford.edu/group/stanfordbirds/text/essays/Polyandry.html

EICHENBAUM, H., DUDCHENKO, P., WOOD, E., SHAPIRO, M., TANILA, H. (1999). The hippocampus, memory, and place cells: Is it spatial memory or a memory space? *Neuron, 23*, 209-226.

EISENBERGER, N. I., & LIEBERMAN, M. D. (2004). Why rejection hurts: A common neural alarm system for physical and social pain. *Trends in Cognitive Sciences, 8*, 294-300.

EISENBERGER, N. I., LIEBERMAN, M. D., & WILLIAMS, K. D. (2003). Does rejection hurt? An fMRI study of social exclusion. *Science, 302*, 290-292.

EKMAN, P. (1982). *Emotion in the human face.* New York: Cambridge University Press.

EKMAN, P. (1994). Strong evidence of universal in facial expressions: A reply to Russell's mistaken critique. *Psychological Bulletin, 115*, 268-287.

EKMAN, P., & FRIESEN, W. V. (1975). *Unmasking the face.* Englewood Cliffs, NJ: Prentice-Hall.

EKMAN, P., FRIESEN, W. V., O'SULLIVAN, M., CHAN, A., DIACOYANNI-TARLATZIS, I., HEIDER, K., KRAUSE, R., LECOMPTE, W. A., PITCAIRN, T., RICCI-BITTI, P. E., SCHERER, K., TOMITA, M., & TZAVARAS, A. (1987). Universals and cultural differences in the judgments of facial expressions of emotion. *Journal of Personality and Social Psychology, 53*, 712-717.

ELFENBEIN, H. A., & AMBADY, N. (2002). On the universality and cultural specificity of emotion recognition: A meta-analysis. *Psychological Bulletin, 128*, 203-235.

ELFENBEIN, H. A., & AMBADY, N. (2003). When familiarity breed accuracy: Cultural exposure and facial emotion recognition. *Journal of Personality and Social Psychology, 85*, 276-290.

ELIAS, C. L., & BERK, L. E. (2002). Self-regulation in young children: Is there a role for sociodramatic play? *Early Childhood Research Quarterly, 17*(2), 216-238.

ELLIOTT, R., & DOLAN, R. J. (1998). Neural response during preference and memory judgments for subliminally presented stimuli: A functional neuroimaging study. *The Journal of Neuroscience, 18*(12), 4697-4704.

ELLIOTT, R., RUBINSZTEIN, J. S., SAHAKIAN, B. J., & DOLAN, R. J. (2002). The neural basis of mood-congruent processing biases in depression. *Archives of General Psychiatry, 59*, 597-604.

ELLIOTT, M. E. (1996). Impact of work, family, and welfare receipt on women's self-esteem in young adulthood. *Social Psychology Quarterly, 59*, 80-95.

ELLIS, L., & BLANCHARD, R. (2001). Birth order, sibling sex ratio, and maternal miscarriages in homosexual and heterosexual men and women. *Personality and Individual Differences, 30*, 543-552.

ERICKSON, K., DREVETS, W. C., CLARK, L., CANNON, D. M., BAIN, E. E., ZARATE, C. A., JR., CHARNEY, D. S., & SAHAKIAN, B. J. (2005). Mood-congruent bias in affective go/no-go performance of unmedicated patients with major depressive disorder. *American Journal of Psychiatry, 162*, 2171-2173.

ERIKSON, E. H. (1963). *Childhood and society.* New York: Norton.

ERON, L. D. (1987). The development of aggressive behavior from the perspective of a developing behaviorism. *American Psychologist, 42*, 435-442.

ERRERA, P. (1972). Statement based on interview with forty "worst cases" in the Milgram obedience experiments. In J. Katz (Ed.), *Experimentation with human beings* (p. 400). New York: Russell Sage Foundation.

EVANS, P. D., GILBERT, S. L., MEKEL-BOBROV, N., VALLENDER, E. J., ANDERSON, J. R., VAEZ-AZIZI, L. M., ET AL. (2005, September 9). Microcephalin, a gene regulating brain size, continues to evolve adaptively in humans. *Science, 309*(5741), 1717-1720.

EVERITT, B. J., & STACEY, P. (1987). Studies of instrumental behavior with sexual reinforcement in male rats (Rattus norvegicus): II. Effects of preoptic area lesions, castration, and testosterone. *Journal of Comparative Psychology, 101*(4), 407-419.

EXPERT: L.A.'S 5.4 QUAKE 'SMALL SAMPLE' OF ONE TO COME. (2008, July 30). CNN. Retrieved August 2, 2008, from http://www.cnn.com/2008/US/07/29/earthquake.ca/

EYSENCK, H. J. (1967). *The biological basis of personality.* Springfield, IL: Thomas.

EYSENCK, H. J., & KAMIN, L. (1981). *The intelligence controversy.* New York: Wiley.

FABBRI-DESTRO, M., & RIZZOLATTI, G. (2008). Mirror neurons and mirror systems in monkeys and humans. *Physiology, 23*, 171-179.

FANTZ, R. L. (1961, May). The origin of form perception. *Scientific America, 204*, 66-72.

FAZIO, R. H., JACKSON, J. R., DUNTON, B. C., & WILLIAMS, C. J. (1995). Variability in automatic activation as an unobtrusive measure of racial attitudes: A *bona fide* pipeline? *Journal of Personality and Social Psychology, 69*, 1013-1027.

FBI. (2004). *Crime in the United States 2003, five-year arrest trends by sex, 1999-2003.* Table 35.

FEDEROFF, I. C., & MACFARLANE, T. (1998). Cultural aspects of eating disorders. In S. S. Kazarian & D. R. Evans (Eds.), *Cultural clinical psychology: Theory, research and practice* (pp. 152-176). New York: Oxford University Press.

FEINGOLD, A. (1992). Good-looking people are not what we think. *Psychological Bulletin, 111*, 304-341.

FERRARI, P. F., ROZZI, S., & FOGASSI, L. (2005). Mirror neurons responding to observation of actions made with tools in monkey ventral premotor cortex. *Journal of Cognitive Neuroscience, 17*, 212-226.

FESTINGER, L. (1957). *A theory of cognitive dissonance.* Stanford, CA: Stanford University Press.

FESTINGER, L., & CARLSMITH, J. M. (1959). Cognitive consequences of forced compliance. *Journal of Abnormal and Social Psychology, 58*, 203-210.

FEUILLET, L., DUFOUR, H., & PELLETIER, J. (2007). Brain of a white-collar worker. *Lancet, 370*(9583), 262.

FIGHTING WITH RUSSIA SPREADS TO CITIES ACROSS GEORGIA. (2008, August 8). CNN. Retrieved August 20, 2008, from http://www.cnn.com/2008/WORLD/europe/08/08/georgia.ossetia/index.html

FLYNN, J. R. (1987). Massive IQ gains in 14 nations: What IQ tests really measure. *Psychological Bulletin, 95,* 29-51.

FLYNN, J. R. (1999). Searching for justice: the discovery of IQ gains over time. *American Psychologist, 54,* 5-20.

FOOD NAVIGATOR. Are you a 'supertaster'? (2003, February 19). Retrieved February 16, 2010, from http://www.foodnavigator.com/Science-Nutrition/Are-you-a-supertaster

FORD, M. R, & WIDIGER, T. A. (1989). Sex bias in the diagnosis of histrionic and antisocial personality disorders. *Journal of Consulting and Clinical Psychology, 57*(2), 301-305.

FOSTER, H., HAGAN, J., & BROOKS-GUNN, J. (2008). Growing up fast: Stress exposure and subjective "weathering" in emerging adulthood. *Journal of Health and Social Behavior, 49,* 162-177.

FOULKES, D. (1982). *Children's dreams.* New York: Wiley.

FOULKES, D. (1999). *Children's dreaming and the development of consciousness.* Cambridge, MA: Harvard University Press.

FOX, E., LESTER, V., RUSSO, R., BOWLES, R. J., PICHLER, A., & DUTTON, K. (2000). Facial expressions of emotion: Are angry faces detected more efficiently? *Cognition and Emotion, 14*(1), 61-92.

FRANCE PUZZLES OVER THE MOTIVES OF THE ROGUE TRADER. (2008, January 25). *The International Herald-Tribune.* Retrieved August 2, 2008, from http://www.iht.com/articles/2008/01/25/business/25sgreacFW.php

FRANK, S. J. (1982). Therapeutic components shared by all psychotherapies. In J. H. Harvey & M. M. Parks (Eds.), *The master lecture series: Vol. 1. Psychotherapy research and behavior change.* Washington, DC: American Psychological Association.

FREDRICKSON, B. L. (2000). Why positive emotions matter in organizations: Lessons from the broaden-and-build theory. *The Psychologist-Manager Journal, 4,* 131-142.

FREED, D. A. (2007). From jokester to jailbird. *The Toronto Star.* Retrieved from http://www.thestar.com/News/article/213298

FREEDMAN, J. L. (1978). *Happy people.* San Diego: Harcourt Brace Jovanovich.

FREQUENTLY ASKED QUESTIONS ABOUT LOBOTOMIES. (2005, November 16). NPR. Retrieved August 4, 2008, from http://www.npr.org/templates/story/story.php?storyId=5014565

FREUD, S. (1960). *A general introduction to psychoanalysis.* New York: Washington Square Press. (Original work published 1935)

FREUD, S. (1961). *Beyond the pleasure principle.* New York: Norton. (Originally published in 1920 as Jenseits des Lustprinzips)

FREUD, S., & GAY, P. (1977). *Inhibitions, symptoms, and anxiety. Standard edition of the complete works of Sigmund Freud.* New York: W. W. Norton.

FRIEDMAN, M., ROSENMAN, R. H., CARROLL, V., & TAT, R. J. (1958). Changes in the serum cholesterol and blood clotting time in men subjected to cyclic variation of occupational stress. *Circulation, 17,* 852.

FRIEDMAN, M., & ULMER, D. (1984). *Treating Type A Behavior—and your heart.* New York: Knopf.

FRISONI, G., TESTA, C., ZORZAN, A., SABATTOLI, F., BELTRAMELLO, A., SOININEN, H., & LAAKSO, M. (2002). Detection of grey matter loss in mild Alzheimer's disease with voxel based morphometry. *The Journal of Neurology, Neurosurgery, and Psychiatry, 73*(6), 657-664.

FRITH, C. D., & FRITH, U. (1999). Interacting minds—a biological basis. *Science, 286,* 1692-1695.

FRY, D. P. (1992, Sept.). Respect for the rights of others is peace: Learning aggression versus nonaggression among the Zapotec. *American Anthropologist, 94*(3), 621-636.

FURMARK, T., TILLFSFORS, M., MARTEINSBOTTIR, I., PISSIOTA, A., LÅNGSTRÖM, B., & FREDRIKSON, M. (2002). Common changes in cerebral blood flow in patients with social phobia treated with citalopram or cognitive-behavioral therapy. *Archives of General Psychiatry, 59,* 425-433.

GABRIELI, J. D. E. (1998). Cognitive neuroscience of human memory. *Annual Review of Psychology 1998, 49,* 87-115.

GALANTER, E. (1962). Contemporary psychophysics. In R. Brown, E. Galanter, E. H. Hess, & G. Mandler (Eds.), *New directions in psychology.* New York: Holt, Rinehart & Winston.

GALANTER, M., HAYDEN, F., CASTANEDA, R., & FRANCO, H. (2005). Group therapy, self-help groups, and network therapy. In R. J. Frances, S. I. Miller, & A. H. Mack (Eds.), *Clinical textbook of addictive disorders* (3rd ed., pp. 502-527). New York: Guilford.

GALEF, B. G., & WIGMORE, S. W. (1983). Transfer of information concerning distant foods: A laboratory investigation of the "information-center" hypothesis. *Animal Behavior, 31,* 748-758.

GALLUP. (2005, May 5). The gender gap: President Bush's handling of Iraq. *The Gallup Poll.*

GARCIA, J., & KOELLING, R. A. (1966). Relation of cue to consequence in avoidance learning. *Psychonomic Science, 4,* 123.

GARDNER, H. (1983). *Frames of mind: Multiple intelligences.* New York: Basic Books, xi.

GARDNER, H., KORNHABER, M. L., & WAKE, W. K. (1996) *Intelligence: Multiple perspectives.* Orlando, FL: Harcourt Brace & Co.

GARLAND, E. J., & SMITH, D. H. (1991). Case study: Simultaneous prepubertal onset of panic disorder, night terrors, and somnambulism. *Journal of the American Academy of Child & Adolescent Psychiatry, 30,* 553-555.

GAUTHIER, I., SKUDLARSKI, P., GORE, J. C., ANDERSON, A. W. (2000). Expertise for cars and birds recruits brain areas involved in face recognition. *Nature Neuroscience, 3*(2): 191-197.

GAZZANIGA, M. S. (1967). The split-brain in man. *Scientific American, 217*(2), 24-29.

GELDARD, F. A. (1972). *The human senses* (2nd ed.). New York: John Wiley & Sons.

GERIN, W., CHAPLIN, W., SCHWARTZ, J. E., HOLLAND, J., ALTER, R., WHEELER, R., DUONG, D., & PICKERING, T. G. (2005). Sustained blood pressure increase after an acute stressor: The effects of the 11 September 2001 attack on the New York City World Trade Center. *Journal of Hypertension, 23,* 279-281.

GERSHOFF, E. (2000). The short and long-term effects of corporal punishment on children: A meta-analytical review. In D. Elliman & M. A. Lynch, *The physical punishment of children, 83,* 196-198.

GIBSON, H. B. (1995, April). Recovered memories. *The Psychologist,* 153-154.

GILBERT, D. T., TAFARODI, R. W., & MALONE, P. S. (1993). You can't not believe everything you read. *Journal of Personality and Social Psychology, 65*(2), 221-233.

GILES, D. E., DAHL, R. E., & COBLE, P. A. (1994). Childbearing, developmental, and familial aspects of sleep. In J. M. Oldham & M. B. Riba (Eds.), *Review of psychiatry* (Vol. 13). Washington, DC: American Psychiatric Press.

GILLIGAN, C. (1982). *In a different voice: Psychological theory and women's development.* Cambridge, MA: Harvard University Press.

GILLIGAN, C., LYONS, N. P., & HAMMER, T. J. (1990). (Eds.). (1990). *Making connections: The relational worlds of adolescent girls at Emma Willard School.* Cambridge, MA: Harvard University Press.

GILOVICH, T. (1991). *How we know what isn't so: The fallibility of human reason in everyday life.* New York: The Free Press.

GINZBURG, K., SOLOMON, Z., KOIFMAN, B., KEREN, G., ROTH, A., KRIWISKY, M., KUTZ, I., DAVID, D., & BLEICH, A. (2003). Trajectories of post-traumatic stress disorder following myocardial infarction: A prospective study. *Journal of Clinical Psychiatry, 64*(10), 1217-1223.

GLASS, R. M. (2001). Electroconvulsive therapy: Time to bring it out of the shadows. *Journal of the American Medical Association, 285,* 1346-1348.

GLATER, J. D. (2001, March 26). Women are close to being majority of law students. *New York Times.* Retrieved September 2, 2008, from http://query.nytimes.com/gst/fullpage.html?res=9806E3D8103CF935A15750C0A9679C8B63

GLICK, P., & FISKE, S. T. (2001). An ambivalent alliance: Hostile and benevolent sexism as complementary justifications for gender inequality. *American Psychologist, 56*(2), 109-118.

GLOBAL POPULATION AND ENVIRONMENT: POPULATION, CONSUMPTION, & OUR ECOLOGICAL FOOTPRINT. (2008). Sierra Club. Retrieved August 20, 2008, from http://www.sierraclub.org/population/consumption/

GODDARD, A. W., MASON, G. F., ROTHMAN, D. L., BEHAR, K. L., PETROFF, O. A. C., & KRYSTAL, J. H. (2004). Family psychopathology and magnitude of reductions in occipital cortex GABA levels in panic disorder. *Neuropsychopharmacology, 29,* 639-640.

GOLDBERG, A. B., & THOMSON, K. N. (2009, June 9). Exclusive: "Pregnant Man" Gives Birth to Second Child. *ABCNews.com.* Retrieved February 16, 2010, from http://abcnews.go.com/2020/story?id=7795344&page=1

GOLDFRIED, M. R., & PADAWER, W. (1982). Current status and future directions in psychotherapy. In M. R. Goldfried (Ed.), *Converging themes in psychotherapy: Trends in psychodynamic, humanistic, and behavioral practice.* New York: Springer.

GOLDMAN, R. (2008, April 3). It's my right to have a kid, pregnant man tells Oprah. *ABC News.* Retrieved September 2, 2008, from http://abcnews.go.com/Health/story? id=4581943&page=1

GOLDSTEIN, I., LUE, T. F., PADMA-NATHAN, H., ROSEN, R. C., STEERS, W. D., & WICKER, P. A. (1998). Oral sildenafil in the treatment of erectile dysfunction. *New England Journal of Medicine, 338,* 1397-1404.

GOOD MORNING AMERICA. (2007, November 19). Parents: Cyber bullying led to teen's suicide. Retrieved February 16, 2010, from http://abcnews.go.com/GMA/Story?id=3882520

GOODE, E. (1999, February 16). Tales of midlife crisis found greatly exaggerated. *New York Times.* Retrieved August 11, 2008, from http://www.nytimes.com

GOODE, E. (2003, January 28). Even in the age of Prozac, some still prefer the couch. *New York Times.* Retrieved September 23, 2008, from http://www.nytimes.com

GOODMAN, A. (2009, June 1). Trash Picking. *Bay Weekly.* Retrieved February 16, 2010, from http://www.bayweekly.com/year09/issue_23/lead_3.html

GOODNOUGH, A. (2002, May 2). Post 9/11 pain found to linger in young minds. *New York Times.* Retrieved September 3, 2008, from http://query.nytimes.com/gst/fullpage.html?res=9E07EFDC1231F931A35756C0A9649C8B63

GORDON, S. K., & CLARK, W. C. (1974a). Adult age differences in word and nonsense syllable recognition memory and response criterion. *Journal of Gerontology, 29,* 659-665.

GORDON, S. K., & CLARK, W. C. (1974b). Application of signal detection theory in prose recall and recognition in elderly and young adults. *Journal of Gerontology, 29,* 64-72.

GORDON, S., & GILGUN, J. F. (1987). Adolescent sexuality. In V. B. Van Hasselt & M. Hersen (Eds.), *Handbook of adolescent psychology.* New York: Pergamon Press.

GORE, A., JR. (1992). *Earth in the balance: Ecology and the human spirit.* Boston: Houghton-Mifflin.

GOSLING, S. D., & JOHN, O. P. (1999). Personality dimensions in nonhuman animals: A cross-species review. *Current Directions in Psychological Science, 8,* 69-75.

GOTTESMAN, I. I. (1991). *Schizophrenia genesis: The origins of madness.* New York: Freeman.

GOULD, S. J. (1996). *The mismeasurement of man.* New York: W. W. Norton.

GRAF, P., & SCHACTER, D. L. (1985). Implicit and explicit memory for new associations in normal and amnesic subjects. *Journal of Experimental Psychology: Learning, Memory, and Cognition, 11,* 501-518.

GRANT, P. R., & GRANT, B. R. (2002). Unpredictable evolution in a 30-year study of Darwin's finches. *Science, 296,* 707-711.

GRAVES, L. A., HELLER, E. A., PACK, A. I., & ABEL, T. (2003). Sleep deprivation selectively impairs memory consolidation for contextual fear conditioning. *Learning & Memory, 10,* 168-176.

GRAY, J. A. (1972). The psychophysiological basis of introversion-extraversion: A modification of Eysenck's theory. In V. D. Nebylitsyn & J. A. Gray (Eds.), *The biological basis of individual behavior.* New York: Academic.

GRAY, K., & ESCHERICH, K. (2008, May 9). Woman who can't forget amazes doctors. *ABCNews.com.* Retrieved February 16, 2010, from http://abcnews.go.com/Health/Story?id=4813052

GREEN, C., & BAVELIER, D. (2003). Action video game modifies visual attention. *Nature, 423,* 534-537.

GREENBERG, M. A., WORTMAN, C. B., & STONE, A. A. (1996). Emotional expression and physical health: Revising traumatic memories or fostering self-regulation? *Journal of Personality and Social Psychology, 71*(3), 588-602.

GREENBERG, M. T., WEISSBERG, R. P., O'BRIEN, M. U., ZINS, J. E., FREDERICKS, L., RESNIK, H., & ELIAS, M. (2003). Enhancing school-based prevention and youth development through coordinated social, emotional, and academic learning. *American Psychologist, 58,* 466-474.

GREENFELD, L. A. (1998). *Alcohol and crime: An analysis of national data on the prevalence of alcohol involvement in crime.* Washington, DC: Document NCJ-168632, Bureau of Justice Statistics. Retrieved August 20, 2008, from http://www.ojp.usdoj.gov/bjs

GREENWALD, A. G., BANAJI, M. R., RUDMAN, L. A., FARNHAM, S. D., NOSEK, B. A., & MELLOTT, D. S. (2002). A unified theory of implicit attitudes, stereotypes, self-esteem, and self-concept. *Psychological Review, 109,* 3-25.

GREENWALD, A. G., MCGHEE, D. E., & SCHWARTZ, J. K. L. (1998). Measuring individual differences in implicit cognition: The Implicit Association Test. *Journal of Personality and Social Psychology, 74,* 1464-1480.

GREENWALD, A. G., OAKES, M. A., & HOFFMAN, H. (2003). Targets of discrimination: Effects of race on responses to weapons holders. *Journal of Experimental Social Psychology, 39,* 399-405.

GRICE, H. P. (1975). Logic and conversation. In P. Cole and J. Morgan, (Eds.), *Syntax and semantics: Vol. 3,* Academic Press, pp. 41-58.

GRILL-SPECTOR, J., & KANWISHER, N. (2005). Visual recognition: As soon as you know it is there, you know what it is. *Psychological Science, 16,* 152-160.

GROSS, C. G., & SERGENT, J. (1992). Face recognition. *Current Opinion in Neurobiology, 2,* 156-161.

GRUZELIER, J. H. (1998). A working model of the neurophysiology of hypnosis: A review of evidence. *Contemporary Hypnosis, 15,* 3-21.

GUERIN, B. (1986). Mere presence effects in humans: A review. *Journal of Personality and Social Psychology, 22,* 38-77.

GUNNEMARK, E. V. (2000). Donald Kenrick as a polyglot: could he be replaced by a machine? *Scholarship and the Gypsy Struggle: Commitment in Romani Studies.* Retrieved February 16, 2010, from http://www.lingua.org.uk/dk&mt.html

GUR, R. C., TURETSKY, B. I., MATSUI, M., YAN, M., BILKER, W., HUGHETT, P., ET AL. (1999). Sex differences in brain gray and white matter in healthy young adults: Correlations with cognitive performance. *The Journal of Neuroscience, 19*(10), 4065-4072.

GUTTMACHER INSTITUTE. (2006). *U.S. teenage pregnancy statistics: National and state trends and trends by race and ethnicity.* Retrieved July 16, 2008, from http://www.guttmacher.org/pubs/2006/09/11/USTPstats.pdf

GUZMAN-MARIN, R., SUNTSOVA, N., METHIPPARA, M. ET AL. (2005). Sleep deprivation suppresses neurogenesis in the adult hippocampus of rats. *European Journal of Neuroscience, 22,* 2111-2116.

GUZMAN-MARIN, R., SUNTSOVA, N., STEWART, D., GONG, H., SZYMUSIAK, R., & MCGINTY, D. (2003). Sleep deprivation reduces proliferation of cells in the dentate gyrus of the hippocampus in rats. *Journal Physiology, 549,* 563-571.

HAIDT, J. (2001). The emotional dog and its rational tail: A social intuitionist approach to moral judgment. *Psychological Review, 108,* 814-834.

HALL, C. (1996). Studies of dreams collected in the laboratory and at home. *Institute of Dream Research Monograph Series* (No. 1). Santa Cruz, CA: Privately printed.

HALL, C. S., & LINDZEY, G. (1978). *Theories of personality.* New York: John Wiley and Sons.

HALL, J. A. (1984). *Nonverbal sex differences: Communication accuracy and expressive style.* Baltimore: Johns Hopkins University Press.

HALL, J. A. (1987). On explaining gender differences: The case of nonverbal communication. In P. Shaver & C. Hencrick (Eds.), *Review of Personality and Social Psychology, 7,* 177-200.

HALLEY, D. (2009, June 8). Growing Organs in the Lab. *Singularity Hub.* Retrieved February 16, 2010, from http://singularityhub.com/2009/06/08/growing-organs-in-the-lab

HAMER, D. H., HU, S., MAGNUSON, V. L., HU, N., & PATTATUCCI, A. M. (1993). A linkage between DNA markers on the X chromosome and male sexual orientation. *Science, 261*(5119), 321-327.

HAMILTON, S. P., SLAGER, S. L., DE LEON, A. B., HEIMAN, G. A., KLEIN, D. F., HODGE, S. E., ET AL. (2004). Evidence for genetic linkage between a polymorphism in the Adenosine 2A receptor and panic disorder. *Neuropsychopharmacology, 29,* 558-565.

HANSEN, C. H., & HANSEN, R. D. (1988). Finding the face in the crowd: an anger superiority effect. *Journal of Personality and Social Psychology, 54*(6), 917-924.

HARBER, K. D. (1998). Feedback to minorities: Evidence of a positive bias. *Journal of Personality and Social Psychology, 74,* 622-628.

HARDER, J. W. (1991). Equity theory versus expectancy theory: The case of major league baseball free agents. *Journal of Applied Psychology, 76,* 458-464.

HARKINS, S. G., & SZYMANSKI, K. (1989). Social loafing and group evaluation. *Journal of Personality and Social Psychology, 56,* 934-941.

HARLOW, H. (1958). The nature of love. *American Psychologist, 13,* 573-685.

HARLOW H. F., DODSWORTH R. O., & HARLOW M. K. (1965). Total social isolation in monkeys. *Proceedings of the National Academy of Sciences of the United States of America, 54,* 90-97.

HART, D., & FEGLEY, S. (1995). Altruism and caring in adolescence: Relations to self-understanding and social judgment. *Child Development, 66,* 1346-1359.

Harvey, S. M. (1987). Female sexual behavior: fluctuations during the menstrual cycle. *Journal of psychosomatic research, 31,* 100-110

Hassed, C. (2001). How humour keeps you well. *Australian Family Physician, 30*(1), 25-28.

Hatfield, E., & Sprecher, S. (1986). *Mirror, mirror . . . the importance of looks in everyday life.* Albany: State University of New York Press.

Havinghurst, R. J. (1957). The leisure activities of the middle-aged. *American Journal of Sociology, 63,* 152-162.

Hayashi, T., Urayama, O., Kawai, K., Hayashi, K., Iwanaga, S., Ohta, M., et al. (2006). Laughter regulates gene expression in patients with type 2 diabetes. *Psychotherapy and Psychosomatics, 75*(1), 62-65.

Hazel, M. T. (2005). Visualization and systematic desensitization: Intervention for habituating and sensitizing patters of public speaking anxiety. *Dissertation Abstracts International Section A: Humanities and Social Sciences, 66,* 30.

Healey, C. G., Booth, K. S., & Enns, J. T. (1996). High-speed visual estimation using preattentive processing. *ACM Transactions on Human Computer Interaction, 3*(2), 107-135.

Hebb, D. O. (1949). *The organization of behavior.* New York: Wiley.

Heider, F. (1958). *The psychology of interpersonal relationships.* New York: Wiley.

Heller, W., Nitschke, J. B., & Miller, G. A. (1998). Lateralization in emotion and emotional disorders. *Current Directions in Psychological Science, 7,* 26-32.

Hellmich, N. (2004, September 16). Nightmare of too little sleep is tied to too much weight. *USA Today.* Retrieved February 16, 2010, from http://www.usatoday.com/news/health/2004-11-16-sleep-weight_x.htm

Henley, N. M. (1989). Molehill or mountain? What we know and don't know about sex bias in language. In M. Crawford & M. Gentry (Eds.), *Gender and thought: Psychological perspectives.* New York: Springer-Verlag.

Henninger, P. (1992). Conditional handedness: Handedness changes in multiple personality disordered subject reflect shift in hemispheric dominance. *Consciousness and Cognition, 1,* 265-287.

Herrnstein, R. J., & Murray, C. (1994). *The bell curve: The reshaping of American life by differences in intelligence.* New York: Free Press.

Herz, R. S. (2001). Ah sweet skunk! Why we like or dislike what we smell. *Cerebrum, 3*(4), 31-47.

Herzog, H., Lele, V. R., Kuwert, T., Langen, K. J., Kops, E. R., & Feinendegen, L. E. (1990/1991). Changed pattern of regional glucose metabolism during Yoga meditative relaxation. *Neuropsychobiology, 23,* 182-187.

Hess, R., Jr. (1965). Sleep and sleep related disturbances in the electroencephalogram. In K. A. Kert, C. Bally, & J. P. Shade (Eds.), *Sleep mechanisms* (pp. 127-139). Amsterdam: Elsevier.

Hilgard, J. R., & LeBaron, S. (1984). *Hypnotherapy of pain in children with cancer.* Lost Altos, CA: Kaufman.

Hill, C. E., & Nakayama, E. Y. (2000). Client-centered therapy: Where has it been and where is it going? A comment on Hathaway. *Journal of Clinical Psychology, 56,* 875-961.

Hillier, L. W., Fulton, R. S., Fulton, L. A., Graves, T. A., Pepin, K. H., Wagner-McPherson, C., et al. (2003). The DNA sequence of human chromosome 7. *Nature, 424,* 157-164.

Hirstein, W., & Ramachandran, V. S. (1997). Capgras syndrome: A novel probe for understanding the neural representation of the identity and familiarity of persons. *Proceedings: Biological Sciences, 264*(1380) 437-444.

HMHL. (2002, January). Disaster and trauma, *Harvard Mental Health Letter,* 1-5.

Hobson, J. A. (1988). *The dreaming brain.* New York: Basic Books.

Hobson, J. A. (1990). Activation, input source, and modulation: A neurocognitive model of the state of the brain mind. In R. R. Bootzin, J. F. Kihlstrom, & D. L. Schachter (Eds.), *Sleep and cognition.* Washington, D.C.: American Psychological Association.

Hobson, J. A., Pace-Schott, E., & Stickgold, R. (2000). Dreaming and the brain: Towards a cognitive neuroscience of conscious states. *Behavioral and Brain Sciences, 23*(6), 793-1121.

Hoffman, D. D. (1998). *Visual Intelligence: How we create what we see.* New York: W. W. Norton.

Holden, C. (1993). Wake-up call for sleep research. *Science, 259,* 305.

Hollon, S. D., Thase, M. E., & Markowitz, J. C. (2002). Treatment and prevention of depression. *Psychological Science in the Public Interest, 3,* 39-77.

Horn, J. L. (1982). The aging of human abilities. In J. Wolman (Ed.), *Handbook of developmental psychology* (p. 128). Englewood Cliffs, NJ: Prentice-Hall.

Horowitz, T. S., Cade, B. E., Wolfe, J. M., & Czeisler, C. A. (2003). Searching night and day: A dissociation of effect of circadian phase and time awake on visual selective attention and vigilance. *Psychological Science, 14,* 549-557.

Hovland, C. I., Lumsdaine, A. A., & Sheffied, F. D. (1949). *Experiments on mass communication.* Princeton, N.J.: Princeton University Press.

Howell, D. Flirting: interview with Monica Moore. *American Way.* Retrieved August 4, 2008, from http://www.geocities.com/marvin_hecht/flirting.html

Hu, S., Pattatucci, A. M. L., Patterson, C., Li, L., Fulker, D. W., Cherny, S. S., et al. (1995). Linkage between sexual orientation and chromosome Xq28 in males but not in females. *Nature Genetics, 11,* 248-256.

Hubel, D. H., & Wiesel, T. N. (1979, September). Brain mechanisms of vision. *Scientific American,* 150-162.

Hughes, T. A. (2007). The advantages of single-sex education. *National Forum of Educational Administration and Supervision Journal, 23*(2), 5-14.

Hull, C. L. (1943). *Principles of behavior: an introduction to behavior theory.* New York: Appleton-Century-Crofts.

Hull, C. L. (1952). *A behavior system: an introduction to behavior theory concerning the individual organism.* New Haven: Yale University Press.

Hunt, E. (1982). Towards new ways of assessing intelligence. *Intelligence, 6,* 231-240.

Huprich, S. K., & Keaschuk, R. A. (2006). Psychodynamic psychotherapy. In F. Andrasik, (Ed.), *Comprehensive handbook of personality and psychopathology: Adult psychopathology* (Vol. 2, pp. 469-486). Hoboken, NJ: John Wiley & Sons.

Ikonomidou, C., Bittigau, P., Ishimaru, M. J., Wozniak, D. F., Koch, C., Genz, K., et al. (2000). Ethanol-induced apoptotic neurodegeneration and fetal alcohol syndrome. *Science, 287,* 1056-1060.

Ilg, R., Wohlschlager, A. M., Gaser, C., Liebau, Y., Dauner, R., Woller, A., Zimmer, C., Zihl, J., & Muhlau, M. (2008). Gray matter increase induced by practice correlates with task-specific activation: A combined functional and morphometric magnetic resonance imaging study. *The Journal of Neuroscience, 28*(16), 4210-4215.

Indian actress Shilpa Shetty wins Britain's Celebrity Big Brother. (2007, January 29). UPI News Service. Retrieved August 11, 2008, from http://www.realitytvworld.com/news/indian-actress-shilpa-shetty-wins-britain-celebrity-big-brother-1011432.php

Irwin, M., Mascovich, A., Gillin, J. C., Willoughby, R., Pike, J., & Smith, T. L. (1994). Partial sleep deprivation reduces natural killer cell activity in humans. *Psychosomatic Medicine, 56,* 493-498.

Ito, M. (2000). Mood-congruent effect in self-relevant information processing. A study using an autobiographical memory recall task. *Japanese Journal of Psychology, 71,* 281-288.

Jackson, J. M., & Williams, K. D. (1988). Social loafing: A review and theoretical analysis. Unpublished manuscript. Fordham University.

James, W. (1890/1950). *Principles of psychology.* New York: Dover.

Jamison, K. R. (1995). *An Unquiet Mind.* New York: Vintage.

Janis, I. L. (1982). *Groupthink: Psychological studies of policy decisions and fiascos.* Boston: Houghton-Mifflin.

Jasper, H., & Penfield, W. (1954). *Epilepsy and the Functional Anatomy of the Human Brain* (2nd ed.). Boston: Little, Brown and Co.

Jensen, A. R. (1969). How much can we boost IQ and scholastic achievement? *Harvard Educational Review, 39,* 1-123.

Jensen, M. R. (1987). Psychobiological factors predicting the course of breast cancer. *Journal of Personality, 55*(2), 317-342.

Jensen-Campbell, L., Graziano, W. G., & West, S. G. (1995). Dominance, prosocial orientation, and female preferences: Do nice guys really finish last? *Journal of Personality & Social Psychology, 68,* 427-440.

Johansson, G. (1973). Visual perception of biological motion and a model for its analysis. *Perception and Psychophysics, 14,* 195-204.

Johansson, P., Hall, Sikström, S., & Olsson, A. (2005). Failure to detect mismatches between intention and outcome in a simple decision task. *Science, 310,* 116-119.

Johnson, J. S, & Newport, E. L. (1991). Critical period effects on universal properties of language: The status of subjacency in the acquisition of a second language. *Cognition, 39,* 215-258.

Johnson, M. E., & Hauck, C. (1999). Beliefs and opinions about hypnosis held by the general public: A systematic evaluation. *American Journal of Clinical Hypnosis, 42,* 10-20.

JOHNSON, W., & KRUEGER, R. F. (2004). Genetic and environmental structure of adjectives describing the domains of the Big Five model of Personality: A nationwide US twin study. *Journal of Research in Personality, 38,* 448-472.

JOHNSTON, T. D., & EDWARDS, L. (2002). Genes, interactions, and the development of behavior. *Psychological Review, 109,* 26-34.

JOSEPH, R. M., & TANAKA, J. (2003). Holistic and part-based face recognition in children with autism. *Journal of Child Psychology and Psychiatry, 44*(4), 529-542.

JUNG-BEEMAN, M., BOWDEN, E. M., HABERMAN, J., FRYMIARE, J. L., ARAMBEL-LIU, S., ET AL. (2004). Neural activity when people solve verbal problems with insight. *Public Library of Science Biology, 2,* e97.

KABAT-ZINN, J., MASSION, A. O., KRISTELLAR, J., PETERSON, L. G., FLETCHER, K. E., PBERT, L., ET AL. (1992). Effectiveness of a meditation-based stress reduction program in the treatment of anxiety disorders. *American Journal of Psychiatry, 149*(7), 936-943.

KAHNEMAN, D., & TVERSKY, A. (1979). Prospect theory: An analysis of decision under risk. *Econometrica, 47,* 263-291.

KANDEL, E. R., & SCHWARTZ, J. H. (1982). Molecular biology of learning: Modulation of transmitter release. *Science, 218,* 433-443.

KANWISHER, N. G., McDERMOTT, J., & CHUN, M. M. (1997). The fusiform face area: A module in human extrastriate cortex specialized for face perception. *Journal of Neuroscience, 17,* 4302-4311.

KAPLAN, H. I., & SADDOCK, B. J. (Eds.). (1989). *Comprehensive textbook of psychiatry, V.* Baltimore, MD: Williams and Wilkins.

KARLINSKY, H. (2008). Grey Gardens: Exploration or exploitation? *Canadian Psychiatry Aujourd'hui, 4*(1). Retrieved from http://publications .cpa-apc.org/browse/documents/312&xwm=true

KASSER, T. (2002). *The high price of materialism.* Cambridge, MA: MIT Press.

KELLER, M. B., McCULLOUGH, J. P., KLEIN, D. N., ARNOW, B., DUNNER, D. L., GELENBERG, A. J., MARKOWITZ, J. C., NEMEROFF, C. B., RUSSELL, J. M., THASE, M. E., TRIVEDI, M. H., & ZAJECKA, J. (2000). A comparison of nefazodone, the cognitive behavioral analysis system of psychotherapy, and their combination for the treatment of chronic depression. *New England Journal of Medicine, 342,* 1462-1470.

KELLER, M. C., & NESSE, R. M. (2005). Is low mood an adaptation? Evidence for subtypes with symptoms that match precipitants. *Journal of Affective Disorders, 86,* 27-35.

KELLEY, H. H. (1967). Attribution theory in social psychology. In D. Levine (Ed.), *Nebraska symposium on motivation* (Vol. 15). Lincoln: University of Nebraska Press.

KELLING, G. L., & COLES, C. M. (1996). *Fixing broken windows.* New York: Free Press.

KELTNER, D., & ANDERSON, C. (2000). Saving face for Darwin: The functions and uses of embarrassment. *Current Directions in Psychological Science, 9,* 187-192.

KENDALL-TACKETT, K. A. (2000). Physiological correlates of childhood abuse: Chronic hyperarousal in PTSD, depression, and irritable bowel syndrome. *Child Abuse and Neglect, 24*(6), 799-810.

KENYON, G. (2002, July 6). Less sleep may cure tiredness. *BBC News.* Retrieved on August 4, 2008, from http://news.bbc.co.uk/1/hi/health/2097666.stm

KERR, N. L., & BRUUN, S. E. (1983). Dispensability of member effort and group motivation losses: Free-rider effects. *Journal of Personality and Social Psychology, 44,* 7-94.

KESSLER, R. C., BERGLUND, P., DEMLER, O., JIN, R., MERIKANGAS, K. R., & WALTERS, E. E. (2005). Lifetime prevalence and age-of-onset distributions of DSM-IV disorders in the National Comorbidity Survey Replication. *Archives of General Psychiatry, 62,* 593-602.

KESSLER, R. C., CHIU, W. T., DEMLER, O., & WALTERS, E. E. (2005). Prevalence, severity, and comorbidity of twelve-month DSM-IV disorders in the National Comorbidity Survey Replication (NCS-R). *Archives of General Psychiatry, 62*(6), 617-627.

KHADEMHOSSEINI, A., VACANTI, J. P., & LANGER, R. (2009. May). How to grow new organs. *Scientific American.* Retrieved February 16, 2010, from http://www.scientificamerican.com/article.cfm?id=how-to-grow-new-organs

KIECOLT-GLASER, J. K., BELURY, M. A., PORTER, K., BEVERSDORF, D. Q., LEMESHOW, S., & GLASER, R. (2007). Depressive symptoms, omega-6: omega-3 fatty acids, and inflammation in older adults. *Psychosomatic Medicine, 69,* 217-224.

KIHLSTROM, J. F., & CANTOR, N. (2000). Social intelligence. In R. J. Sternberg (Ed.), *Handbook of intelligence* (pp. 359-369). New York: Cambridge University Press.

KIM, J. J., RISON, R. A., & FANSELOW, M. S. (1993). Effects of amygdala, hippocampus, and periaqueductal gray lesions on short- and long-term contextual fear. *Behavioral Neuroscience, 107*(6), 1093-8.

KIRSCH, I. (2000). The response set theory of hypnosis. *American Journal of Clinical Hypnosis, 42,* 274-292.

KIRSCH, I., & SAPIRSTEIN, G. (1998, June 26). Listening to Prozac but hearing placebo: A meta-analysis of antidepressant medication. *Prevention & Treatment, 1,* Article 0002a. Retrieved July 9, 2008, from http://journals.apa.org/prevention/volume1/pre0010002a.html

KISILEVSKY, B., HAINS, S., LEE, K., XIE, X., HUANG, H., YE, H., ET AL. (2003). Effects of experience on fetal voice recognition. *Psychological Science, 14,* 220-224.

KLINE, D., & SCHIEBER, F. (1985). Vision and aging. In J. E. Birren & K. W. Schaie (Eds.), *Handbook of the psychology of aging.* New York: Van Nostrand Reinhold.

KLUVER, H., & BUCY, P. C. (1937). "Psychic blindness" and other symptoms following bilateral temporal lobectomy in rhesus monkeys. *American Journal of Physiology, 119,* 352-353.

KOHLBERG, L. (1969). Stage and sequence: The cognitive-developmental approach to socialization. In D. A. Goslin (Ed.), *Handbook of socialization theory and research.* Chicago: Rand McNally.

KOHLBERG, L. (1981). *Essays on moral development: Vol. 1. The philosophy of moral development.* San Francisco: Harper & Row.

KOHLBERG, L. (1984). *Essays on moral development: Vol. 2. The psychology of moral development.* San Francisco: Harper & Row.

KOHN, M. (1977). *Class and conformity: A study in values* (2nd ed.). Chicago: University of Chicago Press.

KOPTA, S. M., LUEGER, R. J., SAUNDERS, S. M., & HOWARD, K. I. (1999). Individual psychotherapy outcome and process research: Challenges leading to greater turmoil or positive transition? *Annual Review of Psychology, 30,* 441-469.

KOUNIOS, J., & HOLCOMB, P. J. (1994). Concreteness effects in semantic processing: ERP evidence supporting dual-coding theory. *Journal of Experimental Psychology: Learning Memory and Cognition, 20,* 804-823.

KRAMER, A. F., HAHN, S., COHEN, N. J., BANICH, M. T., McAULEY, E., HARRISON, C. R., CHASON, J., VAKIL, E., BARDELL, L., BOILEAU, R. A., & COLCOMBE, A. (1999). Ageing, fitness, and neurocognitive function. *Nature, 400,* 418-419.

KRAMER, M. (2006, July 19). Do taste buds make the wine critic? *New York Sun.* Retrieved February 16, 2010, from http://www.nysun.com/food-drink/do-taste-buds-make-the-wine-critic/36343.

KRUGER, A. C. (1992). The effect of peer and adult-child transactive discussions on moral reasoning. *Merrill-Palmer Quarterly, 38,* 191-211.

KUBZANSKY, L. D., SPARROW, D., VOKONAS, P., & KAWACHI, I. (2001). Is the glass half empty or half full? A prospective study of optimism and coronary heart disease in the normative aging study. *Psychosomatic Medicine, 63,* 910-916.

KUHL, P. K., TSAO, F. M., & LIU, H. M. (2003). Foreign-language experience in infancy: Effects of short-term exposure and social interaction on phonetic learning. *Proceedings of the National Academy of Sciences, 100:* 9,096-9,101.

KUIKEN, T. A., LI, G., LOCK, B. A., LIPSCHUTZ, R. D., MILLER, L. A., STUBBLEFIELD, K. A., & ENGLEHART, K. B. (2009). Targeted muscle reinnervation for real-time myoelectric control of multifunction artificial arms. *JAMA, 301*(6): 619-628.

KUIKEN, T. A., MILLER, L. A., LIPSCHUTZ, R. D., LOCK, B. A., STUBBLEFIELD, K., MARASCO, P. D., ZHOU, P., & DUMANIAN, G. A. (2007). Targeted reinnervation for enhanced prosthetic arm function in a woman with a proximal amputation: a case study. *Lancet, 369*(9559), 371-380.

KULIK, J. A., & MAHLER, H. I. M. (1989). Stress and affiliation in a hospital setting: Preoperative roommate preferences. *Personality and Social Psychology Bulletin, 15,* 183—193.

KULIK, J. A., & MAHLER, H. I. M. (1993). Social support and recovery from surgery. *Health Psychology, 8,* 221-238.

KURTZ, L. D. (2004). Support and self-help groups. In C. D. Garvin, L. M. Gutierrez, & M. J. Galinsky (Eds.), *Handbook of social work with groups* (pp. 139-159). New York: Guilford.

KUTAS, M. (1990). Event-related brain potential (ERBP) studies of cognition during sleep: Is it more than a dream? In R. R. Bootzin, J. F. Kihlstrom, & D. Schacter (Eds.), *Sleep and cognition.* Washington, DC: American Psychological Association.

KYLLONEN P. C., & CHRISTAL, R. E. (1990). Reasoning ability is (little more than) working memory capacity? *Intelligence, 14,* 389-433.

LaBerge, S. P., Nagel, L. E., Dement, W. C., & Zarcone, V. P. (1981, June). Lucid dreaming verified by volitional communication during REM sleep. *Perceptual and Motor Skills, 52*(3), 727–732.

Lachman, M. E., & Weaver, S. L. (1998). The sense of control as a moderator of social class differences in health and well-being. *Journal of Personality and Social Psychology, 74*(3), 763–773.

Lagorio, C. (2006, March 3). A new age of celebrity worship. *CBS News.com*. Retrieved February 2, 2010, from http://www.cbsnews.com/stories/2006/03/03/health/webmd/main1366162.shtml?tag=contentMain;contentBody

Lambert, K., & Lilienfeld, S. O. (2007, October/November). Brain stains: Traumatic therapies can have long-lasting effects on mental health. *Scientific American Mind*, 46–53.

Lange, C. (1887). Ueber Gemuthsbewgungen, 3, 8.

Larsen, R. J., Kasimatis, M., & Frey, K. (1992). Facilitating the furrowed brow: An unobtrusive test of the facial feedback hypothesis applied to unpleasant affect. *Cognition and Emotion, 6*, 321–328.

Lashley, K. S. (1950). In search of the engram. In *Symposium of the society for experimental biology* (Vol 4). New York: Cambridge University Press.

Latané, B. (1981). The psychology of social impact. *American Psychologist, 36*, 343–356.

Lavenex, P., Steele, M. A., & Jacobs, L. F. (2000). The seasonal pattern of cell proliferation and neuron number in the dentate gyrus of wild adult eastern grey squirrels. *European Journal of Neuroscience, 12*, 643–648.

Lazar, S. W., Bush, G., Gollub, R. L., Fricchione, G. L., Khalsa, G., & Benson, H. (2000, May 15). Functional brain mapping of the relaxation response and meditation. *Neuroreport, 11*(7), 1581–1585.

Lazarus, R. S. (1991). Cognition and motivation in emotion. *American Psychologist, 46*, 352–357.

Lazarus, R. S. (1998). *Fifty years of the research and theory of R. S. Lazarus. An analysis of historical and perennial issues.* Mahwah, New Jersey: Lawrence Erlbaum Associates.

Leary, W. E. (1998, September 28). Older people enjoy sex, survey says. *New York Times*. Retrieved August 11, 2008, from http://www.nytimes.com

LeDoux, J. E. (1994). Emotion, memory and the brain. *Scientific American, 270*, 32–39.

Lefcourt, H. M. (1982). *Locus of control: Current trends in the theory and research.* New Jersey: Lawrence Erlbaum Associates.

Lehman, A. F., Steinwachs, D. M., Dixon, L. B., Goldman, H. H., Osher, F., Postrado, L., Scott, J. E., Thompson, J. W., Fahey, M., Fischer, P., Kasper, J. A., Lyles, A., Skinner, E. A., Buchanan, R., Carpenter, W. T., Jr., Levine, J., McGlynn, E. A., Roesenheck, R., & Zito, J. (1998). Translating research into practice: The schizophrenic patient outcomes research team (PORT) treatment recommendations. *Schizophrenia Bulletin, 24*, 1–10.

Leming, J. S. (1993). In search of effective character education. *Educational Leadership, 51*, 63–71.

Lemur Center. Duke University. Retrieved August 4, 2008, from http://lemur.duke.edu/animals/whatis.php

Lenneberg, E. (1967). *Biological Foundations of Language.* New York: Wiley.

Lenzenweger, M. F., Dworkin, R. H., & Wethington, E. (1989). Models of positive and negative symptoms in schizophrenia: An empirical evaluation of latent structures. *Journal of Abnormal Psychology, 98*, 62–70.

Leonard, T. (2008, April 5). Winning focus. Retrieved October 7, 2008, from http://www.signonsandiego.com/sports/golf/20080409-9999-1s9tiger.html.

Leproult, R., Copinski, G., Buxton, O., & Van Cauter, E. (1997). Sleepiness, performance, and neuroendocrine function during sleep deprivation: Effects of exposure to bright lights or exercise. *Journal of Biological Rhythms, 12*, 245–258.

LeShan, L. (1942). The breaking of habit by suggestion during sleep. *Abnormal Social Psychology, 37*, 406–408.

LeVay, S. (1991). A difference in hypothalamic structure between heterosexual and homosexual men. *Science, 253*(5023), 1034–1037.

Levin, I. P., & Gaeth, G. J. (1988). Framing of attribute information before and after consuming the product. *Journal of Consumer Research, 15*, 374–378.

Levin, T. (2009, October 23). No Einstein in Your Crib? Get a Refund. *The New York Times*. Retrieved February 16, 2010, from http://www.nytimes.com/2009/10/24/education/24baby.html

Lewis, D. O., Pincus, J. H., Feldman, M., Jackson, L., & Bard, B. (1986). Psychiatric, neurological, and psychoeducational characteristics of 15 death row inmates in the United States. *American Journal of Psychiatry, 143*, 838–845.

Lewis, M., Alessandri, S. M., & Sullivan, M. W. (1990). Violation of expectancy, loss of control, and anger in young infants. *Developmental Psychology, 26*, 745–751.

Lewis, M., & Brooks-Gunn, J. (1979). *Social cognition and the acquisition of self.* New York: Plenum Press.

Lilienfeld, S., & Arkowitz, H. (2008, February/March). Uncovering "brain-scams": In which the authors debunk myths concerning the three-pound organ inside our head. *Scientific American Mind*, 80–81.

Linguist Blogger, The. (2008, May 25). The Many Languages of Ziad Fazah. Retrieved February 16, 2010, from http://thelinguistblogger.wordpress.com/2008/05/25/the-many-languages-of-ziad-fazah/.

Lipsitt, L. P. (2003). Crib death: A biobehavioral phenomenon? *Current Directions in Psychological Science, 12*, 164–170.

Liu, H., & Umberson, D. J. (2008). The times they are a changin': Marital status and health differentials from 1972 to 2003. *Journal of Health and Social Behavior, 49*, 239–253.

Livesley, W. J., Jang, K. L., & Verson, P. A. (2003). Genetic basis of personality structure. In T. Millon & M. J. Lerner, (Eds.), *Handbook of psychology: Personality and social psychology* (Vol. 54, pp. 59–83). New York: John Wiley & Sons.

Livingstone, M., & Hubel, D. (1988). Segregation of form, color, movement, and depth: Anatomy, physiology, and perception. *Science, 240*, 740–749.

Loehlin, J. C., McCrae, R. R., Costa, P. T., Jr., & John, O. P. (1998). Heritabilities of common and measure-specific components of the Big Five personality factors. *Journal of Research in Personality, 32*, 431–453.

Loewenstein, G., & Furstenberg, F. (1991). Is teenage sexual behavior rational? *Journal of Applied Social Psychology, 21*, 957–986.

Loftus, E. F., & Palmer, J. C. (1974). Reconstruction of automobile destruction: An example of the interaction between language and memory. *Journal of Verbal Learning & Verbal Behavior, 13*, 585–589.

Lohr, J., Tolin, D., & Lilienfeld, S. (1998). Efficacy of eye movement desensitization and reprocessing: Implications for behavior therapy. *Behavior Therapy, 29*, 123–56.

Lorenz, K. (1937). The companion in the bird's world. *Auk, 54*, 245–273.

Lorenz, K. (1943). Die angeborenen Formen moeglicher Erfahrung [The innate forms of potential experience]. *Zeitschrift fuer Tierpsychologie, 5*, 233–519.

Louie, K., & Wilson, M. (2001). Temporally structured replay of awake hippocampal ensemble activity during rapid eye movement sleep. *Neuron, 29*, 145–156.

Lovaas, O. I. (1987). Behavioral treatment and normal educational and intellectual functioning in young autistic children. *Journal of Consulting and Clinical Psychology, 55*, 3–9.

Lu, Z.-L., Williamson, S. J., & Kaufman, L. (1992). Behavioral lifetime of human auditory sensory memory predicted by physiological measures. *Science, 258*, 1668–1670.

Luchins, E. A. S. (1946). Classroom experiments on mental set. *American Journal of Psychology, 59*, 295–298.

Ludeke, R. J., & Hartup, W. W. (1983) Teaching behavior of 9- and 11 year-old girls in mixed-age and same-age dyads. *Journal of Educational Psychology, 75*(6), 908–914.

Ludwig, A. M. (1995). *The price of greatness: Resolving the creativity and madness controversy.* New York: Guilford Press.

Lumsden, C. J., & Wilson, E. O. (1983). *Promethean fire: Reflections on the origin of mind.* Cambridge, MA: Harvard University Press.

Lykken, D. T., & Tellegen, A. (1996). Happiness is a stochastic phenomenon. *Psychological Science, 7*(3), 186–189.

Lykken, D. T., Tellegen, A., Bouchard, T. J., Jr., Wilcox, K., Segal, N., & Rich, S. (1988). Personality similarity in twins reared apart and together. *Journal of Personality and Social Psychology, 54*, 1031–1039.

Lynch, G., & Staubli, U. (1991). Possible contributions of long-term potentiation to the encoding and organization of memory. *Brain Research Reviews, 16*, 204–206.

Maas, J. B. (1999). *Power sleep. The revolutionary program that prepares your mind for peak performance.* New York: HarperCollins.

Maccoby, E. E. (1998). *The two sexes: Growing up apart, coming together.* Cambridge, MA: Harvard University Press.

MacFarlane, A. (1978, February). What a baby knows. *Human Nature,* pp. 74-81.

Mack, E. (2008, January 30). A tornado-razed town is rebuilding green. *PlentyMag*.com. Retrieved from http://www.plentymag.com/features/2008/01/greening_greensburg.php.

MacLean, P. (1990). *The triune brain in evolution: Role in Paleocerebral functions.* New York: Springer.

MacWhinney, B. (1998). Models of the emergence of language. *Annual Review of Psychology, 49,* 1999-2227.

Maguire, E. A., Gadian, D. G., Johnsrude, I. S., Good, C. D., Ashburner, J., Frackowiak, R. S. J., & Frith, C. D. (2000, April 11). Navigation-related structural change in the hippocampi of taxi drivers. *Proceedings of the National Academy of Sciences, 97*(8), 4398-4403.

Maguire, E. A., Spiers, H. J., Good, C. D., Hartley, T., Frackowiak, R. S., & Burgess, N. (2003). Navigation expertise and the human hippocampus: A structural brain imaging analysis. *Hippocampus, 13*(2), 250-259.

Mahowald, M. W., & Ettinger, M. G. (1990). Things that go bump in the night: The parsomnias revisited. *Journal of Clinical Neurophysiology, 7,* 119-143.

Maier, N. R. F. (1931). Reasoning in humans II. The solution of a problem and its appearance in consciousness. *Journal of Comparative Psychology, 12,* 181-194.

Main, M., & Hesse, E. (1990). Parents' unresolved traumatic experiences are related to infant disorganized attachment status: Is frightened and/or frightening parental behavior the linking mechanism? In M. T. Greenberg, D. Cicchetti, & E. M. Cummings (Eds.), *Attachment in the preschool years: Theory, research, and intervention* (pp. 161-182). Chicago: University of Chicago Press.

Major, B., Schmidlin, A. M., & Williams, L. (1990). Gender patterns in social touch: The impact of setting and age. *Journal of Personality and Social Psychology Bulletin, 10,* 634-643.

Malnic, B., Hirono, J., Sato, T., & Buck, L. B. (1999). Combinational receptor codes for odors. *Cell, 96,* 713-723.

Manning, R., Levine, M., & Collins, A. (2007). The Kitty Genovese murder and the social psychology of helping: The parable of the 38 witnesses. *American Psychologist, 62*(6), 555-562.

Mansfield, B. K., Haun, H. L., Bownas, J. L., Christen, K., & Mills, M. D. (2008, July 24). Human genome project information. Retrieved August 12, 2008, from http://www.ornl.gov/sci/techresources/Human_Genome/home.shtml

Maquet, P. (2001). The role of sleep in learning and memory. *Science, 294,* 1048-1052.

Maquet, P., & Franck, G. (1996). Functional neuroanatomy of human rapid eye movement sleep and dreaming. *Nature, 383,* 163-166.

Maquet, P., Peters, J-M., Aerts, J., Delfiore, G., Deguildre, C., Luxen, A., & Franck, G. (1996). Functional neuroanatomy of human rapid-eye-movement sleep and dreaming. *Nature, 383,* 163-166.

Marian, V., Shildkrot, Y., Blumenfeld, H. K., Kaushanskaya, M., Faroqi-Shah, Y., & Hirsch, J. (2007). Cortical activation during word processing in late bilinguals: Similarities and differences as revealed by fMRI. *Journal of Clinical and Experimental Neuropsychology, 29*(3), 247-265.

Markus, H., & Kitayama, S. (1991). Culture and the self: Implications for cognition, emotion, and motivation. *Psychological Review, 98,* 224-253.

Marlowe, F. (2000). Paternal investment and the human mating system. *Behavioural Processes, 51,* 45-61.

Martin, C. L., Ruble, D. N., & Szkrybalo, J. (2002). Cognitive theories of early gender development. *Psychological Bulletin, 128,* 903-933.

Maslow, A. H. (1970). *Motivation and personality.* New York: Harper & Row.

Maslow, A. H. (1971). *The farther reaches of human nature.* New York: Viking.

Mason, H. (2003, March 25). Wake up, sleepy teen. *Gallup Poll Tuesday Briefing.*

Mason, H. (2005, January 25). Who dreams, perchance to sleep? *Gallup Poll News Services.*

Mather, M., Canli, T., English, T., Whitfield, S. L., Wais, P., Ochsner, K. N., et al. (2004). Amygdala responses to emotionally valenced stimuli in older and younger adults. *Psychological Science, 15,* 259-263.

Matsumoto, D. (1994). *People: Psychology from a cultural perspective.* Pacific Grove, CA: Brooks/Cole.

Maurer, D., & Maurer, C. (1988). *The world of the newborn.* New York: Basic Books.

Mavromatis, A. (1987). *Hypnagogia: The unique state of consciousness between wakefulness and sleep.* London: Routledge & Kegan Paul.

Mavromatis, A., & Richardson, J. T. E. (1984). Hypnagogic imagery. *International Review of Mental Imagery, 1,* 159-189.

May, C., & Hasher, L. (1998). Synchrony effects in inhibitory control over thought and action. *Journal of Experimental Psychology: Human Perception and Performance, 24,* 363-380.

McAdams, D. P., & Ochberg, R. L. (1988). Psychobiography and life narratives. Durham, NC: Duke University Press.

McCain distances himself from adviser's "nation of whiners" comment. (2008, July 10). The Associated Press. Retrieved August 8, 2008, from http://www.nydailynews.com/news/politics/2008/07/10/2008-07-10_mccain_distances_himself_from_advisers_n.html

McCann, I. L., & Holmes, D. S. (1984). Influence of aerobic exercise on depression. *Journal of Personality and Social Psychology, 46,* 1142-1147.

McClain, D. L. (2008). For hostages, chess can be a solace. *The New York Times.* (2008, July 17). Retrieved August 4, 2008, from http://gambit.blogs.nytimes.com/2008/07/17/for-hostages-chess-is-often-a-solace/

McConkey, K. M. (1995). Hypnosis, memory, and the ethics of uncertainty. *Australian Psychologist, 30,* 1-10.

McCrae, R. R., & Costa, P., Jr. (1994). The stability of personality: Observations and evaluations. *Current Directions in Psycholgoical Science, 3,* 173-175.

McCrae, R. R., & Costa, P., Jr. (1999). A five factor theory of personality. In L. A. Pervin & O. P. John (Eds.), *Handbook of personality: Theory and research* (2nd ed, pp. 139-153). New York: Guilford Press.

McCrae, R. R., Terracciano, A., & 79 members of the Personality Profiles of Cultures Project. (2005). Personality profiles of cultures: Aggregate personality traits. *Journal of Personality and Social Psychology, 89,* 407-425.

McGue, M., Bouchard, T. J., Jr., Iacono, W. G., & Lykken, D. T. (1993). Behavioral genetics of cognitive ability: A life-span perspective. In R. Plomin & G. E. McClearn (Eds.), *Nature, nurture and psychology* (pp. 442-443). Washington, DC: American Psychological Association.

McHugh, P. R. (1995). Witches, multiple personalities, and other psychiatric artifacts. *Nature Medicine, 1*(2), 110-114.

McKellar, J., Stewart, E., & Humphreys, K. (2003). Alcoholics Anonymous involvement and positive alcohol-related outcomes: Cause, consequence, or just a correlate? A prospective 2-year study of 2,319 alcohol-dependent men. *Journal of Consulting and Clinical Psychology, 71,* 302-308.

McMurray, C. (2004, January 13). U.S., Canada, Britain: Who's getting in shape? Gallup Poll Tuesday Briefing. Retrieved September 25, 2008, from http://www.gallup.com/poll/10312/US-Canada-Britain-Whos-Getting-Shape.aspx.

McNeil, D. W., & Zvolensky, M. J. (2000). Systematic desensitization. In A. E. Kazdin (Ed.), *Encyclopedia of psychology* (Vol. 7, pp. 533-535). Washington, DC: American Psychological Association.

Meichenbaum, D. (1977). *Cognitive-behavior modification: An integrative approach.* New York: Plenum Press.

Meichenbaum, D. (1985). *Stress inoculation training.* New York: Pergamon.

Meichenbaum, D. (1996). Stress inoculation training for coping with stressors. *The Clinical Psychologist, 49,* 4-7.

Mekel-Bobrov, N., Gilbert, S. L., Evans, P. D., Vallender, E. J., Anderson, J. R., Hudson, R. R., et al. (2005, September 9). Ongoing adaptive evolution of ASPM, a brain size determinant in *Homo sapiens. Science, 309*(5741), 1720-1722.

Melzack, R. (1980). Psychological aspects of pain. In J. J. Bonica (Ed.), *Pain.* New York: Raven Press.

Melzack, R. (1992, April). Phantom limbs. *Scientific American,* 27-33.

Melzack, R., & Katz, J. (2004). The gate control theory: Reaching for the brain. In T. Hadjistavropoulos & K. Craig (Eds.), *Pain: Psychological perspectives* (pp. 13-34). Mahwah, NJ: Erlbaum.

Merton, R. K., & Kitt, A. S. (1950). Contributions to the theory of reference group behavior. In R. K. Merton & P. F. Lazarsfeld (Eds.), *Continuities in social research: Studies in the scope and method of the American soldier.* Glencoe, IL: Free Press.

Messina, C. R., Lane, D. S., Glanz, K., West, D. S., Taylor, V., Frishman, W., & Powell, L. (2004). Relationship of social support and social burden to repeated breast cancer screening in the Women's Health Initiative. *Health Psychology, 23*(6), 582-594.

Meston, C. M., & Frohlich, P. F. (2000). The neurobiology of sexual function. *Archives of General Psychiatry, 57,* 1012-1030.

METCALFE, J. (1998). Cognitive optimism: Self-deception or memory-based processing heuristics. *Personality and Social Psychology Review, 2,* 100–110.

MEUWISSEN, I., & OVER, R. (1992). Sexual arousal across phases of the humans menstrual cycle. *Archives of Sexual Behavior, 21,* 101–119.

MICHAEL, R. T., GAGNON, J. H., LAUMANN, E. O., KOLATA, G. (1994). *Sex in America: A definitive survey.* Boston: Little, Brown and Company.

MILES, D. R., & CAREY, G. (1997). Genetic and environmental architecture of human aggression. *Journal of Personality and Social Psychology, 72,* 207–217.

MILGRAM, S. (1963). Behavioral study of obedience. *Journal of Abnormal and Social Psychology, 67,* 371–378.

MILGRAM, S. (1964). Issues in the study of obedience: A reply to Baumrind. *American Psychologist, 19,* 848–852.

MILGRAM, S. (1974). *Obedience to authority: An experimental view.* New York: Harper & Row.

MILLER, G. A. (1956). The magical number seven, plus or minus two: Some limits on our capacity for processing information. *Psychological Review, 63,* 81–97.

MILLER, G. A. (2003). The cognitive revolution: A historical perspective. *Trends in Cognitive Sciences, 7*(3), 141–144.

MILLER, M. E., & BOWERS, K. S. (1993). Hypnotic analgesia: Dissociated experience or dissociated control? *Journal of Abnormal Psychology, 102,* 29–38.

MILLER, S. D., BLACKBURN, T., SCHOLES, G., WHITE, G. L., & MAMALIS, N. (1991). Optical differences in multiple personality disorder: A second look. *Journal of Nervous and Mental Disease, 179,* 132–135.

MILLS, M., & MELHUISH, E. (1974). Recognition of mother's voice in early infancy. *Nature, 252,* 123–124.

MISCHEL, W. (1968). *Personality and assessment.* New York: Wiley.

MISCHEL, W. (1984). Converges and challenges in the search for consistency. *American Psychologist, 39,* 351–364.

MISCHEL, W. (2004). Toward an integrative science of the person (Prefatory Chapter). *Annual Review of Psychology, 55,* 1–22.

MIYAKE, K., CHEN, S., & CAMPOS, J. J. (1985). Infant temperament, mother's mode of interaction and attachment in Japan: An interim report. In I. Bretherton & E. Waters (Eds.), *Growing points of attachment theory and research. Monographs of the Society for Research in Child Development,* 50(1–2 Serial No. 109), 276–297.

THE MOMENT OF TRUTH. (2008). YahooTV. Retrieved August 5, 2008, from http://tv.yahoo.com/the-moment-of-truth/show/42401

MONEY, J., BERLIN, F. S., FALCK, A., & STEIN, M. (1983). *Antiandrogenic and counseling treatment of sex offenders.* Baltimore: Department of Psychiatry, Johns Hopkins University School of Medicine.

MONEY, J., & MATTHEWS, D. (1982). Prenatal exposure to virilizing progestins: An adult follow-up study of 12 women. *Archives of Sexual Behavior, 11*(1), 73–83.

MONEY, J., & NORMAN, B. F. (1987). Gender identity and gender transposition: Longitudinal outcome study of 24 male hermaphrodites assigned as boys. *Journal of Sex and Marriage Therapy, 13,* 75–79.

MOODY, R., & PERRY, P. (1993). *Reunions: Visionary encounters with departed loved ones.* London: Little, Brown and Company.

MOORE, D. W. (2004, December 17). Sweet dreams go with a good night's sleep. *Gallup News Service.*

MOORE, M. (2006, July 14). Farinelli's body disinterred to find secrets of castrati. The Telegraph *The Telegraph.* Retrieved August 4, 2008, from http://www.telegraph.co.uk/news/worldnews/europe/italy/1523811/Farinelli's-body-disinterred-to-find-secrets-of-castrati.html

MOORE, P. (1985). *Disguised: A true story.* Texas: Word Books.

MORNIG, R., & SHAR, D. (2008, July 18). False confession expert testifies in Ryan Ferguson hearing. *Columbia Missourian.* Retrieved February 16, 2010, from http://www.columbiamissourian.com/stories/2008/07/18/false-confession-expert-testifies-ryan-ferguson-he/

MORRIS, F. (2007, December 27). Kansas Town's Green Dreams Could Save Its Future. *National Public Radio.* Retrieved from http://www.npr.org/templates/story/story.php?storyId=17643060

MOUCHETANT-ROSTAING, Y., & GIARD, M. H. (2003). Electrophysiological correlates of age and gender perception on human faces. *Journal of Cognitive Neuroscience, 15,* 900–910.

MROCZEK, D. K. (2001). Age and emotion in adulthood. *Current Directions in Psychological Science, 10,* 87–90.

MULLER-OERLINGHAUSEN, B., BERGHOFER, A., & BAUER, M. (2002). Bipolar disorder. *Lancet, 359,* 241–247.

MULROW, C. D. (1999, March). Treatment of depression—newer pharmacotherapies, summary. *Evidence Report/Technology Assessment, 7.* Agency for health care policy and research, Rockville, MD. Retrieved September 23, 2008, from http://www.ahrq.gov/clinic/epcsums/deprsumm.htm

MUNRO, G. D., & DITTO, P. H. (1997). Biased assimilation, attitude polarization, and affect in reactions to stereotype-relevant scientific information. *Personality and Social Psychology Bulletin, 23,* 636–653.

MUNSEY, C. (2007, February). Accentuating the positive—why older people are happier. *Monitor on Psychology, 38*(2), 17.

MURPHY, S. T., MONAHAN, J. L., & ZAJONC, R. B. (1995). Additivity of nonconscious affect: Combined effects of priming and exposure. *Journal of Personality and Social Psychology, 69,* 589–602.

MYERS, D. G. (2000). *The American paradox: Spiritual hunger in an age of plenty.* New Haven: Yale University Press.

NAPOLITAN, D. A., & GOETHALS, G. R. (1979). The attribution of friendliness. *Journal of Experimental Social Psychology, 15,* 105–113.

NASH, M. R. (2001, July) The truth and the hype of hypnosis. *Scientific American,* 47–55.

NATHAN, P. E., & GORMAN, J. M. (2002). Efficacy, effectiveness and the clinical utility of psychotherapy research. In P. E. Nathan and J. M. Gorman (Eds.), *A guide to treatments that work* (2nd ed.). New York: Oxford University Press.

NESTLER, E. J., & MALENKA R. C. (2004). The addicted brain. *Scientific American.* Retrieved July 25, 2008, from http://www.wireheading.com/article/addiction.html

NETTER, S. (2009, June 18). Cloned puppies: A new generation of "Trakrs." *ABCNews.com.* Retrieved December 10, 2009, from http://abcnews.go.com/US/story?id=7871826&page=1

NEUGARTEN, D. A. (Ed.). (1996). *The meanings of age: Selected papers of Bernice L. Neugarten.* Chicago: University of Chicago Press.

NEW ARTICLE CASTS DOUBT ON 'BYSTANDER EFFECT'. (2007, October 1). CNN. Retrieved August 11, 2008, from http://www.cnn.com/2007/HEALTH/10/01/genovese.ap/index.html

NEWBERG, A. B., ALAVI, A., BAIME, M., POURDEHNAD, M., SANTANNA, J., & D'AQUILI, E. (2001). The measurement of regional cerebral blood flow during the complex cognitive task of meditation: A preliminary SPECT study. *Psychiatric Research in Neuroimaging, 106,* 113–122.

NEWCOMBE, N. S., DRUMMEY, A. B., FOX, N. A., LIE, E., & OTTINGER-ALBERTS, W. (2000). Remembering early childhood: How much, how, and why (or why not). *Current Directions in Psychological Science, 9,* 55–58.

NEWELL, A., & SIMON, H. A. (1972). *Human problem solving.* Englewood Cliffs, NJ: Prentice-Hall.

NGUYEN, B., & MORRIS, J. (2009, May 4). After tornado, town rebuilds by going green. *CNN.com.* Retrieved February 16, 2010, from http://www.cnn.com/2009/TECH/science/04/29/green.kansas.town/index.html

NICCOLS, G. A. (1994). Fetal alcohol syndrome: Implications for psychologists. *Clinical Psychology Review, 14,* 91–111.

NICKERSON, R. S., & ADAMS, M. J. (1979). Long-term memory for a common object. *Cognitive Psychology, 11,* 287–307.

NISBETT, R. E., & COHEN, D. (1996). *Culture of honor: The psychology of violence in the South.* Boulder, CO: Westview Press.

NISBETT, R. E., & NORENZAYAN, A. (2002). Culture and cognition. In H. Pashler & D. Medin (Eds.), *Steven's handbook of experimental psychology: Vol 2. Memory and cognitive processes* (3rd ed., pp. 561–597). New York: John Wiley & Sons.

THE NOBEL FOUNDATION. (1986). Elie Wiesel. Retrieved October 7, 2008, from http://nobelprize.org/nobel_prizes/peace/laureates/1986/wiesel-bio.html

NOEL, J. G., FORSYTH, D. R., & KELLEY, K. N. (1987). Improving the performance of failing students by overcoming their self-serving attributional biases. *Basic and Applied Social Psychology, 8,* 151–162.

NORCROSS, J. C. (2002). *Psychotherapeutic relationships that work.* New York: Oxford University Press.

O'CONNOR, A. The struggle for Iraq; Psychology: Pressure to go along with abuse is strong, but some soldiers find strength to refuse. (2004, May 14). *The New York Times.* Retrieved August 12, 2008, from http://query.nytimes.com/gst/fullpage.html?res=9D0CEEDF1F3CF93 7A25756C0A9629C8B63&partner=rssnyt&emc=rss

O'DONNELL, R. (2001). How Rosie O'Donnell beat depression. *ABC News.* Retrieved September 23, 2008, from http://abcnews.go.com/GMA/ Depression/Story?id=126783&page=2

OGAS, O. (2006, November 9). Who wants to be a cognitive neuroscientist millionaire? *Seed.* Retrieved October 17, 2008 from http://www .seedmagazine.com/news/2006/11/who_wants_to_be_a_cognitive_ ne.php

O'KEEFE, J., & NADEL, L. (1978). *The hippocampus as a cognitive map.* Oxford University Press.

OLFSON, M., MARCUS S. C., & SHAFFER, D. (2006). Antidepressant drug therapy and suicide in severely depressed children and adults. *Archives of General Psychiatry, 63,* 865-872.

OLFSON, M., SHAFFER, D., MARCUS, S. C., & GREENBERG, T. (2003). Relationship between antidepressant medication treatment and suicide in adolescents. *Archives of General Psychiatry, 60,* 978-982.

OLSON, I. R., PLOTZKER, A., & EZZYAT, Y. (2007). The enigmatic temporal pole: A review of findings on social and emotional processing. *Brain: A Journal of Neurology, 130*(7), 1718-1731.

O'NEILL, J., SENIOR, T., & CSICSVARI, J. (2006). Place-selective firing of CA1 pyramidal cells during sharp wave/ripple network patterns in exploratory behavior. *Neuron, 49,* 143-155.

O'RAND, A. M. (2004). Women in science: Career processes and outcomes. *Social Forces, 82*(4), 1669-1671.

OREN, D. A., & TERMAN, M. (1998). Tweaking the human circadian clock with light. *Science, 279,* 333-334.

ORNE, M.T., & EVANS, F. J. (1965). Social control in the psychological experiment: Antisocial behavior and hypnosis. *Journal of Personality and Social Psychology, 95,* 189-200.

ORNE, M.T., & HOLLAND, C. H. (1968). On the ecological validity of laboratory deceptions. *International Journal of Psychiatry, 6,* 282-293.

OUIMETTE, P., HUMPHREYS, K., MOOS, R. H., FINNEY, J. W., CRONKITE, R., & FEDERMAN, B. (2001). Self-help group participation among substance use disorder patients with posttraumatic stress disorder. *Journal of Substance Abuse Treatment, 20,* 25-32.

PACKER, C., & PUSEY, A. E. (1983). Adaptations of female lions to infanticide by incoming males. *The American Naturalist, 121*(5), 716-728.

PADECKY, B. (2008, August 3). Going for the gold. *The Press Democrat.* Retrieved August 4, 2008, from http://www.pressdemocrat.com/ article/20080803/NEWS/808030358/1349&title=Going_for_the_gold

PAFFENBARGER, R. S., HYDE, R.T., WING, A. L., LEE, I., JUNG, D. L., & KAMPERT, J. B. (1993, February 25). The association of changes in physical-activity level and other lifestyle characteristics with mortality among men. *New England Journal of Medicine, 328,* 538-545.

PAGE, S. (1977). Effects of the mental illness label in attempts to obtain accommodation. *Canadian Journal of Behavioral Science, 9,* 84-90.

PAIVIO, A. (1986). *Mental representations: A dual coding approach.* New York: Oxford University Press.

PARK, A. (2007, November 1). The science of growing body parts, *Time.* Retrieved February 16, 2010, from http://www.time.com/time/health/ article/0,8599,1679115,00.html

PARK, A. (2008). What's driving Dara Torres. *Time.* Retrieved August 4, 2008, from http://www.time.com/time/specials/packages/article/0,28804, 1819129_1819134_1825304,00.html

PARK, A. (2008). 7. Shawn Johnson. *Time.* Retrieved August 4, 2008, from http://www.time.com/time/specials/packages/article/0, 28804,1819129_1819134_1825314,00.html

PARKER, G., ROY, K., HADZI, P. D., & PEDIC, F. (1992). Psychotic (delusional) depression: A meta-analysis of physical treatments. *Journal of Affective Disorders, 24,* 17-24.

PARKER-POPE, T. (2008, June 5). Summer flip-flops may lead to foot pain. *The New York Times.* Retrieved July 8, 2008, from http://well.blogs. nytimes.com/2008/06/05/summer-flip-flops-may-lead-to-foot-pain/

PARTONEN, T., & LONNQVIST, J. (1998). Seasonal affective disorder. *Lancet, 352*(9137), 1369-1374.

PAULEY, J. (2004). Interview with Matt Lauer. *Today* show. Retrieved September 23, 2008, from http://www.msnbc.msn.com/id/5860105/

PAVLOV, I. P. (1927). *Conditioned reflexes* (G. V. Anrep, Trans.). London: Oxford University Press.

PAYNE, V. G., & ISAACS, L. D. (1987). *Human motor development: A lifespan approach.* Mayfield, CA: Mountainview.

PEDERSEN, N. L., PLOMIN, R., McLEARN, G. E., & FRIBERG, L. (1988). Neuroticism, extraversion, and related traits in adult twins reared apart and reared together. *Journal of Personality and Social Psychology, 55,* 950-957.

PELPHREY, K. A. (2004). Grasping the intentions of others: The perceived intentionality of an action influences activity in the superior temporal sulcus during social perception. *Journal of Cognitive Neuroscience, 16,* 1706-1716.

PELPHREY, K. A., MORRIS, J. P., MICHELICH, C. R., TRUETT, A., & McCARTHY, G. (2005). Functional anatomy of biological motion perception in posterior temporal cortex: An fMRI study of eye, mouth and hand movements. *Cerebral Cortex 15*(12), 1866-1876.

PENG, K., & NISBETT, R. E. (1999). Culture, dialectics, and reasoning about contradiction. *American Psychologist, 54,* 741-754.

PENNEBAKER, J. W., BARGER, S. D., & TIEBOUT, J. (1989). Disclosure of traumas and health among Holocaust survivors. *Psychosomatic Medicine, 51*(5), 577-589.

PENNEBAKER, J. W., & O'HEERON, R. C. (1984). Confiding in others and illness rate among spouses of suicide and accidental-death victims. *Journal of Abnormal Psychology, 93*(4), 473-476.

PEPLAU, L. A., GARNETS, L. D., SPALDING, L. R., CONLEY, T. D., & VENIEGAS, R. C. (1998). A critique of Bem's "Exotic Becomes Erotic" theory of sexual orientation. Psychological Review, 105(2), 387-394.

PERKINS, H. W. (1991). Religious commitment, Yuppie values, and well-being in post-collegiate life. *Review of Religious Research, 32,* 244-251.

PERLS, F. (1969). *Gestalt psychotherapy verbatim.* Lafayette, CA: Real People Press.

PESCHEL, E. R., & PESCHEL, R. E. (1987). Medical insights into the castrati in opera. *American Scientist, 75,* 578-583.

PETERS, T. J., & WATERMAN, R. H., JR. (1982). *In search of excellence: Lessons from America's best-run companies.* New York: Harper & Row.

PETERSON, C., & BARRETT, L. C. (1987). Explanatory style and academic performance among university freshmen. *Journal of personality and social psychology.* 53(3), 603-607.

PETERSON, C., SEMMEL, A., VON BAEYER, C., ABRAMSON, L., METALSKY, G. I., & SELIGMAN, M. E. P. (1982). The attributional style questionnaire. *Cognitive Therapy and Research, 6,* 287-300.

PETITTO, L. A., & MARENTETTE, P. F. (1991). Babbling in the manual mode: Evidence for the ontogeny of language. *Science, 251,* 1493-1493.

PETTEGREW, J. W., KESHAVAN, K. S., & MINSHEW, N. J. (1993). 31P nuclear magnetic resonance spectroscopy: Neurodevelopment and schizophrenia. *Schizophrenia Bulletin, 19,* 35-53.

PETTIGREW, T. F., & TROPP, L. R. (2006). A meta-analytic test of intergroup contact theory. *Journal of Personality and Social Psychology, 90,* 751-783.

PETTY, R. E., & CACIOPPO, J. T. (1986). The elaboration likelihood model of persuasion. In L. Berkowitz (Ed.), *Advances in experimental social psychology, 19,* 123-205. New York: Academic Press.

PFUNGST, O. (2000). *Clever Hans: The horse of Mr. von Osten.* In R. H. Wozniak (Ed.). Bristol: Thoemmes Press. (Original work published 1911)

PHELPS, E. A., O'CONNOR, K. J., CUNNINGHAM, W. A., FUNAYAMA, E. S., GATENBY, J. C., GORE, J. C., & BANAJI, M. (2000). Performance on indirect measures of race evaluation predicts amygdala activation. *Journal of Cognitive Neuroscience, 12*(5), 729-738.

PHILLIPS, P. E. M., STUBER, G. D., HEIEN, M. L. A. V., WIGHTMAN, R. M., & CARELLI, R. M. (2003). Subsecond dopamine release promotes cocaine seeking. *Nature, 422*(6932), 614-618.

PIAGET, J. (1932). *The moral judgment of the child.* New York: Harcourt, Brace & World.

PICKAR, D., LABARCA, R., LINNOILA, M., ROY, A., HOMMER, D., EVERETT, D., & PAYL, S. M. (1984). Neuroleptic-induced decrease in plasma homovanillic acid and antipsychotic activity in schizophrenic patients. *Science, 225,* 954-957.

PLOTNIK, J. M., DE WAAL, F. B. M., & REISS, D. (2006). Self-recognition in an Asian elephant. *Proceedings of the National Academy of Sciences of the United States of America, 103*(45), 17053-17057.

PLUTCHIK, R. (1980). *Emotion: A psychoevolutionary synthesis.* New York: Harper & Row.

POLICE: 10 WITNESS RAPE, DO NOTHING. (2007, August 24). CBS News. Retrieved August 11, 2008, from http://www.cbsnews.com/stories/ 2007/08/24/national/main3200634.shtml?source=RSSattr=U.S._ 3200634

POPULATION DIVISION OF THE DEPARTMENT OF ECONOMIC AND SOCIAL AFFAIRS OF THE UNITED NATIONS SECRETARIAT, WORLD POPULATION PROSPECTS. (2006). Executive summary.

PORTER, L. W., & LAWLER, E. E. (1968). *Managerial attitudes and performance*. Homewood, IL: Irwin.

POSEGATE, ANN. (2009, May 7). A Greener Greensburg Two Years after Tornado. *The Washington Post*. Retrieved February 16, 2010, from http://voices.washingtonpost.com/capitalweathergang/2009/05/green sburg_goes_green_two_year.html

PRESSMAN, S. D., COHEN, S., MILLER, G. E., BARKIN, A., RABIN, B. S., & TREANOR, J. J. (2005). Loneliness, social network size, and immune response to influenza vaccination in college freshman. *Health Psychology, 24*(3), 297-306.

PRESSON, P. K., & BENASSI, V. A. (1996). Illusion of control: A meta-analytic review. *Journal of Social Behavior and Personality, 11*(3), 493-510.

PRIOR, H., SCHWARZ, A., & GÜNTÜRKÜN, O. (2008). Mirror-induced behavior in the magpie (*Pica pica*): Evidence of self-recognition. *PLoS Biology, 6*(8), e202.

QUINN, P. C., BHATT, R. S., BRUSH, D., GRIMES, A., & SHARPNACK, H. (2002). Development of form similarity as a Gestalt grouping principle in infancy. *Psychological Science, 13*, 320-328.

RABINOWITZ, G. (2008, August 3). Stampede kills 145 at remote Hindu temple in India. Associated Press. Retrieved August 3, 2008, from http://ap.google.com/article/ALeqM5inevs3P871iJOyHbjb9rSrpzJEIAD92B10G8

RAINE, A. (1999). Murderous minds: Can we see the mark of Cain? *Cerebrum: The Dana Forum on Brain Science 1*(1), 15-29.

RAINE, A., LENCZ, T., BIHRLE, S., LACASSE, L., & COLLETTI, P. (2000). Reduced prefrontal gray matter volume and reduced autonomic activity in antisocial personality disorder. *Archives of General Psychiatry, 57*, 119-127.

RAINVILLE, P., DUNCAN, G. H., PRICE, D. D., CARRIER, B., & BUSHNELL, M. C. (1997). Pain affect encoded in human anterior cingulated but not somatosensory cortex. *Science, 277*, 968-971.

RAMACHANDRAN, V. S. (2000, June). Mirror neurons and imitation learning as the driving force behind "the great leap forward" in human evolution. *Edge*, 69.

RAMON Y CAJAL, S. (1937). *Recollections of my life* (E. Horne-Craigie, Trans.). Philadelphia: American Philosophical Society.

RAUCH, S. L., & JENIKE, M. A. (1993). Neurobiological models of obsessive-compulsive disorder. *Psychomatics, 34*, 20-32.

RAZRAN, G. (1949). Semantic and phonetographic generalizations of salivary conditioning to verbal stimuli. *Journal of Experimental Psychology, 39*, 642-652.

RECANZONE, G. H., JENKINS, W. M., HRADEK, G. T., & MERZENICH, M. M. (1992). Progressive improvement in discriminative abilities in adult owl monkeys performing a tactile frequency discrimination task. *Journal of Neurophysiology, 67*(5), 1015-1030.

RECHTSCHAFFEN, A., & BERGMAN, B. M. (1965). Sleep deprivation in the rat by the disk-over-water method. *Behavioral Brain Research, 69*, 55-63.

REEVES, J. L., REDD, W. H., STORM, F. K., & MINOGAWA, R. V. (1983). Hypnosis in the control of pain during hyperthermia treatment of cancer. In Bonica, J. J., Lindblom, V., & Iago, A., (Eds.) *Advances in pain research and therapy*. New York: Raven.

REICHMAN, J. (1998). *I'm not in the mood: What every woman should know about improving her libido*. New York: Morrow.

REINER, W. G., & GEARHART, J. P. (2004). Discordant sexual identity in some genetic males with cloacal exstrophy assigned to female sex at birth. *New England Journal of Medicine, 350*, 333-341.

REISS A. L., ABRAMS M. T., SINGER H. S., ROSS J. L., & DENCKLA M. B. (1996). Brain development, gender and IQ in children. A volumetric imaging study. *Brain, 119*, 1763-1774.

RICHARDS, B. J. (2008, September 25). Lack of Sleep, Stress, Adrenals, and Obesity. *Wellness Resources*. Retrieved from http://www.wellness resources.com/weight/articles/lack_of_sleep_stress_adrenals_and_obesity/?source=Email&camp=news092508

RICHESON, J. A., BAIRD, A. A., GORDON, H. L., HEATHERTON, T. F., WYLAND, C. L., TRAWALTER, S., & SHELTON, J. N. (2003). An fMRI investigation of the impact of interracial contact on executive function. *Nature Neuroscience, 6*, 1323-1328.

RICHTER, C. P. (1936). Increased salt appetite in adrenalectomized rats. *American Journal of Physiology, 115*, 155-161.

RICHTER, C. P, & ECKERT, J. F. (1937). Increased calcium appetite of parathyroidectomized rats. *Endocrinology, 21*, 50-54.

RINI, C. K., DUNKEL-SCHETTER, C., WADHWA, P. D., & SANDMAN, C. A. (1999). Psychological adaptation and birth outcomes: The role of personal resources, stress, and sociocultural context in pregnancy. *Health Psychology, 18*, 333-345.

RISSMAN, J., GAZZALEY, A., & D'ESPOSITO, M. (2008). Dynamic adjustments in prefrontal, hippocampal, and inferior temporal interactions with increasing visual working memory load. *Cerebral Cortex, 18*(7), 1618-1629.

ROBINS, L. N., & REGIER, D. A. (1991). *Psychiatric disorders in America: the epidemiologic catchment area study*. New York: The Free Press.

RODIN, J. (1986, September 19). Aging and health: Effects of the sense of control. *Science, 233*(4770), 1271-1276.

ROENNEBERG, T., KUEHNLE, T., PRAMSTALLER, P. P., RICKEN, J., HAVEL, M., GUTH, A., & MERROW, M. (2004). A marker for the end of adolescence. *Current Biology, 14*, R1038-9.

ROGERS, C. R. (1961). *On becoming a person: A therapist's view of psychotherapy*. Boston: Houghton Mifflin.

ROGERS, C. R. (1980). *A way of being*. Boston: Houghton Mifflin.

ROLLINS, B. C., & FELDMAN, H. (1970). Marital satisfaction over the family life cycle. *Journal of Marriage and the Family, 26*, 20-28.

ROSCH, E. (1978). Principles of categorization. In E. Rosch & B. L. Lloyd (Eds.), *Cognition and categorization*. Hillsdale, NJ: Earlbaum.

ROSE, J. S., CHASSIN, L., PRESSON, C. C., & SHERMAN, S. J. (1999). Peer influences on adolescent cigarette smoking: A prospective sibling analysis. *Merrill-Palmer Quarterly, 45*, 62-84.

ROSE, R. L., & WOOD, S. L. (2005). Paradox and the consumption of authenticity through reality television. *Journal of Consumer Research, 32*, 284-296.

ROSE, S., KAMIN, L. J., & LEWONTIN, R. C. (1984). *Not in our genes: Biology, ideology and human nature*. Harmondsworth, UK: Penguin.

ROSEMARY KENNEDY, JFK'S SISTER, DIES AT 86. (2005, January 8). MSNBC. Retrieved August 4, 2008, from http://www.msnbc.msn.com/id/6801152/

ROSEN, W. D., ADAMSON, L. B., & BAKEMAN, R. (1992). An experimental investigation of infant social referencing: Mothers' messages and gender differences. *Developmental Psychology, 28*, 1172-1178.

ROSENBAUM, M. (1986). The repulsion hypothesis: On the nondevelopment of relationships. *Journal of Personality and Social Psychology, 51*, 1156-1166.

ROSENHAN, D. L. (1973). On being sane in insane places. *Science, 179*, 250-258.

ROSENMAN, R. H., BRAND, R. I., JENKINS, C. D., FRIEDMAN, M., STRAUS, R., & WURM, M. (1975). Coronary heart disease in the Western Collaborative Group Study, final follow-up experience of 8½ years. *Journal of the American Medical Association, 233*, 812-817.

ROSENTHAL, R. (1974). *On the social psychology of the self-fulfilling prophecy: Further evidence for Pygmalion effects and their mediating mechanisms*. New York: MSS Modular Publications.

ROSENZWEIG, M. R., BENNETT, E. L., & DIAMOND, M. C. (1972). Brain changes in response to experience. *Scientific American, 226*(2), 22-29.

ROSS, L. (1977). The intuitive psychologist and his shortcomings. In L. Berkowitz (Ed.), *Advances in experimental social psychology*. (Vol. 10, pp. 173-220). New York: Academic Press.

ROSS, L., GREENE, D., & HOUSE, P. (1977). The false consensus effect: An egocentric bias in social perception and attribution processes. *Journal of Experimental Social Psychology, 13*, 279-301.

ROSS, L., LEPPER, M. R., & HUBBARD, M. (1975). Perseverance in self-perception and social perception: Biased attributional process in the debriefing paradigm. *Journal of Personality and Social Psychology, 32*, 880-892.

ROTHBART, M., FULERO, S., JENSEN, C., HOWARD, J., & BIRRELL, P. (1978). From individual to group impressions: Availability heuristics in stereotype formation. *Journal of Experimental Social Psychology, 14*, 237-255.

ROTTER, J. B. (1954). *Social learning and clinical psychology*. Englewood Cliffs, NJ: Prentice-Hall.

ROTTER, J. B. (1966). Generalized expectancies for internal versus external control of reinforcement. *Psychological Monographs, 80*(Whole No. 609).

ROWE, D. C., ALMEIDA, D. M., & JACOBSON, K. C. (1999). School context and genetic influences on aggression in adolescence. *Psychological Science, 10*, 277-280.

RUBIN, P. (1999, July 1). Wake-up Call. *Phoenix New Times*. Retrieved February 16, 2010, from http://www.phoenixnewtimes.com/1999-07-01/news/wake-up-call/1.

RUBY, P., & DECETY, J. (2001). Effect of subjective perspective taking during simulation of action: a PET investigation of agency. *Nature Neuroscience, 4*(5), 546-550.

Ryan, H. (2004, June 10). Dread of fatherhood could be Peterson's motive, witnesses suggest. CNN. Retrieved August 20, 2008, from http://www.cnn.com/2004/LAW/06/10/peterson.case/index.html

Saad, L. (2001, December 17). Americans' mood: Has Sept. 11 made a difference? Gallup Poll News Service.

Sachdev, P., & Sachdev, J. (1997). Sixty years of psychosurgery: Its present status and its future. Australian and New Zealand Journal of Psychiatry, 31, 457-464.

Sadker, D. (2000). Gender equity: Still knocking at the classroom door. Equity & Excellence in Education, 33(1), 80-83.

Sakurai, T., Amemiya, A., Ishii, M., Matsuzaki, I., Chemelli, R. M., Tanaka, H., Williams, S. C., Richardson, J. A., Kozlowski, G. P., Wilson, S., Arch, J. R. S., Buckingham, R. C., Haynes, A. C., Carr, S. A., Annan, R. S., McNulty, D. E., Liu, W. S., Terrett, J. A., Elshourbagy, N. A., Bergsma, D. J., & Yanagisawa, M. (1998). Orexins and orexin receptors: a family of hypothalamic neuropeptides and G-protein coupled receptors that regulate feeding behaviour. Cell, 92, 573-585.

Salleh, A. (2003, August 18). Brain shrinkage: Early sign of schizophrenia? ABC Science Online. Retrieved September 8, 2008, from http://www.abc.net.au/science/news/stories/s925547.htm

Salzinger, S., Ng-Mak, D. S., Feldman, R. S., Kam, C. M., & Rosario, M. (2006). Exposure to community violence: Processes that increase the risk for inner-city middle-school children. Journal of Early Adolescence, 26, 232-266.

Sanford, A. J., Fray, N., Stewart, A., & Moxley, L. (2002). Perspective in statements of quality, with implications for consumer psychology. Psychological Science, 13, 130-134.

Santelli, J., Duberstein Lindberg, L., Finer, L. B., Singh, S. (2007). Explaining recent declines in adolescent pregnancy in the United States: The contribution of abstinence and improved contraceptive use. American Journal of Public Health, 97(10), 150-156.

Sarbin, T. R., & Coe, W. C. (1972). Hypnosis: A social psychological analysis of influence communication. New York: Holt, Rinehart & Winston.

Savic, I., Berglund, H., & Lindström, P. (2005). Brain response to putative pheromones in homosexual men. Proceedings of the National Academy of Sciences of the United States of America, 102(20), 7356-7361.

Saykin, J. A., Gur, R. C., Gur, R. E., et al. (1991). Neuropsychological function in schizophrenia: Selective impairment in memory and learning. Archives of General Psychiatry, 48, 618-624.

Schacter, D. L. (1996). Searching for memory: The brain, the mind, and the past. New York: Basic Books.

Schacter, D. L. (1999). The seven sins of memory: Insights from psychology and cognitive neuroscience. American Psychologist, 54, 182-201.

Schanberg, S., & Field, T. (1988). Maternal deprivation and supplemental stimulation. In T. Field, P. McCabe, & N. Schneiderman (Eds.), Stress and Coping Across Development. Hillsdale, NJ: Erlbaum.

Schachter, S., & Singer, J. E. (1962). Cognitive, social, and physiological determinants of emotional state. Psychological Review, 69, 379-399.

Scheier, M. F., & Carver, C. S. (1985). Optimism, coping, and health: Assessment and implications of generalized outcome expectancies. Health Psychology, 4, 219-247.

Scheier, M. F., & Carver, C. S. (1992). Effects of optimism on psychological and physical well-being: Theoretical overview and empirical update. Cognitive Therapy and Research, 16(2), 201-228.

Schneider Institute for Health Policy, Brandeis University. (2001). Substance abuse: The nation's number one health problem. Princeton: Robert Wood Johnson Foundation. Retrieved August 1, 2008, from http://www.rwjf.org/files/publications/other/SubstanceAbuseChartbook.pdf

Schonfield, D., & Robertson, B. A. (1966). Memory storage and aging. Canadian Journal of Psychology, 20, 228-236.

Schwartz, P. (1994, November 17). Some people with multiple roles are blessedly stressed. The New York Times.

The science of sleep. (n.d.). BBC. Retrieved August 4, 2008, from http://www.bbc.co.uk/science/humanbody/sleep/articles/whatissleep.shtml

Scott, E. Cortisol and stress: How to stay healthy. About.com Guide. Retrieved from http://stress.about.com/od/stresshealth/a/cortisol.htm

Seeman, P., Guan, H-C., & Van Tol, H. H. M. (1993). Dopamine D4 receptors elevated in schizophrenia. Nature, 365, 441-445.

Sei, H., Saitoh, D., Yamamoto, K., Morita, K., & Morita, Y. (2000). Differential effect of short-term REM sleep deprivation on NGF and BDNF protein levels in the rat brain. Brain Research, 877(2), 387-390.

Sekiyama, K., Miyauchi, S., Imaruoka, T., Egusa, H., & Tashiro, T. (2000). Body image as a visuomotor transformation device revealed in adaptation to reversed vision, Nature, 407, 374-377.

Seligman, M. E. P. (1971). Phobias and preparedness. Behavior Therapy, 2, 307-320.

Seligman, M. E. P. (1991). Learned optimism. New York: Knopf.

Seligman, M. E. P. (1995). The effectiveness of psychotherapy: The Consumer Reports study. American Psychologist, 50, 965-974.

Seligman, M. E. P. (2002). Authentic happiness: Using the new positive psychology to realize your potential for lasting fulfillment. New York: Free Press.

Seligman, M. E. P., & Maier, S. F. (1967). Failure to escape traumatic shock. Journal of Experimental Psychology, 74, 1-9.

Seligman, M. E. P., & Yellen, A. (1987). What is a dream? Behavior Research and Therapy, 25, 1-24.

Selinker, L., & Baumgartner-Cohen, B. (1995). Multiple Language Acquisition: 'Damn It, Why Can't I Keep These Two Languages Apart? Language, Culture and Curriculum, 8(2), 115-121.

Semin, G. R., & Manstead, A. S. R. (1982). The social implications of embarrassment displays and restitution behavior. European Journal of Social Psychology, 12, 367-377.

Shadish, W. R., Matt, G. E., Navarro, A. M., & Phillips, G. (2000). The effects of psychological therapies under clinically representative conditions: A meta-analysis. Psychological Bulletin, 126, 512-529.

Shapiro, F. (1989). Efficacy of the eye movement desensitization procedure in the treatment of traumatic memories. Journal of Traumatic Stress, 2, 199-223.

Shapiro, F. (2002). EMDR as an integrative psychotherapy approach: Experts of diverse orientations explore the paradigm prism. Washington, DC: APA Books.

Sheehy, Gail. (1972, January 10). The secret of Grey Gardens. New York Magazine. Retrieved from http://nymag.com/news/features/56102/

Shergill, S. S., Brammer, M. J., Williams, S. C. R., Murray, R. M., & McGuire, P. K. (2000). Mapping auditory hallucinations in schizophrenia using functional magnetic resonance imaging. Archives of General Psychiatry, 57, 1033-1038.

Sherry, D., & Vaccarino, A. L. (1989). Hippocampus and memory for food caches in black-capped chickadees. Behavioral Neuroscience, 103, 308-318.

Shetty wins Celebrity Big Brother. (2007, January 29). BBC News. Retrieved August 11, 2008, from http://news.bbc.co.uk/2/hi/entertainment/6308443.stm

Shields, B. (2005). Down came the rain: My journey through post-partum depression. New York: Christa Incorporated.

Siegel, J. M. (1990, June). Stressful life events and use of physician services among the elderly: The moderating role of pet ownership. Journal of Personality and Social Psychology, 58(6), 1081-1086.

Siegel, S., Hinson, R. E., Krank, M. D, & McCully, J. (1982, April 23). Heroin "overdose" death: Contribution of drug-associated environmental cues. Science, 216(4544), 436-437.

Silva, C. E., & Kirsch, I. (1992). Interpretive sets, expectancy, fantasy proneness, and dissociation as predictors of hypnotic response. Journal of Personality and Social Psychology, 63, 847-856.

Simek, T. C., & O'Brien, R. M. (1981). Total golf: A behavioral approach to lowering your score and getting more out of your game. New York, NY: Doubleday.

Simek, T.C., & O'Brien, R. M. (1988). A chaining-mastery discrimination training program to teach Little Leaguers to hit a baseball. Human Performance, 1, 73-84.

Simons, D. J., & Levin, D. T. (1998). Failure to detect changes to people during a real-world interaction. Psychonomic Bulletin and Review, 5, 644-649.

Singer, E. (2007, November 27). Prosthetic limbs that can feel. Technology Review. Retrieved November 16, 2009, from http://www.technologyreview.com/biomedicine/19759/

Singer, E. (2009, February 10). Patients test an advanced prosthetic arm. Technology Review. Retrieved February 5, 2010, from http://www.technologyreview.com/blog/editors/22730.

Skinner, B. F. (1948). Science and human behavior. New York: Macmillan.

Skinner, B. F. (1957). Verbal behavior. Englewood Cliffs, NJ: Prentice Hall.

Sklar, L. S., & Anisman, H. (1981). Stress and cancer. Psychological Bulletin, 89, 396-406.

SKRE, I., ONSTAD, S., TORGERSEN, S., LYGREN, S., & KRINGLEN, E. (1993). A twin study of DSM-III-R anxiety disorders. *Acta Psychiatrica Scandinavica, 88,* 85-92

SLATER, A., MORISON, V., & SOMERS, M. (1988). Orientation discrimination and cortical function in the human newborn. *Perception, 17,* 597-602.

SLOANE, R. B., STAPLES, F. R., CRISTOL, A. H., YORKSON, N. J., & WHIPPLE, K. (1975). *Psychotherapy versus behavior therapy.* Cambridge, MA: Harvard University Press.

SMITH, D. R., CHARLES D. (2007, April 25). Magnetic Resonance Imaging May Predict Alzheimer's Disease. *Scitizen.* Retrieved February 16, 2010, from http://www.scitizen.com/stories/Neuroscience/2007/04/Magnetic-Resonance-Imaging-May-Predict-Alzheimer-s-Disease

SMITH, M. L., GLASS, G. V., & MILLER, R. L. (1980). *The benefits of psychotherapy.* Baltimore: Johns Hopkins Press.

SNYDER C. R., SYMPSON S. C., YBASCO F. C., BORDERS, T. F., BABYAK, M. A., & HIGGINS, R. L. (1996). Development and validation of the State Hope Scale. *Journal of Personality and Social Psychology 70,* 321-335.

SNYDER, M. (1984). When beliefs create reality. In L. Berkowitz (Ed.), *Advances in experimental social psychology* (Vol. 18, pp. 247-305). New York: Academic Press.

SNYDER, M., & SWANN, W. B. (1978). Hypothesis-testing processes in social interaction. *Journal of Personality and Social Psychology, 36,* 1202-1212.

SO, K. T., & ORME-JOHNSON, D. W. (2001). Three randomized experiments of the longitudinal effects of the Transcendental Meditation technique on cognition. *Intelligence, 29*(5), 419-440.

SOLOMON, D. A., KEITNER, G. I., MILLER, I. W., SHEA, M. T., & KELLER, M. B. (1995). Course of illness and maintenance treatments for patients with bipolar disorder. *Journal of Clinical Psychiatry, 56,* 5-13.

SOLOMON, J. (1996, May 20). Breaking the silence. *Newsweek,* pp. 20-22.

SPERLING, G. (1960). The information available in brief visual presentations. *Psychological Monographs, 74,* 1-29.

SPIEGEL, K., LEPROUL, R., & VAN CAUTER, E. (1999). Impact of sleep debt on metabolic and endocrine function. *Lancet, 345,* 1435-1439.

STALLMAN, J. (2008, July 27). Lab ready for sex tests for female athletes. *The New York Times: Rings.* Retrieved September 2, 2008, from http://olympics.blogs.nytimes.com/2008/07/27/lab-ready-for-sex-tests-for-female-athletes/

STANFORD UNIVERSITY CENTER FOR NARCOLEPSY. (2002). Narcolepsy is a serious medical disorder and a key to understanding other sleep disorders. Retrieved October 7, 2008, from http://www.med.stanford.edu/school/Psychiatry/narcolepsy

STATISTICS CANADA. (2003). Victims and persons accused of homicide, by age and sex. Table 253-0003. Retrieved September 2, 2008, from http://www40.statcan.ca/l01/cst01/legal10a.htm

STEELE, C. M., & ARONSON, J. (1995). Stereotype threat and the intellectual test performance of African-Americans. *Journal of Personality and Social Psychology, 69,* 797-811.

STEIN, E. (1999). *The mismeasure of desire: Science, theory, and the ethics of sexual orientation.* New York: Oxford University Press.

STEPHANOPOULOS, G. (1999). *All too human: A political education.* New York: Little Brown.

STERNBERG, R. J. (1985). *Beyond IQ: A triarchic theory of human intelligence.* New York: Cambridge University Press.

STERNBERG, R. J., & KAUFMAN, J. C. (1998). Human abilities. *Annual Review of Psychology, 49,* 479-502.

STETTER, F., & KUPPER, S. (2002). Autogenic training: A meta-analysis of clinical outcome studies. *Applied Psychophysiology and Biofeedback, 27,* 45-98.

STICKGOLD, R. (2005). Sleep-dependent memory consolidation. *Nature, 437,* 1272-1278.

STICKGOLD, R., HOBSON, J. A., FOSSE, R., & FOSSE, M. (2001, November 2). Sleep, learning, and dreams: Off-line memory reprocessing. *Science, 294*(5544), 1052-1057.

STITH, S. M., ROSEN, K. H., MIDDLETON, K. A., BUSCH, A. L., LUNDEBERG, K., & CARLTON, R. P. (2000). The intergenerational transmission of spouse abuse: A meta-analysis. *Journal of Marriage and the Family, 62,* 640-654.

STONE, A. A., & NEALE, J. M. (1984). Effects of severe daily events on mood. *Journal of Personality and Social Psychology, 46,* 137-144.

ST. ONGE, J. R., & FLORESCO, S. B. (2008, July 30). Dopaminergic modulation of risk-based decision making. *Neuropsychopharmacology.* [Epub ahead of print]

STRACK, F., MARTIN, L., & STEPPER, S. (1988). Inhibiting and facilitating conditions of the human smile: a nonobtrusive test of the facial feedback hypothesis. *Journal of Personality and Social Psychology, 54,* 768-777.

STRATHEARN, L., Li, J., FONAGY, P., & MONTAGUE, P. R. (2008, July). What's in a smile? Maternal brain responses to infant facial cues. *Pediatrics, 122,* 40-51.

STRAYER, D. L, & JOHNSTON, W. A. (2001). Driven to distraction: Dual-task studies of simulated driving and conversing on a cellular telephone. *Psychological Science, 12,* 462-466.

STREISSGUTH, A. P., AASE, J. M., CLARREN, S. K., RANDELS, S. P., LADUE, R. A., & SMITH, D. F. (1991). Fetal alcohol syndrome in adolescents and adults. *Journal of the American Medical Association, 265,* 1961-1967.

STRUPP, H. H. (1986). Psychotherapy: Research, practice, and public policy (How to avoid dead ends). *American Psychologist, 41,* 120-130.

SULLIVAN, H. S. (2008). In Encyclopædia Britannica Online. Retrieved August 21, 2008, from http://www.search.eb.com/eb/article-9070262

SULLIVAN, P. F., NEALE, M. C., & KENDLER, K. S. (2000). Genetic epidemiology of major depression: Review and meta-analysis. *American Journal of Psychiatry, 157,* 1552-1562.

SWERDLOW, N. R., & KOOB, G. F. (1987). Dopamine, schizophrenia, mania, and depression: Toward a unified hypothesis of cortico-statio-pallido-thalamic function (with commentary). *Behavioral and Brain Sciences, 10,* 197-246.

SZABADI, E. (2006). Drugs for sleep disorders: Mechanisms and therapeutic prospects. *British Journal of Clinical Pharamacology, 61*(6), 761-766.

SZASZ, T. (1960). The myth of mental illness. *American Psychologist, 15,* 113-118.

SZATMARI, P., OFFORD, D. R., & BOYLE, M. H. (1989). Ontario child health study: Prevalence of attention deficit disorder with hyperactivity. *Journal of Child Psychology and Psychiatry, 30*(2), 219-223.

TAHERI, S. (2004). The genetics of sleep disorders. *Minerva Medica, 95,* 203-212.

TAJFEL, H. (Ed.). (1982). Social identity and intergroup relations. New York: Cambridge University Press.

TAMRES, L. K., JANICKI, D., & HELGESON, V. S. (2002). Sex differences in coping behavior: A meta-analytic review and an examination of relative coping. Personality and Social Psychology Review, 6(1), 2-30.

TANGNEY, J. P. (1999). The self-conscious emotions: Shame, guilt, embarrassment and pride. In T. Dalgleish & M. J. Power (Eds.), *Handbook of cognition and emotion* (pp. 541-568). Chichester, England: John Wiley & Sons.

TANNEN, D. (1990). *You just don't understand: Women and men in conversation.* New York: William Morrow.

TAUBES, G. (1994). Will new dopamine receptors offer a key to schizophrenia? *Science, 265,* 1034-1035.

TAYLOR, S. E. (2002). *The tending instinct: Women, men, and the biology of our relationships.* New York: Holt.

TEMPLETON, S. (2004, November 14). Women really are hot for chocolate. *The Sunday Times.* Retrieved August 4, 2008, from http://www.timesonline.co.uk/tol/news/uk/article391029.ece

THAYER, R. E. (1978, March). Toward a psychological theory of multidimensional activation (arousal). *Motivation and Emotion, 2*(1), 1-34.

THOMPSON, PAUL M., HAYASHI, KIRALEE M., DE ZUBICARAY, GREIG, JANKE, ANDREW L., ROSE, STEPHEN E., SEMPLE, JAMES, HERMAN, DAVID, HONG, MICHAEL S., DITTMER, STEPHANIE S., DODDRELL, DAVID M., & TOGA, ARTHUR W. (2003). Dynamics of Gray Matter Loss in Alzheimer's Disease. *The Journal of Neuroscience, 23*(3), 994.

THORNDIKE, E. L. (1898). Animal intelligence. *Psychological Review Monograph, 2*(4, Whole No. 8).

TINBERGEN, N. (1951). *The study of instinct.* Oxford: Clarendon.

TOLMAN, E. C., & HONZIK, C. H. (1930). Introduction and removal of reward, and maze learning in rats. *University of California Publications in Psychology, 4,* 257-275.

TORGERSEN, S., KRINGLEN, E., & CRAMER, V. (2001). The prevalence of personality disorders in a community sample. *Archives of General Psychiatry, 58,* 590-596.

TORREY, E. F. (1986). *Witchdoctors and psychiatrists.* New York: Harper & Row.

TRANSGENDER EXPERIENCE LED STANFORD SCIENTIST TO CRITIQUE GENDER DIFFERENCE. (2006, July 14). *ScienceDaily.* Retrieved August 26, 2008, from http://www.science daily.com/releases/2006/07/060714174545.htm

Treisman, A. (1987). Properties, parts, and objects. In K. R. Boff, L. Kaufman, & J. P. Thomas (Eds.), *Handbook of perception and human performance.* New York: Wiley.

Treisman, A. M., & Gelade, G. (1980). A feature-interpretation theory of attention. *Cognitive Psychology, 12,* 97-136.

Tresniowski, A., & Arias, R. (2006, July 14). The boy who sees with sound. *People.* Retrieved July 10, 2008, from http://www.people.com/people/article/0,26334,1212568,00.html

Trivers, R. L. (1971). The evolution of reciprocal altruism. *Quarterly Review of Biology, 46,* 35-57.

Trivers, R. L. (1972). Parental investment and sexual selection. In B. Campbell (Ed.) *Sexual selection and the descent of man.* New York: Aldine de Gruyter.

Trut, L. N. (1999). Early canid domestication: The farm-fox experiment. *New Scientist, 87,* 160-169.

Tryon, R. C. (1940). Studies in individual differences in maze ability VII: The specific components of maze ability and a general theory of psychological components. *Journal of Comparative Psychology, 30,* 283-338.

Tsien, J. Z. (2000, April). Building a brainier mouse. *Scientific American,* 62-68.

Turner, W. J. (1995). Homosexuality, type 1: An Xq28 phenomenon. *Archives of Sexual Behavior, 24*(2), 109-134.

Tuulio-Henriksson, A., Partonen, T., Suvisaari, J., Haukka, J., & Lönnqvist, J. (2004). Age at onset and cognitive functioning in schizophrenia. *The British Journal of Psychiatry, 185,* 215-219.

Tversky, A., & Kahneman, D. (1980). Causal schemata in judgments under uncertainty. In M. Fishbein (Ed.), *Progress in social psychology,* Vol. 1, Hillsdale, NJ, Erlbaum, 49-72.

Twenge, J. M., Baumeister, R. F., Tice, D. M., & Stucke, T. S. (2001). If you can't join them, beat them: Effects of social exclusion on aggressive behavior. *Journal of Personality and Social Psychology, 81,* 1058-1069.

Twenge, J. M., Catanese, K. R., & Baumeister, R. F. (2002). Social exclusion causes selfdefeating behavior. *Journal of Personality and Social Psychology, 83,* 606-615.

UNAIDS. (2008). Report on the global AIDS epidemic: Executive summary. Retrieved September 25, 2008, from http://data.unaids.org/pub/GlobalReport/2008/JC1511_GR08_ExecutiveSummary_en.pdf

Underwood, B. (2008). About ben. Retrieved July 10, 2008, from http://www.benunderwood.com/aboutme.html

United Nations Statistics Division. (2005). World and regional trends. Millennium Indicators Database. Retrieved September 2, 2008, from http://millenniumindicators.un.org/unsd/mdg/

United States Census Bureau, International Programs. Notes on the World POPClock and World Vital Events. Retrieved February 16, 2010, from http://www.census.gov/ipc/www/popwnote.html.

United States Olympic Committee. (2008). Julie Ertel. Retrieved August 4, 2008, from http://www.usatriathlon.org/athlete/athlete/990

USGS Earthquake Hazards Program. Earthquake Summary. Retrieved January 27, 2010, from http://earthquake.usgs.gov/earthquakes/recenteqsww/Quakes/us2010rja6.php#summary.

Valenstein, E. (1998). *Blaming the brain: The truth about drugs and mental health.* New York: The Free Press.

Van de Castle, R. (1994). *Our dreaming mind.* New York: Ballantine Books.

van Engen, M. L., & Willemsen, T. M. (2004). Sex and leadership styles: A meta-analysis of research published in the 1990s. *Psychological Reports, 94*(1), 3-18.

Vemer, E., Coleman, M., Ganang, L. H., & Cooper, H. (1989). Marital satisfaction in remarriage: A meta-analysis. *Journal of Marriage and the Family, 51,* 713-725.

Vitaly, C. (2007, November 14). New Findings on Farinelli, the Famed Castrato. MusicalAmerica.com. Retrieved August 25, 2008, from http://www.comune.bologna.it/iperbole/inglese/testi/riesumazione_del_farinelli-news-ingl.htm

Vogeley, K., Bussfeld, P., Newen, A., Herrmann, S., Happe, F., Falkai, P., Maier, W., Shah, N. J., Fink, G. R., & Zilles, K. (2001). Mind reading: Neural mechanisms of theory of mind and self-perspective. *Neuroimage, 14,* 170-181.

Vogt, B. A., Nimchinsky, E. A., Vogt, L. J., & Hof, P. R. (1995). Human cingulate cortex: Surface features, flat maps, and cytoarchitecture. *Journal of Comparative Neurology, 359*(3), 490-506.

Vokey, J. R., & Read, J. D. (1985). Subliminal messages: Between the devil and the media. *American Psychologist, 40,* 1231-1239.

Volterra, A., & Steinhäuser, C. (2004). Glial modulation of synaptic transmission in the hippocampus. *Glia 47*(3), 249-57.

Von der Heydt, R., Peterhans, E., & Baumgartner, G. (1984). Illusory contours and cortical neuron responses. *Science, 224,* 1260-1262.

von Senden, M. (1932/1960). *Space and sight: The perception of space and shape in the congenitally blind before and after operation* (P. Heath, Trans.). Glencoe, IL: Free Press.

Vroom, V. H. (1964). *Work and motivation.* New York: Wiley

Vyazovskiy, V. V., Cirelli, C., Pfister-Genskow, M., Faraguna, U., & Tononi G. (2008). Molecular and electrophysiological evidence for net synaptic potentiation in wake and depression in sleep. *Nature Neuroscience, 11*(2), 200-208.

Vygotsky, L. (1978). The role of play in development. In M. Cole (Trans.) *Mind in society.* Cambridge, MA: Harvard University Press.

Vyse, S. (2005). The outer limits of belief. *Science, 310,* 1280-1281.

Wade, N. (2006, March 30). Scans show different growth for intelligent brains. *The New York Times.* Retrieved August 29, 2008, from http://www.nytimes.com/2006/03/30/science/30brain.html

Wahlsten, D. (1997). The malleability of intelligence is not constrained by heritability. In B. Devlin, S. E. Fienberg, & K. Roeder, *Intelligence, genes, and success: Scientists respond to the bell curve* (pp. 71-87). New York: Springer.

Walker, J. (2004). The death of David Reimer: A tale of sex, science, and abuse. *Reason Online.* Retrieved September 2, 2008, from http://reason.com/links/links052404.shtml

Wallace, R. K., & Benson, H. (1972). The physiology of meditation. *Scientific American, 226*(2), 84-90.

Wallach, M. A., & Wallach, L. (1983). *Psychology's sanction for selfishness: The error of egoism in theory and therapy.* New York: W. H. Freeman and Company.

Wallis, C. (1996, March 25). The most intimate bond. *Time.* Retrieved August 11, 2008, from http://www.time.com

Walum, H., Westberg, L., Henningsson, S., Neiderhiser, J. M., Reiss, D., Igl, W., Ganiban, J. M., Spotts, E. L., Pederson, N. L., Eriksson, E., & Lichtenstein, P. (2008). Genetic variation in the vasopressin receptor 1a gene (AVPR1A) associates with pair-bonding behavior in humans. *Proceedings of the National Academy of Sciences, 105,* 37, 14153-14156.

Wampold, B. E. (2001). *The great psychology debate: Models, methods, and findings.* Mahwah, NJ: Erlbaum.

Wang, C., & Chen, W. (2000). The efficacy of behavior therapy in 9 patients with phobia. *Chinese Mental Health Journal, 14,* 351-352.

Watson, J. B., & Rayner, R. (1920). Conditioned emotional reactions. *Journal of Experimental Psychology, 3,* 1-14.

Watson, J. S., & Ramey, C. T. (1972). Reactions to response-contingent stimulation in early infancy. *Merrill-Palmer Quarterly, 18,* 219-227.

Wayment, H. A., & Peplau, L. A. (1995). Social support and well-being among lesbian and heterosexual women: A structural modeling approach. *Personality and Social Psychology Bulletin, 21,* 1189-1199.

Weathers, H. (2006, December 31). Abigail and Brittany Hensel: An extraordinary bond. *Mail Online.* Retrieved August 11, 2008, from http://www.dailymail.co.uk

Webb, W. B., & Campbell, S. S. (1983, October). Relationships in sleep characteristics of identical and fraternal twins. *Archives of General Psychiatry, 40*(10), 1093-1095.

Wechsler, D. (1975). *The collected papers of David Wechsler.* New York: Academic Press.

Wehr, T. A., Sack, D. A., Rosenthal, N. E., Cowdry, R. W. (1988). Rapid cycling - affective disorder: Contributing factors and treatment responses in 51 patients. *American Journal of Psychiatry, 145*(2), 179-184.

Weisberg, R. W. (1994). Genius and madness? A quasi-experimental test of the hypothesis that manic-depression increases creativity. *Psychological Science, 5,* 361-367.

Weissman, M. M. (1999). Interpersonal psychotherapy and the health care scene. In D. S. Janowsky (Ed.), *Psychotherapy indications and outcomes.* Washington, DC: American Psychiatric Press.

WEISSMAN, M. M., & OLFSON, M. (1995). Depression in women: Implications for health care research. Science, 269, 799-801.

WELLMAN, H. M., & GELMAN, S. A. (1992). Cognitive development: Foundational theories of core domains. *Annual Review of Psychology, 43,* 337-375.

WESTEN, D. (1998). Unconscious thought, feeling and motivation: The end of a century-long debate. In R. F. Bornstein & J. M. Masling (Eds.), *Empirical perspectives on the psychoanalytic unconscious* (pp. 1-43). Washington, DC: American Psychological Association.

WHITE, H. R., BRICK, J., & HANSELL, S. (1993). A longitudinal investigation of alcohol use and aggression in adolescence. *Journal of Studies on Alcohol,* Supplement no. 11, 62-77.

WHORF, B. L. (1956). Science and linguistics. In J. B. Carroll (Ed.). *Language, thought, and reality: Selected writings of Benjamin Lee Whorf.* Cambridge, MA: MIT Press.

WIENS, A. N., & MENUSTIK, C. E. (1983). Treatment outcomes and patient characteristics in an aversion therapy program for alcoholism. *American Psychologist, 38,* 1089-1096.

WIGMORE, B. (2008, May 8). The woman who can't forget ANYTHING: Widow has ability—and curse—to perfectly remember every single day of her life. *The Daily Mail.* Retrieved February 16, 2010, from http://www.dailymail.co.uk/news/article-564948/The-woman-forget-ANYTHING-Widow-ability–curse–perfectly-remember-single-day-life.html

WILDER, D. A. (1981). Perceiving persons as a group: Categorization and intergroup relations. In D. L. Hamilton (Ed.), *Cognitive processes in stereotyping and intergroup behavior.* Hillsdale, NJ: Erlbaum.

WILLIAMS, J. E., PATON, C. C., SIEGLER, I. C., EIGENBRODT, M. L., NIETO, F. J., & TYROLER, H. A. (2000). Anger proneness predicts coronary heart disease risk: Prospective analysis from the atherosclerosis risk in communities (ARIC) study. *Circulation, 101,* 2034.

WILLIAMS, K. D., CHEUNG, C. K. T., & CHOI, W. (2000). Cyberostracism: Effects of being ignored over the Internet. *Journal of Personality and Social Psychology, 79*(5), 748-762.

WILLING, R. (2003, November 3). Terrorism lends urgency to hunt for better lie detector. *USA Today.* Retrieved August 5, 2008, from http://www.usatoday.com/tech/news/techpolicy/2003-11-04-lie-detect-tech_x.htm

WILSON, R. S. (1979). Analysis of longitudinal twin data: Basic model and applications to physical growth measures. *Acta Geneticae medicae et Gemellologiae, 28,* 93-105.

WILSON, T. D. (2002). *Strangers to ourselves: Discovering the adaptive unconscious.* Cambridge: Harvard University Press.

WISE, R. A. (1978). Catecholamine theories of reward: A critical review. *Brain Research 152,* 215-247.

WITTGENSTEIN, L. (1953). *Philosophical investigations.* Oxford: Blackwell.

WOLFF, E. (2007, September 23). Dual lives of twins separated at birth. *New York Post.* Retrieved August 11, 2008, from http://www.nypost.com/seven/09232007/news/regionalnews/dual_lives_of_twins_separated_.htm?page=0

WOLPE, J. (1958). *Psychotherapy by reciprocal inhibition.* Stanford, CA: Stanford University Press.

WOLPE, J., & PLAUD, J. J. (1997). Pavlov's contributions to behavior therapy: The obvious and the not so obvious. *American Psychologist, 52,* 966-972.

WOOD, W. (1987). Meta-analytic review of sex differences in group performance. *Psychological Bulletin, 102,* 53-71.

WOOD, W., & EAGLY, A. H. (2002). A cross-cultural analysis of the behavior of women and men: Implications for the origins of sex differences. *Psychological Bulletin, 128*(5), 699-727.

WORLD HEALTH ORGANIZATION. (2004). *The World Health Report 2004: Changing History,* Annex Table 3: Burden of disease in DALYs by cause, sex, and mortality stratum in WHO regions, estimates for 2002. Geneva: Author.

WORLDOMETERS. (2010, February). Current World Population. Retrieved from http://www.worldometers.info/population/.

WRIGHT, L. (1997). *Twins: And what they tell us about who we are.* New York: John Wiley and Sons.

WRZESNIEWSKI, A., MCCAULEY, C. R., ROZIN, P., & SCHWARTZ, B. (1997). Jobs, careers, and callings: People's relations to their work. *Journal of Research in Personality, 31,* 21-33.

WYNN, K. (1992). Addition and subtraction by human infants. *Nature, 358,* 749-759.

WYNN, K. (2000). Findings of addition and subtraction in infants are robust and consistent: Reply to Wakeley, Rivera, and Langer. *Child Development, 71,* 1535-1536.

WYON, D. P. (2000). Individual control at each workplace: The means and the potential benefits. In D. J. Croome & D. Clements-Croome *Creating the productive workplace.* New York: Routeledge.

YERKES. R. M., & DODSON, J. D. (1908). The relation of strength of stimulus to rapidity of habit formation. *Journal of Comparative Neurology and Psychology, 18,* 459-482.

YOO, S., HU, P. T., GUJAR, N., JOLESZ, F. A., & WALKER, M. P. (2007, February). A deficit in the ability to form new human memories without sleep. *Nature Neuroscience, 10,* 385-392.

ZAHN-WAXLER, C., FRIEDMAN, R. J., COLE, P. M., MIZUTA, I. & HIRUMA, N. (1996). Japanese and United States preschool children's responses to conflict and distress. *Child Development, 67,* 2462-2477.

ZAJONC, R. B. (1965). Social facilitation. *Science, 149,* 269-274.

ZAJONC, R. B. (1968). Attitudinal effects of mere exposure. *Journal of Personality and Social Psychology, Monograph Supplement, 9,* (2, Part 2) 1-27.

ZAJONC, R. B. (1980). Feeling and thinking. Preferences need no inferences. *American Psychologist, 35,* 151-175.

ZAJONC, R. B. (1984). On the primacy of affect. *American Psychologist, 39,* 117-123.

ZEBROWITZ, L. A., & MCDONALD, S. (1991). The impact of litigants' babyfacedness and attractiveness on adjudications in small claims courts. *Law and Human Behavior, 15,* 603-623.

ZIMBARDO, P. (1971). The pathology of imprisonment. *Society, 9*(6), 4-8.

ZIMBARDO, P. G. (1975). On transforming experimental research into advocacy for social change. In M. Deutsch & H. Hornstein (Eds.), *Applying social psychology: Implications for research, practice, and training* (pp. 33-66). Hillsdale, NJ: Lawrence Erlbaum Associates.

PHOTO CREDITS

COVER: AFP/Newscom.

BACK COVER: Sfkodonnell/istockphoto.

CHAPTER 01 PAGE 2: FilmMagic/Getty Images. **4:** Michael Newman/PhotoEdit, Inc. **5:** Olivier Le Queinec/Shutterstock. **6:** Chris Stowers © Dorling Kindersley. **7:** Library of Congress. **9:** Laura Wickenden © Dorling Kindersley. **10:** pandapaw/Shutterstock. **11:** Ason Reed/Reuters, Corbis/Reuters America LLC. **12:** Edyta Pawlowska/Shutterstock. **13:** Marc Pokempner/Getty Images, Inc.—Stone Allstock.

CHAPTER 02 PAGE 16: Getty Images. **18:** Caroline Purser/Getty Images. **19 (from top):** Kurt Krieger, The Granger Collection, New York; © Pierre Perrin/Sygma/Corbis All Rights Reserved; Yuri Arcurs/Shutterstock; Margo Harrison/Shutterstock; Jupiter Images; istockphoto.com. **22:** Beverly Joubert/Getty—National Geographic Society. **23:** Warren Anatomical Museum, Countway Library of Medicine, Harvard Medical School. **24:** Image Source/Imags.com, IPNStock Royalty Free. **27:** © David Brabyn/Corbis All Rights Reserved. **25:** istockphoto.com. **28:** © Michael Keller/Corbis All Rights Reserved. **32:** Vladimir Yudin/iStockphoto. **34:** Jeff Nagy/iStockphoto.

CHAPTER 03 PAGE 36: AFP/Getty Images. **38:** Yuri Arcurs/Shutterstock. **40:** EPA/Frank May/Corbis RF. **41:** © Franck Seguin/TempSport/Corbis All Rights Reserved. **42:** Altrendo Images/Getty Images. **43 (from top):** Tomasz Trojanowski/Shutterstock; Patrizia Tilly/Shutterstock; Michael Monahan/Shutterstock; Eric Isselee/Shutterstock. **44:** © Dorling Kindersley. **46:** © EPA/Frank May/Corbis All Rights Reserved. **48–49:** Peter Baxter/Shutterstock; © Corbis All Rights Reserved; Anatomical Design/Shutterstock; Alamy Images; Katrina Brown/Shutterstock; © Kurt Kormann/Zefa/Corbis All Rights Reserved; © Roger Ressmeye/Corbis All Rights Reserved; Volker Steger/Peter Arnold, Inc. **52:** Paul Cooklin/Brand X Pictures/Jupiterimages.

CHAPTER 04 PAGE 54: Gabriel Bouys/AFP/Getty Images. **57:** Michel Touraine/Jupiter Images—Pixland Royalty Free. **58:** Gabriel Bouys/AFP/Getty Images. **59:** Getty Images. **72 (from top):** Hans Neleman/Getty Images, Inc.; © Sygma/Corbis All Rights Reserved. **63:** Pearson Education/PH College. **76:** D.J. Peters/AP Wide World Photos.

CHAPTER 05 PAGE 68: Alexander Joe/AFP/Getty Images. **70:** © Dorling Kindersley. **71:** Ammar Awad/Corbis/Reuters America LLC. **72 (clockwise from top):** Patrick Watson/Pearson Education/PH; Jacob Wackerhausen, courtesy of www.istockphoto.com; © Lou Dematteis/Reuters/Corbis All Rights Reserved. **74 (from top):** © 1995, Edward H. Adelson; Maksym Bondarchuk/Shutterstock; Justin Maresch/Shutterstock; LoopAll/Shutterstock; An Nguyen/Shutterstock. **77:** Getty Images. **80:** Mauro Fermariello/Science Photo Library/Photo Researchers, Inc. **82:** Howard Shooter © Dorling Kindersley. **83 (from top):** © Judith Miller/Dorling Kindersley/VinMagCo; © Jared Milgrim/Corbis All Rights Reserved.

CHAPTER 06 PAGE 86: Time & Life Pictures/Getty Images. **88:** Spencer Grant/PhotoEdit, Inc. **89:** Moodboard/Corbis RF. **91:** Fred Goldstein/Shutterstock. **92:** Salvador Dali (1904-1989), "Dream Caused by the Flight of a Bee Around a Pomegranate One Second Before Waking up," 1944, oil on panel/Thyssen-Bornemisza Collection, Madrid, Spain, © DACS/Lauros/Giraudon/The Bridgeman Art Library, © Salvador Dali, Gala-Salvador Dali Foundation/Artists Rights Society (ARS), New York. **93:** Domenico Gelermo/Shutterstock. **94:** Craig Wactor/Shutterstock. **96:** Matthias Clamer/Getty Images. **97:** Chip Simons/Getty Images, Inc. **99:** Mark Harwood © Dorling Kindersley.

CHAPTER 07 PAGE 102: Getty Images. **105:** © Dorling Kindersley. **105:** Dianna Sarto/Corbis. **106:** Steve Gorton © Dorling Kindersley. **107:** Courtesy of Madison Museum of Early Trades and Crafts; Tracy Morgan © Dorling Kindersley; Tracy Morgan © Dorling Kindersley; Tim Ridley © Dorling Kindersley. **109:** Dimitri Vervits/Getty Images, Inc. **110 (clockwise from top left):** Getty Images—Stockbyte, Royalty Free; Jaimie Duplass/Shutterstock; James Shaffer/PhotoEdit, Inc.; Myrleen Ferguson Cate/PhotoEdit, Inc. **111:** © Jultta Klee/Corbis All Rights Reserved. **113:** Richard Hutchings/PhotoEdit, Inc. **115:** © Dorling Kindersley.

CHAPTER 08 PAGE 118: Getty Images. **120:** Photodisc/Getty Images. **122:** Wellcome Dept. of Cognitive Neurology/Science PhotoLibrary/Photo Researchers, Inc. **124:** © Corbis All Rights Reserved. **125:** © Dorling Kindersley. **126 (from top):** Photodisc/Getty Images; © Orjan F. Ellingvag/Corbis All Rights Reserved; Logan Mock-Bunting/Getty Images; © NASA/Corbis All Rights Reserved; © Corbis All Rights Reserved; © T. Mughal/epa/Corbis All Rights Reserved; © Ryan Pyle/Corbis All Rights Reserved; © Scott Olson/Corbis All Rights Reserved. **128:** © MedicalFR.com/Corbis All Rights Reserved. **130:** Courtesy of www.istockphoto.com; © moodboard/Corbis. **131:** © Tetra Images/Tetra Images/Corbis; Courtesy of www.istockphoto.com.

CHAPTER 09 PAGE 134: Said Khatib/AFP/Getty Images. **136 (from top):** Pokaz/Shutterstock; Shutterstock; © Christopher Felver/Corbis; Bettmann Archive, Corbis/Bettmann; argus/Shutterstock; Getty Images, Inc.—Hulton Archive Photos; Shutterstock; Bill Pierce/Time Life Pictures/Getty Images; Lev Dolgachov/Shutterstock; Valentin Mosichev/Shutterstock; Anna Sedneva/Shutterstock; Matka Wariatka/Shutterstock; Getty Images; Shutterstock. **137:** Steve Cukrov/Shutterstock. **139 (clockwise from top):** Bill Burlingham/Prentice Hall School Division; © Dorling Kindersley; Laima Druskis/Pearson Education/PH College; David Mager/Pearson Learning Photo Studio; Andy Crawford © Dorling Kindersley; Pearson Education/PH College; Michael Heron/Pearson Education/PH College; EMG Education Management Group. **141:** Pearson Scott Foresman. **143:** Frank La Bua/Pearson Education/PH College. **144:** AFP/Getty Images. **145:** Getty Images—Stockbyte, Royalty Free. **146:** Pearson Scott Foresman; Ian O'Leary © Dorling Kindersley; Wolfgang Flamisch/Corbis Zefa Collection; Jay Penni/Prentice Hall School Division. **147:** Ariel Skelley/Corbis/Stock Market. **149:** Chad Ehlers/Stock Connection.

CHAPTER 10 PAGE 152: Getty Images. **154:** Getty Images, Inc.—Stone Allstock; G. Moscoso/Photo Researchers, Inc.; James Stevenson/Science Photo Library/Photo Researchers, Inc. **155:** Boris Ryaposiv/Shutterstock. **156:** David Mager/Pearson Learning Photo Studio. **158:** Donna Day/Getty Images, Inc. **159 (from top):** © Dorling Kindersley; Forrest E. Baird, Ph.D. **160:** Bruno De Hogues/Getty Images, Inc.—Taxi. **161:** Ellen Senisi. **163:** Christina Kennedy/PhotoEdit, Inc.

CHAPTER 11 PAGE 166: Getty Images. **168 (from top):** SW Productions/Brand X/Corbis—Brand X Pictures; © Richard Heinzen/Bureau L.A. Collection/Corbis All Rights Reserved. **170:** Katelyn Metzger/Merrill Education. **171:** © Raed Outena/epa/Corbis All Rights Reserved. **172:** © Liao Yujie/Corbis All Rights Reserved. **173:** Kim Sayer © Dorling Kindersley. **175:** © Dorling Kindersley.

CHAPTER 12 PAGE 178: Getty Images/Yellow Dog Productions. **180:** Thomas McAvoy/Getty Images/Time Life Pictures. **181:** Christina Kennedy/Photodisc/Getty Images. **182:** Don Nichols/iStockPhoto; Bill Noll/iStockPhoto; Pakhnyushcha/Shutterstock; © Dorling Kindersley; Vanessa Davies © Dorling Kindersley; George Dodson/Pearson Education/PH College; Cultura/Corbis RF. **183:** Ethel Wolovitz/The Image Works. **184:** Richard Heinzen/SuperStock, Inc. **185:** EyeWire Collection/Getty Images/Photodisc. **186:** Mandy Godbehear/Shutterstock. **187:** Jamie Grill/Corbis RF. **188:** Silver Burdett Ginn. **189:** © Anna Peisl/zefa/Corbis All Rights Reserved.

CHAPTER 13 PAGE 192: Getty Images/Yellow Dog Productions. **194:** Erik Dreyer/Getty Images, Inc.—Stone Allstock. **197 (from top):** Jurgen Vogt/Getty Images, Inc.—Image Bank; 2happy/Shutterstock; Photodisc/Getty Images; Photos 12/Alamy Images. **198:** Alpha/Landov. **200:** Dave King © Dorling Kindersley. **201:** Alan Keohane © Dorling Kindersley. **203:** Michael Buckner/Getty Images Entertainment.

CHAPTER 14 PAGE 206: APF/Getty Images. **208:** © Bob Anderson/ Masterfile. **210:** SW Productions/Getty Images, Inc.—Photodisc. **211:** Getty Images. **212–213:** Andresr/Shutterstock. **214:** istockphoto.com. **216:** © Tannen Maury/epa/Corbis All Rights Reserved. **218:** © Somos Images/Corbis All Rights Reserved. **219:** Yuri Arcurs/Shutterstock; Carla Donofrio/Shutterstock. **220:** © Petty Officer 2nd Class Samuel C. Peterson/Reuters/Corbis All Rights Reserved. **224:** Suparpics/Alamy Images.

CHAPTER 15 PAGE 226: TIM SLOAN/AFP/Getty Images. **229:** Caren Firouz/Corbis/Reuters America LLC. **230:** JGI/Blend Images/Corbis RF. **231:** Elnur/Shutterstock. **232:** © Bettmann/Corbis All Rights Reserved. **234:** Randy Faris/Corbis RF. **235:** iStockPhoto. **236:** James Steidl/Shutterstock. **237:** Trish Gant

TEXT, TABLE, AND FIGURE CREDITS

INDEX